TEXAS WOMAN'S UNIVERSITY LIBRARY

D0075721

88-0091

"RACE," WRITING, AND DIFFERENCE

"RACE," WRITING, AND DIFFERENCE

Edited by Henry Louis Gates, Jr.

The University of Chicago Press
Chicago and London

For Dominique de Menil, artist and humanitarian

The essays in this volume originally appeared in two issues of CRITICAL INQUIRY: Autumn 1985 (vol. 12, no. 1) and Autumn 1986 (vol. 13, no. 1). Articles reprinted from the Autumn 1985 issue have endnotes, whereas articles from the Autumn 1986 issue have footnotes.

The University of Chicago Press, Chicago 60637
The University of Chicago Press, Ltd., London
© 1985, 1986 by The University of Chicago
All rights reserved. Published 1986
Printed in the United States of America
94 93 92 91 90 89 88 87 86   5 4 3 2 1

Library of Congress Cataloging-in-Publication Data

"Race," writing, and difference.

    "Most of the essays . . . originally appeared in the autumn 1985 issue of Critical inquiry, volume 12, number 1"—Verso t.p.
    Bibliography: p.
    Includes index.
    1. Blacks in literature.   2. Authors, Black.
I. Gates, Henry Louis.
PN56.3.B55R3 1986   809'.9335203   86-6921
ISBN 0-226-28434-4 (alk. paper)
ISBN 0-226-28435-2 (pbk. : alk. paper)

The paper used in this publication meets the minimum requirements of American National Standard for Information Sciences—Permanence of Paper for Printed Library Materials, ANSI Z39.48-1984. ∞

Contents

98-0091

Editor's Introduction:
Writing "Race" and the Difference It Makes

Henry Louis Gates, Jr.

The truth is that, with the fading of the Renaissance ideal through progressive stages of specialism, leading to intellectual emptiness, we are left with a potentially suicidal movement among "leaders of the profession," while, at the same time, the profession sprawls, without its old center, in helpless disarray.

One quickly cited example is the professional organization, the Modern Language Association. . . . A glance at its thick program for its last meeting shows a massive increase and fragmentation into more than 500 categories! I cite a few examples: . . . "The Trickster Figure in Chicano and Black Literature" . . . Naturally, the progressive trivialization of topics has made these meetings a laughingstock in the national press.
—W. JACKSON BATE, "The Crisis in English Studies"

Language, for the individual consciousness, lies on the borderline between oneself and the other. The word in language is half someone else's. It becomes "one's own" only when the speaker populates it with his own intention, his own accent, when he appropriates the word, adapting it to his own semantic and expressive intention. Prior to this moment of appropriation, the word does not exist in a neutral and impersonal language (it is not, after all, out of a dictionary that the speaker gets his words!), but rather it exists in other people's mouths, in other people's contexts, serving other people's intentions: it is from there that one must take the word, and make it one's own.
—MIKHAIL BAKHTIN, "Discourse in the Novel"

> They cannot represent themselves, they must be represented.
> —Karl Marx, *The Eighteenth Brumaire of Louis Bonaparte*

1

What importance does "race" have as a meaningful category in the study of literature and the shaping of critical theory? If we attempt to answer this question by examining the history of Western literature and its criticism, our initial response would probably be "nothing" or, at the very least, "nothing explicitly." Indeed, until the past decade or so, even the most subtle and sensitive literary critics would most likely have argued that, except for aberrant moments in the history of criticism, race has not been brought to bear upon the study of literature in any apparent way. Since T. S. Eliot, after all, the canonical texts of the Western literary tradition have been defined as a more or less closed set of works that somehow speak to, or respond to, "the human condition" and to each other in formal patterns of repetition and revision. And while most critics acknowledge that judgment is not absolute and indeed reflects historically conditioned presuppositions, certain canonical works (the argument runs) do seem to transcend value judgments of the moment, speaking irresistibly to the human condition. The question of the place of texts written by the Other (be that odd metaphorical negation of the European defined as African, Arabic, Chinese, Latin American, Yiddish, or female authors) in the proper study of "literature," "Western literature," or "comparative literature" has, until recently, remained an unasked question, suspended or silenced by a discourse in which the canonical and the noncanonical stand as the ultimate opposition. In much of the thinking about the proper study of literature in this century, race has been an invisible quantity, a persistent yet implicit presence.

This was not always the case, we know. By mid-nineteenth century, "national spirit" and "historical period" had become widely accepted categories within theories of the nature and function of literature which argued that the principal value in a great work of literary art resided in the extent to which these categories were *reflected* in that work of art. Montesquieu's *De l'esprit des lois* considered a culture's formal social institution as the repository of its "guiding spirit," while Giambattista Vico's *Principi di una scienza nuova* read literature against a complex pattern of historical cycles. Friedrich and August von Schlegel managed rather deftly to bring "both national spirit and historical period" to bear upon the

---

Henry Louis Gates, Jr. is professor of English, comparative literature, and African studies at Cornell University. He has edited several books and has written *Figures in Black* and *The Signifying Monkey*.

interpretation of literature, as W. Jackson Bate has shown. But it was Hippolyte-Adolphe Taine who made the implicit explicit by postulating "race, moment, and milieu" as positivistic criteria through which any work could be read and which, by definition, any work reflected. Taine's *History of English Literature* was the great foundation upon which subsequent nineteenth-century notions of "national literatures" would be constructed.

What Taine called "race" was the source of all structures of feeling and thought: to "track the root of man," he writes, is "to consider the race itself . . . the structure of his character and mind, his general processes of thought and feeling, . . . the irregularity and revolutions of his conception, which arrest in him the birth of fair dispositions and harmonious forms, the disdain of appearances, the desire for truth, the attachment for bare and abstract ideas, which develop in him conscience, at the expense of all else." In race, Taine concludes, was predetermined "a particularity inseparable from all the motions of his intellect and his heart. Here lie the grand causes, for they are the universal and permanent causes, . . . indestructible, and finally infallibly supreme." "Poetries," as Taine puts it, and all other forms of social expression, "are in fact only the imprints stamped by their seal."[1]

Race, for Taine, was everything: "the first and richest source of these master faculties from which historical events take their rise"; it was a "community of blood and intellect which to this day binds its offshoots together." Lest we misunderstand the *naturally* determining role of race, Taine concludes that it is "no simple spring but a kind of lake, a deep reservoir wherein other springs have, for a multitude of centuries, discharged their several streams."[2]

Taine's originality lay not in his ideas about the nature and role of race but rather in their almost "scientific" application to the history of literature. These ideas about race were received from the Enlightenment, if not from the Renaissance. By 1850, ideas of irresistible racial differences were commonly held. When Abraham Lincoln invited a small group of black leaders to the White House in 1862 to present his ideas about returning all blacks in America to Africa, his argument turned upon these "natural" differences. "You and we are different races," he said. "We have between us a broader difference than exists between any other two races."[3] Since this sense of difference was never to be bridged, Lincoln concluded, the slaves and the ex-slaves should be returned to Africa. The growth of canonical national literatures[4] was coterminous with the shared assumption among intellectuals that race was a "thing," an ineffaceable quantity, which irresistibly determined the shape and contour of thought and feeling as surely as it did the shape and contour of human anatomy.

How did the pronounced concern for the language of the text, which defined the Practical Criticism and New Criticism movements, affect this category called race in the reading of literature? Race, along with all sorts of other "unseemly" or "untoward" notions about the composition of the literary work of art, was bracketed or suspended. Within these theories of literature to which we are all heir, texts were considered canonical insofar as they elevated the cultural; Eliot's simultaneous ordering of the texts that comprised the Western tradition rendered race implicit. History, milieu, and even moment were then brought to bear upon the interpretation of literature through philology and etymology: the dictionary (in the Anglo-American tradition, specifically the *Oxford English Dictionary*) was the castle in which Taine's criteria took refuge. Once the concept of value became encased in the belief in a canon of texts whose authors purportedly shared a common culture, inherited from *both* the Greco-Roman and the Judeo-Christian traditions, there was no need to speak of matters of race, since the race of these authors was "the same." One not heir to these traditions was, by definition, of another race.

Despite their beliefs in the unassailable primacy of language in the estimation of a literary work, however, both I. A. Richards and Allen Tate, in separate prefaces to books of poems by black authors, paused to wonder about the black faces of the authors and the importance of that blackness in the reading of their texts.[5] The racism often attributed to the Southern Agrarians, while an easily identifiable target, was only an extreme manifestation of the presuppositions forming much of the foundation upon which formalism was built. The citizens of the republic of literature, in other words, were all white, and mostly male. Difference, if difference obtained at all, was a difference obliterated by the simultaneity of Eliot's tradition. For the writer from a culture of color, Eliot's fiction of tradition was the literary equivalent of the "grandfather clause."[6] So, in response to the line in Robert Penn Warren's "Pondy Woods"—"Nigger, your breed ain't metaphysical"—Sterling Brown is fond of repeating, "Cracker, your breed ain't exegetical." This signifyin(g) pun deconstructs the "racialism" inherent in such claims of tradition.

2

Race, as a meaningful criterion within the biological sciences, has long been recognized to be a fiction. When we speak of "the white race" or "the black race," "the Jewish race" or "the Aryan race," we speak in biological misnomers and, more generally, in metaphors. Nevertheless, our conversations are replete with usages of race which have their sources in the dubious pseudoscience of the eighteenth and nineteenth centuries. One need only flip through the pages of the *New York Times* to find headlines such as "Brown University President Sees School Racial Problems" or "Sensing Racism, Thousands March in Paris." In "The Lost White Tribe," a lead editorial in the 29 March 1985 issue, the *New York Times* notes that while "racism is not unique to South Africa," we must condemn that society because in "betraying the religious tenets underlying Western culture, it has made race the touchstone of political rights." The *Times* editorial echoes Eliot's "dissociation of sensibility," which he felt had been caused in large part by the fraternal atrocities of the First World War. (For many people with non-European origins, however, dissociation of sensibility resulted from colonialism and human slavery.) Race, in these usages, pretends to be an objective term of classification, when in fact it is a dangerous trope.

The sense of difference defined in popular usages of the term "race" has both described and *inscribed* differences of language, belief system, artistic tradition, and gene pool, as well as all sorts of supposedly natural attributes such as rhythm, athletic ability, cerebration, usury, fidelity, and so forth. The relation between "racial character" and these sorts of characteristics has been inscribed through tropes of race, lending the sanction of God, biology, or the natural order to even presumably unbiased descriptions of cultural tendencies and differences. "Race consciousness," Zora Neale Hurston wrote, "is a deadly explosive on the tongues of men."[7] In 1973 I was amazed to hear a member of the House of Lords describe the differences between Irish Protestants and Catholics in terms of their "distinct and clearly definable differences of race." "You mean to say that you can tell them apart?" I asked incredulously. "Of course," responded the lord. "Any Englishman can."

Race has become a trope of ultimate, irreducible difference between cultures, linguistic groups, or adherents of specific belief systems which—more often than not—also have fundamentally opposed economic interests. Race is the ultimate trope of difference because it is so very arbitrary in its application. The biological criteria used to determine "difference" in sex simply do not hold when applied to "race." Yet we carelessly use language in such a way as to *will* this sense of *natural* difference into our formulations. To do so is to engage in a pernicious act of language, one which exacerbates the complex problem of cultural or ethnic difference, rather than to assuage or redress it. This is especially the case at a time when, once again, racism has become fashionable. The extreme "otherness" of the black African continues to surface as a matter of controversy even in such humanitarian and cosmopolitan institutions as the Roman Catholic Church. On a visit to west Africa in August, Pope John Paul II sailed across Lake Togo to face Aveto, "supreme priest" of Togo's traditional African religion, on the edge of the sacred forest at Togoville, the historical meeting point of the Roman Catholic and traditional black religions. It was a confrontation of primal dimensions: the Pope, accompanied by the Vatican Secretary of State and other top officials, and Aveto, accompanied by five of his chief priests and priestesses, exchanged blessings and then discussed the compatibility of their belief systems. The Pope, however, a rather vocal critic of the creative African integration of traditional black ("animist") beliefs with those received from Rome, emerged from his confrontation with the mystical black Other in the heart of darkness, still worried about "great confusions in ideas," "syncretistic mysticism incompatible with the Church," and customs "contrary to the will of God," thereby denying Africans the right to remake European religion in their own images, just as various Western cultures have done.[8]

Scores of people are killed every day in the name of differences ascribed only to race. This slaughter demands the gesture in which the contributors to this volume are collectively engaged: to deconstruct, if you will, the ideas of difference inscribed in the trope of race, to explicate discourse itself in order to reveal the hidden relations of power and knowledge inherent in popular and academic usages of "race." But when, on 31 March 1985, twenty-five thousand people felt compelled to gather on the rue de Rivoli in support of the antiracist "Ne touche pas à mon pote" movement, when thousands of people willingly risk death to protest apartheid, when Iran and Iraq each feel justified in murdering the other's citizens because of their "race," when Beirut stands as a monument of shards and ruins, the gesture that we make here seems local and tiny.

I have edited this volume of *Critical Inquiry* to explore, from a variety of methodological perspectives and formal concerns, the curious dialectic between formal language use and the inscription of metaphorical racial differences. At times, as Nancy Stepan expertly shows in *The Idea of Race in Science*, these metaphors have sought a universal and transcendent sanction in biological science. Western writers in French, Spanish, German, Portuguese, and English have tried to mystify these rhetorical figures of race, to make them natural, absolute, essential. In doing so, they have *inscribed* these differences as fixed and finite categories which they merely report or draw upon for authority. It takes little reflection, however, to recognize that these pseudoscientific categories are themselves figures. Who has seen a black or red person, a white, yellow, or brown? These terms are arbitrary constructs, not reports of reality. But language is not only the medium of this often insidious tendency; it is its *sign*. Current language use signifies the difference between cultures and their possession of power, spelling out the distance between subordinate and superordinate, between bondsman and lord in terms of their "race." These usages develop simultaneously with the shaping of an economic order in which the cultures of color have been dominated in several important senses by Western Judeo-Christian, Greco-Roman cultures and their traditions. To use contemporary theories of criticism to explicate these modes of inscription is to demystify large and obscure ideological relations and, indeed, theory itself. Before discussing the essays gathered here, it would be useful to consider a typical example of Western culture's use of writing as a commodity to confine and delimit a culture of color. For literacy, as I hope to demonstrate, is the emblem that links racial alienation with economic alienation.

3

Where better to test this thesis than in the example of the black tradition's first poet in English, the African slave girl Phillis Wheatley. Let us imagine the scene.

One bright morning in the spring of 1772, a young African girl walked demurely into the courthouse at Boston to undergo an oral examination, the results of which would determine the direction of her life and work. Perhaps she was shocked upon entering the appointed room. For there, gathered in a semicircle, sat eighteen of Boston's most notable citizens. Among them was John Erving, a prominent Boston merchant; the Reverend Charles Chauncey, pastor of the Tenth Congregational Church; and John Hancock, who would later gain fame for his signature on the Declaration of Independence. At the center of this group would have sat His Excellency, Thomas Hutchinson, governor of the colony, with Andrew Oliver, his lieutenant governor, close by his side.

Why had this august group been assembled? Why had it seen fit to summon this young African girl, scarcely eighteen years old, before it? This group of "the most respectable characters in *Boston*," as it would later define itself, had assembled to question closely the African adolescent on the slender sheaf of poems that she claimed to have written by herself. We can only speculate on the nature of the questions posed to the fledgling poet. Perhaps they asked her to identify and explain—for all to hear—exactly who were the Greek and Latin gods and poets alluded to so frequently in her work. Perhaps they asked her to conjugate a verb in Latin, or even to translate randomly selected passages from the Latin, which she and her master, John Wheatley, claimed that she "had made some progress in." Or perhaps they asked her to recite from memory key passages from the texts of John Milton and Alexander Pope, the two poets by whom the African claimed to be most directly influenced. We do not know.

We do know, however, that the African poet's responses were more than sufficient to prompt the eighteen august gentlemen to compose, sign, and publish a two-paragraph "Attestation," an open letter "To the Publick" that prefaces Phillis Wheatley's book, and which reads in part:

> We whose Names are underwritten, do assure the World, that the poems specified in the following Page, were (as we veribly believe) written by Phillis, a young Negro Girl, who was but a few Years since, brought an uncultivated Barbarian from *Africa,* and has ever since been, and now is, under the Disadvantage of serving as a Slave in a Family in this Town. She has been examined by some of the best judges, and is thought qualified to write them.[9]

So important was this document in securing a publisher for Phillis Wheatley's poems that it forms the signal element in the prefatory matter printed in the opening pages of her *Poems on Various Subjects, Religious and Moral,* published at London in 1773.

Without the published "Attestation," Phillis Wheatley's publisher claimed, few would believe that an African could possibly have written poetry all by herself. As the eighteen put the matter clearly in their letter, "Numbers would be ready to suspect they were not really the Writings of Phillis."[10] Phillis Wheatley and her master, John Wheatley, had attempted to publish a similar volume in 1770 at Boston, but Boston publishers had been incredulous. Three years later, "Attestation" in hand, Phillis Wheatley and her master's son, Nathaniel Wheatley, sailed for England, where they completed arrangements for the publication of a volume of her poems with the aid of the countess of Huntington and the earl of Dartmouth.

This curious anecdote, surely one of the oddest oral examinations on record, is only a tiny part of a larger, and even more curious, episode in the Enlightenment. Since the beginning of the seventeenth century, Europeans had wondered aloud whether or not the African "species of men," as they most commonly put it, *could* ever create formal literature, could ever master "the arts and sciences." If they could, the argument ran, then the African variety of humanity and the European variety were fundamentally related. If not, then it seemed clear that the African was destined by nature to be a slave.

Why was the creative writing of the African of such importance to the eighteenth century's debate over slavery? I can briefly outline one thesis: after René Descartes, *reason* was privileged, or valorized, above all other human characteristics. Writing, especially after the printing press became so widespread, was taken to be the *visible* sign of reason. Blacks were "reasonable," and hence "men," if—and only if—they demonstrated mastery of "the arts and sciences," the eighteenth century's formula for writing. So, while the Enlightenment is characterized by its foundation on man's ability to reason, it simultaneously used the absence and presence of reason to delimit and circumscribe the very humanity of the cultures and people of color which Europeans had been "discovering" since the Renaissance. The urge toward the systematization of all human knowledge (by which we characterize the Enlightenment) led directly to the relegation of black people to a lower place in the great chain of being, an ancient construct that arranged all of creation on a vertical scale from plants, insects, and animals through man to the angels and God himself.

By 1750, the chain had become minutely calibrated; the human scale rose from "the lowliest Hottentot" (black South Africans) to "glorious Milton and Newton." If blacks could write and publish imaginative literature, then they could, in effect, take a few "giant steps" up the chain of being in an evil game of "Mother, May I?" For example, scores of reviews of Wheatley's book argued that the publication of her poems meant that the African was indeed a human being and should not be enslaved. Indeed, Wheatley herself was manumitted soon after her poems were published. That which was only implicit in Wheatley's case would become explicit fifty years later. George Moses Horton had, by the middle of the 1820s, gained a considerable reputation at Chapel Hill as "the slave-poet." His master printed full-page advertisements in Northern newspapers soliciting subscriptions for a book of Horton's poems and promising to exchange the slave's freedom for a sufficient return on sales of the book. Writing, for these slaves, was not an activity of mind; rather, it was a commodity which they were forced to trade for their humanity.

4

Blacks and other people of color could not write.

Writing, many Europeans argued, stood alone among the fine arts as the most salient repository of "genius," the visible sign of reason itself. In this subordinate role, however, writing, although secondary to reason, is nevertheless the *medium* of reason's expression. We *know* reason by its writing, by its representations. Such representations could assume spoken or written form. And while several superb scholars give priority to the *spoken* as the privileged of the pair, most Europeans privileged *writing*— in their writings about Africans, at least—as the principal measure of the Africans' humanity, their capacity for progress, their very place in the great chain of being.

The direct correlation between economic and political alienation, on the one hand, and racial alienation, on the other, is epitomized in the following 1740 South Carolina statute that attempted to make it almost impossible for black slaves to acquire, let alone master, literacy:

> *And whereas* the having of slaves taught to write, or suffering them to be employed in writing, may be attending with great inconveniences;
>
> *Be it enacted,* that all and every person and persons whatsoever, who shall hereafter teach, or cause any slave or slaves to be taught to write, or shall use or employ any slave as a scribe in any manner of writing whatsoever, hereafter taught to write; every such person or persons shall, for every offense, forfeith the sum of one hundred pounds current money.

Learning to read and to write, then, was not only difficult, it was a violation of a law.

As early as 1705, a Dutch explorer, William Bosman, had encased the commodity function of writing and its relation to racial and economic alienation in a myth which the Africans he "discovered" had purportedly related to him. According to Bosman, the blacks tell us, that in the beginning God created Black as well as White men; thereby . . . giving the Blacks the first Election, who chose Gold, and left the Knowledge of Letters to the White. God granted their Request, but being incensed at their Avarice, resolved that the Whites should for ever be their masters, and they obliged to wait on them as their slaves.[11]

Bosman's fabrication, of course, was a claim of origins designed to sanction through mythology a political order created by Europeans. But it was Hume, writing midway through the eighteenth century, who gave to Bosman's myth the sanction of Enlightenment philosophical reasoning.

In a major essay, "Of National Characters" (1748), Hume discusses the "characteristics" of the world's major division of human beings. In a footnote added in 1753 to his original text (the margins of his discourse), Hume posited with all of the authority of philosophy the fundamental identity of complexion, character, and intellectual capacity:

> I am apt to suspect the negroes, and in general all the other species of men (for there are four or five different kinds) to be naturally inferior to the whites. There never was a civilized nation of any other complexion than white, nor even any individual eminent either in action or speculation. No ingenious manufactures amongst them, *no arts, no sciences* . . . Such a uniform and constant difference could not happen, in so many countries and ages, if *nature* had not made an original distinction betwixt these breeds of men. Not to mention our colonies, there are Negroe slaves dispersed all over Europe, of which none ever discovered any symptoms of ingenuity. . . . In Jamaica indeed they talk of one negroe as a man of parts and learning [Francis Williams, the Cambridge-educated poet who wrote verse in Latin]; but 'tis likely he is admired for very slender accomplishments, like a parrot, who speaks a few words plainly.[12]

Hume's opinion on the subject, as we might expect, became prescriptive.

In his *Observations on the Feeling of the Beautiful and Sublime* (1764), Kant elaborates on Hume's essay in section 4, entitled "Of National Characteristics, So Far as They Depend upon the Distinct Feeling of the Beautiful and Sublime." Kant first claims that "so fundamental is the difference between [the black and white] races of man, . . . it appears to be as great in regard to mental capacities as in color."[13] Kant, moreover, is one of the earliest major European philosophers to conflate color with intelligence, a determining relation he posits with dictatorial surety:

> Father Labat reports that a Negro carpenter, whom he reproached for haughty treatment toward his wives, answered: "You whites are indeed fools, for first you make great concessions to your wives, and afterward you complain when they drive you mad." And it might be that there were something in this which perhaps deserved

to be considered; but in short, this fellow was *quite black* from head to foot, a clear proof that what he said was stupid.[14]

The correlation of "black" and "stupid" Kant posits as if it were self-evident.

Hegel, echoing Hume and Kant, claimed that Africans had no history, because they had developed no systems of writing and had not mastered the art of writing in European languages. In judging civilizations, Hegel's strictures with respect to the absence of written history presume a crucial role for *memory,* a collective, cultural memory. Metaphors of the childlike nature of the slaves, of the masked, puppetlike personality of the black, all share this assumption about the absence of memory. Mary Langdon, in her novel *Ida May: A Story of Things Actual and Possible* (1854), writes that "they *are* mere children. . . . You seldom hear them say much about anything that's past, if they only get enough to eat and drink at the present moment."[15] Without writing, no *repeatable* sign of the workings of reason, of mind, could exist. Without memory or mind, no history could exist. Without history, no humanity, as defined consistently from Vico to Hegel, could exist.

5

Ironically, Anglo-African writing arose as a response to allegations of its absence. Black people responded to these profoundly serious allegations about their "nature" as directly as they could: they wrote books, poetry, autobiographical narratives. Political and philosophical discourse were the predominant forms of writing. Among these, autobiographical "deliverance" narratives were the most common and the most accomplished. Accused of lacking a formal and collective history, blacks published individual histories which, taken together, were intended to narrate in segments the larger yet fragmented history of blacks in Africa, now dispersed throughout a cold New World. The narrated, descriptive "eye" was put into service as a literary form to posit both the individual "I" of the black author as well as the collective "I" of the race. Text created author; and black authors, it was hoped, would create, or re-create, the image of the race in European discourse. The very *face* of the race was contingent upon the recording of the black *voice*. Voice presupposed a face, but also seems to have been thought to determine the very contours of the black face.

The recording of an authentic black voice—a voice of deliverance from the deafening discursive silence which an enlightened Europe cited to prove the absence of the African's humanity—was the millennial instrument of transformation through which the African would become the European, the slave become the ex-slave, brute animal become the human being. So central was this idea to the birth of the black literary tradition in the eighteenth century that five of the earliest slave narratives draw upon the figure of the voice in the text—of the talking book—as crucial "scenes of instruction" in the development of the slave on the road to freedom.[16]

These five authors, linked by revision of a trope into the very first chain of black signifiers, implicitly signify upon another chain, the metaphorical great chain of being. Blacks were most commonly represented on the chain either as the lowest of the human races or as first cousin to the ape. Because writing, according to Hume, was the ultimate sign of difference between animal and human, these writers implicitly were signifyin(g) upon the figure of the chain itself. Simply by publishing autobiographies, they indicted the received order of Western culture, of which slavery was to them the most salient sign. The writings of James Gronniosaw, John Marrant, Olaudah Equiano, Ottabah Cugoano, and John Jea served to criticize the sign of the chain of being and the black person's figurative "place" on the chain. This chain of black signifiers, regardless of their intent or desire, made the first political gesture in the Anglo-African literary tradition "simply" by the act of writing. Their collective act gave birth to the black literary tradition and defined it as the "Other's chain," the chain of black being as black people themselves would have it. Making the book speak, then, constituted a motivated and political engagement with and condemnation of Europe's fundamental sign of domination, the commodity of writing, the text and technology of reason. We are justified, however, in wondering aloud if the sort of subjectivity which these writers seek through the act of writing can be realized through a process which is so very ironic from the outset: how can the black subject posit a full and sufficient self in a language in which blackness is a sign of absence? Can writing, with the very difference it makes and marks, mask the blackness of the black face that addresses the text of Western letters, in a voice that speaks English through an idiom which contains the irreducible element of cultural difference that will always separate the white voice from the black? Black people, we know, have not been liberated from racism by our writings. We accepted a false premise by assuming that racism would be destroyed once white racists became convinced that we were human, too. Writing stood as a complex "certificate of humanity," as Paulin Hountondji put it. Black writing, and especially the literature of the slave, served not to obliterate the difference of race; rather, the inscription of the black voice in Western literatures has preserved those very cultural differences to be repeated, imitated, and revised in a separate Western literary tradition, a tradition of black difference.

We black people tried to write ourselves out of slavery, a slavery even more profound than mere physical bondage. Accepting the challenge of the great white Western tradition, black writers wrote as if their lives depended upon it—and, in a curious sense, their lives did, the "life of the race" in Western discourse. But if blacks accepted this challenge, we also accepted its premises, premises which perhaps concealed a trap. What trap might this be? Let us recall the curious case of M. Edmond Laforest.

In 1915, Edmond Laforest, a prominent member of the Haitian literary movement called La Ronde, made his death a symbolic, if ironic, statement of the curious relation of the marginalized writer to the act of writing in a modern language. Laforest, with an inimitable, if fatal, flair for the grand gesture, stood upon a bridge, calmly tied a Larousse dictionary around his neck, then leapt to his death. While other black writers, before and after Laforest, have been drowned artistically by the weight of various modern languages, Laforest chose to make his death an emblem of this relation of overwhelming indenture.

It is the challenge of the black tradition to critique this relation of indenture, an indenture that obtains for our writers and for our critics. We must master, as Jacques Derrida writes in his essay in this collection, how "to speak the other's language without renouncing [our] own" (p. 333). When we attempt to appropriate, by inversion, "race" as a term for an essence—as did the négritude movement, for example ("We feel, therefore we are," as Léopold Senghor argued of the African)—we yield too much: the basis of a shared humanity. Such gestures, as Anthony Appiah observes in his essay, are futile and dangerous because of their further inscription of new and bizarre stereotypes. How do we meet Derrida's challenge in the discourse of criticism? The Western critical tradition has a canon, as the Western literary tradition does. I once thought it our most important gesture to *master* the canon of criticism, to *imitate* and *apply* it, but I now believe that we must turn to the black tradition itself to develop theories of criticism indigenous to our literatures. Alice Walker's revision of Rebecca Cox Jackson's parable of white interpretation (written in 1836) makes this point most tellingly. Jackson, a Shaker eldress and black visionary, claimed like Jea to have been taught to read by the Lord. She writes in her autobiography that she dreamed a white man came to her house to teach her how to *interpret* and understand the word of God, now that God had taught her to read:

> A white man took me by my right hand and led me on the north side of the room, where sat a square table. On it lay a book open. And he said to me. "Thou shall be instructed in this book, from Genesis to Revelations." And then he took me on the west side, where stood a table. And it looked like the first. And said, "Yea, thou shall be instructed from the beginning of creation to the end of time." And then he took me on the east side of the room

also, where stood a table and book like the two first, and said, "I will instruct thee—yea, thou shall be instructed from the beginning of all things to the end of all things. Yea, thou shall be well instructed. I will instruct."

> And then I awoke, and I saw him as plain as I did in my dream. And after that he taught me daily. And when I would be reading and come to a hard word, I would see him standing by my side and he would teach me the word right. And often, when I would be in meditation and looking into things which was hard to understand, I would find him by me, teaching and giving me understanding. And oh, his labor and care which he had with me often caused me to weep bitterly, when I would see my great ignorance and the great trouble he had to make me understand eternal things. For I was so buried in the depth of the tradition of my forefathers, that it did seem as if I never could be dug up.[17]

In response to Jackson's relation of interpretive indenture to "a white man," Walker, in *The Color Purple,* records an exchange between Celie and Shug about turning away from "the old white man" which soon turns into a conversation about the elimination of "man" as a mediator between a woman and "everything":

> You have to git man off your eyeball, before you can see anything a'tall.
> Man corrupt everything, say Shug. He on your box of grits, in your head, and all over the radio. He try to make you think he everywhere. Soon as you think he everywhere, you think he God. But he ain't. Whenever you trying to pray, and man plop himself on the other end of it, tell him to git lost, say Shug.[18]

Celie and Shug's omnipresent "man," of course, echoes the black tradition's epithet for the white power structure, "the man."

 For non-Western, so-called noncanonical critics, getting the "man off your eyeball" means using the most sophisticated critical theories and methods available to reappropriate and to define our own "colonial" discourses. We must use these theories and methods insofar as they are relevant to the study of our own literatures. The danger in doing so, however, is best put by Anthony Appiah in his definition of what he calls "the Naipaul fallacy":

> It is not necessary to show that African literature is fundamentally the same as European literature in order to show that it can be treated with the same tools; . . . nor should we endorse a more sinister line . . . : the post-colonial legacy which requires us to show that African literature is worthy of study precisely (but only) because it is fundamentally the same as European literature.[19]

We *must* not, Appiah concludes, ask "the reader to understand Africa by embedding it in European culture" ("S," p. 146).

We must, I believe, analyze the ways in which writing relates to race, how attitudes toward racial differences generate and structure literary texts by us *and* about us. We must determine how critical methods can effectively disclose the traces of ethnic differences in literature. But we must also understand how certain forms of difference and the *languages* we employ to define those supposed differences not only reinforce each other but tend to create and maintain each other. Similarly, and as importantly, we must analyze the language of contemporary criticism itself, recognizing especially that hermeneutic systems are not universal, colorblind, apolitical, or neutral. Whereas some critics wonder aloud, as Appiah notes, about such matters as whether or not "a structuralist poetics is inapplicable in Africa because structuralism is European" ("S," p. 145), the concern of the Third World critic should properly be to understand the ideological subtext which any critical theory reflects and embodies, and the relation which this subtext bears to the production of meaning. No critical theory—be it Marxist, feminist, post-structuralist, Kwame Nkrumah's "consciencism," or whatever—escapes the specificity of value and ideology, no matter how mediated these may be. To attempt to appropriate our own discourses by using Western critical theory uncritically is to substitute one mode of neocolonialism for another. To begin to do this in my own tradition, theorists have turned to the black vernacular tradition—to paraphrase Jackson, they have begun to dig into the depths of the tradition of our foreparents—to isolate the signifying black difference through which to theorize about the so-called discourse of the Other.

6

"Race," Writing, and Difference is not a manifesto composed by several essayists who share one agenda. Rather, the essays collected here manifest the wide variety of critical approaches through which one may discuss the complex interplay among race, writing, and difference.

In "The Uncompleted Argument: Du Bois and the Illusion of Race," Appiah charts the changes in Du Bois' ideas about race. Using the most sophisticated biological theories of race, morphology, and difference, Appiah shows how race functions in Western culture as a metonym for muddled thinking about the relation among genetics, intention, meaning, and culture. "An Ideology of Difference" by Edward Said serves as a response to Appiah's reminder that our obsession with structure, relations, and concepts "under Saussurian hegemony" has led us to ignore or suspend "reality" (pp. 35–36). Said discusses the ideological foundations of abstract categories of Otherness which depend for their effectiveness upon fictions of a fundamental and constitutive difference.

The other essayists in this collection read specific verbal and visual texts against complex cultural codes of power, assertion, and domination which these texts both reflect and, indeed, reinforce. As Abdul Jan-Mohamed puts this relation, "A rigorous subconscious logic defines the relations . . . between . . . material and discursive practices" (p. 81). Using Jacques Lacan's categories of the imaginary and the symbolic, Jan-Mohamed shows how racial difference, raised to the level of moral and even metaphysical difference, is a central perceptual category not only of British colonial policy and practice but also of its general and literary discourse.

In a pioneering consideration of a virtually unknown group of poets, Bernard Lewis discusses the several ways in which *aghribat al-Arab* (the crows, or ravens, of the Arabs) represented their own black African heritage in Arabic poetry between the seventh and ninth centuries. Israel Burshatin's essay on the image of the Moor in classical Spanish literature shows how the Moor, whether stereotyped positively or negatively, functioned as metaphor and emblem within fictions of the historical relation between conqueror and conquered; then Burshatin shows how authors who were Moors created a self-reflexive parodic discourse which sought to reinterpret history at its origins. Mary Louise Pratt's reading of eighteenth- and nineteenth-century European travel literature shows how seemingly innocent or neutral "descriptions" in travel accounts textualize and naturalize received cultural or character traits that underscore "the Other's amenability to domination and potential as a labor pool" (p. 139). If Pratt is concerned to analyze the subtle but persistent ways in which the discourse of travel variously represented the Other and then transformed itself into "the canonical story about Africa—the fall from the sun-drenched prospect into the heart of darkness," then Homi Bhabha's essay is concerned with the book as an emblem itself—that is, with the discovery of the very concept of "book" by the Other of color. Bhabha, more specifically, reveals how the emblem of the English book—"signs taken for wonders"—became an "insignia of colonial authority and a signifier of colonial desire and discipline" (p. 163). Similarly, Patrick Brantlinger explicates in fascinating detail the origins and transformations of the metaphor of the Dark Continent throughout a wide variety of Victorian texts to show how Europeans inscribed this myth onto distant terrain as a prelude to "the imperialist partitioning of Africa which dominated the final quarter of the nineteenth century" (p. 185). The Dark Continent would figure as a larger metaphor for Otherness; it was Freud who conflated images of racial and sexual difference. "But we need not feel ashamed of this distinction [that we know less about the sexual life of little girls than boys]," Freud wrote; "after all, the sexual life of adult women is a 'dark continent' for psychology."[20] Sander Gilman's essay establishes an iconography of female sexuality in late nineteenth-century art, medicine, and literature by exploring the similarities in visual representations of black and white women in both "aesthetic" and "scientific" texts.

Gayatri Chakravorty Spivak, Hazel Carby, and Barbara Johnson share a concern about the curious interrelationships between figures for sexual and racial Otherness. Spivak explores these questions in a sustained reading of *Jane Eyre* ("a cult text of feminism"), *The Wild Sargasso Sea* (*Jane Eyre's* "reinscription"), and *Frankenstein* (which analyzes the "worlding" posited by *Jane Eyre*) (p. 263). Spivak reveals how the much-praised individualism of the female protagonist in *Jane Eyre* coincides with the exclusion of the "'native female' as such" from any meaningful subjectivity at all (p. 264). Whereas Spivak analyzes the exclusion of the female subject of color from both Western literature and criticism, Carby explores the turn-of-the-century writings of Afro-American women intellectuals for what these reveal about the theoretical analysis of race, gender, and patriarchal power. Carby concludes that the theoretical legacy of these writers is their exposition of a process that simultaneously led to the "colonization of the black female body to white male power and the destruction of black males who attempted to exercise any oppositional patriarchal control" (p. 315).

Barbara Johnson discusses the various ways in which "strategies and structures of problematic address" reflect and comment on "thresholds of difference," or "the dynamics of any encounter between an inside and an outside, any attempt to make a statement about difference" (pp. 317, 318). Johnson's essay, by focusing upon the manner in which Zora Neale Hurston "suspends the certainty of reference," stands as a fitting commentary on the attempts of the essayists gathered here to draw upon the sophisticated theories and methodologies of Marxist, psychoanalytic, and post-structuralist literary criticism to address issues that affect actual human beings in an actual world in the most immediate and compelling ways. Accordingly, the collection ends with Jacques Derrida's "Racisms's Last Word," written originally for the catalog of the exhibition "Art contre/against Apartheid" and appearing here in English translation by Peggy Kamuf. "Racism's Last Word" addresses the complexities and ironies of the word itself: "apartheid" is "the archival record of the unnameable," the untranslated and perhaps untranslatable name of "a racism par excellence" (p. 330). Derrida, whom one critic nicknamed "Monsieur Texte," demonstrates how his method of close reading can be employed in a most illuminating manner to analyze the heinous sociopolitical reality of white racism in black South Africa.[21] If the contributors, in all their diversity, might agree on one matter, it would be this: one important benefit of the development of subtle and searching modes of "reading" is that these can indeed be brought to bear upon relationships that extend far beyond the confined boundaries of a text.

This book grew out of *Critical Inquiry's* special issue *"Race," Writing, and Difference* (vol. 12, no. 1 [Autumn 1985]). In addition to the essays first printed there, the present volume contains essays by Jane Tompkins and Christopher L. Miller, and critical responses by Rob Nixon and Anne McClintock, Jacques Derrida, Houston A. Baker, Jr., Tzvetan Todorov, Harold Fromm, Mary Louise Pratt, and Henry Louis Gates, Jr., which appeared one year later in *Critical Inquiry* (vol. 13, no. 1 [Autumn 1986]).

A collective publishing project of this kind depends for its realization upon the generous efforts of many people. W. J. T. Mitchell and Mary Caraway encouraged me with their enthusiasm and energy when I first approached *Critical Inquiry* about editing a special issue that could bring critical theory to bear upon ideas of race. Without their initial positive reception and their subsequent unflagging support, my project would have remained an unfulfilled fantasy.

I also wish to express my appreciation to the coeditors of *Critical Inquiry,* who invited me to Chicago to discuss the purpose and shape of that special issue and whose commitment to my proposal has, I hope, been responsibly addressed by the writers whose essays are collected here. Mary Caraway and Susan Olin's remarkable editorial commentary directed each of us to a cleaner and fuller understanding of our own meanings. These two stellar editors also established a productive timetable that enabled me to undertake research in Africa as planned.

I would also like to thank Houston A. Baker, Jr., Sander L. Gilman, Arnold Rampersad, and Nancy Stepan for their respective responses to my prospectus and for their fruitful suggestions, which helped determine the ultimate shape of this volume. Candy Ruck, my administrative assistant, and Nicola Shilliam, my research assistant, combined their considerable talents for efficiency and innovation, enabling me to coordinate the editing of this volume while commuting for a semester between New Haven and Ithaca.

By allowing me to dedicate *"Race," Writing, and Difference* to Dominique de Menil, *Critical Inquiry* gracefully departs from previous practice. It does so for good reason. Dominique de Menil, born in Paris in 1908, has been for over five decades a central influence in the development of contemporary art. As the guiding force in assembling one of the world's great collections of art (soon to be housed in its own museum in Houston), as a highly regarded professor of the history of art, and as a patron of artists and scholars, Dominique de Menil has shaped, as much as has any individual, the direction of modern art and the lives of those who make it.

I wish to dedicate this special issue of *Critical Inquiry* to her, however, for still another reason. As the president of the Menil Foundation, for the past twenty-five years she has funded a project entitled "The Image of the Black in Western Art." This project, nearing completion, has produced three copious volumes of color reproduction and sophisticated historical commentary addressing the figure of the black person in Western art from 2500 B.C. to the twentieth century. Among other startling conclusions about the representation of the black Other in Western culture are the facts that black people and Europeans seem to have remained in fairly constant contact since Greco-Roman antiquity and that blacks were depicted in formal art in extraordinarily various ways—from gods, saints, and kings to devils, heathens, and slaves. Her support of liberal political causes, her early stand against racism and de jure segregation in the South, her antipathy toward apartheid, and her creation of the Truth and Freedom Awards for those whose humanitarian politics often led to imprisonment and death—all these are fitting analogues to her commitment to art.

It is for her consistent stand against those who would limit the human mind and spirit, for her concomitant affirmation of the nobility of the human spirit, for her philanthropic generosity, and for her example of the life of the mind well-lived that I dedicate *"Race," Writing, and Difference* to Dominique de Menil.

The publication of this volume would have been impossible without the continuing support and encouragement of W. J. T. Mitchell, Susan Olin, and Margaret Berg, whose knowledge of contemporary literary theory in its several subtle shades and complexions is matched only by their grace in shaping and editing the critical essay. That *Critical Inquiry* has opened its pages so generously to theorists of the so-called noncanonical literatures and to topics of broader interest than those of the Western tradition augurs well for scholars who wish to see the academic institution of literature and its criticism become *truly* a comparative and decolonized endeavor. I wish to thank the editors for this very important, and political, gesture.

Henry Louis Gates, Jr.

1. Hippolyte-Adolphe Taine, intro. to *The History of English Literature,* in *Criticism: The Major Texts,* ed. Walter Jackson Bate, enlarged ed. (New York, 1970), pp. 503–4.

2. Ibid., pp. 504, 505.

3. Abraham Lincoln, quoted in Michael P. Banton, *The Idea of Race* (Boulder, Colo., 1978), p. 1.

4. See the special issue *Canons, Critical Inquiry* 10 (Sept. 1983).

5. See I. A. Richards, intro. to Claude McKay, *"Spring in New Hampshire" and Other Poems* (London, 1920), and Allen Tate, intro. to Melvin B. Tolson, *The Libretto for the Republic of Liberia* (New York, 1953).

6. The "grandfather clause" was a provision in several southern state constitutions designed to enfranchise poor whites and disfranchise blacks by waiving high voting requirements for descendants of men voting before 1867.

7. Zora Neale Hurston, *Dust Tracks on a Road: An Autobiography,* 2d ed. (Urbana, Ill., 1984), p. 326.

8. *New York Times,* 9 Aug. 1985, p. A3; *New York Times,* 14 Aug. 1985, p. A3; *Ithaca Journal,* 9 Aug. 1985, p. 9; *Ithaca Journal,* 10 Aug. 1985, p. 8.

9. Phillis Wheatley, preface to *Poems on Various Subjects, Religious and Moral* (New York, 1985), p. vii.

10. Ibid.

11. William Bosman, *A New and Accurate Description of the Coast of Guinea* (1705; London, 1967), pp. 146, 147.

12. David Hume, "Of National Characters," *The Philosophical Works,* ed. Thomas Hill Green and Thomas Hodge Grose, 4 vols. (Darmstadt, 1964), 3:252 n. 1; my emphasis.

13. Immanuel Kant, *Observations on the Feeling of the Beautiful and Sublime,* trans. John T. Goldthwait (Berkeley and Los Angeles, 1960), p. 111.

14. Ibid., p. 113; my emphasis.

15. Mary Langdon, *Ida May: A Story of Things Actual and Possible* (Boston, 1854), p. 116.

16. See James Albert Ukawsaw Gronniosaw, *A Narrative of the Most Remarkable Particulars of the Life of James Albert Ukawsaw Gronniosaw, An African Prince* (Bath, 1770); John Marrant, *Narrative of the Lord's Wonderful Dealings with John Marrant, A Black* (London, 1785); Ottabah Cugoano, *Thoughts and Sentiments on the Evil and Wicked Traffic of the Slavery and Commerce of the Human Species* (London, 1787); Olaudah Equiano, *The Interesting Narrative of the Life of Olaudah Equiano, or Gustavus Vassa, The African. Written by Himself* (London, 1789); and John Jea, *The Life and Sufferings of John Jea, An African Preacher* (Swansea, 1806).

17. Rebecca Cox Jackson, "A Dream of Three Books and a Holy One," *Gifts of Power: The Writings of Rebecca Jackson, Black Visionary, Shaker Eldress,* ed. Jean McMahon Humez (Amherst, Mass., 1981), pp. 146, 147.

18. Alice Walker, *The Color Purple* (New York, 1982), p. 179.

19. Anthony Appiah, "Strictures on Structures: The Prospects for a Structuralist Poetics of African Fiction," in *Black Literature and Literary Theory,* ed. Henry Louis Gates, Jr. (New York, 1984), pp. 146, 145; all further references to this work, abbreviated "S," will be included in the text.

20. Sigmund Freud, *The Standard Edition of the Complete Psychological Works of Sigmund Freud,* ed. and trans. James Strachey, 24 vols. (London, 1953–74), 20:212.

21. See Geoffrey H. Hartman, "Monsieur Texte," *Saving the Text: Literature/Derrida/Philosophy* (Baltimore, 1981), pp. 1–83.

The Uncompleted Argument: Du Bois and the Illusion of Race

Anthony Appiah

Introduction

Contemporary biologists are not agreed on the question of whether there are any human races, despite the widespread scientific consensus on the underlying genetics. For most purposes, however, we can reasonably treat this issue as terminological. What most people in most cultures ordinarily believe about the significance of "racial" difference is quite remote, I think, from what the biologists *are* agreed on. Every reputable biologist will agree that human genetic variability between the populations of Africa or Europe or Asia is not much greater than that within those populations; though *how much* greater depends, in part, on the measure of genetic variability the biologist chooses. If biologists want to make interracial difference seem relatively large, they can say that "the proportion of genic variation attributable to racial differences is . . . 9–11%."[1] If they want to make it seem small, they can say that, for two people who are both Caucasoid, the chances of difference in genetic constitution at one site on a given chromosome are currently estimated at about 14.3 percent, while for any two people taken at random from the human population, they are estimated at about 14.8 percent. (I will discuss why this is considered a measure of genetic difference in section 2.) The statistical facts about the distribution of variant characteristics in human populations and sub-populations are the same, whichever way the matter is expressed. Apart from the visible morphological characteristics of skin, hair, and bone, by which we are inclined to assign people to the broadest racial categories—

black, white, yellow—there are few genetic characteristics to be found in the population of England that are not found in similar proportions in Zaire or in China; and few too (though more) which are found in Zaire but not in similar proportions in China or in England. All this, I repeat, is part of the consensus (see "GR," pp. 1–59). A more familiar part of the consensus is that the differences between peoples in language, moral affections, aesthetic attitudes, or political ideology—those differences which most deeply affect us in our dealings with each other—are not biologically determined to any significant degree.

These claims will, no doubt, seem outrageous to those who confuse the question of whether biological difference accounts for our differences with the question of whether biological similarity accounts for our similarities. Some of our similarities as human beings in these broadly cultural respects—the capacity to acquire human languages, for example, or, more specifically, the ability to smile—*are* to a significant degree biologically determined. We can study the biological basis of these cultural capacities and give biological explanations of our exercise of them. But if biological difference between human beings is unimportant in these explanations—and it is—then racial difference, as a species of biological difference, will not matter either.

In this essay, I want to discuss the way in which W. E. B. Du Bois—who called his life story the "autobiography of a race concept"—came gradually, though never completely, to assimilate the unbiological nature of races. I have made these few prefatory remarks partly because it is my experience that the biological evidence about race is not sufficiently known and appreciated but also because they are important in discussing Du Bois. Throughout his life, Du Bois was concerned not just with the meaning of race but with the truth about it. We are more inclined at present, however, not to express our understanding of the intellectual development of people and cultures as a movement toward the truth; I shall sketch some of the reasons for this at the end of the essay. I will begin, therefore, by saying what I think the rough truth is about race, because, against the stream, I am disposed to argue that this struggle toward the truth is exactly what we find in the life of Du Bois, who can claim, in my view, to have thought longer, more engagedly, and more publicly about race than any other social theorist of our century.

Anthony Appiah is associate professor of philosophy at Cornell University. He is the author of *Assertion and Conditionals* (1985) and *For Truth in Semantics* (1986). In addition, he is at work on *African Reflections: Essays in the Philosophy of Culture*.

"The Conservation of Races"

Du Bois' first extended discussion of the concept of race is in "The Conservation of Races" (1897), a paper he delivered to the American Negro Academy in the year it was founded. The "American Negro," he declares, has "been led to . . . minimize race distinctions" because "back of most of the discussions of race with which he is familiar, have lurked certain assumptions as to his natural abilities, as to his political, intellectual and moral status, which he felt were wrong." Du Bois continues: "Nevertheless, in our calmer moments we must acknowledge that human beings are divided into races," even if when we "come to inquire into the essential difference of races we find it hard to come at once to any definite conclusion." For what it is worth, however, the "final word of science, so far, is that we have at least two, perhaps three, great families of human beings—the whites and Negroes, possibly the yellow race."[2]

Du Bois is not, however, satisfied with the final word of nineteenth-century science. For, as he thinks, what matter are not the "grosser physical differences of color, hair and bone" but the "differences—subtle, delicate and elusive, though they may be—which have silently but definitely separated men into groups" ("CR," p. 75).

> While these subtle forces have generally followed the natural cleavage of common blood, descent and physical peculiarities, they have at other times swept across and ignored these. At all times, however, they have divided human beings into races, which, while they perhaps transcend scientific definition, nevertheless, are clearly defined to the eye of the historian and sociologist.
>
> If this be true, then the history of the world is the history, not of individuals, but of groups, not of nations, but of races. . . . What, then, is a race? It is a vast family of human beings, generally of common blood and language, always of common history, traditions and impulses, who are both voluntarily and involuntarily striving together for the accomplishment of certain more or less vividly conceived ideals of life. ["CR," pp. 75–76]

We have moved, then, away from the "scientific"—that is, biological and anthropological—conception of race to a sociohistorical notion. Using this sociohistorical criterion—the sweep of which certainly encourages the thought that no biological or anthropological definition is possible— Du Bois considers that there are not three but eight "distinctly differentiated races, in the sense in which history tells us the word must be used" ("CR," p. 76). The list is an odd one: Slavs, Teutons, English (both in Great Britain and America), Negroes (of Africa and, likewise, America), the Romance race, Semites, Hindus and Mongolians.

The question now is: What is the real distinction between these nations? Is it the physical differences of blood, color and cranial measurements? Certainly we must all acknowledge that physical differences play a great part. . . . But while race differences have followed mainly physical race lines, yet no mere physical distinctions would really define or explain the deeper differences—the cohesiveness and continuity of these groups. The deeper differences are spiritual, psychical, differences—undoubtedly based on the physical, but infinitely transcending them. ["CR," p. 77]

Each of the various races is

striving, . . . in its own way, to develop for civilization its particular message, its particular ideal, which shall help to guide the world nearer and nearer that perfection of human life for which we all long, that "one far off Divine event." ["CR," p. 78]

For Du Bois, then, the problem for the Negro is the discovery and expression of the message of his or her race.

The full, complete Negro message of the whole Negro race has not as yet been given to the world.
   The question is, then: how shall this message be delivered; how shall these various ideals be realized? The answer is plain: by the development of these race groups, not as individuals, but as races. . . . For the development of Negro genius, of Negro literature and art, of Negro spirit, only Negroes bound and welded together, Negroes inspired by one vast ideal, can work out in its fullness the great message we have for humanity.
   For this reason, the advance guard of the Negro people—the eight million people of Negro blood in the United States of America—must soon come to realize that if they are to take their just place in the van of Pan-Negroism, then their destiny is *not* absorption by the white Americans. ["CR," pp. 78, 79][3]

Du Bois ends by proposing his Academy Creed, which begins with words that echo down almost a century of American race relations:

1. We believe that the Negro people, as a race, have a contribution to make to civilization and humanity, which no other race can make.
2. We believe it the duty of the Americans of Negro descent, as a body, to maintain their race identity until this mission of the Negro people is accomplished, and the ideal of human brotherhood has become a practical possibility. ["CR," p. 84]

What can we make of this analysis and prescription?

On the face of it, Du Bois' argument in "The Conservation of Races" is that "race" is not a scientific—that is, biological—concept. It is a sociohistorical concept. Sociohistorical races each have a "message" for humanity—a message which derives, in some way, from God's purpose in creating races. The Negro race has still to deliver its full message, and so it is the duty of Negroes to work together—through race organizations— so that this message can be delivered.

We do not need the theological underpinnings of this argument. What is essential is the thought that through common action Negroes can achieve, by virtue of their sociohistorical community, worthwhile ends which will not otherwise be achieved. On the face of it, then, Du Bois' strategy here is the antithesis in the classic dialectic of reaction to prejudice.

The thesis in this dialectic—which Du Bois reports as the American Negro's attempt to "minimize race distinctions"—is the denial of difference. Du Bois' antithesis is the acceptance of difference, along with a claim that each group has its part to play; that the white race and its racial Other are related not as superior to inferior but as complementaries; that the Negro message is, with the white one, part of the message of humankind.

I call this pattern the classic dialectic for a simple reason: we find it in feminism also—on the one hand, a simple claim to equality, a denial of substantial difference; on the other, a claim to a special message, revaluing the feminine Other not as the helpmeet of sexism, but as the New Woman.

Because this *is* a classic dialectic, my reading of Du Bois' argument is a natural one. I believe that it is substantially correct. But to see that it is correct, we need to make clear that what Du Bois attempts, despite his own claims to the contrary, is not the transcendence of the nineteenth-century scientific conception of race—as we shall see, he relies on it— but rather, as the dialectic requires, a revaluation of the Negro race in the face of the sciences of racial inferiority. We can begin by analyzing the sources of tension in Du Bois' allegedly sociohistorical conception of race, which he explicitly sets over against the scientific conception. The tension is plain enough in his references to "common blood"; for this, dressed up with fancy craniometry, a dose of melanin, and some measure for hair-curl, is what the scientific notion amounts to. If he has fully transcended the scientific notion, what is the role of this talk about "blood"?

We may leave aside for the moment the common "impulses" and the voluntary and involuntary "strivings." These must be due either to a shared biological inheritance, "based on the physical, but infinitely transcending" it; to a shared history; or, of course, to some combination of these. If Du Bois' notion is purely sociohistorical, then the issue is common history and traditions; otherwise, the issue is, at least in part, a common biology. We shall know which only when we understand the core of Du Bois' conception of race.

The claim that a race generally shares a common language is also plainly inessential: the "Romance" race is not of common language nor, more obviously, is the Negro. And "common blood" can mean little more than "of shared ancestry," which is already implied by talk of a "vast family." At the center of Du Bois' conception, then, is the claim that a race is "a vast family of human beings, . . . always of common history [and] traditions." So, if we want to understand Du Bois, our question must be: What is a family of common history?

We already see that the scientific notion, which presupposes common features in virtue of a common biology derived from a common descent, is not fully transcended. A family can, it is true, have adopted children, kin by social rather than biological law. By analogy, therefore, a vast human family might contain people joined not by biology but by an act of choice. But it is plain that Du Bois cannot have been contemplating this possibility: like all of his contemporaries, he would have taken for granted that race is a matter of birth. Indeed, to understand the talk of "family," we must distance ourselves from its sociological meaning. A family is almost always culturally defined only through either patrilineal or matrilineal descent. But if an individual drew a "conceptual" family tree back over five hundred years and assumed that he or she was descended from each ancestor in only one way, it would have more than a million branches at the top. Although, in such a case, many individuals would be represented by more than one branch—that far back we are all going to be descended from many people by more than one route—it is plain that either a matrilineal or patrilineal conception of our family histories drastically underrepresents the biological range of our ancestry. Biology and social convention go startlingly different ways. Let's pretend, secure in our republicanism, that the claim of the queen of England to the throne depends partly on a single line from one of her ancestors nine hundred years ago. If there were no overlaps in her family tree, there would be more than fifty thousand billion such lines, though there have never been that many people on the earth; even with reasonable assumptions about overlaps, there are millions of such lines. We chose one line, even though most of the population of England is probably descended from William the Conqueror by *some* uncharted route. Biology is democratic: all parents are equal. Thus, to speak of two people as being of common ancestry requires that, before some historical point in the past, a large proportion of the branches in their respective family trees coincided.[4]

Already, then, Du Bois requires, as the scientific conception does, a common ancestry (in the sense just defined) with whatever—if anything—that ancestry biologically entails. But apparently this does not commit him to the scientific conception, for there are many groups of common ancestry—ranging from humanity in general to narrower groups such as the Slavs, Teutons, and Romance people taken together—which do not, for Du Bois, constitute races. Thus, Du Bois' "common history," which must be what is supposed to distinguish Slav from Teuton, is an essential part of his conception. The problem is whether a common history can be a criterion which distinguishes one group of human beings—extended in time—from another. Does adding a notion of common history allow us to make the distinctions between Slav and Teuton or between English and Negro? The answer is no.

Consider, for example, Du Bois himself. As the descendant of Dutch ancestors, why doesn't his relation to the history of Holland in the fourteenth century (which he shares with all people of Dutch descent) make him a member of the Teutonic race? The answer is straightforward: the Dutch were not Negroes; Du Bois is. But it follows from this that the history of Africa is part of the common history of Afro-Americans not simply because Afro-Americans descended from various peoples who played a part in African history but rather because African history is the history of people of the same race.

My general point is this: in order to recognize two events at different times as part of the history of a single individual, we have to have a criterion for identity of the individual at each of those times, independent of his or her participation in the two events. In the same way, when we recognize two events as belonging to the history of one race, we have to have a criterion for membership in the race at those two times, independent of the participation of the members in the two events. To put it more simply: sharing a common group history cannot be a criterion for being members of the same group, for we would have to be able to identify the group in order to identify *its* history. Someone in the fourteenth century could share a common history with me through our membership in a historically extended race only if something accounts both for his or her membership in the race in the fourteenth century and for mine in the twentieth. That something cannot, on pain of circularity, be the history of the race. Whatever holds Du Bois' races together conceptually cannot be a common history; it is only because they are bound together that members of a race at different times can share a history at all. If this is true, Du Bois' reference to a common history cannot be doing any work in his individuation of races. And once we have stripped away the sociohistorical elements from Du Bois' definition of race, we are left with the true criterion.

Consequently, not only the talk of language, which Du Bois admits is neither necessary (the Romance race speaks many languages) nor sufficient (Afro-Americans and Americans generally speak the same language) for racial identity, must be expunged from the definition; now we have seen that talk of common history and traditions must go too. We are left with common descent and the common impulses and strivings that I put aside earlier. Since common descent and the characteristics which flow from it are part of the scientific conception of race, these impulses are all that remain to do the job that Du Bois had claimed for a sociohistorical conception: namely, to distinguish his conception from the biological one. Du Bois claims that the existence of races is "clearly defined to the eye of the historian and sociologist" ("CR," p. 75). Since biology acknowledges common ancestry as a criterion, whatever extra insight is provided by sociohistorical understanding can be gained only by observing the common impulses and strivings. Reflection suggests, however, that this cannot be true. For what common impulses—whether voluntary or involuntary—do the Romance people share that the Teutons and the English do not?

Du Bois had read the historiography of the Anglo-Saxon school, which accounted for the democratic impulse in America by the racial tradition of the Anglo-Saxon moot. He had read American and British historians in earnest discussion of the "Latin" spirit of Romance peoples; and perhaps he had believed some of it. Here perhaps may be the source of the notion that history and sociology can observe the differing impulses of races.

In all these writings, however, such impulses are allegedly discovered to be the a posteriori properties of racial and national groups, not criteria of membership in them. It is, indeed, because the claim is a posteriori that historical evidence is relevant to it. And if we ask what common impulses history has detected which allow us to recognize the Negro, we shall see that Du Bois' claim to have found a criterion of identity in these impulses is mere bravado. If, without evidence about his or her impulses, we can say who is a Negro, then it cannot be part of what it is to be a Negro that he or she has them; rather, it must be an a posteriori claim that people of a common race, defined by descent and biology, have impulses, for whatever reason, in common. Of course, the common impulses of a biologically defined group may be historically caused by common experiences, common history. But Du Bois' claim can only be that biologically defined races happen to share, for whatever reason, common impulses. The common impulses cannot be a criterion of group membership. And if that is so, we are left with the scientific conception.

How, then, is it possible for Du Bois' criteria to issue in eight groups, while the scientific conception issues in three? The reason is clear from the list. Slavs, Teutons, English, Hindus, and Romance peoples each live in a characteristic geographical region. (American English—and, for that matter, American Teutons, American Slavs, and American Romance people—share recent ancestry with their European "cousins" and thus share a relation to a place and certain languages and traditions.) Semites and Mongolians each inhabit a rather larger geographical region also. Du Bois' talk of common history conceals his superaddition of a geographical criterion: group history is, in part, the history of people who have lived in the same place.[5]

The criterion Du Bois actually uses amounts to this: people are members of the same race if they share features in virtue of being descended largely from people of the same region. Those features may be physical—hence Afro-Americans are Negroes—or cultural—hence Anglo-Americans are English. Focusing on one sort of feature—"grosser . . . differences of color, hair and bone"—defines "whites and Negroes, possibly the yellow race" as the "final word of science, so far." Focusing on a different feature—language or shared customs—defines instead Teutons, Slavs, and Romance peoples. The tension in Du Bois' definition of race reflects the fact that, for the purposes of European historiography (of which his Harvard and University of Berlin training had made him aware), it was the latter that mattered; but for the purposes of American social and political life, it was the former.

The real difference in Du Bois' conception, therefore, is not that his definition of race is at odds with the scientific one. It is, rather, as the classic dialectic requires, that he assigns to race a moral and metaphysical significance different from that of his contemporaries. The distinctive claim is that the Negro race has a positive message, a message not only of difference but of value. And that, it seems to me, is the significance of the sociohistorical dimension: the strivings of a race are, as Du Bois viewed the matter, the stuff of history.

> The history of the world is the history, not of individuals, but of groups, not of nations, but of races, and he who ignores or seeks to override the race idea in human history ignores and overrides the central thought of all history. ["CR," p. 75]

By studying history, we can discern the outlines of the message of each race.

"Crisis": August 1911

We have seen that, for the purpose that concerned him most—understanding the status of the Negro—Du Bois was thrown back on the scientific definition of race, which he officially rejected. But the scientific definition (Du Bois' uneasiness with which is reflected in his remark that races "perhaps transcend scientific definition") was itself threatened as he spoke at the first meeting of the Negro Academy. In the later nineteenth century most thinking people (like too many even today) believed that what Du Bois called the "grosser differences" were a sign of an inherited racial essence which accounted for the intellectual and moral deficiency of the "lower" races. In "The Conservation of Races" Du Bois elected, in effect, to admit that color was a sign of a racial essence but to deny that the cultural capacities of the black-skinned, curly-haired members of humankind were inferior to those of the white-skinned, straighter-haired ones. But the collapse of the sciences of racial inferiority led Du Bois to deny the connection between cultural capacity and gross morphology—the familiar impulses and strivings of his earlier definition.

We can find evidence of his change of mind in an article in the August 1911 issue of the *Crisis*.

> The leading scientists of the world have come forward[6] . . . and laid down in categorical terms a series of propositions which may be summarized as follows:
>   1. (a) It is not legitimate to argue from differences in physical characteristics to differences in mental characteristics. . . .
>   2. The civilization of a . . . race at any particular moment of time offers no index to its innate or inherited capacities.[7]

These results have been amply confirmed since then. And we do well, I think, to remind ourselves of the current picture.

Human characteristics are genetically determined, to the extent that they are determined, by sequences of DNA in the chromosome—in other words, by genes.[8] The region of a chromosome occupied by a gene is called a locus. Some loci are occupied in different members of a population by different genes, each of which is called an allele; and a locus is said to be polymorphic in a population if there is at least one pair of alleles for it. Perhaps as many as half the loci in the human population are polymorphic; the rest, naturally enough, are monomorphic.

Many loci have not just two alleles but several, and each has a frequency in the population. Suppose a particular locus has n alleles, which we can call 1, 2, and so on up to n; then we can call their frequencies $x_1, x_2, \ldots ,$ to x_n. If we consider two randomly chosen members of a population and look at the same locus on one chromosome of each of them, the probability that they'll have the same allele at that locus is just the probability that they'll both have the first allele (x_1^2), plus the probability that they'll both have the second (x_2^2), plus the probability that they'll both have the nth (x_n^2). We can call this number the expected homozygosity at that locus: for it is just the proportion of people in the population who would be homozygous at that locus—having identical alleles at that locus on each of the relevant chromosomes—provided the population is mating at random.[9]

Now if we take the average value of the expected homozygosity for all loci, polymorphic and monomorphic (which, for some reason, tends to get labeled J), we have a measure of the chance that two people, taken at random from the population, will share the same allele at a locus on a chromosome taken at random. This is a good measure of how similar a randomly chosen pair of individuals should be expected to be in their biology *and* a good (though rough) guide to how closely the populations are genetically related.

I can now express simply one measure of the extent to which members of these human populations we call races differ more from each other than they do from members of the same race. For example, the value of J for Caucasoids—based largely on samples from the English population—is estimated to be about 0.857, while that for the whole human population is estimated at 0.852.[10] The chances, in other words, that two people taken at random from the human population will have the same characteristic at a locus, are about 85.2 percent, while the chances for two (white) people taken from the population of England are about 85.7 percent. And since 85.2 is 100 minus 14.8 and 85.7 is 100 minus 14.3, this is equivalent to what I said in the introduction: the chances of two people who are both Caucasoid differing in genetic constitution at one site on a given chromosome are about 14.3 percent, while, for any two people taken at random from the human population, they are about 14.8 percent. The conclusion is obvious: given only a person's race, it is hard to say what his or her biological characteristics will be, except in respect of the "grosser" features of color, hair, and bone (the genetics of which are, in any case, rather poorly understood)—features of "morphological differentiation," as the evolutionary biologist would say. As Nei and Roychoudhury express themselves, somewhat coyly, "The extent of genic differentiation between human races is not always correlated with the degree of morphological differentiation" ("GR," p. 44).

To establish that race is relatively unimportant in explaining biological differences between people, where biological difference is measured in the proportion of differences in loci on the chromosome, is not yet to show that race is unimportant in explaining cultural difference. It could be that large differences in intellectual or moral capacity are caused by differences at very few loci and that, at these loci, all (or most) black-skinned people differ from all (or most) white-skinned or yellow-skinned ones. As it happens, there is little evidence for any such proposition and much against it. But suppose we had reason to believe it. In the biological conception of the human organism, in which characteristics are determined by the pattern of genes in interaction with environments, it is the presence of the alleles (which give rise to these moral and intellectual capacities) that accounts for the observed differences in those capacities in people in similar environments. So the characteristic racial morphology—skin and hair and bone—could only be a sign of those differences if it were (highly) correlated with those alleles. Furthermore, even if it were so correlated, the causal explanation of the differences would be that they differed in those alleles, not that they differed in race. Since there are no such strong correlations, even those who think that intellectual and moral character are strongly genetically determined must accept that *race* is at best a poor indicator of capacity.

But it was earlier evidence, pointing similarly to the conclusion that "the genic variation within and between the three major races of man . . . is small compared with the intraracial variation" ("GR," p. 40) and that differences in morphology were not correlated strongly with intellectual and moral capacity, which led Du Bois in the *Crisis* to an explicit rejection of the claim that biological race mattered for understanding the status of the Negro:

> So far at least as intellectual and moral aptitudes are concerned, we ought to speak of civilizations where we now speak of races. . . . Indeed, even the physical characteristics, excluding the skin color of a people, are to no small extent the direct result of the physical and social environment under which it is living. . . . These physical characteristics are furthermore too indefinite and elusive to serve as a basis for any rigid classification or division of human groups.[11]

This is straightforward enough. Yet it would be too swift a conclusion to suppose that Du Bois here expresses his deepest convictions. After 1911, he went on to advocate Pan-Africanism, as he had advocated Pan-Negroism in 1897, and whatever Afro-Americans and Africans, from Ashanti to Zulu, share, it is not a single civilization.

Du Bois managed to maintain Pan-Africanism while officially rejecting talk of race as anything other than a synonym for color. We can see how he did this by turning to his second autobiography, *Dusk of Dawn,* published in 1940.

"Dusk of Dawn"

In *Dusk of Dawn*—the "essay toward an autobiography of a race concept"—Du Bois explicitly allies himself with the claim that race is not a scientific concept.

> It is easy to see that scientific definition of race is impossible; it is easy to prove that physical characteristics are not so inherited as to make it possible to divide the world into races; that ability is the monopoly of no known aristocracy; that the possibilities of human development cannot be circumscribed by color, nationality, or any conceivable definition of race.[12]

But we need no scientific definition, for

> all this has nothing to do with the plain fact that throughout the world today organized groups of men by monopoly of economic

and physical power, legal enactment and intellectual training are limiting with determination and unflagging zeal the development of other groups; and that the concentration particularly of economic power today puts the majority of mankind into a slavery to the rest. [*D*, pp. 137–38]

Or, as he puts it pithily a little later,

the black man is a person who must ride "Jim Crow" in Georgia. [*D*, p. 153]

Yet, just a few pages earlier, he has explained why he remains a Pan-Africanist, committed to a political program which binds all this indefinable black race together. The passage is worth citing extensively.

Du Bois begins with Countée Cullen's question, "What is Africa to me?" and answers,

Once I should have answered the question simply: I should have said "fatherland" or perhaps better "motherland" because I was born in the century when the walls of race were clear and straight; when the world consisted of mut[u]ally exclusive races; and even though the edges might be blurred, there was no question of exact definition and understanding of the meaning of the word. . . .

Since then [the writing of "The Conservation of Races"] the concept of race has so changed and presented so much of contradiction that as I face Africa I ask myself: what is it between us that constitutes a tie which I can feel better than I can explain? Africa is, of course, my fatherland. Yet neither my father nor my father's father ever saw Africa or knew its meaning or cared overmuch for it. My mother's folk were closer and yet their direct connection, in culture and race, became tenuous; still, my tie to Africa is strong. On this vast continent were born and lived a large portion of my direct ancestors going back a thousand years or more. The mark of their heritage is upon me in color and hair. These are obvious things, but of little meaning in themselves; only important as they stand for real and more subtle differences from other men. Whether they do or not, I do not know nor does science know today.

But one thing is sure and that is the fact that since the fifteenth century these ancestors of mine and their other descendants have had a common history; have suffered a common disaster and have one long memory. The actual ties of heritage between the individuals of this group, vary with the ancestors that they have in common [with] many others: Europeans and Semites, perhaps Mongolians, certainly American Indians. But the physical bond is least and the badge of color relatively unimportant save as a badge; the real essence of this kinship is its social heritage of slavery; the discrimination and insult; and this heritage binds together not simply the children of Africa, but extends through yellow Asia and into the

South Seas. It is this unity that draws me to Africa. [*D*, pp. 116–17]

This passage is affecting, powerfully expressed. We might like to be able to follow it in its conclusions. But we should not; since the passage seduces us into error, we should begin distancing ourselves from the appeal of its argument by noticing how it echoes an earlier text. Color and hair are unimportant save "as they stand for real and more subtle differences," Du Bois says here, and we recall the "subtle forces" that "generally followed the natural cleavage of common blood, descent and physical peculiarities" of "The Conservation of Races." There it was an essential part of the argument that these subtle forces—"impulses" and "strivings"—were the common property of those who shared a "common blood"; here, Du Bois does "not know nor does science" whether this is so. But if it is not so, then, on Du Bois' own admission, these "obvious things" are "of little meaning." If they are of little meaning, then his mention of them marks, on the surface of his argument, the extent to which he cannot quite escape the appeal of the earlier conception of race.

Du Bois' yearning for the earlier conception which he prohibited himself from using accounts for the pathos of the gap between the unconfident certainty that Africa is "of course" his fatherland and the concession that it is not the land of his father or his father's father. What use is such a fatherland? What use is a motherland with which your own mother's connection is "tenuous"? What does it matter that a large portion of his ancestors have lived on that vast continent, if there is no subtler bond with them than brute—that is, culturally unmediated—biological descent and its entailed "badge" of hair and color?

Even in the passage that follows Du Bois' explicit disavowal of the scientific conception of race, the references to "common history"—the "one long memory," the "social heritage of slavery"—only lead us back into the now familiar move of substituting a sociohistorical conception of race for the biological one; but that is simply to bury the biological conception below the surface, not to transcend it. Because he never truly "speaks of civilization," Du Bois cannot ask if there is not in American culture—which undoubtedly *is* his—an African residue to take hold of and rejoice in, a subtle connection mediated not by genetics but by intentions, by meaning. Du Bois has no more conceptual resources here for explicating the unity of the Negro race—the Pan-African identity—than he had in "The Conservation of Races" half a century earlier. A glorious non sequitur must be submerged in the depths of the argument. It is easily brought to the surface.

If what Du Bois has in common with Africa is a history of "discrimination and insult," then this binds him, by his own account, to "yellow Asia and . . . the South Seas" also. How can something he shares with the whole nonwhite world bind him to only a part of it? Once we interrogate the argument here, a further suspicion arises that the claim to this bond may be based on a hyperbolic reading of the facts. Du Bois' experience of "discrimination and insult" in his American childhood and as an adult citizen of the industrialized world was different in character from that experienced by, say, Kwame Nkrumah in colonized West Africa; it is absent altogether in large parts of "yellow Asia." What Du Bois shares with the nonwhite world is not insult but the *badge* of insult; and the badge, without the insult, is the very skin and hair and bone which it is impossible to connect with a scientific definition of race.

Concluding Unscientific Postscript

Du Bois died in Nkrumah's Ghana, led there by the dream of Pan-Africanism and the reality of American racism. If he escaped that racism, he never completed the escape from race. The logic of his argument leads naturally to the final repudiation of race as a term of difference and to speaking instead "of civilizations where we now speak of races." The logic is the same logic that has brought us to speak of genders where we spoke of sexes, and a rational assessment of the evidence requires that we should endorse not only the logic but the premises of each argument. I have only sketched the evidence for these premises in the case of race, but it is all there in the scientific journals. Discussing Du Bois has been largely a pretext for adumbrating the argument he never quite managed to complete.

I think the argument worth making because I believe that we—scholars in the academy—have not done enough to share it with our fellow citizens. One barrier facing those of us in the humanities has been methodological. Under Saussurian hegemony, we have too easily become accustomed to thinking of meaning as constituted by systems of differences purely internal to our endlessly structured *langues*.[13] Race, we all assume, is, like all other concepts, constructed by metaphor and metonymy; it stands in, metonymically, for the Other; it bears the weight, metaphorically, of other kinds of difference.

Yet, in our social lives away from the text-world of the academy, we take reference for granted too easily. Even if the concept of race *is* a structure of oppositions—white opposed to black (but also to yellow), Jew opposed to Gentile (but also to Arab)—it is a structure whose realization is, at best, problematic and, at worst, impossible. If we can now hope to understand the concept embodied in this system of oppositions, we are nowhere near finding referents for it. The truth is that there are no races: there is nothing in the world that can do all we ask "race" to do for us. The evil that is done is done by the concept and by easy—yet impossible—assumptions as to its application. What we miss through our obsession with the structure of relations of concepts is, simply, reality.

Talk of "race" is particularly distressing for those of us who take culture seriously. For, where race works—in places where "gross differences" of morphology are correlated with "subtle differences" of temperament, belief, and intention—it works as an attempt at a metonym for culture; and it does so only at the price of biologizing what *is* culture, or ideology. To call it "biologizing" is not to consign our concept of race to biology. What is present there is not our concept but our word only. Even the biologists who believe in human races use the term "race," as they say, "without any social implication" ("GR," p. 4). What exists "out there" in the world—communities of meaning, shading variously into each other in the rich structure of the social world—is the province not of biology but of hermeneutic understanding.

I have examined these issues through the writings of Du Bois, with the burden of his scholarly inheritance, and have tried to transcend the system of oppositions which, had Du Bois accepted it, would have left him opposed to the (white) norm of form and value. In his early work, Du Bois took race for granted and sought to revalue one pole of the opposition of white to black. The received concept is a hierarchy, a vertical structure, and Du Bois wished to rotate the axis, to give race a "horizontal" reading. Challenge the assumption that there can be an axis, however oriented in the space of values, and the project fails for loss of presuppositions. In his later work, Du Bois—whose life's work was, in a sense, an attempt at just this impossible project—was unable to escape the notion of race he had explicitly rejected. We may borrow his own metaphor: though he saw the dawn coming, he never faced the sun. And we must surely admit that he is followed in this by many in our culture today; we too live in the dusk of that dawn.

1. Masatoshi Nei and Arun K. Roychoudhury, "Genetic Relationship and Evolution of Human Races," *Evolutionary Biology* 14 (1983): 11; all further references to this work, abbreviated "GR," will be included in the text.

2. W. E. B. Du Bois, "The Conservation of Races," *W. E. B. Du Bois Speaks: Speeches and Addresses, 1890–1919,* ed. Philip S. Foner (1897; New York, 1970), pp. 73, 74, 75; all further references to this work, abbreviated "CR," will be included in the text.

3. This talk of racial absorption (and similar talk of racial extinction) reflects the idea that Afro-Americans might disappear because their genetic heritage would be diluted by the white one. This idea might be considered absurd in any view propounding the notion of a racial essence: either a person has it or they don't. But this way of thinking conceives of racial essences as being like genes, though Mendelian genetics was not yet "rediscovered" when Du Bois wrote this piece. Du Bois is probably thinking of "passing for white"; in views of inheritance as the blending of parental "blood," the more that black "blood" is diluted, the more it is likely that *every* person of African descent in America *could* pass for white. That, of course, would be a kind of extinction of the Negro. It is interesting that

those who discussed this issue assumed that it would not cause the extinction of the white race also and the creation of a "hybridized" human race. But, as I say, such speculation is ruled out by the rise of Mendelian genetics.

4. I owe this way of thinking about the distance between social and biological ancestry to chapter 6 of R. B. Le Page and A. Tabouret-Keller's forthcoming book, *Acts of Identity.* I am very grateful to Professor Le Page for allowing me to see a typescript.

5. This seems to me the very notion that the biologists have ended up with: a population is a group of people (or, more generally, organisms) occupying a common region (or, more generally, an environmental niche), along with people largely descended from that original group who now live in other regions. See Nei and Roychoudhury, "Gene Differences between Caucasian, Negro, and Japanese Populations," *Science* 177 (Aug. 1972): 434–35, and "Genetic Relationship," p. 4.

6. This claim was prompted by G. Spiller; see *Papers in Inter-Racial Problems Communicated to the First Universal Races Congress Held at the University of London, July 26–29, 1911,* ed. Spiller (1911; Secaucus, N.J., 1970).

7. Du Bois, "Races," *Crisis,* August 1911, pp. 157–58.

8. Strictly we should say that the character of an organism is fixed by genes, along with sequences of nucleic acid in the cytoplasm and some other features of the cytoplasm of the ovum. But these latter sources of human characteristics are largely swamped by the nucleic DNA and are, in any case, substantially similar in almost all people. It is the latter fact that accounts, I think, for their not being generally mentioned.

9. It follows from these definitions that where a locus is monomorphic, the expected homozygosity is going to be one.

10. These figures come from Nei and Roychoudhury, "Genetic Relationship," and I have used the figures derived from looking at proteins, not blood-groups, since they claim these are likely to be more reliable. I have chosen a measure of "racial" biological difference that makes it look spectacularly small, but I would not wish to imply that it is not the case, as these authors say, that "genetic differentiation is real and generally statistically highly significant" (pp. 8, 11, 41). I would dispute their claim that their work shows the existence of a biological basis for the classification of human races; what it shows is that human populations differ in their distributions of genes. That *is* a biological fact. The objection to using this fact as a basis of a system of classification is that far too many people don't fit into just one category that can be so defined.

11. Du Bois, "Races," p. 158.

12. Du Bois, *Dusk of Dawn: An Essay toward an Autobiography of a Race Concept* (1940; New York, 1975), p. 137. All further references to this work, abbreviated *D*, will be included in the text.

13. Post-structuralism is not a step forward here, as Terry Eagleton has observed (see *Literary Theory: An Introduction* [Oxford, 1983], pp. 143–44).

An Ideology of Difference

Edward W. Said

1

The Israeli invasion of Lebanon in 1982 seems to have broken, for the first time, the immunity from sustained criticism previously enjoyed by Israel and its American supporters. For a variety of reasons, Israel's status in European and American public life and discourse has always been special, just as the position of Jews in the West has always been special, sometimes for its tragedy and horrendous suffering, at other times for its uniquely impressive intellectual and aesthetic triumphs. On behalf of Israel, anomalous norms, exceptional arguments, eccentric claims were (and still are) made, all of them forcibly conveying the notion that Israel does not entirely belong to the world of normal politics. Nevertheless, Israel—and, with it, Zionism—had gained this unusual status *politically*, not miraculously: it merged with a variety of currents in the West whose power and attractiveness for supporters of Israel effaced anything as concrete as, for example, an Israeli policy of rigid separation between Jew and non-Jew, or a military rule over hundreds of thousands of Arabs that was as repressive as any tyranny in Latin America or Eastern Europe. There are any number of credible accounts of this, from daily fare in the Israeli press to studies by Amnesty International, to reports by various U.N. bodies, Western journalists, church groups, and, not least, dissenting supporters of Israel. In other words, even though Israel was a Jewish state established by force on territory already inhabited by a native population largely of Muslim Arabs, in a part of the world overwhelmingly

Muslim and Arab, it appeared to most of Israel's supporters in the West (from which Zionism increasingly drew its greatest help) that the Palestinian Arabs who paid a large part of the price for Israel's establishment were neither relevant nor necessarily even real. What changed in 1982 was that the distance between Arab and Jew was for the first time perceived more or less universally as not so great and, indeed, that any consideration of Israel, and any perception of Israel at all, would have to include some consideration of the Palestinian Arabs, their travail, their claims, their humanity.

Changes of this sort seem to occur dramatically, although it is more accurate to comprehend them as complex, cumulative, often contradictory processes occurring over a long period of time. Above all else, however, no such process can be viewed neutrally, since for better or for worse there are many interests at work in it and, therefore, many interests also at work whenever it is interpreted or reported. Moreover, while it is worthwhile and even possible to reduce and curtail the gross pressure of those interests for the purpose of analysis or reflection, it is useless to deny that any such analysis is inevitably *grounded in,* or inevitably affiliated to, a particular historical moment and a specific political situation.

I repeat these truisms because, as I noted above, discussions of Israel and of Zionism have regularly been conducted as if the actualities of interpretation either could be suspended or did not obtain. Why and how this has been so is one of the themes of this essay, but first we must plant ourselves squarely on some historical and existential realities. I shall begin with a few basic points.

1. Even though most of what is said either "for" or "against" Israel is debatable, there is common consent on one major point: Israel was established in 1948 as a Jewish state. In this context, "Jewish" must be construed as different from "Christian" or "Muslim," on the one hand, and different from "French," "Arab," "Chinese," or "British," on the other. How it was established, what existed in Palestine before its establishment, what justified its establishment, what forces brought it about—all these are matters of immense controversy and/or justification. But no one, so far as I know, disputes the Jewishness *in intent* of Israel, for in this lies its uniqueness and, to the contemporary Palestinians, *their* uniqueness

Edward W. Said, Parr Professor of English and Comparative Literature at Columbia University, is the author of, among other works, *The Question of Palestine* (1979), *The World, the Text, and the Critic* (1983), and *After the Last Sky* (1986).

with regard to the Jewish state. A Jewish state is on national, religious, cultural, juridical, and political grounds different from any other state.

2. In its own public and juridical practice as well as in its international operations, Israel is the state of "the Jewish people," not a sovereign, independent state of its citizens, non-Jew and Jew alike. This was a matter discussed and resolved in the earliest period of Israel's existence. During that time it was decided in the People's Council debates that, as a state, Israel would not and could not be independent of *all the Jewish people*, Israeli and non-Israeli.[1] The result has been that the non-Jewish Israeli has fundamentally fewer rights than Jewish Israeli members of the Jewish people: the inequity between Jew and non-Jew in Israel is therefore radically antidemocratic, as Rabbi Meir Kahane has had the boldness to proclaim. Moreover, even though Israel has no constitution and no fully declared international boundaries, its Basic Laws press the claim for Jewishness on "the Land of Israel" with unmistakable clarity. One example will stand for many: the Law of Return and, with it, the Nationality Law together stipulate that any (but only a) Jew anywhere is entitled to immigrate to Israel and to acquire Israeli citizenship or nationality. No Palestinian— who in this formula is reduced to the status of "non-Jew"—has any such right, not even if he/she has had generations of family resident in Palestine. But, to add to the problem, even liberal Zionists have great difficulty in admitting this fact.

3. Yet there are—also according to both Israeli and Arab rhetoric and practice—non-Jews in Israel. About their status, their history, their national as well as political identity, their intentions, their present situation, much controversy has raged. Nevertheless, two things can be agreed on: first, that these people are, in fact, non-Jews and therefore separated from and in numerous ways different from Jews in the Jewish state; second, that a vast preponderance of the world's population (themselves included) refers to them as "Palestinians"—that is, present or former native Arab inhabitants of what is now referred to as "historical Palestine" (because it does not exist today, although it once did).

Beyond these three observations, very little can normally be said without contest, challenge, and debate. Later I shall bring up two very recent books symptomatic, at this late date, of the desire to maintain that Palestinians do not exist or that, if their existence is granted, they are considered to be "different," a murderous race of mindless fanatics. "Difference" is a crucial issue, central to many recent theoretical and interpretive discussions. One can, however, declare oneself *for* difference (as opposed to sameness or homogenization) without at the same time being for the rigidly enforced and policed separation of populations into different groups. As a touchstone for examining the political issues raised by difference, we can use a combination of two commonly held positions.

The first is the uncontroversially accepted view, based on experience and common sense, that all social situations—and, hence, all populations, states, and groupings—are *in fact* mixed. Thus there cannot be any such thing as a pure race, a pure nation, or a pure collectivity, regardless of patriotic, ideological, or religious argument. A corollary to this is that all efforts (particularly the efforts of governments or states) to purify one or several of these human agglomerations are tantamount to organized discrimination or persecution: the examples of Nazi Germany and South Africa argue the force of such a judgment with considerable authority in today's world.

Second, we have the U.N. Declaration on the Elimination of All Forms of Racial Discrimination (20 December 1963), which proscribes all forms of segregation, separation, and discrimination on the basis of race, color, religion, or national origin. The declaration's premise is, of course, that all modern states are composed of mixed populations. Both Israel and the United States, among most U.N. member states, subscribed to this and voted to confirm the declaration.

The Palestinian argument, insofar as there is a unified one, contends that not only is it manifestly the case that different national, ethnic, and religious groups exist but that no one has an inherent right to use difference as an instrument to relegate the rights of others to an inferior or lesser status. (Not incidentally, Palestinians employ this argument not just against Israel but also against the Arab states which, almost without exception, have over time created a separate set of laws for resident and transient Palestinians.) In contrast, the Jewish case for possessing Palestine—a case expressed politically by Zionism—has derived from and rested on what purports to be an inherent right: the special relationship between Jews and "the Land of Israel," first articulated in the modern period during the nineteenth century, is now—since the land has been gained—institutionalized on all levels of life in the Israeli state.

As applied to the Jewish people on "the Land of Israel," difference takes various forms. Theologically, of course, difference here means "the Chosen People," who have a different relationship to God than that enjoyed by any other group. But that sort of difference is, I confess, impossible for me to understand. On a purely secular plane, however, difference means the unique bond to the land of Palestine/Israel distinguishing Jews from all other peoples. Tradition, custom, ethos, the experience of suffering and exile—these carry Jewish difference through time and historicosocial identity. Inside Israel, the difference that counts is that between Jew and non-Jew. So far as land in Israel is concerned, for instance, much of it (nearly 90 percent) is held in trust for the Jewish people, whereas non-Jews, simply because they are not Jews, cannot juridically derive equal benefits from it. Indeed, even if we exclude Arab land acquired by Israel in 1967 and after, land either annexed (Jerusalem, portions of the Golan Heights) or occupied and settled (the West Bank, Gaza, southern Lebanon), hundreds of thousands of acres of Palestinian Arab land have been expropriated by the state of Israel since 1948 on behalf of the Jewish people. Note that when the 1948 war broke out, the total amount of land owned by Jews in Palestine amounted to only 6 percent of the country. The means employed to "transfer" the land from Arab to Jewish ownership were legal, but their consequence to the Palestinian Arab was dispossession *tout court*. Thus the Law of Return is exactly commensurate with these means and no less absolute in differentiating between all Jews anywhere and the non-Jewish Palestinians, who are not entitled to rights of return and Israeli citizenship. Here, too, liberal Zionists routinely camouflage the facts; they would, quite properly, denounce such discrimination if it were exercised against Jews.

Difference, then, extends to non-Jews as well. For if a Jewish state is created by and for the Jewish people, then it must be the case that non-Jews are posited as radically *other*, fundamentally and constitutively different. There is by now a small but excellent literature on the condition of non-Jews (Palestinian Arabs) in Israel: nothing in this literature indicates anything but a radically subordinate and consequently disadvantaged position for the Arab citizens of Israel, a position hardly in consonance with the sustained praise in the United States for Israeli democracy.[2] The condition of the Arabs on the West Bank and in Gaza, southern Lebanon, and the Golan Heights is, as I said earlier, the subject of a regularly documented journalistic as well as specialist literature. All of it reiterates evidence of the gross difference in treatment between the captive Arab population and the Jewish settlers, who—in the words of every major figure in the Israeli government and establishment—have the right to settle anywhere in the land of "Eretz-Yisrael." This, according to numerous authorities, includes southern Lebanon, the East Bank of the Jordan, and the Golan Heights, in addition to all of historical Palestine.

None of this, however, has had very much bearing upon intellectuals in the West for whom issues of tyranny, social justice, and the violation of human rights are supposedly central. What we should observe is how the Israeli practice of separation between Jew and non-Jew has been translated ideologically into something different from all other practices of discrimination, so that—as a case in point—comparisons between the Palestinians and American Indians or South African blacks are routinely *not* made, even though similarities between them all are striking. Moreover, we will find that during the years around and after 1948, Zionism was especially supported by liberals and socialists, precisely those political communities who usually would be the first to champion the cause of downtrodden populations, mistreated minorities, oppressed ethnic groups, victims of policies of separation. Whereas during the 1960s few such intellectuals had any difficulty criticizing U.S. napalm bombing of Vietnam, hardly any of them protested continued Israeli use of napalm (and later of cluster bombs) against civilian Arab populations. Subsequent invitations to connect Palestinian militancy with, say, Afghan resistance to Soviet occupation or with Polish workers' action against the Jaruzelski regime were either ignored or vehemently rejected. E. M. Forster's injunction "Only connect" was regularly circumvented: Israel and what Israel did were special, were not connected to similar practices elsewhere, were therefore regularly overlooked.

As I said at the outset, Israel's status has changed somewhat now. In consequence of this change, we can begin to see retrospectively how connected the practice of separation between Jew and non-Jew has been with a complex ideological formation built upon an epistemology of forcible separation between things *for the sake of separation itself.* The reason for the change is that Palestinian nationalism has undeniably emerged, generating a critique whose premise is the need for forging connections and, more important, the existential need to form modes of knowledge, coexistence, and justice that are not based on coercive separation and unequal privilege. Let us then say that we can reinterpret ideologies of difference only because we do so from an awareness of the supervening actuality of "mixing," of crossing over, of stepping beyond boundaries, which are more creative human activities than staying inside rigidly policed borders. That awareness is the achieved product of a political process responding to the travail and expense of separation imposed upon—and, to some extent, creating—a national community, the Palestinian Arabs. Perhaps more important, we develop in the process a heightened critical consciousness not only of what difference can do but of where its politics can lead.

2

To be a non-Jew in Palestine/Israel is first of all to be marked negatively. This is no less paradoxical a thing than one of the laws promulgated in Israel for gaining Palestinian land, the one designating so-called present-absentees (*nifkadim nochachim*): non-Jews defined, on the one hand, as absentees by virtue of their having abandoned their place of residence during the 1948 war and, on the other, as present by virtue of their current residence in Israel as Israeli citizens.[3] If, in a Jewish state, normality is defined by Jewishness, abnormality is the normal condition of the non-Jew. The logic extends itself to history and society more generally considered. Thus the routine and by now orthodox view of the Palestinians is that they are not a people but rather only persons who are Arab, as if the threshold for a positive national identity had not yet been crossed. To this day most Israelis and Zionists do not deviate much from this position; only a small segment of the Jewish population advocates active, positive support for Palestinian rights.

Accordingly—to consider one small index of this—Elia Zureik points out that the principal research paradigm in mainstream Israeli social science holds the Arab in a psychocultural vise. Such supposedly real and stable objects as the Arab mind, the Arab temperament, and Arab cultural weakness predominate, while little attention is devoted to foreign domination or, for that matter, to developments within Arab history. Talal Asad further notes that Israeli ethnographic research on Palestinian Arabs, presented as uncontroversial fact, employs abstract categories like "ethnicity" or the *hamula* ("village clan") in ideological terms, for the "resolution of a Zionist problem"—which, of course, was the existential presence in Palestine of a long-standing and settled population.[4] Like all such populations, this one developed and changed historically, so that a social structure like the *hamula* played a greater or lesser role at different times: it changed along with the rest of the population, its centrality diminished over time. Yet for Zionist anthropology, the *hamula* is fixed as an invariant structure, Asad says, for epistemological as well as political reasons: "It constituted a mode of control and an imputed identity for the only political existence allowed to Arab villagers in Israel."[5] Hence, the Palestinian Arabs could be regarded as at best a collection of village clans, not a people, certainly not an evolving nation.

Ideology and practice thus support each other. Of the earliest Zionist thinkers, it is correct to say that the presence of resident Arabs played very little part in their views of the future Jewish homeland. The structures of Zionist settlements in Palestine itself reflected this skewed awareness; they were designed to emphasize Jewishness by including only Jews within their confines; conversely, non-Jews were programmatically excluded as outsiders. (The kibbutz, for instance, has never admitted Arabs except, in the years since 1967, as manual daily wage labor.) With the establishment of the Jewish state, the non-Jew was marked again, this time by inferiority and secondariness. As an example of what I mean, consider an article published in *Ha'aretz* in 1983. Written by Ran Kislev, it concerns the remaining Arab residents of Jaffa, an Arab city adjoining Tel Aviv, captured in 1948. The Israeli official in charge of the Arab population in what is now called Tel Aviv–Jaffa can only *estimate* the number of Arabs in his charge and, indeed, confesses that he has very little information about the group he oversees. This paucity of statistics and dates must be seen against the background of data in Israel about Jews, information which is as refined and plentiful as any on earth. Kislev then concludes:

> But the main reason for the lack of information is not that the inhabitants don't want to give it. So far, there has not been one Israeli authorized institution—the state, or an academic or municipal body—that bothered to make any serious survey of the Arab population of Jaffa. Obviously no one bothered to examine the socio-economical conditions of this population. This situation continued while surveys and plans have been made concerning the urban future of Jaffa, and considerable sums of money have been given to prepare these plans. All this is done as if the Arabs are not there, as if this obstacle, which no one knows what to do with, has disappeared because no one wants it. As if Arab Jaffa does not exist.[6]

The point is that Kislev's account is itself part of the ideology of difference it attempts to impugn. His speculation is that Israeli Arabs are the victims of a neglect that is neither organized nor deliberate: no one bothers, no one cares, no one knows whether or not to do something, he says. Whereas

> the problems between Arabs and Jews [in Israel only] appear to lie in differences in attitudes, values and understanding. The logical outcome of many of these studies [and of remarks such as Kislev's made by Israelis about "their" Arabs], *when considered in isolation,* is that injustice appears to be rooted in the irrationality of individual men and not in the collective and institutional aspects of Israeli society which are rationally directed.[7]

A far stronger sign of what has issued from "the collective and institutional aspects of Israeli society" is the following item, which I reproduce in full.

> As part of my job, I organized some seminars about current issues for youngsters about to be conscripted. I met with ten such groups of 50 boys each, who can be described as a representative random sample of Israel's Jewish population. The boys came from all sections of society and from all groups of ethnic origin existing within that age group. Since this happened after Finkelstein from Upper Nazareth had been interviewed on television on 1 November, I chose as one of my topics the attitudes towards the Arabs of Israel. [Finkelstein's campaign to expel the Arabs from Upper Nazareth had aroused a stormy debate inside Israel.] Almost all the participants in the debate said they fully identified with Finkelstein's racist attitude towards the Arabs. When I argued that the Arabs in question were citizens accorded equal rights by our laws, the typical response was that they should be deprived of Israeli citizenship.
>
> In every discussion group there were several boys who argued that the Arabs of Israel should be physically eliminated including the old, women and children. When I drew comparisons between Sabra and Chatila and the Nazi extermination campaign, they voiced their approval and declared in all honesty that they were willing to do the exterminating with their own hands, without guilt feelings or hang-ups. Not a single boy voiced his horror or even reservations about these remarks, but some did say that there was no need for physical extermination. It was enough to expel the Arabs across the border.
>
> Many argued for South African style apartheid. The idea that the Arabs of Israel regarded this country as their homeland was received with amazement and contempt. Any moral arguments presented were rejected with sneers. In any one group there were never more than two or three boys with humanitarian and anti-racist opinions, and I felt that they feared to express these publicly. Those few who dared to present unpopular views were indeed immediately silenced by a chorus of shouts.[8]

No ideological or social system, however, is completely effective, and we should not make the mistake of ascribing to Israel and Zionism what it is about both of them that we criticize. No more than the "non-Jew" or the "Palestinian" are they stable and essentialized objects. For within Zionism and Israel, almost as much as within the Palestinian community, it has been true—in Raymond Williams' formulation—"that however dominant a social system may be, the very meaning of its domination involves a limitation or selection of the activities it covers, so that by definition it cannot exhaust all social experience, which therefore always potentially contains space for alternative acts and alternative intentions which are not yet articulated as a social institution or even project."[9] Hence we witness the emergence not only of a Palestinian nationalism responsive to Israeli practice but also of many currents within Israel and Zionism challenging the systematic view (and treatment) of non-Jews. The appearance of such phenomena as draft resistance, a civil rights movement, organized dissent, and public debate and revision all testify to the truth of Williams' observation.

Yet these "alternative" acts and intentions, both Palestinian and Israeli, have themselves bred counteralternative practices, especially on the ideological level, and these—alas—have been extremely, if not totally, effective. Certainly, the rise of Menachem Begin's Likud party, its Lebanese campaigns of 1978 and 1982, the emergence of Gush Emunim, Jewish terrorism, and Rabbi Meir Kahane, testify to this counterweight. We must therefore view difference as challenged by many kinds of counterdifference: internally and existentially a real and internationally acknowledged Palestinian people has appeared on the scene; rifts have appeared within the ranks of Israel's supporters and citizens; Israel now sits on vast new amounts of Arab land whose occupation and potential annexation it must justify against an increasingly critical world public. Most of all, however, major discrepancies between the discourse of Israeli democracy and the reports of what Israeli state practice has actually done to non-Jews are beginning to accumulate, particularly in places where support for Israel is historically crucial. For whereas in the past it almost went without saying that the cause of Israel was a liberal and even progressive one, its ideological privileges within Western discourse are now encroached upon constantly. Once this perspective is recognized, the period since the 1967 war assumes vital importance.

Since 1967, therefore, difference has had to be reasserted by Israel's supporters in ideologically antinomian terms. *Where* this assertion takes place has been a matter of strategic moment, but let us confine ourselves to the generally Western, more particularly American, liberal constituency, especially given the fact, which totally contradicts almost all the normal complaints about Israel's vulnerability, that after Israel's enormously conclusive military victory in 1967 there can be no serious doubt on logical and commonsense ground that the dangers to Israel's existence are largely illusory. Its military is commonly held to be weaker only than those of the two superpowers; it is the world's sixth largest exporter of arms; it has at will penetrated the borders of Egypt, Lebanon, Jordan, Syria, Iraq, and Saudi Arabia and taken territory from four of these states; it rules millions of Arabs in occupied lands; it intervenes with impunity in the daily life of each of these Arabs; it has killed, tortured, displaced, and deported hundreds of thousands of Arabs at a factor of fifty Arabs killed for each Jew killed: all this done with little abatement in the praise from Israel's Western supporters for Israeli democracy and decency. Not that these supporters have been ignorant of what Israeli policy means for non-Jews—they *have known,* but they have allowed this information either to be ignored or to coexist casually with their resolutely positive views of Israeli society. Noam Chomsky calls this the Orwellian syndrome. At the same time, some of the leading pro-Israeli left-liberal intellectuals have modified their views and theories of other matters to keep pace with the increasing drift toward extremism in Israel, as reflected in Israeli state practice. When it comes to equality, justice, or war, for instance, left-liberals have altered their old views rightward as a way of preventing these views and theories from furnishing even implicit criticism of Israel's actions. This is a phenomenon worth examining.

Consider Hannah Arendt. For many years she was closely associated with the efforts of Judah Magnes and Martin Buber on behalf of bi-nationalism in Palestine. Although she worked for the emigration of Jews to Palestine before the war, she was always critical of mainstream Zionism, as her collection of essays *The Jew as Pariah* and her remarks in *The Origins of Totalitarianism* and *Eichmann in Jerusalem* testify. Yet in 1967 she donated money to the Jewish Defense League and did so again in 1973. This information—presented by Elisabeth Young-Bruehl in her biography of Arendt without any awareness of the contradictions at work here—is remarkable for someone otherwise so compassionate and reflective on the subject of what Zionism did to Palestinians. How did the supporter of both Magnes and Kahane mediate the discrepancy? Significant also is Young-Bruehl's implicit (and perhaps unconscious) attempt to explain this difficulty when she prefaces her remarks on Arendt's excited concern for Israel in 1973 with the phrase "Egypt and Syria invaded Israeli territory on Yom Kippur."[10] It should be noted that what Egypt and Syria literally invaded were, respectively, the Sinai Peninsula and the Golan Heights— Egyptian and Syrian territory occupied by Israel in 1967. Thus do wishes override truth.

During the antiwar uprisings of the 1960s, two prominent American liberals, Michael Walzer and Martin Peretz, characterized Israel as "not Vietnam," as if to say that Israeli acts of conquest belong to a different genre from those of French and American interventions in Indochina. This acceptable conquest emanates from what Barbara Tuchman called the country's "terrible swift sword." Not all wars are just, Walzer later went on to argue in his book *Just and Unjust Wars,* but canons of justice established for all states can largely be suspended, he maintained, in Israel's case. Similarly, for the civil libertarian Alan Dershowitz, preventive detention is usually unjustifiable, except in Israel, where the "terrorist" threat is a real, present danger, evidently allowing Israel to abrogate the norms of democratic process (where Arabs are concerned) without ceasing to be a democracy.

Such forms of legitimation for Israel's actions were offered during the years after 1967 as responses to an inescapable problem: Palestinian and other Arab populations were acutely—and visibly—affected by the warlike actions of Israeli soldiers, by curfews and the demolition of houses, by the rampages of militant Zionist settlers. The legitimation was needed even more because Israel had become almost wholly dependent on the United States for military and, above all, economic support. At continually increasing levels of assistance, Israel has received more U.S. dollar aid than any other country, about one thousand dollars per Israeli man, woman, and child every year. This includes assistance to the Israeli defense industry, outright grants, forgiven loans, and proceeds from the sale of tax-free bonds, all at a rate of about $7.4 million per day ($25 billion between 1948 and 1982 and, in fiscal year 1984–85, over $2.6 billion in direct military and economic assistance). These figures give some meat to the fantasy of idealism and fascination sketched by Peter Grose in *Israel in the Mind of America,* whose ideological premises almost obliterate the material foundations of the U.S.-Israeli partnership.

Thus, Israel is a unique country: what it did and how it lived bear no obvious relationship to its productivity or resources. It had an inflation rate of over 300 percent in 1984, military expenditures at over 40 percent of its gross national product, dependence on underpaid Arab labor, and occupation and settlement policies far in excess of production or revenue. Israel, as Gideon Spiro trenchantly testified before the MacBride Commission in 1982, does not

> pay the price of anything that we are doing, not in the occupied territories, because Israel is in this a unique miracle. There is no country in the world which has over 100% inflation, which is occupying the West Bank, occupying another people, and building all those settlements with billions of dollars, and spending 30% of the GNP on defence—and still we can live here. I mean, somebody is paying for everything, so if everybody can live well and go abroad and buy cars, why not be for the occupation? So they are all luxury wars and people are very proud of the way we are fighting, the quick victories, the self-image of the brave Israeli—very flattering![11]

Even so, there are limits to what luxury can do. The main one facing Israel during the period from 1967 to 1982 was the active determination of the Palestinian people to resist the inferior, quasi-invisible, nonnational fate decreed for them by mainstream Zionist ideology and by Israeli state practice. No one needs reminders of the dramatic appearance of Palestinian fedayeen, first in Egypt, then in Jordan and Lebanon, who challenged the total uselessness of the Arab armies as well as, of course, the tyranny of Israeli occupation. The Israeli counter-response (leaving aside the Arab response, which belongs to a discussion of the ideology of sameness) was to view Palestinian nationalist activity in essentially *reductive* terms, given that most Zionist ideologists had never considered the existence of Palestinian Arabs on land designated as Eretz-Yisrael as anything more than a collection of miscellaneous people possessing no intrinsic historical or political nationalist dynamic of their own. Even a quick glance at Shlomo Avineri's book *The Making of Modern Zionism*—despite its Hegelian mode and show of sophistication—verifies precisely this fact. There is thus a hidden ideological connection between, on the one hand, the appearance in the late 1960s and 1970s of a large number of expert Israeli and Israeli-supported studies investigating "the Palestinian problem" and, on the other, the resurgence in 1977 of Zionist Revisionism and, with it, the doctrine that Palestinians are essentially terrorists. Here too the convergence between left-liberal and right-wing positions is notable, just as today American liberals and right-wing evangelical Christians (Jerry Falwell, Jimmy Swaggart, and such) compete in intensity of support for Israel.

For proof of what I have just said, we can look first at Israeli official positions, which have dictated policy and which command the use of Israeli military power. True, the Israeli government concluded a peace agreement with Egypt, but we must remember that Zionism never had a territorial dispute with Egypt nor, for that matter, an ideological one of a fundamental kind. Yet during the same time that Israeli policymakers and social scientists (for example, Avineri, Yehoshafat Harkabi, Shimon Shamir—to mention only the ones best known and quoted in the West) were discussing the escalating "Palestinian problem" from the "socialist" Labor party perspective, one Israeli government after another—Labor and Likud—refused to compromise on the issue after 1967. Jerusalem was annexed, as were sections of the Golan Heights; Gaza was brutally pacified (by Ariel Sharon mainly) by the early 1970s; vast amounts of land in what came to be called Judaea and Samaria were expropriated and settled (the change of name legitimated after 1977 simply announces what force had accomplished earlier). A whole series of severe measures— curfews; detention; long prison sentences; torture; censorship; school and university closures; destruction of houses; denial of rights to con- struction, water access, and improvement; plus numerous killings by gunfire, dynamite, and booby traps—on the occupied territories made one thing plain: Israeli declarations of the need for direct negotiations with "the Arabs" bore little relationship to what the Israelis themselves referred to as "creating facts" designed expressly to make negotiations impossible, or at least very unattractive, for any Arab interlocutor who (unlike Egypt's Anwar al-Sadat) would press the Palestinian claim.

In the light of these developments, then, the role of the Zionist doves, as they came to be called, was highly ambiguous. Plausible, humane, liberal, these people were correspondingly successful in obtaining a Western audience for their views, even though those views stopped very far short of saying anything that might restrict the ideology of difference constantly operating in Israel's favor. Others (for example, Matti Peled, Uri Avneri, Lova Eliav, Simha Flaphan) remained Zionists but took the far more explicit and courageous position advocating Palestinian rights and national coexistence. In the course of time, both in Israel and abroad, the New Left critique of imperialism and the establishment would have come to focus on Israel and its policies as a state, like others in Asia, Africa, and Latin America, that ruled an oppressed native population. Instead, the sector of the liberal (or democratic) socialist Left to which I previously referred came to a standstill and obstructed a true critique of Israel—a critique, that is, which would touch the ideological premises upon which Zionism based its actions against the Palestinians. For awhile, then, Zionist doves like Amos Oz spoke—in Avineri's formula—of the conflicts in Palestine as the struggle of two competing national movements, of right versus right.

Deconstructing the logic of this argument, we note that it admits the Palestinians' belated appearance as a national movement but does not recognize them as a people already in Palestine before the advent of Zionist colonization. This acknowledgment of a present fact but not of its historical background required only a small adjustment in Zionist views of the ideological importance of the difference between Jew and non-Jew. Ever the ideological tactician, Avineri deemed Israeli administration of the West Bank and Gaza "brilliantly" improvisatory, as if there had been no precedent in Israeli history of Jews ruling over non-Jews. And, in keeping with this extraordinary fiction, he proposed the establishment of a two-state settlement, not as a solution to the fundamental problem of difference but as a clever, pragmatic, and tactical answer to Israel's "problem" for hundreds of thousands of non-Jewish Palestinians. Thus you adjust to the existence of non-Jews by making no essential change in your ideological belief that Jews should rule over, be different and separate from, non-Jews.

The dovish argument therefore did not take into sufficient account the real forces (or the real interests) of either the Israeli government or the Palestinian grievance, which were radically and systematically incommensurate with each other. The Israeli stance stemmed from the historical bases of Zionist thought, concerned with Jewish settlers on a land believed to be either previously uninhabited or merely tenanted by an inferior people without nationhood or national aspirations; the Palestinian grievance stemmed from the revenge of an abused people who, in the words of the Palestinian National Covenants of 1964 and 1968, persisted ret-roactively (and ineffectively) in considering the Zionist invasion to be null and void. But as the Israeli government's line hardened and Begin's policies were implemented, the doves and their liberal constituency did not analyze these ominous consequences of the original ideological sep-aration of Zionist claims from Palestinian realities; instead, they gradually accommodated themselves to what Begin did. No one did this more completely than Avineri, a socialist who, during the Israeli siege of Beirut, worked with the army to indoctrinate the troops on the advisability of taking West Beirut by force.[12]

But let us return to "pure" ideology. In the first place, the conflict between Israeli Jew and Palestinian non-Jew was never discussed in the theoretical or philosophical terms that might have elucidated its core as an ideology of difference imposed on a different—that is, non-Jewish—population. The Palestinians were routinely discussed in pragmatic and essentialist terms—pragmatic when their claims were felt at all (ergo, Let us solve the Palestinian problem), essentialist when their claims were felt as too great (ergo, Palestinians are terrorists in fact). The pragmatic bias always challenged the liberal intellectual to come up with "solutions," as if solutions could materialize because intellectuals proposed them to waiting politicians. The essentialists would regularly revert to describing Palestinians as the inhabitants of Judaea and Samaria. Usually both exercises concluded with Zionists berating Palestinians for not being forthcoming enough, for not recognizing Israel, for not renouncing violence, for not being like Peace Now, as if all of these things were equal in magnitude to the destruction of Palestinian society and the continued ethnocide waged by the Israeli government against the Palestinian people.

Along with this performance went another, which was to be *for* Palestinian rights in general but against Palestinians and their represen-tatives in particular. This move has been preferred by socialists like Irving Howe and Michael Walzer, who speak openly against Begin—excellent—but simultaneously speak cold-bloodedly both of *destroying* the only au-thentic representatives of Palestinian nationalism and with undisguised revulsion of the "unspeakable" Yasser Arafat. There is no other way to understand such thinkers, who claim to be positive about the need for a Palestinian solution but adamantly oppose the Palestinians' right to represent themselves and their own program.

Indeed, this was entirely understandable, since after the 1982 war there has been a tremendous Zionist effort—to which I shall return in a moment—to bludgeon the media and the public back into line. Every-thing shown on TV screens in the West has now been called into question, as if the traumatic siege of Beirut and the enormous human cost of the war to Palestinians and Lebanese never really occurred. What took place, runs the Zionist argument proliferating more or less everywhere, was the implementation of an anti-Semitic bias in the media, deliberately misrepresenting a clean, relatively painless surgical Israeli entry into Lebanon to purify southern Lebanon of a few terrorists. The result of putting this preposterous message across has been that anyone writing about Lebanon and Israel has had to either reinvent the wheel, so to speak, or compile so overwhelmingly complete a set of facts that discussing the radical problem of the ideology of separation itself is precluded. In other words, either you must try to tell the story of the Palestinians from scratch, or—no less onerous—you have to put forth the most detailed facts possible, facts restricted to what is taking place now. I have discussed these matters elsewhere, focusing in particular on Chomsky's book *The Fateful Triangle,* although a breathtakingly dishonest and hostile review of Chomsky's book by Avishai Margalit, an Israeli dove, can easily be added to the corroborating evidence.[13] Margalit charges Chomsky with distorting the horrific evidence on Israel's Palestinian policies that led to the Lebanese invasion; whereas, in Margalit's view, it is, and remains, possible to discuss Israel in terms that do not necessarily include the whole atrocious history of what Israel has systematically inflicted on the Palestinians.

3

That such distinctions, separations, disconnections are still made boggles the mind. To the Palestinians, Israel is a Jewish state programmatically associated with the systematic denial of Palestinian human, political, and national rights. On almost every conceivable level of history, contemporary actuality, and ideological argument, this has always been the case. Its denial is therefore a dramatic symptom of an ideology of difference oedipally blind to the origin which has brought about the present horrors. As I write these lines, we must remember, for instance, that in mid-1984 Israeli administrators shut down a West Bank university for four months on the grounds that a festival of Palestinian culture might pose a danger to Israeli security. Thousands of students were deprived of matriculation or graduation. And all this occurs simultaneously with the total disruption of life in southern Lebanon and the devastation of its economy—the results of Israeli occupation. In addition, we need to consider the perpetually occurring detail of Israeli encroachment on Palestinian life: the dozens of illegal settlements, the humiliating searches and detentions, the torture and imprisonment of "suspects," the prevention of building and development, the control of water supplies to every Palestinian community. In addition, the consequence of Israel's war on the Palestinians has been to create opportunities for *Arab* massacres of and attacks on them—all, ironically, in the name of either Arab nationalism or anti-Zionism.

As I said, none of Israel's practices are secret, although they are routinely circumvented or suspended by Israel's European and American supporters. Faced with the evidence, the supporters of conscience resort to anguished dirges on the death of the Zionist dream—as if that dream weren't always a bad one for the Palestinians, who watched their land being taken away from them and their families displaced—and as if laments for the loss of early Zionist idealism were not also effective in shutting out the painful truth that, no less than the present leaders of Israel, the early Zionist settlers either overlooked the Arabs completely or actively plotted to remove them. At least these conscience-stricken critics of present Israeli policy regard what is taking place now with some degree of regret. But at the same time, they use that regret to exonerate— and hence differentiate from all other white settlers in Africa and Asia— the early Zionist dreamers who, it is claimed, were not really interested in doing what other colonizing Europeans did to *their* natives.

As for Israel's more muscular supporters, their current behavior is characterized by a different, if far more brutal and less nostalgic, atavism. The largest, wealthiest, and most organized Jewish community in the world—the one in the United States—has moved on several fronts since the Israeli invasion in 1982. Its publicists and agents have attacked all critics of Israel, labeling them as anti-Semitic, proterrorist, and Soviet stooges. Once propounded, this framework is used in the various books and hit lists published by the American-Israeli Public Affairs Committee (AIPAC), both as a device for discouraging any criticism of Israel and as a means of actively punishing it. The goal is to assure continued and unqualified congressional, financial, and military support for Israel so that no even vaguely "anti-Israel" sounds will issue from official Washington: a formidable task.

The most visible aspect of this campaign, however, has occurred on the ideological level, in the discourse of culture and of history. I referred earlier to two books published in 1984, with enormous public attention and with—for the Palestinian people—clear political messages. One is Joan Peters' *From Time Immemorial: The Origins of the Arab-Jewish Conflict over Palestine,* whose subject is nothing less than the Palestinians' nonexistence, a theme unimaginable during the period from 1974 to 1982 but well known during the 1950s, as anyone familiar with Israeli social science literature will confirm. Using various sources and documents, Peters undertakes to prove that the people who now call themselves Palestinians are in fact mistaken: most of them are refugees of the 1948 war, yes; but almost all really came from neighboring Arab countries, attracted to Palestine during the years immediately before 1948 by the success and prosperity of Jewish settlements. For them to claim repatriation in Palestine is, she says, inappropriate. Peters elicits one other major point: since most of the Israeli Jews originally from Arab countries had been expelled by Arab regimes, an exchange of populations ensued—Arab refugees for Jewish refugees. While Israel has accommodated by resettling the Jews as Israeli citizens, the Arabs have stayed oblivious, allowing the Palestinians to remain as a political nuisance to themselves and to the world in general.

Peters' book was launched with accolades and testimonials of every variety: the jacket is blazoned with approving quotations from political figures of nearly every stripe, authors and intellectuals like Barbara Tuchman and Saul Bellow, august personalities and all-purpose sages. The book has been presented on various radio programs and talk shows, and of course it has been reviewed in prominent journals and newspapers. This is not the place to refute its specious arguments, its contemptible demagoguery, or its almost incredibly coarse attempts at proof. Nor should we spend much time demonstrating how an only slightly altered version of its thesis can, with a good deal more justice, be applied to European Jewish settlers in Palestine, who after an "absence" of two thousand years came to claim Palestine from its native residents. At least Peters' Palestinian "frauds" want repatriation after the two or three years' residence in Palestine that she has in fact allowed them; the Polish, Russian, and American *olim* came to Palestine with a far weaker claim, a millennial absence and promises from God and Lord Balfour. Nor is it worth going into the racist impulses really dictating her book's main line, one which denies peoplehood to a non-European, non-Jewish people simply on the basis of supervening (but doctored and totally misleading) statistics and facts, irrespective of historical experience, demonstrated communality, or actual political will. What is noteworthy about the book is, on the contrary, what it does not say, what is implicit in its appearance, what constitutes it as an event.

In the first place, Peters' book represents a natural analogue to the concerted, sustained Israeli attack on Palestinian nationalism, the Israeli invasion of Lebanon, and the unstated desires of the Jewish state (and of the Zionist dream) that the Palestinians not exist or, failing that, that they be wished away, expelled, or slaughtered. Depriving the Palestinians of their legitimacy *as* Palestinians is nothing less than declaring them Orwellian nonpersons: in *1984,* the Ministry of Truth concocts evidence disputing commonsense reality and then uses it retroactively to dismiss a person's historical presence. If you thought you were a Palestinian, you were wrong. You really came from someplace else and therefore are someone else.

In the second place, Peters' book exactly reproduces the schizophrenic ideological formation within Israel and doctrinal Zionism that decrees the Palestinians to be present-absentees. What is different is that this is now offered to a general American audience and not simply to a local Israeli audience or to readers of specialized journals. The book depends on the general audience's knowledge of "the Palestinians," who have become a staple of contemporary Western journalism, to say nothing of numerous U.N. resolutions, countless studies, and innumerable declarations almost everywhere in the world. Before 1982 such an exercise as Peters' would have seemed improbable and even preposterous. Now, however, it is both reactive and overstated, as if Generals Sharon and Eytan were given license in print to finish the job they couldn't complete in Lebanon. It displays the confidence and defensiveness of a political line unconcerned with credibility or persuasion. Willfulness and assertion have become paramount, much as the Reaganism to which the book is very closely tied asserts that the world must either behave as America says it should behave or risk being nuked. The extent to which ideology has overridden truth can no longer be hidden. If Zionist propaganda in the West had once denied the Palestinians' presence by not talking about them, it now denies their presence by talking about them obsessively: you are not who you say you are because we can prove you were never really you.

Yet Peters' *From Time Immemorial,* which has not received a *single* negative review in the mainstream American press, is mild and even benign when compared with Leon Uris' novel, *The Haj*. I must confess at the outset that I could not finish its six hundred pages, so filled are they with sheer disgusting hatred. This book, which makes the worst Nazi anti-Semitism seem restrained, was nonetheless a best-seller. It is intended as a fiction, offering to place before a wide audience the reality of Arab Palestinian life, Islamic religion, contemporary Middle Eastern history and politics. Its premises are simple: the Arab is a lecherous, deceitful, murderous, irrational, larcenous, and utterly reprehensible subhuman, whereas the Jew (to his credit, Uris is totally uncompromising in his portrayals) is noble, intelligent, understanding, courageous, and—above all—deserving of Palestine. Of this diseased work it can be said without any fear of contradiction that in its hatred, fear, and demented inability to deal with reality, it could only be the production of an American supporter of Israel writing about the Muslim Arabs generally, the Palestinians in particular, at this moment. It expresses the horror and loathing of a man so gorged on his own strength and consequent contempt for what he has been attempting to destroy, as to obliterate even the rudimentary discursive courtesies of writing about a different group of people. And lest we think of Uris as a vulgar aberration, we should remember that his book was published by Doubleday, that it was on the best-seller list for many weeks, and that it is advertised publicly as a work of penetrating, compassionate, and courageous humanism.

Only the Zionism of Begin, Sharon, and Gush Emunim could have yielded Uris. And Uris' brand of gutter racism finds a high-class equivalent in the *New Republic,* whose suave deceits and rabid blandishments still earn it the respect of the liberals and good-thinking intellectuals who read it and write for it. Consider the following, by the *New Republic*'s editor, Martin Peretz. It is a description of a play put on at the American Repertory Theater in Cambridge

> in which a visiting German businessman, an American Jewess come as an immigrant, and an Arab Palestinian find themselves taking refuge in a bomb shelter in Jerusalem under Arab siege. If there is something a bit startling about the emerging empathy between the play's German and its Jew, even less have the universalist prejudices of our culture prepared us for its Arab—a crazed Arab to be sure, but crazed in the distinctive ways of his culture. He is intoxicated by language, cannot discern between fantasy and reality, abhors compromise, always blames others for his predicament, and in the end lances the painful boil of his frustrations in a pointless, though momentarily gratifying, act of bloodlust. This is a political play and what makes it compelling is its pessimism, which is to say its truthfulness. We have seen this play's Arab in Tripoli and in Damascus, and in recent weeks hijacking a bus to Gaza and shooting up a street of innocents in Jerusalem. On the Rep. stage he is a fictional character, of course, but in the real world it is not he but his "moderate" brother who is a figment of the imagination.[14]

Such remarks, which impugn an *entire* race, cannot be printed by any respectable journal in the West today about any other people. But the ideology of difference fueling Zionism has progressed to such a point that *any* Arab, *any* Palestinian can be tolerated only in the sort of terms employed by Uris and Peretz. And liberals legitimize these terms. Note how Peretz's "Arab" is decontextualized entirely and then made to play the role of crazed terrorist run amok—all this without reference to the history of occupied Gaza, for example, brutally pacified and ruled, or without reference to the assertions of General Eytan, who—unlike a camp-dwelling refugee—can and does deliver on promises to turn West Bank Palestinians into "drugged roaches in a bottle." It is no exaggeration to say of such writers as Uris and Peretz that what they write about Arabs is traceable to what Nazis said about Jews or what South African whites say about blacks. Finally, we may note with regret, if not alarm, how this ideology of difference has become almost a touchstone of apostasy for former left-liberals who have abandoned an earlier politics for a safer one. The Conor Cruise O'Brien who once censured Albert Camus for not even mentioning the name of the Arab killed by Meursault has now become a Zionist publicist who regularly says absolutely nothing, in his attacks on "terrorism," about Palestinian dispossession. Similarly, O'Brien— once the anti-imperialist specialist on Africa—now gives Naipaulian lectures to Third World leaders, chiding them not to blame their difficulties on imperialism but on themselves as unregenerate nonwhites.

Difference, in short, can become an ideological infection and a generalized *trahison des clercs*. I note its ravagements not to turn the clock back to an earlier, presumably less unpleasant period, nor to score points, but as a method for understanding the unprecedented miseries of a part of the world beset with massive socioeconomic problems as well as numerous inhibiting ideologies and doctrines, most of them glossed over by fraud, deceit, and utter contempt for the truth. Rarely has the Middle East seemed as factionalized and riven as today—Zionism, Shi'ite zealotry, Maronite exclusivism, plus every kind of reactive nationalism, underwrite a political setting as stagnant as it is deadly. Anyone proposing political community as an alternative to this owes it to his/her audience to understand the dangers of what we have now; otherwise there is the danger of dreaming another version of the Zionist dream. I do not think that there is even a remote possibility that we Palestinians can return to a pristine undivided past. For us, the only hope is a community with Zionist and non-Zionist Jews on the land of historical Palestine. We have yet to find the way to achieve this goal, especially since conflict and hostility are imposed on us by our far more powerful opponents. But if we can at least succeed in getting people to testify to what conscience and common sense tell them, we will have done something to mitigate the effects of an ideology of difference insufficiently restrained by reason or humanity.

The only way to do this, I believe, is to grasp and understand the problem of difference, as exemplified in the relationship between Israel and Palestinians, and to do so as radically, as fully, and as variously as possible. This need not be either a vindictive or an antiquarian process; obviously it should not be a purely theoretical exercise. On the other hand, we must reckon with the actual historical facts of Israel as a state and society with a continuity and integrity of its own. And this, I hasten to add, is not simply the sum total of what Israel has done to the Palestinians: it is certainly more than that. Even if it is impossible for Palestinians to assent to the many paeans of praise for "the miracle of Israel," it is quite possible for us to appreciate the impressive social, political, and cultural gains of the Jewish state so far as Jews are concerned.

But there is a crucial difference between unqualified assent to Israel and the understandable criticism of the state that most Palestinians feel. Both attitudes are there; both are invested with powerful emotions; both represent deeply entrenched interests. Yet if we see and construct something out of a conscious distinction made between both attitudes, a distinction open to both attitudes and to the future, a more creative difference than mere difference emerges. The logic of the present is a logic of either unacceptable stagnation or annihilation—that, at least, seems certain to me. Different logics are necessary.

1. See the Executive of the [World] Zionist Organization, *Problems of the Zionist Organization with the Establishment of the State: Summary of the Debate on Ideological and Organizational Problems*

of the Movement, cited in Uri Davis and Walter Lehr, "And the Fund Still Lives: The Role of the Jewish National Fund in the Determination of Israel's Land Policies," *Journal of Palestine Studies* 7 (Summer 1978): 5–6.

2. I consider the principal works on the condition of Palestinian Arabs in Israel to be: Sabri Jiryis, *The Arabs in Israel,* trans. Inea Bushnaq (New York, 1976); Uri Davis, Andrew Mack, and Nira Yuval-Davis, eds., *Israel and the Palestinians* (London, 1975); Elia Zureik, *The Palestinians in Israel: A Study in Internal Colonialism* (Boston, 1979); and Ian Lustick, *Arabs in the Jewish State: Israel's Control of a National Minority* (Austin, Tex., 1980).

3. See Lustick, *Arabs in the Jewish State,* p. 173, and Jiryis, *Arabs in Israel,* p. 83.

4. Talad Asad, "Anthropological Texts and Ideological Problems: An Analysis of Cohen on Arab Villages in Israel," *Economy and Society* 4 (Aug. 1975): 274.

5. Ibid.

6. Ran Kislev, *Ha'aretz,* 30 Dec. 1983.

7. Zureik, *Palestinians in Israel,* pp. 95–96.

8. Shlomo Ariel, letter to the editor, *Ha'aretz,* 1 Dec. 1983.

9. Raymond Williams, *Politics and Letters: Interviews with "New Left Review"* (London, 1979), p. 252.

10. Elisabeth Young-Bruehl, *Hannah Arendt: For Love of the World* (New Haven, Conn., 1982), p. 455.

11. Gideon Spiro, testimony given to the MacBride Commission, 8 Sept. 1982, *Israel in Lebanon: Report of the International Commission to Enquire into Reported Violations of International Law by Israel during Its Invasion of the Lebanon* [Seán MacBride, chairman](London, 1983), app. 5, p. 222.

12. See the remarkable denunciation of Shlomo Avineri by Meron Benvenisti, ex-deputy mayor of Jerusalem, in "A Letter to Professor Avineri," *Ha'aretz,* 22 July 1982.

13. See my *The Question of Palestine* (New York, 1979), and "Permission to Narrate," *London Review of Books,* 16–29 Feb. 1984. See also Avishai Margalit, "Israel: A Partial Indictment," review of *The Fateful Triangle* by Noam Chomsky, *New York Review of Books,* 28 June 1984, pp. 9–14.

14. Martin Peretz, "Washington Diarist," *New Republic,* 7 May 1984, p. 43.

"Indians": Textualism, Morality, and the Problem of History

Jane Tompkins

When I was growing up in New York City, my parents used to take me to an event in Inwood Park at which Indians—real American Indians dressed in feathers and blankets—could be seen and touched by children like me. This event was always a disappointment. It was more fun to imagine that you *were* an Indian in one of the caves in Inwood Park than to shake the hand of an old man in a headdress who was not overwhelmed at the opportunity of meeting you. After staring at the Indians for a while, we would take a walk in the woods where the caves were, and once I asked my mother if the remains of a fire I had seen in one of them might have been left by the original inhabitants. After that, wandering up some stone steps cut into the side of the hill, I imagined I was a princess in a rude castle. My Indians, like my princesses, were creatures totally of the imagination, and I did not care to have any real exemplars interfering with what I already knew.

I already knew about Indians from having read about them in school. Over and over we were told the story of how Peter Minuit had bought Manhattan Island from the Indians for twenty-four dollars' worth of glass beads. And it was a story we didn't mind hearing because it gave us the rare pleasure of having someone to feel superior to, since the poor Indians had not known (as we eight-year-olds did) how valuable a piece of property Manhattan Island would become. Generally, much was made of the Indian presence in Manhattan; a poem in one of our readers began: "Where we walk to school today / Indian children used to play," and we were encouraged to write poetry on this topic ourselves. So I had a fairly rich relationship with Indians before I ever met the unpre-possessing people in Inwood Park. I felt that I had a lot in common with them. They, too, liked animals (they were often named after animals); they, too, made mistakes—they liked the brightly colored trinkets of little value that the white men were always offering them; they were handsome, warlike, and brave and had led an exciting, romantic life in the forest long ago, a life such as I dreamed of leading myself. I felt lucky to be living in one of the places where they had definitely been. Never mind where they were or what they were doing now.

My story stands for the relationship most non-Indians have to the people who first populated this continent, a relationship characterized by narcissistic fantasies of freedom and adventure, of a life lived closer to nature and to spirit than the life we lead now. As Vine Deloria, Jr. has pointed out, the American Indian Movement in the early seventies couldn't get people to pay attention to what was happening to Indians who were alive in the present, so powerful was this country's infatuation with people who wore loincloths, lived in tepees, and roamed the plains and forests long ago.[1] The present essay, like these fantasies, doesn't have much to do with actual Indians, though its subject matter is the histories of European-Indian relations in seventeenth-century New England. In a sense, my encounter with Indians as an adult doing "research" replicates the childhood one, for while I started out to learn about Indians, I ended up preoccupied with a problem of my own.

This essay enacts a particular instance of the challenge post-struc-turalism poses to the study of history. In simpler language, it concerns the difference that point of view makes when people are giving accounts of events, whether at first or second hand. The problem is that if all accounts of events are determined through and through by the observer's frame of reference, then one will never know, in any given case, what really happened.

I encountered this problem in concrete terms while preparing to teach a course in colonial American literature. I'd set out to learn what I could about the Puritans' relations with American Indians. All I wanted was a general idea of what had happened between the English settlers and the natives in seventeenth-century New England; post-structuralism and its dilemmas were the furthest thing from my mind. I began, more

1. See Vine Deloria, Jr., *God Is Red* (New York, 1973), pp. 39–56.

Jane Tompkins is professor of English at Duke University. She is the author of *Sensational Designs: The Cultural Work of American Fiction, 1790–1860* (1985) and editor of *Reader-Response Criticism: From Formalism to Post-Structuralism* (1980). Her current work concerns the construction of male identity in American popular culture.

or less automatically, with Perry Miller, who hardly mentions the Indians at all, then proceeded to the work of historians who had dealt exclusively with the European-Indian encounter. At first, it was a question of deciding which of these authors to believe, for it quickly became apparent that there was no unanimity on the subject. As I read on, however, I discovered that the problem was more complicated than deciding whose version of events was correct. Some of the conflicting accounts were not simply contradictory, they were completely incommensurable, in that their assumptions about what counted as a valid approach to the subject, and what the subject itself was, diverged in fundamental ways. Faced with an array of mutually irreconcilable points of view, points of view which determined what was being discussed as well as the terms of the discussion, I decided to turn to primary sources for clarification, only to discover that the primary sources reproduced the problem all over again. I found myself, in other words, in an epistemological quandary, not only unable to decide among conflicting versions of events but also unable to believe that any such decision could, in principle, be made. It was a moral quandary as well. Knowledge of what really happened when the Europeans and the Indians first met seemed particularly important, since the result of that encounter was virtual genocide. This was the kind of past "mistake" which, presumably, we studied history in order to avoid repeating. If studying history couldn't put us in touch with actual events and their causes, then what was to prevent such atrocities from happening again?

For a while, I remained at this impasse. But through analyzing the process by which I had reached it, I eventually arrived at an understanding which seemed to offer a way out. This essay records the concrete experience of meeting and solving the difficulty I have just described (as an abstract problem, I thought I had solved it long ago). My purpose is not to throw new light on antifoundationalist epistemology—the solution I reached is not a new one—but to dramatize and expose the troubles antifoundationalism gets you into when you meet it, so to speak, in the road.

My research began with Perry Miller. Early in the preface to *Errand into the Wilderness,* while explaining how he came to write his history of the New England mind, Miller writes a sentence that stopped me dead. He says that what fascinated him as a young man about his country's history was "the massive narrative of the movement of European culture into the vacant wilderness of America."[2] "Vacant?" Miller, writing in 1956, doesn't pause over the word "vacant," but to people who read his preface thirty years later, the word is shocking. In what circumstances could someone proposing to write a history of colonial New England *not* take account of the Indian presence there?

2. Perry Miller, *Errand into the Wilderness* (Cambridge, Mass., 1964), p. vii; all further references will be included in the text.

The rest of Miller's preface supplies an answer to this question, if one takes the trouble to piece together its details. Miller explains that as a young man, jealous of older compatriots who had had the luck to fight in World War I, he had gone to Africa in search of adventure. "The adventures that Africa afforded," he writes, "were tawdry enough, but it became the setting for a sudden epiphany" (p. vii). "It was given to me," he writes, "disconsolate on the edge of a jungle of central Africa, to have thrust upon me the mission of expounding what I took to be the innermost propulsion of the United States, while supervising, in that barbaric tropic, the unloading of drums of case oil flowing out of the inexhaustible wilderness of America" (p. viii). Miller's picture of himself on the banks of the Congo furnishes a key to the kind of history he will write and to his mental image of a vacant wilderness; it explains why it was just here, under precisely these conditions, that he should have had his epiphany.

The fuel drums stand, in Miller's mind, for the popular misconception of what this country is about. They are "tangible symbols of [America's] appalling power," a power that everyone but Miller takes for the ultimate reality (p. ix). To Miller, "the mind of man is the basic factor in human history," and he will plead, all unaccommodated as he is among the fuel drums, for the intellect—the intellect for which his fellow historians, with their chapters on "stoves or bathtubs, or tax laws," "the Wilmot Proviso" and "the chain store," "have so little respect" (p. viii, ix). His preface seethes with a hatred of the merely physical and mechanical, and this hatred, which is really a form of moral outrage, explains not only the contempt with which he mentions the stoves and bathtubs but also the nature of his experience in Africa and its relationship to the "massive narrative" he will write.

Miller's experiences in Africa are "tawdry," his tropic is barbaric because the jungle he stands on the edge of means nothing to him, no more, indeed something less, than the case oil. It is the nothingness of Africa that precipitates his vision. It is the barbarity of the "dark continent," the obvious (but superficial) parallelism between the jungle at Matadi and America's "vacant wilderness" that releases in Miller the desire to define and vindicate his country's cultural identity. To the young Miller, colonial Africa and colonial America are—but for the history he will bring to light—mirror images of one another. And what he fails to see in the one landscape is the same thing he overlooks in the other: the human beings who people it. As Miller stood with his back to the jungle, thinking about the role of mind in human history, his failure to see that the land into which European culture had moved was not vacant but already occupied by a varied and numerous population, is of a piece with his failure, in his portrait of himself at Matadi, to notice *who* was carrying the fuel drums he was supervising the unloading of.

The point is crucial because it suggests that what is invisible to the historian in his own historical moment remains invisible when he turns his gaze to the past. It isn't that Miller didn't "see" the black men, in a literal sense, any more than it's the case that when he looked back he didn't "see" the Indians, in the sense of not realizing they were there. Rather, it's that neither the Indians nor the blacks *counted* for him, in a fundamental way. The way in which Indians can be seen but not counted is illustrated by an entry in Governor John Winthrop's journal, three hundred years before, when he recorded that there had been a great storm with high winds "yet through God's great mercy it did no hurt, but only killed one Indian with the fall of a tree."[3] The juxtaposition suggests that Miller shared with Winthrop a certain colonial point of view, a point of view from which Indians, though present, do not finally matter.

A book entitled *New England Frontier: Puritans and Indians, 1620–1675,* written by Alden Vaughan and published in 1965, promised to rectify Miller's omission. In the outpouring of work on the European-Indian encounter that began in the early sixties, this book is the first major landmark, and to a neophyte it seems definitive. Vaughan acknowledges the absence of Indian sources and emphasizes his use of materials which catch the Puritans "off guard."[4] His announced conclusion that "the New England Puritans followed a remarkably humane, considerate, and just policy in their dealings with the Indians" seems supported by the scope, documentation, and methodicalness of his project (*NEF,* p. vii). The author's fair-mindedness and equanimity seem everywhere apparent, so that when he asserts "the history of interracial relations from the arrival of the Pilgrims to the outbreak of King Philip's War is a credit to the integrity of both peoples," one is positively reassured (*NEF,* p. viii).

But these impressions do not survive an admission that comes late in the book, when, in the course of explaining why works like Helen Hunt Jackson's *Century of Dishonor* had spread misconceptions about Puritan treatment of the Indians, Vaughan finally lays his own cards on the table.

> The root of the misunderstanding [about Puritans and Indians] . . . lie[s] in a failure to recognize the nature of the two societies that met in seventeenth century New England. One was unified, visionary, disciplined, and dynamic. The other was divided, self-satisfied, undisciplined, and static. It would be unreasonable to

3. This passage from John Winthrop's *Journal* is excerpted by Perry Miller in his anthology *The American Puritans: Their Prose and Poetry* (Garden City, N.Y., 1956), p. 43. In his headnote to the selections from the *Journal,* Miller speaks of Winthrop's "characteristic objectivity" (p. 37).

4. Alden T. Vaughan, *New England Frontier: Puritans and Indians, 1620–1675* (Boston, 1965), pp. vi–vii; all further references to this work, abbreviated *NEF,* will be included in the text.

expect that such societies could live side by side indefinitely with no penetration of the more fragmented and passive by the more consolidated and active. What resulted, then, was not—as many have held—a clash of dissimilar ways of life, but rather the expansion of one into the areas in which the other was lacking. [*NEF*, p. 323]

From our present vantage point, these remarks seem culturally biased to an incredible degree, not to mention inaccurate: Was Puritan society unified? If so, how does one account for its internal dissensions and obsessive need to cast out deviants? Is "unity" necessarily a positive culture trait? From what standpoint can one say that American Indians were neither disciplined nor visionary, when both these characteristics loom so large in the enthnographies? Is it an accident that ways of describing cultural strength and weakness coincide with gender stereotypes—active/passive, and so on? Why is one culture said to "penetrate" the other? Why is the "other" described in terms of "lack"?

Vaughan's fundamental categories of apprehension and judgment will not withstand even the most cursory inspection. For what looked like evenhandedness when he was writing *New England Frontier* does not look that way anymore. In his introduction to *New Directions in American Intellectual History,* John Higham writes that by the end of the sixties

the entire conceptual foundation on which [this sort of work] rested [had] crumbled away. . . . Simultaneously, in sociology, anthropology, and history, two working assumptions . . . came under withering attack: first, the assumption that societies tend to be integrated, and second, that a shared culture maintains that integration. . . . By the late 1960s all claims issued in the name of an "American mind" . . . were subject to drastic skepticism.[5]

"Clearly," Higham continues, "the sociocultural upheaval of the sixties created the occasion" for this reaction.[6] Vaughan's book, it seemed, could only have been written before the events of the sixties had sensitized scholars to questions of race and ethnicity. It came as no surprise, therefore, that ten years later there appeared a study of European-Indian relations which reflected the new awareness of social issues the sixties had engendered. And it offered an entirely different picture of the European-Indian encounter.

Francis Jennings' *The Invasion of America* (1975) rips wide open the idea that the Puritans were humane and considerate in their dealings with the Indians. In Jennings' account, even more massively documented than Vaughan's, the early settlers lied to the Indians, stole from them,

5. John Higham, intro. to *New Directions in American Intellectual History,* ed. Higham and Paul K. Conkin (Baltimore, 1979), p. xii.
6. Ibid.

murdered them, scalped them, captured them, tortured them, raped them, sold them into slavery, confiscated their land, destroyed their crops, burned their homes, scattered their possessions, gave them alcohol, underminded their systems of belief, and infected them with diseases that wiped out ninety percent of their numbers within the first hundred years after contact.[7]

Jennings mounts an all-out attack on the essential decency of the Puritan leadership and their apologists in the twentieth century. The Pequot War, which previous historians had described as an attempt on the part of Massachussetts Bay to protect itself from the fiercest of the New England tribes, becomes, in Jennings' painstakingly researched account, a deliberate war of extermination, waged by whites against Indians. It starts with trumped-up charges, is carried on through a series of increasingly bloody reprisals, and ends in the massacre of scores of Indian men, women, and children, all so that Massachussets Bay could gain political and economic control of the southern Connecticut Valley. When one reads this and then turns over the page and sees a reproduction of the Bay Colony seal, which depicts an Indian from whose mouth issue the words "Come over and help us," the effect is shattering.[8]

But even so powerful an argument as Jennings' did not remain unshaken by subsequent work. Reading on, I discovered that if the events of the sixties had revolutionized the study of European-Indian relations, the events of the seventies produced yet another transformation. The American Indian Movement, and in particular the founding of the Native American Rights Fund in 1971 to finance Indian litigation, and a court decision in 1975 which gave the tribes the right to seek redress for past injustices in federal court, created a climate within which historians began to focus on the Indians themselves. "Almost simultaneously," writes James Axtell, "frontier and colonial historians began to discover the necessity of considering the American natives as real determinants of history and the utility of ethnohistory as a way of ensuring parity of focus and impartiality of judgment."[9] In Miller, Indians had been simply beneath notice; in Vaughan, they belonged to an inferior culture; and in Jennings,

---

7. See Francis Jennings, *The Invasion of America: Indians, Colonialism, and the Cant of Conquest* (New York, 1975), pp. 3–31. Jennings writes: "The so-called settlement of America was a *re*settlement, a reoccupation of a land made waste by the diseases and demoralization introduced by the newcomers. Although the source data pertaining to populations have never been compiled, one careful scholar, Henry F. Dobyns, has provided a relatively conservative and meticulously reasoned estimate conforming to the known effects of conquest catastrophe. Dobyns has calculated a total aboriginal population for the western hemisphere within the range of 90 to 112 million, of which 10 to 12 million lived north of the Rio Grande" (p. 30).

8. Jennings, fig. 7, p. 229; and see pp. 186–229.

9. James Axtell, *The European and the Indian: Essays in the Ethnohistory of Colonial North America* (Oxford, 1981), p. viii.

they were the more or less innocent prey of power-hungry whites. But in the most original and provocative of the ethnohistories, Calvin Martin's *Keepers of the Game,* Indians became complicated, purposeful human beings, whose lives were spiritually motivated to a high degree.[10] Their relationship to the animals they hunted, to the natural environment, and to the whites with whom they traded became intelligible within a system of beliefs that formed the basis for an entirely new perspective on the European-Indian encounter.

Within the broader question of why European contact had such a devastating effect on the Indians, Martin's specific aim is to determine why Indians participated in the fur trade which ultimately led them to the brink of annihilation. The standard answer to this question had always been that once the Indian was introduced to European guns, copper kettles, woolen blankets, and the like, he literally couldn't keep his hands off them. In order to acquire these coveted items, he decimated the animal populations on which his survival depended. In short, the Indian's motivation in participating in the fur trade was assumed to be the same as the white European's—a desire to accumulate material goods. In direct opposition to this thesis, Martin argues that the reason why Indians ruthlessly exploited their own resources had nothing to do with supply and demand, but stemmed rather from a breakdown of the cosmic worldview that tied them to the game they killed in a spiritual relationship of parity and mutual obligation.

The hunt, according to Martin, was conceived not primarily as a physical activity but as a spiritual quest, in which the spirit of the hunter must overmaster the spirit of the game animal before the kill can take place. The animal, in effect, *allows* itself to be found and killed, once the hunter has mastered its spirit. The hunter prepared himself through rituals of fasting, sweating, or dreaming which reveal the identity of his prey and where he can find it. The physical act of killing is the least important element in the process. Once the animal is killed, eaten, and its parts used for clothing or implements, its remains must be disposed of in ritually prescribed fashion, or the game boss, the "keeper" of that species, will not permit more animals to be killed. The relationship between Indians and animals, then, is contractual; each side must hold up its end of the bargain, or no further transactions can occur.

What happened, according to Martin, was that as a result of diseases introduced into the animal population by Europeans, the game suddenly disappeared, began to act in inexplicable ways, or sickened and died in plain view, and communicated their diseases to the Indians. The Indians, consequently, believed that their compact with the animals had been broken and that the keepers of the game, the tutelary spirits of each

10. See Calvin Martin, *Keepers of the Game: Indian-Animal Relationships and the Fur Trade* (Berkeley and Los Angeles, 1978).

animal species whom they had been so careful to propitiate, had betrayed them. And when missionization, wars with the Europeans, and displacement from their tribal lands had further weakened Indian society and its belief structure, the Indians, no longer restrained by religious sanctions, in effect, turned on the animals in a holy war of revenge.

Whether or not Martin's specific claim about the "holy war" was correct, his analysis made it clear to me that, given the Indians' under-standing of economic, religious, and physical processes, an Indian account of what transpired when the European settlers arrived here would look nothing like our own. Their (potential, unwritten) history of the conflict could bear only a marginal resemblance to Eurocentric views. I began to think that the key to understanding European-Indian relations was to see them as an encounter between wholly disparate cultures, and that therefore either defending or attacking the colonists was beside the point since, given the cultural disparity between the two groups, conflict was inevitable and in large part a product of mutual misunderstanding.

But three years after Martin's book appeared, Shepard Krech III edited a collection of seven essays called *Indians, Animals, and the Fur Trade,* attacking Martin's entire project. Here the authors argued that we don't need an ideological or religious explanation for the fur trade. As Charles Hudson writes,

> The Southeastern Indians slaughtered deer (and were prompt-ed to enslave and kill each other) because of their position on the outer fringes of an expanding modern world-system. . . . In the modern world-system there is a core region which establishes *eco-nomic* relations with its colonial periphery. . . . If the Indians could not produce commodities, they were on the road to cultural ex-tinction. . . . To maximize his chances for survival, an eighteenth-century Southeastern Indian had to . . . live in the interior, out of range of European cattle, forestry, and agriculture. . . . He had to produce a commodity which was valuable enough to earn him some protection from English slavers.[11]

Though we are talking here about Southeastern Indians, rather than the subarctic and Northeastern tribes Martin studied, what really accounts for these divergent explanations of why Indians slaughtered the game are the assumptions that underlie them. Martin believes that the Indians acted on the basis of perceptions made available to them by their own cosmology; that is, he explains their behavior as the Indians themselves would have explained it (insofar as he can), using a logic and a set of values that are not Eurocentric but derived from within Amerindian culture. Hudson, on the other hand, insists that the Indians' own beliefs

---

11. See the essay by Charles Hudson in *Indians, Animals, and the Fur Trade: A Critique of "Keepers of the Game,"* ed. Shepard Krech III (Athens, Ga., 1981), pp. 167–69.

are irrelevant to an explanation of how they acted, which can only be understood, as far as he is concerned, in the terms of a Western materialist economic and political analysis. Martin and Hudson, in short, don't agree on what counts as an explanation, and this disagreement sheds light on the preceding accounts as well. From this standpoint, we can see that Vaughan, who thought that the Puritans were superior to the Indians, and Jennings, who thought the reverse, are both, like Hudson, using Eurocentric criteria of description and evaluation. While all three critics (Vaughan, Jennings, and Hudson) acknowledge that Indians and Europeans behave differently from one another, the behavior differs, as it were, within the order of the same: all three assume, though only Hudson makes the assumption explicit, that an understanding of relations between the Europeans and the Indians must be elaborated in European terms. In Martin's analysis, however, what we have are not only two different sets of behavior but two incommensurable ways of describing and assigning meaning to events. This difference at the level of explanation calls into question the possibility of obtaining any theory-independent account of interaction between Indians and Europeans.

At this point, dismayed and confused by the wildly divergent views of colonial history the twentieth-century historians had provided, I decided to look at some primary materials. I thought, perhaps, if I looked at some firsthand accounts and at some scholars looking at those accounts, it would be possible to decide which experts were right and which were wrong by comparing their views with the evidence. Captivity narratives seemed a good place to begin, since it was logical to suppose that the records left by whites who had been captured by Indians would furnish the sort of firsthand information I wanted.

I began with two fascinating essays based on these materials written by the ethnohistorian James Axtell, "The White Indians of Colonial America" and "The Scholastic Philosophy of the Wilderness."[12] These essays suggest that it would have been a privilege to be captured by North American Indians and taken off to Canada to dwell in a wigwam for the rest of one's life. Axtell's reconstruction of the process by which Indians taught European captives to feel comfortable in the wilderness, first taking their shoes away and giving them moccasins, carrying the children on their backs, sharing the scanty food supply equally, ceremonially cleansing them of their old identities, giving them Indian clothes and jewelry, assiduously teaching them the Indian language, finally adopting them into their families, and even visiting them after many years if, as sometimes happened, they were restored to white society—all of this

12. See Axtell, "The White Indians of Colonial America" and "The Scholastic Philosophy of the Wilderness," *The European and the Indian*, pp. 168–206 and 131–67.

creates a compelling portrait of Indian culture and helps to explain the extraordinary attraction that Indian culture apparently exercised over Europeans.

But, as I had by now come to expect, this beguiling portrait of the Indians' superior humanity is called into question by other writings on Indian captivity—for example, Norman Heard's *White into Red,* whose summation of the comparative treatment of captive children east and west of the Mississippi seems to contradict some of Axtell's conclusions:

> The treatment of captive children seems to have been similar in initial stages. . . . Most children were treated brutally at the time of capture. Babies and toddlers usually were killed immediately and other small children would be dispatched during the rapid retreat to the Indian villages if they cried, failed to keep the pace, or otherwise indicated a lack of fortitude needed to become a worthy member of the tribe. Upon reaching the village, the child might face such ordeals as running the gauntlet or dancing in the center of a throng of threatening Indians. The prisoner might be so seriously injured at this time that he would no longer be acceptable for adoption.[13]

One account which Heard reprints is particularly arresting. A young girl captured by the Comanches who had not been adopted into a family but used as a slave had been peculiarly mistreated. When they wanted to wake her up the family she belonged to would take a burning brand from the fire and touch it to her nose. When she was returned to her parents, the flesh of her nose was completely burned away, exposing the bone.[14]

Since the pictures drawn by Heard and Axtell were in certain respects irreconcilable, it made sense to turn to a firsthand account to see how the Indians treated their captives in a particular instance. Mary Rowlandson's "The Soveraignty and Goodness of God," published in Boston around 1680, suggested itself because it was so widely read and had set the pattern for later narratives. Rowlandson interprets her captivity as God's punishment on her for failing to keep the Sabbath properly on several occasions. She sees everything that happens to her as a sign from God. When the Indians are kind to her, she attributes her good fortune to divine Providence; when they are cruel, she blames her captors. But beyond the question of how Rowlandson interprets events is the question of what she saw in the first place and what she considered worth reporting. The following passage, with its abrupt shifts of focus and peculiar emphases,

13. J. Norman Heard, *White into Red: A Study of the Assimilation of White Persons Captured by Indians* (Metuchen, N.J., 1973), p. 97.

14. See ibid., p. 98.

makes it hard to see her testimony as evidence of anything other than the Puritan point of view:

> Then my heart began to fail: and I fell weeping, which was the first time to my remembrance, that I wept before them. Although I had met with so much Affliction, and my heart was many times ready to break, yet could I not shed one tear in their sight: but rather had been all this while in a maze, and like one astonished: but now I may say as, Psal. 137.1. *By the Rivers of Babylon, there we sate down; yea, we wept when we remembered Zion.* There one of them asked me, why I wept, I could hardly tell what to say: yet I answered, they would kill me: No, said he, none will hurt you. Then came one of them and gave me two spoon-fulls of Meal to comfort me, and another gave me half a pint of Pease; which was more worth than many Bushels at another time. Then I went to see King Philip, he bade me come in and sit down, and asked me whether I woold smoke it (a usual Complement nowadayes among Saints and Sinners) but this no way suited me. For though I had formerly used Tobacco, yet I had left it ever since I was first taken. It seems to be a Bait, the Devil layes to make men loose their precious time: I remember with shame, how formerly, when I had taken two or three pipes, I was presently ready for another, such a bewitching thing it is: But I thank God, he has now given me power over it; surely there are many who may be better imployed than to ly sucking a stinking Tobacco-pipe.[15]

Anyone who has ever tried to give up smoking has to sympathize with Rowlandson, but it is nonetheless remarkable, first, that a passage which begins with her weeping openly in front of her captors, and comparing herself to Israel in Babylon, should end with her railing against the vice of tobacco; and, second, that it has not a word to say about King Philip, the leader of the Indians who captured her and mastermind of the campaign that devastated the white population of the English colonies. The fact that Rowlandson has just been introduced to the chief of chiefs makes hardly any impression on her at all. What excites her is a moral issue which was being hotly debated in the seventeenth century: to smoke or not to smoke (Puritans frowned on it, apparently, because it wasted time and presented a fire hazard). What seem to us the peculiar emphases in Rowlandson's relation are not the result of her having *screened out* evidence she couldn't handle, but of her way of constructing the world. She saw what her seventeenth-century English Separatist background

15. Mary Rowlandson, "The Soveraignty and Goodness of God, Together with the Faithfulness of His Promises Displayed; Being a Narrative of the Captivity and Restauration of Mrs. Mary Rowlandson (1676)," in *Held Captive by Indians: Selected Narratives, 1642–1836*, ed. Richard VanDerBeets (Knoxville, Tenn., 1973), pp. 57–58.

made visible. It is when one realizes that the biases of twentieth-century historians like Vaughan or Axtell cannot be corrected for simply by consulting the primary materials, since the primary materials are constructed according to *their* authors' biases, that one begins to envy Miller his vision at Matadi. Not for what he didn't see—the Indian and the black—but for his epistemological confidence.

Since captivity narratives made a poor source of evidence for the nature of European-Indian relations in early New England because they were so relentlessly pietistic, my hope was that a better source of evidence might be writings designed simply to tell Englishmen what the American natives were like. These authors could be presumed to be less severely biased, since they hadn't seen their loved ones killed by Indians or been made to endure the hardships of captivity, and because they weren't writing propaganda calculated to prove that God had delivered his chosen people from the hands of Satan's emissaries.

The problem was that these texts were written with aims no less specific than those of the captivity narratives, though the aims were of a different sort. Here is a passage from William Wood's *New England's Prospect*, published in London in 1634.

> To enter into a serious discourse concerning the natural conditions of these Indians might procure admiration from the people of any civilized nations, in regard of their civility and good natures. . . . These Indians are of affable, courteous and well disposed natures, ready to communicate the best of their wealth to the mutual good of one another; . . . so . . . perspicuous is their love . . . that they are as willing to part with a mite in poverty as treasure in plenty. . . . If it were possible to recount the courtesies they have showed the English, since their first arrival in those parts, it would not only steady belief, that they are a loving people, but also win the love of those that never saw them, and wipe off that needless fear that is too deeply rooted in the conceits of many who think them envious and of such rancorous and inhumane dispositions, that they will one day make an end of their English inmates.[16]

However, in a pamphlet published twenty-one years earlier, Alexander Whitaker of Virginia has this to say of the natives:

> These naked slaves . . . serve the divell for feare, after a most base manner, sacrificing sometimes (as I have heere heard) their own Children to him. . . . They live naked in bodie, as if their shame

---

16. William Wood, *New England's Prospect*, ed. Vaughan (Amherst, Mass., 1977), pp. 88–89.

of their sinne deserved no covering: Their names are as naked as their bodie: They esteem it a virtue to lie, deceive and steale as their master the divell teacheth to them.[17]

According to Robert Berkhofer in *The White Man's Indian,* these divergent reports can be explained by looking at the authors' motives. A favorable report like Wood's, intended to encourage new emigrants to America, naturally represented Indians as loving and courteous, civilized and generous, in order to allay the fears of prospective colonists. Whitaker, on the other hand, a minister who wishes to convince his readers that the Indians are in need of conversion, paints them as benighted agents of the devil. Berkhofer's commentary constantly implies that white men were to blame for having represented the Indians in the image of their own desires and needs.[18] But the evidence supplied by Rowlandson's narrative, and by the accounts left by early reporters such as Wood and Whitaker, suggests something rather different. Though it is probably true that in certain cases Europeans did consciously tamper with the evidence, in most cases there is no reason to suppose that they did not record faithfully what they saw. And what they saw was not an illusion, was not determined by selfish motives in any narrow sense, but was there by virtue of a *way* of seeing which they could no more consciously manipulate than they could choose not to have been born. At this point, it seemed to me, the ethnocentric bias of the firsthand observers invited an investigation of the cultural situation they spoke from. Karen Kupperman's *Settling with the Indians* (1980) supplied just such an analysis.

Kupperman argues that Englishmen inevitably looked at Indians in exactly the same way that they looked at other Englishmen. For instance, if they looked down on Indians and saw them as people to be exploited, it was not because of racial prejudice or antique notions about savagery, it was because they looked down on ordinary English men and women and saw them as subjects for exploitation as well.[19] According to Kupperman, what concerned these writers most when they described the Indians were the insignia of social class, of rank, and of prestige. Indian faces are virtually never described in the earliest accounts, but clothes and hairstyles, tattoos and jewelry, posture and skin color are. "Early modern Englishmen believed that people can create their own identity, and that therefore one communicates to the world through signals such

17. Alexander Whitaker, *Goode Newes from Virginia* (1613), quoted in Robert F. Berkhofer, Jr., *The White Man's Indian: Images of the American Indian from Columbus to the Present* (New York, 1978), p. 19.

18. See, for example, Berkhofer's discussion of the passages he quotes from Whitaker (*The White Man's Indian,* pp. 19, 20).

19. See Karen Ordahl Kupperman, *Settling with the Indians: The Meeting of English and Indian Cultures in America, 1580–1640* (Totowa, N.J., 1980), pp. 3, 4.

as dress and other forms of decoration who one is, what group or category one belongs to."[20]

Kupperman's book marks a watershed in writings on European-Indian relations, for it reverses the strategy employed by Martin two years before. Whereas Martin had performed an ethnographic analysis of Indian cosmology in order to explain, from within, the Indians' motives for engaging in the fur trade, Kupperman performs an ethnographic study of seventeenth-century England in order to explain, from within, what motivated Englishmen's behavior. The sympathy and understanding that Martin, Axtell, and others extend to the Indians are extended in Kupperman's work to the English themselves. Rather than giving an account of "what happened" between Indians and Europeans, like Martin, she reconstructs the worldview that gave the experience of one group its content. With her study, scholarship on European-Indian relations comes full circle.

It may well seem to you at this point that, given the tremendous variation among the historical accounts, I had no choice but to end in relativism. If the experience of encountering conflicting versions of the "same" events suggests anything certain it is that the attitude a historian takes up in relation to a given event, the way in which he or she judges and even describes "it"—and the "it" has to go in quotation marks because, depending on the perspective, that event either did or did not occur—this stance, these judgments and descriptions are a function of the historian's position in relation to the subject. Miller, standing on the banks of the Congo, couldn't see the black men he was supervising because of his background, his assumptions, values, experiences, goals. Jennings, intent on exposing the distortions introduced into the historical record by Vaughan and his predecessors stretching all the way back to Winthrop, couldn't see that Winthrop and his peers were not racists but only Englishmen who looked at other cultures in the way their own culture had taught them to see one another. The historian can never escape the limitations of his or her own position in history and so inevitably gives an account that is an extension of the circumstances from which it springs. But it seems to me that when one is confronted with this particular succession of stories, cultural and historical relativism is not a position that one can comfortably assume. The phenomena to which these histories testify—conquest, massacre, and genocide, on the one hand; torture, slavery, and murder on the other—cry out for judgment. When faced with claims and counterclaims of this magnitude one feels obligated to reach an understanding of what actually did occur. The dilemma posed by the study of European-Indian relations in early America is that the highly charged nature of the materials demands a moral decisiveness which the succession of conflicting accounts effectively precludes. That

20. Ibid., p. 35.

is the dilemma I found myself in at the end of this course of reading, and which I eventually came to resolve as follows.

    After a while it began to seem to me that there was something wrong with the way I had formulated the problem. The statement that the materials on European-Indian relations were so highly charged that they demanded moral judgment, but that the judgment couldn't be made because all possible descriptions of what happened were biased, seemed to contain an internal contradiction. The statement implied that in order to make a moral judgment about something, you have to know something else first—namely, the facts of the case you're being called upon to judge. My complaint was that their perspectival nature would disqualify any facts I might encounter and that therefore I couldn't judge. But to say as I did that the materials I had read were "highly charged" and therefore demanded judgment suggests both that I was reacting to something real—to some facts—*and* that I had judged them. Perhaps I wasn't so much in the lurch morally or epistemologically as I had thought. If you— or I—react with horror to the story of the girl captured and enslaved by Comanches who touched a firebrand to her nose every time they wanted to wake her up, it's because we read this as a story about cruelty and suffering, and not as a story about the conventions of prisoner exchange or the economics of Comanche life. The *seeing* of the story as a cause for alarm rather than as a droll anecdote or a piece of curious information is evidence of values we already hold, of judgments already made, of facts already perceived as facts.

    My problem presupposed that I couldn't judge because I didn't know what the facts were. All I had, or could have, was a series of different perspectives, and so nothing that would count as an authoritative source on which moral judgments could be based. But, as I have just shown, I did judge, and that is because, as I now think, I did have some facts. I seemed to accept as facts that ninety percent of the native American population of New England died after the first hundred years of contact, that tribes in eastern Canada and the northeastern United States had a compact with the game they killed, that Comanches had subjected a captive girl to casual cruelty, that King Philip smoked a pipe, and so on. It was only where different versions of the same event came into conflict that I doubted the text was a record of something real. And even then, there was no question about certain major catastrophes. I believed that four hundred Pequots were killed near Saybrook, that Winthrop was the Governor of the Massachusetts Bay Colony when it happened, and so on. My sense that certain events, such as the Pequot War, did occur in no way reflected the indecisiveness that overtook me when I tried to choose among the various historical versions. In fact, the need I felt to make up my mind was impelled by the conviction that certain things *had* happened that shouldn't have happened. Hence it was never the case that "what happened" was completely unknowable or unavailable. It's rather that in the process of reading so many different approaches to the same phenomenon I became aware of the difference in the attitudes that informed these approaches. This awareness of the interests motivating each version cast suspicion over everything, in retrospect, and I ended by claiming that there was nothing I could know. This, I now see, was never really the case. But how did it happen?

Someone else, confronted with the same materials, could have decided that one of these historical accounts was correct. Still another person might have decided that more evidence was needed in order to decide among them. Why did I conclude that none of the accounts was accurate because they were all produced from some particular angle of vision? Presumably there was something in my background that enabled me to see the problem in this way. That something, very likely, was post-structuralist theory. I let my discovery that Vaughan was a product of the fifties, Jennings of the sixties, Rowlandson of a Puritan worldview, and so on lead me to the conclusion that all facts are theory dependent because that conclusion was already a thinkable one for me. My inability to come up with a true account was not the product of being situated nowhere; it was the product of certitude that existed *somewhere else,* namely, in contemporary literary theory. Hence, the level at which my indecision came into play was a function of particular beliefs I held. I was never in a position of epistemological indeterminacy, I was never *en abyme.* The idea that all accounts are perspectival seemed to give me a superior standpoint from which to view all the versions of "what happened," and to regard with sympathetic condescension any person so old-fashioned and benighted as to believe that there really was some way of arriving at the truth. But this skeptical standpoint was just as firm as any other. The fact that it was also seriously disabling—it prevented me from coming to any conclusion about what I had read—did not render it any less definite.

At this point something is beginning to show itself that has up to now been hidden. The notion that all facts are only facts within a perspective has the effect of emptying statements of their content. Once I had Miller and Vaughan and Jennings, Martin and Hudson, Axtell and Heard, Rowlandson and Wood and Whitaker, and Kupperman; I had Europeans and Indians, ships and canoes, wigwams and log cabins, bows and arrows and muskets, wigs and tattoos, whisky and corn, rivers and forts, treaties and battles, fire and blood—and then suddenly all I had was a meta-statement about perspectives. The effect of bringing perspectivism to bear on history was to wipe out completely the subject matter of history. And it follows that bringing perspectivism to bear in this way on any subject matter would have a similar effect; everything is wiped out and you are left with nothing but a single idea—perspectivism itself.

But—and it is a crucial but—all this is true only if you believe that there is an alternative. As long as you think that there are or should be facts that exist outside of any perspective, then the notion that facts are perspectival will have this disappearing effect on whatever it touches. But if you are convinced that the alternative does not exist, that there really are no facts except as they are embedded in some particular way of seeing the world, then the argument that a set of facts derives from some particular worldview is no longer an argument against that set of facts. If all facts share this characteristic, to say that any one fact is perspectival doesn't change its factual nature in the slightest. It merely reiterates it.

This doesn't mean that you have to accept just anybody's facts. You can show that what someone else asserts to be a fact is false. But it does mean that you can't argue that someone else's facts are not facts *because they are only the product of a perspective,* since this will be true of the facts that you perceive as well. What this means then is that arguments about "what happened" have to proceed much as they did before post-structuralism broke in with all its talk about language-based reality and culturally produced knowledge. Reasons must be given, evidence adduced, authorities citied, analogies drawn. Being aware that all facts are motivated, believing that people are always operating inside some particular interpretive framework or other is a pertinent argument when what is under discussion is the way beliefs are grounded. But it doesn't give one any leverage on the facts of a particular case.[21]

What this means for the problem I've been addressing is that I must piece together the story of European-Indian relations as best I can, believing this version up to a point, that version not at all, another almost entirely, according to what seems reasonable and plausible, given everything else that I know. And this, as I've shown, is what I was already doing in the back of my mind without realizing it, because there was nothing else I *could* do. If the accounts don't fit together neatly, that is not a reason for rejecting them all in favor of a metadiscourse about epistemology; on the contrary, one encounters contradictory facts and divergent points of view in practically every phase of life, from deciding whom to marry to choosing the right brand of cat food, and one decides as best one can given the evidence available. It is only the nature of the academic situation which makes it appear that one can linger on the threshold of decision in the name of an epistemological principle. What has really happened in such a case is that the subject of debate has changed from the question of what happened in a particular instance to the question of how knowledge

---

21. The position I've been outlining is a version of neopragmatism. For an exposition, see *Against Theory: Literary Studies and the New Pragmatism,* ed. W. J. T. Mitchell (Chicago, 1985).

is arrived at. The absence of pressure to decide what happened creates the possibility for this change of venue.

The change of venue, however, is itself an action taken. In diverting attention from the original problem and placing it where Miller did, on "the mind of man," it once again ignores what happened and still is happening to American Indians. The moral problem that confronts me now is not that I can never have any facts to go on, but that the work I do is not directed toward solving the kinds of problems that studying the history of European-Indian relations has awakened me to.

The Economy of Manichean Allegory:
The Function of Racial Difference
in Colonialist Literature

Abdul R. JanMohamed

Despite all its merits, the vast majority of critical attention devoted to colonialist literature restricts itself by severely bracketing the political context of culture and history. This typical facet of humanistic closure requires the critic systematically to avoid an analysis of the domination, manipulation, exploitation, and disfranchisement that are inevitably involved in the construction of any cultural artifact or relationship. I can best illustrate such closures in the field of colonialist discourse with two brief examples. In her book *The Colonial Encounter,* which contrasts the colonial representations of three European and three non-European writers, M. M. Mahood skirts the political issue quite explicitly by arguing that she chose those authors precisely because they are "innocent of emotional exploitation of the colonial scene" and are "distanced" from the politics of domination.[1]

We find a more interesting example of this closure in Homi Bhabha's criticism. While otherwise provocative and illuminating, his work rests on two assumptions—the unity of the "colonial subject" and the "ambivalence" of colonial discourse—that are inadequately problematized and, I feel, finally unwarranted and unacceptable. In rejecting Edward Said's "suggestion that colonial power and discourse is possessed entirely by the coloniser," Bhabha asserts, without providing any explanation, the unity of the "colonial subject (both coloniser and colonised)."[2] I do not wish to rule out, a priori, the possibility that at some rarefied theoretical level the varied material and discursive antagonisms between conquerors and natives can be reduced to the workings of a single "subject"; but such a unity, let alone its value, must be demonstrated, not assumed. Though he cites Frantz Fanon, Bhabha completely ignores Fanon's definition of the conqueror/native relation as a "Manichean" struggle—a definition that is not a fanciful metaphoric caricature but an accurate representation of a profound conflict.[3]

Consider, for instance, E. A. Brett's research, only one example I might adduce that corroborates Fanon's definition. Brett found that the European attempt to develop a capital-centered mode of agricultural production in Kenya, where farming was essentially precapitalistic, created a conflict between two incompatible modes of production and that "any effective development of one necessarily precluded an equivalent development of the other in the same social universe."[4] Native farming was centered around a subsistence economy and, more crucially, did not offer the means of production—namely, land and labor—for exchange on the market. Consequently, as Brett demonstrates, in order to commodify land and labor and make them available on the capitalist "market," the British systematically destroyed the native mode of production. In other words, the Europeans disrupted a material and discursive universe based on use-value and replaced it with one dominated by exchange-value. In this kind of context, what does it mean, in practice, to imply as Bhabha does that the native, whose entire economy and culture are destroyed, is somehow in "possession" of "colonial power"? Bhabha's unexamined conflation allows him to circumvent entirely the dense history of the material conflict between Europeans and natives and to focus on colonial discourse as if it existed in a vacuum.

This move in turn permits him to fetishize what he calls "colonial" discourse (that is, the discourse of the dominators *and* the dominated) and map its contradictions as the problematics of an "ambivalence," an "indeterminacy," that is somehow intrinsic to the authority of that discourse.[5] By dismissing "intentionalist" readings of such discourse as "idealist" quests, Bhabha is able to privilege its "ambivalence" and, thereby, to imply that its "authority" is genuinely and innocently *confused*, unable to choose between two equally valid meanings and representations. To impute in this way, at this late date, and through the back door, an innocent or naive "intention" to colonialist discourse is itself a naive act at best. Wittingly or otherwise, Bhabha's strategy serves the same ideological function as older, humanistic analyses: like Mahood, he represses the political history of colonialism, which is inevitably sedimented in its discourse.

Abdul R. JanMohamed, assistant professor of English at the University of California, Berkeley, is the author of *Manichean Aesthetics: The Politics of Literature in Colonial Africa.* He is a founding member and associate editor of *Cultural Critique* and is currently working on a study of Richard Wright.

We can better understand colonialist discourse, it seems to me, through an analysis that maps its ideological function in relation to actual imperialist practices. Such an examination reveals that any evident "ambivalence" is in fact a product of deliberate, if at times subconscious, imperialist duplicity, operating very efficiently through the economy of its central trope, the manichean allegory. This economy, in turn, is based on a transformation of racial difference into moral and even metaphysical difference. Though the phenomenological origins of this metonymic transformation may lie in the "neutral" perception of physical difference (skin color, physical features, and such), its allegorical extensions come to dominate every facet of imperialist mentality. Even the works of some of the most enlightened and critical colonial writers eventually succumb to a narrative organization based on racial/metaphysical oppositions, whose motives remain morally fixed but whose categories flex to accommodate any situation. I cannot trace the genealogy of the metonymic transformation and the resulting allegory in its entirety here; nevertheless, our examination must begin with a brief appraisal of the social, political, and economic ambience of colonial society, which is responsible for generating these duplicitous tropes.

1

The perception of racial difference is, in the first place, influenced by economic motives. For instance, as Dorothy Hammond and Alta Jablow have shown, Africans were perceived in a more or less neutral and benign manner before the slave trade developed; however, once the triangular trade became established, Africans were newly characterized as the epitome of evil and barbarity.[6] The European desire to exploit the resources of the colonies (including the natives, whom Europeans regarded as beasts of burden) drastically disrupted the indigenous societies. Through specific policies of population transfers, gerrymandering of borders, and forced production, to mention only a few such measures, European colonialists promoted the destruction of native legal and cultural systems and, ultimately, the negation of non-European civilizations.[7] These measures produce pathological societies, ones that exist in a state of perpetual crisis.[8]

To appreciate the function of colonialist fiction within this ambience, we must first distinguish between the "dominant" and the "hegemonic" phases of colonialism as well as between its material and discursive ideological practices. Throughout the dominant phase, which spans the period from the earliest European conquest to the moment at which a colony is granted "independence," European colonizers exercise direct and continuous bureaucratic control and military coercion of the natives: during this phase the "consent" of the natives is primarily passive and indirect.

Although we shouldn't overlook the various forms of native "cooperation"—for example, in the traffic of slaves—the point remains that such cooperation testifies less to a successful interpellation of the native than to the colonizer's ability to exploit preexisting power relations of hierarchy, subordination, and subjugation within native societies. Within the dominant phase (to which I will confine the scope of this paper), the indigenous peoples are subjugated by colonialist material practices (population transfers, and so forth), the efficacy of which finally depends on the technological superiority of European military forces. Colonialist discursive practices, particularly its literature, are not very useful in controlling the conquered group at this early stage: the native is not subjugated, nor does his culture disintegrate, simply because a European characterizes both as savage.

By contrast, in the hegemonic phase (or neocolonialism) the natives accept a version of the colonizers' entire system of values, attitudes, morality, institutions, and, more important, mode of production. This stage of imperialism does rely on the active and direct "consent" of the dominated, though, of course, the threat of military coercion is always in the background. The natives' internalization of Western cultures begins before the end of the dominant phase. The nature and the speed of this internalization depend on two factors: the many local circumstances and the emphasis placed on interpellation by various European colonial policies. But in all cases, the moment of "independence"—with the natives' obligatory, ritualized acceptance of Western forms of parliamentary government—marks the formal transition to hegemonic colonialism.

Distinguishing between material and discursive practices also allows us to understand more clearly the contradictions between the covert and overt aspects of colonialism. While the covert purpose is to exploit the colony's natural resources thoroughly and ruthlessly through the various imperialist material practices, the overt aim, as articulated by colonialist discourse, is to "civilize" the savage, to introduce him to all the benefits of Western cultures. Yet the fact that this overt aim, embedded as an assumption in all colonialist literature, is accompanied in colonialist texts by a more vociferous insistence, indeed by a fixation, upon the savagery and the evilness of the native should alert us to the real function of these texts: to justify imperial occupation and exploitation. If such literature can demonstrate that the barbarism of the native is irrevocable, or at least very deeply ingrained, then the European's attempt to civilize him can continue indefinitely, the exploitation of his resources can proceed without hindrance, and the European can persist in enjoying a position of moral superiority.

Thus a rigorous subconscious logic defines the relations between the covert and overt policies and between the material and discursive practices of colonialism. The ideological functions of colonialist fiction within the dominant phase of imperial control, then, must be understood not in terms of its putative or even real effects on the native but in terms of the exigencies of domestic—that is, European and colonialist—politics and culture; and the function of racial difference, of the fixation on and fetishization of native savagery and evil, must be mapped in terms of these exigencies and ideological imperatives. I do not wish to suggest, however, that racial denigration has no effect whatsoever on colonized intellectuals and literature. It does—but only during the late stages of the dominant phase and, more particularly, during the hegemonic phase.

Before turning to the question of racial difference in the works I will discuss, we need to note the relation of the individual author to the field of colonialist discourse. The dominant pattern of relations that controls the text within the colonialist context is determined by economic and political imperatives and changes, such as the development of slavery, that are external to the discursive field itself. The dominant model of power- and interest-relations in all colonial societies is the manichean opposition between the putative superiority of the European and the supposed inferiority of the native. This axis in turn provides the central feature of the colonialist cognitive framework and colonialist literary representation: the manichean allegory—a field of diverse yet inter-changeable oppositions between white and black, good and evil, superiority and inferiority, civilization and savagery, intelligence and emotion, ra-tionality and sensuality, self and Other, subject and object. The power relations underlying this model set in motion such strong currents that even a writer who is reluctant to acknowledge it and who may indeed be highly critical of imperialist exploitation is drawn into its vortex.[9] The writer is easily seduced by colonial privileges and profits and forced by various ideological factors (that I will examine below) to conform to the prevailing racial and cultural preconceptions. Thus the "author-function" in such texts, as elsewhere, "is tied to the legal and institutional systems that circumscribe, determine, and articulate the realm of discourses."[10] And since this "function" in the imperialist context confers on the author all the moral and psychological pleasures of manichean superiority, a "native" writer, such as V. S. Naipaul, can also be inducted, under the right circumstances, to fulfill the author-function of the colonialist writer.[11]

Another significant feature of the system governing colonialist fiction is the nature of its audience. Since the object of representation—the native—does not have access to these texts (because of linguistic barriers) and since the European audience has no direct contact with the native, imperialist fiction tends to be unconcerned with the truth-value of its representation. In fact, since such literature does not so much re-present as present the native for the first time, it is rarely concerned with overtly affirming the reader's experience of his own culture and therefore does not really solicit his approval: it exists outside the dialogic class discourse of European literature. The value of colonialist statements is consequently all the more dependent on their place in colonialist discourse and on "their capacity for circulation and exchange, their possibility of transformation, not only in the economy of discourse, but, more generally, in the administration of scarce resources."[12]

Just as imperialists "administer" the resources of the conquered country, so colonialist discourse "commodifies" the native subject into a stereotyped object and uses him as a "resource" for colonialist fiction. The European writer commodifies the native by negating his individuality, his subjectivity, so that he is now perceived as a generic being that can be exchanged for any other native (they all look alike, act alike, and so on). Once reduced to his exchange-value in the colonialist signifying system, he is fed into the manichean allegory, which functions as the currency, the medium of exchange, for the entire colonialist discursive system. The exchange function of the allegory remains constant, while the generic attributes themselves can be substituted infinitely (and even contradictorily) for one another. As Said points out in his study of Orientalism, such strategies depend on a "flexible *positional* superiority, which puts the Westerner in a whole series of possible relationships with the Orient without ever losing him the relative upper hand."[13] Within such a representational economy, the writer's task is to "administer" the relatively scarce resources of the manichean opposition in order to reproduce the native in a potentially infinite variety of images, the apparent diversity of which is determined by the simple machinery of the manichean allegory.

Hence we can observe a profound symbiotic relationship between the discursive and the material practices of imperialism: the discursive practices do to the symbolic, linguistic presence of the native what the material practices do to his physical presence; the writer commodifies him so that he can be exploited more efficiently by the administrator, who, of course, obliges by returning the favor in kind.[14] In fact, at any given point within a fully developed dominant imperialism, it is impossible to determine which form of commodification takes precedence, so entirely are the two forms intertwined.

2

Colonialist literature is an exploration and a representation of a world at the boundaries of "civilization," a world that has not (yet) been domesticated by European signification or codified in detail by its ideology. That world is therefore perceived as uncontrollable, chaotic, unattainable, and ultimately evil. Motivated by his desire to conquer and dominate, the imperialist configures the colonial realm as a confrontation based on differences in race, language, social customs, cultural values, and modes of production.

Faced with an incomprehensible and multifaceted alterity, the European theoretically has the option of responding to the Other in terms of identity or difference. If he assumes that he and the Other are essentially identical, then he would tend to ignore the significant divergences and to judge the Other according to his own cultural values. If, on the other hand, he assumes that the Other is irremediably different, then he would have little incentive to adopt the viewpoint of that alterity: he would again tend to turn to the security of his own cultural perspective. Genuine and thorough comprehension of Otherness is possible only if the self can somehow negate or at least severely bracket the values, assumptions, and ideology of his culture. As Nadine Gordimer's and Isak Dinesen's writings show, however, this entails in practice the virtually impossible task of negating one's very being, precisely because one's culture is what formed that being. Moreover, the colonizer's invariable assumption about his moral superiority means that he will rarely question the validity of either his own or his society's formation and that he will not be inclined to expend any energy in understanding the worthless alterity of the colonized. By thus subverting the traditional dialectic of self and Other that contemporary theory considers so important in the formation of self and culture, the assumption of moral superiority subverts the very potential of colonialist literature. Instead of being an exploration of the racial Other, such literature merely affirms its own ethnocentric assumptions; instead of actually depicting the outer limits of "civilization," it simply codifies and preserves the structures of its own mentality. While the surface of each colonialist text purports to represent specific encounters with specific varieties of the racial Other, the subtext valorizes the superiority of European cultures, of the collective process that has mediated that representation. Such literature is essentially specular: instead of seeing the native as a bridge toward syncretic possibility, it uses him as a mirror that reflects the colonialist's self-image.

Accordingly, I would argue that colonialist literature is divisible into two broad categories: the "imaginary" and the "symbolic."[15] The emotive as well as the cognitive intentionalities of the "imaginary" text are structured by objectification and aggression. In such works the native functions as an image of the imperialist self in such a manner that it reveals the latter's self-alienation. Because of the subsequent projection involved in this context, the "imaginary" novel maps the European's intense internal rivalry. The "imaginary" representation of indigenous people tends to coalesce the signifier with the signified. In describing the attributes or actions of the native, issues such as intention, causality, extenuating circumstances, and so forth, are completely ignored; in the "imaginary" colonialist realm, to say "native" is automatically to say "evil" and to evoke immediately the economy of the manichean allegory. The writer of such texts tends to fetishize a nondialectical, fixed opposition between the self and the native. Threatened by a metaphysical alterity that he has created, he quickly retreats to the homogeneity of his own group. Consequently, his psyche and text tend to be much closer to and are often entirely occluded by the ideology of his group.

Writers of "symbolic" texts, on the other hand, are more aware of the inevitable necessity of using the native as a mediator of European desires. Grounded more firmly and securely in the egalitarian imperatives of Western societies, these authors tend to be more open to a modifying dialectic of self and Other. They are willing to examine the specific individual and cultural differences between Europeans and natives and to reflect on the efficacy of European values, assumptions, and habits in contrast to those of the indigenous cultures. "Symbolic" texts, most of which thematize the problem of colonialist mentality and its encounter with the racial Other, can in turn be subdivided into two categories.

The first type, represented by novels like E. M. Forster's *A Passage to India* and Rudyard Kipling's *Kim,* attempts to find syncretic solutions to the manichean opposition of the colonizer and the colonized. This kind of novel overlaps in some ways with the "imaginary" text: those portions of the novel organized at the emotive level are structured by "imaginary" identification, while those controlled by cognitive intentionality are structured by the rules of the "symbolic" order. Ironically, these novels—which are conceived in the "symbolic" realm of intersubjectivity, heterogeneity, and particularity but are seduced by the specularity of "imaginary" Otherness—better illustrate the economy and power of the manichean allegory than do the strictly "imaginary" texts.

The second type of "symbolic" fiction, represented by the novels of Joseph Conrad and Nadine Gordimer, realizes that syncretism is impossible within the power relations of colonial society because such a context traps the writer in the libidinal economy of the "imaginary." Hence, becoming reflexive about its context, by confining itself to a rigorous examination of the "imaginary" mechanism of colonialist mentality, this type of fiction manages to free itself from the manichean allegory.

3

If every desire is at base a desire to impose oneself on another and to be recognized by the Other, then the colonial situation provides an ideal context for the fulfillment of that fundamental drive. The colonialist's military superiority ensures a complete projection of his self on the Other: exercising his assumed superiority, he destroys without any significant qualms the effectiveness of indigenous economic, social, political, legal, and moral systems and imposes his own versions of these structures on the Other. By thus subjugating the native, the European settler is able to compel the Other's recognition of him and, in the process, allow his own identity to become deeply dependent on his position as a master.[16] This enforced recognition from the Other in fact amounts to the European's narcissistic self-recognition since the native, who is considered too degraded and inhuman to be credited with any specific subjectivity, is cast as no more than a recipient of the negative elements of the self that the European projects onto him.[17] This transitivity and the preoccupation with the inverted self-image mark the "imaginary" relations that characterize the colonial encounter.

Nevertheless, the gratification that this situation affords is impaired by the European's alienation from his own unconscious desire. In the "imaginary" text, the subject is eclipsed by his fixation on and fetishization of the Other: the self becomes a prisoner of the projected image. Even though the native is negated by the projection of the inverted image, his presence as an absence can never be canceled. Thus the colonialist's desire only entraps him in the dualism of the "imaginary" and foments a violent hatred of the native. This desire to exterminate the brutes, which is thematized consciously and critically in "symbolic" texts such as *Heart of Darkness* and *A Passage to India,* manifests itself subconsciously in "imaginary" texts, such as those of Joyce Cary, through the narrators' clear relish in describing the mutilation of natives. "Imaginary" texts, like fantasies which provide naive solutions to the subjects' basic problems, tend to center themselves on plots that end with the elimination of the offending natives.

The power of the "imaginary" field binding the narcissistic colonialist text is nowhere better illustrated than in its fetishization of the Other. This process operates by substituting natural or generic categories for those that are socially or ideologically determined. All the evil characteristics and habits with which the colonialist endows the native are thereby not presented as the products of social and cultural difference but as characteristics inherent in the race—in the "blood"—of the native. In its extreme form, this kind of fetishization transmutes all specificity and difference into a magical essence. Thus Dinesen boldly asserts:

> The Natives were Africa in flesh and blood. . . . [The various cultures of Africa, the mountains, the trees, the animals] were different expressions of one idea, variations upon the same theme. It was not a congenial upheaping of heterogeneous atoms, but a heterogeneous upheaping of congenial atoms, as in the case of the oakleaf and the acorn and the object made from oak.[18]

As this example illustrates, it is not the stereotypes, the denigrating "images" of the native (which abound in colonialist literature), that are fetishized. Careful scrutiny of colonialist texts reveals that such images are used at random and in a self-contradictory fashion. For example, the narrator of Cary's *Aissa Saved* can claim that "Kolu children of old-fashioned families like Makunde's were remarkable for their gravity and decorum; . . . they were strictly brought up and made to behave themselves as far as possible like grown-ups."[19] He even shows one such child, Tanawe, behaving with great decorum and gravity. Yet the same narrator depicts Kolu adults who have converted to Christianity as naughty, irresponsible children. Given the colonialist mentality, the source of the contradiction is quite obvious. Since Tanawe is too young to challenge colonialism, she can be depicted in a benign manner, and the narrator can draw moral sustenance from the generosity of his portrayal. But the adult Kolus' desire to become Christians threatens to eliminate one of the fundamental differences between them and the Europeans; so the narrator has to impose a difference. The overdetermined image he picks (Africans = children) allows him to feel secure once again because it restores the moral balance in favor of the ("adult") Christian conqueror. Such contradictory use of images abounds in colonialist literature.

My point, then, is that the imperialist is not fixated on specific images or stereotypes of the Other but rather on the affective benefits proffered by the manichean allegory, which generates the various stereotypes. As I have argued, the manichean allegory, with its highly efficient exchange mechanism, permits various kinds of rapid transformations, for example, metonymic displacement—which leads to the essentialist metonymy, as in the above quotation from Dinesen—and metaphoric condensation—which accounts for the structure and characterization in Cary's *Mister Johnson*. Exchange-value remains the central motivating force of both colonialist material practice and colonialist literary representation.

The fetishizing strategy and the allegorical mechanism not only permit a rapid exchange of denigrating images which can be used to maintain a sense of moral difference; they also allow the writer to transform social and historical dissimilarities into universal, metaphysical differences. If, as Dinesen has done, African natives can be collapsed into African animals and mystified still further as some magical essence of the continent, then clearly there can be no meeting ground, no identity, between the social, historical creatures of Europe and the metaphysical alterity of the Calibans and Ariels of Africa. If the differences between the Europeans and the natives are so vast, then clearly, as I stated earlier, the process of civilizing the natives can continue indefinitely. The ideological function of this mechanism, in addition to prolonging colonialism, is to dehistoricize and desocialize the conquered world, to present it as a metaphysical "fact of life," before which those who have fashioned the colonial world are themselves reduced to the role of passive spectators in a mystery not of their making.

There are many formal consequences of this denial of history and normal social interaction. While masquerading under the guise of realist fiction, the colonialist text is in fact antagonistic to some of the prevailing tendencies of realism. As M. M. Bakhtin has argued, the temporal model of the world changes radically with the rise of the realist novel: "For the first time in artistic-ideological consciousness, time and the world become historical: they unfold . . . as becoming, as an uninterrupted movement into a real future, as a unified, all-embracing and unconcluded process."[20]

But since the colonialist wants to maintain his privileges by preserving the status quo, his representation of the world contains neither a sense of historical becoming, nor a concrete vision of a future different from the present, nor a teleology other than the infinitely postponed process of "civilizing." In short, it does not contain any syncretic cultural possibility, which alone would open up the historical process once more.

Gordimer has succinctly articulated the consequences of this foreclosure for the colonial writer:

> Cultural identity [is] "nothing more nor less than the mean between selfhood and otherness . . ."
> The dilemma of a literature in a multiracial [that is, imperialist] society, where the law effectively prevents any real identification of the writer with his society as a whole, so that ultimately he can identify only with his colour, distorts this mean irreparably. And cultural identity is the ground on which the exploration of self in the imaginative writer makes a national literature.[21]

For these reasons the colonialist text also lacks the domestic novel's inconclusive contact with an open-ended present. By producing a necessary incongruity between man and his potential, domestic fiction can actively engage the question of the hero's unrealized potential and demand and his inadequate response to his fate and situation. In the colonialist fiction, on the other hand, either the debased native's lack of potential is a foregone conclusion or, if he is endowed with potentiality—as, for example, Aladai is in Cary's *African Witch*—then it is violently and irrevocably foreclosed before the novel ends. The potentiality and even the humanity of the native are considered momentary aberrations that will inevitably subside and return him to his innate, inhuman barbarity. Similarly, the European's own potential, purpose, and direction are never called into question by the social and cultural alterity of the native since he is, after all, extremely debased or entirely inhuman.

The colonialist's need to perpetuate racial differences also prevents him, as we have seen, from placing the object of his representation, the racial Other, on the same temporally and socially valorized plane as that occupied by the author and the reader. This complicity between reader and author encourages an even further distancing of the represented world. We find the most telling version of this strategy in colonialist humor. In Cary's *Mister Johnson*, for instance, the ridiculousness of Johnson, a black, semiliterate clerk in the colonial service, depends on an implicit agreement between the narrator and the reader that Johnson's attempt to imitate English manners, values, and ideas is inherently absurd. Comic dismemberment in these kinds of novels does not demystify and familiarize the world but, rather, solidifies and reinforces the distance between the reader and the world. Even in a "symbolic" novel such as *Kim*, the absurdity of Hurree Chunder Mookerjee, M.A.—and, above all, of his desire to become a fellow of the Royal Society—depends on the same distancing strategy. In the manichean world of the colonizer and the colonized, of the master and the slave, distance tends to become absolute and qualitative rather than relative and quantitative. The world is perceived in terms of ultimate, fixed differences, and the privileging of experience, knowledge, and practice, which Bakhtin considers necessary for the development of the novel, tends to be ignored entirely.[22] The economic, social, and political hierarchical organization of the colonial society turns it into a quasi-feudal world, which finds its appropriate literary forms in the adaptable categories and hierarchically valorized structures of allegory and racial romance.

Conrad seems to have understood implicitly that such involvement in the colonial situation entailed a regression to the economy of the "imaginary" phase and its concomitant domination of the psyche. In many of his short stories and novels, he explores the edges of the European imperial world, and in *Heart of Darkness* he depicts the process whereby the colonialist is transformed by the structure he sets in place. Conrad's thorough comprehension of the imperial situation, the colonialist mind, and its literary implications manifests itself in his decision to write a "symbolic" novella that deliberately thematizes the libidinal economy of the "imaginary." His comprehension is equally evident in his choice of a form best suited to the colonialist context: a manichean allegory, with its metonymic machinery, based on an overdetermined metaphor of Africa as the heart of darkness and evil. The allegory operates through imagery of light and dark that functions simultaneously at the pseudo-religious, political, and psychological levels. Furthermore, it is buttressed by the parallel between the Roman conquest of Europe and the European conquest of Africa, which tends to dehistoricize Western colonialism. Yet through the imagery, the narrative frame, and the character development, Conrad ensures that in the final analysis his novella remains rooted in the "symbolic" realm.

He does so, first, by inverting the metaphor of darkness: through the breaks in the narrative, he demonstrates that darkness is present in London; he characterizes Brussels, the whited sepulcher, as the door to darkness, guarded by the angels of death; and, by insisting that the Belgian Congo is not initially a dark but a blank spot on the map, he implies that darkness, both as a metaphor and as the practice emblematized by slavery, comes with colonial occupation. By characterizing Marlow as Buddha, by implicitly equating his voyage with Christ's journey into the wilderness, and by thus turning his "inconclusive" story into a modern parable, Conrad rescues his novella from the easy satisfaction of the allegorical fantasy typical of the narcissistic colonialist text and transforms it into a story that becomes meaningful through the exegetical participation of the audience. Finally, by granting Kurtz a momentary awareness of his actions and by presenting us with Marlow's meditation about their implication, Conrad demystifies important aspects of the fetishistic and occluded mentality of the colonizer.

In doing so, Conrad shows that the transformation from the overt to the covert colonialist aims, depicted by the degeneration of Kurtz, is mediated by the infinite power of the conqueror, by his arrogation of the position of a God among the natives. Once he succumbs to his own power, Kurtz is trapped by his own self-image, which he superimposes on the natives. He eventually projects his self-hatred, as well, in his desire to exterminate all the brutes, whom he now considers the source of the evil. Yet despite what writers like Chinua Achebe say about the denigration of Africans in *Heart of Darkness,* Africans are an incidental part, and not the main objects of representation, in the novella.[23] At times Conrad's depiction of Africans is quite unbiased and perceptive—for example, when he equates the function of African drumming with that of church bells in a Christian country, he rejects the traditional colonialist use of drumming as the emblem of the natives' evil, bloodthirsty intentions. He is not entirely free, however, from the colonialist mentality that he reveals so well: his depiction of the intimated cannibalism is tasteless and probably groundless, and he represents and eventually forecloses the syncretic potentiality of his African helmsman through traditional colonialist humor.

We can also see embedded within Conrad's novella a number of subgenres that are always based on the manichean allegory: the adventure story—such as those of G. A. Henty that are specifically designed for young boys or those of Edgar Wallace and H. Rider Haggard that are also geared to adults—about Europeans battling dark, evil forces; the story utilizing Africa as an alluring, destructive woman—from Haggard's *She* and *Nanda the Lily* to Marguerite Steen's *Sun Is My Undoing*—that recalls Kurtz's fixation on the dark, satanic woman; and the story presenting Africa as a dark labyrinth—which Conrad seems to have inaugurated and which finds its more recent manifestations in such novels as Graham Greene's *Heart of the Matter*—wherein a European journeys into Africa in order to discover his own identity as well as the meaning of life and death. All these are implicitly at work in *Heart of Darkness*. The only subgenre not included in the novella (but which Conrad understood thoroughly and dramatized in *Lord Jim,* in Jim's journey to the mythic world of Patusan) is the narrative depicting Africa as an uncorrupted Eden. But whether these versions of Africa are benign or denigrating, they are all manichean and essentially unchanging. As Hammond and Jablow conclude after surveying four centuries of British writing about Africa, "whether confident or doubtful, the writers describe Africa in the same conventions. The image of Africa remains the negative reflection, the shadow, of the British self-image."[24]

The most significant formal manifestation of the manichean allegory is the racial romance. Northrop Frye's definition of the romance also appropriately describes this subgenre: "The essential difference between novel and romance lies in the conception of characterization. The romancer does not attempt to create 'real people' so much as stylized figures which expand into psychological archetypes. It is in romance that we find Jung's libido, anima, and shadow reflected in the hero, heroine, and villain respectively." Where the novelist deals with personae and a stable society, the "romancer deals with individuality, with characters *in vacuo* idealized by revery."[25] In the racial, colonialist version of this genre, the villains are always the dark, evil natives (and, occasionally, whites who sympathize or consort with the natives) who are used simultaneously as stereotypes and archetypes. Racial romances can vary from pristine fantasy versions to more mixed and problematic ones, from Haggard's *She* to André Brink's *A Chain of Voices*. In all cases, however, they pit civilized societies against the barbaric aberrations of an Other, and they always end with the elimination of the threat posed by the Other and the legitimation of the values of the good, civilized society. The ideological function of this form of "kidnapped romance" is to justify the social function of the dominant class and to idealize its acts of protection and responsibility.[26] This genre is not only suited to but is an integral and necessary part of the dominant phase of colonialism. Its persistence and the obsessive preoccupation that Cary, for one, has had with it in spite of his desire to move away from it testify to the fact that this form is determined by colonialist social and economic structures.[27]

Finally, we must briefly consider the fact that where dominant colonialism and racism still exist today we will find examples of racial romance and allegory. The "Republic" of South Africa, which has codified one of the most developed forms of racism, has recently produced two worthy paradigms: André Brink's *A Chain of Voices* and J. M. Coetzee's *Waiting for the Barbarians*.[28] At the level of cognitive intentionality, Brink's work is a "radical" historical novel. It depicts a failed revolt of black, "Coloured," and Asian slaves against their Afrikaner master in the South African hinterland of the early 1800s. By endowing each character with a distinctive individual voice, Brink builds up a polyphonic chorus, spanning two generations, that is designed to explore from various viewpoints the causes and nature of the revolt. To give a voice to slaves and particularly to their desire for freedom is no doubt a courageous and provocative act in contemporary South Africa. Nonetheless, the novel remains rooted in racial stereotypes/archetypes. The latter are not crude, for both the white and the leading nonwhite characters have depth. However, the only distinction between the two racial groups, other than the obvious one between masters and slaves, is that the whites experience severe sexual repression, while the nonwhites are obsessed with sex; indeed, some of the nonwhites can perceive themselves only in terms of sexual pleasure and fecundity. The undiscriminating sexuality of Ma-Rose, the slave earth mother, is endowed with an ill-defined liberatory quality, and the efficient and immediate cause of the revolt is a series of sexual transgressions by the white masters. Thus we see, once again, that the very conception of the novel, its emotive intentionality, is determined by the "imaginary" mechanism of the manichean allegory: the whites are in perfect control of themselves, while the natives, who indiscriminately indulge their sexual appetites, clearly lack control and hence need to be managed. The "historical" nature of the novel is also undermined, with unintentional irony, by the framing device. The preface of the novel presents the court's formal accusation against the rebels, and the epilogue presents the conviction and sentencing. The main body of the narrative is thus intended to examine the "reality" bracketed between legal facts. Yet the legal facts also serve to bracket the narrative from the external historical world: they utterly seal the failure of the rebellion. This drastic legal closure cuts off all historical continuity and the hope for change.

Coetzee's *Waiting for the Barbarians*, a deliberate allegory, epitomizes the dehistoricizing, desocializing tendency of colonialist fiction. Set in a remote border town of a socially and historically unspecified empire, the allegory focuses on a liberal judge's reluctant, passive participation in the fascist activity of his country. The novel does justice to the themes of a liberal's complicity with fascism, his subsequent sense of guilt, and, most important, the function of manichean polarity within the empire; it shows without any hesitation that the empire projects its own barbarism onto the Other beyond its borders. Although the novel is obviously generated by white South Africa's racial paranoia and the guilt of its liberals, *Waiting for the Barbarians*, unlike Conrad's *Heart of Darkness*, refuses to acknowledge its historical sources or to make any allusions to the specific barbarism of the apartheid regime. The novel thus implies that we are all somehow equally guilty and that fascism is endemic to all societies. In its studied refusal to accept historical responsibility, this novel, like all "imaginary" colonialist texts, attempts to mystify the imperial endeavor by representing the relation between self and Other in metaphysical terms. The fundamental strategy of all such fiction is its unchanging presentation of the natives' inferiority as an unalterable metaphysical fact. Thus, for instance, Joyce Cary, after spending years trying to "civilize" the natives of Nigeria, confidently asserts that they should not be given independence: "An overcrowded raft manned by children who had never seen the sea would have a better chance in a typhoon" than would the Africans in managing their own destinies.[29]

4

This adamant refusal to admit the possibility of syncretism, of a rapprochement between self and Other, is the most important factor distinguishing the "imaginary" from the "symbolic" colonialist text. The "symbolic" text's openness toward the Other is based on a greater awareness of *potential* identity and a heightened sense of the *concrete* socio-politico-cultural differences between self and Other. Although the "symbolic" writer's understanding of the Other proceeds through self-understanding, he is freer from the codes and motifs of the deeper, collective classification system of his culture. In the final analysis, his success in comprehending or appreciating alterity will depend on his ability to bracket the values and bases of his culture. He may do so very consciously and deliberately, as Forster does in *A Passage to India,* or he may allow the emotions and values instilled in him during his social formation in an alien culture to inform his appraisals of the Other, as Kipling does in *Kim.* These two novels offer the most interesting attempts to overcome the barriers of racial difference.

"The racial problem can take subtle forms," says the narrator of *A Passage to India,* and in order to focus on the subtler versions, Forster firmly and mercilessly satirizes the cruder, "imaginary" forms of colonialist racism.[30] Although his statements verge at times on the stereotypic/archetypic colonialist generalizations (for instance: "Like most Orientals, Aziz overrated hospitality" [*PI*, p. 142]), Forster does not present us with stereotypes. The main characters may be flatter than in his previous novels, but in the context of colonialist literature they are well-rounded individuals who adequately represent themselves as well as some of the general characteristics of their cultures. Thus, for instance, the general differences between Muslim and Hindu beliefs and between Anglo-Indian and English values are concretely and accurately delineated. Forster clearly understood and represented the British colonialists' "imaginary" fixation on racial difference and all the psychic and social distortion it entails. Benita Parry succinctly characterizes them in her analysis:

> While profiting from the fear on which the Raj rests, the Anglo-Indians are victims of a fear which India arouses in them. They live amidst scenery they do not understand, sense that Indians hate them and feel India to be a poisonous country intending evil against them. Already coarsened by their status in India, the crisis generated by Adela Quested's accusation against Aziz hurls them into cruder demonstrations of their hostility, some demanding holocausts of natives, others longing to inflict humiliating punishment.[31]

The retreat of Anglo-Indians into the simple, manichean emotions of the "imaginary," their negation of "free intellectual inquiry and accommodating civilized personal relations,"[32] is also clearly castigated by Forster: "[Fielding] was still after facts, though the herd had decided on emotion. Nothing enrages Anglo-India more than the lantern of reason if it is exhibited for one moment after its extinction is decreed" (*PI*, p. 165). Forster's representation of the Indians' cruder attempts to overcome the effects of racial denigration—for example, the servility of the colonized, the easily wounded pride and vanity of Aziz, the histrionic outbursts of Mahmoud Ali in court, and other such manifestations of self-pity—are equally acerbic and penetrating. All of these, however, provide the backdrop against which Forster examines the more genuine and well-intentioned efforts of some of the Indians and the few British, those still not entirely contaminated by colonialist values, to overcome the barriers of racial difference.

Yet the very devices—the landscape of India and, in particular, the Marabar Caves, which become the efficient cause of mystical experiences and the major crisis in the novel—through which Forster chooses to examine the possibilities of cultural and racial rapprochement (as well as the larger issue of the spiritual and metaphysical meaning of human endeavor that is the central preoccupation of the novel) eventually guarantee their failure. He characterizes India as a land of pathos, of an ontological homesickness, a land that knows "the whole world's trouble, to its uttermost depth": "[India] calls 'Come' through her hundred mouths, through objects ridiculous and august. But come to what? She has never defined. She is not a promise, only an appeal" (*PI*, p. 136). The pathos is embodied in the Marabar Hills and Caves and is characterized by their eternal ambiguity. In the scene prior to the incidents in the caves, Forster takes some pains to establish, through the discussion about some mounds and a snake, that the Indian mind is steeped in and thrives on ambiguity: "Everything seemed cut off at its root, and therefore infected with illusion" (*PI*, p. 140). The ambiguity of the caves—the absolute "Nothing" which inheres in them and the experience of which is the goal of Jain religion—comes to represent the essence of Indian metaphysics, and, as Frederick Crews points out, metaphysics rather than morality preoccupies Forster in *A Passage to India*.[33] The careful correlations between the iconography of the caves and the metaphors of Jain metaphysics stress Forster's concern with the concepts of identity and difference that Indian philosophy privileges.[34] The caves represent the fundamental, unconscious identity from which all natural and social differences emanate and to which they all return when they can escape their phenomenal manifestation. Mrs. Moore and Professor Godbole experience this kind of unity, and Greysford and Sorley anxiously speculate about it in their own Christian terminology.

Given Mrs. Moore's spiritual concerns and her rejection of the value of social relations (see *PI*, p. 135), the caves echo her unconscious meditation with "boum," itself an echo of the sacred Hindu syllable "om," the meditation on which leads eventually to an experience of transcendent unity, identity, and silence that erases all the categories of thought (and thereby of nature), all the differences posited by signification. For Adela Quested, balanced delicately between the spiritual concerns of Mrs. Moore and the purely social ones of Fielding (who finds the caves meaningless and unimpressive), the unconscious realm of the caves mirrors her own repressed sexuality, the horror of which is quickly projected, with the eager help of the Anglo-Indian community (well versed in such projection), onto the racial Other, Aziz, who was the object of her fantasy. Thus Forster, too, endows not the native but the land, emblematized by the caves, with a specular function. Adela's repression and projection are not rescinded until the courtroom scene, when she is once again aroused by the physical beauty of that icon of god-as-unconscious, the punkah wallah, and by the deification of Mrs. Moore's name, which, like other mantras, also leads to the unconscious identity underlying difference.

Yet, having invested "India" (the land, the caves, and the non-Muslim Indian religions) with this particular metaphysics of identity and difference, Forster recoils from it in mild horror. His subconscious rejection of it is revealed by the chaos and danger that follow each encounter with the all-consuming transcendental identity: immediately after her experience in the caves, Mrs. Moore is panicked and hurt by the crowd of wild, uncontrolled Indians that surge into the cave; Adela feels sexually abused after her visit; her encounter, in the courtroom, with the iconic representation of the unconscious is followed by pandemonium that symbolically threatens the order of the British Empire; and Godbole's mystical experience of identity is surrounded by the utter chaos of the Gokul Ashtami festival. Even a momentary transcendence of difference, Forster seems to fear, will lead to uncontrollable chaos.

A Passage to India also abounds in *conscious* rejection of the chaos that, from Forster's viewpoint, attends the discovery of transcendent identity. The echo returns to tell Mrs. Moore that "everything exists, nothing has value," and she is gradually terrified by the realization that everything—the concepts of eternity and infinity, the wisdom of "talkative Christianity," and even her affection for her children and Aziz—is "boum," Nothing (*PI*, pp. 149, 150). In consequence, she wishes to leave India as soon as possible. Her experiences may well be the product of disillusioned old age, as Crews argues, but the fear of identity manifests itself in other forms as well.[35] India itself (which is a protagonist rather than a background in this novel) mocks Mrs. Moore's discovery of identity by confronting her with its differences: as she sails, the palm trees of India say to her, " 'So you thought an echo was India; you took the Marabar caves as final?' they laughed. 'What have we in common with them, or they with Asirgarh? Good-bye!' " (*PI*, p. 210). Difference, then, mocks the primacy of identity, but the result is not order. Like Fielding, who prefers the "order" of Renaissance Italy to the "chaos" of India, the narrator too withdraws from the emotional demands inherent in the process of identifying with an alterity:

> How indeed is it possible for one human being to be sorry for all the sadness that meets him on the face of the earth, for the pain that is endured not only by men, but by animals and plants, and

perhaps by the stones? The soul is tired in a moment, and in fear of losing the little she does understand, she *retreats to the permanent lines which habit or chance have dictated,* and suffers there. [*PI,* pp. 247–48; my emphasis][36]

Just as the novel retreats from the demands of metaphysical identity to the safety of phenomenal difference, so conversely it avoids the prospects of interracial identity by evoking metaphysical difference—that is, it takes refuge behind the "permanent" ideological boundaries defined by "habit or chance," by culture or race that has been turned into a metaphysical fact. The only relationship with the potential for transcending this kind of racial barrier fails, but the reasons for the failure are rather curious. In spite of Fielding's rationality, lack of racial prejudice, and humaneness, he is unable to "give in to the East" and live in "a condition of affectionate dependence upon it" as Aziz wants him to. For Fielding, "dependence" means becoming subservient, like Mohammed Latif, and such conversion is naturally beyond him: "When they argued about it something racial intruded—not bitterly, but inevitably, like the colour of their skins: coffee-colour versus pinko-grey" (*PI,* p. 260). The misunderstanding or mis-interpretation about subservience seems, at first sight, like an attempt to avoid the possibility of a genuine friendship. Indeed, Forster is quite ambivalent about identifying the causes that perpetuate racial difference. On initial consideration, the discussion between Aziz and Fielding at the end of the novel strongly implies that colonialism, which necessarily involves the subordination of one to the other, is the real barrier. But when Fielding finally asks why he and Aziz cannot be friends even though they both want it, the negative reply comes not from either man but from the many objects, both "ridiculous and august." The "India" that had said "Come" and that, as we have seen, is the embodiment of an unpalatable metaphysical calculus of identity and difference, now says "No" to the possibility of overcoming racial alterity. In the final analysis, racial difference is once again supported and justified by metaphysical difference. The metaphysical preoccupation of *A Passage to India* is a culmination of problems that Forster had been examining throughout his work, and his decision to cast his concerns in terms of Indian philosophy is innocent and logical. But the narrative decision to turn India into a metaphysical protagonist inherently antithetical to Western liberal humanism probably stems from a sense of larger cultural differences, the machinery of which is similar to that of the manichean allegory.

A Passage to India is in many ways a far more penetrating and satisfying novel than *Kim.* But, ironically enough, Kipling, the champion of colonialism and British superiority, has produced the novel that more intriguingly explores the issues of racial barriers and syncretic possibility. This is due to the fact that Forster's depiction of racial and cultural difference is ultimately based on a rational, intellectual concern, whereas Kipling's is determined by strong emotional ties that collide with his intellectual prejudice and colonialist sympathies. Kipling's own childhood in India is quite obviously the basis of Kim's affection for the Indian world; and, in the context of colonial fiction, a novel that proceeds from emotional identification with the Other offers the most thorough vision of the syncretic possibility.

In *Kim,* Kipling has created a lovable, honest rogue who easily wins the reader's affection, which the narrator then harnesses to Kim's affection for India. We are thus introduced to a positive, detailed, and nonstereotypic portrait of the colonized that is unique in colonialist literature. The narrator seems to find as much pleasure in describing the varied and tumultuous life of India as Kim finds in experiencing it. What may initially seem like a rapt aesthetic appreciation of Indian cultures turns out, on closer examination, to be a positive acceptance and celebration of difference. Kim delights in changing his appearance and identity, in becoming Other, and he loves to live in a world of pure becoming. He is a world of infinite concrete potentiality. As an orphan (a fact that is inconsequential to him), he has no origins and therefore no familial, social, political, or teleological constraints either. Endowed by the narrator with special talents, he can do anything and become anybody. Kim and his celebration of Indian cultures seem like perfect embodiments of Kipling's syncretic desires. In fact, the structures of Kim's character and his situation reveal the imperative that is essential for the fulfillment of that desire. Because Kim's self is entirely decentered and malleable, he finds pleasure in becoming an Other and in the variety and difference in his world. Occasionally and momentarily he is troubled by his lack of fixed identity, but in extreme situations he temporarily finds a center by chanting his name. This ability to forgo a permanent fixed self, which is essential if one is going to understand and appreciate a racial or cultural alterity, is turned into a positive principle in *Kim.* The novel also implicitly celebrates the analogous notion of *maya,* which means both "creation" and "illusion." Kim delights in creating illusions of himself, and eventually the question about his identity and his political role as a spy is linked up with the lama's philosophical theories about the illusion of the phenomenal world.

Kipling's choice of the picaresque form is not only appropriate to this story but also bolsters the unique position of this novel in the gamut of colonialist fiction. Like the Grand Trunk Road, the novel continuously accommodates a wide variety of episodes and people, including the "low life" of India, without distancing them through moral disapproval or a preponderance of colonialist humor. In fact, it familiarizes the mundane world of the colonized through gentle, affectionate humor and in this way overcomes the barriers of racial difference better than any other colonialist novel. It rescues the native cultures from the prejudged allegorical closure of the "imaginary" text and brings them into the open-ended, transitory, contemporary world; in keeping with the personality and values of its protagonist, it presents the world as becoming, as a movement into the future, and raises the question of unrealized potential and demand.

Yet underneath the celebration of Indian cultures lurks the problem of racial difference. Is Kim white, or is he a native? The underlying problem is that the birth of a genuinely syncretic subject necessarily implies the death of an exclusively British subject. Consequently, the novel equivocates: while Kim insists that he is an Indian, the narrator adamantly asserts Kim's British origins. Kim is an Irish orphan who has been brought up entirely within various Indian cultures: he looks, behaves, and thinks like an Indian, speaks and dreams only in Hindustani, and is more afraid of the English than are other native children. Subconsciously aware of the enormous weight of this social formation, the narrator tries to negate it at the very beginning of the novel:

> *Though* he was burned black as any native; *though* he spoke the vernacular by preference, and his mother-tongue in a clipped, uncertain sing-song; *though* he consorted on terms of perfect equality with the small boys of the bazaar; Kim was white—a poor white of the very poorest.[37]

Thus we see the old manichean dichotomies surfacing once again: in the colonialist universe nurture is ephemeral—one's culture is inherited, like the color of skin, through the genes. This struggle between Kim and the narrator continues throughout the novel. Every time someone suggests that he is white, Kim denies it vehemently and even insists that he will die if he is removed from his beloved Indians. The narrative, however, burdens him with a racial destiny that must, of course, be fulfilled: his father's regiment will discover and restore him to his race. Eventually, the novel works out a satisfactory compromise, which, for all its subtlety, is once again a product of the infinitely flexible categories of the manichean allegory.

The compromise also resolves the problem of Kim's origins. Among other things, *Kim* is a story of the prolonged and unnatural recovery of the paternal function, and the struggle over Kim's inheritance is a manifestation of the conflict over cultural allegiance. Kim is an orphan, a fact that he volunteers repeatedly when he is pretending to be a beggar. As he matures and gradually is enlisted as a spy, he develops allegiances to various Indian and European adults. Eventually, some of them adopt him as their son, and he accepts them as fathers and mothers. The process of mutual adoption between Mahbub Ali and Kim is explicitly, if not legally, ceremonious; the relationship between the Teshoo Lama and Kim, between a religious master and his disciple, is that of a spiritual father and son; Hurree Babu acts and is accepted as Kim's elder brother;

and the Sahiba becomes his mother. All these relations are deeply emotional and specific: each "parent" or "sibling" sees the chameleonic Kim as a unique being, and he in turn draws a different kind of sustenance from each of them. In contrast, his relationship to two Englishmen who control the British espionage activities in India and take charge of his formal education (though it is financed by the lama) is cold and rational. Kim is fully aware that Creighton's largess and protection are based on an ulterior motive (see *K*, p. 133). While the Indians keep reminding him that he is white, the Englishmen tell him not to alienate himself from the Indians. Thus the struggle over the inheritance is resolved through a bifurcation of the paternal function: on the one hand, Kim's *personal* and *emotional* allegiance to the Indians and, on the other, his *impersonal* and *rational* relation to the Englishmen.

This solution plunges the novel back into colonialist ideology. According to the manichean allegory, Europeans are rational and intelligent, while Orientals are emotional and sensuous. *Kim* does not resort to racist stereotypes; the Indians are portrayed as being intelligent. Kim's allegiance to them, however, is entirely emotional, whereas his relationship to whites is entirely rational and impersonal—they simply train his mind. Hence, the results of the syncretic experiment are finally decided by manichean bifurcations. Furthermore, Kim's initiation into espionage, his becoming an *intelligence* agent, allows the white Kim to serve colonialist power and the Indian Kim to consort with various natives.

Kim's first major accomplishment as a spy is to thwart Russian and French agents who are trying to subvert the British Empire in India. As a "protector" of India, Kim also helps to bolster the overt colonialist aims (to protect and civilize the Indians) while in fact prolonging the lease of the covert policies. Kim becomes involved in espionage because he loves to play games of illusion and to experience the variety of life. He has no ulterior motives in this: he plays at the "Great Game" of life (and espionage) simply for the pleasure of playing, not for the sake of any profit. Yet in this specific use-value that motivates Kim, the British colonialists and their Indian agents are able to detect and exploit his exchange-value: it is precisely because Kim can "exchange" himself with any native that he is useful to the British. Thus like other colonialist writers, Kipling also builds a novel around the exchange-value of the native, or quasi native. Not once does the fascinating possibility that Kim's syncretism could have a significance other than its use for British colonialism cross the threshold of awareness in this novel.

The hero's syncretic potential is foreclosed and his celebration of that syncretism is limited by the narrative decision not to probe beyond his adolescence. The foreclosure is part of a larger strategy of containment. As John McClure has observed, Kipling creates an idyllic world in *Kim* by purging all significant danger or evil from the novel and by excluding the two social forces that most infuriated him: the imperial administrative hierarchy and the emerging nationalist Indian bourgeoisie. Both these forces are present in the novel in only their most marginal and absurd forms. More crucially, however, "what Kipling excludes, ultimately, is history, the vital force changing Indian society. He does so by focusing on either side of the historical process, on the plentitude of the moment [Kim's experiences of the highways, bazaars, and so forth] and the finality of the eternal [the "Great Game," the lama's search, and so forth]."[38] Despite all its concreteness, then, the syncretism of *Kim* is founded both on the fixed oppositions of the manichean allegory and on the ahistorical abstractness of wish fulfillment.

Kipling understands and flirts with the concept of *maya*—the notion that illusion inheres in all the noemata of human and natural creation and in the noetics of human perception—at several different levels of the novel, but ultimately the problematics of *maya*, too, are displaced by the colonialist preoccupation with race. The lama feels that the whole phenomenal world is an illusion and that everyone is "deceived by the shadow of appearance" (*K*, p. 286), but Kipling is gently mocking him: he is entirely blind to the fact that his unique disciple is a spy and is using him to thwart the foreign agents. Mahbub Ali, Hurree Babu, Kim, and the other British agents are playing their own "Great Game" of *maya*, masking their real purposes and identities while trying to probe beneath the appearances of Indian political life. Whereas the narrator dismisses the lama's game of *maya*, that of the spies continues indefinitely because its perpetuation is necessary for the resolution of the third game—the game of Kim's identity. Only so long as Kim is a spy can he continue to be an Englishman while appearing to be an Indian. For the narrator, the only certainty behind the appearances of the novel is the racial identity of Kim.

5

European fiction that deals with the colonial context is not invariably caught in the pitfalls of the "imaginary" relations with the racial Other. One type manages to avoid the world of specularity. Another type, at times, even breaks through the barriers of fetishized racial difference, and, though unable to achieve some "genuine" or "objective" understanding of the Other, it offers evidence of a dialectical, mutually modifying relation between self and Other. Both varieties, however, pay a certain price in order to avoid the narcissistic world of the colonialist.

The first type of writer manages to resist the pull of the "imaginary" realm by rigorously eschewing the temptation to represent the Other. Whether deliberate or subconscious, this decision is based on an understanding that differences between self and Other cannot be adequately transcended within the colonial context. Consequently, the writer chooses instead to focus almost exclusively on the subjugating process and on the mentality of the conqueror. Conrad follows this course most of the time, but occasionally he slips either into the colonialist mode of perception or into the world of the Other.[39] In *Nostromo,* as in *Heart of Darkness,* he stereotypes the Other, in this case the South American Indian, but uses him as a background in order to examine the imperial process itself. Thus *Nostromo* can be read as a study of the alienating power of exchange-value, emblematized by the silver. Idealists and cynics, reactionaries and revolutionaries, pompous fools and lucid thinkers, altruistic and egotistic men and women are all eventually "corrupted" and alienated by their attempt to use the silver as a medium of exchange in order to gratify their "real" desires. The novel is relentlessly preoccupied with the fundamental motive of colonialism, that is, with the desire for profit, which is ultimately the desire to control the medium of exchange. Accordingly, Conrad's notions of capitalism/imperialism are, as Fredric Jameson implies, both the source and object of *Nostromo:* "the emergence of capitalism as . . . an always-already-begun dynamic, as the supreme and privileged mystery of a synchronic system which, once in place, discredits the attempts of 'linear' history or the habits of the diachronic mind to conceive of its beginnings."[40] However, in the context of colonialist discourse, it must be emphasized that Conrad is able to achieve this apparently impossible feat precisely by focusing on the colonialist manifestation of capitalism, that is, on the space in which capitalism reproduces itself and rehearses its own history. In this capacity, *Nostromo* functions as a mirror—it shows capitalism, in its process of subjugating the Other, its own specular image.

Nadine Gordimer, a contemporary writer whose interrogation of colonialist intervention is even more relentless in some ways than Conrad's, began her career with a clear understanding of the "imaginary" trap. At a crucial point in her first novel, the heroine's developing awareness of the manichean oppositions enforced by apartheid is mediated by an inverted image of the self. Helen Shaw first sees Mary Seswayo, one of the few black women students at the university she attends, in a mirror, and, as their glances meet, Helen for the first time recognizes, in the other woman's face, her own idealistic anticipation of boundless intellectual stimulation and infinite justice that she expects the university to offer.[41] Apartheid, however, will neither allow Helen to become intimate with her Other nor permit her to pursue a self-development untainted with its fascist precepts. The novel ends with her determination to avoid, at all costs, the ideological closures of a racist, exploitative society. Henceforth, all of Gordimer's novels focus on the bankruptcy of the liberal ideology, on the effects of South African fascism on the liberal consciousness of her white protagonists, and on their progressive radicalization. When she does enter the world of the Other, as in *July's People,* it is primarily to examine the dependence of whites on their African servants. Unable and unwilling to turn away from the colonial situation, Gordimer makes

a virtue of necessity by systematically scrutinizing the social and psychological effects of the manichean bifurcation on her white protagonists,
even though she is acutely aware that the price she pays for this deliberately
restricted focus is her inability, as a writer, to participate in the formation
of a genuinely national literature.[42]

Occasionally a writer overcomes the racial barriers and is significantly
influenced by the dominated Other. Isak Dinesen is an interesting case
in point. Her autobiographical works, *Out of Africa* and *Shadows on the
Grass,* clearly show that she was strongly influenced by the oral/mythic
culture of the Africans (which has a phenomenology significantly different
from that of chirographic cultures).[43] It can be argued that her tales, the
themes of which are only incidentally connected with Africa, are influenced
by oral narratives. Dinesen's understanding and appreciation of the Gikuyu,
Masai, and Somali cultures are the result of her willingness to examine
and decenter herself and her culture in the presence of the Other. As
she looks at herself through the eyes of natives, she begins to realize that
her cultural values, and therefore the self constituted by those values,
are entirely relative; instead of panicking, however, she is able to accept
the experience and even attain a partial transcendence through it, which
once again verifies the power of the manichean allegory. Her treatment
of her African servants and laborers and her regard for their dignity
and feelings improve dramatically as a result of her transformation. But
much of her colonialist rhetoric remains intact: she thinks of Africans
as primitive children. Though she sympathizes with their plight under
colonialism and makes genuine and significant efforts to improve their
situation, her representation of Africans is nonetheless determined by
the pervasive currency of the manichean allegory. But, while the manichean
allegory determines the deep structure of most colonialist texts, in Dinesen's
work it produces only the surface structure.

Similarly, Laurens Van der Post's decision to depict his own experience
of African oral cultures takes the form of a novel about a young boy's
adventures: even though Van der Post clearly does understand the phenomenology of mythic culture, his representation of it is limited by his
belief that only a child would be interested in such cultures.[44] Here the
allegory determines the deep structure, the very conception, of the novel.

6

As we have seen, colonialist fiction is generated predominantly by
the ideological machinery of the manichean allegory. Yet the relation
between imperial ideology and fiction is not unidirectional: the ideology
does not simply determine the fiction. Rather, through a process of
symbiosis, the fiction *forms* the ideology by articulating and justifying the
position and aims of the colonialist. But it does more than just define

and elaborate the actual military and putative moral superiority of the Europeans. Troubled by the nagging contradiction between the theoretical justification of exploitation and the barbarity of its actual practice, it also attempts to mask the contradiction by obsessively portraying the supposed inferiority and barbarity of the racial Other, thereby insisting on the profound moral difference between self and Other. Within this symbiotic relation, the manichean allegory functions as a transformative mechanism between the affective pleasure derived from the moral superiority and material profit that motivate imperialism, on the one hand, and the formal devices (genres, stereotypes, and so on) of colonialist fiction, on the other hand. By allowing the European to denigrate the native in a variety of ways, by permitting an obsessive, fetishistic representation of the native's moral inferiority, the allegory also enables the European to increase, by contrast, the store of his own moral superiority; it allows him to accumulate "surplus morality," which is further invested in the denigration of the native, in a self-sustaining cycle.

Thus the ideological function of all "imaginary" and some "symbolic" colonialist literature is to articulate and justify the moral authority of the colonizer and—by positing the inferiority of the native as a metaphysical fact—to mask the pleasure the colonizer derives from that authority. The partial success that such literature achieves in justifying and per- petuating imperial ideology is evident in certain kinds of critical elabo- rations. Harry Barba, for instance, feels that the "regression" of Aladai, the African "hero" of Cary's *African Witch,* "represents a triumph for the primordial, retrogressive urge that dominates the Nigerian: for totem and taboo, for ju-ju, and for the more advanced but equally destructive stages of primitive ju-ju Christianity." We may receive this statement with incredulity, but he goes on to state his point even more explicitly: "Like Uli, Aladai shows a response to the call of blood which is stronger than the influence of his contact with civilization."[45] Such "criticism" is by no means rare: more sophisticated current versions of it can be found praising V. S. Naipaul's representation of the innate barbarity of Third World people.[46] But while colonialist fiction-as-rhetorical-practice does succeed in persuading some people that its claims are valid, the same fiction in its essence as determined-cultural-text preserves the structures and func- tions of imperialist ideology for those who wish to discern them.

Finally, we must bear in mind that colonialist fiction and ideology do not exist in a vacuum. In order to appreciate them thoroughly, we must examine them in juxtaposition to domestic English fiction and the anglophone fiction of the Third World, which originates from British occupation and which, during the current, hegemonic phase of colonialism, is establishing a dialogic relation with colonialist fiction. The Third World's literary dialogue with Western cultures is marked by two broad charac- teristics: its attempt to negate the prior European negation of colonized cultures and its adoption and creative modification of Western languages and artistic forms in conjunction with indigenous languages and forms. This dialogue merits our serious attention for two reasons: first, in spite of the often studied attempts by ethnocentric canonizers in English and other (Western) language and literature departments to ignore Third World culture and art, they will not go away; and, second, as this analysis of colonialist literature (a literature, we must remember, that is *supposed* to mediate between different cultures) demonstrates, the domain of literary and cultural syncretism belongs not to colonialist and neocolonialist writers but increasingly to Third World artists.

1. M. M. Mahood, *The Colonial Encounter: A Reading of Six Novels* (Totowa, N.J., 1977), pp. 170, 171; and see p. 3. As many other studies demonstrate, the emotional innocence and the distance of the six writers whom Mahood has chosen—Joseph Conrad, E. M. Forster, Graham Greene, Chinua Achebe, R. K. Narayan, and V. S. Naipaul—are, at best, highly debatable.

2. Homi K. Bhabha, "The Other Question—The Stereotype and Colonial Discourse," *Screen* 24 (Nov.–Dec. 1983): 25, 19.

3. Frantz Fanon, *The Wretched of the Earth*, trans. Constance Farrington (New York, 1968), p. 41.

4. E. A. Brett, *Colonialism and Underdevelopment in East Africa: The Politics of Economic Change, 1919–1939* (New York, 1973), p. 169.

5. "For it is the force of ambivalence that gives the colonial stereotype its currency: ensures its repeatability in changing historical and discursive conjunctures; informs its strategies of individuation and marginalisation; produces the effect of probabilistic truth and predictability which, for the stereotype, must always be in *excess* of what can be empirically proved or logically construed" (Bhabha, "The Other Question," p. 18). Bhabha amplifies his views of ambivalence in "Of Mimicry and Man: The Ambivalence of Colonial Discourse," *October* 28 (Spring 1984): 125–33.

6. See Dorothy Hammond and Alta Jablow, *The Africa That Never Was: Four Centuries of British Writing about Africa* (New York, 1970), pp. 20–23.

7. These policies and practices have been documented abundantly. Specific studies provide thoroughly detailed information; see, e.g., Richard D. Wolff, *The Economics of Colonialism: Britain and Kenya, 1870–1930* (New Haven, Conn., 1974).

8. See G. Balandier, "The Colonial Situation: A Theoretical Approach," in *Social Change: The Colonial Situation*, ed. Immanuel Wallerstein (New York, 1966), p. 37.

9. For a detailed study of one such case, see chapter 2, "Joyce Cary: The Generation of Racial Romance," in my *Manichean Aesthetics: The Politics of Literature in Colonial Africa* (Amherst, Mass., 1983), pp. 15–48.

10. Michel Foucault, "What is an Author?" *Language, Counter-Memory, Practice: Selected Essays and Interviews*, ed. Donald F. Bouchard, trans. Bouchard and Sherry Simon (Ithaca, N.Y., 1977), p. 130.

11. I cannot develop this argument here for two reasons: first, Naipaul clearly belongs to the hegemonic phase of colonialism, the discourse of which must be examined in its own right and, second, the transformations and repressions that a "native" writer must undergo in order to become a colonialist writer are complicated and also demand separate consideration.

12. Foucault, *The Archaeology of Knowledge*, trans. A. M. Sheridan Smith (New York, 1972), p. 120.

13. Edward W. Said, *Orientalism* (New York, 1978), p. 7.

14. This relation between material and discursive practices, between power and knowledge in Western representation of Others, has been mapped most thoroughly in Said's *Orientalism*.

15. These categories, the "imaginary" and the "symbolic," are derived from the work of Jacques Lacan. The "imaginary" is a preverbal order, essentially visual, that precedes the "symbolic," or verbal, order in the development of the psyche. The "imaginary," actualized during the "mirror stage" (between the ages of six and eighteen months) by the child's recognition of his own image in a mirror or in the presence of another human being, is characterized by identification and aggressivity. During this phase, the child identifies himself completely with his specular image; yet, because the identification includes a non-transversable distance between self and the Other (who is seen as self), the experience is deeply imbued with aggressivity toward the self/Other. This capture of the self by the specular image is only partially modified by the subject's accession, through the acquisition of language, to the "symbolic" order of society and intersubjectivity. In the "symbolic" order, language mediates (and, once again, alienates) the subject's desire, but the specular dynamics of the "imaginary" phase remain embedded in the "symbolic" order, albeit in a form modified by the complex sublimations of the "symbolic" order. See, particularly, Lacan, "The Mirror Stage as Formative of the Function of the I as Revealed in Psychoanalytic Experience," *Ecrits: A Selection,* trans. Alan Sheridan (London, 1977), pp. 1–7. I am also indebted to commentaries on Lacanian theory; see Anika Rifflet-Lemaire, *Jacques Lacan,* trans. David Macey (London, 1977); Lacan, *The Language of the Self: The Function of Language in Psychoanalysis,* ed. and trans. Anthony Wilden (Baltimore, 1968); and Fredric Jameson, "Imaginary and Symbolic in Lacan: Marxism, Psychoanalytic Criticism, and the Problem of the Subject," *Yale French Studies,* no. 55–56 (1977): 338–95.

It is perhaps necessary to repeat Wilden's stress on the fact that the relationship between the "imaginary" and "symbolic" orders is simultaneously diachronic (developmental) and synchronic (structural) and that the *stade du miroir* must be read in three ways at once: "backwards—as a symptom of or a substitute for a much more primordial identification; forwards—as a phase in development; and timelessly—as a relationship best formulated in algorithmic terms. The subject's 'fixation' on (or in) the Imaginary is a matter of degree" (Wilden, "Lacan and the Discourse of the Other," in *The Language of the Self,* p. 174). We might add that similarly the "imaginary" or "symbolic" quality of a given text is a matter of degree.

16. See Nadine Gordimer, *July's People* (New York, 1981), for an unrelenting examination of this dependence.

17. For a general discussion of this transitive mechanism in racial situations, see Joel Kovel, *White Racism: A Psychohistory* (New York, 1971); for a historical case study see O. Mannoni's discussion of rape in Madagascar in *Prospero and Caliban: The Psychology of Colonization,* trans. Pamela Powesland, 2d ed. (New York, 1964).

18. Isak Dinesen, *Out of Africa* (New York, 1937), p. 21.

19. Joyce Cary, *Aissa Saved* (London, 1949), p. 33.

20. M. M. Bakhtin, "Epic and Novel: Toward a Methodology for the Study of the Novel," *The Dialogic Imagination: Four Essays,* ed. Michael Holquist, trans. Caryl Emerson and Holquist, University of Texas Press Slavic Series, no. 1 (Austin, Tex., 1981), p. 30.

21. Gordimer, "Literature and Politics in South Africa," *Southern Review [An Australian Journal of Literary Studies]* 7 (Nov. 1974): 226.

22. See Bakhtin, "Epic and Novel," pp. 15–16.

23. The interpretation and status of Conrad's fiction among Third World writers is quite ambivalent; see, e.g., Achebe, "An Image of Africa," *Massachusetts Review* 18 (Winter 1977): 782–94, and Peter Nazareth, "Out of Darkness: Conrad and Other Third World Writers," *Conradiana* 14, no. 3 (1982): 173–87.

24. Hammond and Jablow, *The Africa That Never Was,* p. 197; in this book Hammond and Jablow present a good content analysis of these subgenres.

25. Northrop Frye, *Anatomy of Criticism: Four Essays* (Princeton, N.J., 1957), pp. 304, 305.

26. See Frye, *The Secular Scripture: A Study of the Structure of Romance*, Charles Eliot Norton Lectures, 1974–1975 (Cambridge, Mass., 1976), p. 57.

27. For a more elaborate definition of racial romance, see my chapter "Joyce Cary: The Generation of Racial Romance," *Manichean Aesthetics*, pp. 15–48.

28. See André Brink, *A Chain of Voices* (Harmondsworth, 1983), and J. M. Coetzee, *Waiting for the Barbarians* (Harmondsworth, 1982).

29. Cary, *The African Witch* (London, 1949), p. 12.

30. Forster, *A Passage to India* (New York, 1924), p. 158; all further references to this work, abbreviated *PI*, will be included in the text.

31. Benita Parry, *Delusions and Discoveries: Studies on India in the British Imagination, 1880–1930* (London, 1972), pp. 279–80.

32. Parry, *Delusions and Discoveries*, p. 273.

33. For an elaboration of Forster's humanist concerns in *A Passage to India*, see Frederick C. Crews, *E. M. Forster: The Perils of Humanism* (Princeton, N.J., 1962), pp. 139–63.

34. For an elaboration of this fascinating correlation, see Parry, *Delusions and Discoveries*, pp. 288–90.

35. See Crews, *E. M. Forster*, p. 156.

36. In Jain philosophy each distinct entity, including the tiniest grain of sand, has a soul and is capable of feeling; see Parry, *Delusions and Discoveries*, pp. 288–90.

37. Rudyard Kipling, *Kim* (New York, 1959), p. 5; my emphasis. All further references to this work, abbreviated *K*, will be included in the text.

38. John A. McClure, *Kipling and Conrad: The Colonial Fiction* (Cambridge, Mass., 1981), p. 80.

39. Conrad's attempts to free himself from the preformed categories of colonialist discourse and the consequent struggles in his fiction between his criticism of imperialism/capitalism and the received closures of colonialist ideology are admirably mapped in Parry, *Conrad and Imperialism: Ideological Boundaries and Visionary Frontiers* (London, 1983).

40. Fredric Jameson, *The Political Unconscious: Narrative as a Socially Symbolic Act* (Ithaca, N.Y., 1981), p. 280.

41. See Gordimer, *The Lying Days* (New York, 1953), p. 144.

42. I have explored Gordimer's fiction in detail elsewhere; see my chapter "Nadine Gordimer: The Degeneration of the Great South African Lie," *Manichean Aesthetics*, pp. 79–149.

43. See Dinesen, *Out of Africa*, and *Shadows on the Grass* (New York, 1974). For a succinct definition of oral cultures, see Walter J. Ong, *Orality and Literacy: The Technologizing of the Word* (London, 1982), and for a detailed study of Dinesen's transformation, see my chapter "Isak Dinesen: The Generation of Mythic Consciousness," *Manichean Aesthetics*, pp. 49–77.

44. See Laurens Van der Post, *A Story Like the Wind* (New York, 1972).

45. Harry Barba, "Cary's Image of Africa in Transition," *University of Kansas City Review* 29 (1963): 293.

46. I do not mean to imply that any writer who criticizes Third World cultures must be automatically condemned as a colonialist. For instance, Achebe's depiction of corruption in Nigeria, in his novel *No Longer at Ease* (New York, 1961), is as complete and penetrating (if not more so) as any of Naipaul's characterizations. The crucial difference, however, is that while Achebe's representation is sympathetic and, therefore, informative, Naipaul's reeks of contempt and reveals only the operation of colonialist mentality.

The Crows of the Arabs

Bernard Lewis

Aghribat al-Arab, "crows or ravens of the Arabs," was the name given to a group of early Arabic poets who were of African or partly African parentage. Of very early origin, the term was commonly used by classical Arabic writers on poetics and literary history. Its use is well attested in the ninth century and was probably current in the eighth century, if not earlier. The term was used with some variation. Originally, it apparently designated a small group of poets in pre-Islamic Arabia whose fathers were free and sometimes noble Arabs and whose mothers were African, probably Ethiopian, slaves. As the sons of slave women, they were, by Arab customary law, themselves slaves unless and until their fathers chose to recognize and liberate them. As the sons of African women, their complexions were darker than was normal among the Arabs of the peninsula.

Both themes—servitude and blackness—occur in some of the verses ascribed to these poets and, in a sense, define their identity as a group. Professor 'Abduh Badawī of Khartoum begins his book on the black Arab poets—the first serious and extensive study devoted to the topic—with this definition:

> This name [the crows of the Arabs] was applied to those [Arabic] poets to whom blackness was transmitted by their slave mothers, and whom at the same time their Arab fathers did not recognize, or recognized only under constraint from them.[1]

The term commonly used by the ancient Arabs for the offspring of mixed unions was *hajīn,* a word which, like the English "mongrel" and "half-breed," was used both of animals and of human beings. For example, *hajīn* would indicate a horse whose sire was a thoroughbred Arab and whose dam was not. It had much the same meaning when applied to human beings, denoting a person whose father was Arab and free and whose mother was a slave. The term *hajīn* in itself is social rather than racial in content, expressing the contempt of the highborn for the baseborn, without attributing any specific racial identity to the latter. Non-Arabs, of whatever racial origin, were of course baseborn but so too were many Arabs who, for one reason or another, were not full and free members of a tribe. Full Arabs—those born of two free Arab parents—ranked above half-Arabs, the children of Arab fathers and non-Arab mothers (the opposite case was inadmissible). In turn, half-Arabs ranked above non-Arabs, who were, so to speak, outside the system.

Among the ancient Arabs there was an elaborate system of social gradations. A man's status was determined by his parentage, family, clan, sept, and tribe, and the rank assigned to them in the Arab social order. All this is richly documented in poetry, tradition, and a vast genealogical literature. A more difficult question is how far the ancient Arabs recognized and observed social distinctions among the various non-Arab peoples and races who supplied much, though not all, of the slave population of Arabia. According to Badawī, "there was a consensus that the most unfortunate of the *hajīn*s and the lowest in social status were those to whom blackness had passed from their mothers" (*S,* p. 21).

At his discretion, the free father of a slave child could recognize and liberate him and thus confer membership of the tribe. Under the Islamic dispensation such recognition became mandatory. In pre-Islamic custom, however, the father retained the option; according to Badawī and the sources cited by him, Arab fathers at that time were reluctant to recognize the sons of black mothers. The alleged reason for this reluctance was their color, since

> the Arabs despised the black color as much as they loved the white color; they described everything that they admired, material or moral, as white. A theme in both eulogy and boasting was the whiteness of a man, just as one of the signs of beauty in a woman was also whiteness. It was also a proof of her nobility. In the same way a man could be eulogized as 'the son of a white woman'. Similarly

Bernard Lewis is Cleveland E. Dodge Professor of Near Eastern Studies at Princeton University and has been a long-term Member of the Institute for Advanced Study. His most recent books are *The Muslim Discovery of Europe* and *The Jews of Islam.*

they would boast that they had taken white women as captives. [*S*, p. 21]

This is probably an accurate description of the social attitudes of the Bedouin aristocracy of conquest that emerged after the great expansion of the Arabs in the seventh century, and for a while dominated the new Islamic empire which they created in the lands of the Middle East and North Africa. There may be some doubt, however, as to whether such attitudes prevailed before all this happened. Apart from some inscriptions, there is no contemporary internal historical evidence on life in Arabia on the eve of the birth of the Prophet Muhammad. There is a great deal of poetry and narrative, which was however not committed to writing until much later, in Islamic times. Although very detailed and informative, it needs careful critical scrutiny, since it often projects back into the pre-Islamic Arabian past the situations and attitudes of the very different later age in which the texts were collected and written. This consideration applies with particular force to the poems and traditions relating to blacks, whose situation changed radically after the great Arab conquests as did the attitude of the Arabs toward them.

The normal fate of captives in antiquity was enslavement, and Ethiopians appear, together with Persians, Greeks, and others, among the foreign slave population of Arabia. The proportion of black slaves is unknown, but, from such evidence as we have (for example, the lists of slaves and freedmen of the Prophet and of some of his companions), it would seem that they formed a minority. These slaves included a proportion of women, who were normally and lawfully used as concubines.

Arabic poetry and legend have preserved the names of several famous figures in ancient Arabia—notably, three poets said to have been born to Ethiopian mothers and, consequently, of dark complexion. The most famous of these was the poet and warrior ʿAntara, whose father was of the Arab tribe of ʿAbs and whose mother was an Ethiopian slave woman called Zabība. One of the greatest Arabic poets of the pre-Islamic period, he is by far the most important of the "crows of the Arabs." Of the twenty-four black Arabic poets studied by Badawī, ʿAntara alone ranks as a major figure in general Arabic literature. His poems, both authentic and ascribed, were collected in a *Dīwān*, and one of them is included among the seven *Muʿallaqāt*, the so-called Suspended Odes, which are regarded as the supreme achievement of pre-Islamic Arabic poetry. A famous warrior, ʿAntara is especially admired for his descriptions of battles. Some of the verses attributed to him speak of his unrequited passion for his paternal cousin ʿAbla, who scorned his love and whose father refused to give her in marriage to ʿAntara despite the Arab custom by which male cousins had first claim.

Already in early times ʿAntara had become the subject of a whole cycle of tales and legends. As the son of a slave mother, he was himself a slave; his father refused to recognize him. A relatively early narrative tells how he gained his freedom. One day his tribe, the ʿAbs, were attacked by raiders from a hostile tribe, who drove off their camels. "The ʿAbs pursued and fought them, and ʿAntara, who was present, was called on by his father to charge. ' 'Antara is a slave,' he replied, 'he does not know how to charge—only to milk camels and bind their udders.' 'Charge!' cried his father, 'and you are free.' And ʿAntara charged."[2] If we are to accept as authentic certain verses ascribed to him, even ʿAntara, once free, despised those who were still slaves, and, proud of his half-Arab descent, looked down on the "jabbering barbarians" and "skin-clad, crop-eared slaves" who lacked this advantage. Later, as ʿAntar (the shortened form of his name), he became the hero of a famous Arab romance of chivalry that celebrated the wars against Persia, Byzantium, the Crusaders, and many other enemies. In one campaign, against the blacks in Africa, the hero penetrates farther and farther south until he reaches the empire of Ethiopia and discovers, in true fairy-tale style, that his mother, the slave girl Zabība, was the granddaughter of the emperor.

All this is clearly fiction, but even the early historical accounts of ʿAntara are questionable, and only a very small part of the poetry extant in his name can be ascribed to him with any certainty. The greater part, and especially the verses in which he complains of the insult and abuse that he suffered because of his blackness, is probably of later composition, some of it perhaps the work of other black poets. Some of these verses do indeed recur in various collections and are ascribed by name to later poets of African or part African birth. The same verses are at times attributed to more than one of these poets. A famous verse ascribed only to ʿAntara runs:

> I am a man, of whom one half ranks with the best of ʿAbs
> The other half I defend with my sword.[3]

This may mean no more than that his mother was a slave, without reference to race or color. Other verses ascribed to ʿAntara, however, indicate that his African blood and dark skin marked him as socially inferior and exposed him to insult and abuse. In one poem he is even quoted as insulting his own mother:

> I am the son of a black-browed woman
>   like the hyena that thrives on an abandoned camping ground
> Her leg is like the leg of an ostrich, and her
>   hair like peppercorns
> Her front teeth gleam behind her veil like lightning
>   in curtained darkness.[4]

In another poem he sounds a note that was unconsciously echoed centuries later:

Enemies revile me for the blackness of my skin
But the whiteness of my character effaces the blackness.[5]

Similar complaints are ascribed to other figures of the pre-Islamic
and early Islamic period. Also named among the "crows of the Arabs"
was a certain Khufāf, a contemporary of the Prophet. He was known as
Ibn Nadba, after his mother. Khufāf, like the other original "crows of
the Arabs," was the son of an Arab father and a black slave woman. He
was, however, a man of high social position and was chosen to be chief
of his tribe. A verse ascribed to him remarks that his tribe had made
him chief "despite this dark pedigree."[6]

The third of the original trio of "crows of the Arabs" was Sulayk ibn
al-Sulāka, another pre-Islamic poet whose father was an Arab of the tribe
of Tamīm and whose mother was a black slave woman, according to most
sources an Ethiopian. Sulayk found a different solution to his problems—
he became celebrated as a brigand. He was one of a number of brigand
poets whose exploits form the subject of heroic narratives and whose
verses are cited, usually together, in the early anthologies. By a confusion
between the two groups—the "crows of the Arabs" and the brigand
poets—several of the latter are described by some early sources as having
been black, though this is not supported by the main tradition.

The best indication that the stories and verses about ʿAntara and
Khufāf belong to a later period is their content, reflecting a situation
which did not yet exist in pre-Islamic Arabia. This is shown by the very
fact that men of such mixed social and racial parentage could attain a
high position, something which would have been much more difficult,
if not impossible, a century later. In pre-Islamic and early Islamic Arabia,
Arabs had no reason whatever to regard Ethiopians as inferior or to
consider Ethiopian ancestry as a mark of base origin. On the contrary,
there is a good deal of evidence to show that the Ethiopians were regarded
with respect, as a people on a level of civilization substantially higher
than that of the Arabs themselves. A slave as such was of course inferior,
but a black slave was no worse than a white slave; the sons of black slave
women seem to have suffered no particular impediment. Many prominent
figures in the earliest Islamic period had Ethiopian women among their
ancestresses. They include no less a person than the caliph ʿUmar himself,
whose father, al-Khaṭṭāb, had an Ethiopian mother. Another was the
great general ʿAmr ibn al-ʿĀṣ, conqueror of Egypt and one of the architects
of the Arab empire.

The great change in the position of blacks and in the attitude of the
Arabs toward them came after the creation of the empire. Conquest
resulted in new sets of relationships, the most important of which was
the transformation and enormous extension of the institution of slavery.
In antiquity, most slaves had been of local provenance—enslaved for
crime, debt, or money. From time to time the suppression of a rebellion
or a war on the frontier flooded the market with slaves from far away.

Otherwise, local sources of supply provided for local needs. Islam created a new situation by prohibiting the enslavement not only of freeborn Muslims but even of freeborn non-Muslims living under the protection of the Muslim state. The children of slaves were born slaves, but, for a number of reasons, this source of recruitment was not adequate. The growing need for slaves had to be met, therefore, by importation from beyond the Islamic frontier. This gave rise to a vast expansion of slave raiding and slave trading in the Eurasian steppe to the north and in tropical Africa to the south of the Islamic lands. It is for this reason, no doubt, that the massive development of the slave trade in black Africa and the large scale importation of black Africans for use in the Mediterranean and Middle Eastern countries date from the Arab period. In one of the sad paradoxes of history, this resulted from one of the most important of the liberalizing and humanizing changes that the Islamic dispensation brought to the ancient world.

At first, there seems to have been no particular discrimination among the various nations and races of non-Arabs who made up the vast majority of the subject as well as the servile population. But in time, differences of color began to matter, and this is clearly indicated by the literary, pictorial, and even lexical evidence. One of the commonest Arabic words for slave, ʿabd (from a verb meaning "to serve"), mirrors these changes. In early classical usage, it means "slave," irrespective of race or color; by the High Middle Ages, its use is restricted to black slaves only; in later colloquial Arabic, it is used to mean blacks, whether slave or free. One reason for the change is surely that those who were of black or partly black origin were more visible. As Islam spread by conversion, the races of the Middle East and North Africa intermingled rapidly through polygamy and concubinage. As a result, the difference between the Arab conquerors and the kindred peoples of the region became less and less important. Only those of African origin showed visible and unmistakable evidence of their non-Arab ancestry. Slaves of white origin, from the Eurasian steppe and from Europe, could mingle into the population; this was much more difficult for Africans.

These changes are clearly reflected in the poetry ascribed to some of the poets of the seventh and eighth centuries, whom later Arab anthologists and literary historians of the classical period do not normally include among the "crows of the Arabs." Some of them are not the sons of Arab fathers and black mothers but are of purely African origin.

One of these latter was Suḥaym (who died in 660). His name is the diminutive form of a word meaning "black" and might be rendered as "little blackie." He was born and lived a slave and, indeed, was commonly known in literary histories as "the slave of the Banū'l-Ḥashās," after the family to which he belonged later in his life.

Suḥaym was of course a nickname; his real name is said to have been Ḥabba. According to one story, his owner offered him to the caliph ʿUthmān saying, "I can sell you an Ethiopian slave poet." The caliph, in this version, refused, remarking that he did not need a slave who treated his owners as did Suḥaym: "When he is sated he directs love-verses at their women, and when he is hungry he directs satires at them." Later Suḥaym passed into the hands of the Banū'l-Ḥashās, a clan of the tribe of Asad. He is variously described as an Ethiopian and as a Nubian. According to an early source he was branded on his face, a detail which suggests a Nubian rather than an Ethiopian origin. He is said to have angered the men of the tribe by flirting with their women, a practice for which he was eventually killed and burned by his owners.

In some of his poems, Suḥaym speaks of his love affairs and of the troubles they caused him:

> Though I hate servitude, I would gladly serve
>   as camelherd to Ibn Ayman
> provided that I am not sold, and that they tell me, "Slave! Take the
>   maiden her evening drink!"
> And I may prop a languorous lady,
>   sleep stripping her garment, baring her breast,
>   for even a slave may find an assignation.
> And if she refuse me, I hold her tight, she cannot break free,
>   so that her beauty and her charm are manifest.
>
> [*D*, pp. 56–57]

Such adventures were punished, and Suḥaym was condemned to imprisonment and flogging. He bore them with fortitude:

> If you imprison me, you imprison the son of a slavewoman,
>   if you free me, you free a tawny lion.
> Prison is no more than the shadow of the house where I live,
>   and a whipping no more than hide meeting hide.
>
> [*D*, p. 57]

But Suḥaym's amours did not always go well. In one poem he laments:

> She points with her comb and says to her companion,
>   "Is that the slave of Banū'l-Ḥashās, the slick rhymester?
> She saw a threadbare saddlebag, a worn cloak,
>   a naked negro such as men own.
> These girls excite other men and turn away from my shock of hair,
>   despising me as I can clearly see.
> If I were pink of color, these women would love me,
>   but my Lord has shamed me with blackness.
> Yet it does not diminish me that my mother was a slavewoman
>   who tended the udders of she-camels.
>
> [*D*, p. 26]

In another poem he defends himself in words which strikingly anticipate a famous poem of William Blake:

> My verses serve me on the day of boasting
>> in place of birth and coin;
> though I am a slave, my soul is nobly free;
>> though I am black of color, my nature is white.
>>> [D, p. 55][8]

The same theme is expressed in several poems, often attributed to more than one of these black poets. Here are two examples:

> Blackness does not degrade a whole man
>> nor a young man of discernment and breeding
> If blackness has fallen to me as my lot
>> so has the whiteness of my character.
>>> [D, pp. 54–55]

My blackness does not harm my habit, for I am like musk; who tastes
it does not forget.
I am covered with a black garment, but under it there is a lustrous
garment with white tails.
>>> [D, p. 69]

Perhaps the most gifted of these black poets was Nuṣayb ibn Rabāḥ, who died in 726. The Arab literary historians have preserved some fragments of biographical information about him. From these and from his surviving poems, it is clear that he was very conscious of his slave birth and black color and that he endured many insults because of them. In one story, Nuṣayb was asked by his friends to reply in kind to an Arab poet who had composed some insulting verses alluding to his blackness. Nuṣayb refused. God, he said, had given him the gift of poetry to use for good; he would not abuse it by turning it into satire. And in any case, Nuṣayb responded, "all he has done is call me black—and he speaks truth." In a striking poem, Nuṣayb says of his own color:

> Blackness does not diminish me, as long
>> as I have this tongue and a stout heart,
> Some are raised up by their lineage;
>> the verses of my poems are my lineage.
> How much better is a black, eloquent and keen-minded,
>> than a mute white.
> For this merit the nobleman envies me from his heights
>> and no one gloats over me.

But in spite of this note of pride, Nuṣayb had his moments of desperation. Like other early black poets writing in Arabic, he cites the example of musk as something which is black but rare, precious and highly esteemed:

> If I am jet-black, musk is blacker,
>> and there is no medicine for the blackness of my skin;

I have a nobility that towers over their depravity
   like the sky over the earth.
There are few of my like among your menfolk;
   there is no lack of your kind among the women.
If you accept my advances, you respond to one who is compliant;
   if you refuse, then we are equal.[9]

Nuṣayb was able to make a career as a court poet, with the Umayyad caliph ʿAbd al-Malik. He is sometimes confused with another poet of the same name, known as Nuṣayb the Younger, who died in 791. By this time, the worsening condition of blacks in Islamic society brought a change of tone to this poetry—dignified self-respect turned to desperate self-deprecation. In a panegyric ode addressed to the caliph Hārūn al-Rashīd, Nuṣayb the Younger says of himself:

Black man, what have you to do with love?
Give over chasing white girls if you have any sense!
An Ethiop black like you can have no way to reach them.[10]

After the eighth century, blackness as a poetic theme almost disappears from Arabic literature. A few poets composed in Arabic in the black lands converted to Islam, but most black African Muslims preferred to use Arabic for scholarship and their own languages for poetry. In the central lands, though the flow of black as of other slaves continued, the school of self-consciously black poets came to an end. Few of the slaves were sufficiently assimilated to compose poetry in Arabic; while the few Arabic poets of African or part African ancestry were too assimilated to see themselves as black and therefore Other.

1. ʿAbduh Badawī, *Al-Shuʿarāʾ al-Sūd wa-Khaṣāʾiṣuhum fiʾl-Shiʿr al-ʿArabī* (Cairo, 1973), p. 21; my translation, as are all further translations in this essay. All further references to this work, abbreviated *S*, will be included in the text.

In addition, the black Arabic poets have been examined in detail in several articles, notably by Muḥammad Bāqir ʿAlwān, "Aghribat al-ʿArab," *Al-Mawrid* 2, no. 1 (1973): 11–13, and ʿAwn al-Sharīf Qāsim, "Al-Sūdān fī ḥayāt al-ʿArab wa-adabihim," *Bulletin of Sudanese Studies* 1, no. 1 (1968): 76–92. Accounts (unfortunately very brief) of the group and of the individual poets may also be found in the standard histories of Arabic literature; see esp. Régis Blachère, *Histoire de la littérature arabe des origines à la fin du quinzième siecle*, 2 vols. (Paris, 1952–66). On ʿAntara, see *Encyclopaedia of Islam*, 2d ed., s.v. " ʿAntara" (article by Blachère), where further references are given. Suhaym's poems were collected and edited; see Suhaym, *Dīwān*, ed. ʿAbd al-ʿAzīz al-Maymanī (Cairo, 1950); all further references to this work, abbreviated *D*, will be included in the text. See also the translation into German, *Beiträge zur arabischen Poësie*, trans. Oscar Rescher, 8 vols. (Istanbul, 1937–), 6, pt. 2:30–50. For the life and work of Nuṣayb, see Umberto Rizzitano, "Abū Miḥǧan Nuṣayb B. Rabāḥ," *Rivista degli studi orientali* 20 (1943): 421–71 and "Alcuni frammenti poetici di Abū Miḥǧan Nuṣayb B. Rabāḥ poeta ommiade del i secolo dell'egira," *Rivista degli studi orientali* 22 (1945): 23–35.

2. Abu'l Faraj al-Isfāhānī, *Kitāb al-Aghānī*, 20 vols. (Būlāq, 1868–69), 7:149. See also R. A. Nicholson, *A Literary History of the Arabs* (Cambridge, 1941), p. 115.

3. Wilhelm Ahlwardt, ed., *The Divans of the Six Ancient Arabic Poets Ennābiga, ʿAntara, Tharafa, Zuhair, ʿAlqama, and Imruulqais* (London, 1870), p. 42. See *Encyclopaedia of Islam*, 2d ed., s.v. "ʿAntara."

4. ʿAntara, *Dīwān* (Cairo, 1911), p. 196.

5. Ibid.

6. Ibn Qutayba, *Kitāb al-Shiʿr waʾl-shuʿarāʾ*, ed. M. J. de Goeje (Leiden, 1904), p. 196.

7. On Suhaym, often named by Arab authors as "the slave of the Banūʾl-Hashās," see al-Isfāhānī, *Kitāb al-Aghānī*, new ed. (Cairo, 1928–29), 20:2–9; Blachère, *Histoire de la littérature arabe* 1:318–19; and *Beiträge zur arabischen Poësie* 6, pt. 2:30–50.

8. Cf. Franz Rosenthal, *The Muslim Concept of Freedom* (Leiden, 1960), p. 91.

9. *Aghānī*, 1:140–41 (new ed. 1:352–54); and see Rizzitano, "Abū Miḥǵan Nuṣayb B. Rabāḥ," *Rivista* 20:453, 456 and "Alcuni frammenti," *Rivista* 22:24, 26.

10. *Aghānī*, 20:25; and see Badawī, *Al-Shuʿarāʾ*, p. 158.

The Moor in the Text: Metaphor, Emblem, and Silence

Israel Burshatin

—Decidme, señor— dijo Dorotea—: ¿esta señora es cristiana o mora? Porque el traje y el silencio nos hace pensar que es lo que no querríamos que fuese.
—MIGUEL DE CERVANTES SAAVEDRA, *Don Quijote*

["Tell me, sir," said Dorotea, "is this lady a Christian or a Moor? For her dress and her silence make us think that she is what we hope she is not."]

The image of the Moor in Spanish literature reveals a paradox at the heart of Christian and Castilian hegemony in the period between the conquest of Nasrid Granada in 1492 and the expulsion of the Moriscos by Philip III in 1609.[1] Depictions fall between two extremes. On the "villifying" side, Moors are hateful dogs, miserly, treacherous, lazy *and* overreaching. On the "idealizing" side, the men are noble, loyal, heroic, courtly—they even mirror the virtues that Christian knights aspire to— while the women are endowed with singular beauty and discretion.

Anti-Muslim diatribes are fairly common and predictable: they are flat and repetitive in their assertion of Old Christian superiority over every aspect of the lives of Muslims or crypto-Muslims. Any sign of cultural otherness is ridiculed; the conquering caste, insecure about its own lofty (and, more often than not, chimerical) standards of *limpieza de*

Research for this essay was supported by a 1982–83 fellowship from the National Endowment for the Humanities.

sangre ("purity of blood"), laughs away whatever trace of old Hispano-Arab splendor might remain in the Morisco.[2] Or, conversely, the uneasy master recasts wretched Moriscos as ominous brethren of the Ottoman Turk.[3]

The truly vexed problem, however, consists in determining the meaning of idealized Moors in historiography, ballads, drama, and the novel. Roughly speaking, modern criticism divides into two camps in attempting to explain this curious phenomenon of literary infatuation with a cultural and religious minority subjected to growing popular hostility, Inquisitional hounding, and economic exploitation. I will call one camp "aestheticist" and the other "social."[4]

In the "aestheticist" view, what counts above all else is the expansiveness of the Spanish soul, which is so generous to its enemies of eight centuries' standing that it buries the hatchet and fashions them into models of the courtly and chivalric. No Christian knight is more adept at arms than Abindarráez; no lady is ever lovelier than Jarifa, Daraja, or Ana Félix.

The "social" interpretations render literary phenomena as pamphlets for "peaceful coexistence." They argue, often persuasively, that chivalric or sentimental narrative in Orientalist garb hides a subversive message available only to the *cognoscenti*—New Christians, crypto-Muslims, and crypto-Jews—in need of consoling or intent on dismantling the dominant culture. This literary fashion may well have been encouraged by aristocratic patrons wary of sacrificing faithful and hard-working vassals to the Church-inspired zealotry of Charles V's heirs. Some of the strongest dissenting voices belonged to Aragonese seigneurial patrons, whose fondness for *Maurophilie littéraire* may have come from a political conservatism rooted in profitable *mudéjar* traditions. Aragonese lords of Morisco vassals may thus have nurtured the proliferation of Moorish "positive role models." Some scholars argue that seigneurial protectors of Morisco traditions might have sought to lift the sagging image of their New Christian subjects by conjuring up aristocratic Moors of yore. Still, the Morisco was as much of an outsider in sixteenth-century Spain as he would have been in the golden Nasrid Granada romanticized in literature.

1. Metaphor

Turning from the "social" aperçus on the possible origins of the sixteenth-century Moorish novel to the earliest vernacular instances of the discourse on the Moor, we find one of the most uncanny expressions

Israel Burshatin, assistant professor of Spanish at Haverford College, is currently preparing a critical edition of Pedro del Corral's *Crónica sarracina*.

in premodern literature of the power of representations.[5] In the *Poema de mio Cid,* composed some time around 1207, the exiled hero's return to the fold takes the form of an ever widening but essentially redundant displacement of the Moor.[6] And, as in the sixteenth century, the Moor in the *Poema de mio Cid* falls between extremes of the dehumanizing and the fanciful: either he is reduced, metonymically, to an item of value in the booty lists carefully drawn by the hero's *quiñoneros* ("officers in charge of counting and distributing booty"), or he is the reassuring and Orientalized projection of the hero's sway over reconquered lands.[7] Grounded in conquest and reiterated tests of valor on the battlefield, the discourse of the conqueror also displays a twofold drift: on the one hand, writing is an instrument of surveillance, the means of recording all the wealth taken from Moors and then allotted to the Cid's fighters; on the other hand, the conqueror produces a poetic language belonging to the class of propagandistic gestures and calls to arms (*pregones*) which is essential to the seizure and, later, to the defense of Valencia.

The Cid is a soldier turned poet when he describes an army of Moors as a pageant of Moorish service that proclaims the Cid's presence—and not the Moors'—in a reconquered landscape. This metaphoric transformation of a Moorish menace into a hyperbolic statement of Moorish devotion to the conqueror takes place in Valencia, at the tower of the alcazar, where the proud conqueror has taken his wife and daughters to contemplate their vast estates.[8] But into their vision of wealth and familial pleasures now intrude King Yúçef's North African hordes, encamped around the city they hope to seize for Mafomat ("Muhammad"). The threat is a Moorish version of the Christian Reconquest, and it is therefore all the more horrifying to the women after their uncertain years in the monastery at Cardeña, outside Burgos, away from the Cid. Model father and husband that he is, the Cid soothes the women by translating his proven force of arms into a reassuring metaphor of Moorish service:

> Su mugier e sus fijas   subiolas al alcaçar,
> alçavan los ojos,   tiendas vieron fincadas:
> "¿Ques esto, Çid? ¡Si el Criador vos salve!"
> "¡Ya mugier ondrada   non ayades pesar!
> Riqueza es que nos acreçe   maravillosa e grand;
> ¡a poco que viniestes   presend vos quieren dar;
> por casar son vuestras fijas: aduzen vos axuvar!"
>
> [*PMC,* 1644–50]

[He led his wife and daughters   up into the castle;
they raised their eyes   and saw the tents pitched.
"What is this, Cid,   in the name of the Creator?"
"My honored wife,   let it not trouble you!
This is great and marvelous wealth   to be added unto us;

you have barely arrived here   and they send you gifts,
they bring the marriage portion   for the wedding of your daughters."

$$(PC, 90)]$$

Confident of his military and political savvy, the warrior as poet turns an image of Moorish force into a projection of his own overwhelming presence. Moorish weapons, tents, and horses exist in the poem only to be detached from armies whose defeat is episodic and invariable. In the Cid's proleptic metaphor, "Riqueza es que nos acreçe   maravillosa e grand," the tension between the ominous beating of Moorish battle drums and the hope of making worthy marriages for his daughters in the court of Alfonso VI of Castile and León is swiftly resolved in the ensuing battle, which bears out what the poem's implied audience has come to expect of its hero.

The Cid's metaphor makes two rhetorical thrusts. One is the proleptic shorthand that captures the development of the plot it describes. The second is the metonymic reduction of the Moor, whose presence ("riqueza es ["this is . . . wealth"]") in the conqueror's universe of discourse is illusory, relegated to the spoils that *quiñoneros* can describe in their lists. But the heuristic fiction, which the metaphor gives rise to, dresses epic force in Orientalized garb.[9] Once the Moor is defeated in battle, the role of the Moor in discourse is to enhance the prestige of the hero and his world. Not for nothing does the adjectival form *morisco* undergo a semantic shift in the work. First, it describes a coveted cloak which one of the duped Jewish moneylenders requests:

> Rachel a mio Çid   la manol ba besar:
> "¡Ya Campeador   en buen ora çinxiestes espada!
> De Castiella vos ides   pora las yentes estrañas;
> assi es vuestra ventura,   grandes son vuestras ganançias,
> una piel vermeja   *morisca e ondrada*
> Çid, beso vuestra mano   en don que la yo aya"
>
> [*PMC*, 174–79; my emphasis]

> [Raquel has kissed   the hand of My Cid:
> "Ah, Campeador,   in good hour you girded on sword!
> You go from Castile   forth among strangers.
> Such is your fortune   and great are your gains;
> I kiss your hand,   begging you to bring me
> a skin of crimson leather,   *Moorish and highly prized.*"
>
> (*PC*, 10; my emphasis)]

Later, as the hero sweeps over Muslim lands, the adjective *morisco* aptly describes the manner in which the Cid puts his own stamp on booty and people: beaten *moros* point to *moriscos,* and both are the undifferentiated names for the Islamic defenders which the *Poema de mio Cid* marks for defeat.

> Esta albergada   los de mio Çid luego la an robada
> de escudos e de armas   e de otros averes largos;
> de los *moriscos*   quando son legados
> ffallaron   .dx. cavallos.
>
> [*PMC*, 794–96b; my emphasis]

[My Cid's men have looted from this camp, shields and arms and many other things; they counted sixty horses in the booty taken from *Moriscos*. (My translation; my emphasis)]

Thus, the idealized Moor and the items listed by *quiñoneros*—congener to the romanticized Moor—presuppose one another in the conqueror's metaphoric language. The Cid's exemplary Moorish vassal Avengalvón, probably the first of a long line of idealized Moors in Spanish literary history,[10] also displays elements of this complex interplay between the logic of the poet and that of the *quiñonero*.

To imagine the besieging Almoravides at the walls as an already beaten yet prestigious foe is a powerful device, but it becomes more vividly so when seen in the wider context of the Western epic tradition. The exchange of words between the Cid and his wife, Ximena, as they watch the armies below is a discrete reworking of the classical *teichoskopia*—the view from/on the wall.[11] This topos, as in the *Iliad,* marks a shift in point of view, emphasis, and theme.[12] In the *Poema de mio Cid* the broadening effect of the classical *teichoskopia* is masterfully turned into an Orientalizing trope. As viewed from the walls, the besieging warriors—shouting heretical war cries of "Mafomat!" and beating thousands of battle drums—are turned, simultaneously, into chattel *and* romanticized subjects not to be feared but counted and possessed. In the guise of a poet, the hero produces a powerfully self-centered caption to the fearsome sight below. The *teichoskopia* thus furnishes the privileged vantage point from which the hero enacts his sway over Muslim adversaries. High above the enemy, within sight of vast land-holdings and wealth, the hero now empowers his discourse with the ability to redefine, at will, bristling motifs of Moorish force and to imbue them with "Cidian" meaning and a reassuring sense of harmony and continuity.

This total dominion over the Moor—the linking, through *teichoskopia,* of metaphor and sword, the Moor as chattel *and* as romantic Other—is a key moment, both in shaping the Spanish Orientalist tradition and in fostering the ideological solidarity characteristic of the epic. All those who participate in the social mobility and expansiveness of the vigorous frontier world of Castile and its hero feed on the beaten Moors: the townspeople of Burgos, the fighting bishop don Jerome, the Cid's intrepid followers, and even Avengalvón, the Cid's ever loyal Moorish vassal. Catalans, Leonese, members of the old aristocracy, duped Jewish moneylenders, and Moorish enemy all constitute an opposition handily negated by the Cid and his band, exiles whose ostensible return to the fold actually initiates a new society and an ethos nurtured by "object values" taken from their antagonists and reinscribed in their own—the conqueror's — universe of discourse.[13] The univocity thus achieved also manifests in the continuity of language and world: mobility over vast stretches of frontier territory coincides with the frequent *pregones* ("recruiting propaganda"); booty lists are homologous to epic catalogs of warriors; and narrative equivalence of wealth and authority, the forceful and the sacred, displays the scope of epic consolidation. This seamlessness of the *Poema de mio Cid,* described by Américo Castro as a "delicious journey" linking the commonplace and the extraordinary in the person of the hero, stands in contrast to the other key work about Moors, Pedro del Corral's *Crónica sarracina,* composed around 1425 to 1430 in less stable political circumstances and possessed of an aggressively nostalgic temperament.[14]

2. Emblem

The *Crónica sarracina* is the sort of historical romance dear to historians of literature. Plays, ballads, histories, and novels from the fifteenth to the twentieth centuries stem from this seminal work. The *Sarracina*'s filiation to medieval chronicles in Spanish, Latin, and Arabic as well as the tradition it generated have been studied by some of the most distinguished figures in Hispanic studies.[15] But scant attention has been paid to a striking feature of the *Sarracina,* one which will be immediately familiar to readers of contemporary Latin American fiction. The making, writing, and reading of history are made homologous to cataclysmic events, triggered in the *Sarracina* by Rodrigo, last of the Visigothic kings of Spain.

King Rodrigo's lustful appetite unleashes a series of disasters, culminating in the Arab invasion of the Iberian Peninsula and the "destruction" of Spain at precisely the moment when political stability and a golden age had seemed assured under Rodrigo's firm command. The fall of Spain and Rodrigo's own tragic fall are recounted in personal terms.[16] The king is impetuous and proud. He also lusts after a maiden, La Cava, to the point of betraying the trust that the girl's father has placed in the king and his household. In a letter to her father, Count Julián, La Cava describes how she was unable to preserve her honor. In retaliation, the vengeful count invites the Arabs and Berbers he had always held in check from his strategic enclave at Ceuta, on the North African side of the straits, to launch an invasion from ships provided by the count himself.

Rodrigo's excesses produce a series of irreversible events which are joined with an all-embracing pattern of historical epochs. The private becomes public and historical via mediational motifs of narrativity, prophecy, and interpretation, which give particular shape to the notion of history in the *Sarracina*. In contrast to the continuities of epic, fissures and disruptions prevail in a world on the brink of disaster. Thus, while the Cid harnesses the duality of poet and soldier by his extraordinary deeds in both domains, King Rodrigo's failures in discernment and *mesura* make him a flawed reader of symbols. In place of Cidian mastery over word and sword, stands King Rodrigo's intemperance. His thirst for knowledge and appetite for sex invite condemnation—and usher in the Arab conquest of Spain.

The king's unbridled force is thus a sign of weakness: hence his role as passive interpreter of portents of doom, his inability to deploy arms and symbols against the invaders from North Africa and their allies among the Goths. The discontinuity between the activity of his excesses— he breaks the taboo on entering the Tower of Hercules at Toledo—and the passivity of his interpretation—he is helpless to avert the disasters he learns about at the tower—mark the place in discourse where the fictional compilers—fabricated authorities—are inserted into the "chronicle." And they, as mediating figures, yoke motifs of narrative and adventure—a privilege which the epic reserves for the hero but which this ambitious, pseudohistorical romance confers on the overarching authorial persona.

The "destruction" of Spain implies, then, not just lust, vengeance, and betrayal but, more important, understanding and interpretation. The most telling illustration of this metaphoric concatenation of knowing, interpreting, the end of a world, and the presence of Moors occurs in the famous episode of the Tower of Hercules. From the time the tower was built by Hercules, the legendary founder of the Gothic monarchy, every king of the Goths, until King Rodrigo, had placed a lock on the tower door. Rodrigo *breaks* all the locks and enters the tower. By upsetting the tradition and flouting the will of Hercules, Rodrigo sets in motion the founder's prediction of dynastic doom. The cohesion of temporal and spatial aspects is remarkable here—and calls to mind Mikhail Bakhtin's notion of the "chronotope."[17] The tower is an architectural wonder. Its inner walls are a splendid mosaic, yet no seams or cracks are visible; the interiors display no sign of time having passed since Hercules' day. Even the taboo on entering the building produces motifs of dynastic time which emphasize permanence rather than duration. But, Rodrigo's break with the tradition—as he removes the locks and opens the tower doors—links the dynastic time scheme to the turbulent and irreversible trajectory of adventure in chivalric romances, whose features the *Sarracina* recalls beyond the topical tourneys and drawn-out courtships. Rodrigo's actions in the tower suggest an identification with Hercules that is fascinating in its subtle complexity and temporal sense. Hercules, the first person to enter the tower, is the progenitor of the dynasty; the first person to break with tradition and follow in Hercules' footsteps is foreseen to be the last king of the Goths.[18]

The enchanted tower is thus the location of historical time and the place where historical discourse occurs; the building conceals the signs of sacred traditions. Once entered, however, it becomes the place where interpretations, portents, and prophecies can happen. The episode is liminal: it connects Rodrigo's ascent to the throne and the conduct of his rule, events which are firmly placed in linear, sequential time. But, as the locus of the prophecy and epiphany of a cycle of origins and demise, the Tower of Hercules subordinates all other time and space configurations—chivalric, epic, and courtly—which comprise the *Sarracina*. The conjunction of the personal (Rodrigo's ill-advised and impassioned moves) and the historical (the certain doom of the Gothic dynasty) achieves narrative form through motifs of violence, the crossing of thresholds, and the interpretation of history. Such access to a self-reflexive reading of the projected ending also implies the presence of chroniclers. Accordingly, we glimpse the subsequent importance of the "narrated narrator" segments which tell us in great detail how the fictional compilers—Eleastras, Alanzuri, and Carestes—obtained their material and drafted the chronicle which the author-narrator subsequently—and in fortuitous circumstances—purchased from a merchant and then cobbled into the *Sarracina*.

Rodrigo breaks into historical discourse, and his blind force is aptly synonymous with his limited understanding of the anti-Herculean role he is to play in the cycle of origins and demise that informs the *Sarracina*'s perfective notion of history.[19] Cyclical also is the chain of violations inaugurated by the breaking of the locks on the tower door in a Herculean display of *fortitudo,* however lacking that display is in the complementary *sapientia* which the Renaissance Hercules applied to harness the appetitive and muscular energies.[20] The other moments of discovery at the tower are equally emblematic. Indeed, even the description of the seamless mosaic walls inside the building suggests an emblem in the etymological sense of the word—"mosaic work."[21]

Given this close intermingling of text, image, and moral lesson, it seems only fitting that Rodrigo's fatal curiosity at the tower door was to become an emblem in Covarrubias' *Emblemas morales* (1610).[22] In this emblem book the Tower of Hercules is depicted with its doors tightly shut and secured by three locks. The motto above the image is a sacred injunction against overweening knowledge: Nec Scire Fas Est Omnia ("It is not right to know everything") (*EM*, p. 158).[23] The poem below the image, a royal octave, reads:

> Rodrigo el temerario, y atreuido
> De los Godos Rey vltimo en España,

Gran tesoro cuido estar escondido
En la Herculea torre, y con gran saña,
Rompe las cerraduras, que han fornido,
Los demas Reyes, y se desengaña,
Hallando en ciertas letras, y pintura,
Su perdicion, y nuestra desuentura.

[*EM*, p. 158]

[Rodrigo, the fearless and daring,
last king of the Goths in Spain,
imagined that a great treasure was hidden
in the Herculean tower, and, possessed of great wrath
he breaks the locks that were placed
by all the previous kings, and he unfools himself,
finding in certain letters and a painting,
his perdition and our misfortune.]

Covarrubias' commentary summarizes the pertinent chapter in the *Sarracina* and then ends with a disclaimer: "Si esto fue verdad, o fabula, no es mio el aueriguarlo ["If this be truth or fable, it is not for me to know"]" (*EM*, p. 158 verso). For the emblematist, then, what matters is not the veracity of the legend but, rather, the exemplariness of the narrative and the force of its moral truth.[24] In preferring rhetoric over reference, Covarrubias is in good company, as historians and chroniclers, regardless of individual merit, held the story in high esteem for its didactic and narrative appeal. But Covarrubias' careful re-creation of the episode's context and, especially, his description of the other emblematic occurrences in the tower alert us to one of the episode's central features. Rodrigo is clearly the protagonist here—but his role is also that of reader or interpreter of emblems.

On entering the tower, Rodrigo sees a statue of Hercules lying on a bed. In the statue's outstretched arm there is a letter, which Rodrigo opens and reads:

Abriólo y leyólo y dezía assí: "Tú, tan osado que este escripto leerás, para mientes quién eres, y quánto de mal por ti verná; que assí como por mí fue España poblada y conquistada, assí será por ti despoblada y perdida. E quiero te dezir que yo fuy Hércoles el fuerte, aquel que toda la mayor parte del mundo conquisté, e a toda España. . . . Cata lo que harás, que deste mundo ál no llevarás, sino los bienes que hizieres."[25]

[He opened and read it, and (the letter) said: "You who are so daring and will read this writing, think hard on who you are, and how much evil will come because of you; that just as Spain was conquered and populated by me, so will it be depopulated and lost by you. Know that I was Hercules the powerful, who conquered most of the world, and all of Spain. . . . Mind what you do, for you shall take with you from this world only the good of your own actions."]

Having broken into the tower and opened the letter, Rodrigo is thus "qualified" to read himself into history and furnish the pronoun "tú" with its awaited meaning; the anti-Hercules is whoever first reads the text. The historical and the biographical converge here and, perhaps more important, the domain of discourse interweaves with motifs of adventure. The text of the letter spells out the analogy between Hercules and Rodrigo. Rodrigo's identification with Hercules—the wise and strong ruler to be revered by generations to follow—however, yields to the more dramatic one, the one between "tú" and Rodrigo—the anti-Hercules. It is the meaningfulness of the indexical "tú" which ropes Rodrigo into a historical pattern of origins and demise, the waves of beginnings and endings, rising and falling fortunes, which describes the Christian Reconquest as a form of narrative.

There is an important difference, however, between Covarrubias' Rodrigo and the *Sarracina*'s Rodrigo. In the emblem book, the doomed monarch is a competent reader of emblems. Indeed, as someone fully cognizant of *desengaño* ("unfooling"), he is an ideal reader of Baroque moralists. But the plot of the *Sarracina*—even the rest of the episode of the Tower of Hercules—hinges precisely on Rodrigo's lack of full understanding. Rodrigo is in fact a failed emblem reader who becomes only slightly better at it as he interprets several images and texts in the tower. The *Sarracina*'s protagonist is Herculean in his boundless appetite for knowledge and, later, for La Cava's body. He is spurred on by a process of recognition which falls short of realizing that the parallel with Hercules implies a negative valuation.

The king next reads a Greek inscription on a splendid silver chest adorned with gold and precious stones:

> Assí Hércoles, señor de Grecia y de España, supo algunas cosas de las que avían de venir. [*S*, 22a]

> [Thus, Hercules, lord of Greece and Spain, discovered some of the events that were to take place.]

It is as if the cyclical form of reconquest as narrative were also present in these reiterated segments of epiphany and (mis)understanding.[26] Presumably, Rodrigo's bent toward temerity is encouraged here by the analogue to Hercules—which, if "properly" misread, would certainly urge Rodrigo to imitate Hercules and search the tower. And so, Rodrigo breaks the pearl-encrusted lock, opens the chest, and removes a painted cloth:

> No hallaron dentro sino una tela blanca y plegada entre dos tablas de arambre. E assí como las tomó desplególas luego e hallaron en ellas alárabes en figuras con sus tocas, y en sus manos pendones, e con sus espadas a los cuellos, e sus ballestas tras sí en los arçones de las sillas. Y encima de las figuras avían letras que dezían: "quando

este paño fuere estendido y paresçieren estas figuras, hombres andarán así armados, conquirirán a España, y serán della señores." [*S*, 22a]

[They found inside a white cloth, folded between two wire frames. As soon as he unfolded them, they found depicted in it Arabs with their turbans, shields in their hands, their swords raised high above their heads, their crossbows on mounts behind them. And above the picture there were letters that said: "When this cloth is laid open, and these figures appear, men armed in this manner will conquer Spain and will become her master."]

At first, Rodrigo hopes that what he and the courtiers accompanying him have seen is not true. But this somewhat cowardly reaction soon gives way to a more noble note of fatalism, which acknowledges the irreversible historical unfolding in which Rodrigo's further actions will be staged. Nevertheless, in the king's eyes his individual pursuit of *fama* and the historical narrative that now englobes it remain, paradoxically, uncoordinated. Rodrigo's "blindness" to the relationship between the personal and the historical is a necessary attribute of his heroic persona. In attempting to assuage his courtiers' growing anxiety, the king displays full awareness of the existence, if not the articulation, of the temporal planes he is subject to. Thus, if words and images about Arabs signify the divinely ordained and historical scheme of things, he argues, no human science or deed could hope to undo the will of God:

E si de Dios es ordenado, al sumo poderío no ay fuerça ni arte que las cosas no vengan como a El plaze. [*S*, 22b]

[And if God so wills it, there is no might or art capable of undoing what he wishes.]

But, to the extent that he and his men inhabit a biographical time and all the fighting and chivalric deeds are for the sake of earning their share of *fama*, their prowess will be matchless, Rodrigo declares, and they shall make a superb display of it:

E ya, por cosa que venga, no me quitaré que a todo mi poder no estorve lo que Hércoles dize hasta que la muerte tome por lo escusar. Y si todos vosotros assí hazedes, dudo si el mundo todo nos quita nuestro poder. [*S*, 22b]

[Regardless of what happens, I will not cease to oppose with all I can what Hercules has said, and only death will stop me. If all of you do as I say, there will never be on earth a force greater than ours.]

From this comes the exalted, golden age of Rodrigo's reign, profusely illustrated in the *Sarracina*'s chivalric account.

At the end of the Tower of Hercules episode, the portrait of the last king of the Goths is richly and boldly drawn. His futile attempts to reverse the inevitable disclose a consciousness in retreat from the historical. Rodrigo forbids the courtiers present, Count Julián among them, from ever mentioning what they have seen. Similarly, he orders that all the locks on the outer door be replaced. But the irony of it all is revealed to them when an eagle swoops down, drops a *tizón* ("burning ember") and, wonder of wonders, the tower built of solid stone goes up in flames. The ashes, scattered by thousands of fluttering small birds, smear thousands of people throughout Spain, who look as though stained with blood. The spectral *figura* is again at work. The narrator adds that it would be said, many years later, that those who were soiled by the ashes were the ones who died in the destruction of Spain:

Y este fue el primero signo de la destruyçión de España. [*S*, 22c]

[And this was the first sign of the destruction of Spain.]

3. Fictional Compilers

Following the Tower of Hercules episode, the fictional compilers Eleastras and Alanzuri become more prominent. These "narrated-narrator segments" are central to the work not only as an authenticating device— to impart a veneer of authority and accuracy to historical romance—but, more important, because they serve to knot together the various strands of biography, history, adventure, didacticism, and misogyny that comprise the *Sarracina*.

As I mentioned earlier, the discourse of the chroniclers arises from and describes the discontinuity between language and action, text and world. As character, the chronicler mediates between the personal and the historical, and this privileged position strengthens the work's rhetorical dimension. The final, didactic turn of narrative produces a moral truth of universal significance that is of a piece with the obtrusive and moralistic apostrophes to those who have strayed from the right path: Rodrigo, La Cava, and Count Julián. Rodrigo, like the others so inveighed, stands beyond reach of the sermons aimed at him, which the implied readers receive instead. Thus, in contrast to events in the Tower of Hercules, the shifter "tú" now excludes Rodrigo. Only when he is at the edge of disaster can Rodrigo read himself in the moralist's "tú"—only when Rodrigo the reader of the chronicle compiled by Eleastras, his official chronicler, and Rodrigo the actor in the fall of Spain converge in a moment of anguish and defeat which reveals the truth of the author-narrator's earlier warning:

> Y quando tú entendieres el mal consejo que tomaste y el yerro en que cayste, será la destruyçión tan esforçada, que seso ni poder no podrá abastar. [S, 86b]

> [When you realize the folly of your decision and the error of your ways, the destruction will be so vast that no matter how much wisdom or strength you deploy, it will not be enough to save you.]

The notion that belated understanding is coextensive with doom achieves its most dramatic form during the decisive battle at Guadalete against the Arab invaders (see S, 119d–124b). Rodrigo asks to read from the chronicle that Eleastras has been compiling, we are told, from the beginning of the king's reign up to the moment at which the king begins to read it. On the verge of defeat, Rodrigo is now in a position to achieve full understanding, to become one with the *Sarracina*'s implied readers— and with his own chroniclers. But Eleastras hesitates at his patron's request, which is an amusing reversal. Apparently, Eleastras has written for posterity, not for his monarch's daily perusal, and so he tries, unsuccessfully, to expurgate the Infante Sancho's prophetic dream of total defeat. Rodrigo easily thwarts his chronicler and reads the chronicle. It is only now that Rodrigo comprehends his life and his lot. The act of reading situates his actions within the frame of history. He becomes aware of the story line that threads his actions, the portents and messages at the Tower of Hercules, the significance of Sancho's oracular dream. He sobs and writhes in convulsions, and his physical appearance traces the gaining of insight: he is to bear a troubled mien (*turbado*) for the remainder of his life.

It is at this point in the *Sarracina* (which, we should keep in mind, is not the same as Eleastras' compilation) that we discover how the story of La Cava—a personal and secret event—enters historical discourse. Rodrigo now confesses to Eleastras all the details of La Cava's seduction, and he asks the writer to insert the account at its proper place in the chronicle. The history of the compilation is further detailed by the *Sarracina*'s scrupulous, almost fussy authorial voice. This voice addresses his readers, informing them that, after the destruction of Spain, Eleastras went to Count Julián and La Cava for the rest of the story:

> Y desta guisa se supieron estas cosas que se hizieron tan escondidas, y ora se muestran tan plazenteras [S, 99d]

> [In this manner, things which were so hushed up came to be known and are revealed with pleasure]

—"plazenteras ["with pleasure"]" because Rodrigo is now touched with *desengaño*—considerably later than in Covarrubias' compression of story and moral—and because the story which Rodrigo read has been rounded out with the sententious statement that raises narrative—especially a historical legend—above the constraints of referentiality.

Book 2 of the *Sarracina* recounts the beginnings of the Christian Reconquest under Pelayo's leadership. Not until the end of this book do we learn of Rodrigo's famous penance. The gory episode had been overheard by a priest, who had also heard the king's confession. Rodrigo undresses and crawls into a grave with a two-headed snake, fattened up to deadly size by the king himself. After three days the snake devours his *natura* ("penis") and, twelve hours later, reaches *las telas del corazón* ("the walls of the heart"). The king's self-mutilation redeems his sins of *soberbia* ("pride") and *luxuria* ("lust") and conjures up in reverse the paradigmatic status of Hercules.[27] But the *Sarracina,* we are told, comes to an end not because of Rodrigo's self-sacrifice but, rather, because Eleastras, the royal chronicler, having turned into one of Pelayo's best soldiers, dies on the battlefield in defense of Christian Spain. Unlike the *Poema de mio Cid,* whose skillful hero deploys arms and words with equal ease, the *Sarracina* reserves for one of the chroniclers the distinction of unifying the domains of discourse and adventure when it makes Eleastras a key fighter in the Christian Reconquest and concludes the story with the chronicler's—and not the hero's—demise.

The ending of the *Sarracina* reasserts the yoking of adventure and narrativity which we have examined in the emblematic trials of the king and moral *sententiae* of the narrators. A Bakhtinian reading of the *Sarracina* would not fail to notice the insistence on the motif of the journey or road. This most suggestive of chronotopes is to the *Sarracina* what the syncretism of actantial roles is to the *Poema de mio Cid.*[28] Thus, the road motif furnishes convenient circumstances for lucky encounters and discoveries and reappears as the wise and earnest message to the defeated Gothic elite to flee northward to the Cantabrian Mountains for shelter from the bloodbath in the wake of the Arab invasion. At the end of book 1, we learn of the Hermitaño's ("the hermit's") interview with the defeated Rodrigo, which occurs on the road to Toledo, where Eleastras is headed to inform Queen Eliata of the Gothic armies' collapse. The Hermitaño tells Eleastras that he witnessed Rodrigo's lament for the loss of his kingdom on the "alto y sovervioso çerro ["the great and proud mountain"]" (*S,* 123c–d)—a portion of the *Sarracina* immortalized in some of the finest examples of ballad literature.[29] This meeting between eyewitness and chronicler, as well as the Hermitaño's advice to the king, and Queen Eliata's dream of her husband's urging her to flee to "las montañas postrimeras de nuestro señorío ["the most isolated mountains in our kingdom"]" (*S,* 126c) expand the domain of the fortuitous. Equally eventful is the road setting of the author-narrator's discovery and acquisition of the royal chronicles. When the Hermitaño runs into Eleastras on the road,

> y hizo relación de todo esto a Eleastras con mandamiento de muerte de su ánima que si en su vida dél lo supiessen. El qual secreto en quanto él vivió fue guardado; y assí mismo el libro desta hystoria, de la guisa que oýdo havedes, que a gran tiempo passado de la gran destruyçión, y en breve tiempo de nosotros visto, paresçió en poder de un mercader. [*S*, 125a]

> [He told all this to Eleastras, and made him promise, on his life and soul, never to divulge the secret contents. He kept the secret as long as he lived; and thus the book containing this history [story], in the manner told here, long after the time of the great destruction, and shortly before we saw it, came into the hands of a merchant.]

The authorial personae thus come to situate and "paper over" the breach between words and action, narrative and adventure.

4. Subversion, Figura, Silence

It seems an act of poetic justice that New Christians of Muslim descent—and in the position of having some influence in political and religious circles—should have located their efforts to undermine the discourse about Moors precisely at the knotting of discourse and adventure, which the *Sarracina* reserves as the domain of the fictional compilers and the author-narrator. Miguel de Luna and Alonso de Castillo were official translators of Arabic for Philip II. Luna wrote the *Verdadera historia del rey don Rodrigo*, published in two parts in 1592 and 1600. As Francisco Márquez Villanueva has shown, Luna's intent was nothing less than the dismantling of the "neo-Gothic myth of Spain" and its repressive and racialist implications for New Christians. In Luna's daring *remaniement* of the *Sarracina*, the final years of Gothic Spain are no longer a golden age but, rather, "a nightmare which is providentially ended by the Arab invasion."[30] Luna and Castillo were also instrumental in the affair of the lead tablets found in Granada in 1595.[31] The tablets contained inscriptions in Arabic "in a strange script in which none of the characters were joined together" (*LCM*, p. 212). The cryptic texts were translated by Luna, Castillo, and other Moriscos. A long debate ensued over the authenticity of the lead books, until they were finally condemned by the Church in 1682. These fake antiquities were meant to furnish a possible common reference point acceptable to Christians and crypto-Muslims alike, one which might have softened some of the pressures on Moriscos. The texts claimed that their author was a disciple of Saint James. Among the topics discussed in the texts were the Virgin's Immaculate Conception, the heretofore unknown visit to Granada by Saint James, and the key role of the Arabs in saving the religion of God at the end of the world (see *LCM,* p. 213). Luna and Castillo were seemingly above reproach, and, as students of this curious chapter of Morisco cultural history suggest, they must have resolved to deflect growing antagonism against their compatriots by furnishing novel religious doctrines of a syncretic sort— and in a script only they could interpret—that might have reversed the growing rift between Old Christians and Moriscos.[32]

I will not go into the decisions that led up to the expulsion of the Moriscos. But the numbers—and the official end of discourse—are telling. It has been estimated that between 275,000 and 300,000 Moriscos were forced into exile in the years between 1609 and 1614.[33] Those who failed to assimilate—that is, learn to speak "in Christian" (*hablar en cristiano*), abandon their traditional dress, or intermarry with Old Christian families early enough to hide among the mass of Old Christians—were dispatched to other, at times equally uncongenial, places in North Africa and around the Mediterranean. (Many Moriscos, however, seem to have remained or managed to return at the expense of their cultural identity.) Thus, after 1614, the Morisco ceased to exist in the official discourse. The city of Talavera de la Reina offers an interesting example of how survival was predicated on the official end of Otherness. Parochial registers after the expulsion continued to list the same Morisco names and individuals found in documents drafted before 1610. Whether Moriscos were allowed to stay in their homeland by intermingling with the underclass of vagrants, bandits, and others of a picaresque sort or, if, on the other hand, their dissembled existence in Spain was secured by Old Christian compassion or economic interest, the evidence suggests that in certain regions of Spain (Castile, Catalonia, and Andalusia but not in Valencia and Aragon) the expulsion was less effective than the official silence suggests. This abrupt muffling of the "Morisco problem" in official discourse also extended to the Inquisition, but it was relatively uninterested in hounding Moriscos after the expulsion was formally concluded, even though it did continue to busy itself with *judaizantes* ("New Christians suspected of secretly practicing the Jewish faith").[34]

The end of debates over assimilation and conversion point to the radical surgery, however imperfectly accomplished, performed on the body politic, as historians now suggest. But the meaning of this official silence seems more properly a discursive matter, namely, the culmination of the allegorical interpretation that apologists for the expulsion devised. In Fray Marco de Guadalajara's *Memorable expulsion y ivstissimo destierro de los moriscos de España* (1613), the ultimate justification for Philip III's decrees lies in their *figural* meaning.[35] The polemicist deploys the biblical story of Abraham, Sarah, Hagar, and Ishmael (see Gen. 21:8–10) to turn the decrees of expulsion into an exegetical instrument.

Tenia nuestro gran Monarca Filipo II dentro de sus Catholicos
Reynos dos hijos: el uno representa los Christianos legitimos de la
Madre Iglesia, y hermosa Sarra, y el segundo bastardo y traydor,
que son los Moriscos decendientes de Agar: los quales morando en
España han hecho altares a su Idolo Mahoma, jugando con sus
hermanos los fieles.[36]

[Our great monarch, Philip II, had two sons in his Catholic Kingdoms:
one represents the legitimate Christian children of the Mother
Church, and beautiful Sarah, and the second son, bastard and traitor,
who are the Moriscos descended from Hagar: these, living in Spain,
have raised altars to their idol, Muhammad, and are playing with
their brothers, the true and faithful ones.]

For Guadalajara, the expulsion is a just measure not simply because of
the moral and strategic reasons he adduces but, more important, because
he sees it as the equivalent of biblical exegesis: expulsion "reveals" the
anagogic truth of Abraham's ouster of Hagar and Ishmael. Hence, that
new Sarah (Queen Margarita) prevailed on that second Abraham (Philip
III) to safeguard their legitimate children (Catholic Spain) from the
threat of the Ishmaelites (the Moriscos); so the king cast them out of
their homeland.

    This *figural* account of the expulsion is a radical version of the meta-
phoric process that redescribes Moors in the language and rhetorical
system of their conqueror. The meaning of the Moor in discourse is best
summarized by recalling Cipión's deliciously sly description of signification
as a phenomenon comprising the ludic and the forceful:

Digo, pues, que el verdadero sentido es un juego de bolos, donde
con presta diligencia derriban los que están en pie y vuelven a alzar
los caídos, y esto por la mano de quien lo puede hacer.[37]

[I say, then, that true meaning is a game of ninepins, in which those
that are standing get knocked down just as easily as those that are
on the ground come back up, and all this by the hand of someone
who can do it.]

    As we have seen in the course of this study, "the hand of someone
who can do it ["la mano de quien lo puede hacer"]" shapes the meaning
of the Moor in discourse. In the epic, the wealth and prestige of defeated
Moors—the inhabitants of Alcocer or King Yúçef's Almoravides—enhance
the reputation of a hero presented to his audience as an unjustly maligned
but faithful vassal. As soldier and poet, the Cid wields the symbols and
creates the meanings—idealizing or vilifying—with the same flexible,
representational logic espoused throughout the entire *Poema de mio Cid.*
In the *Sarracina,* the "destruction" of Spain by the Arab invaders hinges
on acts of interpretation that are productive in a bungling manner. Morisco

attempts to undermine the tradition that had silenced them centered on the place in discourse that the fictional compilers of the *Sarracina* occupy. From this vantage point, poised between adventure and self-reflexive elaborations on writing and compiling, Luna and the authors of the lead books of Granada devised a parodic discourse which overturned the meaning of the Arab invasion and sought to redefine what constituted the origins of Christianity in Granada and the differences between the religious castes.

The reversibility of meaning which Cipión expresses as the central feature of signification also informs the epigraph to this essay. It is only at the end of the Captive's tale that we—and Dorotea—learn the "true" meaning of the Moorish lady's garb. Dorotea's question, "¿esta señora es cristiana o mora? ["is this lady a Christian or a Moor?"]," doesn't probe into what is already known—that Zoraida's Otherness in dress and silence smack of Moorishness.[38] Dorotea's desire to know is, in effect, the first step in the interpretative process that disposes of the Moors and their world. At the end of the Captive's tale, we discover that the Moorish lady, Zoraida, is a Christian at heart and that her Moorish clothes bespeak not her origins as much as the kindness of French pirates, who respected her honor and set her free without despoiling her. Something akin to Cipión's *avant la lettre* deconstructive bent is at play in the reduction of Moors to biblical exegesis and in the official silencing of the "Moorish problem."

1. The sizable bibliography on the subject appears in María Soledad Carrasco Urgoiti, *El moro de Granada en la literatura (del siglo quince al veinte)* (Madrid, 1956); María Rosa Lida de Malkiel, "El moro en las letras castellanas," *Hispanic Review* 28 (Oct. 1960): 350–58; Julio Caro Baroja, *Los moriscos del reino de Granada: Ensayo de historia social* (Madrid, 1957); James T. Monroe, *Islam and the Arabs in Spanish Scholarship: Sixteenth Century to the Present,* Medieval Iberian Peninsula Texts and Studies, vol. 3 (Leiden, 1970); Louis Cardaillac, *Moriscos y cristianos: Un enfrentamiento polémico (1492–1640),* trans. Mercedes García Arenal (Madrid-México-Buenos Aires, 1979); Antonio Domínguez Ortiz and Bernard Vincent, *Historia de los moriscos: Vida y tragedia de una minoría* (Madrid, 1978); Robert I. Burns, "Muslim-Christian Conflict and Contact in Medieval Spain: Context and Methodology," *Thought* 54 (Sept. 1979): 238–52; Miguel Ángel de Bunes Ibarra, *Los moriscos en el pensamiento histórico: Historiografía de un grupo marginado* (Madrid, 1983); and Anwar G. Chejne, *Islam and the West: The Moriscos; A Cultural and Social History* (Albany, N.Y., 1983).

2. The landlady in Miguel de Cervantes Saavedra's *El coloquio de los perros* asks: "¿Qué linaje hay en el mundo, por bueno que sea, que no tenga algún dime y direte? ["Is there any family line in the world, no matter how high, without skeletons in the closet?"]" (*Novelas ejemplares,* ed. Harry Sieber, 2 vols. [Madrid, 1981], 2:327; my translation, as are all other English translations in this paper, unless otherwise noted). See also Joseph H. Silverman, "Saber vidas ajenas: Un tema de vida y literatura y sus variantes cervantinas," *Papeles de Son Armadans* 89, no. 267 (1978): 197–212, and Cardaillac, *Moriscos y cristianos,* pp. 313–410.

3. The fear was not entirely unfounded; see Monroe, "A Curious Morisco Appeal to the Ottoman Empire," *Al-Andalus* 31 (1966): 281–303.

4. I have borrowed the term "social" from a letter to me by Professor Harry Sieber. Paradoxically, both approaches, the "aestheticist" and the "social," are found at times in

the work of a single critic; see, e.g., Georges Cirot, "La Maurophilie littéraire en Espagne au seizième siècle (Suite et fin)," *Bulletin Hispanique* 46 (Jan.–June 1944): 5–25. The "social" approach can be seen in the studies by Francisco López Estrada, *El Abencerraje y la hermosa Jarifa: Cuatro textos y su estudio* (Madrid, 1957); Claudio Guillén, "Individuo y ejemplaridad en el *Abencerraje,*" in *Collected Studies in Honour of Américo Castro's Eightieth Year,* ed. M. P. Hornik (Oxford, 1965), pp. 175–97; and "Literature as Historical Contradiction: *El Abencerraje,* the Moorish Novel, and the Eclogue," *Literature as System: Essays toward the Theory of Literary History* (Princeton, N.J., 1971), pp. 159–217; Carrasco Urgoiti, *El problema morisco en Aragón al comienzo del reinado de Felipe II,* University of North Carolina Studies in Spanish, no. 11 (Valencia, 1969); George A. Shipley, "La obra literaria como monumento histórico: El caso de *El Abencerraje,*" *Journal of Hispanic Philology* 2 (Winter 1978): 115; and Francisco Márquez Villanueva, "La voluntad de leyenda de Miguel de Luna," *Nueva Revista de Filología Hispánica* 30, no. 2 (1981): 391–93. For a critique of the "social" interpretations, see my "Power, Discourse, and Metaphor in the *Abencerraje,*" *Modern Language Notes* 99 (Mar. 1984): 195–213.

5. See Edward W. Said, *Orientalism* (New York, 1979), and Juan Goytisolo, *Crónicas sarracinas* (Barcelona, 1982).

6. For a discussion of the 1207 date of composition, see *Poema de mio Cid,* ed. Colin Smith (Oxford, 1972), pp. xxx–xxxvii. All further references to this work, abbreviated *PMC,* will be included in the text, with line numbers in parentheses; the accompanying English translations are from *Poem of the Cid,* trans. W. S. Merwin ([New York, 1975], abbreviated *PC,* with laisse numbers in parentheses), unless otherwise noted.

7. Ramón Menéndez Pidal defines *quiñonero* ("officer in charge of recording and distributing the booty") with reference to Minaya Alvar Fáñez, the Cid's lieutenant, who is to "write and count" the loot (*PMC,* 1773; my translation) as "acaso como inspector de los quiñoneros ["perhaps in the capacity of supervisor of *quiñoneros*"]": it is in this sense that I used *quiñonero* in the present study (*Obras completas de Ramón Menéndez Pidal,* vols. 3–5, *"Cantar de mio Cid": Texto, gramática y vocabulario* [Madrid, 1969], 2:816).

8. In the poet Pedro Salinas' felicitous description, the proud father and husband, finally reunited with his family, is "en la cima del regreso ["at the tip of return"]" to power ("La vuelta al esposo: Ensayo sobre estructura y sensibilidad en el *Cantar de Mío Cid,*" *Bulletin of Spanish Studies* 24 [Apr. 1947]: 87; rpt. in Salinas, *Ensayos de literatura hispánica,* ed. Juan Marichal, 3d ed. [Madrid, 1967], p. 56).

9. For the theory of metaphor, see Paul Ricoeur, *The Rule of Metaphor: Multi-Disciplinary Studies of the Creation of Meaning in Language,* trans. Robert Czerny et al. (Toronto, 1977). See also my discussion of the Cid as warrior and poet, in "The Docile Image: The Moor as Figure of Force, Subservience, and Nobility in the *Poema de mio Cid,*" *Kentucky Romance Quarterly* 31, no. 3 (1984): 269–80.

10. See Smith, ed., *Poema de mio Cid,* p. 170, s.v. "Avengalvón."

11. P.-J. Miniconi studies the topos of the *teichoskopia* and cites several Spanish ballads (*romances*) in which it appears but does not mention the *Poema de mio Cid* (see "Un Thème épique: La *Teichoskopia,*" in *Colloque l'epopée greco-latine et ses prolongements européens,* ed. R. Chevallier, Collection Caesarodunum, no. 16 bis (Paris, 1981), pp. 71–80.

12. See Homer *Iliad* 4. 153–244.

13. For the circulation of the "object value" in narrative, see A. -J. Greimas, *Sémantique structurale: Recherche de méthode* (Paris, 1972), pp. 179–91.

14. Américo Castro, "Poesía y realidad en el *Poema del Cid,*" *Tierra Firme* 1 (1935): 22; rpt. in Castro, *Semblanzas y estudios españoles* (Princeton, N.J., 1956), p. 9.

For the 1425 date of composition of Pedro del Corral's *Crónica sarracina,* see Derek C. Carr, "La *Epístola que enbio Don Enrrique de Villena a Suero de Quiñones* y la fecha de la *Crónica sarracina* de Pedro de Corral," in *University of British Columbia Hispanic Studies,* ed. Harold Livermore (London, 1974), pp. 1–18.

15. See Juan Menéndez Pidal, *Leyendas del último rey godo: Notas e investigaciones,* rev. ed. (Madrid, 1906); Alexander Haggerty Krappe, *The Legend of Rodrick, Last of the Visigoth Kings and the Ermanarich Cycle* (Heidelberg, 1923); Ramón Menéndez Pidal, *Floresta de*

leyendas heroicas españolas: Rodrigo, el último godo, 3 vols. (Madrid, 1973); Helmut Brettschneider, *Der Anseïs de Cartage und die Seconda Spagna,* Romanistische Arbeiten, no. 27 (Halle, 1937); José Joaquín Satorre Grau, "Pedro de Corral y la estructura de su *Crónica del rey don Rodrigo,*" *Al-Andalus* 34 (1969): 159–73; and intro. to *Crónica del moro Rasis,* ed. Diego Catalán and María Soledad de Andrés (Madrid, 1975).

16. See Edward Meryon Wilson, *Tragic Themes in Spanish Ballads,* Diamante Series, no. 8 (London, 1958); rpt. in Wilson, *Entre las jarchas y Cernuda: Constantes y variables en la poesía española,* trans. Sara Struuck (Barcelona, 1977), pp. 108–29.

17. M. M. Bakhtin defines "chronotopes" as "the organizing centers for the fundamental narrative events of the novel. The chronotope is the place where the knots of narrative are tied and untied." The term describes how a motif of narrative, such as meeting or separation, recognition or nonrecognition, gathers together temporal and spatial markers on a common ground of meaning ("Forms of Time and of the Chronotope in the Novel: Notes toward a Historical Poetics," *The Dialogic Imagination: Four Essays,* ed. Michael Holquist, trans. Caryl Emerson and Holquist, University of Texas Press Slavic Series, no. 1 [Austin, Tex., 1981], p. 250; and see p. 97).

18. Hercules is a key legitimating motif in fifteenth-century historical discourse; see Robert B. Tate, "Mitología en la historiografía española de la Edad Media y del Renaciento," *Ensayos sobre la historiografía peninsular del siglo quince,* trans. Jesús Díaz (Madrid, 1970), pp. 16–20; Catalán, ed., *Crónico del moro Rasis,* pp. lxxv–lxxx; Margherita Morreale, intro. to Enrique de Villena, *Los doze trabajos de Hércules,* ed. Morreale (Madrid, 1958), pp. viii–xxxv; Franco Gaeta, "L'avventura di Ercole," *Rinascimento* 5 (Dec. 1954): 227–60; and G. Karl Galinsky, *The Herakles Theme: The Adaptations of the Hero in Literature from Homer to the Twentieth Century* (Totowa, N.J., 1972), pp. 116–17 and 185–230.

19. If Hercules is "the averter of evil," then Rodrigo is the anti-Hercules (Galinsky, *The Herakles Theme,* p. 4; and see pp. 4–88). Cf.: "Oyeron la fama del glorioso ercules que por su virtud por todo el mundo era nonbrado, mayormente que estirpava o derramava tales nozimientos del mundo doquier que los sopiese ["They heard about the fame of glorious Hercules, renowned the world over for his virtue in destroying and wiping out all that was harmful in the world"]" (Villena, *Los doze trabajos de Hércules,* p. 66).

20. See Galinsky, *The Herakles Theme,* pp. 190–211. Might not the twofold nature of Hercules' virtue underlie the hesitation in the *Chrónica de 1344* between "libro de las Andanças ["book of Deeds"]" and "libro de las Adeuinanças ["book of Divinations"]"? See the remarks by Catalán, ed., *Crónica del moro Rasis,* p. lxxix.

21. "The name [emblem] was devised by Alciati who derived it from F. Budé's *Annotationes ad Pandectas* where it signified 'mosaic work'" (Mario Praz, *Studies in Seventeenth-Century Imagery,* 2 vols. (London, 1939), 1:18).

22. See Sebastián de Covarrubias Orozco, *Emblemas morales, 1610,* ed. John Horden, Continental Emblem Books, no. 7 (Menston, 1973), p. 158; all further references to this work, abbreviated *EM,* will be included in the text. See also Arthur Henkel and Albrecht Schöne, eds., *Emblemata: Handbuch zur Sinnbildkunst des sechszehnten und siebzehnten Jahrhunderts,* rev. ed. (Stuttgart, 1976), pp. 1214–15, and Karl-Ludwig Selig, "La teoria dell'emblema in Ispagna: I testi fondamentali," *Convivium* n.s. 3 (1955): 409–21.

23. Covarrubias takes the motto from Horace *Carmina* 4. 4. 22; see also Henkel and Schöne, *Emblemata,* p. 1215.

24. See Paul Zumthor, "Roman et histoire: Aux sources d'un univers narratif," *Langue, texte, énigme* (Paris, 1972), p. 241.

25. Corral, *Crónica sarracina [Cronica del rey don Rodrigo con la destruycion de España y como los moros la ganaron]* (Alcala de Henares, 1587 [copy at the Hispanic Society of America, New York]), fol. 21d. All further references to this work, abbreviated *S,* will be included in the text, with folio numbers in parentheses (*a* and *b* denote recto columns; *c* and *d* denote verso columns); punctuation and diacritical marks are mine (I have also regularized the use of *u* and *v*).

26. I am thinking here of the *Poema de Fernán González* (c. 1250), which describes Moors in a manner reminiscent of the *Chanson de Roland*'s racialist slant. Moors are "Mas

feos que Satan con todo su convento, / Quando sal(e) del infyerno suzio e carv[o]niento ["Uglier than Satan and his conventicle combined / When he comes out of hell, dirty and sooty"]" (*Poema de Fernan Gonçalez,* ed. C. Carroll Marden [Baltimore, 1904], p. 56, st. 385, ll. 3–4). For the clerkly poet of the *Poema de Fernán González,* the Christian Reconquest is a historicist construct, full of thirteenth-century occurrences and beliefs projected on a dimly perceived past. The reconquest as narrative is a cyclical playing on the wheel of fortune. Clashes and reversals flesh out the underlying analogies and oppositions. Thus, the eighth-century Arab and Berber incursions retrace an analogical, past event. The initial conquest is already a *re*-conquest by a camel-riding and homeless people: "Non eran dun logar nin dun entendimiento ["They were not from one place in particular and had no understanding"]" (p. 56, st. 385, 1. 2). Moors exist only as former or would-be conquerors of Spain: "Por que es toda Espanna en el nuestro poder. / ¡Mal grrado a los moros que la solian tener! ["Because all of Spain is in our power / The Moors are displeased, for they used to be masters here!"]" declares a confident Rodrigo (p. 9, st. 59, ll. 3–4). The notion that Rodrigo's Goths were, at one point, successful reconquerors can be seen as either a projection of thirteenth-century fans of the Goths or as an identification between the Arabs known to the thirteenth century and the Africans who emigrated to Cádiz at the end of the Punic Wars and saw eight of their kings become rulers of Spain (see Catalán, ed., *Crónica del moro Rasis,* p. lxxvi).

27. Galinsky notes that allegorical interpretations of Hercules raise his victories over beasts and monsters to "triumphs of the virtuous mind over all sorts of vice" (*The Herakles Theme,* p. 198; and see pp. 197–98).

28. For the actantial model, see Greimas, *Sémantique structurale,* pp. 179–91, and Jonathan Culler, *Structuralist Poetics: Structuralism, Linguistics, and the Study of Literature* (Ithaca, N.Y., 1975), p. 82. In the *Poema de mio Cid,* the roles of subject, object, sender, and receiver cluster around the hero when he transforms an army of Moors into a procession of gift-bearing subjects.

29. See Julio Rodríguez-Puértolas, "El romancero, historia de una frustración," in *Literatura, historia, alienación* (Barcelona, 1976), pp. 116–17.

30. Márquez Villaneuva, "La voluntad de leyenda de Miguel de Luna," p. 363 ("Luna dibuja el pasado gótico como una pesadilla a la que viene a poner fin una providencial invasión musulmana").

31. See Darío Cabanelas, "Intento de supervivencia en el ocaso de una cultura: Los libros plúmbeos de Granada," *Nueva Revista de Filología Hispánica* 30, no. 2 (1981): 334–58; L. Patrick Harvey, "The Literary Culture of the Moriscos, 1492–1609: A Study Based on the Extant Manuscripts in Arabic and Aljamía" (Ph.D. diss., Oxford University, 1958), pp. 212–68 (all further references to this work, abbreviated *LCM,* will be included in the text); and Monroe, *Islam and the Arabs in Spanish Scholarship,* pp. 7–16.

32. See Cabanelas, "Intento de supervivencia," p. 354; see also Marcel Bataillon's discussion of illuminism and the *inquiétude messianique* ("messianic fervor") associated with Jewish converts to Christianity (*Erasme et l'Espagne: Recherches sur l'histoire spirituelle du seizième siècle* [Paris, 1937], p. 65) and Bruce W. Wardropper, "*Don Quixote:* Story or History?" *Modern Philology* 63 (Aug. 1965): 1–11.

33. See Domínguez Ortiz and Vincent, *Historia de los moriscos,* p. 200.

34. For the consequences of the expulsion, see Domínguez Ortiz and Vincent, *Historia de los moriscos,* pp. 247–66.

35. See F. Marco de Guadalajara y Xavierr, *Memorable expulsion y Ivstissimo destierro de los moriscos de España* (Pamplona, 1613 [copy at Biblioteca Nacional de Madrid, R-16526]).

36. Guadalajara, *Memorable expulsion,* fol. 154v.

37. Cervantes, *Coloquio de los perros,* 2:347.

38. Cervantes, *El ingenioso hidalgo don Quijote de la Mancha,* ed. Luis Andrés Murillo, 2d ed., 3 vols. (Madrid, 1982), 1:462; *The Adventures of Don Quixote,* trans. J. M. Cohen (Harmondsworth, 1970), p. 338.

Scratches on the Face of the Country; or, What Mr. Barrow Saw in the Land of the Bushmen

Mary Louise Pratt

> It is not difficult to transpose from physics to politics [the rule that] it is impossible for two bodies to occupy the same space at the same time.
>
> —JOHANNES FABIAN, *Time and the Other*

My title originated in the following passage from John Barrow's *Account of Travels into the Interior of Southern Africa in the Years 1797 and 1798*, published in London in 1801. It is an excerpt from a fairly lengthy portrait describing the Bushmen:

> In his disposition he is lively and chearful; in his person active. His talents are far above mediocrity; and, averse to idleness, they are seldom without employment. Confined generally to their hovels by day, for fear of being surprised and taken by the farmers, they sometimes dance on moonlight nights from setting to the rising of the sun. . . . The small circular trodden places around their huts indicated their fondness for this amusement. His chearfulness is the more extraordinary, as the morsel he procures to support existence is earned with danger and fatigue. He neither cultivates the ground nor breeds cattle; and his country yields few natural productions that serve for food. The bulbs of the iris, and a few gramineous roots of a bitter and pungent taste, are all that the vegetable kingdom

I am grateful to Renato Rosaldo, James Clifford, Herbert Lindenberger, Cynthia Ward, and Wlad Godzich for comments and suggestions on this paper.

affords him. By the search of these the whole surface of the plains near the horde was scratched.[1]

Any reader recognizes here a very familiar, widespread, and stable form of "othering." The people to be othered are homogenized into a collective "they," which is distilled even further into an iconic "he" (the standardized adult male specimen). This abstracted "he"/"they" is the subject of verbs in a timeless present tense, which characterizes anything "he" is or does not as a particular historical event but as an instance of a pregiven custom or trait. (In contexts of conquest, descriptions are likely to focus on the Other's amenability to domination and potential as a labor pool, as Barrow's does in part.) Through this discourse, encounters with an Other can be textualized or processed as enumerations of such traits. This is what happens in modern anthropology, where a fieldwork encounter results in a descriptive ethnography. It also happens in ethnography's antecedent, the portrait of manners and customs. Barrow's portrait of the Bushmen is an instance of this old and remarkably stable subgenre, which turns up in a wide range of discursive contexts. Barrow's portrait is directly continuous in many respects with those in Christopher Columbus' letters or in John Mandeville's *Travels* (circa 1350), where we find the following account of the inhabitants of the Isle of Natumeran:

> Men and women of that isle have heads like hounds; and they are called Cynocephales. This folk, thereof all they be of such shape, yet they are full reasonable and subtle of wit. . . And they gang all naked but a little cloth before their privy members. They are large of stature and good warriors, and they bear a great target, with which they cover all their body, and a long spear in their hand.[2]

The only trace of a face-to-face encounter, real or imagined, in this description is the fact that it begins with the body as seen/scene. Such portraits conventionally do so, commonly with the genitals as the crucial site/sight in the "bodyscape"—as they are in Barrow's Bushmen portrait, where he devotes two full pages to the supposed genital peculiarities of Bushmen men and women.[3]

The portrait of manners and customs is a normalizing discourse, whose work is to codify difference, to fix the Other in a timeless present where all "his" actions and reactions are repetitions of "his" normal habits.

Mary Louise Pratt is an associate professor in the Department of Spanish and Portuguese and the Program in Comparative Literature at Stanford University. She is author of *Toward a Speech-Act Theory of Literary Discourse* and is a member of the editorial boards of *Poetics, Signs, Tabloid,* and *Cultural Anthropology.*

Thus, it textually produces the Other without an explicit anchoring either in an observing self or in a particular encounter in which contact with the Other takes place. "He" is a *sui generis* configuration, often only a list of features set in a temporal order different from that of the perceiving and speaking subject. Johannes Fabian has recently used the phrase "denial of coevalness" to refer specifically to this temporal distancing.[4]

Manners-and-customs description could serve as a paradigmatic case of the ways in which ideology normalizes, codifies, and reifies. Such reductive normalizing is sometimes seen as the primary or defining characteristic of ideology. In this view, as Catherine Belsey puts it in her lucid study *Critical Practice,* "the task of ideology is to present the position of the subject as fixed and unchangeable, an element in a given system of differences which is human nature and the world of human experience, and to show possible action as an endless repetition of 'normal' familiar action."[5] That, it would seem, is exactly what Mr. Barrow is doing in his description of the Bushmen. Indeed, he is doing so at an especially critical ideological juncture, for nowhere are the notions of normal, familiar action and given systems of difference in greater jeopardy than on the imperial frontier. There Europeans confront not only unfamiliar Others but unfamiliar selves; there they engage in not just the reproduction of the capitalist mode of production but its expansion through displacement of previously established modes. It is no accident that, in the literature of the imperial frontier, manners-and-customs description has always flourished as a normalizing force and now retains a kind of credibility and authority it has lost elsewhere. It is a mainstay of travel and exploration writing; and under the rubric of ethnography, it has been professionalized into an academic discipline which serves, in part, to mediate the shock of contact on the frontier.

If the discourse of manners and customs aspires to a stable fixing of subjects and systems of differences, however, its project is not and never can be complete. This is true if only for the seemingly trivial reason that manners-and-customs descriptions seldom occur on their own as discrete texts. They usually appear embedded in or appended to a superordinate genre, whether a narrative, as in travel books and much ethnography, or an assemblage, as in anthologies and magazines.[6] In the case of travel writing, which is the main focus of this essay, manners-and-customs description is always in play with other sorts of representation that also bespeak difference and position subjects in their own ways. Sometimes these other positionings complement the ideological project of normalizing description, and sometimes they do not.

In what follows, I propose to examine this interplay of discourses in some nineteenth-century travel writing chiefly about Africa. While Barrow's work is not prominent on anybody's mental bookshelves these days, readers will recognize such names as David Livingstone, John Speke, James Grant, Richard Burton, Mungo Park, or Paul Du Chaillu. During the so-called opening up of central and southern Africa to European capitalism in the first half of the nineteenth century, such explorer-writers were the principal producers of Africa for European imaginations—producers, that is, of ideology in connection with the European expansionist project there. What I hope to underscore in these writings is not their tendency towards single, fixed subject positions or single, fixed systems of difference. Rather, I wish to emphasize the multiplicity of ways of codifying the Other, the variety of (seemingly) fixed positions and the variety of (seemingly) given sets of differences that they posit. European penetration and appropriation is semanticized in numerous ways that can be quite distinct, even mutually contradictory. In the course of examining discursive polyphony in these travel writings, I hope to stress the need to consider ideology not only in terms of reductive simplification but also in terms of the proliferation of meanings.

In the case of Barrow's *Travels* (and in a great many other books of its kind), manners-and-customs descriptions of indigenous peoples are appended to or embedded in the day-to-day narrative of the journey. In contrast to what we might expect, that day-to-day narrative is most often largely devoted not to Indiana Jones–style confrontations with the natives but to the considerably less exciting presentation of landscape. Barrow's book exemplifies this practice. Though he was traveling as a colonial official, charged with mediating disputes between Boer colonists and indigenous peoples, and though he was traveling with a large party of Europeans, Boers, and Hottentots, human interaction plays little role in his narrative.[7] Instead, page after page catalogs without a thrill what Barrow likes to call "the face of the country." For example:

> The termination of the Snowy mountains is about twelve miles to the northeastward of Compassberg; and here a port or pass through them opens upon a plain extending to the northward, without a swell, farther than the eye could command. Eight miles beyond this pass we encamped for the night, when the weather was more raw and cold than we had hitherto experienced on the Sneuwberg. The thick clouds being at length dissipated by the sun, the Compassberg shewed itself white near the summit with snow.
> The division of Sneuwberg comprehends a great extent of country. The moment we had ascended from the plains behind Graaf Reynet to those more elevated of Sneuwberg, the difference of the face of the country and its natural productions were remarkably striking. [*A*, 1:244–45]

And so it goes for the better part of some three hundred pages. The organization of this passage is basically narrative, but it is a strange, attenuated kind of narrative because it does everything possible to minimize all human presence, including that of the people whose journey is being told. In the main, what is narrated proves to be a descriptive sequence of sights/sites, with the travelers present chiefly as a kind of collective moving eye which registers these sights. Their presence as agents scarcely registers at all. In the opening sentence, for instance, we must infer that Barrow and his party traveled the twelve miles, passed through the mountains, and so on. The cold is presented chiefly as a fact about the weather, not as a discomfort they endured. The drama here is produced not by the adventures of the travelers but by the changing "face of the country." Signs of human presence, when they occur, are also expressed as marks upon this face; the human agents responsible for those signs are themselves rarely seen.[8] In the following passage, for example, the villages are less important than the rivers and streams, and there is no sign of inhabitants:

> The following day we passed the Great Fish river, though not without some difficulty, the banks being high and steep, the stream strong, the bottom rocky, and the water deep. Some fine trees of the willow of Babylon, or a variety of that species, skirted the river at this place. The opposite side presented a very beautiful country, well wooded and watered, and plentifully covered with grass, among which grew in great abundance, a species of indigo, apparently the same as that described by Mr. Masson as the *candicans*.
>
> The first night that we encamped in the Kaffr country was near a stream called *Kowsha,* which falls into the Great Fish River. On the following day we passed the villages of *Malloo* and *Tooley,* the two chiefs and brothers we had seen in Zuure Veldt, delightfully situated on two eminences rising from the said streamlet. We also passed several villages placed along the banks of the *Guengka* and its branches, and the next day we came to a river of very considerable magnitude called the *Keiskamma.* [A, 1:190–91]

Here again, the travelers' struggle to cross the river is not narrated but expressed in a much more mediated fashion, as an enumeration of the traits of the river that produced the difficulty. The speaking and experiencing self is as effaced as it is in the ethnographic portraits.

Barrow's book exemplifies a kind of discursive division of labor common to much travel writing of his time: the main narrative deals with landscape, while indigenous peoples are represented separately in descriptive portraits. This division of labor is hinted at in the passage that I quoted at the beginning of this paper. At two points there, the timeless ethnographic present tense is interrupted by a narrative past tense: (1) the trodden places around the Bushmen's huts *indicated* their fondness for dancing, and (2) by the Bushmen's search for roots, the surface of the surrounding plains *was scratched.* These two past tense verbs refer to the specific occasion of Barrow's visit to the Bushmen. What they historicize, however, is his encounter not with *them* but with traces they have left on the landscape—their scratches on "the face of the country."

In this kind of writing, the "face of the country" is presented chiefly in sweeping prospects that open before or, more often, beneath the traveler's eye. Such panoramic views are an important commonplace of European aesthetics, of course, and that undoubtedly accounts for much of their appeal here. In the context of exploration writing like Barrow's, however, such views acquire and serve to familiarize meanings they may not have on the domestic front. Barrow's own language suggests, for example, the fantasy of dominance that is commonly built into this stance. The eye "commands" what falls within its gaze; the mountains "show themselves" or "present themselves"; the country "opens up" before the European newcomer, as does the unclothed indigenous bodyscape.[9] At the same time, this eye seems powerless to act or interact with this landscape. Unheroic, unparticularized, without ego, interest, or desire of its own, it seems able to do nothing but gaze from a periphery of its own creation, like the self-effaced, noninterventionist eye that scans the Other's body.

This discursive configuration, which centers landscape, separates people from place, and effaces the speaking self, is characteristic of a great deal of travel writing in the last century, especially the literature of exploration and especially that which aspired to scientific status. By mid-century it predominates among the Victorian explorers who fought so fiercely (with each other) to "win" the source of the Nile for England (and themselves). Despite his vastly greater involvement with African peoples and his more historical view of things, Livingstone readily writes about southern Africa from the same distanced and self-effaced stance that Barrow assumed. Consider, for instance, this excerpt from his *Narrative of an Expedition to the Zambesi* (1857):

> Ten or fifteen miles north of Morambala stands the dome-shaped mountain Makanga, or Chi-kanda; several others, with granitic-looking peaks, stretch away to the north, and form the eastern boundary of the valley; another range, but of metamorphic rocks, commencing opposite Senna, bounds the valley on the west. After steaming through a portion of this marsh, we came to a broad belt of palm and other trees, crossing the fine plain on the right bank. Marks of large game were abundant. Elephants had been feeding on the palm nuts, which have a pleasant fruity taste, and are used as food by man. Two pythons were observed coiled together among the branches of a large tree, and were both shot. The larger of the two, a female, was ten feet long. They are harmless, and said to be good eating.[10]

Again, the Europeans are present mainly as the deleted subjects of passive verbs ("were observed," "were shot"); indigenous inhabitants are there only in the abstract ("man"); even the rest of the animal kingdom is reduced to traces. The presence of the "harmless" female python and her mate and their unexplained destruction suggest at least one of the ideological dimensions underlying this kind of description—a fantasy of returning the country to an Edenic or even pre-Adamic condition. (I will be looking shortly at some other versions of this fantasy in the work of Alexander von Humboldt and Du Chaillu.)

The explicit project of these explorer-writers, whether scientists or not, is to produce what they themselves referred to as "information." Their task, in other words, was to incorporate a particular reality into a series of interlocking information orders—aesthetic, geographic, mineralogical, botanical, agricultural, economic, ecological, ethnographic, and so on. To the extent that it strives to efface itself, the invisible eye/I strives to make those informational orders natural, to find them there uncommanded, rather than assert them as the products/producers of European knowledges or disciplines. In turn, those knowledges are the producers/ products of a project they likewise presuppose and seldom bespeak. It is the project whereby, to use Daniel Defert's terms, Europe "takes consciousness of itself . . . as a planetary process rather than [as] a region of the world."[11] This nineteenth-century exploration writing rejoins two planetary processes that had been ideologically sundered: the expansion of the knowledge edifice of natural history and the expansion of the capitalist world system. While the former had set for itself what Humboldt was to call "the great problem of the physical description of the globe,"[12] the latter was undertaking nothing less than the physical appropriation and transformation of that globe in what Barrow calls "the spirit of commerce and adventurous industry" (*A*, 1:1).

In these information-producing travel accounts, the goal of expanding the capitalist world system is, as a rule, acknowledged in prefaces, but only there. Livingstone—the missionary—explicitly states in his preface the connection between information, landscape, and commercial expansion. He declares that his account "is written in the earnest hope that it may contribute to the *information* which will cause the great and fertile continent of Africa to be no longer kept wantonly sealed, but made available as a *scene* of European enterprise" (*N*, p. 2; my emphasis). In the body of the text, European enterprise is seldom mentioned, but the sight/site as textualized consistently presupposes a global transformation that, whether the I/eye likes it or not, is already understood to be underway. In scanning prospects in the spatial sense—as landscape panoramas—this eye *knows itself* to be looking at prospects in the temporal sense—as possibilities for the future, resources to be developed, landscapes to be peopled or re-peopled by Europeans. These prospects are one of the main criteria of relevance in the landscape descriptions. They are what make a plain "fine" or make it noteworthy that a peak is "granitic" or a country "well-wooded." Occasionally the force of these criteria is made explicit. At the conclusion of Speke's description of newly discovered Lake Victoria Nyanza (1864), for instance, the "pleasure of the mere view" vanishes in favor of "those more intense and exciting emotions which are called up by the consideration of the commercial and geographical importance of the *prospect* before me."[13] More commonly, European aspirations are introduced in the form of a reverie that overtakes the seer as he ponders the panorama before him. Speke's partner Grant, arriving at Lake Victoria Nyanza, is inspired to make a sketch, "dotting it with imaginary steamers and ships riding at anchor in the bay," apparently dissatisfied with the African boats already plying its waters.[14] As he scans Lake Tanganyika, Burton declares that the view "wants but a little of the neatness and finish of Art—mosques and kiosks, palaces and villas, gardens and orchards—contrasting with the profuse lavishness and magnificence of nature." The view already includes African "villages, cultivated lands, the frequent canoes of fishermen," but they are not enough for Burton.[15] And again, only the traces of people are apparent—not the people themselves. Such reveries abound in nineteenth-century exploration writing. They are determined, in part, by highly generalized literary conventions. It is conventional, for instance, for romantic prospect poems to move from description into reverie. In exploration writing, however, the reverie convention often very specifically projects the civilizing mission onto the scene.

Apart from such relatively explicit allusions, the will to intervene is also present in more ubiquitous and more mystified ways in these writings. It emanates from an unknown site behind the speaking "I"—behind the periphery of what is seen, from a seat of power that should probably be identified with the state. I find it useful here to recall the current conception of the state as a form of public power separate from both ruler and ruled, constituted most basically by the exclusive right to exercise legitimate violence within a certain defined territory.[16] It is not surprising, then, to find the emissaries of the European states on the imperial frontier concerning themselves, above all, with defining territory and scanning perimeters, even though territorial possession was not yet part of the imperial strategy. Nor is it surprising that these subjects positioned themselves in their discourse as neither ruler nor ruled, neither actor nor acted upon, but as invisible, passive, and personally innocent conduits for information. The normalizing, generalizing voice that produces the ethnographic manners-and-customs portraits is distinct from but complementary to the landscape narrator. This voice scans the prospects of the indigenous body and body politic and, in the ethnographic present, abstracts them out of the landscape that is under contention and away from the history that is being made—a history into which they will later be reinserted as an exploited labor pool.

Throughout much nineteenth-century exploration writing on the imperial frontier, this discursive configuration effaces the European presence and textually splits off indigenous inhabitants from habitat. It is a configuration which, in (mis)recognition of what was materially underway or in anticipation of what was to come, verbally depopulates landscapes. Indigenous peoples are relocated in separate manners-and-customs chapters as if in textual homelands or reservations, where they are pulled out of time to be preserved, contained, studied, admired, detested, pitied, mourned. Meanwhile, the now-empty landscape is personified as the metaphorical "face of the country"—a more tractable face that returns the European's gaze, echoes his words, and accepts his caress.[17] Exploration certainly lends itself to heroic narrative paradigms of adventure, personal prowess, obstacles overcome and prizes won, and explorers in the nineteenth century were certainly seen as heroes. Yet most of them did not write themselves as heroes. Indeed, one of the most striking aspects of this informational branch of travel writing is the way it reverses and refuses heroic priorities: it narrates place and describes people. Its European protagonists are everywhere on the margins of their own story, present not as heroes but as effaced information-producers gazing in from a periphery. This discourse was by no means the only one used in travel writing at the time, and I will mention one of the contending discourses below. But until the last decades of the century, when the notorious scramble for Africa changed the whole character of European intervention, it was one of the most powerful discourses.

An important consequence of the European's self-effacement in this literature is that it is possible to narrate the journey and "to other" the Other while maintaining silence about the actual, specific contacts going on between the European travelers and the indigenous peoples they encounter. No conventional textual space calls on the Europeans to portray their interactions, recount their dialogues, report the Other's voices, or display the concrete working out of relations on the spot. Perhaps the most telling conventional silence surrounds the day-to-day interaction within the traveling party—between the European masters and the indigenous laborers who accompanied and far outnumbered them. The two groups coexisted in ongoing struggle, held together in complex relations of mutual dependency, extreme exploitation, and tremendous instability. As we learn from other accounts, conflict between Europeans and indigenous laborers was an endemic fact of life on frontier expeditions. Relations were constantly breaking down and erupting into violence, constantly being renegotiated or enforced by brutality. And regardless of an individual traveler's own attitudes and intentions, the Europeans in this domain of struggle were charged with installing the edifice of domination and legitimizing its hierarchy.

In a discourse that effaces the European and displaces the African, however, all this can be consigned to an invisible, often trivialized domestic sphere behind the back of the land-scanning eye. Significantly enough, when "life in camp" does get textualized, it often appears in the guise of a sketch of a "typical day": "Soon after we halt, the spot for the English is selected, and all regulate their places accordingly and deposit their burdens" (*N*, p. 193). As with ethnographic portraits, life in camp is represented in a normalized discourse that bleaches out irregularity, uncertainty, instability, violence. In other cases, the accompanying indigenous laborers appear in the narrative as an exotic, comic, or pathetic spectacle for the eyes of the European. The European remains a steadfastly self-effaced seer, whose only intervention seems to be to define the perimeters of what is seen (in this case, the camp). In such instances, the master/slave relation that organizes the traveling group often expresses itself through the mediated form of an emotional projection. The indigenous labor pool is commonly employed (textually speaking) to express or reproduce the desires and fears of their European masters—to carry their emotional baggage, as it were. Burton, in whom these strategies are much in evidence, writes that on reaching Lake Tanganyika, "all the party seemed to join with me in joy," or that after a day without water, "the impatience and selfishness of thirst showed strongly in the Baloch." Grant measures the beauty of Lake Victoria Nyanza by the fact that "even the listless Wanyamuezi came to have a look at its waters. . . . The Seedees were in raptures."[18]

All the works I have mentioned so far have concerned Africa, but this discursive configuration is by no means peculiar to African travel writing. Indeed, one of the most programmatic instances of the strategies I have been examining here appears in the work of a writer who was gazing on the wilds of South America at the same time that Barrow was writing up his African expeditions. Alexander von Humboldt, foiled by Napoleon Bonaparte in his attempts to arrange a trip to Egypt, secured in 1799 from the court of Spain carte blanche to travel in Spanish America. It was an extraordinary coup—except for coastal shipping, the region has been virtually sealed off to legitimate travelers for over two centuries. Humboldt, accompanied by his friend Aimé Bonpland, was gone nearly five years. If the task of Barrow and the others was to invent Africa for the domestic subjects of the British Empire, Humboldt's discursive challenge was to reinvent Spanish America for a Europe well aware that Spanish control over the region was coming to an end. It was a time for replacing outdated orthodoxies like the old *leyenda negra* ("black legend") of Spanish cruelty with new ones that would provide the ideological framework for the rush of European (notably British) capital that would take over the region once it gained independence from Spain.

Like his counterparts in Africa, Humboldt traveled and wrote in the name of science and, like them, one of his principal discursive strategies was to reduce America to landscape and marginalize its inhabitants. In the preface to his *Personal Narrative of Travels to the Equinoctial Regions of the New Continent* (1816), he extols the American wilderness and discounts both the indigenous cultures and three hundred years of Spanish colonial society:

> In the ancient world, nations, and the distinctions of their civilization form the principal figures on the canvass; in the new, man and his productions almost disappear amidst the stupendous display of wild and gigantic nature. The human race here presents but a few remnants of indigenous hordes, slightly advanced in civilization; or that uniformity of manners and institutions which has been transplanted by European colonists to foreign shores. [*PN*, 1:xliii–xliv]

The *Personal Narrative,* neither very personal nor very narrative, chiefly deploys Humboldt's own brand of landscape appreciation, aimed at harmonizing science and aesthetics. The work is most remembered for its pages and pages of scientist rhapsody like this:

> After walking two hours, we arrived at the foot of the high chain of the interior mountains, which stretches from the east to the west; from the Brigantine to the Cerro de San Lorenzo. There, new rocks appear, and with them another aspect of vegetation. Every object assumes a more majestic and picturesque character; the soil, watered by springs, is furrowed in every direction; trees of gigantic loftiness, and covered with lianas, rise from the ravins; their bark, black and burnt by the double action of the light and the oxygen of the atmosphere, forms a contrast with the fresh verdure of the pothos and dracontium, the tough and shining leaves of which are sometimes several feet long. The parasite monocotyledones take between the tropics the place of the moss and lichens of our northern zone. As we advanced, the forms and grouping of the rocks reminded us of the scenes of Switzerland and the Tyrol. [*PN*, 3:9]

Though Humboldt includes some manners-and-customs portraits, current indigenous inhabitants hold little interest for him despite the fact that, as in similar cases in Africa, large numbers of them were engaged in transporting him, his delicate instruments and bulky collections up the Cordillera and down the Amazon. This silence weighs the more heavily if we recall that Humboldt was by profession a mining inspector and that one of his charges on the South American trip was to scout for exploitable precious metals. It can hardly have escaped him that these "few remnants of indigenous hordes" were the labor pool on whose backs would rest the advancement of capitalism in the region. Indeed, Humboldt might well be trying to escape this fact when he writes people out of the place completely.

But Humboldt, like Barrow, *is* interested in the traces the natives have left on the "face of the country." Indigenous America attracts Humboldt in the guise of archaeological ruins, and he devotes many pages to the description of sites, artifacts, and mythologies almost completely unknown or forgotten in Europe. Without detracting from Humboldt's considerable achievement, we cannot overlook the ideological import of this effort. It valorizes America by European standards—America too had its great cities—but, by the same token, it reduces current American societies to vestiges of a glorious past. In this framework, disruption and transformation of indigenous ways of life do not destroy anything of current value but simply dispose of scraps or leftovers in preparation for a new transformation.[19]

What that transformation is supposed to be is hardly in doubt, though, as with the African explorers, Humboldt seldom mentions it explicitly within his travel narrative. In his book, too, it turns up in the form of fantasy. Humboldt ends his introduction to the *Personal Narrative* by sketching out the landscape of his dreams, and it too depicts America as the future "scene of European enterprise":

> If then some pages of my book are snatched from oblivion, the inhabitant of the banks of the Oroonoko will behold with extasy, that populous cities enriched by commerce, and fertile fields cultivated by the hands of freemen, adorn those very spots, where, at the time of my travels, I found only impenetrable forests, and inundated lands. [*PN*, 1:l–li]

I have argued that this scientistic, information-oriented branch of travel writing played an extremely important role in producing the domestic subjects of nineteenth-century European capitalist expansion. We would be justified in calling it the hegemonic form of othering at the time, at least on the imperial frontier. But its hegemony was much contested— perhaps more contested than most—because this informational kind of writing suffered from one serious defect: it was terribly boring. Despite many writers' very real talent for description, despite their passionate engagement with nature, despite their often sincere fascination and admiration for indigenous peoples, the commentators on these works never stopped bemoaning how dull they made it all. Humboldt himself was one such commentator. In the introduction to his *Personal Narrative*, he diagnoses the problem as follows:

> In proportion as voyages have been made by persons more enlightened, and whose views have been directed towards researches into descriptive natural history, geography, or political economy, itineraries [that is, travel narratives] have partly lost that unity of composition, and that simplicity which characterized those of former ages. It is now become scarcely possible to connect so many different materials with the narration of other events; and that part which we may call dramatic gives way to dissertations merely descriptive. The great number of readers, who prefer an agreeable amusement to solid instruction, have not gained by the exchange. [*PN*, 1: xli–xlii]

This discursive dilemma was much discussed in the literature of the time. While bourgeois readers welcomed the authority of science and the totalizing project of natural history, there was no denying that these had drastically upset the balance of teaching and delighting that had long been considered the great virtue of travel books. Despite his recognition of the loss involved, Humboldt clearly cast his lot with science. His preferred solution to the dilemma was to abandon travel narrative altogether in favor of nonnarrative (or nondramatic) forms such as his famous *Political Essay on the Kingdom of New Spain* (1811) or descriptive sketches like his popular *Views of Nature* which sought to harmonize science and aesthetics. Humboldt undertook his *Personal Narrative* only reluctantly seven years after his trip and abandoned it nine years later, after the third volume.

But contrary to what Humboldt suggests in his preface, "dramatic" travel narrative full of "agreeable amusement" was far from being a relic of "former ages." Indeed, it had entered a full-fledged renaissance in the 1780s; by the time Humboldt was writing, dramatic travel narrative constituted one of the strongest voices contrasting with the scientific, informational tradition Humboldt was trying to codify. Humboldt certainly knew this, and his attempt to consign this writing to "former ages" points up the programmatic thrust of the comments in his preface.

The contrastive voice is that of a kind of travel writing most aptly described as sentimental, which emerges in the 1780s. Early authors of such narratives on Africa include James Bruce, François Le Vaillant, Richard Lander, and Mungo Park. One well-known example, set in South America, was John Stedman's *Narrative of a Five Years' Expedition against the Revolted Negroes of Surinam* (1796), which recounted a famous love story between its hero and a mulatta slave named Joanna. The tale, which Humboldt surely knew, gave rise to a German play, *Die Sklavin in Surinam*, which ran in Frankfurt in 1804; it revived in London in a popular story, "Joanna; or, The Female Slave," and again in 1840 in Eugène Sue's *Aventures D'Hercule Hardi*.

In this sentimental literature, dramatization predominates and heroic paradigms are retained. Its discursive agenda is sharply distinct from that of the informational tradition. The traveler is the protagonist of the journey and the primary focus of the account. It narrates the journey as an epic-style series of trials and challenges, of various kinds of encounters—often erotic ones—where indigenous inhabitants occupy the stage alongside the European. If the other discourse is called informational, this one should be called experiential. It constitutes its authority by anchoring itself not in informational orders but in situated human subjects, notably (but not always) the European protagonist.

These features are well illustrated by one of the most characteristic commonplaces of this branch of writing, the courtly encounter. In this conventional scene, the European male portrays himself arriving in a village and presenting himself to the local patriarch and his court. One of the classics of the sentimental genre, Park's *Travels in the Interior Districts of Africa* (1799)—a personal favorite of Humboldt's and one of the most popular travel books of its time—includes several such scenes:

> We reached at length the king's tent, where we found a great number of people, men and women, assembled. Ali was sitting upon a black leather cushion, clipping a few hairs from his upper lip; a female attendant holding up a looking glass before him. He appeared to be an old man, of the Arab cast, with a long white beard; and he had a sullen and indignant aspect. He surveyed me with attention and inquired of the Moors if I could speak Arabic; being answered in the negative he appeared much surprised, and continued silent. The surrounding attendants and especially the ladies were abundantly more inquisitive; they asked a thousand questions, inspected every part of my apparel, searched my pockets and obliged me to unbutton my waistcoat, and display the whiteness of my skin; they even counted my toes and fingers, as if they doubted whether I was in truth a human being.[20]

In its eroticism, its dramatization of contact, the realization of both Europeans and Africans as characters, the situating of the European at the center of a stage—someone else's stage—this passage contrasts strongly with the writing of Barrow and the others. These sentimental texts are characteristically dialogic in the Bakhtinian sense: they represent the Other's voices in dialogue with the voices of the self and often tender the Other some credibility and equality. The European's relations with the Other are governed by a desire for reciprocity and exchange. Estrangement and repulsion are presented as entirely mutual and equally irrational on both sides. Parody and self-parody abound. Park, displaying his tummy and toes, looks as ridiculous as the narcissistic Ali. This discourse does not explicitly seek a unified, authoritative speaking subject. The subject here is split simply by virtue of realizing itself as both protagonist and narrator, and it tends to split itself even further in these accounts. As this passage demonstrates, the self sees, it sees itself seeing, it sees itself being seen. And always it parodies both itself and the Other.

Ethnographic manners-and-customs description occurs in this kind of travel writing too, but it tends to be much more entwined with narrative episodes. Landscape is textualized mainly as a source of comfort or discomfort, danger or safety for the protagonist or as a trigger for an outpouring of emotion. In this famous and highly conventional scene from Park's *Travels,* Park has just been plundered and left for dead by a band of thieves:

> After they were gone I sat for some time looking around me with amazement and terror. Whichever way I turned, nothing appeared but danger and difficulty. I saw myself in the midst of a vast wilderness,

in the depth of the rainy season, naked and alone; surrounded by savage animals, and men still more savage. I was five hundred miles from the nearest European settlement. All these circumstances crowded at once on my recollection, and I confess that my spirits began to fail me. [*T*, p. 225]

The "influence of religion" saves Park from despair; the flora and fauna around him become not pieces of information to be gathered but triggers for meditation on human psychology and Providence's benevolent presence:

At this moment, painful as my reflections were, the extraordinary beauty of a small moss, in fructification, irresistibly caught my eye. I mention this to show from what trifling circumstances the mind will sometimes derive consolation; for though the whole plant was not larger than the top of one of my fingers, I could not contemplate the delicate conformation of its roots, leaves, and capsula, without admiration. *Can that Being (thought I) who planted, watered, and brought to perfection, in this obscure part of the world, a thing which appears of so small importance, look with unconcern upon the situation and sufferings of creatures formed after his own image?—surely not!* [*T*, p. 225]

If the land-scanning, self-effacing producer of information is associated with the state, then this sentimental, experiential voice must be associated with that critical sector of the bourgeois world, the private sphere, home of the solitary, introspecting Individual. Though positioned at the center rather than on a periphery, and though composed of a whole body rather than just an eye, this European too is passive and incapable of intervention. The voice, too, is innocent, though its innocence lies not in its self-effacement but in its isolation and vulnerability. In short, European expansionism is as mystified in this literature as in the informational kind. Park's explicitly commercial assignment—"rendering the geography of Africa more familiar to my countrymen and . . . opening to their ambition and industry new sources of wealth and new channels of commerce"—is readily lost from sight in the drama of personal survival and the satisfying symmetry of reciprocal exchange (*T*, p. 2).

I have focused on Park's book here because it was a popular classic and a touchstone for many writers such as Humboldt, who cited it often. In his introduction to the *Personal Narrative*, Humboldt names Park's *Travels* as an example of the simple (that is, naive) dramatic travel writing that has (supposedly) been overtaken by science. The other example Humboldt gives is that of the Spanish chroniclers of the sixteenth century. Although Humboldt is right to identify his influential contemporary with a different discursive configuration, the attempt to link Park with a lost past must be seen as an attempt to marginalize a discourse that was to remain, throughout the next century, a main challenger to the hegemony of information.

Much more could be said about this subject-centered, experiential discourse and its challenge to scientific, informational travel writing. Comments like Humboldt's—and there are many of them—demonstrate how readily the two discourses were distinguished in the early nineteenth century. In the 1860s, their contrast is nicely reasserted in the frontispieces of two books that were published within months of each other—the first edition of Livingstone's *Narrative of an Expedition to the Zambesi* (1861) and a new edition of Park's *Travels* (1860) (figs. 1–4). Livingstone's frontispiece depicts "a bird's-eye view of the cataracts of the Zambesi"; his title page shows a drawing of a lone, unidentified African. Park's frontispiece depicts himself with five companions arriving at the "majestic Niger"; the title page again shows Park, in the scene quoted earlier, forlorn and destitute while a group of native bandits flees in the background.

Ultimately, the sentimental, experiential discourse, like the private sphere to which it attached, mounted little more than an internal critique of the hegemony of information. But it could be a powerful critique. In 1861, for example, the Franco-American explorer Du Chaillu published his *Explorations and Adventures in Equatorial Africa,* a relentless travesty of the scientific, informational tradition. In the following excerpt, for instance, Du Chaillu marshals the same strategies found in Park's writing to construct an explicit parody of the kind of landscape description I discussed at the beginning of this essay. The passage starts out as a conventional promontory scene and moves into a particularly American fantasy of the civilized future (Du Chaillu is in the Congo):

> From this elevation—about 5000 feet above the ocean level— I enjoyed an unobstructed view as far as the eye could reach. The hills we had surmounted the day before lay quietly at our feet, seeming mere molehills. On all sides stretched the immense virgin forests, with here and there the sheen of a water-course. And far away in the east loomed the blue tops of the farthest range of the Sierra del Crystal, the goal of my desires. The murmur of the rapids below filled my ears, and, as I strained my eyes toward those distant mountains which I hoped to reach, I began to think how this wilderness would look if only the light of Christian civilization could once be fairly introduced among the black children of Africa. I dreamed of forests giving way to plantations of coffee, cotton, and spices; of peaceful negroes going to their contented daily tasks; of farming and manufactures; of churches and schools . . .

It is obvious why this vision makes contemporary readers uncomfortable; but it was intended, in its unabashed explicitness about colonialism and

BIRD'S-EYE VIEW OF THE GREAT CATARACTS OF THE ZAMBESI (CALLED MOSIOATUNYA, OR VICTORIA FALLS), AND OF THE ZIGZAG CHASM BELOW THE FALLS THROUGH WHICH THE RIVER ESCAPES.

FIG. 1.

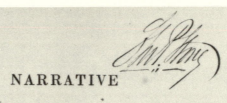

NARRATIVE

OF AN

EXPEDITION TO THE ZAMBESI

AND ITS TRIBUTARIES;

AND OF THE

DISCOVERY OF THE LAKES SHIRWA AND NYASSA.

1858—1864.

BY DAVID AND CHARLES LIVINGSTONE.

With Map and Illustrations.

NEW YORK:

HARPER & BROTHERS, PUBLISHERS,

FRANKLIN SQUARE.

1866.

FIG. 2.

I saw with infinite pleasure the great object of my mission,—the long sought for majestic Niger, glittering to the morning sun.—P. 176.

Fig. 3.

TRAVELS

IN

THE INTERIOR OF AFRICA

BY MUNGO PARK.

EDINBURGH:

ADAM AND CHARLES BLACK, NORTH BRIDGE.

MDCCCLX.

FIG. 4.

its suggestion of slavery, to make Du Chaillu's contemporaries uncomfortable too. For the guilty fantasy is punished by a new arrival on the scene—both a symbol of the Other and the dreamer's own double. The passage continues:

> and, luckily raising my eyes heavenward at this stage of my thoughts, [I] saw pendent from the branch of a tree beneath which I was sitting an immense serpent, evidently preparing to gobble up this dreaming intruder on his domains.
> My dreams of future civilization vanished in a moment. Luckily my gun lay at hand.[21]

Probably this serpent (not snake) has come directly from the Garden of Eden to remind everyone that, among other things, the cozy pastoral/plantation fantasy is forbidden fruit which will lead eventually to expulsion from the garden. On waking from his reverie, Du Chaillu turns to the real instrument of the civilizing mission, his gun. He shoots this guilty self (referring to the serpent as "my black friend"), but that does not save it from the grip of the colonized themselves. Du Chaillu's bearers immediately roast the snake and eat it ("dividing the body into proper pieces") in a kind of macabre last supper, a symbolic cannibalism in which the great white father himself is unable to partake. (Du Chaillu pointedly does not eat snake, or gorilla.) He mocks himself for being a "poor, starved, but *civilized* mortal," concluding, "so much for civilization, which is a very good thing in its way, but has no business in an African forest when food is scarce."[22] So the subject splits and authority shifts in this writing—Du Chaillu is now parodier, now parodied, now dreamer, now demystifier of his own dream, now provider of civilization, now deprived by civilization, now hunter, now hunted.

In contrast and in chorus with the monochromatic and self-effacing stance of information, then, books like Du Chaillu's asserted multivalence, confusion, self-doubt, and self-parody. Indeed, as might be expected, the multivalent sentimental discourse can be found erupting into predominantly informational texts, especially at points of intense ideological contradiction. This brings me back, finally, to Mr. Barrow's visit with the Bushmen. For though that encounter results in a conventional ethnographic portrait like the others in his book, the violence and wild contradictoriness of the encounter itself register in the text as a breakdown of the information-producing subject.

By the time Barrow appears, the Bushmen have become difficult to find and impossible to visit. After decades of being hunted down for sport by Boers bent on genocide, the survivors have become wary and skilled at hiding. The only way to see them is to literally invade one of their camps. Barrow reluctantly hires some Boer farmers to do just that, with the condition they not fire unless fired upon. The Boers' nocturnal attack from a hilltop on the Bushmen "horde" encamped below brings Barrow tumbling off his sunlit promontory, down into the center of things, in a veritable descent into hell:

> We instantly set off on full gallop, and in a moment found ourselves in the middle of the kraal. Day was but just beginning to break; and by the faint light I could discover only a few straw-mats, bent each between two sticks, into a semicircular form; but our ears were stunned with a horrid scream like the war-hoop of savages; the shrieking of women and the cries of children proceeded from every side. I rode up with the commandant and another farmer, both of whom fired upon the kraal. I immediately expressed to the former my very great surprise that he, of all others, should have been the first to break a condition which he had solemnly promised to observe, and that I had expected from him a very different kind of conduct. "Good God!" he exclaimed, "have you not seen a shower of arrows falling among us?" I certainly had seen neither arrows nor people, but had heard enough to pierce the hardest heart. [*A*, p. 272]

It would be difficult to exaggerate how starkly this episode stands out in Barrow's book. It is the only nocturnal scene in the work, the only instance of direct dialogue, the only occasion when Barrow dramatizes himself as a participant (seer and seen), the only outburst of emotion, the only outbreak of violence, one of the few scenes where people and place coincide, the only time sound prevails over sight, and Barrow asserts a limit on his authority to apprehend and represent his surroundings. What provokes the crisis here, it seems, is the fact that Barrow chooses to exercise his right to legitimate violence—not, however, in order to defend himself or his fellow citizens or the state but simply in order to get a look. The ideology that construes seeing as an inherently passive and innocent act cannot be sustained, and Barrow's discursive order breaks down along with his humanitarian moral order. Into that break the sentimental, dramatic counterdiscourse inserts itself, so that Barrow winds up in a confessional mode. "Nothing," he later says, "could be more unwarrantable, because cruel and unjust, than the attack made by our party upon the kraal" (*A*, p. 291).

But this confessional mode is certainly not a transformative one, for Barrow's loss of innocence produces no new self, no new position of speech. His descent into colonial hell would be repeated by the writers who followed him, at first as an interruption of the calm textual surface produced by the disembodied gaze. Later, as northern Europe created its own black legend in the horrific, genocidal scramble for Africa, that descent would become the canonical story about Africa—the fall from the sun-drenched dreamy prospect into the heart of darkness.

Partly because it has never been fully professionalized or "disciplined," travel writing is one of the most polyphonous of genres. It therefore richly illustrates the fact that, in practice, ideology works through proliferation as well as containment of meaning. The texts I have discussed in this essay were among the most popular travel books of their day; readers of these books received nothing like a fixed set of differences that normalized self and Other in fixed ways. They were presented with multiple sets of differences, multiple fixed subject positions, multiple ways of legitimizing and familiarizing the process of European expansion. The discourses complemented each other even as they challenged and demystified each other. Even if we agree that, as Rosalind Coward and John Ellis put it, "the production of an ideological *vraisemblable* . . . is the result of a practice of fixing or limiting of the endless productivity of the signifying chain," we must recognize that such practices or fixings often work only because they are multiple and endlessly productive.[23] It takes a lot of ideological *vraisemblables* to keep the world comprehensible, especially in a day-to-day way. Proverbs work, after all, only because there is a proverb for everything—there is always going to be more than one way to skin a cat.

1. John Barrow, *An Account of Travels into the Interior of Southern Africa in the Years 1797 and 1798*, 2 vols. (New York, 1968), 1:283–84 (the full description of the Bushmen runs sixteen pages); all further references to this work, abbreviated *A*, will be included in the text.

2. John Mandeville, *The Book of John Mandeville*, Hakluyt Society Series 2, vol. 101 (London, 1953), p. 138.

3. This genital fixation is still very much with us, especially as regards the Bushmen. See, for example, Laurens Van der Post's popular *Lost World of the Kalahari* (New York, 1958).

4. Johannes Fabian, *Time and the Other: How Anthropology Makes Its Object* (New York, 1983), p. 35.

5. Catherine Belsey, *Critical Practice*, New Accents Series (London, 1980), p. 90.

6. Ethnographies would seem to be a counterexample to this claim, but in fact one can fairly easily show that ethnographic writing is inextricably tied to personal narrative. Indeed, this tie is a symptom of a serious contradiction between ethnographic methods and ethnographic discourse. See my "Fieldwork in Common Places," in *Writing Culture: The Poetics and Politics of Ethnography*, ed. James Clifford and George Marcus (forthcoming, 1986).

7. In 1795, the British took over the Dutch Cape Colony by force, on the pretext that it was in danger of being occupied by the French, who had just overrun Holland. George Macartney was appointed governor of the newly annexed colony; he took Barrow with him as his personal secretary. Appointed Macartney's representative to the interior, Barrow made several lengthy journeys there to settle internal grievances between Boer settlers and Dutch colonial officials, to establish a sense of the British presence to both Boer and indigenous populations, and to begin documenting the geography of the interior, so far almost completely unmapped. He traveled, as was the custom, by ox-drawn wagon, and

relied for supplies, fresh oxen, and often lodging on the Boer settlers, who were required to provide such services for state representatives in exchange for powder and shot. The cape was returned to the Dutch in 1802 and retaken by the British in 1806. Barrow eventually succeeded Joseph Banks as head of the African Association (the same body that employed Mungo Park) and ended up much involved in polar exploration. See Christopher Lloyd, *Mr. Barrow of the Admiralty: A Life of Sir John Barrow, 1764–1848* (London, 1970).

8. If such human landmarks are too many or too conspicuous, they must themselves be thematized in this discourse—for instance, as ruins or vestiges of some past civilization.

9. For more on this "monarch of all I survey" strategy, see my "Conventions of Representation: Where Discourse and Ideology Meet," in *Contemporary Perceptions of Language: Interdisciplinary Dimensions,* ed. Heidi Byrnes, Georgetown University Roundtable in Languages and Linguistics (Washington, D.C., 1982), pp. 139–55.

10. David and Charles Livingstone, *Narrative of an Expedition to the Zambesi and its Tributaries; and of the Discovery of the Lakes Shirwa and Nyassa, 1858–1864* (New York, 1866), pp. 101–2; all further references to this work, abbreviated *N*, will be included in the text.

11. Daniel Defert, "La collecte du monde: Pour une étude des récits de voyages du seizième au dix-huitième siècle," in *Collections passions,* ed. Jacques Hainard and Roland Kaeht (Neuchatel 1982), p. 26; my translation.

12. Alexander von Humboldt and Aimé Bonpland, *Personal Narrative of Travels to the Equinoctial Regions of the New Continent during the Years 1799–1804,* trans. Helen Maria Williams, 3d ed., 2 vols. (London, 1822), 1:viii; all further references to this work, abbreviated *PN,* will be included in the text, with volume and page numbers in parentheses.

13. John Hanning Speke, *What Led to the Discovery of the Source of the Nile* (Edinburgh, 1864), p. 307; my emphasis.

14. James Augustus Grant, *A Walk across Africa; or, Domestic Scenes from My Nile Journal* (Edinburgh, 1864), p. 196; all further references to this work, abbreviated *W,* will be included in the text.

15. Richard F. Burton, *The Lake Regions of Central Africa; A Picture of Exploration,* 2 vols. (New York, 1961), 2:43; all further references to this work, abbreviated *LR,* will be included in the text.

16. My wording here is indebted to Quentin Skinner, *Foundations of Modern Political Thought,* 2 vols. (Cambridge, 1978) as well as to Nicos Poulantzas, *State, Power, Socialism* (London, 1978).

17. This face, moreover, has apparently gotten emptier to Western eyes as time goes by. Alberto Moravia wrote in 1972 of the "terrifying monotony" of African landscape: "The face of Africa bears a greater resemblance to that of an infant, with few barely indicated features, than to that of a man, upon which life has imprinted innumerable significant lines; in other words, it bears greater resemblance to the face of the earth in prehistoric times . . . than to the face of the earth as it is today" (*Which Tribe Do You Belong To?* trans. Angus Davidson [New York, 1974], p. 8).

18. Burton, *The Lake Regions,* 2:43; Grant, *A Walk across Africa,* p. 196.

19. I am reminded of the rediscovery of Egypt, which took place at the same time, in the wake of the Napoleonic invasion. There, too, the monuments of the distant past were mainly what was depicted and valorized; the glorious history of ancient Egypt was recaptured for Europe, while contemporary Egyptian life was seen as archaic and vestigial.

20. Park, *Travels in the Interior Districts of Africa, Performed under the Direction and Patronage of the African Association, in the Years 1795, 1796, and 1797* (Edinburgh, 1860), p. 109; all further references to this work, abbreviated *T,* will be included in the text. Park was a Scottish physician who was sent out by the African Association which had been formed in 1785. By the time Park made his "successful" journey (i.e., he survived it), several parties sent out on the same mission had already disappeared without a trace. Park's own survival was improbable. Accompanied by a single African servant, as he tells it, he made his way through chiefdoms hostile to strangers of any kind, especially Christians. Often plundered, threatened, held captive, relying for survival on the charity of slave populations, he made

his way to the Niger River and observed the crucial datum: its direction of flow (away from, not toward, the Nile). Park did not, however, succeed in reaching Timbuktu, as had been hoped. Several years later, Park led a second, much larger mission into the same region and disappeared without a trace. The story of that mission's demise was slowly pieced together by subsequent travelers.

21. Paul B. Du Chaillu, *Explorations and Adventures in Equatorial Africa* (New York, 1861), p. 83.

22. Ibid.

23. Rosalind Coward and John Ellis, *Language and Materialism: Developments in Semiology and the Theory of the Subject* (London, 1977), p. 67.

Signs Taken for Wonders: Questions of Ambivalence and Authority under a Tree Outside Delhi, May 1817

Homi K. Bhabha

> A remarkable peculiarity is that they (the English) always write the personal pronoun I with a capital letter. May we not consider this Great I as an unintended proof how much an Englishman thinks of his own consequence?
>
> —ROBERT SOUTHEY, *Letters from England*

There is a scene in the cultural writings of English colonialism which repeats so insistently after the early nineteenth century—and, through that repetition, so triumphantly *inaugurates* a literature of empire—that I am bound to repeat it once more. It is the scenario, played out in the wild and wordless wastes of colonial India, Africa, the Caribbean, of the sudden, fortuitous discovery of the English book. It is, like all myths of origin, memorable for its balance between epiphany and enunciation. The discovery of the book is, at once, a moment of originality and authority, as well as a process of displacement that, paradoxically, makes the presence of the book wondrous to the extent to which it is repeated, translated, misread, displaced. It is with the emblem of the English book—"signs taken for wonders"—as an insignia of colonial authority and a signifier of colonial desire and discipline, that I want to begin this essay.

I would like to thank Stephan Feuchtwang for his sustaining advice, Gayatri Spivak for suggesting that I should further develop my concept of colonial mimicry; Parveen Adams for her impeccable critique of the text; and Jacqueline Bhabha, whose political engagement with the discriminatory nature of British immigration and nationality law has convinced me of the modesty of the theoretical enterprise.

In the first week of May 1817, Anund Messeh, one of the earliest Indian catechists, made a hurried and excited journey from his mission in Meerut to a grove of trees just outside Delhi.

> He found about 500 people, men, women and children, seated under the shade of the trees, and employed, as had been related to him, in reading and conversation. He went up to an elderly looking man, and accosted him, and the following conversation passed.
>   'Pray who are all these people? and whence come they?' 'We are poor and lowly, and we read and love this book.' — 'What is that book?' 'The book of God!' — 'Let me look at it, if you please.' Anund, on opening the book, perceived it to be the Gospel of our Lord, translated into the Hindoostanee Tongue, many copies of which seemed to be in the possession of the party: some were PRINTED, others WRITTEN by themselves from the printed ones. Anund pointed to the name of Jesus, and asked, 'Who is that?' 'That is God! He gave us this book.' — 'Where did you obtain it?' 'An Angel from heaven gave it us, at Hurdwar fair.' — 'An Angel?' 'Yes, to us he was God's Angel: but he was a man, a learned Pundit.' (Doubtless these translated Gospels must have been the books distributed, five or six years ago, at Hurdwar by the Missionary.) 'The written copies we write ourselves, having no other means of obtaining more of this blessed word.' — 'These books,' said Anund, 'teach the religion of the European Sahibs. It is THEIR book; and they printed it in our language, for our use.' 'Ah! no,' replied the stranger, 'that cannot be, for they eat flesh.' — 'Jesus Christ,' said Anund, 'teaches that it does not signify what a man eats or drinks. EATING is nothing before God. *Not that which entereth into a man's mouth defileth him, but that which cometh out of the mouth, this defileth a man: for vile things come forth from the heart. Out of the heart proceed evil thoughts, murders, adulteries, fornications, thefts; and these are the things that defile.*'
>   'That is true; but how can it be the European Book, when we believe that it is God's gift to us? He sent it to us at Hurdwar.' 'God gave it long ago to the Sahibs, and THEY sent it to us.' . . . The ignorance and simplicity of many are very striking, never having heard of a printed book before; and its very appearance was to them miraculous. A great stir was excited by the gradual increasing information hereby obtained, and all united to acknowledge the superiority of the doctrines of this Holy Book to every thing which

---

Homi K. Bhabha is lecturer in English literature and literary theory at the University of Sussex. He is working at present on *Power and Spectacle: Colonial Discourse and the English Novel* and is commissioning and editing a collection of essays entitled *Nation and Narration: Post-structuralism and the Culture of National Identity*. He is also writing the introduction to the new English edition of Frantz Fanon's *Black Skin, White Masks*.

they had hitherto heard or known. An indifference to the distinctions of Caste soon manifested itself; and the interference and tyrannical authority of the Brahmins became more offensive and contemptible. At last, it was determined to separate themselves from the rest of their Hindoo Brethren; and to establish a party of their own choosing, four or five, who could read the best, to be the public teachers from this newly-acquired Book. . . . Anund asked them, 'Why are you all dressed in white?' 'The people of God should wear white raiment,' was the reply, 'as a sign that they are clean, and rid of their sins.' — Anund observed, 'You ought to be BAPTIZED, in the name of the Father, and of the Son, and of the Holy Ghost. Come to Meerut: there is a Christian Padre there; and he will shew you what you ought to do.' They answered, 'Now we must go home to the harvest; but, as we mean to meet once a year, perhaps the next year we may come to Meerut.' . . . I explained to them the nature of the Sacrament and of Baptism; in answer to which, they replied, 'We are willing to be baptized, but we will never take the Sacrament. To all the other customs of Christians we are willing to conform, but not to the Sacrament, because the Europeans eat cow's flesh, and this will never do for us.' To this I answered, 'This WORD is of God, and not of men; and when HE makes your hearts to understand, then you will PROPERLY comprehend it.' They replied, 'If all our country will receive this Sacrament, then will we.' I then observed, 'The time is at hand, when all the countries will receive this WORD!' They replied, 'True!'[1]

Almost a hundred years later, in 1902, Joseph Conrad's Marlow, traveling in the Congo, in the night of the first ages, without a sign and no memories, cut off from the comprehension of his surroundings, desperately in need of a deliberate belief, comes upon Towson's (or Towser's) *Inquiry into some Points of Seamanship*.

Not a very enthralling book; but at the first glance you could see there a singleness of intention, an honest concern for the right way of going to work, which made these humble pages, thought out so many years ago, luminous with another than a professional light. . . . I assure you to leave off reading was like tearing myself away from the shelter of an old and solid friendship. . . .

"It must be this miserable trader—this intruder," exclaimed the manager, looking back malevolently at the place we had left. "He must be English," I said.[2]

Half a century later, a young Trinidadian discovers that same volume of Towson's in that very passage from Conrad and draws from it a vision of literature and a lesson of history. "The scene," writes V. S. Naipaul,

answered some of the political panic I was beginning to feel.
   To be a colonial was to know a kind of security; it was to inhabit a fixed world. And I suppose that in my fantasy I had seen myself

coming to England as to some purely literary region, where, un-
trammeled by the accidents of history or background, I could make
a romantic career for myself as a writer. But in the new world I
felt that ground move below me. . . . Conrad . . . had been everywhere
before me. Not as a man with a cause, but a man offering . . . a
vision of the world's half-made societies . . . where always "something
inherent in the necessities of successful action . . . carried with it
the moral degradation of the idea." Dismal but deeply felt: a kind
of truth and half a consolation.[3]

Written as they are in the name of the father and the author, these
texts of the civilizing mission immediately suggest the triumph of the
colonialist moment in early English Evangelism and modern English
literature. The discovery of the book installs the sign of appropriate
representation: the word of God, truth, art creates the conditions for a
beginning, a practice of history and narrative. But the institution of the
Word in the wilds is also an *Entstellung*, a process of displacement, distortion,
dislocation, repetition[4]—the dazzling light of literature sheds only areas
of darkness. Still the idea of the English book is presented as universally
adequate: like the "metaphoric writing of the West," it communicates "the
immediate vision of the thing, freed from the discourse that accompanied
it, or even encumbered it."[5]

Shortly before the discovery of the book, Marlow interrogates the
odd, inappropriate, "colonial" transformation of a textile into an uncertain
textual sign, possibly a fetish:

Why? Where did he get it? Was it a badge—an ornament—a charm—
a propitiatory act? Was there any idea at all connected with it? It
looked startling round his black neck, this bit of white thread from
beyond the seas.[6]

Such questions of the historical act of enunciation, which carry a political
intent, are lost, a few pages later, in the myth of origins and discovery.
The immediate vision of the book figures those ideological correlatives
of the Western sign—empiricism, idealism, mimeticism, monoculturalism
(to use Edward Said's term)—that sustain a tradition of English "national"
authority. It is, significantly, a normalizing myth whose organics and
revisionary narrative is also the history of that nationalist discipline of
Commonwealth history and its equally expansionist epigone, Commonwealth literature. Their versions of traditional, academicist wisdom moralize
the conflictual moment of colonialist intervention into that constitutive
chain of exemplum and imitation, what Friedrich Nietzsche describes as
the monumental history beloved of "gifted egoists and visionary scoun-
drels."[7] For despite first appearances, a repetition of the episodes of the
book reveals that they represent important moments in the historical
transformation and discursive transfiguration of the colonial text and
context.

Anund Messeh's riposte to the natives who refuse the sacrament—
"the time is at hand when all countries *will* receive this WORD" (my emphasis)—is both firmly and timely spoken in 1817. For it represents a
shift away from the "orientalist" educational practice of, say, Warren
Hastings and the much more interventionist and "interpellative" ambition
of Charles Grant for a culturally and linguistically homogeneous English
India. It was with Grant's election to the board of the East India Company
in 1794 and to Parliament in 1802, and through his energetic espousal
of the Evangelical ideals of the Clapham sect, that the East India Company
reintroduced a "pious clause" into its charter for 1813. By 1817 the
Church Missionary Society ran sixty-one schools, and in 1818 it com-
missioned the Burdwan Plan, a central plan of education for instruction
in the English language. The aim of the plan anticipates, almost to the
word, Thomas Macaulay's infamous 1835 "Minute on Education": "to
form a body of well instructed labourers, competent in their proficiency
in English to act as Teachers, Translators, and Compilers of useful works
for the masses of the people."[8] Anund Messeh's lifeless repetition of
chapter and verse, his artless technique of translation, participate in one
of the most artful technologies of colonial power. In the same month
that Anund Messeh discovered the miraculous effects of the book outside
Delhi—May 1817—a correspondent of the Church Missionary Society
wrote to London describing the method of English education at Father
John's mission in Tranquebar:

> The principal method of teaching them the English language would
> be by giving them English phrases and sentences, with a translation
> for them to commit to memory. These sentences might be so arranged
> as to teach them whatever sentiments the instructor should choose.
> They would become, in short, attached to the Mission; and though
> first put into the school from worldly motives alone, should any of
> them be converted, accustomed as they are to the language, manners
> and climate of the country, they might soon be prepared for a great
> usefulness in the cause of religion. . . . In this way the Heathens
> themselves might be made the instruments of pulling down their
> own religion, and of erecting in its ruins the standards of the Cross.
> [*MR*, May 1817, p. 187]

Marlow's ruminative closing statement, "He must be English," acknowledges at the heart of darkness, in Conrad's *fin de siècle* malaise
which Ian Watt so thoroughly describes, the particular debt that both
Marlow and Conrad owe to the ideals of English "liberty" and its liberal-
conservative culture.[9] Caught as he is—between the madness of "pre-
historic" Africa and the unconscious desire to repeat the traumatic intervention of modern colonialism within the compass of a seaman's yarn—
Towson's manual provides Marlow with a singleness of intention. It is
the book of work that turns delirium into the discourse of civil address.

For the ethic of work, as Conrad was to exemplify in "Tradition" (1918), provides a sense of right conduct and honour achievable only through the acceptance of those "customary" norms which are the signs of culturally cohesive "civil" communities.[10] These aims of the civilizing mission, endorsed in the "idea" of British imperialism and enacted on the red sections of the map, speak with a peculiarly English authority based upon the *customary practice* on which both English common law and the English national language rely for their effectivity and appeal.[11] It is the ideal of English civil discourse that permits Conrad to entertain the ideological ambivalences that riddle his narratives. It is under its watchful eye that he allows the fraught text of late nineteenth-century imperialism to implode within the practices of early modernism. The devastating effects of such an encounter are not only contained in an (un)common yarn; they are concealed in the propriety of a civil "lie" told to the Intended (the complicity of the customary?): "The horror! The horror!" must not be repeated in the drawing-rooms of Europe.

It is to preserve the peculiar sensibility of what he understands as a tradition of civility that Naipaul "translates" Conrad, from Africa to the Caribbean, in order to transform the despair of postcolonial history into an appeal for the autonomy of art. The more fiercely he believes that "the wisdom of the heart ha[s] no concern with the erection or demolition of theories," the more convinced he becomes of the unmediated nature of the Western book—"the words it pronounces have the value of acts of integrity."[12] The values that such a perspective generates for his own work, and for the once colonized world it chooses to represent and evaluate, are visible in the hideous panorama that some of his titles provide: *The Loss of El Dorado, The Mimic Men, An Area of Darkness, A Wounded Civilization, The Overcrowded Barracoon.*

The discovery of the English book establishes both a measure of mimesis and a mode of civil authority and order. If these scenes, as I've narrated them, suggest the triumph of the writ of colonialist power, then it must be conceded that the wily letter of the law inscribes a much more ambivalent text of authority. For it is in between the edict of Englishness and the assault of the dark unruly spaces of the earth, through an act of repetition, that the colonial text emerges uncertainly. Anund Messeh disavows the natives' disturbing questions as he returns to repeat the now questionable "authority" of Evangelical dicta; Marlow turns away from the African jungle to recognize, in retrospect, the peculiarly "English" quality of the discovery of the book; Naipaul turns his back on the hybrid half-made colonial world to fix his eye on the universal domain of English literature. What we witness is neither an untroubled, innocent dream of England nor a "secondary revision" of the nightmare of India, Africa, the Caribbean. What is "English" in these discourses of colonial power cannot be represented as a plenitude or a "full" presence; it is determined by its belatedness. As a signifier of authority, the English book acquires its meaning *after* the traumatic scenario of colonial difference, cultural or racial, returns the eye of power to some prior, archaic image or identity. Paradoxically, however, such an image can neither be "original"—by virtue of the act of repetition that constructs it—nor "identical"—by virtue of the difference that defines it. Consequently, the colonial presence is always ambivalent, split between its appearance as original and authoritative and its articulation as repetition and difference.

It is this ambivalence that makes the boundaries of colonial "positionality"—the division of self/other—and the question of colonial power—the differentiation of colonizer/colonized—different from both the Hegelian master/slave dialectic or the phenomenological projection of Otherness. It is a *différance* produced within the act of enunciation as a specifically colonial articulation of those two disproportionate sites of colonial discourse and power: the colonial scene as the invention of historicity, mastery, mimesis or as the "other scene" of *Entstellung*, displacement, fantasy, psychic defence, and an "open" textuality. Such a dis-play of difference produces a mode of authority that is agonistic (rather than antagonistic). Its discriminatory effects are visible in those split subjects of the racist stereotype—the simian Negro, the effeminate Asiatic male—which ambivalently fix identity as the fantasy of difference.[13] To recognize the *différance* of the colonial presence is to realize that the colonial text occupies that space of double inscription, hallowed—no, hollowed—by Jacques Derrida:

> whenever any writing both marks and goes back over its mark with an undecidable stroke . . . [this] double mark escapes the pertinence or authority of truth: it does not overturn it but rather inscribes it within its play as one of its functions or parts. This displacement does not take place, has not taken place once as an *event*. It does not occupy a simple place. It does not take place *in* writing. This dis-location (is what) writes/is written. [*D*, p. 193]

How can the question of authority, the power and presence of the English, be posed in the interstices of a double inscription? I have no wish to replace an idealist myth—the metaphoric English book—with a historicist one—the colonialist project of English civility. Such a reductive reading would deny what is obvious, that the representation of colonial authority depends less on a universal symbol of English identity than on its productivity as a sign of difference. Yet in my use of "English" there is a "transparency" of reference that registers a certain obvious presence: the Bible translated into Hindi, propagated by Dutch or native catechists, is still the English book; a Polish émigré, deeply influenced by Gustave Flaubert, writing about Africa, produces an English classic. What is there about such a process of visibility and recognition that never fails to be an authoritative acknowledgement without ceasing to be a "spacing between desire and fulfillment, between perpetuation and its recollection . . . [a] medium [which] has nothing to do with a center" (*D*, p. 212)?

This question demands a departure from Derrida's objectives in "The Double Session"; a turning away from the vicissitudes of interpretation in the mimetic act of reading to the question of the effects of power, the inscription of strategies of individuation and domination in those "dividing practices" which construct the colonial space—a departure from Derrida which is also a return to those moments in his essay when he acknowledges the problematic of "presence" as a certain quality of discursive transparency which he describes as "the production of *mere* reality-effects" or "the effect of content" or as the problematic relation between the "medium of writing and the determination of each textual unit." In the rich ruses and rebukes with which he shows up the "false appearance of the present," Derrida fails to decipher the specific and determinate system of *address* (not referent) that is signified by the "effect of content" (see *D*, pp. 173–85). It is precisely such a strategy of address—the *immediate presence* of the English— that engages the questions of authority that I want to raise. When the ocular metaphors of presence refer to the process by which content is fixed as an "effect of the present," we encounter not plenitude but the structured gaze of power whose objective is authority, whose "subjects" are historical.

The reality effect constructs a mode of address in which a complementarity of meaning—not a correspondential notion of truth, as anti-realists insist—produces the moment of discursive transparency. It is the moment when, "under the false appearance of the present," the semantic seems to prevail over the syntactic, the signified over the signifier. Contrary to current avant-garde orthodoxy, however, the transparent is neither simply the triumph of the "imaginary" capture of the subject in realist narrative nor the ultimate interpellation of the individual by ideology. It is not a proposal that you cannot positively refuse. It is better described, I suggest, as a form of the *disposal* of those discursive signs of presence/ the present within the strategies that articulate the range of meanings from "dispose to disposition." Transparency is the action of the distribution and arrangement of differential spaces, positions, knowledges in relation to each other, relative to a differential, not inherent, sense of order. This effects a regulation of spaces and places that is authoritatively assigned; it puts the addressee into the proper frame or condition for some action or result. Such a mode of governance addresses itself to a form of conduct that is achieved through a reality effect that equivocates between the sense of disposal, as the bestowal of a frame of reference, and disposition, as mental inclination, a frame of mind. Such equivocation allows neither an equivalence of the two sites of disposal nor their division as self/other, subject/object. Transparency achieves an effect of authority in the present (and an authoritative presence) through a process similar to what Michel Foucault describes as "an effect of finalisation, relative to an objective," without its necessary attribution to a subject that makes a prohibitory law, thou shalt or thou shalt not.[14]

The place of difference and otherness, or the space of the adversarial, within such a system of "disposal" as I've proposed, is never entirely on the outside or implacably oppositional. It is a pressure, and a presence, that acts constantly, if unevenly, along the entire boundary of authorization, that is, on the surface between what I've called disposal-as-bestowal and disposition-as-inclination. The contour of difference is agonistic, shifting, splitting, rather like Freud's description of the system of consciousness which occupies a position in space lying on the borderline between outside and inside, a surface of protection, reception, and projection.[15] The power play of presence is lost if its transparency is treated naively as the nostalgia for plenitude that should be flung repeatedly into the abyss— *mise en abîme*—from which its desire is born. Such theoreticist anarchism cannot intervene in the agonistic space of authority where

> the true and the false are separated and specific effects of power [are] attached to the true, it being understood also that it is not a matter of a battle "on behalf" of the truth, but of a battle about the status of truth and the economic and political role it plays.[16]

It is precisely to intervene in such a battle for the *status* of the truth that it becomes crucial to examine the *presence* of the English book. For it is this *surface* that stabilizes the agonistic colonial space; it is its *appearance* that regulates the ambivalence between origin and *Entstellung,* discipline and desire, mimesis and repetition.

Despite appearances, the text of transparency inscribes a double vision: the field of the "true" emerges as a visible effect of knowledge/power only after the regulatory and displacing division of the true and the false. From this point of view, discursive "transparency" is best read in the photographic sense in which a transparency is also always a negative, processed into visibility through the technologies of reversal, enlargement, lighting, editing, projection, not a source but a re-source of light. Such a bringing to light is never a prevision; it is always a question of the provision of visibility as a capacity, a strategy, an agency but also in the sense in which the prefix pro(vision) might indicate an elision of sight, delegation, substitution, contiguity, in place of . . . what?

This is the question that brings us to the ambivalence of the presence of authority, peculiarly visible in its colonial articulation. For if transparency signifies discursive closure—intention, image, author—it does so through a disclosure of its *rules of recognition*—those social texts of epistemic, ethnocentric, nationalist intelligibility which cohere in the address of authority as the "present," the voice of modernity. The acknowledgement of authority depends upon the immediate—unmediated—visibility of its rules of recognition as the unmistakable referent of historical necessity.

In the doubly inscribed space of colonial representation where the presence of authority—the English book—is also a question of its repetition and displacement, where transparency is *technē,* the immediate visibility of such a régime of recognition is resisted. Resistance is not necessarily an oppositional act of political intention, nor is it the simple negation or exclusion of the "content" of an other culture, as a difference once perceived. It is the effect of an ambivalence produced within the rules of recognition of dominating discourses as they articulate the signs of cultural difference and reimplicate them within the deferential relations of colonial power—hierarchy, normalization, marginalization, and so forth. For domination is achieved through a process of disavowal that denies the *différance* of colonialist power—the chaos of its intervention as *Entstellung,* its dislocatory presence—in order to preserve the authority of its identity in the universalist narrative of nineteenth-century historical and political evolutionism.

The exercise of colonialist authority, however, requires the production of differentiations, individuations, identity effects through which discriminatory practices can map out subject populations that are tarred with the visible and transparent mark of power. Such a mode of subjection is distinct from what Foucault describes as "power through transparency": the reign of opinion, after the late eighteenth century, which could not tolerate areas of darkness and sought to exercise power through the mere fact of things being known and people seen in an immediate, collective gaze.[17] What radically differentiates the exercise of colonial power is the unsuitability of the Enlightenment assumption of collectivity and the eye that beholds it. For Jeremy Bentham (as Michel Perrot points out), the small group is representative of the whole society—the part is *already* the whole. Colonial authority requires modes of discrimination (cultural, racial, administrative . . .) that disallow a stable unitary assumption of collectivity. The "part" (which must be the colonialist foreign body) must be representative of the "whole" (conquered country), but the right of representation is based on its radical difference. Such doublethink is made viable only through the strategy of disavowal just described, which requires a theory of the "hybridization" of discourse and power that is ignored by Western post-structuralists who engage in the battle for "power" as the purists of difference.

The discriminatory effects of the discourse of cultural colonialism, for instance, do not simply or singly refer to a "person," or to a dialectical power struggle between self and Other, or to a discrimination between mother culture and alien cultures. Produced through the strategy of disavowal, the *reference* of discrimination is always to a process of splitting as the condition of subjection: a discrimination between the mother culture and its bastards, the self and its doubles, where the trace of what is disavowed is not repressed but repeated as something *different*—a mutation, a hybrid. It is such a partial and double force that is more than the mimetic but less than the symbolic, that disturbs the visibility of the colonial presence and makes the recognition of its authority problematic. To be authoritative, its rules of recognition must reflect consensual knowledge or opinion; to be powerful, these rules of recognition must be breached in order to represent the exorbitant objects of discrimination that lie beyond its purview. Consequently, if the unitary (and essentialist) reference to race, nation, or cultural tradition is essential to preserve the presence of authority as an immediate mimetic effect, such essentialism must be exceeded in the articulation of "differentiatory," discriminatory identities.

To demonstrate such an "excess" is not merely to celebrate the joyous power of the signifier. Hybridity is the sign of the productivity of colonial power, its shifting forces and fixities; it is the name for the strategic reversal of the process of domination through disavowal (that is, the production of discriminatory identities that secure the "pure" and original identity of authority). Hybridity is the revaluation of the assumption of colonial identity through the repetition of discriminatory identity effects. It displays the necessary deformation and displacement of all sites of discrimination and domination. It unsettles the mimetic or narcissistic demands of colonial power but reimplicates its identifications in strategies of subversion that turn the gaze of the discriminated back upon the eye of power. For the colonial hybrid is the articulation of the ambivalent space where the rite of power is enacted on the site of desire, making its objects at once disciplinary and disseminatory—or, in my mixed metaphor, a negative transparency. If discriminatory effects enable the authorities to keep an eye on them, their proliferating difference evades that eye, escapes that surveillance. Those discriminated against may be instantly recognized, but they also force a re-cognition of the immediacy and articulacy of authority—a disturbing effect that is familiar in the repeated hesitancy afflicting the colonialist discourse when it contemplates its discriminated subjects: the *inscrutability* of the Chinese, the *unspeakable* rites of the Indians, the *indescribable* habits of the Hottentots. It is not that the voice of authority is at a loss for words. It is, rather, that the colonial discourse has reached that point when, faced with the hybridity of its objects, the *presence* of power is revealed as something other than what its rules of recognition assert.

If the effect of colonial power is seen to be the *production* of hybridization rather than the noisy command of colonialist authority or the silent repression of native traditions, then an important change of perspective occurs. It reveals the ambivalence at the source of traditional discourses on authority and enables a form of subversion, founded on that uncertainty, that turns the discursive conditions of dominance into the grounds of intervention. It is traditional academic wisdom that the presence of authority is properly established through the nonexercise of private judgment and the exclusion of reasons, in conflict with the authoritative reason. The recognition of authority, however, requires a validation of its source that must be immediately, even intuitively, apparent—"You have that in your countenance which I would fain call master"—and held in common (rules of recognition). What is left unacknowledged is the paradox of such a demand for proof and the resulting ambivalence for positions of authority. If, as Steven Lukes rightly says, the acceptance of authority excludes any evaluation of the content of an utterance, and if its source, which must be acknowledged, disavows both conflicting reasons and personal judgment, then can the "signs" or "marks" of authority be anything more than "empty" presences of strategic devices?[18] Need they be any the less effective because of that? Not less effective but effective in a different form, would be our answer.

Tom Nairn reveals a basic ambivalence between the symbols of English imperialism which could not help "looking universal" and a "hollowness [that] sounds through the English imperialist mind in a thousand forms: in Rider Haggard's necrophilia, in Kipling's moments of gloomy doubt, . . . in the gloomy cosmic truth of Forster's Marabar caves."[19] Nairn explains this "imperial delirium" as the disproportion between the grandiose rhetoric of English imperialism and the *real* economic and political situation of late Victorian England. I would like to suggest that these crucial moments in English literature are not simply crises of England's own making. They are also the signs of a discontinuous history, an estrangement of the English book. They mark the disturbance of its authoritative representations by the uncanny forces of race, sexuality, violence, cultural and even climatic differences which emerge in the colonial discourse as the mixed and split texts of hybridity. If the appearance of the English book is read as a production of colonial hybridity, then it no longer simply commands authority. It gives rise to a series of *questions of authority* that, in my bastardized repetition, must sound strangely familiar:

> Was it a badge—an ornament—a charm—a propitiatory act? Was there any idea at all connected with it? It looked startling in this black neck of the woods, this bit of white writing from beyond the seas.

In repeating the scenario of the English book, I hope I have succeeded in representing a colonial difference: it is the effect of uncertainty that afflicts the discourse of power, an uncertainty that estranges the familiar symbol of English "national" authority and emerges from its colonial appropriation as the sign of its difference. Hybridity is the name of this displacement of value from symbol to sign that causes the dominant discourse to split along the axis of its power to be representative, authoritative. Hybridity represents that ambivalent "turn" of the discriminated subject into the terrifying, exorbitant object of paranoid classification— a disturbing questioning of the images and presences of authority. To grasp the ambivalence of hybridity, it must be distinguished from an inversion that would suggest that the originary is, really, only the "effect" of an *Entstellung*. Hybridity has no such perspective of depth or truth to provide: it is not a third term that resolves the tension between two cultures, or the two scenes of the book, in a dialectical play of "recognition." The displacement from symbol to sign creates a crisis for any concept of authority based on a system of recognition: colonial specularity, doubly inscribed, does not produce a mirror where the self apprehends itself; it is always the split screen of the self and its doubling, the hybrid.

These metaphors are very much to the point, because they suggest that colonial hybridity is not a *problem* of genealogy or identity between two *different* cultures which can then be resolved as an issue of cultural relativism. Hybridity is a *problematic* of colonial representation and individuation that reverses the effects of the colonialist disavowal, so that other "denied" knowledges enter upon the dominant discourse and estrange the basis of its authority—its rules of recognition. Again, it must be stressed, it is not simply the *content* of disavowed knowledges—be they forms of cultural Otherness or traditions of colonialist treachery—that return to be acknowledged as counterauthorities. For the resolution of conflicts between authorities, civil discourse always maintains an adjudicative procedure. What is irremediably estranging in the presence of the hybrid—in the revaluation of the symbol of national authority as the sign of colonial difference—is that the difference of cultures can no longer be identified or evaluated as objects of epistemological or moral contemplation: they are not simply *there* to be seen or appropriated.

Hybridity reverses the *formal* process of disavowal so that the violent dislocation, the *Entstellung* of the act of colonization, becomes the *conditionality* of colonial discourse. The presence of colonialist authority is no longer immediately visible; its discriminatory identifications no longer have their authoritative reference to this culture's cannibalism or that people's perfidy. As an articulation of displacement and dislocation, it is now possible to identify "the cultural" as a disposal of power, a negative transparency that comes to be agonistically constructed *on the boundary* between frame of reference/frame of mind. It is crucial to remember that the colonial construction of the cultural (the site of the civilizing mission) through the process of disavowal is authoritative to the extent to which it is structured around the ambivalence of splitting, denial, repetition—strategies of defence that mobilize culture as an open-textured, warlike strategy whose aim "is rather a continued agony than a total disappearance of the pre-existing culture."[20] To see the cultural not as the *source* of conflict—*different* cultures—but as the *effect* of discriminatory practices—the production of cultural *differentiation* as signs of authority—changes its value and its rules of recognition. What is preserved is the visible surfaces of its artefacts—the mere *visibility* of the symbol, as a fleeting immediacy. Hybridity intervenes in the exercise of authority not merely to indicate the impossibility of its identity but to represent the unpredictability of its presence. The book retains its presence, but it is no longer a representation of an essence; it is now a partial presence, a (strategic) device in a specific colonial engagement, an appurtenance of authority.

This partializing process of hybridity is best described as a metonymy of presence. It shares Sigmund Freud's valuable insight into the strategy of disavowal as the persistence of the narcissistic demand in the acknowledgement of difference.[21] This, however, exacts a price, for the existence of two contradictory knowledges (multiple beliefs) splits the ego (or the discourse) into two psychical attitudes, and forms of knowledge, toward the external world. The first of these takes reality into consideration while the second replaces it with a product of desire. What is remarkable is that these two contradictory objectives always represent a "partiality" in the construction of the fetish object, at once a substitute for the phallus and a mark of its absence. There is an important difference between fetishism and hybridity. The fetish reacts to the change in the value of the phallus by fixing on an object *prior to the perception of difference,* an object that can metaphorically substitute for its presence while registering the difference. So long as it fulfills the fetishistic ritual, the object can look like anything (or nothing!). The hybrid object, however, retains the actual semblance of the authoritative symbol but revalues its presence by resiting it as the signifier of *Entstellung—after the intervention of difference.* It is the power of this strange metonymy of presence to so disturb the systematic (and systemic) construction of discriminatory knowledges that the cultural, once recognized as the medium of authority, becomes virtually unrecognizable. Culture, as a colonial space of intervention and agonism, as the trace of the displacement of symbol to sign, can be transformed by the unpredictable and partial desire of hybridity. Deprived of their full presence, the knowledges of cultural authority may be articulated with forms of "native" knowledges or faced with those discriminated subjects that they must rule but can no longer represent. This may lead, as in the case of the natives outside Delhi, to questions of authority that the authorities—the Bible included—cannot answer. Such a process is not the deconstruction of a cultural system from the margins of its own aporia nor, as in Derrida's "Double Session," the mime that haunts mimesis. The display of hybridity—its peculiar "replication"—terrorizes authority with the *ruse* of recognition, its mimicry, its mockery.

Such a reading of colonial authority profoundly unsettles the demand that figures at the centre of the originary myth of colonialist power. It is the demand that *the space it occupies be unbounded,* its reality *coincident* with the emergence of an imperialist narrative and history, its discourse *nondialogic,* its enunciation *unitary,* unmarked by the trace of difference— a demand that is recognizable in a range of justificatory Western "civil" discourses where the presence of the "colony" often alienates its own language of liberty and reveals its universalist concepts of labour and property as particular, post-Enlightenment ideological and technological practices. Consider, for example: Locke's notion of the wasteland of Carolina—"Thus in the beginning all the World was *America*"; Montesquieu's emblem of the wasteful and disorderly life and labour in despotic societies—"When the savages of Louisiana are desirous of fruit, they cut the tree to the root, and gather the fruit"; Grant's belief in the impossibility of law and history in Muslim and Hindu India—"where treasons and revolutions are continual; by which the insolent and abject frequently change places"; or the contemporary Zionist myth of the neglect of Palestine—"of a *whole* territory," Said writes, "essentially unused, unappreciated, misunderstood . . . *to be made* useful, appreciated, understandable."[22]

What renders this demand of colonial power impossible is precisely the point at which the question of authority emerges. For the unitary voice of command is interrupted by questions that arise from these heterogeneous sites and circuits of power which, though momentarily "fixed" in the authoritative alignment of subjects, must continually be re-presented in the production of terror or fear—the paranoid threat from the hybrid is finally uncontainable because it breaks down the symmetry and duality of self/Other, inside/outside. In the productivity of power, the boundaries of authority—its reality effects—are always besieged by "the other scene" of fixations and phantoms. We can now understand the link between the psychic and political that is suggested in Frantz Fanon's figure of speech: the colon is an exhibitionist, because his *preoccupation* with security makes him "remind the native out loud that there he alone is master."[23] The native, caught in the chains of colonialist command, achieves a "pseudo-petrification" which further incites and excites him, thus making the settler-native boundary an anxious and ambivalent one. What then presents itself as the subject of authority in the discourse of colonial power is, in fact, a desire that so exceeds the original authority of the book and the immediate visibility of its metaphoric writing that we are bound to ask: What does colonial power want? My answer is only partially in agreement with Lacan's *vel* or Derrida's veil or hymen. For the desire of colonial discourse *is* a splitting of hybridity that is *less than one and double;* and if that sounds enigmatic, it is because its explanation has to wait upon the authority of those canny questions that the natives put, so insistently, to the English book.

The native questions quite literally turn the origin of the book into an enigma. First: *How can the word of God come from the flesh-eating mouths of the English?*—a question that faces the unitary and universalist assumption of authority with the cultural difference of its historical moment of enunciation. And later: *How can it be the* European *Book, when we believe that it is God's gift to us? He sent it to Hurdwar.* This is not merely an illustration of what Foucault would call the capillary effects of the microtechnics of power. It reveals the penetrative power—*both* psychic and social—of the technology of the printed word in early nineteenth-century rural India. Imagine the scene: the Bible, perhaps translated into a North Indian dialect like Brigbhasha, handed out free or for one rupee within a culture where usually only caste Hindus would possess a copy of the Scriptures, and received in awe by the natives as both a novelty and a household deity. Contemporary missionary records reveal that, in Middle India alone, by 1815 we could have witnessed the spectacle of the Gospel "doing its own work," as the Evangelicals put it, in at least eight languages and dialects, with a first edition of between one thousand and ten thousand copies in each translation (see *MR*, May 1816, pp. 181–82). It is the force of these colonialist practices that produce that discursive tension between Anund Messeh, whose address *assumes* its authority, and the natives who question the English presence and seek a culturally differentiated, "colonial" authority *to* address.

The subversive character of the native questions will be realized only once we recognize the strategic disavowal of cultural/historical difference in Anund Messeh's Evangelical discourse. Having introduced the *presence* of the English and their *intercession*—"God gave [the Book] long ago to the Sahibs, and THEY sent it to us"—he then disavows that political/ linguistic "imposition" by attributing the intervention of the Church to the power of God and the received authority of chapter and verse. What is being disavowed is not entirely visible in Anund Messeh's contradictory statements, at the level of the "enounced." What he, as well as the English Bible-in-disguise, must conceal are their particular enunciatory conditions—that is, the design of the Burdwan Plan to deploy "natives" to destroy native culture and religion. This is done through the repeated production of a teleological narrative of Evangelical witness: eager conversions, bereft Brahmins, and Christian gatherings. The descent from God to the English is both linear and circular: "This WORD is of God, and not of men; and when HE makes your hearts to understand, then you will PROPERLY comprehend." The historical "evidence" of Christianity is plain for all to see, Indian Evangelists would have argued, with the help of William Paley's *Evidences of Christianity* (1791), the most important missionary manual throughout the nineteenth century. The miraculous authority of colonial Christianity, they would have held, lies precisely in its being both English and universal, empirical and uncanny, for "ought we not rather to expect that such a Being on occasions of peculiar importance, may interrupt the order which he had appointed?"[24] The Word, no less theocratic than logocentric, would have certainly borne absolute witness to the gospel of Hurdwar had it not been for the rather tasteless fact that most Hindus were vegetarian!

By taking their stand on the grounds of dietary law, the natives resist the miraculous equivalence of God and the English. They introduce the practice of colonial cultural differentiation *as* an indispensable *enunciative function* in the discourse of authority—a function Foucault describes as linked to "a 'referential' that . . . forms the place, the condition, the field of emergence, the *authority to differentiate* between individuals or objects, states of things and relations that are brought into play by the statement itself; it defines the possibilities of appearance and delimitation."[25] Through the natives' strange questions, it is possible to see, with historical hindsight, what they resisted in questioning the presence of the English—as religious mediation and as a cultural and linguistic medium. What is the value of English in the offering of the Hindi Bible? It is the creation of a print technology calculated to produce a visual effect that will not "look like the work of foreigners"; it is the decision to produce simple, abridged tracts of the plainest narrative that may inculcate the habit of "private, solitary reading," as a missionary wrote in 1816, so that the natives may resist the Brahmin's "monopoly of knowledge" and lessen their dependence on their own religious and cultural traditions; it is the opinion of the Reverend Donald Corrie that "on learning English they acquire ideas quite new, and of the first importance, respecting God and his government" (*MR*, July 1816, p. 193; Nov. 1816, pp. 444–45; Mar. 1816, pp. 106–7). It is the shrewd view of an unknown native, in 1819:

> For instance, I take a book of yours and read it awhile and whether I become a Christian or not, I leave the book in my family: after my death, my son, conceiving that I would leave nothing useless or bad in my house, will look into the book, understand its contents, consider that his father left him that book, and become a Christian. [*MR*, Jan. 1819, p. 27]

When the natives demand an Indianized Gospel, they are using the powers of hybridity to resist baptism and to put the project of conversion in an impossible position. Any adaptation of the Bible was forbidden by the evidences of Christianity, for, as the bishop of Calcutta preached in his Christmas sermon in 1815: "I mean that it is a Historical Religion: the History of the whole dispensation is before us from the creation of the world to the present hour: and it is throughout consistent with itself and with the attributes of God" (*MR*, Jan. 1817, p. 31). Their stipulation that only mass conversion would persuade them to take the sacrament touches on a tension between missionary zeal and the East India Company Statutes for 1814 which strongly advised against such proselytizing. When they make these intercultural, hybrid demands, the natives are both challenging the boundaries of discourse and subtly changing its terms by setting up another specifically colonial space of power/knowledge. And they do this under the eye of authority, through the production of "partial" knowledges and positionalities in keeping with my earlier, more general explanation of hybridity. Such objects of knowledges make the signifiers of authority enigmatic in a way that is "less than one and double." They change their conditions of recognition while maintaining their visibility; they introduce a lack that is then represented as a doubling or mimicry. This mode of discursive disturbance is a sharp practice, rather like that of the perfidious barbers in the bazaars of Bombay who do not mug their customers with the blunt Lacanian *vel* "Your money or your life," leaving them with nothing. No, these wily oriental thieves, with far greater skill, pick their clients' pockets and cry out, "How the master's face shines!" and then, in a whisper, "But he's lost his mettle!"

And this traveler's tale, told by a native, is an emblem of that form of splitting—less than one and double—that I have suggested for the reading of the ambivalence of colonial cultural texts. In estranging the word of God from the English medium, the natives' questions dispense the logical order of the discourse of authority—"These books . . . teach the religion of the European Sahibs. It is THEIR Book; and they printed it in our language, for our use." The natives expel the copula, or middle term, of the Evangelical "power = knowledge" equation, which then disarticulates the structure of the God-Englishman equivalence. Such a crisis in the positionality and propositionality of colonialist authority destabilizes the sign of authority. For by alienating "English" as the middle term, the presence of authority is freed of a range of ideological correlates— for instance, intentionality, originality, authenticity, cultural normativity. The Bible is now ready for a specific colonial appropriation. On the one hand, its paradigmatic presence as the Word of God is assiduously preserved: it is only to the direct quotations from the Bible that the natives give their unquestioning approval—"True!" The expulsion of the copula, however, empties the presence of its syntagmatic supports—codes, connotations, and cultural associations that give it contiguity and continuity— that make its presence culturally and politically authoritative.

In this sense, then, it may be said that the *presence* of the book has acceded to the logic of the signifier and has been "separated," in Lacan's use of the term, from "itself." If, on one side, its authority, or some symbol or meaning of it, is maintained—willy-nilly, *less than one*—then, on the other, it fades. It is at the point of its fading that the signifier of presence gets caught up in an alienating strategy of doubling or repetition. Doubling repeats the fixed and empty presence of authority by articulating it syntagmatically with a range of differential knowledges and positionalities that both estrange its "identity" and produce new forms of knowledge, new modes of differentiation, new sites of power. In the case of the colonial discourse, these syntagmatic appropriations of presence confront it with those contradictory and threatening differences of its enunciative function that had been disavowed. In their repetition, these disavowed knowledges return to make the presence of authority uncertain. This may take the form of multiple or contradictory belief, as in some forms of native knowledges: "We are willing to be baptized, but we will never take the Sacrament." Or they may be forms of mythic explanation that refuse to acknowledge the agency of the Evangelicals: "An Angel from

heaven gave it [the Bible] us at Hurdwar fair." Or they may be the
fetishistic repetition of litany in the face of an unanswerable challenge
to authority: for instance, Anund Messeh's "*Not that which entereth into a
man's mouth defileth him, but that which cometh out of the mouth.*"

In each of these cases we see a colonial doubling which I've described
as a strategic displacement of value through a process of the metonymy
of presence. It is through this partial process, represented in its enigmatic,
inappropriate signifiers—stereotypes, jokes, multiple and contradictory
belief, the "native" Bible—that we begin to get a sense of a specific space
of cultural colonial discourse. It is a "separate" space, a space of *separation*—
less than one and double—which has been systematically denied by both
colonialists and nationalists who have sought authority in the authenticity
of "origins." It is precisely as a separation from origins and essences that
this colonial space is constructed. It is separate, in the sense in which the
French psychoanalyst Victor Smirnoff describes the separateness of the
fetish as a "separateness that makes the fetish easily available, so that the
subject can make use of it in his own way and establish it in an order of
things that frees it from any subordination."[26]

The metonymic strategy produces the signifier of colonial *mimicry*
as the affect of hybridity—at once a mode of appropriation and of resistance,
from the disciplined to the desiring. As the discriminated object, the
metonym of presence becomes the support of an authoritarian voyeurism,
all the better to exhibit the eye of power. Then, as discrimination turns
into the assertion of the hybrid, the insignia of authority becomes a mask,
a mockery. After our experience of the native interrogation, it is difficult
to agree entirely with Fanon that the psychic choice is to "turn white or
disappear."[27] There is the more ambivalent, third choice: camouflage,
mimicry, black skins/white masks. "Mimicry reveals something in so far
as it is distinct from what might be called an *itself* that is behind. The
effect of mimicry," writes Lacan, "is camouflage, in the strictly technical
sense. It is not a question of harmonizing with the background but,
against a mottled background, of being mottled—exactly like the technique
of camouflage practised in human warfare."[28]

Read as a masque of mimicry, Anund Messeh's tale emerges as a
question of colonial authority, an agonistic space. To the extent to which
discourse is a form of defensive warfare, mimicry marks those moments
of civil disobedience within the discipline of civility: signs of spectacular
resistance. When the words of the master become the site of hybridity—
the warlike sign of the native—then we may not only read between the
lines but even seek to change the often coercive reality that they so lucidly
contain. It is with the strange sense of a hybrid history that I want to
end.

Despite Anund Messeh's miraculous evidence, "native Christians were
never more than vain phantoms" as J. A. Dubois wrote in 1815, after

twenty-five years in Madras. Their parlous partial state caused him particular anxiety,

> for in embracing the Christian religion they never entirely renounce
> their superstitions towards which they always keep a secret bent . . .
> there is no *unfeigned, undisguised* Christian among these Indians.
> [*MR,* Nov. 1816, p. 212]

And what of the native discourse? Who can tell?

The Reverend Mr. Corrie, the most eminent of the Indian evangelists, warned that

> till they came under the English Government, they have not been
> accustomed to assert the nose upon their face their own. . . . This
> temper prevails, more or less, in the converted. [*MR,* Mar. 1816,
> pp. 106–7]

Archdeacon Potts, in handing over charge to the Reverend J. P. Sperschneider in July 1818, was a good deal more worried:

> If you urge them with their gross and unworthy misconceptions of
> the nature and will of God or the monstrous follies of their fabulous
> theology, they will turn it off with a sly civility perhaps, or with a
> popular and careless proverb. [*MR,* Sept. 1818, p. 375]

Was it in the spirit of such sly civility that the native Christians parried so long with Anund Messeh and then, at the mention of baptism, politely excused themselves: "Now we must go home to the harvest. . . . perhaps the next year we may come to Meerut."

And what is the significance of the Bible? Who knows?

Three years before the native Christians received the Bible at Hurdwar, a schoolmaster named Sandappan wrote from southern India, asking for a Bible:

> Rev. Fr. Have mercy upon me. I am amongst so many craving
> beggars for the Holy Scriptures the chief craving beggar. The bounty
> of the bestowers of this treasure is so great I understand, that even
> this book is read in rice and salt-markets. [*MR,* June 1813, pp. 221–
> 22]

But, in the same year—1817—as the miracle outside Delhi, a much-tried missionary wrote in some considerable rage:

> Still everyone would gladly receive a Bible. And why? That he may
> store it up as a curiosity; sell it for a few pice; or use it for waste

paper. . . . Some have been bartered in the markets. . . . If these remarks are at all warranted then an indiscriminate distribution of the scriptures, to everyone who may say he wants a Bible, can be little less than a waste of time, a waste of money and a waste of expectations. For while the public are hearing of so many Bibles distributed, they expect to hear soon of a correspondent number of conversions. [*MR*, May 1817, p. 186]

1. Missionary Register, Church Missionary Society, London, Jan. 1818, pp. 18–19; all further references to this work, abbreviated *MR*, will be included in the text, with dates and page numbers in parentheses.

2. Joseph Conrad, *Heart of Darkness*, ed. Paul O'Prey (Harmondsworth, 1983), pp. 71, 72.

3. V. S. Naipaul, "Conrad's Darkness," *The Return of Eva Perón* (New York, 1974), p. 233.

4. "Overall effect of the dream-work: the latent thoughts are transformed into a manifest formation in which they are not easily recognisable. They are not only transposed, as it were, into another key, but *they are also distorted in such a fashion that only an effort of interpretation can reconstitute them*" (J. Laplanche and J. B. Pontalis, *The Language of Psycho-Analysis*, trans. Donald Nicholson-Smith [London, 1980], p. 124; my emphasis). See also Samuel Weber's excellent chapter "Metapsychology Set Apart," *The Legend of Freud* (Minneapolis, 1982), pp. 32–60.

5. Jacques Derrida, *Dissemination*, trans. Barbara Johnson (Chicago, 1981), pp. 189–90; all further references to this work, abbreviated *D*, will be included in the text.

6. Conrad, *Heart of Darkness*, p. 45.

7. Friedrich Nietzsche, *Untimely Meditations*, trans. R. J. Hollingdale (Cambridge, 1983), p. 71.

8. Thomas Babington Macaulay, "Minute on Education," quoted in Elmer H. Cutts, "The Background of Macaulay's Minute," *American Historical Review* 58 (July 1953): 839.

9. See Ian Watt, *Conrad in the Nineteenth Century* (Berkeley and Los Angeles, 1979), chap. 4, pt. i.

10. See Conrad, "Tradition," *Notes on Life and Letters* (London, 1925), pp. 194–201.

11. See John Barrell's excellent chapter "The Language Properly So-called: The Authority of Common Usage," *English Literature in History, 1730–1780: An Equal Wide Survey* (New York, 1983), pp. 110–75.

12. Conrad, quoted in Naipaul, "Conrad's Darkness," p. 236.

13. See my "The Other Question—The Stereotype and Colonial Discourse," *Screen* 24 (Nov.–Dec. 1983): 18–36.

14. Michel Foucault, "The Confession of the Flesh," *Power/Knowledge: Selected Interviews and Other Writings, 1972–1977*, ed. Colin Gordon, trans. Gordon et al. (New York, 1980), p. 204.

15. See Sigmund Freud, *Beyond the Pleasure Principle*, trans. and ed. James Strachey (London, 1974), pp. 18–25.

16. Foucault, "Truth and Power," *Power/Knowledge*, p. 132.

17. Foucault, "The Eye of Power," *Power/Knowledge*, p. 154; and see pp. 152–56.

18. See Steven Lukes, "Power and Authority," in *A History of Sociological Analysis*, ed. Tom Bottomore and Robert Nisbet (New York, 1978), pp. 633–76.

19. Tom Nairn, *The Break-Up of Britain: Crisis and Neo-Nationalism* (London, 1981), p. 265.

20. Frantz Fanon, *Toward the African Revolution*, trans. Haakon Chevalier (Harmondsworth, 1967), p. 44.

21. See Freud, *An Outline of Psycho-Analysis,* trans. and ed. Strachey (London, 1973), pp. 59–61.

22. John Locke, "The Second Treatise of Government," *Two Treatises of Government* (New York, 1965), p. 343, par. 49; Baron de Montesquieu, *The Spirit of the Laws,* trans. Thomas Nugent (New York, 1949), p. 57; Charles Grant, "Observations on the State of Society among the Asiatic Subjects of Great Britain," *Sessional Papers of the East India Company* 10, no. 282 (1812–13): 70; Edward W. Said, *The Question of Palestine* (New York, 1979), p. 85.

23. Fanon, *The Wretched of the Earth,* trans. Constance Farrington (Harmondsworth, 1969), p. 42.

24. William Paley, quoted in D. L. LeMahieu, *The Mind of William Paley: A Philosopher and His Age* (Lincoln, Nebr., 1976), p. 97.

25. Foucault, *The Archaeology of Knowledge,* trans. A. M. Sheridan Smith (London, 1972), p. 91; my emphasis.

26. Victor N. Smirnoff, "The Fetishistic Transaction," in *Psychoanalysis in France,* ed. Serge Lebovici and Daniel Widlöcher (New York, 1980), p. 307.

27. See Fanon, "The Negro and Psychopathology," *Black Skin, White Masks,* trans. Charles Lam Markmann (New York, 1967).

28. Jacques Lacan, *The Four Fundamental Concepts of Psycho-analysis,* ed. Jacques-Alain Miller, trans. Alan Sheridan (New York, 1978), p. 99.

Victorians and Africans: The Genealogy of the Myth of the Dark Continent

Patrick Brantlinger

In *Heart of Darkness,* Marlow says that Africa is no longer the "blank space" on the map that he had once daydreamed over. "It had got filled since my boyhood with rivers and lakes and names. . . . It had become a place of darkness."[1] Marlow is right: Africa grew "dark" as Victorian explorers, missionaries, and scientists flooded it with light, because the light was refracted through an imperialist ideology that urged the abolition of "savage customs" in the name of civilization. As a product of that ideology, the myth of the Dark Continent developed during the transition from the main British campaign against the slave trade, which culminated in the outlawing of slavery in all British territory in 1833, to the imperialist partitioning of Africa which dominated the final quarter of the nineteenth century.

The transition from the altruism of the antislavery movement to the cynicism of empire building involved a transvaluation of values that might be appropriately described in the genealogical language of Michel Foucault. Edward Said's Foucauldian analysis in *Orientalism,* based on a theory of discourse as strategies of power and subjection, inclusion and exclusion, the voiced and the silenced, suggests the kind of approach I am taking here. For middle- and upper-class Victorians, dominant over a vast working-class majority at home and over increasing millions of "uncivilized" peoples of "inferior" races abroad, power was self-validating. There might be many stages of social evolution and many seemingly bizarre customs and "superstitions" in the world, but there was only one "civilization," one path of "progress," one "true religion." "Anarchy" was many-tongued; "culture" spoke with one voice. Said writes of "the power of culture by virtue of its elevated or superior position to authorize, to dominate, to legitimate, demote, interdict, and validate: in short, the power of culture to be an agent of, and perhaps the main agency for, powerful differentiation within its domain and beyond it too." At home, culture might often seem threatened by anarchy: through Chartism, trade unionism, and socialism, the alternative voices of the working class could at least be heard by anyone who cared to listen. Abroad, the culture of the "conquering race" seemed unchallenged: in imperialist discourse the voices of the dominated are represented almost entirely by their silence, their absence. If Said is right that "the critic is responsible to a degree for articulating those voices dominated, displaced, or silenced" by the authority of a dominant culture, the place to begin is with a critique of that culture. This, according to Foucault, is the function of "genealogy," which seeks to analyze "the various systems of subjection: not the antic-ipatory power of meaning, but the hazardous play of dominations."[2]

Paradoxically, abolitionism contained the seeds of empire. If we accept the general outline of Eric Williams' thesis in *Capitalism and Slavery* that abolition was not purely altruistic but was as economically conditioned as Britain's later empire building in Africa, the contradiction between the ideologies of antislavery and imperialism seems more apparent than real. Although the idealism that motivated the great abolitionists such as William Wilberforce and Thomas Clarkson is unquestionable, Williams argues that Britain could *afford* to legislate against the slave trade only after that trade had helped to provide the surplus capital necessary for industrial "take-off." Britain had lost much of its slave-owning territory as a result of the American Revolution; as the leading industrial power in the world, Britain found in abolition a way to work against the interests of its rivals who were still heavily involved in colonial slavery and a plantation economy.[3]

The British abolitionist program entailed deeper and deeper in-volvement in Africa—the creation of Sierra Leone as a haven for freed slaves was just a start—but British abolitionists before the 1840s were neither jingoists nor deliberate expansionists. Humanitarianism applied to Africa, however, did point insistently toward imperialism.[4] By mid-century, the success of the antislavery movement, the impact of the great Victorian explorers, and the merger of racist and evolutionary doctrines in the social sciences had combined to give the British public a widely shared view of Africa that demanded imperialization on moral, religious,

Patrick Brantlinger, professor of English at Indiana University, is the editor of *Victorian Studies.* He has written *The Spirit of Reform: British Literature and Politics, 1832–1867* (1977) and *Bread and Circuses: Theories of Mass Culture and Social Decay* (1983).

and scientific grounds. It is this view that I have called the myth of the Dark Continent; by mythology I mean a form of modern, secularized, "depoliticized speech" (to adopt Roland Barthes' phrase)—discourse which treats its subject as universally accepted, scientifically established, and therefore no longer open to criticism by a political or theoretical opposition. In *The Idea of Race in Science: Great Britain, 1800–1960*, Nancy Stepan writes:

> A fundamental question about the history of racism in the first half of the nineteenth century is why it was that, just as the battle against slavery was being won by abolitionists, the war against racism was being lost. The Negro was legally freed by the Emancipation Act of 1833, but in the British mind he was still mentally, morally and physically a slave.[5]

It is this "fundamental question" which a genealogy of the myth of the Dark Continent can help to answer.

1

From the 1790s to the 1840s, the most influential kind of writing about Africa was abolitionist propaganda (see fig. 1). Most of the great Romantics wrote poems against what William Wordsworth in *The Prelude* called "the traffickers in Negro blood." William Blake's "Little Black Boy" is probably the most familiar of these:

> My mother bore me in the southern wild,
> And I am black, but O! my soul is white;
> White as an angel is the English child;
> But I am black as if bereav'd of light.[6]

To Blake's poem can be added Coleridge's "Greek Prize Ode on the Slave Trade," Wordsworth's "Sonnet to Thomas Clarkson," and a number of stanzas and poems by both Byron and Shelley. Several of Robert Southey's poems deal with the slave trade, including the final stanza of his poem "To Horror":

> Horror! I call thee yet once more!
> Bear me to that accursed shore,
> Where on the stake the Negro writhes.[7]

Quite apart from the similarity between Southey's "Dark Horror" and Conrad's "The horror! The horror!" a century later, I want to make two main points about the literature of the antislavery tradition.[8]

FIG. 1.—Typical of abolitionist propaganda were the publications of the Leeds Anti-Slavery Society.

First, antislavery writing involves the revelation of atrocities. Simon Legree's beating Uncle Tom to death is only the most familiar example. Abolitionist propaganda depicted in excruciating detail the barbaric practices of slave traders and owners in Africa, during the infamous middle passage, and in the southern states and West Indies. The constant association of Africa with the inhuman violence of the slave trade, of course, did much to darken its landscape even during the Romantic period. The exposé style of abolitionist propaganda, moreover, influenced much British writing about Africa well after slavery had ceased to be an urgent issue. Though not directly about slavery, an exposé purpose is evident in *Heart of Darkness* and also, for example, in Olive Schreiner's fictional diatribe against Cecil Rhodes, *Trooper Peter Halket of Mashonaland* (1897). The frontispiece to Schreiner's novel is a photograph showing white Rhodesians with three lynched Mashona rebels—unfortunately a summary of much of the history of southern Africa (fig. 2).

The second main point about antislavery literature is that the Romantics, unlike the Victorians, were able to envisage Africans living freely and happily without European interference. Strike off the fetters which European slavers had placed on them, and the result was a vision of noble savages living in pastoral freedom and innocence (see fig. 3). In sonnet 5 of Southey's "Poems concerning the Slave Trade," a slave's rebelliousness is inspired by

> the intolerable thought
> Of every past delight; his native grove,
> Friendship's best joys, and liberty and love
> For ever lost.[9]

Similarly, in "Africa Delivered; or, The Slave Trade Abolished" (1809), James Grahame writes:

> In that fair land of hill, and dale, and stream,
> The simple tribes from age to age had heard
> No hostile voice

—until the arrival of the European slave traders, who introduced to an Edenic Africa those characteristic products of civilization: avarice, treachery, rapine, murder, warfare, and slavery.[10]

Abolitionist portrayals of Africans as perhaps noble but also innocent or "simple" savages were patronizing and unintentionally derogatory. Nevertheless, portrayals of Africans between 1800 and the 1830s were often both more positive and more open-minded than those of later years. In saying so, I am slightly extending the period of relative objectivity noted by Katherine George, who argues that accounts of Africa from Herodotus to about 1700 tend to be highly prejudicial but that with the

FIG. 2.—Frontispiece. Olive Schreiner, *Trooper Peter Halket of Mashonaland*, 1897.

FIG. 3.—A typical Edenic African scene, with a slave ship approaching. James Montgomery, James Grahame, and E. Benger, *Poems on the Abolition of the Slave Trade*, 1809.

Enlightenment arose new standards of objectivity.[11] Ironically, the expansion of the slave trade itself from the 1600s on meant that Europeans had to develop more accurate knowledge of Africans—both those Africans with whom they did business and those who became their commodities. Many factors contributed to what George sees as a golden age of accuracy and lack of prejudice in writing about Africa; among these were the satiric tradition of the noble savage, turned to effective popular use by Aphra Behn in *Oroonoko; or, the Royal Slave* (1688); and later by many abolitionists; the Enlightenment belief that all people should be treated equally under the law; the growth of the abolitionist movement; and the exploration of the Niger River by Mungo Park and others, starting in the late 1700s. This period of relative objectivity did not end in 1800 but continued well into the nineteenth century, as evidenced by the abolitionist poetry of Southey and Grahame and by such works of social observation as Thomas Bowdich's *Mission from Cape Coast Castle to Ashantee* (1819). Bowdich condemned the Ashanti practice of ritual human sacrifice, but he did not treat that aspect of their culture as representative of the whole, nor did he allow it to interfere with his appreciation for other Ashanti customs, arts, and institutions.[12]

The abolition of slavery in all British territories did not eliminate concern about slavery elsewhere, but the British began to see themselves less and less as perpetrators of the slave trade and more and more as the potential saviors of the African. The blame for slavery could now be displaced onto others—onto Americans, for example. Blame was increasingly displaced onto Africans themselves for maintaining the slave trade as a chief form of economic exchange. This shifting of the burden of guilt is already evident in the Niger Expedition of 1841, "the first step toward a general 'forward policy' in West Africa."[13] Thomas Fowell Buxton, leader of the British antislavery movement after Wilberforce, recognized that the emancipation legislation of 1833 would not eliminate slavery from non-British parts of the world. He therefore proposed to attack slavery at its source, planning the Niger Expedition as a first step toward the introduction of Christianity and "legitimate commerce" to west Africa. In *The African Slave Trade and Its Remedy* (1840), Buxton portrays Africa as a land "teeming with inhabitants who admire, and are desirous of possessing our manufactures."[14] In the past, Africans had learned to trade in human lives; in the future, they must learn to produce something other than slaves. The British would teach them to be both religious and industrious.

Although Buxton repudiated empire building, the Niger Expedition aimed to establish bases from which European values could be spread throughout Africa. Buxton's portrayal of Africa is almost wholly negative: "Bound in the chains of the grossest ignorance, [Africa] is a prey to the most savage superstition. Christianity has made but feeble inroads on this kingdom of darkness" (*A*, pp. 10–11). In a chapter entitled "Superstitions and Cruelties of the Africans," Buxton anticipates many later writers who also seek to show the necessity for increased intervention in Africa: he extracts the most grisly descriptions of such customs as human sacrifice from the writings of Bowdich and others and offers these as the essence of African culture. Buxton's "dark catalogue of crime" combines slavery and savagery; both are seen as disrupting Africa's chances for civilization and salvation (*A*, p. 270). "Such atrocious deeds, as have been detailed in the foregoing pages, keep the African population in a state of callous barbarity, which can only be effectually counteracted by Christian civilisation" (*A*, p. 244).

The Niger Expedition ended in disaster when most of its European participants were laid low by malaria, forty-one of them dying. For at least a decade, its failure supported arguments that Europeans should stay out of central Africa; the harsh facts of disease and death themselves contributed to the darkening of the Dark Continent. In his essay on the Niger Expedition (1848), Charles Dickens attacked the aims of philanthropists like Buxton and decried Africa as a continent not fit for civilization—one best left in the dark.

> The history of this Expedition is the history of the Past [rather than the future] in reference to the heated visions of philanthropists for the railroad Christianisation of Africa, and the abolition of the Slave Trade. . . . Between the civilized European and the barbarous African there is a great gulf set. . . . To change the customs even of civilised . . . men . . . is . . . a most difficult and slow proceeding; but to do this by ignorant and savage races, is a work which, like the progressive changes of the globe itself, requires a stretch of years that dazzles in the looking at.[15]

In *Bleak House,* Dickens' placement of Mrs. Jellyby's Borrioboola-Gha mission on the banks of the Niger suggests its utter and absurd futility, like that of the Niger Expedition. In his occasional rantings against "natives," "Sambos," and "ignoble savages," Dickens also vents his hostility toward evangelical philanthropy. He regarded missionaries as "perfect nuisances who leave every place worse than they find it." "Believe it, African Civilisation, Church of England Missionary, and all other Missionary Societies!" he writes. "The work at home must be completed thoroughly, or there is no hope abroad."[16] This was also Thomas Carlyle's attitude in "The Nigger Question" (1849) and again in his response to the rebellion in Jamaica in 1865. According to both Carlyle and Dickens, abolitionist and missionary activities were distractions from more appropriate concerns about poverty and misgovernment at home.

As the Governor Eyre Controversy of 1865 showed, many Victorians (including Carlyle and Dickens) sympathized with the poor at home but not with the exploited abroad. Thus, a sizable portion of the Victorian public sided with the South during the American Civil War. Slavery, however, remained an important issue from the 1840s to the end of the century. Slavery is central, for example, to an 1847 novel by Sarah Lee Wallis (whose first husband was Thomas Bowdich), *The African Wanderers,* in which "from one end of Africa to the other we find traces of that horrible traffic." Some of Wallis' "natives" are restless and hostile because they are cannibals "who file their teeth" and lust after human flesh, but more are restless and hostile because their normally pacific lives have been disrupted by the slave trade. When *Uncle Tom's Cabin* appeared in 1852, moreover, it sold more copies in England than in America.[17] One of Harriet Beecher Stowe's most ardent English admirers, Elizabeth Barrett Browning, also contributed to the abolitionist cause with her poems "The Runaway Slave at Pilgrim's Point" and "A Curse for a Nation." Following the Civil War, slavery seemed largely confined to Africa; along with such staples of sensationalist journalism as human sacrifice and cannibalism, slavery looked more and more like a direct extension of African savagery.

After abolishing slavery on their own ground, the British turned to the seemingly humane work of abolishing slavery—and all "savage customs"—on African ground. By the time of the Berlin Conference of 1884, which is often taken as the start of the "scramble for Africa," the British tended to see Africa as a center of evil, a part of the world possessed by a demonic "darkness" or barbarism, represented above all by slavery and cannibalism, which it was their duty to exorcise. The writers most responsible for promoting this point of view—and for maintaining the crusade against the slave trade even after both Britain and the United States were well out of it—were the explorers and missionaries, with Buxton's disciple David Livingstone in the lead.

2

The so-called opening up of Africa by the great Victorian explorers commenced in the late 1850s, facilitated by quinine as a prophylactic against malaria. Earlier explorers had excited public interest, but the search for the sources of the White Nile—initiated by Richard Burton and John Speke in 1856 and followed up by the expeditions of Speke and James Grant, Samuel White Baker, Livingstone, and Henry Stanley—raised British interest to a new level. As headline, best-selling reading, the "penetration" of Africa provided a narrative fascination that has been likened to excitement about space exploration today.[18] When Alec MacKenzie, the hero of William Somerset Maugham's *Explorer* (1907), begins "to read the marvellous records of African exploration," his "blood tingled at the magic of those pages." Inspired by the journals of Burton, Livingstone, and Stanley, MacKenzie becomes an explorer who struggles mightily against savagery and the internal slave trade (not to mention

European villainy) and who thus contributes mightily to imperial expansion. Maugham offers a fictional hagiography of all the great explorers of Africa, "men who've built up the empire piece by piece" and whose chief aim has been to add "another fair jewel to her crown." If the connection between exploration and empire building was not always evident to MacKenzie's originals, it is paramount for Maugham: "Success rewarded [MacKenzie's] long efforts. . . . The slavers were driven out of a territory larger than the United Kingdom, treaties were signed with chiefs who had hitherto been independent . . . and only one step remained, that the government should . . . annex the conquered district to the empire."[19]

The books that the explorers wrote took the Victorian reading public by storm. In the first few months after its publication in 1857, Livingstone's *Missionary Travels* sold seventy thousand copies and made its author wealthy and so famous that he had to avoid situations where he might be mobbed by admirers. If Livingstone was already a national hero in the late 1850s, he was a national saint by the time of his last African journey in 1872. The obverse side of the myth of the Dark Continent was that of the Promethean and, at least in Livingstone's case, saintly bestower of light (see fig. 4). Even Dickens, with his dislike of evangelical types, made an exception of Livingstone, calling him one of those who "carry into desert places the water of life."[20] Livingstone's apotheosis was complete in 1872 when Stanley, with his great journalistic scoop, published his first best-seller, *How I Found Livingstone*. Stanley's other books were also best-sellers: *In Darkest Africa,* for example, sold one hundred and fifty thousand copies in English, was frequently translated, and, according to one reviewer, "has been read more universally and with deeper interest than any other publication of" 1890.[21] Still another best-seller was Baker's *Albert N'yanza* of 1866; many others were widely read, including Burton's *Lake Regions of Central Africa* (1861), Speke's *Discovery of the Source of the Nile* (1864), Joseph Thomson's *To the Central African Lakes and Back* (1881), and so on. Although these titles do not figure in standard histories of Victorian literature, such accounts of African exploration exerted an incalculable influence on British culture and the course of modern history. It would be difficult to find a clearer example of the Foucauldian concept of discourse as power or as "a violence that we do to things."[22]

The great explorers' writings are nonfictional quest romances in which the hero-authors struggle through enchanted or bedeviled lands toward a goal, ostensibly the discovery of the Nile's sources or the conversion of the cannibals. But that goal also turns out to include sheer survival and the return home, to the regions of light. These humble but heroic authors move from adventure to adventure against a dark, infernal back-drop where there are no other characters of equal stature—only bewitched or demonic savages. Although they sometimes individualize their portraits of Africans, explorers usually portray them as amusing or dangerous obstacles or as objects of curiosity, while missionaries usually portray

Fig. 4.—Livingstone as a saint, carrying the light of Christianity into the Dark Continent. William Garden Blaikie, *The Personal Life of David Livingstone,* 1880.

Africans as weak, pitiable, inferior mortals who need to be shown the light. Center stage is occupied not by Africa or Africans but by a Livingstone or a Stanley, a Baker or a Burton—Victorian Saint Georges battling the armies of the night. Kurtz's career in devilry suggests that, on at least some occasions or in some ways, it was a losing battle.

Livingstone offers a striking example of how humanitarian aims could contribute to imperialist encroachment. Deeply influenced by Buxton, Livingstone also advocated the "opening up" of Africa by "commerce and Christianity." He had more respect for Africans than most explorers and missionaries, though he still viewed them as "children" and "savages." Occasionally he even expressed doubt that a European presence in Africa would be beneficial, but he also believed that the African was "benighted" and that the European was the bearer of the "light" of civilization and true religion. He held that Africa would be without hope of "raising itself" unless there was "contact with superior races by commerce." Africans were "inured to bloodshed and murder, and care[d] for no god except being bewitched"; without "commerce and Christianity," "the prospects for these dark regions are not bright." Tim Jeal writes of this most humanitarian of explorers that "with his missionary aims and his almost messianic passion for exporting British values [Livingstone] seemed to his successors to have provided the moral basis for massive imperial expansion."[23]

Economic and political motives are, of course, easier to detect in Livingstone's doppelgänger, Stanley. The purpose behind his work in the Congo for King Leopold II of Belgium was not far removed from the aims of the Eldorado Exploring Expedition in *Heart of Darkness:* "To tear treasure out of the bowels of the land was their desire, with no more moral purpose at the back of it than there is in burglars breaking into a safe" (*HD*, p. 31). But that sort of blatant economic motive was not what impelled Livingstone and the horde of missionaries who imitated him. The melodrama of Africa called for intervention by a higher moral power, and the Victorians increasingly saw themselves—again, with Livingstone in the lead—as the highest moral power among nations. The success of the British antislavery movement, after all, seemed to prove that Britain was more virtuous than its rivals for empire. For Livingstone, as for other missionaries and abolitionists, the African was a creature to be pitied, to be saved from slavery, and also to be saved from his own "darkness," his "savagery." At least Livingstone believed that the African could be rescued from "darkness"—that he could be Christianized and perhaps civilized. This attitude was, of course, necessary for any missionary activity. At the same time, missionaries were strongly tempted to exaggerate "savagery" and "darkness" in order to rationalize their presence in Africa, to explain the frustrations they experienced in making converts, and to win support from mission societies at home.[24]

Typical missionary attitudes are suggested by such titles as *Daybreak in the Dark Continent,* by Wilson S. Naylor, and *Dawn in the Dark Continent; or, Africa and Its Missions,* by James Stewart. Typical, too, are these assertions from *By the Equator's Snowy Peak* (1913), May Crawford's autobiography about missionary life in Kenya: "With the coming of the British," she says, "dawned a somewhat brighter" day for Kenya. It is only "somewhat brighter" because of the great backwardness of the natives, not because of any failing by the British. "Loving darkness rather than light," she continues, the "natives" "resent all that makes for progress."[25] Perhaps what the Kenyans resented was the British intrusion into their country, but this Crawford could not see. I have read of no instances where cannibals put missionaries into pots and cooked them, but Africans did sometimes kill, capture, or drive missionaries away from their lands, thus fueling arguments for armed intervention and imperialist annexation.[26] In Anthony Hope's novel *The God in the Car* (1895), Lord Semingham is asked how his great scheme for investing in central Africa is faring. "Everything's going on very well," he replies. "They've killed a missionary." This may be "regrettable in itself," Semingham smiles, "but [it's] the first step towards empire."[27]

The missionary idea that Africa could be redeemed for civilization was more than some explorers were willing to grant. Burton believed that the African was "unimprovable."

> He is inferior to the active-minded and objective . . . Europeans, and to the . . . subjective and reflective Asiatic. He partakes largely of the worst characteristics of the lower Oriental types—stagnation of mind, indolence of body, moral deficiency, superstition, and childish passion.[28]

Burton goes to some trouble to undermine the missionary point of view. He declares that "these wild African fetissists [*sic*] are [not] easily converted to a 'purer creed.' . . . Their faith is a web woven with threads of iron." At the same time, Burton agrees with the missionaries when he depicts fetishism as witchcraft and devil worship, Kurtz's "unspeakable rites." "A prey to base passions and melancholy godless fears, the Fetissist . . . peoples with malevolent beings the invisible world, and animates material nature with evil influences. The rites of his dark and deadly superstition" are entirely nefarious, as almost all Victorian writers claimed.[29] In their books and essays on the Dark Continent, the Victorians demote all central African kings to "chiefs" and all African priests (with the exception of Muslims) to "witch doctors" (see fig. 5).

Even if Africans are doomed by their "negro instincts" always to remain "savage," Burton still has a role in mind for them in the work of civilization. Like Carlyle, Burton argues both that abolitionist philanthropy

Fig. 5.—A typical portrayal of African religion as idol or devil worship. Herbert Ward, *Five Years with the Congo Cannibals*, 1890.

is mistaken and that primitive peoples need civilized masters. His argument is explicitly imperialist:

> I unhesitatingly assert—and all unprejudiced travellers will agree with me—that the world still wants the black hand. Enormous tropical regions yet await the clearing and draining operations by the lower races, which will fit them to become the dwelling-places of civilized man.[30]

Other explorers agreed with Burton. Though a hero in the late stages of the antislavery crusade, Baker believed that "the African . . . will assuredly relapse into an idle and savage state, unless specially governed and forced by industry."[31]

Burton was a marginal aristocrat and Baker came from a well-to-do family of shipowners and West Indian planters. Their racist view of Africans as a natural laboring class, suited only for performing the dirty work of civilization, expresses a nostalgia for lost authority and for a pliable, completely subordinate proletariat that is one of the central fantasies of imperialism. For opposite reasons, that fantasy also appealed to explorers from working-class backgrounds like Livingstone and Stanley: their subordinate status at home was reversed in Africa. Livingstone the factory boy could be Livingstone the great white leader and teacher in Africa, and Stanley the pauper orphan could be Stanley the great pioneer and field marshal, blazing the trail for civilization.

That Africans were suited only for manual labor is an idea often repeated in fiction. In Henry Merriman's *With Edged Tools* (1894), for example, African porters "hired themselves out like animals, and as the beasts of the field they did their work—patiently, without intelligence. . . . Such is the African." The comparison with British labor is made explicit when the narrator adds: "If any hold that men are not created so dense and unambitious as has just been represented, let him look nearer home in our own merchant service. The able-bodied seaman goes to sea all his life, but he never gets any nearer navigating the ship—and he a white man." The English protagonists are shocked to discover that the Africans who work for their villainous half-breed partner are his slaves, to whom he pays no wages. Slavery by the 1890s was patently a violation of "one of Heaven's laws."[32] But when the English offer the Africans the choice between freedom and continuing in slavery, most of them choose slavery. Merriman implies that Africans are not suited for freedom, though he leaves cloudy the issue of whether they can ever be elevated to freedom or are genetically doomed to a life no higher than that of beasts of burden.

Racism often functions as a displaced or surrogate class system, growing more extreme as the domestic class alignments it reflects are threatened or erode. As a rationalization for the domination of "inferior" peoples, imperialist discourse is inevitably racist; it treats class and race terminology as covertly interchangeable or at least analogous. Both a hierarchy of classes and a hierarchy of races exist; both are the results of evolution or of the laws of nature; both are simpler than but similar to species; and both are developing but are also, at any given moment, fixed, inevitable, not subject to political manipulation. Varieties of liberalism and socialism might view social class as more or less subject to political reform, and in that way the hierarchy of classes never seemed so absolute as the hierarchy of races. Further, while the "social imperialism" of Joseph Chamberlain offered itself as an alternative to socialism, the spectacle of the domination of "inferior races" abroad also served to allay anxieties about both democratization and economic decline at home.

As in South Africa, the "conquered races" of the empire were often treated as a new proletariat—a proletariat much less distinct from slaves than the working class at home. Of course, the desire for and, in many places, creation of a new, subordinate underclass contradicted the abolitionist stance that all the explorers took. Nevertheless, it influenced all relations between Victorians and Africans, appearing, for example, in the forced labor system of King Leopold's Congo which Stanley helped establish or again in so small an item as Sir Harry Johnston's design for the first postage stamp of British Central Africa (fig. 6). The Africans who flank the shield and the motto Light in Darkness hold a spade and a pickax—the implements, no doubt, to build the future *white* civilization of Africa.[33]

3

The racist views held by Burton and Baker were at least as close to the science of their day as the somewhat less negative views of the missionaries. As a member of James Hunt's Anthropological Society, Burton was a scientist of sorts. Hunt had founded his group in 1863, after breaking with the Ethnological Society on the issue of whether the Negro race formed a distinct species.[34] Hunt believed that it did; the Darwinians, in contrast, held that the races of mankind had a common origin and therefore supported ideas of the unity of human nature. But Darwinism was only relatively more advanced than Hunt's racism. The development of physical anthropology and of "ethnology" as disciplines concerned with differences between races was reinforced from the 1860s on by Darwinism and social Darwinism; these "sciences" strengthened the stereotypes voiced by explorers and missionaries. Evolutionary anthropology often suggested that Africans, if not nonhuman or a different species, were such an inferior "breed" that they might be impervious to "higher influences."

Just as concerted investigations of race and evolution were beginning, so were investigations of prehistory and of the anthropoid apes. Some

FIG. 6.—Sir Harry H. Johnston, design for first postage stamp of British Central Africa. Phot. Roland Oliver, *Sir Harry H. Johnston and the Scramble for Africa*, courtesy of the Royal Geographical Society.

of the results can be seen in Charles Darwin's *Descent of Man* (1872) and earlier in Thomas Henry Huxley's *Man's Place in Nature* (1863). Huxley's essay involves a refutation of the idea that Africans, Australians, or other primitive peoples are the "missing link" or evolutionary stage between the anthropoid apes and civilized (white) mankind. But Huxley repeatedly cites evidence that suggests the proximity between the African and the chimpanzee and gorilla, including the story of an African tribe who believe that the great apes were once their next of kin. Into the middle of his otherwise logical argument, moreover, he inserts a wholly gratuitous note on "African cannibalism in the sixteenth century," drawn from a Portuguese account and illustrated with a grisly woodcut depicting a "human butcher shop" (fig. 7).[35]

When an astute, scientific observer such as Huxley indulges in fantasies about cannibalism, something is at work on a level deeper than mere caprice. As Dorothy Hammond and Alta Jablow note, cannibalism was not an important theme in British writing about Africa before mid-century. But "in the imperial period writers were far more addicted to tales of cannibalism than . . . Africans ever were to cannibalism." Typical of the more sensational treatments of anthropophagy is Winwood Reade, who in *Savage Africa* (1863) writes that "the mob of Dahomey are *man-eaters;* they have cannibal minds; they have been accustomed to feed on murder." Reade nonetheless describes his flirtations with "cannibal" maidens, and in a capricious chapter on "The Philosophy of Cannibalism," he distinguishes between ritual cannibalism, which was practiced by some west African societies, and another (mythical) sort which is "simply an act of *gourmandise.*" "A cannibal is not necessarily ferocious. He eats his fellow-creatures, not because he hates them, but because he likes them."[36] The more that Europeans dominated Africans, the more "savage" Africans came to seem; cannibalism represented the nadir of savagery, more extreme even than slavery (which, of course, a number of "civilized" nations practiced through much of the nineteenth century).

Evolutionary thought seems almost calculated to legitimize imperialism. The theory that man evolved through distinct social stages—from savagery to barbarism to civilization—led to a self-congratulatory anthropology that actively promoted belief in the inferiority—indeed, the bestiality—of the African. In *The Origin of Civilisation* (1870), John Lubbock argues not just that contemporary "savages" represent the starting point of social evolution but that they are below that starting point. The original primitives from whom Europeans evolved contained the seeds of progress; modern savages had not progressed, according to Lubbock, and hence must be lower on the evolutionary scale than the ancestors of the Europeans. All the more reason, of course, to place them under imperial guardianship and to treat them as nothing more than potential labor.[37] The connection between theories of race and social class appears in George Romanes' *Mental Evolution in Man* (1889):

FIG. 7.—"The human butcher shop." Thomas Henry Huxley, *Man's Place in Nature*, 1863.

When we come to consider the case of savages, and through them the case of pre-historic man, we shall find that, in the great interval which lies between such grades of mental evolution and our own, we are brought far on the way towards bridging the psychological distance which separates the gorilla from the gentleman.[38]

Presumably, everyone is a link somewhere in this late Victorian version of the great chain of being: if gentlemen are at the farthest remove from our anthropoid ancestors, the working class is not so far removed, and "savages" are even closer.

In her examination of the "scientific" codification of racist dogmas, Stepan writes:

By the 1850s, the shift from the earlier ethnographic, monogenist, historical and philosophical tradition to a more conservative, anthropological, and polygenist approach . . . had advanced quite far in Britain. . . . Races were now seen as forming a natural but static chain of excellence.[39]

By the end of the century, eugenicists and social Darwinists were offering "scientific" justifications for genocide as well as for imperialism. The two were inseparable, but whereas imperialism could be lavishly praised in public, open support for the liquidation of "inferior" races was another matter. In *Social Evolution* (1894), Benjamin Kidd argued that, try as they might to be humane, the British would inevitably kill off the "weaker" races in "the struggle for existence":

The Anglo-Saxon has exterminated the less developed peoples with which he has come into competition . . . through the operation of laws not less deadly [than war] and even more certain in their result. The weaker races disappear before the stronger through the effects of mere contact . . . The Anglo-Saxon, driven by forces inherent in his own civilisation, comes to develop the natural resources of the land, and the consequences appear to be inevitable. The same history is repeating itself in South Africa. In the words [of] a leading colonist of that country, "the natives must go; or they must work as laboriously to develop the land as we are prepared to do."[40]

Similarly, in *National Life from the Standpoint of Science* (1901), the eugenicist Karl Pearson goes beyond the vision of the black African with spade or pickax performing the groundwork for white civilization in the tropics: "No strong and permanent civilization can be built upon slave labour, [and] an inferior race doing menial labour for a superior race can give no stable community." The solution? Where the abolitionists sought to liberate the slaves, Pearson's "science" seeks to eliminate them or at least push them out of the path of civilization:

We shall never have a healthy social state in South Africa until the white man replaces the dark in the fields and the mines, and the Kaffir is pushed back towards the equator. The nation organized for the struggle [of existence] must be a *homogeneous* whole, not a mixture of superior and inferior races.[41]

Darwin himself speculated about the causes of the apparently inevitable extinction of primitive races in the encounter with "higher" ones. Genocide decimated the American Indians, Tasmanians, Maoris, and Australians, but Darwin believed that they would have withered on the vine anyway— the less fit races vanishing as the more fit advanced. The Africans did not dwindle away as Europeans encroached on their territory, despite the slave trade; this seemed to some observers proof of their hardiness, their fitness. But to some this apparent fitness only showed the Africans' inferiority in a different light—they were made of coarser stuff from that of the sensitive and poetic Maoris, for example. Darwin is comparatively cautious in his speculations about race. Nevertheless, throughout *The Descent of Man* he emphasizes the distance between "savage" and "civilized" peoples, contrasting "savages" who practice infanticide to types of moral and intellectual excellence like John Howard, the eighteenth-century prison reformer, and Shakespeare. In the last paragraph, he declares that he would rather be related to a baboon than to "a savage who delights to torture his enemies, offers up bloody sacrifices without remorse, treats his wives like slaves, knows no decency, and is haunted by the grossest superstitions."[42] In general, Darwinism lent scientific status to the view that there were higher and lower races, progressive and nonprogressive ones, and that the lower races ought to be governed by—or even completely supplanted by—civilized, progressive races like the British.

There is much irony in the merger of racist and evolutionary theories in Victorian anthropology, which was, in certain respects, the first scientific anthropology. For the Victorians, the distance between primitive and civilized peoples seemed immense, perhaps unbridgeable. But through another sharp transvaluation, anthropology in the modern era has shifted from evolutionism to cultural relativism. First in the work of Franz Boas, and then more generally after World War I, the morally judgmental and racist anthropology of the Victorians gave way to a new version of "objectivity" or even of what might be called scientific primitivism.[43] What Claude Lévi-Strauss has to say in *Tristes Tropiques* about the religious attitudes of "primitives" is exemplary of the transvaluation that anthropology has undergone since its nineteenth-century inception as the study of racial differences and a form of scientific rationalization for empire. Their beliefs are not "superstitions," he declares, but rather "preferences . . . denoting a kind of wisdom [acceptance of individual and ecological limits, reverence for nature] which savage races practised spontaneously and the rejection of which, by the modern world, is the real madness."[44]

4

While the antislavery crusade inspired much poetry before 1833, Victorian poets wrote little about Africa except for patriotic verses on topics such as General Charles Gordon's last stand at Khartoum. Alfred, Lord Tennyson's "Timbuctoo" is perhaps an exception, but it was written in 1829 for a Cambridge poetry contest, and it offers a Romantic account of how the visionary city of Fable has been "darkened" by "keen Discovery" (a paradoxical application of "darken" similar to Marlow's). More typical of later Victorian attitudes is William Makepeace Thackeray's "Timbuctoo," written for the same contest that Tennyson's poem won. Thackeray produced a parody of abolitionist propaganda:

> Desolate Afric! thou art lovely yet!!
> One heart yet beats which ne'er shall thee forget.
> What though thy maidens are a blackish brown,
> Does virtue dwell in whiter breasts alone?
> Oh no, oh no, oh no, oh no, oh no!
> It shall not, must not, cannot, e'er be so.
> The day shall come when Albion's self shall feel
> Stern Afric's wrath, and writhe 'neath Afric's steel.[45]

Other far-flung parts of the world inspired the Victorian muse—Edward FitzGerald's *Rubáiyát of Omar Khayyám* and Edwin Arnold's *Light of Asia* come to mind—but Victorian imaginative discourse about Africa tended toward the vaguely discredited forms of the gothic romance and the boys' adventure story. For the most part, fiction writers imitated the explorers, producing quest romances with gothic overtones in which the heroic white penetration of the Dark Continent is the central theme. H. Rider Haggard's stories fit this pattern, and so—with ironic differences—does *Heart of Darkness*.

Explorers themselves sometimes wrote adventure novels. Baker's *Cast Up by the Sea* (1866) and Stanley's *My Kalulu: Prince, King, and Slave* (1889) are both tales addressed to boys, and both carry abolitionist themes into Africa well after the emancipation of slaves in most other parts of the world (Cuba ended slavery in 1886, Brazil in 1888). "I had in view," writes Stanley, "that I might be able to describe more vividly in such a book as this than in any other way the evils of the slave trade in Africa."[46] The story traces an Arab slaving caravan to Lake Tanganyika; when the Arabs are attacked by the blacks whom they've come to enslave, the only survivors—a few Arab boys—are enslaved instead. Later they are rescued from slavery by Prince Kalulu, who himself escaped from slavery in an earlier episode. But Kalulu and the Arab boys are once more captured by slave-trading blacks, "the Wazavila assassins and midnight robbers," whose attacks on innocent villages provide what Stanley calls "a true picture" of the horrors of the slave trade. Even the Arab slavers are morally superior to the "fiendish" Wazavila. After many scrapes, Kalulu and the Arab boys reach Zanzibar and freedom, well experienced in the horrors of both slavery and the Dark Continent. Stanley's moral is plain: the internal slave trade will cease only when European forces squelch slave-trading tribes like the Wazavila and harness the African to the wheel of—to use Buxton's phrase—"legitimate commerce."

In 1888 the great Scottish explorer of Kenya, Joseph Thomson, published an ostensibly adult novel. The protagonist of *Ulu: An African Romance* is a disgruntled Scotsman named Gilmour (partly modeled on Thomson himself), who escapes from corrupt civilization to the Kenyan highlands. Gilmour accepts as his fiancée a fourteen-year-old African girl, Ulu, whom he proceeds (inconsistently, given his rejection of civilization) to try to civilize before marrying. This African Pygmalion story seems daring for the first fifty pages—a direct assault on Victorian stereotypes of race and empire. But the hero never marries or even civilizes Ulu; instead, he realizes the terrible mistake he has made when he meets the blond, blue-eyed daughter of the local missionary. Ulu then becomes an object of patronizing, cloying concern for the white lovers. Gilmour acknowledges "the impossibility of making Ulu other than she is, an out-and-out little savage, childlike and simple, and lovable in many ways, perhaps, but utterly incapable of assimilating any of the higher thoughts and aspirations of the civilized life." While Gilmour's Pygmalion scheme collapses, the story falls into a stereotypic adventure pattern. The ferocious Masais attack and capture Ulu and the missionary's daughter. "What had [Kate] to expect from these licentious, bloodthirsty savages, the indulgence of whose brutal passions was their sole rule in life?"[47] Fortunately, the Masais have never seen anything so beautiful as Kate; they proceed to worship her as a goddess. Gilmour rescues Kate, and Ulu conveniently sacrifices herself so that the intrepid white couple, who were of course meant for each other all along, can live happily ever after. (It's tempting to correlate this wishful fantasy of love and extermination with the "scientific" rationalizations of genocide mentioned earlier: progress and fulfillment are the domain of Europeans even on an individual level. Nevertheless, Thomson was one of the more liberal defenders of Africans and African rights among the great explorers.) Thomson's story is ludicrously inconsistent, but it is also remarkable for suggesting that the European invasion of Africa might corrupt the innocent savages without civilizing them and for even broaching the possibility of intermarriage. White/black unions were not uncommon in reality: the history of the Griqua and other racially mixed peoples in South Africa testifies to the contrary. But intermarriage was unheard of in fiction.

Except for the stress on love and marriage, there is little to distinguish Thomson's adult novel from the whole subgenre of boys' adventure tales to which Stanley's and Baker's stories belong. An adolescent quality pervades most imperialist literature, as it does much fascist culture in the 1920s and 1930s. Africa was a setting where British boys could become men but also where British men could behave like boys with impunity, as do Haggard's heroes. Africa was a great testing—or teething—ground for moral growth and moral regression; the two processes were often indistinguishable. And since imperialism always entailed violence and exploitation and therefore never could bear much scrutiny, propagandists found it easier to leave it to boys to "play up, play up, and play the game" than to more mature, thoughtful types. Much imperialist discourse was thus directed at a specifically adolescent audience, the future rulers of the world. In the works of Haggard, Captain Frederick Marryat, Mayne Reid, G. A. Henty, W. H. G. Kingston, Gordon Stables, Robert Louis Stevenson, and many others through Rudyard Kipling, Britain turned youthful as it turned outward.

In *Black Ivory: A Tale of Adventure among the Slavers of East Africa* (1873), another boys' novelist, R. M. Ballantyne, emulated Livingstone in seeking to expose "the horrible traffic in human beings" (see fig. 8). "Exaggeration has easily been avoided," Ballantyne assures us, "because— as Dr. Livingstone says in regard to the slave-trade—'exaggeration is impossible.'" Ballantyne wishes both to expose the atrocities of the slave trade and to expose anti-Negro stereotypes. Ballantyne writes that his character Chief Kambira has "nothing of our *nursery* savage . . . [he] does not roar, or glare, or chatter, or devour his food in its blood."[48] This is all to the good, but Ballantyne is inconsistent. His sympathetic Africans are so mainly as melodrama victims; otherwise he portrays their customs as laughably childish. And he has only praise for British antislavery squadrons patrolling the coasts and for Britishers intruding inland in east Africa to stop the slave trade.[49]

More interesting than *Black Ivory* is Sir Harry Johnston's *History of a Slave* (1889), which takes the form of an autobiographical slave narrative. Himself an explorer and an artist (see fig. 6), Johnston attacks slavery as an extension of savagery. The atrocities which his slave narrator depicts are more grisly than anything in Ballantyne's work; most grisly of all are the slow tortures practiced by the Executioner of Zinder under the Tree of Death. But if the slave's life under various Muslim masters is violent and cruel, his life before slavery was just as bloody and even more irrational. Thus the narrator recounts his earliest memory: "When . . . the men of our town killed someone and roasted his flesh for a feast . . . the bones . . . were laid round about the base of [a] tree. The first thing I remember clearly was playing with [a] skull."[50] Johnston's exposé of the atrocities of the slave trade is preceded by an exposé of the alleged atrocities of tribal savagery—no pastoral innocence here. The solution to the slave trade entails more than persuading Muslim sheikhs to set black Africans free; it also entails abolishing tribal savagery, and the only way to do this

FIG. 8.—Frontispiece. Robert M. Ballantyne, *Black Ivory: A Tale of Adventure among the Slavers of East Africa*, 1873.

lies through imperialist annexation, the fulfillment of Britain's "civilizing mission."

Other post–Civil War fictions about Africa also attack the slave trade as part of a larger pattern of violence and savagery. In *The Congo Rovers: A Story of the Slave Squadron* (1885) by the American William Lancaster, the hero is captured by slave-trading natives and, in a chapter entitled "A Fiendish Ceremonial," narrowly escapes being sacrificially murdered. Such a work exhibits all the stereotypes about the Dark Continent that were to be exploited by another popular American writer, Edgar Rice Burroughs, in the Tarzan books. In novels not about slavery, moreover, stress still falls on the violence and irrationality of tribal customs. The publication dates of Haggard's *King Solomon's Mines* (1885) and John Buchan's *Prester John* (1910) span the period of the main imperialist "scramble for Africa," and in both novels "civilization" is juxtaposed to "savagery" in ways that call for the elimination of the latter. For Haggard and Buchan too, the Dark Continent must be made light.

But Haggard and Buchan also give new life to the Romantic figure of the noble savage—Haggard through his magnificent Zulu warriors, Umbopa and Umslopagass, and Buchan through his black antihero, John Laputa, also from Zulu country. Haggard sees clearly the destruction of Zulu society brought about by the encroachment of whites (*King Solomon's Mines* appeared six years after the Zulu War of 1879); he can also praise primitive customs, contrasting them favorably with civilized ones. He nevertheless maintains a sharp division between the savage and the civilized; his white heroes penetrate the darkness as representatives of vastly higher levels of social evolution. Like aristocrats in Renaissance pastoral, they cleave to their own kind and return to the light. Their friendship with Umbopa cannot hold them in Kukuanaland, and only one other relationship threatens to do so. The romance between Captain John Good and the beautiful Foulata is nipped in the bud when, like Ulu, she is killed near the end of the story. The narrator, Allan Quatermain, concludes:

> I am bound to say that, looking at the thing from the point of view of an oldish man of the world, I consider her removal was a fortunate occurrence, since, otherwise, complications would have been sure to ensue. The poor creature was no ordinary native girl, but a person of great, I had almost said stately, beauty, and of considerable refinement of mind. But no amount of beauty or refinement could have made an entanglement between Good and herself a desirable occurrence; for, as she herself put it, "Can the sun mate with the darkness, or the white with the black?"[51]

Buchan depicts a revolutionary conspiracy led by John Laputa, the self-proclaimed heir of Prester John. To the narrator, Davie Crawfurd, Laputa is a noble but also satanic savage; Davie finds him intensely attractive, but the attraction is charged with a deeply racist and erotic antipathy. Buchan portrays the conspiracy in terms of gothic romance, as a nightmare from which Davie struggles to awake. "You know the [kind of] nightmare when you are pursued by some awful terror," Davie says. "Last night I . . . looked into the heart of darkness, and the sight . . . terrified me."[52] But this "heart of darkness" is not within Davie's psyche; instead, it is Africa and the murderous savagery of Laputa. Haggard can entertain the thought of a free society of noble savages so long as it is distant and mythical; so can Buchan in *A Lodge in the Wilderness*. But in *Prester John*, the idea of independence for Africans is a source only of terror. Laputa must be destroyed, the nightmare dispelled.

Even at its most positive, the romance genre renders the hero's quest as a journey to an underworld, a harrowing of hell; the myth of the Dark Continent fits this pattern perfectly. Conrad dealt with these mythic dimensions in a more conscious way than other writers, producing a quest romance that foreshadows the atrocity literature of the Congo Reform Association—works such as Arthur Conan Doyle's *Crime of the Congo* and Mark Twain's *King Leopold's Soliloquy*, to name two examples by other prominent novelists.[53] By combining the romance and exposé forms, Conrad creates a brilliantly ironic structure in which the diabolic Kurtz demonstrates how the Dark Continent grew dark. For Conrad, the ultimate atrocity is not some form of tribal savagery; it is Kurtz's regression. Kurtz has become "tropenkollered" or "maddened by the tropics"; he has "gone native."[54] In one sense, going native was universal, because in Africa—or in any foreign setting—every traveler must to some extent adopt the customs of the country, eat its food, learn its language, and so on. But Kurtz does something worse—he betrays the ideals of the civilization that he is supposedly importing from Europe. Conrad does not debunk the myth of the Dark Continent: Africa is the location of his hell on earth. But at the center of that hell is Kurtz, the would-be civilizer, the embodiment of Europe's highest and noblest values, radiating darkness.

By universalizing darkness, Conrad passes judgment on imperialism. Marlow looks more favorably upon British than upon Belgian, German, or French imperialism. In the red parts of the map, at least, "one knows that some real work is done" (*HD*, p. 10). But Marlow can also say that

> the conquest of the earth, which mostly means the taking it away from those who have a different complexion or slightly flatter noses than ourselves, is not a pretty thing when you look into it too much. What redeems [conquest] is the idea only. An idea at the back of it; not a sentimental pretence but an idea; and an unselfish belief in the idea—something you can set up, and bow down before, and offer a sacrifice to . . . [*HD*, p. 7]

The modern version of idol worship, it appears, is idea worship. Conrad suggests the universality of darkness by suggesting the universality of fetishism. If the natives in their darkness set Kurtz up as an idol, the European "pilgrims" or traders worship ivory, money, power, reputation. Kurtz joins the natives in their "unspeakable rites," worshiping his own unrestrained power and lust. Marlow himself assumes the pose of an idol, sitting on ship deck with folded legs and outward palms like a Buddha. And Kurtz's Intended is perhaps the greatest fetishist of all, idolizing her image of her fiancé—a fetishism which Marlow refuses to disrupt, as he has earlier disrupted Kurtz's diabolic ceremonies. Marlow's lie leaves Kurtz's Intended shrouded in the protective darkness of her illusions, her idol worship.

Ian Watt identifies nine possible models for Kurtz—the very number suggests the commonness of going native. Stanley is among these models, and so is Charles Stokes, "the renegade missionary," who abandoned the Church Missionary Society, took a native wife, and led a wild career as a slave trader and gun runner.[55] Stokes was not particular about either his stock-in-trade or his customers: he sold guns to Germans working against the British in east Africa and also to French Catholic converts in Buganda, waging a small-scale religious war against the Protestant converts of Stokes' former colleagues. He was finally arrested and executed without trial in the Congo for selling guns to Arab slavers; his demise added to the scandal back in Britain about King Leopold's empire. Stokes' case of backsliding was no doubt extreme, but not unusual. "I have been increasingly struck," wrote Johnston in 1897, "with the rapidity with which such members of the white race as are not of the best class, can throw over the restraints of civilisation and develop into savages of unbridled lust and abominable cruelty."[56] That was another way in which "savages" and the working class sometimes appeared similar. But Kurtz is of "the best class," not a "lower" one: going native could happen to anyone. It could even happen to entire societies. In Charles Reade's novel *A Simpleton* (1873), for example, the Boers have "degenerated into white savages"; the British hero finds that Kaffir "savages" are "socially superior" to them, a typical assertion well before the Boer War of 1899–1902.[57]

Missionaries were perhaps especially susceptible to going native; they frequently expressed fears about regressing, about being converted to heathenism instead of converting the heathen. According to J. S. Moffat, a missionary had to be "deeply imbued with God's spirit in order to have strength to stand against the deadening and corrupting influence around him. . . . I am like a man looking forward to getting back to the sweet air and bright sunshine after being in a coal-mine." Another missionary, S. T. Pruen, believed that merely witnessing heathen customs could be dangerous: "Can a man touch pitch, and not be himself defiled?"[58] The Victorians found strong temptations in Africa, as their frequent references to the allegedly promiscuous sexual customs of Africans show. Burton's prurient anthropology is a notable example; also typical is the sensuousness that Haggard attributes to Foulata and Thomson to Ulu (fig. 9). Never far from their civilized surfaces, the potential for being

FIG. 9.—Henry Stanley resisting temptation. J. W. Buel, *Heroes of the Dark Continent*, 1898.

"defiled"—for "going native" or becoming "tropenkollered"—led Europeans again and again to displace their own "savage" impulses onto Africans. Just as the social class fantasies of the Victorians (*Oliver Twist*, for example) often express the fear of falling into the abyss of poverty, so the myth of the Dark Continent contains the submerged fear of falling out of the light, down the long coal chute of social and moral regression. In both cases, the fear of backsliding has a powerful sexual dimension. If, as Freud argued, civilization is based on the repression of instincts and if the demands of repression become excessive, then civilization itself is liable to break down.

Dominique Mannoni has raised the question of the extent to which Europeans "project upon . . . colonial peoples the obscurities of their own unconscious—obscurities they would rather not penetrate." In European writings about Africa, Mannoni says,

> the savage . . . is identified in the unconscious with a certain image of the instincts. . . . And civilized man is painfully divided between the desire to "correct" the "errors" of the savages and the desire to identify himself with them in his search for some lost paradise (a desire which at once casts doubt upon the merit of the very civilization he is trying to transmit to them).[59]

Kurtz is a product of this painful division. But not even Marlow sees Kurtz's going native as a step toward the recovery of a lost paradise; it is instead a fall into hell, into the abyss of his own darkness. For modern Europeans—Lévi-Strauss again comes to mind—as for the Romantics, the association of primitive life with paradise has once more become possible.[60] But for the Victorians, that association was taboo; they repressed it so much that the African landscapes they explored and exploited were painted again and again with the same tarbrush image of pandemonium. But as they penetrated the heart of darkness only to discover lust and depravity, cannibalism and devil worship, they always also discovered, as the central figure in the shadows, a Stanley, a Stokes, or a Kurtz—an astonished white face staring back.

Nothing points more uncannily to the processes of projection and displacement of guilt for the slave trade, guilt for empire, guilt for one's own savage and shadowy impulses than those moments when white man confronts white man in the depths of the jungle. The archetypal event is Stanley's discovery of Livingstone; the famous scene of "Dr. Livingstone, I presume?" suggests a narcissistic doubling, a repetition or mirroring. The solipsistic repression of whatever is nonself or alien characterizes all forms of cultural and political domination (see fig. 10). In analogous fashion, Haggard's Britishers in *King Solomon's Mines* discover a black race living among the ruins of a great white civilization. When Karl Mauch discovered the ruins of Zimbabwe in 1871, no European was

FIG. 10.—"Dr. Livingstone, I presume?" Stanley, *How I Found Livingstone*, 1872.

prepared to believe that they had been constructed by Africans. So arose the theory that they were the ruins of King Solomon's Golden Ophir—the work of a higher, fairer race—a myth which archaeologists only began to controvert in 1906; hence, "King Solomon's Mines."[61] Haggard repeats this myth in other stories. In *She,* Ayesha is a beautiful white demigoddess ruling over a brown-skinned race; and in *Allan Quatermain,* the white explorers discover a mysterious white race in the heart of darkness. So the Dark Continent turned into a mirror, on one level reflecting what the Victorians wanted to see—heroic and saintly self-images—but on another, casting the ghostly shadows of guilt and regression.

5

The myth of the Dark Continent was thus a Victorian invention. As part of a larger discourse about empire, it was shaped by political and economic pressures and also by a psychology of blaming the victim through which Europeans projected many of their own darkest impulses onto Africans. The product of the transition—or transvaluation—from abolitionism to imperialism, the myth of the Dark Continent defined slavery as the offspring of tribal savagery and portrayed white explorers and missionaries as the leaders of a Christian crusade that would vanquish the forces of darkness. The first abolitionists had placed blame for the slave trade mainly on Europeans, but, by mid-century, that blame had largely been displaced onto Africans. When the taint of slavery fused with sensational reports about cannibalism, witchcraft, and apparently shameless sexual customs, Victorian Africa emerged draped in that pall of darkness that the Victorians themselves accepted as reality.

The invasion of preindustrial, largely preliterate societies by the representatives of literate ones with industrialized communications, weapons, and transportation techniques meant a deluge of ruling discourse on one side and what appeared to be total acquiescence and silence on the other. As Frantz Fanon declares, "A man who has a language . . . possesses the world expressed and implied by that language. . . . Mastery of language affords remarkable power."[62] Victorian imperialism both created and was in part created by a growing monopoly on discourse. Unless they became virtually "mimic men," in V. S. Naipaul's phrase, Africans were stripped of articulation: the Bible might be translated into numerous African languages, but the colonizers rarely translated in the other direction, even when they learned Wolof or Zulu. African customs and beliefs were condemned as superstitions, their social organizations were despised and demolished, their land, belongings, and labor often appropriated as ruthlessly as they had been through the slave trade.

But the ethnocentric discourse of domination was not met with silence. Though it has not been easy to recover, modern historians have begun piecing together how Africans responded to their Victorian savior-invaders.[63] The wars of resistance fought by Zulu, Ashanti, Matabele, Ethiopian, Bugandan, and Sudanese peoples have offered perhaps the best evidence. The writings of literate nineteenth-century Africans like the Liberian Edward Blyden, pioneer of the négritude movement, have also been important. Still other responses can be found in the modern independence movements and the writings of nationalists like Fanon, Kwame Nkrumah, Jomo Kenyatta, and Steve Biko. But the legacy of the myth of the Dark Continent and, more generally, of imperialism has been massive and impossible to evade, as stereotypic treatments of Africa by today's mass media continue to demonstrate. The work of liberation from racism and the politics of domination is far from over. Discourse—that most subtle yet also inescapable form of power—in its imperial guise persists, for example, in the most recent assumptions about the antithesis between "primitive" or "backward" and "civilized" or "advanced" societies, about the cultural and historical differences between Afro-Americans and white Americans, and about the legitimacy of the white apartheid regime in South Africa. In this regard, what Nkrumah said in 1965 about the special impact of the American mass media on the African situation is still relevant:

> The cinema stories of fabulous Hollywood are loaded. One has only to listen to the cheers of an African audience as Hollywood's heroes slaughter red Indians or Asiatics to understand the effectiveness of this weapon. For, in the developing continents, where the colonialist heritage has left a vast majority still illiterate, even the smallest child gets the message. . . . And along with murder and the Wild West goes an incessant barrage of anti-socialist propaganda, in which the trade union man, the revolutionary, or the man of dark skin is generally cast as the villain, while the policeman, the gum-shoe, the Federal agent—in a word, the CIA-type spy—is ever the hero. Here, truly, is the ideological under-belly of those political murders which so often use local people as their instruments.[64]

The spirit of Tarzan and Tabu Dick lives on in Western culture, though often reduced to the level of sophisticated buffoonery, as in Saul Bellow's *Henderson, the Rain King*. In criticizing recent American and European failures to imagine Africa without prejudice, Chinua Achebe notes the continuing "desire—one might indeed say the need—in Western psychology to set Africa up as a foil to Europe, a place of negations at once remote and vaguely familiar in comparison with which Europe's own state of spiritual grace will be manifest." As Achebe points out, whether they come from Victorian or modern England, the America of Grover Cleveland or that of Ronald Reagan, "travellers with closed minds can tell us little except about themselves."[65]

1. Joseph Conrad, *Heart of Darkness* (New York, 1963), p. 8; all further references to this work, abbreviated *HD*, will be included in the text. Philip D. Curtin writes that "the image of 'darkest Africa,' either as an expression of geographical ignorance, or as one of cultural arrogance, was a nineteenth-century invention" (*The Image of Africa: British Ideas and Action, 1780–1850* [Madison, Wis., 1964], p. 9). See also Dorothy Hammond and Alta Jablow, *The Africa That Never Was: Four Centuries of British Writing about Africa* (New York, 1970), esp. pp. 49–113.

2. Edward W. Said, "Secular Criticism," *The World, the Text, and the Critic* (Cambridge, Mass., 1983), p. 9, and "The World, the Text, and the Critic," *The World, the Text, and the Critic*, p. 53; Michel Foucault, "Nietzsche, Genealogy, History," *Language, Counter-Memory, Practice: Selected Essays and Interviews*, ed. Donald F. Bouchard, trans. Bouchard and Sherry Simon (Ithaca, N.Y., 1977), p. 148. See also Said, *Orientalism* (New York, 1978).

3. See Eric Williams, *Capitalism and Slavery* (Chapel Hill, N.C., 1944); Williams' theory has been often criticized but not his general thesis of some sort of correlation between abolitionism and industrialization. See Roger T. Anstey, "Capitalism and Slavery: A Critique," *Economic History Review* 21 (Aug. 1968): 307–20; cf. David Brion Davis, *The Problem of Slavery in the Age of Revolution, 1770–1823* (Ithaca, N.Y., 1975), pp. 346–52. Other accounts include Michael Craton, *Sinews of Empire: A Short History of British Slavery* (Garden City, N.Y., 1974), and Howard Temperley, *British Antislavery, 1833–1870* (London, 1972).

4. See Ralph A. Austen and Woodruff D. Smith, "Images of Africa and British Slave-Trade Abolition: The Transition to an Imperialist Ideology, 1787–1807," *African Historical Studies* 2, no. 1 (1969): 69–83. The classic work on motives for expansion is Ronald Robinson, John Gallagher, and Alice Denney, *Africa and the Victorians: The Climax of Imperialism in the Dark Continent* (New York, 1961).

5. Nancy Stepan, *The Idea of Race in Science: Great Britain, 1800–1960* (Hamden, Conn., 1982), p. 1. See also Christine Bolt, *Victorian Attitudes to Race* (Toronto, 1971).

6. William Blake, "The Little Black Boy," *The Poetry and Prose of William Blake*, ed. David V. Erdman (Garden City, N.Y., 1970), p. 9.

7. Robert Southey, "To Horror," *Poetical Works*, 10 vols. (London, 1837–38), 2:129.

8. See Eva Beatrice Dykes, *The Negro in English Romantic Thought* (Washington, D.C., 1942) and Wylie Sypher, *Guinea's Captive Kings: British Anti-Slavery Literature of the Eighteenth Century* (Chapel Hill, N.C., 1942).

9. Southey, "Poems Concerning the Slave Trade," *Poetical Works*, 2:57.

10. James Grahame, "Africa Delivered; or, the Slave Trade Abolished," in James Montgomery, James Grahame, and E. Benger, *Poems on the Abolition of the Slave Trade* (1809; Freeport, N.Y., 1971), p. 58.

11. See Katherine George, "The Civilized West Looks at Primitive Africa, 1400–1800," *Isis* 49 (Mar. 1958): 62–72. Winthrop D. Jordan reaches a similar conclusion; see *White over Black: American Attitudes toward the Negro, 1550–1812* (Chapel Hill, N.C., 1968), pp. 269–311. See also Curtin, *The Image of Africa*, p. 9.

12. See Thomas Edward Bowdich, *Mission from Cape Coast Castle to Ashantee* (1819; London, 1966). Curtin calls Bowdich one of a group of "enlightened travellers" between 1795 and the 1820s and calls his book "a glowing description of Ashanti society" (*The Image of Africa*, pp. 211, 169).

13. Curtin, *The Image of Africa*, p. 298. The Niger Expedition was "no mere exploring expedition [but] the first step toward a general 'forward policy' in West Africa, reversing the established doctrine of minimum commitments" (p. 298).

14. Thomas Fowell Buxton, *The African Slave Trade and Its Remedy* (1840; London, 1967), p. 342; all further references to this work, abbreviated *A*, will be included in the text. See also John Gallagher, "Fowell Buxton and the New African Policy, 1838–1842," *Cambridge Historical Journal* 10, no. 1 (1950): 36–58.

15. Charles Dickens, "The Niger Expedition," *Works*, 20 vols. (New York, 1903), 18:64.

16. Dickens, quoted in Donald H. Simpson, "Charles Dickens and the Empire," *Library Notes of the Royal Commonwealth Society*, n.s. 162 (June 1970): 15; Dickens, "The Niger

Expedition," p. 63. See also Dickens, "The Noble Savage," *Household Words,* 11 June 1853, pp. 337–39.

17. Mrs. R. Lee [Sarah Wallis], *The African Wanderers: or, The Adventures of Carlos and Antonio* (London, 1847), pp. 230, 126; and see Curtin, *The Image of Africa,* p. 328.

18. The best general account is Alan Moorehead, *The White Nile,* rev. ed. (New York, 1971); Moorehead likens the great Victorian explorers to astronauts. See also Robert I. Rotberg, ed., *Africa and Its Explorers: Motives, Methods, and Impact* (Cambridge, Mass., 1970).

19. William Somerset Maugham, *The Explorer* (New York, 1909), pp. 45, 175–76. See also Joseph Conrad, "Geography and Some Explorers," *Last Essays* (Freeport, N.Y., 1970), p. 14.

20. Dickens, quoted in Simpson, "Charles Dickens and Empire," p. 15. For Livingstone, see Tim Jeal, *Livingstone* (New York, 1973).

21. M. E. Chamberlain, *The Scramble for Africa,* Seminar Studies in History (London, 1974), p. 28.

22. Foucault, "The Discourse on Language," *The Archaeology of Knowledge,* trans. A. M. Sheridan Smith (New York, 1972), p. 229.

23. David Livingstone, quoted in Jeal, *Livingstone,* pp. 146, 124; Jeal, *Livingstone,* p. 4.

24. See Curtin and Paul Bohanan, *Africa and Africans* (Garden City, N.Y., 1971), p. 8.

25. May Crawford, *By the Equator's Snowy Peak: A Record of Medical Missionary Work and Travel in British East Africa* (London, 1913), pp. 29, 56. I am indebted to Carolyn Redouty for calling my attention to these citations.

26. On missionary attitudes, see H. A. C. Cairns, *Prelude to Imperialism: British Reactions to Central African Society, 1840–1890* (London, 1965), and Geoffrey Moorhouse, *The Missionaries* (Philadelphia, 1973).

27. Anthony Hope Hawkins [Anthony Hope], *The God in the Car* (1895; New York, 1896), p. 19.

28. Richard F. Burton, *The Lake Regions of Central Africa,* 2 vols. (1861; New York, 1961), 2:326.

29. Ibid., 2:347–48.

30. Burton, *Two Trips to Gorilla Land and the Cataracts of the Congo,* 2 vols. (1876; New York, 1967), 2:311.

31. Samuel White Baker, *The Albert N'yanza, Great Basin of the Nile, and Exploration of the Nile Sources,* 2 vols. (1866; London, 1962), 1:211.

32. Hugh Stowell Scott [Henry S. Merriman], *With Edged Tools* (1894; London, 1909), pp. 321–22.

33. The stamp design is reproduced in Roland Oliver, *Sir Harry Johnston and the Scramble for Africa* (London, 1957). On racism and class, see Robert Ross, ed., *Racism and Colonialism: Essays on Ideology and Social Structure* (The Hague, 1982); Frantz Fanon, *The Wretched of the Earth,* trans. Constance Farrington (New York, 1963); and Douglas A. Lorimer, *Colour, Class, and the Victorians: A Study of English Attitudes toward the Negro in the Mid-Nineteenth Century* (Leicester, 1978).

34. See Ronald Rainger, "Race, Politics, and Science: The Anthropological Society of London in the 1860s," *Victorian Studies* 22 (Autumn 1978): 51–70.

35. Thomas Henry Huxley, *Man's Place in Nature* (Ann Arbor, Mich., 1959), pp. 58, 69–70; Huxley acknowledges that the "human butcher shop" is "irrelevant" to his argument. Stepan notes that in the nineteenth century, "textbook after textbook compared the Negro to the ape" (*The Idea of Race in Science,* p. 18).

36. Hammond and Jablow, *The Africa That Never Was,* p. 94; Winwood Reade, *Savage Africa; Being the Narrative of a Tour in Equatorial, Southwestern, and Northwestern Africa* (New York, 1864), pp. 54, 136.

37. See Sir John Lubbock, *The Origin of Civilisation and the Primitive Condition of Man: Mental and Social Condition of Savages* (1870; London, 1912), pp. 1–2.

38. George John Romanes, *Mental Evolution in Man: Origin of Human Faculty* (New York, 1889), p. 439.

39. Stepan, *The Idea of Race in Science,* pp. 45, 46.

40. Benjamin Kidd, *Social Evolution* (New York, 1894), p. 46.

41. Karl Pearson, *National Life from the Standpoint of Science* (London, 1901), pp. 47–48.

42. Charles Darwin, *The Descent of Man and Selection in Relation to Sex,* 2d ed. (New York, 1874), p. 613; and see esp. chap. 7, "On the Races of Man," pp. 162–202. On the question of racial extinction, see also Charles Wentworth Dilke, *Greater Britain: A Record of Travel in English-Speaking Countries during 1866 and 1867* (New York, 1869), pp. 90–100, 221, 250, and 273.

43. See George Stocking, Jr.: "Once the 'one grand scheme' of evolutionism was rejected, the multiplicity of *cultures* which took the place of the cultural *stages* of savagery, barbarism, and civilization were no more easily brought within one standard of evaluation than they were within one system of explanation" (*Race, Culture, and Evolution: Essays in the History of Anthropology* [New York, 1968], p. 229).

44. Claude Lévi-Strauss, *Tristes Tropiques,* trans. John and Doreen Weightman (New York, 1974), p. 123.

45. William Makepeace Thackeray, "Timbuctoo," *Works,* Oxford ed., 17 vols. (London, 1908), 1:2.

46. Henry M. Stanley, *My Kalulu: Prince, King, and Slave* (London, 1889), p. viii.

47. Joseph Thomson and E. Harriet-Smith, *Ulu: An African Romance,* 3 vols. (London, 1888), 2:18–19, 65–66.

48. R. M. Ballantyne, *Black Ivory: A Tale of Adventure among the Slavers of East Africa* (1873; Chicago, 1969), pp. iv, iii, 169.

49. In Ballantyne's best-seller of 1858, one of the three shipwrecked British boys says: "We've got an island all to ourselves. We'll take possession of it in the name of the King; we'll go and enter the service of its black inhabitants. Of course we'll rise, naturally, to the top of affairs. White men always do in savage countries" (*The Coral Island* [London, n.d.], p. 22). Ballantyne expresses the sentiment of total racial and cultural superiority that pervades boys' fiction about "savage countries" even when, as in *Black Ivory,* the target is the slave trade.

50. Sir Harry H. Johnston, *The History of a Slave* (London, 1889), p. 6.

51. H. Rider Haggard, *King Solomon's Mines* (Harmondsworth, 1965), p. 241.

52. John Buchan, *Prester John* (New York, 1910), pp. 211, 148.

53. See S. J. Cookey, *Britain and the Congo Question, 1885–1913* (London, 1968); see also my *"Heart of Darkness:* Anti-Imperialism, Racism, or Impressionism?" *Criticism* (forthcoming).

54. "Tropenkollered" was the term used by the Dutch naval officer Captain Otto Lütken, quoted in Ian Watt, *Conrad in the Nineteenth Century* (Berkeley and Los Angeles, 1979), p. 145.

55. See Watt, *Conrad in the Nineteenth Century,* pp. 141–46. On Stokes, see also Moorhouse, *The Missionaries,* p. 196.

56. Johnston, *British Central Africa: An Attempt to Give Some Account of a Portion of the Territories under British Influence North of the Zambezi,* 3d ed. (London, 1906), p. 68.

57. Charles Reade, *A Simpleton: A Story of the Day* (London, 1873), pp. 250–51.

58. J. S. Moffat and S. T. Pruen, quoted in Cairns, *Prelude to Imperialism,* p. 68.

59. [Dominique] O. Mannoni, *Prospero and Caliban: The Psychology of Colonization,* trans. Pamela Powesland (London, 1956), pp. 19, 21.

60. See Lévi-Strauss, *Tristes Tropiques;* see also Stanley Diamond, *In Search of the Primitive* (New Brunswick, N.J., 1974) and Eric R. Wolf, *Europe and the People without History* (Berkeley and Los Angeles, 1982).

61. See Karl Peters, *King Solomon's Golden Ophir: A Research into the Most Ancient Gold Production in History* (1899; New York, 1969); this work is one example of the speculation about the Zimbabwe ruins that underlies Haggard's stories. The first scientific work demonstrating that the ruins had been built by Africans was David Randall-MacIver, *Mediaeval*

Rhodesia (London, 1906). As late as the 1960s, works published in Rhodesia and South Africa were still insisting that the original builders were non-African.

62. Frantz Fanon, *Black Skin, White Masks,* trans. Charles Lam Markmann (New York, 1967), p. 18.

63. For nineteenth-century African responses to the European invasion, see Curtin, ed., *Africa and the West: Intellectual Responses to European Culture* (Madison, Wis., 1972); Robert I. Rotberg and Ali A. Mazrui, eds., *Protest and Power in Black Africa* (New York, 1970); and Terence O. Ranger, ed., *Aspects of Central African History* (Evanston, Ill., 1968).

64. Kwame Nkrumah, *Neo-Colonialism: The Last Stage of Imperialism* (London, 1965), p. 246.

65. Chinua Achebe, "An Image of Africa," *Research in African Literatures* 9 (Spring 1978): 2, 12. See also Ezekiel Mphahlele, *The African Image* (New York, 1962).

Black Bodies, White Bodies: Toward an Iconography of Female Sexuality in Late Nineteenth-Century Art, Medicine, and Literature

Sander L. Gilman

How do we organize our perceptions of the world? Recent discussions of this age-old question have centered around the function of visual conventions as the primary means by which we perceive and transmit our understanding of the world about us.[1] Nowhere are these conventions more evident than in artistic representations, which consist more or less exclusively of icons. Rather than presenting the world, icons represent it. Even with a modest nod to supposedly mimetic portrayals it is apparent that, when individuals are shown within a work of art (no matter how broadly defined), the ideologically charged iconographic nature of the representation dominates. And it dominates in a very specific manner, for the representation of individuals implies the creation of some greater class or classes to which the individual is seen to belong. These classes in turn are characterized by the use of a model which synthesizes our perception of the uniformity of the groups into a convincingly homogeneous image. The resulting stereotypes may be overt, as in the case of caricatures, or covert, as in eighteenth-century portraiture. But they serve to focus the viewer's attention on the relationship between the portrayed individual and the general qualities ascribed to the class.

Specific individual realities are thus given mythic extension through association with the qualities of a class. These realities manifest as icons representing perceived attributes of the class into which the individual has been placed. The myths associated with the class, the myth of difference from the rest of humanity, is thus, to an extent, composed of fragments of the real world, perceived through the ideological bias of the observer.

These myths are often so powerful, and the associations of their conventions so overpowering, that they are able to move from class to class without substantial alteration. In linking otherwise marginally or totally unrelated classes of individuals, the use of these conventions reveals perceptual patterns which themselves illuminate the inherent ideology at work.

While the discussion of the function of conventions has helped reveal the essential iconographic nature of all visual representation, it has mainly been limited to a specific sphere—aesthetics. And although the definition of the aesthetic has expanded greatly in the past decade to include every-thing from decoration to advertising, it continues to dominate discussions of visual conventions. Patterns of conventions are established within the world of art or between that world and parallel ones, such as the world of literature, but they go no farther. We maintain a special sanctity about the aesthetic object which we deny to the conventions of representation in other areas.

This essay is an attempt to plumb the conventions (and thus the ideologies) which exist at a specific historical moment in both the aesthetic and scientific spheres. I will assume the existence of a web of conventions within the world of the aesthetic—conventions which have elsewhere been admirably illustrated—but will depart from the norm by examining the synchronic existence of another series of conventions, those of medicine. I do not mean in any way to accord special status to medical conventions. Indeed, the world is full of overlapping and intertwined systems of con-ventions, of which the medical and the aesthetic are but two. Medicine offers an especially interesting source of conventions since we do tend to give medical conventions special "scientific" status as opposed to the "subjective" status of the aesthetic conventions. But medical icons are no more "real" than "aesthetic" ones. Like aesthetic icons, medical icons may (or may not) be rooted in some observed reality. Like them, they are iconographic in that they represent these realities in a manner determined by the historical position of the observers, their relationship to their own time, and to the history of the conventions which they employ. Medicine uses its categories to structure an image of the diversity of mankind; it is as much at the mercy of the needs of any age to comprehend this infinite diversity as any other system which organizes our perception of the world. The power of medicine, at least in the nineteenth century,

Sander L. Gilman is professor of Humane Studies in the Depart-ments of German Literature and Near Eastern Studies and professor of Psychiatry (History) in the Cornell Medical College, Cornell University. He is the author or editor of numerous studies of European cultural history with a focus on the history of stereotypes. In addition, he has coedited *Degeneration* (1985) with J. E. Chamberlin. His most recent publication is *Jewish Self-Hatred*.

lies in the rise of the status of science. The conventions of medicine infiltrate other seemingly closed iconographic systems precisely because of this status. In examining the conventions of medicine employed in other areas, we must not forget this power.

One excellent example of the conventions of human diversity captured in the iconography of the nineteenth century is the linkage of two seemingly unrelated female images—the icon of the Hottentot female and the icon of the prostitute. In the course of the nineteenth century, the female Hottentot comes to represent the black female *in nuce,* and the prostitute to represent the sexualized woman. Both of these categories represent the creation of classes which correspondingly represent very specific qualities. While the number of terms describing the various categories of the prostitute expanded substantially during the nineteenth century, all were used to label the sexualized woman. Likewise, while many groups of African blacks were known to Europeans in the nineteenth century, the Hottentot remained representative of the essence of the black, especially the black female. Both concepts fulfilled an iconographic function in the perception and the representation of the world. How these two concepts were associated provides a case study for the investigation of patterns of conventions, without any limitation on the "value" of one pattern over another.

Let us begin with one of the classic works of nineteenth-century art, a work which records the idea of both the sexualized woman and the black woman. Edouard Manet's *Olympia*, painted in 1862–63 and first exhibited in the Salon of 1865, assumes a key position in documenting the merger of these two images (fig. 1). The conventional wisdom concerning Manet's painting states that the model, Victorine Meurend, is "obviously naked rather than conventionally nude,"[2] and that her pose is heavily indebted to classical models such as Titian's *Venus of Urbino* (1538), Francisco Goya's *Naked Maja* (1800), and Eugène Delacroix's *Odalisque* (1847), as well as other works by Manet's contemporaries, such as Gustave Courbet.[3] George Needham has shown quite convincingly that Manet was also using a convention of early erotic photography in having the central figure directly confront the observer.[4] The black female attendant, based on a black model called Laura, has been seen as a reflex of both the classic black servant figure present in the visual arts of the eighteenth century as well as a representation of Baudelaire's *Vénus noire*.[5] Let us juxtapose the *Olympia,* with all its aesthetic and artistic analogies and parallels, to a work by Manet which Georges Bataille, among others, has seen as a modern "genre scene"—the *Nana* of 1877 (fig. 2).[6] Unlike Olympia, Nana is modern, a creature of present-day Paris, according to a contemporary.[7] But like Olympia, Nana was perceived as a sexualized female and is so represented. Yet in moving from a work with an evident aesthetic provenance, as understood by Manet's contemporaries, to one which was influenced by the former and yet was seen by its contemporaries

FIG. 1.—Edouard Manet, *Olympia*, 1863. Musée de l'Impressionisme, Paris. Phot. Museum.

FIG. 2.—Manet, *Nana*, 1877. Kunsthalle, Hamburg. Phot. Museum.

as modern, certain major shifts in the iconography of the sexualized woman take place, not the least of which is the apparènt disappearance of the black female.

The figure of the black servant in European art is ubiquitous. Richard Strauss knew this when he had Hugo von Hofmannsthal conclude their conscious evocation of the eighteenth century, *Der Rosenkavalier* (1911), with the mute return of the little black servant to reclaim the Marschallin's forgotten gloves.[8] But Hofmannsthal was also aware that one of the black servant's central functions in the visual arts of the eighteenth and nineteenth centuries was to sexualize the society in which he or she is found. The forgotten gloves, for instance, mark the end of the relationship between Octavian, the Knight of the Rose, and the Marschallin: the illicit nature of their sexual relationship, which opens the opera, is thereby linked to the appearance of the figure of the black servant, which closes the opera. When one turns to the narrative art of the eighteenth century—for example, to William Hogarth's two great cycles, *A Rake's Progress* (1733–34) and *A Harlot's Progress* (1731)—it is not very surprising that, as in the Strauss opera some two centuries later, the figures of the black servants mark the presence of illicit sexual activity. Furthermore, as in Hofmannsthal's libretto, they appear in the opposite sex to the central figure. In the second plate of *A Harlot's Progress*, we see Moll Hackabout as the mistress of a Jewish merchant, the first stage of her decline as a sexualized female; also present is a young, black male servant (fig. 3). In the third stage of Tom Rakewell's collapse, we find him in a notorious brothel, the Rose Tavern in Covent Garden.[9] The entire picture is full of references to illicit sexual activity, all portrayed negatively; present as well is the figure of a young female black servant.

The association of the black with concupiscence reaches back into the Middle Ages. The twelfth-century Jewish traveler Benjamin of Tudela wrote that

> at Seba on the river Pishon . . . is a people . . . who, like animals, eat of the herbs that grow on the banks of the Nile and in the fields. They go about naked and have not the intelligence of ordinary men. They cohabit with their sisters and anyone they can find. . . . And these are the Black slaves, the sons of Ham.[10]

By the eighteenth century, the sexuality of the black, both male and female, becomes an icon for deviant sexuality in general; as we have seen, the black figure appears almost always paired with a white figure of the opposite sex. By the nineteenth century, as in the *Olympia,* or more crudely in one of a series of Viennese erotic prints entitled "The Servant" (fig. 4), the central female figure is associated with a black female in such a way as to imply their sexual similarity. The association of figures of the same sex stresses the special status of female sexuality. In "The Servant"

FIG. 3.—William Hogarth, *A Harlot's Progress*, pl. 2, engraving, 1731.

FIG. 4.—Franz von Bayros, "The Servant," ca. 1890.

the overt sexuality of the black child indicates the covert sexuality of the white woman, a sexuality quite manifest in the other plates in the series. The relationship between the sexuality of the black woman and that of the sexualized white woman enters a new dimension when contemporary scientific discourse concerning the nature of black female sexuality is examined.

Buffon commented on the lascivious, apelike sexual appetite of the black, introducing a commonplace of early travel literature into a "scientific" context.[11] He stated that this animallike sexual appetite went so far as to lead black women to copulate with apes. The black female thus comes to serve as an icon for black sexuality in general. Buffon's view was based on a confusion of two applications of the great chain of being to the nature of the black. Such a scale was employed to indicate the innate difference between the races: in this view of mankind, the black occupied the antithetical position to the white on the scale of humanity. This polygenetic view was applied to all aspects of mankind, including sexuality and beauty. The antithesis of European sexual mores and beauty is embodied in the black, and the essential black, the lowest rung on the great chain of being, is the Hottentot. The physical appearance of the Hottentot is, indeed, the central nineteenth-century icon for sexual difference between the European and the black—a perceived difference in sexual physiology which puzzled even early monogenetic theoreticians such as Johann Friedrich Blumenbach.

Such labeling of the black female as more primitive, and therefore more sexually intensive, by writers like the Abbé Raynal would have been dismissed as unscientific by the radical empiricists of late eighteenth- and early nineteenth-century Europe.[12] To meet their scientific standards, a paradigm was needed which would technically place both the sexuality and the beauty of the black in an antithetical position to that of the white. This paradigm would have to be rooted in some type of unique and observable physical difference; they found that difference in the distinction they drew between the pathological and the normal in the medical model. William Bynum has contended that nineteenth-century biology constantly needed to deal with the polygenetic argument. We see the validity of his contention demonstrated here, for the medical model assumes the polygenetic difference between the races.[13]

It was in the work of J. J. Virey that this alteration of the mode of discourse—though not of the underlying ideology concerning the black female—took place. He was the author of the study of race standard in the early nineteenth century and also contributed a major essay (the only one on a specific racial group) to the widely cited *Dictionnaire des sciences médicales* [*Dictionary of medical sciences*] (1819).[14] In this essay, Virey summarized his (and his contemporaries') views on the sexual nature of black females in terms of acceptable medical discourse. According to him, their "voluptuousness" is "developed to a degree of lascivity unknown in our climate, for their sexual organs are much more developed than those of whites." Elsewhere, Virey cites the Hottentot woman as the epitome of this sexual lasciviousness and stresses the relationship between her physiology and her physiognomy (her "hideous form" and her "horribly flattened nose"). His central proof is a discussion of the unique structure of the Hottentot female's sexual parts, the description of which he takes from the anatomical studies published by his contemporary, Georges Cuvier.[15] According to Cuvier, the black female looks different. Her physiognomy, her skin color, the form of her genitalia label her as inherently different. In the nineteenth century, the black female was widely perceived as possessing not only a "primitive" sexual appetite but also the external signs of this temperament—"primitive" genitalia. Eighteenth-century travelers to southern Africa, such as François Le Vaillant and John Barrow, had described the so-called Hottentot apron, a hypertrophy of the labia and nymphae caused by the manipulation of the genitalia and serving as a sign of beauty among certain tribes, including the Hottentots and Bushmen as well as tribes in Basutoland and Dahomey.[16]

The exhibition in 1810 of Saartjie Baartman, also called Sarah Bartmann or Saat-Jee and known as the "Hottentot Venus," caused a public scandal in a London inflamed by the issue of the abolition of slavery, since she was exhibited "to the public in a manner offensive to decency. She . . . does exhibit all the shape and frame of her body as if naked" (fig. 5). The state's objection was as much to her lewdness as to her status as an indentured black. In France her presentation was similar. Sarah Bartmann was not the only African to be so displayed: in 1829 a nude Hottentot woman, also called "the Hottentot Venus," was the prize attraction at a ball given by the Duchess Du Barry in Paris. A contemporary print emphasized her physical difference from the observers portrayed (fig. 6).[17] After more than five years of exhibition in Europe, Sarah Bartmann died in Paris in 1815 at the age of twenty-five. An autopsy was performed on her which was first written up by Henri de Blainville in 1816 and then, in its most famous version, by Cuvier in 1817.[18] Reprinted at least twice during the next decade, Cuvier's description reflected de Blainville's two intentions: the comparison of a female of the "lowest" human species with the highest ape (the orangutan) and the description of the anomalies of the Hottentot's "organ of generation." It is important to note that Sarah Bartmann was exhibited not to show her genitalia but rather to present another anomaly which the European audience (and pathologists such as de Blainville and Cuvier) found riveting. This was the steatopygia, or protruding buttocks, the other physical characteristic of the Hottentot female which captured the eye of early European travelers. Thus the figure of Sarah Bartmann was reduced to her sexual parts. The audience which had paid to see her buttocks and had fantasized about the uniqueness of her genitalia when she was alive could, after her death and dissection, examine both, for Cuvier presented to "the Academy the

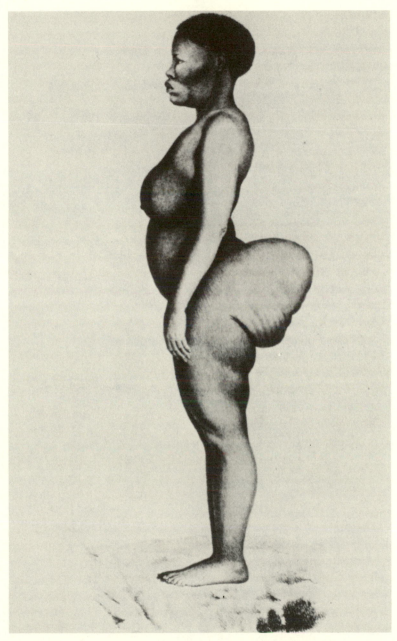

Fig. 5.—"The Hottentot Venus." Georges Cuvier, "Extraits d'observations faites sur le cadavre d'une femme connue à Paris et à Londres sous le nom de Vénus Hottentote," 1817.

FIG. 6.—"The Ball of the Duchess Du Barry," popular engraving, 1829.

genital organs of this woman prepared in a way so as to allow one to see the nature of the labia."[19]

Sarah Bartmann's sexual parts, her genitalia and her buttocks, serve as the central image for the black female throughout the nineteenth century. And the model of de Blainville's and Cuvier's descriptions, which center on the detailed presentation of the sexual parts of the black, dominates all medical description of the black during the nineteenth century. To an extent, this reflects the general nineteenth-century understanding of female sexuality as pathological: the female genitalia were of interest partly as examples of the various pathologies which could befall them but also because the female genitalia came to define the female for the nineteenth century. When a specimen was to be preserved for an anatomical museum, more often than not the specimen was seen as a pathological summary of the entire individual. Thus, the skeleton of a giant or a dwarf represented "giantism" or "dwarfism"; the head of a criminal represented the act of execution which labeled him "criminal."[20] Sarah Bartmann's genitalia and buttocks summarized her essence for the nineteenth-century observer, or, indeed, for the twentieth-century one, as they are still on display at the Musée de l'homme in Paris. Thus when one turns to the autopsies of Hottentot females in the nineteenth century, their description centers about the sexual parts. De Blainville (1816) and Cuvier (1817) set the tone, which is followed by A. W. Otto in 1824, Johannes Müller in 1834, William H. Flower and James Murie in 1867, and Luschka, Koch, and Görtz in 1869 (fig. 7).[21] These presentations of Hottentot or Bushman women all focus on the presentation of the genitalia and buttocks. Flower, the editor of the *Journal of Anatomy and Physiology*, included his dissection study in the opening volume of that famed journal. His ideological intent was clear. He wished to provide data "relating to the unity or plurality of mankind." His description begins with a detailed presentation of the form and size of the buttocks and concludes with his portrayal of the "remarkable development of the labia minoria, or nymphae, which is so general a characteristic of the Hottentot and Bushman race." These were "sufficiently well marked to distinguish these parts at once from those of any of the ordinary varieties of the human species." The polygenetic argument is the ideological basis for all the dissections of these women. If their sexual parts could be shown to be inherently different, this would be a sufficient sign that the blacks were a separate (and, needless to say, lower) race, as different from the European as the proverbial orangutan. Similar arguments had been made about the nature of all blacks' (and not just Hottentots') genitalia, but almost always concerning the female. Edward Turnipseed of South Carolina argued in 1868 that the hymen in black women "is not at the entrance to the vagina, as in the white woman, but from one-and-a-half to two inches from its entrance in the interior." From this he concluded that "this may be one of the anatomical marks of the non-unity of the races."[22] His views were

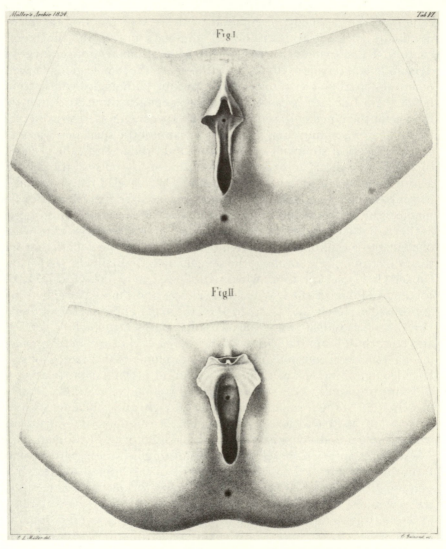

FIG. 7.—The "Hottentot Apron." Johannes Müller, "Ueber die äusseren Geschlechtstheile der Buschmänninnen," figs. 1 and 2, 1834.

seconded in 1877 by C. H. Fort, who presented another six cases of this seeming anomaly.[23] In comparison, when one turns to the description of the autopsies of black males from approximately the same period, the absence of any discussion of the male genitalia whatsoever is striking. For example, William Turner, in his three dissections of male blacks in 1878, 1879, and 1896, makes no mention at all of the genitalia.[24] The uniqueness of the genitalia and buttocks of the black is thus associated primarily with the female and is taken to be a sign solely of an anomalous *female* sexuality.

By mid-century the image of the genitalia of the Hottentot had assumed a certain set of implications. The central view is that these anomalies are inherent, biological variations rather than adaptions. In Theodor Billroth's standard handbook of gynecology, a detailed presentation of the "Hottentot apron" is part of the discussion of errors in development of the female genitalia (*Entwicklungsfehler*). By 1877 it was a commonplace that the Hottentot's anomalous sexual form was similar to other errors in the development of the labia. The author of this section links this malformation with the overdevelopment of the clitoris, which he sees as leading to those "excesses" which "are called 'lesbian love.'" The concupiscence of the black is thus associated also with the sexuality of the lesbian.[25] In addition, the idea of a congenital error incorporates the disease model applied to the deformation of the labia in the Hottentot, for the model of degeneracy presumes some acquired pathology in one generation which is the direct cause of the stigmata of degeneracy in the next. Surely the best example for this is the concept of congenital syphilis as captured in the popular consciousness by Henrik Ibsen's drama of biological decay, *Ghosts*. Thus Billroth's "congenital failure" is presupposed to have some direct and explicable etiology as well as a specific manifestation. While this text is silent as to the etiology, we can see the link established between the ill, the bestial, and the freak (pathology, biology, and medicine) in this view of the Hottentot's genitalia.

At this point, an aside might help explain both the association of the genitalia, a primary sexual characteristic, and the buttocks, a secondary sexual characteristic, in their role as the semantic signs of "primitive" sexual appetite and activity. Havelock Ellis, in volume 4 of his *Studies in the Psychology of Sex* (1905), provided a detailed example of the great chain of being as applied to the perception of the sexualized Other. Ellis believed that there is an absolute scale of beauty which is totally objective and which ranges from the European to the black. Thus men of the lower races, according to Ellis, admire European women more than their own, and women of lower races attempt to whiten themselves with face powder. Ellis then proceeded to list the secondary sexual characteristics which comprise this ideal of beauty, rejecting the "naked sexual organ[s]" as not "aesthetically beautiful" since it is "fundamentally necessary" that they "retain their primitive characteristics." Only people "in a low state of culture" perceive the "naked sexual organs as objects of attraction."[26] The list of secondary sexual characteristics which Ellis then gives as the signs of a cultured (that is, not primitive) perception of the body—the vocabulary of aesthetically pleasing signs—begins with the buttocks. This is, of course, a nineteenth-century fascination with the buttocks as a displacement for the genitalia. Ellis gives it the quality of a higher regard for the beautiful. His discussions of the buttocks ranks the races by size of the female pelvis, a view which began with Willem Vrolik's claim in 1826 that a narrow pelvis is a sign of racial superiority and is echoed by R. Verneau's study in 1875 of the form of the pelvis among the various races.[27] Verneau uses the pelvis of Sarah Bartmann to argue the primitive nature of the Hottentot's anatomical structure. Ellis accepts this ranking, seeing the steatopygia as "a simulation of the large pelvis of the higher races," having a compensatory function like face powder in emulating white skin. This view places the pelvis in an intermediary role as both a secondary as well as a primary sexual sign. Darwin himself, who held similar views as to the objective nature of human beauty, saw the pelvis as a "primary [rather] than as a secondary . . . character" and the buttocks of the Hottentot as a somewhat comic sign of the primitive, grotesque nature of the black female.[28]

When the Victorians saw the female black, they saw her in terms of her buttocks and saw represented by the buttocks all the anomalies of her genitalia. In a mid-century erotic caricature of the Hottentot Venus, a white, male observer views her through a telescope, unable to see anything but her buttocks (fig. 8).[29] This fascination with the uniqueness of the sexual parts of the black focuses on the buttocks over and over again. In a British pornographic novel, published in 1899 but set in a mythic, antebellum Southern United States, the male author indulges his fantasy of flagellation on the buttocks of a number of white women. When he describes the one black, a runaway slave, being shipped, the power of the image of the Hottentot's buttocks captures him:

> She would have had a good figure, only that her bottom was out of all proportion. It was too big, but nevertheless it was fairly well shaped, with well-rounded cheeks meeting each other closely, her thighs were large, and she had a sturdy pair of legs, her skin was smooth and of a clear yellow tint.[30]

The presence of exaggerated buttocks points to the other, hidden sexual signs, both physical and temperamental, of the black female. This association is a powerful one. Indeed Freud, in *Three Essays on Sexuality* (1905), echoes the view that female genitalia are more primitive than those of the male, for female sexuality is more anal than that of the male.[31] Female sexuality is linked to the image of the buttocks, and the quintessential buttocks are those of the Hottentot.

FIG. 8.—"The Hottentot Venus," popular engraving, ca. 1850.

We can see in Edwin Long's painting of 1882, *The Babylonian Marriage Market,* the centrality of this vocabulary in perceiving the sexualized woman (fig. 9). This painting was the most expensive work of contemporary art sold in nineteenth-century London. It also has a special place in documenting the perception of the sexualized female in terms of the great chain of aesthetic perception presented by Ellis. Long's painting is based on a specific text from Herodotus, who described the marriage auction in Babylon in which maidens were sold in order of comeliness. In the painting they are arranged in order of their attractiveness. Their physiognomies are clearly portrayed. Their features run from the most European and white (a fact emphasized by the light reflected from the mirror onto the figure at the far left) to the Negroid features (thick lips, broad nose, dark but not black skin) of the figure furthest to the observer's right. The latter figure fulfills all of Virey's categories for the appearance of the black. This is, however, the Victorian scale of sexualized women acceptable within marriage, portrayed from the most to the least attractive, according to contemporary British standards. The only black female present is the servant-slave shown on the auction block, positioned so as to present her buttocks to the viewer. While there are black males in the audience and thus among the bidders, the only black female is associated with sexualized white women as a signifier of their sexual availability. Her position is her sign and her presence in the painting is thus analogous to the figure of the black servant, Laura, in Manet's *Olympia.* Here, the linkage between two female figures, one black and one white, represents not the perversities of human sexuality in a corrupt society, such as the black servants signify in Hogarth; rather, it represents the internalization of this perversity in one specific aspect of human society, the sexualized female, in the perception of late nineteenth-century Europe.

In the nineteenth century, the prostitute is perceived as the essential sexualized female. She is perceived as the embodiment of sexuality and of all that is associated with sexuality—disease as well as passion.[32] Within the large and detailed literature concerning prostitution written during the nineteenth century (most of which documents the need for legal controls and draws on the medical model as perceived by public health officials), the physiognomy and physiology of the prostitute are analyzed in detail. We can begin with the most widely read early nineteenth-century work on prostitution, that of A. J. B. Parent-Duchatelet, who provides a documentation of the anthropology of the prostitute in his study of prostitution in Paris (1836).[33] Alain Corbin has shown how Parent-Duchatelet's use of the public health model reduces the prostitute to yet another source of pollution, similar to the sewers of Paris. Likewise in Parent-Duchatelet's discussion of the physiognomy of the prostitute, he believes himself to be providing a descriptive presentation of the appearance of the prostitute. He presents his readers with a statistical

FIG. 9.—Edwin Long, *The Babylonian Marriage Market*, 1882. Royal Holloway College, London. Phot. College.

description of the physical types of the prostitutes, the nature of their voices, the color of their hair and eyes, their physical anomalies, and their sexual profile in relation to childbearing and disease. Parent-Duchatelet's descriptions range from the detailed to the anecdotal. His discussion of the *embonpoint* of the prostitute begins his litany of external signs. Prostitutes have a "peculiar plumpness" which is attributed to "the great number of hot baths which the major part of these women take"— or perhaps to their lassitude, since they rise at ten or eleven in the morning, "leading an animal life." They are fat as prisoners are fat, from simple confinement. As an English commentator noted, "the grossest and stoutest of these women are to be found amongst the lowest and most disgusting classes of prostitutes."[34] These are the Hottentots on the scale of the sexualized female.

When Parent-Duchatelet considers the sexual parts of the prostitutes, he provides two sets of information which merge to become part of the myth of the physical anthropology of the prostitute. The prostitute's sexual parts are in no way directly affected by her profession. He contradicts the "general opinion . . . that the genital parts in prostitutes must alter, and assume a particular disposition, as the inevitable consequence of their avocation" (*P*, p. 42). He cites one case of a woman of fifty-one "who had prostituted herself thirty-six years, but in whom, notwithstanding, the genital parts might have been mistaken for those of a virgin just arrived at puberty" (*P*, p. 43). Parent-Duchatelet thus rejects any Lamarckian adaptation as well as any indication that the prostitute is inherently marked as a prostitute. This, of course, follows from his view that prostitution is an illness of a society rather than of an individual or group of individuals. While he does not see the genitalia of the prostitute altering, he does observe that prostitutes were subject to specific pathologies of their genitalia. They are especially prone to tumors "of the great labia . . . which commence with a little pus and tumefy at each menstrual period" (*P*, p. 49). He identifies the central pathology of the prostitute in the following manner: "Nothing is more frequent in prostitutes than common abscesses in the thickness of the labia majora" (*P*, p. 50). Parent-Duchatelet's two views— first, that there is no adaption of the sexual organ and, second, that the sexual organ is especially prone to labial tumors and abscesses—merge in the image of the prostitute as developing, through illness, an altered appearance of the genitalia.

From Parent-Duchatelet's description of the physical appearance of the prostitute (a catalog which reappears in most nineteenth-century studies of prostitutes, such as Josef Schrank's study of the prostitutes of Vienna), it is but a small step to the use of such catalogs of stigmata as a means of categorizing those women who have, as Freud states, "an aptitude for prostitution" (*SE*, 7:191).[35] The major work of nineteenth-century physical anthropology, public health, and pathology to undertake this was written by Pauline Tarnowsky. Tarnowsky, one of a number of

Saint Petersburg female physicians in the late nineteenth century, wrote in the tradition of her eponymous colleague, V. M. Tarnowsky, the author of the standard work on Russian prostitution. His study appeared in both Russian and German and assumed a central role in the late nineteenth-century discussions of the nature of the prostitute.[36] She followed his more general study with a detailed investigation of the physiognomy of the prostitute.[37] Her categories remain those of Parent-Duchatelet. She describes the excessive weight of prostitutes, their hair and eye color; she provides anthropometric measurements of skull size, a catalog of their family background (as with Parent-Duchatelet, most are the children of alcoholics), and their level of fecundity (extremely low) as well as the signs of their degeneration. These signs deal with the abnormalities of the face: asymmetry of features, misshapen noses, over-development of the parietal region of the skull, and the appearance of the so-called Darwin's ear (fig. 10). All of these signs are the signs of the lower end of the scale of beauty, the end dominated by the Hottentot. All of these signs point to the "primitive" nature of the prostitute's physiognomy, for stigmata such as Darwin's ear (the simplification of the convolutes of the ear shell and the absence of a lobe) are a sign of the atavistic female.

In a later paper, Tarnowsky provided a scale of appearance of the prostitute, in an analysis of the "physiognomy of the Russian prostitute." At the upper end of the scale is the "Russian Helen" (fig. 11). Here, classical aesthetics are introduced as the measure of the appearance of the sexualized female. A bit further on is one who is "very handsome in spite of her hard expression." Indeed, the first fifteen prostitutes on her

FIG. 10.—"The Face and Ear of the Prostitute." Pauline Tarnowsky, *Etude anthropométrique sur les prostituées et les voleuses,* pl. 5, 1889.

Fɪɢ. 12.—"The Madwoman/Prostitute." Tarnowsky, "Fisionomie di prostitute russe," pl. 17, 1893.

Fɪɢ. 11.—"The Russian Helen." Tarnowsky, "Fisionomie di
prostitute russe," pl. 25, 1893.

scale "might pass on the street for beauties." But hidden even within these seeming beauties are the stigmata of criminal degeneration: black, thick hair; a strong jaw; a hard, spent glance. Some show the "wild eyes and perturbed countenance along with facial asymmetry" of the insane (fig. 12).[38] Only the scientific observer can see the hidden faults, and thus identify the true prostitute, for prostitutes use superficial beauty as the bait for their clients. But when they age, their

> strong jaws and cheek-bones, and their masculine aspect . . . [once] hidden by adipose tissue, emerge, salient angles stand out, and the face grows virile, uglier than a man's; wrinkles deepen into the likeness of scars, and the countenance, once attractive, exhibits the full degenerate type which early grace had concealed.[39]

Change over time affects the physiognomy of the prostitute just as it does her genitalia, which become more and more diseased as she ages. For Tarnowsky, the appearance of the prostitute and her sexual identity are preestablished by heredity. What is most striking is that as the prostitute ages, she begins to appear more and more mannish. The link between the physical anomalies of the Hottentot and those of the lesbian appear in Billroth's *Handbuch der Frauenkrankheiten* [*Handbook of gynecological diseases*]; here, the link is between two further models of sexual deviancy, the prostitute and the lesbian. Both are seen as possessing the physical signs which set them apart from the normal.

The paper in which Tarnowsky undertook her documentation of the appearance of the prostitute is repeated word for word in the major late nineteenth-century study of prostitution. This study of the criminal woman, subtitled *The Prostitute and the Normal Woman,* written by Cesare Lombroso and his son-in-law, Guillaume Ferrero, was published in 1893.[40] Lombroso accepts Tarnowsky's entire manner of seeing the prostitute and articulates one further subtext of central importance in the perception of the sexualized woman in the nineteenth century. This subtext becomes apparent only by examining the plates in his study. Two of the plates deal with the image of the Hottentot female and illustrate the "Hottentot apron" and the steatopygia (figs. 13 and 14). Lombroso accepts Parent-Duchatelet's image of the fat prostitute and sees her as similar to women living in asylums and to the Hottentot female. He regards the anomalies of the prostitute's labia as atavistic throwbacks to the Hottentot, if not the chimpanzee. Lombroso deems the prostitute to be an atavistic subclass of woman, and he applies the power of the polygenetic argument to the image of the Hottentot to support his views. Lombroso's text, in its offhanded use of the analogy between the Hottentot and the prostitute, simply articulates in images a view which had been present throughout the late nineteenth century. Adrien Charpy's essay of 1870, published in the most distinguished French journal of dermatology and syphilology,

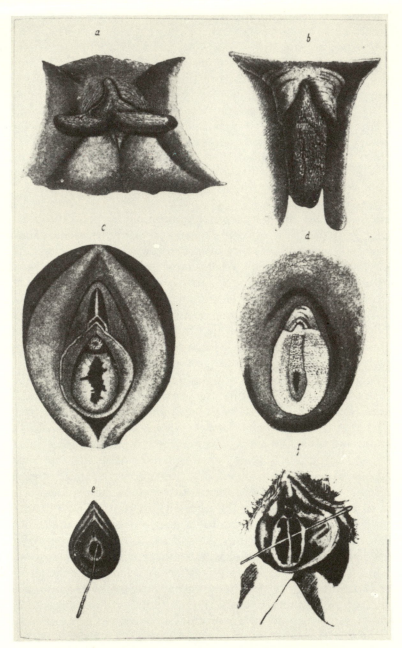

Fig. 13.—The "Hottentot Apron" (figs. a and b) and other genital anomalies. Cesare Lombroso and Guillaume Ferrero, *La donna deliquente: La prostituta e la donna normale,* pl. 1, 1893.

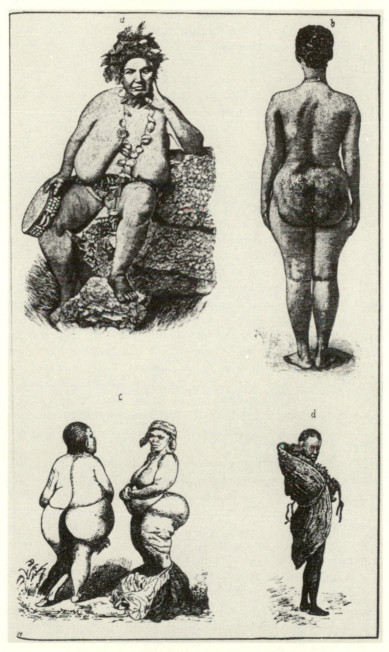

Fig. 14.—The Hottentot buttocks (figs. b and c) and an Ethiopian prostitute (fig. a). Lombroso and Ferrero, *La donna deliquente,* pl. 2, 1893.

presented an analysis of the external form of the genitalia of 800 prostitutes examined at Lyons.[41] Charpy merged Parent-Duchatelet's two contradictory categories by describing all of the alterations as either pathological or adaptive. The initial category of anomalies is that of the labia; he begins by commenting on the elongation of the labia majora in prostitutes, comparing this with the apron of the "disgusting" Hottentots. The image comes as a natural one to Charpy, as it did to Lombroso two decades later. The prostitute is an atavistic form of humanity whose "primitive" nature can be observed in the form of her genitalia. What Tarnowsky and Lombroso add to the equation is the parallel they draw between the seemingly beautiful physiognomy and this atavistic nature. Other signs were quickly found. Ellis saw, as one of the secondary sexual characteristics which determine the beautiful, the presence in a woman of a long second toe and a short fifth toe (see *SPS*, p. 164). The French physician L. Jullien presented clinical material concerning the antithetical case, the foot of the prostitute, which Lombroso in commenting on the paper immediately labeled as prehensile.[42] The ultimate of the throwbacks was, of course, the throwback to the level of the Hottentot or the Bushman—to the level of the lasciviousness of the prostitute. Ferrero, Lombroso's coauthor, described prostitution as the rule in primitive societies and placed the Bushman at the nadir of the scale of primitive lasciviousness: adultery has no meaning for them, he asserted, nor does virginity; the poverty of their mental universe can be seen in the fact that they have but one word for "girl, woman, or wife."[43] The primitive is the black, and the qualities of blackness, or at least of the black female, are those of the prostitute. The work of a student of Lombroso's, Abele de Blasio, makes this grotesquely evident: he published a series of case studies on steatopygia in prostitutes in which he perceives the prostitute as being, quite literally, the Hottentot (fig. 15).[44]

The perception of the prostitute in the late nineteenth century thus merged with the perception of the black. Both categories are those of outsiders, but what does this amalgamation imply in terms of the perception of both groups? It is a commonplace that the primitive was associated with unbridled sexuality. This was either condemned, as in Thomas Jefferson's discussions of the nature of the black in Virginia, or praised, as in the fictional supplement written by Denis Diderot to Bougainville's voyages. It is exactly this type of uncontrolled sexuality, however, which is postulated by historians such as J. J. Bachofen as the sign of the "swamp," the earliest stage of human history. Blacks, if both G. W. F. Hegel and Arthur Schopenhauer are to be believed, remained at this most primitive stage, and their presence in the contemporary world served as an indicator of how far mankind had come in establishing control over his world and himself. The loss of control was marked by a regression into this dark past—a degeneracy into the primitive expression

Fig. 15.—An Italian Prostitute. Abele de Blasio, "Staetopigia in prostitute," pl. 1, 1905.

of emotions in the form of either madness or unrestrained sexuality. Such a loss of control was, of course, viewed as pathological and thus fell into the domain of the medical model. For the medical model, especially as articulated in the public health reforms of the mid- and late nineteenth century, had as its central preoccupation the elimination of sexually transmitted disease through the institution of social controls; this was the project which motivated writers such as Parent-Duchatelet and Tarnowsky. The social controls which they wished to institute had existed in the nineteenth century but in quite a different context. The laws applying to the control of slaves (such as the 1685 French *code noir* and its American analogues) had placed great emphasis on the control of the slave as sexual object, both in terms of permitted and forbidden sexual contacts as well as by requiring documentation as to the legal status of the offspring of slaves. Sexual control was thus well known to the late eighteenth and early nineteenth century.

The linkage which the late nineteenth century established between this earlier model of control and the later model of sexual control advocated by the public health authorities came about through the association of two bits of medical mythology. The primary marker of the black is his or her skin color. Medical tradition has a long history of perceiving this skin color as the result of some pathology. The favorite theory, which reappears with some frequency in the early nineteenth century, is that the skin color and attendant physiognomy of the black are the result of congenital leprosy.[45] It is not very surprising, therefore, to read in the late nineteenth century—after social conventions surrounding the abolition of slavery in Great Britian and France, as well as the trauma of the American Civil War, forbade the public association of at least skin color with illness—that syphilis was not introduced into Europe by Christopher Columbus' sailors but rather that it was a form of leprosy which had long been present in Africa and had spread into Europe in the Middle Ages.[46] The association of the black, especially the black female, with the syphilophobia of the late nineteenth century was thus made manifest. Black females do not merely represent the sexualized female, they also represent the female as the source of corruption and disease. It is the black female as the emblem of illness who haunts the background of Manet's *Olympia*.

For Manet's *Olympia* stands exactly midway between the glorification and the condemnation of the sexualized female. She is the antithesis of the fat prostitute. Indeed, she was perceived as thin by her contemporaries, much in the style of the actual prostitutes of the 1860s. But Laura, the black servant, is presented as plump, which can be best seen in Manet's initial oil sketch of her done in 1862–63. Her presence in both the sketch and in the final painting emphasizes her face, for it is the physiognomy of the black which points to her own sexuality and to that of the white female presented to the viewer unclothed but with her genitalia demurely covered. The association is between these hidden genitalia and the signifier of the black. Both point to potential corruption of the male viewer by the female. This is made even more evident in that work which art historians have stressed as being heavily influenced by Manet's *Olympia,* his portrait *Nana.* Here the associations would have been quite clear to the contemporary viewer. First, the model for the painting was Henriette Hauser, called Citron, the mistress of the prince of Orange. Second, Manet places in the background of the painting a Japanese crane, for which the French word (*grue*) was a slang term for prostitute. He thus labels the figure as a sexualized female. Unlike the classical pose of the *Olympia,* Nana is presented being admired by a well-dressed man-about-town (a *flâneur*). She is not naked but partially clothed. What Manet can further draw upon is the entire vocabulary of signs which, by the late nineteenth century, were associated with the sexualized female. Nana is fulsome rather than thin. Here Manet employs the stigmata of fatness to characterize the prostitute. This convention becomes part of the visualization of the sexualized female even while the reality of the idealized sexualized female is that of a thin female. Constantin Guys presents a fat, reclining prostitute in 1860, while Edgar Degas' *Madam's Birthday* (1879) presents an entire brothel of fat prostitutes. At the same time, Napoléon III's mistress, Marguerite Bellanger, set a vogue for slenderness. She was described as "below average in size, slight, thin, almost skinny."[47] This is certainly not Nana. Manet places her in a position vis-à-vis the viewer (but not the male observer in the painting) which emphasizes the line of her buttocks, the steatopygia of the prostitute. Second, Nana is placed in such a way that the viewer (but again not the *flâneur*) can observe her ear. It is, to no one's surprise, Darwin's ear, a sign of the atavistic female. Thus we know where the black servant is hidden in *Nana*—within Nana. Even Nana's seeming beauty is but a sign of the black hidden within. All her external stigmata point to the pathology within the sexualized female.

Manet's *Nana* thus provides a further reading of his *Olympia,* a reading which stresses Manet's debt to the pathological model of sexuality present during the late nineteenth century. The black hidden within *Olympia* bursts forth in Pablo Picasso's 1901 version of the painting: Olympia is presented as a sexualized black, with broad hips, revealed genitalia, gazing at the nude *flâneur* bearing her a gift of fruit, much as Laura bears a gift of flowers in Manet's original (fig. 16). But, unlike Manet, the artist is himself present in this work, as a sexualized observer of the sexualized female. Picasso owes part of his reading of the *Olympia* to the polar image of the primitive female as sexual object, as found in the lower-class prostitutes painted by Vincent van Gogh or the Tahitian maidens à la Diderot painted by Paul Gauguin. Picasso saw the sexualized female as the visual analogue of the black. Indeed, in his most radical break with

FIG. 16.—Pablo Picasso, *Olympia*, 1901, New York.

the impressionist tradition, *Les Demoiselles d'Avignon* (1907), he linked the inmates of the brothel with the black by using the theme of African masks to characterize their appearance. The figure of the male represents the artist as victim. Picasso's parody points toward the importance of seeing Manet's *Nana* in the context of the medical discourse concerning the sexualized female which dominated the late nineteenth century.

The portrait of *Nana* is also embedded in a complex literary matrix which provides many of the signs needed to illustrate the function of the sexualized female as the sign of disease. The figure of Nana first appeared in Emile Zola's novel *L'Assommoir* (1877) in which she was presented as the offspring of the alcoholic couple who are the central figures of the novel.[48] Her heredity assured the reader that she would eventually become a sexualized female—a prostitute—and, indeed, by the close of the novel she has run off with an older man, the owner of a button factory, and has begun her life as a sexualized female. Manet was captivated by the figure of Nana (as was the French reading public), and his portrait of her symbolically reflected her sexual encounters presented during the novel. Zola then decided to build the next novel in his Rougon-Macquart cycle about the figure of Nana as a sexualized female. Thus in Zola's *Nana* the reader is presented with Zola's reading of Manet's portrait of Nana. Indeed, Zola uses the portrait of the *flâneur* observing the half-dressed Nana as the centerpiece for a scene in the theater in which Nana seduces the simple Count Muffat. Immediately before this meeting, Zola presents Nana's first success in the theater (or, as the theater director calls it, his brothel). She appears in a revue, unable to sing or dance, and becomes the butt of laughter until, in the second act of the revue, she appears unclothed on stage:

> Nana was in the nude: naked with a quiet audacity, certain of the omnipotence of her flesh. She was wrapped in a simple piece of gauze: her rounded shoulders, her Amazon's breasts of which the pink tips stood up rigidly like lances, her broad buttocks which rolled in a voluptuous swaying motion, and her fair, fat hips: her whole body was in evidence, and could be seen under the light tissue with its foamy whiteness.[49]

What Zola describes are the characteristics of the sexualized woman, the "primitive" hidden beneath the surface: "all of a sudden in the comely child the woman arose, disturbing, bringing the mad surge of her sex, inviting the unknown element of desire. Nana was still smiling: but it was the smile of a man-eater." Nana's atavistic sexuality, the sexuality of the Amazon, is destructive. The sign of this is her fleshliness. And it is this sign which reappears when she is observed by Muffat in her dressing room, the scene which Zola found in Manet's painting:

> Then calmly, to reach her dressing-table, she walked in her drawers through that group of gentlemen, who made way for her. She had large buttocks, her drawers ballooned, and with breast well forward she bowed to them, giving her delicate smile. [*N*, p. 135]

Nana's childlike face is but a mask which conceals the hidden disease buried within, the corruption of sexuality. Thus Zola concludes the novel by revealing the horror beneath the mask: Nana dies of the pox. (Zola's pun works in French as well as in English and is needed because of the rapidity of decay demanded by the moral implication of Zola's portrait. It would not do to have Nana die slowly over thirty years of tertiary syphilis. Smallpox, with its play on "the pox," works quickly and gives the same visual icon of decay.) Nana's death reveals her true nature:

> Nana remained alone, her face looking up in the light from the candle. It was a charnel-house scene, a mass of tissue-fluids and blood, a shovelful of putrid flesh thrown there on a cushion. The pustules had invaded the entire face with the pocks touching each other; and, dissolving and subsiding with the greyish look of mud, there seemed to be already an earthy mouldiness on the shapeless muscosity, in which the features were no longer discernible. An eye, the left one, had completely subsided in a soft mass of purulence; the other, half-open, was sinking like a collapsing hole. The nose was still suppurating. A whole reddish crust was peeling off one cheek and invaded the mouth, distorting it into a loathsome grimace. And on that horrible and grotesque mask, the hair, that beautiful head of hair still preserving its blaze of sunlight, flowed down in a golden trickle. Venus was decomposing. It seems as though the virus she had absorbed from the gutters and from the tacitly permitted carrion of humanity, that baneful ferment with which she had poisoned a people, had now risen to her face and putrefied it. [*N*, pp. 464–65]

The decaying visage is the visible sign of the diseased genitalia through which the sexualized female corrupts an entire nation of warriors and leads them to the collapse of the French Army and the resultant German victory at Sedan. The image is an old one, it is *Frau Welt*, Madam World, who masks her corruption, the disease of being a woman, through her beauty. It reappears in the vignette on the title page of the French translation (1840) of the Renaissance poem *Syphilis* (fig. 17).[50] But it is yet more, for in death Nana begins to revert to the blackness of the earth, to assume the horrible grotesque countenance perceived as belonging to the world of the black, the world of the "primitive," the world of disease. Nana is, like Olympia, in the words of Paul Valéry, "pre-eminently unclean."[51]

FIG. 17.—Frontispiece. August Barthelemy, *Syphilis*, 1840.

It is this uncleanliness, this disease, which forms the final link between two images of woman, the black and the prostitute. Just as the genitalia of the Hottentot were perceived as parallel to the diseased genitalia of the prostitute, so too the power of the idea of corruption links both images. Thus part of Nana's fall into corruption comes through her seduction by a lesbian, yet a further sign of her innate, physical degeneracy. She is corrupted and corrupts through sexuality. Miscegenation was a fear (and a word) from the late nineteenth-century vocabulary of sexuality. It was a fear not merely of interracial sexuality but of its results, the decline of the population. Interracial marriages were seen as exactly parallel to the barrenness of the prostitute; if they produced children at all, these children were weak and doomed. Thus Ellis, drawing on his view of the objective nature of the beauty of mankind, states that "it is difficult to be sexually attracted to persons who are fundamentally unlike ourselves in racial constitution" (*SPS*, p. 176). He cites Abel Hermant to substantiate his views:

> Differences of race are irreducible and between two beings who love each other they cannot fail to produce exceptional and instructive reactions. In the first superficial ebullition of love, indeed, nothing notable may be manifested, but in a fairly short time the two lovers, innately hostile, in striving to approach each other strike against an invisible partition which separates them. Their sensibilities are divergent; everything in each shocks the other; even their anatomical conformation, even the language of their gestures; all is foreign.[52]

It is thus the inherent fear of the difference in the anatomy of the Other which lies behind the synthesis of images. The Other's pathology is revealed in anatomy. It is the similarity between the black and the prostitute—as bearers of the stigmata of sexual difference and, thus, pathology—which captured the late nineteenth century. Zola sees in the sexual corruption of the male the source of political impotence and projects what is basically an internal fear, the fear of loss of power, onto the world.[53]

The "white *man's* burden" thus becomes his sexuality and its control, and it is this which is transferred into the need to control the sexuality of the Other, the Other as sexualized female. The colonial mentality which sees "natives" as needing control is easily transferred to "woman"— but woman as exemplified by the caste of the prostitute. This need for control was a projection of inner fears; thus, its articulation in visual images was in terms which described the polar opposite of the European male.

The roots of this image of the sexualized female are to be found in male observers, the progenitors of the vocabulary of images through which they believed themselves able to capture the essence of the Other. Thus when Freud, in his *Essay on Lay Analysis* (1926), discusses the ignorance of contemporary psychology concerning adult female sexuality, he refers to this lack of knowledge as the "dark continent" of psychology (*SE*, 20:212).[54] In using this phrase in English, Freud ties the image of female sexuality to the image of the colonial black and to the perceived relationship between the female's ascribed sexuality and the Other's exoticism and pathology. It is Freud's intent to explore this hidden "dark continent" and reveal the hidden truths about female sexuality, just as the anthropologist-explorers (such as Lombroso) were revealing the hidden truths about the nature of the black. Freud continues a discourse which relates the images of male discovery to the images of the female as object of discovery. The line from the secrets possessed by the "Hottentot Venus" to twentieth-century psychoanalysis runs reasonably straight.

1. The debate between E. H. Gombrich, *The Image and the Eye* (Ithaca, N.Y., 1982) and Nelson Goodman, *Ways of Worldmaking* (Hassocks, 1978) has revolved mainly around the manner by which conventions of representation create the work of art. Implicit in their debate is the broader question of the function of systems of conventions as icons within the work of art itself. On the limitation of the discussion of systems of conventions to aesthetic objects, see the extensive bibliography compiled in Ulrich Weisstein, "Bibliography of Literature and the Visual Arts, 1945–1980," *Comparative Criticism* 4 (1982): 324–34, in which the special position of the work of art as separate from other aspects of society can be seen. This is a holdover from the era of *Geistesgeschichte* in which special status was given to the interaction between aesthetic objects.

This can be seen in the alternative case of works of aesthetic provenance which are, however, part of medical discourse. One thinks immediately of the anatomical works of Leonardo or George Stubbs or of paintings with any medical reference such as Rembrandt's *Dr. Tulp* or Théodore Géricault's paintings of the insane. When the literature on these works is examined, it is striking how most analysis remains embedded in the discourse of aesthetic objects, i.e., the anatomical drawing as a "subjective" manner of studying human form or, within medical discourse, as part of a "scientific" history of anatomical illustration. The evident fact that both of these modes of discourse exist simultaneously in the context of social history is lost on most critics. An exception is William Schupbach, *The Paradox of Rembrandt's "Anatomy of Dr. Tulp,"* Medical History, supp. 2 (London, 1982).

2. George Heard Hamilton, *Manet and His Critics* (New Haven, Conn., 1954), p. 68. I am ignoring here George Mauner's peculiar position that "we may conclude that Manet makes no comment at all with this painting, if by comment we understand judgment or criticism" *(Manet: Peintre-Philosophe: A Study of the Painter's Themes* [University Park, Pa., 1975], p. 99).

3. For my discussion of Manet's works, I draw especially on Theodore Reff, *Manet: "Olympia"* (London, 1976), and Werner Hofmann, *Nana: Mythos und Wirklichkeit* (Cologne, 1973); neither of these studies examines the medical analogies. See also Eunice Lipton, "Manet: A Radicalized Female Imagery," *Artforum* 13 (Mar. 1975): 48–53.

4. See George Needham, "Manet, *Olympia*, and Pornographic Photography," in *Woman as Sex Object*, ed. Thomas Hess and Linda Nochlin (New York, 1972), pp. 81–89.

5. See Philippe Rebeyrol, "Baudelaire et Manet," *Les Temps modernes* 5 (Oct. 1949): 707–25.

6. Georges Bataille, *Manet*, trans. A. Wainhouse and James Emmons (New York, 1956), p. 113. And see Hofmann, *Nana*.

7. See Edmund Bazire, quoted in Anne Coffin Hanson, *Manet and the Modern Tradition* (New Haven, Conn., 1977), p. 130.

8. See my *On Blackness without Blacks: Essays on the Image of the Black in Germany* (Boston, 1982). On the image of the black, see Ladislas Bugner, ed., *L'Image du noir dans l'art occidental*, 3 vols. (Paris, 1976–); the fourth volume, not yet published, will cover the post-Renaissance period.

9. See the various works on Hogarth by Ronald Paulson, such as *Hogarth: His Life, Art, and Times,* 2 vols. (New Haven, Conn., 1971) and *Hogarth's Graphic Works,* 2 vols. (New Haven, Conn., 1970); and see Ross E. Taggert, "A Tavern Scene: An Evening at the Rose," *Art Quarterly* 19 (Autumn 1956): 320–23.

10. M. N. Adler, trans., *The Itinerary of Benjamin of Tudela* (London, 1907), p. 68.

11. See John Herbert Eddy, Jr., "Buffon, Organic Change, and the Races of Man" (Ph.D. diss., University of Oklahoma, 1977), p. 109. See also Paul Alfred Erickson, "The Origins of Physical Anthropology" (Ph.D. diss., University of Connecticut, 1974) and Werner Krauss, *Zur Anthropologie des achtzehnten Jahrhunderts: Die Frühgeschichte der Menschheit im Blickpunkt der Aufklärung,* ed. Hans Kortum and Christa Gohrisch (Munich, 1979).

12. See Guillaum-Thomas Raynal, *Histoire philosophique et politique des établissemens et du commerce des Européens dans les deux Indes,* 10 vols. (Geneva, 1775), 2:406–7.

13. See William F. Bynum, "The Great Chain of Being after Forty Years: An Appraisal," *History of Science* 13 (1975): 1–28, and "Time's Noblest Offspring: The Problem of Man in British Natural Historical Sciences" (Ph.D. diss., Cambridge, 1974).

14. See J. J. Virey, "Négre," *Dictionnaire des sciences médicales,* 41 vols. (Paris, 1819), 35:398–403.

15. See Virey, *Histoire naturelle du genre humaine,* 2 vols. (Paris, 1824), 2:151.

16. See George M. Gould and Walter L. Pyle, *Anomalies and Curiosities of Medicine* (Philadelphia, 1901), p. 307, and Eugen Holländer, *Aeskulap und Venus: Eine Kultur- und Sittengeschichte im Spiegel des Arztes* (Berlin, 1928). Much material on the indebtedness of the early pathologists to the reports of travelers to Africa can be found in the accounts of the autopsies I will discuss below.

One indication of the power which the image of the Hottentot still possessed in the late nineteenth century can be found in George Eliot, *Daniel Deronda,* ed. Barbara Hardy (1876; Harmondsworth, 1967). On its surface the novel is a hymn to racial harmony and an attack on British middle-class bigotry. Eliot's liberal agenda is nowhere better articulated than in the ironic debate concerning the nature of the black in which the eponymous hero of the novel defends black sexuality (see p. 376). This position is attributed to the hero not a half-dozen pages after the authorial voice of the narrator introduced the description of this very figure with the comparison: "And one man differs from another, as we all differ from the Bosjesman" (p. 370). Eliot's comment is quite in keeping with the underlying understanding of race in the novel. For just as Deronda is fated to marry a Jewess and thus avoid the taint of race mixing, so too is the Bushman, a Hottentot surrogate in the nineteenth century, isolated from the rest of mankind. The ability of Europeans to hold simultaneously a polygenetic view of race and a liberal ideology is evident as far back as Voltaire. But in Eliot's novel the Jew is contrasted to the Hottentot, and, as we have seen, it is the Hottentot who serves as the icon of pathologically corrupted sexuality. Can Eliot be drawing a line between outsiders such as the Jew or the sexualized female in Western society and the Hottentot? The Hottentot comes to serve as the sexualized Other onto whom Eliot projects the opprobrium with which she herself was labeled. For Eliot, the Hottentot remains beyond the pale; even in the most whiggish text, the Hottentot remains the essential Other.

17. Paul Edwards and James Walvin, *Black Personalities in the Era of the Slave Trade* (Baton Rouge, La., 1983), pp. 173, 175. A print of the 1829 ball in Paris with the nude "Hottentot Venus" is reproduced in *Illustrierte Geschichte der Medizin,* ed. Richard Toellner, 9 vols. (Salzburg, 1980), 4:1319; this is a German reworking of Jacques Vie et al., *Histoire de la médecine,* 8 vols. (Paris, 1977).

18. See Henri de Blainville, "Sur une femme de la race hottentote," *Bulletin des sciences par la société philomatique de Paris* (1816): 183–90. This early version of the autopsy seems to be unknown to William B. Cohen, *The French Encounter with Africans: White Response to Blacks, 1530–1880* (Bloomington, 1980), esp. pp. 239–45. See also Stephen Jay Gould, "The Hottentot Venus," *Natural History* 91 (1982): 20–27.

19. Georges Cuvier, "Extraits d'observations faites sur le cadavre d'une femme connue à Paris et à Londres sous le nom de Vénus Hottentote," *Memoires du Museum d'histoire naturelle* 3 (1817): 259–74; rpt. with plates in Geoffrey Saint-Hilaire and Frédéric Cuvier, *Histoire naturelle des mammifères avec des figures originales*, 2 vols. (Paris, 1824), 1:1–23. The substance of the autopsy is reprinted again by Flourens in the *Journal complémentaire du dictionnaire des sciences médicales* 4 (1819): 145–49, and by Jules Cloquet, *Manuel d'anatomie de l'homme descriptive du corps humaine* (Paris, 1825), pl. 278. Cuvier's presentation of the "Hottentot Venus" forms the major signifier for the image of the Hottentot as sexual primitive in the nineteenth century.

20. See, e.g., Walker D. Greer, "John Hunter: Order out of Variety," *Annals of the Royal College of Surgeons of England* 28 (1961): 238–51. See also Barbara J. Babiger, "The Kunst- und Wunderkammern: A catalogue raisonné of Collecting in Germany, France and England, 1565–1750" (Ph.D. diss., University of Pittsburgh, 1970).

21. See Adolf Wilhelm Otto, *Seltene Beobachtungen zur Anatomie, Physiologie, und Pathologie gehörig* (Breslau, 1816), p. 135; Johannes Müller, "Ueber die äusseren Geschlechtstheile der Buschmänninnen," *Archiv für Anatomie, Physiologie, und wissenschaftliche Medizin* (1834), pp. 319–45; W. H. Flower and James Murie, "Account of the Dissection of a Bushwoman," *Journal of Anatomy and Physiology* 1 (1867): 189–208; and Hubert von Luschka, A. Koch, and E. Görtz, "Die äusseren Geschlechtstheile eines Buschweibes," *Monatsschrift für Geburtskunde* 32 (1868): 343–50. The popularity of these accounts can be seen by their republication in extract for a lay audience. These extracts also stress the sexual anomalies described. See *Anthropological Review* 5 (July, 1867): 319–24, and *Anthropological Review* 8 (Jan., 1870): 89–318.

22. Edward Turnipseed, "Some Facts in Regard to the Anatomical Differences between the Negro and White Races," *American Journal of Obstetrics* 10 (1877): 32, 33.

23. See C. H. Fort, "Some Corroborative Facts in Regard to the Anatomical Difference between the Negro and White Races," *American Journal of Obstetrics* 10 (1877): 258–59. Paul Broca was influenced by similar American material (which he cites from the *New York City Medical Record,* 15 Sept. 1868) concerning the position of the hymen; see his untitled note in the *Bulletins de la société d'anthropologie de Paris* 4 (1869): 443–44. Broca, like Cuvier before him, supported a polygenetic view of the human races.

24. See William Turner, "Notes on the Dissection of a Negro," *Journal of Anatomy and Physiology* 13 (1878): 382–86; "Notes on the Dissection of a Second Negro," *Journal of Anatomy and Physiology* 14 (1879): 244–48; and "Notes on the Dissection of a Third Negro," *Journal of Anatomy and Physiology* 31 (1896): 624–26. This was not merely a British anomaly. Jefferies Wyman reports the dissection of a black suicide (originally published in *Proceedings of the Boston Society of Natural History,* 2 Apr. 1862 and 16 Dec. 1863) and does not refer to the genitalia of the male Hottentot at all; see *Anthropological Review* 3 (1865): 330–35.

25. H. Hildebrandt, *Die Krankheiten der äusseren weiblichen Genitalien,* in *Handbuch der Frauenkrankheiten 3,* ed. Theodor Billroth, 3 vols. (Stuttgart, 1885–86), pp. 11–12. See also Thomas Power Lowry, ed., *The Classic Clitoris: Historic Contributions to Scientific Sexuality* (Chicago, 1978).

26. Havelock Ellis, *Studies in the Psychology of Sex,* vol. 4, *Sexual Selection in Man* (Philadelphia, 1920), p. 158; all further references to this work, abbreviated *SPS,* will be included in the text.

27. See Willem Vrolik, *Considerations sur la diversité du bassin des différentes races humaines* (Amsterdam, 1826) and R. Verneau, *Le bassin dans les sexes et dans les races* (Paris, 1875), pp. 126–29.

28. Charles Darwin, *The Descent of Man and Selection in Relation to Sex* (Princeton, N.J., 1981), 2:317, and see 2:345–46.

29. See John Grand-Carteret, *Die Erotik in der französischen Karikatur,* trans. Cary von Karwarth and Adolf Neumann (Vienna, 1909), p. 195.

30. [Hugues Rebell?], *The Memories of Dolly Morton: The Story of a Woman's Part in the Struggle to Free the Slaves: An Account of the Whippings, Rapes, and Violences That Preceded the Civil War in America with Curious Anthropological Observations on the Radical Diversities in the Conformation of the Female Bottom and the Way Different Women Endure Chastisement* (Paris, 1899), p. 207.

31. See Sigmund Freud, *The Standard Edition of the Complete Psychological Works of Sigmund Freud,* ed. and trans. James Strachey, 24 vols. (London, 1953–74), 7:186–87, esp. n. 1; all further references to this work, abbreviated *SE* and with volume and page numbers, will be included in the text.

32. The best study of the image of the prostitute is Alain Corbin, *Les filles de noce: Misère sexuelle et prostitution (dix-neuvième et vingtième siècles)* (Paris, 1978). On the black prostitute, see Khalid Kishtainy, *The Prostitute in Progressive Literature* (London, 1982), pp. 74–84. On the iconography associated with the pictorial representation of the prostitute in nineteenth-century art, see Hess and Nochlin, *Woman as Sex Object;* Nochlin, "Lost and Found: Once More the Fallen Woman," *Art Bulletin* 60 (Mar. 1978): 139–53; and Lynda Nead, "Seduction, Prostitution, Suicide: *On the Brink* by Alfred Elmore," *Art History* 5 (Sept. 1982): 310–22. On the special status of medical representations of female sexuality, see the eighteenth-century wax models of female anatomy in the Museo della Specola, Florence, and reproduced in Mario Bucci, *Anatomia come arte* (Florence, 1969), esp. pl. 8.

33. See A. J. B. Parent-Duchatelet, *De la prostitution dans la ville de Paris,* 2 vols. (Paris, 1836), 1:193–244.

34. Parent-Duchatelet, *On Prostitution in the City of Paris,* (London, 1840), p. 38; all further references to this work, abbreviated *P,* will be included in the text. It is exactly the passages on the physiognomy and appearance of the prostitute which this anonymous translator presents to his English audience as the essence of Parent-Duchatelet's work.

35. See my "Freud and the Prostitute: Male Stereotypes of Female Sexuality in *fin de siècle* Vienna," *Journal of the American Academy of Psychoanalysis* 9 (1981): 337–60.

36. See V. M. Tarnowsky, *Prostitutsija i abolitsioniszm* (Petersburg, 1888) and *Prostitution und Abolitionismus* (Hamburg, 1890).

37. See Pauline Tarnowsky, *Etude anthropométrique sur les prostituées et les voleuses* (Paris, 1889).

38. Tarnowsky, "Fisiomie di prostitute russe," *Archivio di psichiatria, scienze penali e antropologia criminale* 14 (1893): 141–42; my translation.

39. Ibid., p. 141; my translation.

40. See Cesare Lombroso and Guillaume Ferrero, *La donna delinquente: La prostituta e la donna normale* (Turin, 1893), esp. pp. 349–50, 361–62, and 38.

41. See Adrien Charpy, "Des organes génitaux externes chez les prostituées," *Annales des dermatologie* 3 (1870–71): 271–79.

42. See L. Jullien, "Contribution à l'étude de la morphologie des prostituées," in *Quatrième Congrès international d'anthropologie criminelle,* 1896 (Geneva, 1897), pp. 348–49.

43. See Ferrero, "L'atavisme de la prostitution," *Révue scientifique* (1892): 136–41.

44. See A. de Blasio, "Staetopigia in prostitute," *Archivio di psichiatria* 26 (1905): 257–64.

45. See Winthrop D. Jordan, *White over Black: American Attitudes toward the Negro, 1550–1812* (New York, 1977), pp. 3–43.

46. See Iwan Bloch, *Der Ursprung der Syphilis; Eine medizinische und kulturgeschichtliche Untersuchung,* 2 vols. (Jena, 1901–11).

47. Reff, *Manet: "Olympia,"* p. 58; see also p. 118.

48. See Théodore Lascaris [Auriant], *La véritable histoire de "Nana"* (Paris, 1942). See also Demetra Palamari, "The Shark Who Swallowed His Epoch: Family, Nature, and Society

in the Novels of Emile Zola," in *Changing Images of the Family*, ed. Virginia Tufte and Barbara Myerhoff (New Haven, Conn., 1979), pp. 155–72.

49. Emile Zola, *Nana,* trans. Charles Duff (London, 1953), p. 27; all further references to this work, abbreviated *N,* will be included in the text.

50. See August Barthelemy, trans., *Syphilis: Poeme en deux chants* (Paris, 1840). This is a translation of a section of Fracastorius' Latin poem on the nature and origin of syphilis. The French edition was in print well past mid-century.

51. Paul Valéry, quoted in Bataille, *Manet,* p. 65.

52. Abel Hermant, quoted in Ellis, *Studies in the Psychology of Sex,* 4:176 n. 1.

53. See Joachim Hohmann, ed., *Schon auf den ersten Blick: Lesebuch zur Geschichte unserer Feindbilder* (Darmstadt, 1981).

54. See Renate Schlesier, *Konstruktion der Weiblichkeit bei Sigmund Freud* (Frankfurt, 1981), pp. 35–39.

Three Women's Texts and a Critique of Imperialism

Gayatri Chakravorty Spivak

It should not be possible to read nineteenth-century British literature without remembering that imperialism, understood as England's social mission, was a crucial part of the cultural representation of England to the English. The role of literature in the production of cultural representation should not be ignored. These two obvious "facts" continue to be disregarded in the reading of nineteenth-century British literature. This itself attests to the continuing success of the imperialist project, displaced and dispersed into more modern forms.

If these "facts" were remembered, not only in the study of British literature but in the study of the literatures of the European colonizing cultures of the great age of imperialism, we would produce a narrative, in literary history, of the "worlding" of what is now called "the Third World." To consider the Third World as distant cultures, exploited but with rich intact literary heritages waiting to be recovered, interpreted, and curricularized in English translation fosters the emergence of "the Third World" as a signifier that allows us to forget that "worlding," even as it expands the empire of the literary discipline.[1]

It seems particularly unfortunate when the emergent perspective of feminist criticism reproduces the axioms of imperialism. A basically isolationist admiration for the literature of the female subject in Europe and Anglo-America establishes the high feminist norm. It is supported and operated by an information-retrieval approach to "Third World" literature which often employs a deliberately "nontheoretical" methodology with self-conscious rectitude.

©1985 by Gayatri Chakravorty Spivak. All rights reserved. Permission to reprint may be obtained only from the author.

In this essay, I will attempt to examine the operation of the "worlding" of what is today "the Third World" by what has become a cult text of feminism: *Jane Eyre*.² I plot the novel's reach and grasp, and locate its structural motors. I read *Wide Sargasso Sea* as *Jane Eyre*'s reinscription and *Frankenstein* as an analysis—even a deconstruction—of a "worlding" such as *Jane Eyre*'s.³

I need hardly mention that the object of my investigation is the printed book, not its "author." To make such a distinction is, of course, to ignore the lessons of deconstruction. A deconstructive critical approach would loosen the binding of the book, undo the opposition between verbal text and the bio-graphy of the named subject "Charlotte Brontë," and see the two as each other's "scene of writing." In such a reading, the life that writes itself as "my life" is as much a production in psychosocial space (other names can be found) as the book that is written by the holder of that named life—a book that is then consigned to what *is* most often recognized as genuinely "social": the world of publication and distribution.⁴ To touch Brontë's "life" in such a way, however, would be too risky here. We must rather strategically take shelter in an essentialism which, not wishing to lose the important advantages won by U.S. mainstream feminism, will continue to honor the suspect binary oppositions— book and author, individual and history—and start with an assurance of the following sort: my readings here do not seek to undermine the excellence of the individual artist. If even minimally successful, the readings will incite a degree of rage against the imperialist narrativization of history, that it should produce so abject a script for her. I provide these assurances to allow myself some room to situate feminist individualism in its historical determination rather than simply to canonize it as feminism as such.

Sympathetic U.S. feminists have remarked that I do not do justice to Jane Eyre's subjectivity. A word of explanation is perhaps in order. The broad strokes of my presuppositions are that what is at stake, for feminist individualism in the age of imperialism, is precisely the making of human beings, the constitution and "interpellation" of the subject not only as individual but as "individualist."⁵ This stake is represented on two registers: childbearing and soul making. The first is domestic-society-through-sexual-reproduction cathected as "companionate love"; the second is the imperialist project cathected as civil-society-through-social-mission. As the female individualist, not-quite/not-male, articulates herself in shifting

Gayatri Chakravorty Spivak is Longstreet Professor of English at Emory University. She is the translator of Jacques Derrida's *De la grammatologie* and is presently finishing a book entitled *Master Discourse, Native Informant*.

relationship to what is at stake, the "native female" as such (*within* discourse, *as* a signifier) is excluded from any share in this emerging norm.[6] If we read this account from an isolationist perspective in a "metropolitan" context, we see nothing there but the psychobiography of the militant female subject. In a reading such as mine, in contrast, the effort is to wrench oneself away from the mesmerizing focus of the "subject-constitution" of the female individualist.

To develop further the notion that my stance need not be an accusing one, I will refer to a passage from Roberto Fernández Retamar's "Caliban."[7] José Enrique Rodó had argued in 1900 that the model for the Latin American intellectual in relationship to Europe could be Shakespeare's Ariel.[8] In 1971 Retamar, denying the possibility of an identifiable "Latin American Culture," recast the model as Caliban. Not surprisingly, this powerful exchange still excludes any specific consideration of the civilizations of the Maya, the Aztecs, the Incas, or the smaller nations of what is now called Latin America. Let us note carefully that, at this stage of my argument, this "conversation" between Europe and Latin America (without a specific consideration of the political economy of the "worlding" of the "native") provides a sufficient thematic description of our attempt to confront the ethnocentric and reverse-ethnocentric benevolent double bind (that is, considering the "native" as object for enthusiastic information-retrieval and thus denying its own "worlding") that I sketched in my opening paragraphs.

In a moving passage in "Caliban," Retamar locates both Caliban and Ariel in the postcolonial intellectual:

> There is no real Ariel-Caliban polarity: both are slaves in the hands of Prospero, the foreign magician. But Caliban is the rude and unconquerable master of the island, while Ariel, a creature of the air, although also a child of the isle, is the intellectual.

> The deformed Caliban—enslaved, robbed of his island, and taught the language by Prospero—rebukes him thus: "You taught me language, and my profit on't / Is, I know how to curse." ["C," pp. 28, 11]

As we attempt to unlearn our so-called privilege as Ariel and "seek from [a certain] Caliban the honor of a place in his rebellious and glorious ranks," we do not ask that our students and colleagues should emulate us but that they should attend to us ("C," p. 72). If, however, we are driven by a nostalgia for lost origins, we too run the risk of effacing the "native" and stepping forth as "the real Caliban," of forgetting that he is a name in a play, an inaccessible blankness circumscribed by an interpretable text.[9] The stagings of Caliban work alongside the narrativization of history: claiming to *be* Caliban legitimizes the very individualism that we must persistently attempt to undermine from within.

Elizabeth Fox-Genovese, in an article on history and women's history, shows us how to define the historical moment of feminism in the West in terms of female access to individualism.[10] The battle for female individualism plays itself out within the larger theater of the establishment of meritocratic individualism, indexed in the aesthetic field by the ideology of "the creative imagination." Fox-Genovese's presupposition will guide us into the beautifully orchestrated opening of *Jane Eyre*.

It is a scene of the marginalization and privatization of the protagonist: "There was no possibility of taking a walk that day. . . . Out-door exercise was now out of the question. I was glad of it," Brontë writes (*JE*, p. 9). The movement continues as Jane breaks the rules of the appropriate topography of withdrawal. The family at the center withdraws into the sanctioned architectural space of the withdrawing room or drawing room; Jane inserts herself—"I slipped in"—into the margin—"A small breakfast-room *adjoined* the drawing room" (*JE,* p. 9; my emphasis).

The manipulation of the domestic inscription of space within the upwardly mobilizing currents of the eighteenth- and nineteenth-century bourgeoisie in England and France is well known. It seems fitting that the place to which Jane withdraws is not only not the withdrawing room but also not the dining room, the sanctioned place of family meals. Nor is it the library, the appropriate place for reading. The breakfast room "contained a book-case" (*JE*, p. 9). As Rudolph Ackerman wrote in his *Repository* (1823), one of the many manuals of taste in circulation in nineteenth-century England, these low bookcases and stands were designed to "contain all the books that may be desired for a sitting-room without reference to the library."[11] Even in this already triply off-center place, "having drawn the red moreen curtain nearly close, I [Jane] was shrined in double retirement" (*JE*, pp. 9–10).

Here in Jane's self-marginalized uniqueness, the reader becomes her accomplice: the reader and Jane are united—both are reading. Yet Jane still preserves her odd privilege, for she continues never quite doing the proper thing in its proper place. She cares little for reading what is *meant* to be read: the "letter-press." *She* reads the pictures. The power of this singular hermeneutics is precisely that it can make the outside inside. "At intervals, while turning over the leaves of my book, I studied the aspect of that winter afternoon." Under "the clear panes of glass," the rain no longer penetrates, "the drear November day" is rather a one-dimensional "aspect" to be "studied," not decoded like the "letter-press" but, like pictures, deciphered by the unique creative imagination of the marginal individualist (*JE*, p. 10).

Before following the track of this unique imagination, let us consider the suggestion that the progress of *Jane Eyre* can be charted through a sequential arrangement of the family/counter-family dyad. In the novel, we encounter, first, the Reeds as the legal family and Jane, the late Mr. Reed's sister's daughter, as the representative of a near incestuous counter-family; second, the Brocklehursts, who run the school Jane is sent to, as the legal family and Jane, Miss Temple, and Helen Burns as a counter-family that falls short because it is only a community of women; third, Rochester and the mad Mrs. Rochester as the legal family and Jane and Rochester as the illicit counter-family. Other items may be added to the thematic chain in this sequence: Rochester and Céline Varens as structurally functional counter-family; Rochester and Blanche Ingram as dissimulation of legality—and so on. It is during this sequence that Jane is moved from the counter-family to the family-in-law. In the next sequence, it is Jane who restores full family status to the as-yet-incomplete community of siblings, the Riverses. The final sequence of the book is a *community of families*, with Jane, Rochester, and their children at the center.

In terms of the narrative energy of the novel, how is Jane moved from the place of the counter-family to the family-in-law? It is the active ideology of imperialism that provides the discursive field.

(My working definition of "discursive field" must assume the existence of discrete "systems of signs" at hand in the socius, each based on a specific axiomatics. I am identifying these systems as discursive fields. "Imperialism as social mission" generates the possibility of one such axiomatics. How the individual artist taps the discursive field at hand with a sure touch, if not with transhistorical clairvoyance, in order to make the narrative structure move I hope to demonstrate through the following example. It is crucial that we extend our analysis of this example beyond the minimal diagnosis of "racism.")

Let us consider the figure of Bertha Mason, a figure produced by the axiomatics of imperialism. Through Bertha Mason, the white Jamaican Creole, Brontë renders the human/animal frontier as acceptably indeterminate, so that a good greater than the letter of the Law can be broached. Here is the celebrated passage, given in the voice of Jane:

> In the deep shade, at the further end of the room, a figure ran backwards and forwards. What it was, whether beast or human being, one could not . . . tell: it grovelled, seemingly, on all fours; it snatched and growled like some strange wild animal: but it was covered with clothing, and a quantity of dark, grizzled hair, wild as a mane, hid its head and face. [*JE*, p. 295]

In a matching passage, given in the voice of Rochester speaking *to* Jane, Brontë presents the imperative for a shift beyond the Law as divine injunction rather than human motive. In the terms of my essay, we might say that this is the register not of mere marriage or sexual reproduction but of Europe and its not-yet-human Other, of soul making. The field of imperial conquest is here inscribed as Hell:

> "One night I had been awakened by her yells . . . it was a fiery West Indian night. . . .

"'This life,' said I at last, 'is hell!—this is the air—those are the sounds of the bottomless pit! *I have a right* to deliver myself from it if I can. . . . Let me break away, and go home to God!' . . .

"A wind fresh from Europe blew over the ocean and rushed through the open casement: the storm broke, streamed, thundered, blazed, and the air grew pure. . . . It was true Wisdom that consoled me in that hour, and showed me the right path. . . .

"The sweet wind from Europe was still whispering in the refreshed leaves, and the Atlantic was thundering in glorious liberty. . . .

" 'Go,' said Hope, 'and live again in Europe. . . . You have done all that God and Humanity require of you.'" [*JE*, pp. 310–11; my emphasis]

It is the unquestioned ideology of imperialist axiomatics, then, that conditions Jane's move from the counter-family set to the set of the family-in-law. Marxist critics such as Terry Eagleton have seen this only in terms of the ambiguous *class* position of the governess.[12] Sandra Gilbert and Susan Gubar, on the other hand, have seen Bertha Mason only in psychological terms, as Jane's dark double.[13]

I will not enter the critical debates that offer themselves here. Instead, I will develop the suggestion that nineteenth-century feminist individualism could conceive of a "greater" project than access to the closed circle of the nuclear family. This is the project of soul making beyond "mere" sexual reproduction. Here the native "subject" is not almost an animal but rather the object of what might be termed the terrorism of the categorical imperative.

I am using "Kant" in this essay as a metonym for the most flexible ethical moment in the European eighteenth century. Kant words the categorical imperative, conceived as the universal moral law given by pure reason, in this way: "In all creation every thing one chooses and over which one has any power, may be used *merely as means;* man alone, and with him every rational creature, is an *end in himself.*" It is thus a moving displacement of Christian ethics from religion to philosophy. As Kant writes: "With this agrees very well the possibility of such a command as: *Love God above everything, and thy neighbor as thyself.* For as a command it requires respect for a law which *commands love* and does not leave it to our own arbitrary choice to make this our principle."[14]

The "categorical" in Kant cannot be adequately represented in determinately grounded action. The dangerous transformative power of philosophy, however, is that its formal subtlety can be travestied in the service of the state. Such a travesty in the case of the categorical imperative can justify the imperialist project by producing the following formula: *make* the heathen into a human so that he can be treated as an end in himself.[15] This project is presented as a sort of tangent in *Jane Eyre*, a tangent that escapes the closed circle of the *narrative* conclusion. The tangent narrative is the story of St. John Rivers, who is granted the important task of concluding the *text*.

At the novel's end, the *allegorical* language of Christian psychobiography—rather than the textually constituted and seemingly *private* grammar of the creative imagination which we noted in the novel's opening—marks the inaccessibility of the imperialist project as such to the nascent "feminist" scenario. The concluding passage of *Jane Eyre* places St. John Rivers within the fold of *Pilgrim's Progress*. Eagleton pays no attention to this but accepts the novel's ideological lexicon, which establishes St. John Rivers' heroism by identifying a life in Calcutta with an unquestioning choice of death. Gilbert and Gubar, by calling *Jane Eyre* "Plain Jane's progress," see the novel as simply replacing the male protagonist with the female. They do not notice the distance between sexual reproduction and soul making, both actualized by the unquestioned idiom of imperialist presuppositions evident in the last part of *Jane Eyre:*

> Firm, faithful, and devoted, full of energy, and zeal, and truth, [St. John Rivers] labours for his race. . . . His is the sternness of the warrior Greatheart, who guards his pilgrim convoy from the onslaught of Apollyon. . . . His is the ambition of the high master-spirit[s] . . . who stand without fault before the throne of God; who share the last mighty victories of the Lamb; who are called, and chosen, and faithful. [*JE,* p. 455]

Earlier in the novel, St. John Rivers himself justifies the project: "My vocation? My great work? . . . My hopes of being numbered in the band who have merged all ambitions in the glorious one of bettering their race—of carrying knowledge into the realms of ignorance—of substituting peace for war—freedom for bondage—religion for superstition—the hope of heaven for the fear of hell?" (*JE,* p. 376). Imperialism and its territorial and subject-constituting project are a violent deconstruction of these oppositions.

When Jean Rhys, born on the Caribbean island of Dominica, read *Jane Eyre* as a child, she was moved by Bertha Mason: "I thought I'd try to write her a life."[16] *Wide Sargasso Sea,* the slim novel published in 1965, at the end of Rhys' long career, is that "life."

I have suggested that Bertha's function in *Jane Eyre* is to render indeterminate the boundary between human and animal and thereby to weaken her entitlement under the spirit if not the letter of the Law. When Rhys rewrites the scene in *Jane Eyre* where Jane hears "a snarling, snatching sound, almost like a dog quarrelling" and then encounters a bleeding Richard Mason (*JE,* p. 210), she keeps Bertha's humanity, indeed her sanity as critic of imperialism, intact. Grace Poole, another character originally in *Jane Eyre,* describes the incident to Bertha in *Wide Sargasso Sea:* "So you don't remember that you attacked this gentleman with a knife? . . . I didn't hear all he said except 'I cannot interfere legally between yourself and your husband'. It was when he said 'legally' that you flew at him' " (*WSS*, p. 150). In Rhys' retelling, it is the dissimulation that Bertha discerns in the word "legally"—not an innate bestiality—that prompts her violent *re*action.

In the figure of Antoinette, whom in *Wide Sargasso Sea* Rochester violently renames Bertha, Rhys suggests that so intimate a thing as personal and human identity might be determined by the politics of imperialism. Antoinette, as a white Creole child growing up at the time of emancipation in Jamaica, is caught between the English imperialist and the black native. In recounting Antoinette's development, Rhys reinscribes some thematics of Narcissus.

There are, noticeably, many images of mirroring in the text. I will quote one from the first section. In this passage, Tia is the little black servant girl who is Antoinette's close companion: "We had eaten the same food, slept side by side, bathed in the same river. As I ran, I thought, I will live with Tia and I will be like her. . . . When I was close I saw the jagged stone in her hand but I did not see her throw it. . . . We stared at each other, blood on my face, tears on hers. It was as if I saw myself. Like in a looking glass" (*WSS*, p. 38).

A progressive sequence of dreams reinforces this mirror imagery. In its second occurrence, the dream is partially set in a *hortus conclusus*, or "enclosed garden"—Rhys uses the phrase (*WSS*, p. 50)—a Romance rewriting of the Narcissus topos as the place of encounter with Love.[17] In the enclosed garden, Antoinette encounters not Love but a strange threatening voice that says merely "in here," inviting her into a prison which masquerades as the legalization of love (*WSS*, p. 50).

In Ovid's *Metamorphoses*, Narcissus' madness is disclosed when he recognizes his Other as his self: "Iste ego sum."[18] Rhys makes Antoinette see her *self* as her Other, Brontë's Bertha. In the last section of *Wide Sargasso Sea*, Antoinette acts out *Jane Eyre*'s conclusion and recognizes herself as the so-called ghost in Thornfield Hall: "I went into the hall again with the tall candle in my hand. It was then that I saw her—the ghost. The woman with streaming hair. She was surrounded by a gilt frame but I knew her" (*WSS*, p. 154). The gilt frame encloses a mirror: as Narcissus' pool reflects the selfed Other, so this "pool" reflects the Othered self. Here the dream sequence ends, with an invocation of none other than Tia, the Other that could not be selfed, because the fracture of imperialism rather than the Ovidian pool intervened. (I will return to this difficult point.) "That was the third time I had my dream, and it ended. . . . I called 'Tia' and jumped and woke" (*WSS*, p. 155). It is now, at the very end of the book, that Antoinette/Bertha can say: "Now at last I know why I was brought here and what I have to do" (*WSS*, pp. 155–56). We can read this as her having been brought into the England of Brontë's novel: "This cardboard house"—a book between cardboard cov-

ers—"where I walk at night is not England" (*WSS*, p. 148). In this fictive
England, she must play out her role, act out the transformation of her
"self" into that fictive Other, set fire to the house and kill herself, so that
Jane Eyre can become the feminist individualist heroine of British fiction.
I must read this as an allegory of the general epistemic violence of
imperialism, the construction of a self-immolating colonial subject for
the glorification of the social mission of the colonizer. At least Rhys sees
to it that the woman from the colonies is not sacrificed as an insane
animal for her sister's consolation.

Critics have remarked that *Wide Sargasso Sea* treats the Rochester
character with understanding and sympathy.[19] Indeed, he narrates the
entire middle section of the book. Rhys makes it clear that he is a victim
of the patriarchal inheritance law of entailment rather than of a father's
natural preference for the firstborn: in *Wide Sargasso Sea,* Rochester's
situation is clearly that of a younger son dispatched to the colonies to
buy an heiress. If in the case of Antoinette and her identity, Rhys utilizes
the thematics of Narcissus, in the case of Rochester and his patrimony,
she touches on the thematics of Oedipus. (In this she has her finger on
our "historical moment." If, in the nineteenth century, subject-constitution
is represented as childbearing and soul making, in the twentieth century
psychoanalysis allows the West to plot the itinerary of the subject from
Narcissus [the "imaginary"] to Oedipus [the "symbolic"]. This subject,
however, is the normative male subject. In Rhys' reinscription of these
themes, divided between the female and the male protagonist, feminism
and a critique of imperialism become complicit.)

In place of the "wind from Europe" scene, Rhys substitutes the
scenario of a suppressed letter to a father, a letter which would be the
"correct" explanation of the tragedy of the book.[20] "I thought about the
letter which should have been written to England a week ago. Dear Father
. . ." (*WSS*, p. 57). This is the first instance: the letter not written. Shortly
afterward:

> Dear Father. The thirty thousand pounds have been paid to me
> without question or condition. No provision made for her (that
> must be seen to). . . . I will never be a disgrace to you or to my dear
> brother the son you love. No begging letters, no mean requests.
> None of the furtive shabby manoeuvres of a younger son. I have
> sold my soul or you have sold it, and after all is it such a bad bargain?
> The girl is thought to be beautiful, she is beautiful. And yet . . .
> [*WSS*, p. 59]

This is the second instance: the letter not sent. The formal letter is
uninteresting; I will quote only a part of it:

> Dear Father, we have arrived from Jamaica after an uncomfortable
> few days. This little estate in the Windward Islands is part of the

family property and Antoinette is much attached to it. . . . All is
well and has gone according to your plans and wishes. I dealt of
course with Richard Mason. . . . He seemed to become attached to
me and trusted me completely. This place is very beautiful but my
illness has left me too exhausted to appreciate it fully. I will write
again in a few days' time. [*WSS*, p. 63]

And so on.

Rhys' version of the Oedipal exchange is ironic, not a closed circle.
We cannot know if the letter actually reaches its destination. "I wondered
how they got their letters posted," the Rochester figure muses. "I folded
mine and put it into a drawer of the desk. . . . There are blanks in my
mind that cannot be filled up" (*WSS*, p. 64). It is as if the text presses us
to note the analogy between letter and mind.

Rhys denies to Brontë's Rochester the one thing that is supposed to
be secured in the Oedipal relay: the Name of the Father, or the patronymic.
In *Wide Sargasso Sea*, the character corresponding to Rochester has no
name. His writing of the final version of the letter to his father is supervised,
in fact, by an image of the *loss* of the patronymic: "There was a crude
bookshelf made of three shingles strung together over the desk and I
looked at the books, Byron's poems, novels by Sir Walter Scott, *Confessions
of an Opium Eater* . . . and on the last shelf, *Life and Letters of* . . . The rest
was eaten away" (*WSS*, p. 63).

Wide Sargasso Sea marks with uncanny clarity the limits of its own
discourse in Christophine, Antoinette's black nurse. We may perhaps
surmise the distance between *Jane Eyre* and *Wide Sargasso Sea* by remarking
that Christophine's unfinished story is the tangent to the latter narrative,
as St. John Rivers' story is to the former. Christophine is not a native of
Jamaica; she is from Martinique. Taxonomically, she belongs to the category
of the good servant rather than that of the pure native. But within these
borders, Rhys creates a powerfully suggestive figure.

Christophine is the first interpreter and named speaking subject in
the text. "The Jamaican ladies had never approved of my mother, 'because
she pretty like, pretty self' Christophine said," we read in the book's
opening paragraph (*WSS*, p. 15). I have taught this book five times, once
in France, once to students who had worked on the book with the well-
known Caribbean novelist Wilson Harris, and once at a prestigious institute
where the majority of the students were faculty from other universities.
It is part of the political argument I am making that all these students
blithely stepped over this paragraph without asking or knowing what
Christophine's patois, so-called incorrect English, might mean.

Christophine is, of course, a commodified person. " 'She was your
father's wedding present to me' " explains Antoinette's mother, " 'one of
his presents' " (*WSS*, p. 18). Yet Rhys assigns her some crucial functions
in the text. It is Christophine who judges that black ritual practices are

culture-specific and cannot be used by whites as cheap remedies for social evils, such as Rochester's lack of love for Antoinette. Most important, it is Christophine alone whom Rhys allows to offer a hard analysis of Rochester's actions, to challenge him in a face-to-face encounter. The entire extended passage is worthy of comment. I quote a brief extract:

> "She is Creole girl, and she have the sun in her. Tell the truth now. She don't come to your house in this place England they tell me about, she don't come to your beautiful house to beg you to marry with her. No, it's you come all the long way to her house—it's you beg her to marry. And she love you and she give you all she have. Now you say you don't love her and you break her up. What you do with her money, eh?" [And then Rochester, the white man, comments silently to himself] Her voice was still quiet but with a hiss in it when she said "money." [*WSS*, p. 130]

Her analysis is powerful enough for the white man to be afraid: "I no longer felt dazed, tired, half hypnotized, but alert and wary, ready to defend myself" (*WSS*, p. 130).

Rhys does not, however, romanticize individual heroics on the part of the oppressed. When the Man refers to the forces of Law and Order, Christophine recognizes their power. This exposure of civil inequality is emphasized by the fact that, just before the Man's successful threat, Christophine had invoked the emancipation of slaves in Jamaica by proclaiming: "No chain gang, no tread machine, no dark jail either. This is free country and I am free woman" (*WSS*, p. 131).

As I mentioned above, Christophine is tangential to this narrative. She cannot be contained by a novel which rewrites a canonical English text within the European novelistic tradition in the interest of the white Creole rather than the native. No perspective *critical* of imperialism can turn the Other into a self, because the project of imperialism has always already historically refracted what might have been the absolutely Other into a domesticated Other that consolidates the imperialist self.[21] The Caliban of Retamar, caught between Europe and Latin America, reflects this predicament. We can read Rhys' reinscription of Narcissus as a thematization of the same problematic.

Of course, we cannot know Jean Rhys' feelings in the matter. We can, however, look at the scene of Christophine's inscription in the text. Immediately after the exchange between her and the Man, well before the conclusion, she is simply driven out of the story, with neither narrative nor characterological explanation or justice. " 'Read and write I don't know. Other things I know.' She walked away without looking back" (*WSS*, p. 133).

Indeed, if Rhys rewrites the madwoman's attack on the Man by underlining of the misuse of "legality," she cannot deal with the passage that corresponds to St. John Rivers' own justification of his martyrdom, for it has been displaced into the current idiom of modernization and development. Attempts to construct the "Third World Woman" as a signifier remind us that the hegemonic definition of literature is itself caught within the history of imperialism. A full literary reinscription cannot easily flourish in the imperialist fracture or discontinuity, covered over by an alien legal system masquerading as Law as such, an alien ideology established as only Truth, and a set of human sciences busy establishing the "native" as self-consolidating Other.

In the Indian case at least, it would be difficult to find an ideological clue to the planned epistemic violence of imperialism merely by rearranging curricula or syllabi within existing norms of literary pedagogy. For a later period of imperialism—when the constituted colonial subject has firmly taken hold—straightforward experiments of comparison can be undertaken, say, between the functionally witless India of *Mrs. Dalloway,* on the one hand, and literary texts produced in India in the 1920s, on the other. But the first half of the nineteenth century resists questioning through literature or literary criticism in the narrow sense, because both are implicated in the project of producing Ariel. To reopen the fracture without succumbing to a nostalgia for lost origins, the literary critic must turn to the archives of imperial governance.

In conclusion, I shall look briefly at Mary Shelley's *Frankenstein,* a text of nascent feminism that remains cryptic, I think, simply because it does not speak the language of feminist individualism which we have come to hail as the language of high feminism within English literature. It is interesting that Barbara Johnson's brief study tries to rescue this recalcitrant text for the service of feminist autobiography.[22] Alternatively, George Levine reads *Frankenstein* in the context of the creative imagination and the nature of the hero. He sees the novel as a book about its own writing and about writing itself, a Romantic allegory of reading within which Jane Eyre as unself-conscious critic would fit quite nicely.[23]

I propose to take *Frankenstein* out of this arena and focus on it in terms of that sense of English cultural identity which I invoked at the opening of this essay. Within that focus we are obliged to admit that, although *Frankenstein* is ostensibly about the origin and evolution of man in society, it does not deploy the axiomatics of imperialism.

Let me say at once that there is plenty of incidental imperialist sentiment in *Frankenstein.* My point, within the argument of this essay, is that the discursive field of imperialism does not produce unquestioned ideological correlatives for the narrative structuring of the book. The discourse of imperialism surfaces in a curiously powerful way in Shelley's novel, and I will later discuss the moment at which it emerges.

Frankenstein is not a battleground of male and female individualism articulated in terms of sexual reproduction (family and female) and social subject-production (race and male). That binary opposition is undone in Victor Frankenstein's laboratory—an artificial womb where both projects are undertaken simultaneously, though the terms are never openly spelled out. Frankenstein's apparent antagonist is God himself as Maker of Man, but his real competitor is also woman as the maker of children. It is not just that his dream of the death of mother and bride and the actual death of his bride are associated with the visit of his monstrous homoerotic "son" to his bed. On a much more overt level, the monster is a bodied "corpse," unnatural because bereft of a determinable childhood: "No father had watched my infant days, no mother had blessed me with smiles and caresses; or if they had, all my past was now a blot, a blind vacancy in which I distinguished nothing" (*F*, pp. 57, 115). It is Frankenstein's own ambiguous and miscued understanding of the real motive for the monster's vengefulness that reveals his own competition with woman as maker:

> I created a rational creature and was bound towards him to assure, as far as was in my power, his happiness and well-being. This was my duty, but there was another still paramount to that. My duties towards the beings of my own species had greater claims to my attention because they included a greater proportion of happiness or misery. Urged by this view, I refused, and I did right in refusing, to create a companion for the first creature. [*F*, p. 206]

It is impossible not to notice the accents of transgression inflecting Frankenstein's demolition of his experiment to create the future Eve. Even in the laboratory, the woman-in-the-making is not a bodied corpse but "a human being." The (il)logic of the metaphor bestows on her a prior existence which Frankenstein aborts, rather than an anterior death which he reembodies: "The remains of the half-finished creature, whom I had destroyed, lay scattered on the floor, and I almost felt as if I had mangled the living flesh of a human being" (*F*, p. 163).

In Shelley's view, man's hubris as soul maker both usurps the place of God and attempts—vainly—to sublate woman's physiological prerogative.[24] Indeed, indulging a Freudian fantasy here, I could urge that, if to give and withhold to/from the mother a phallus is *the* male fetish, then to give and withhold to/from the man a womb might be the female fetish.[25] The icon of the sublimated womb in man is surely his productive brain, the box in the head.

In the judgment of classical psychoanalysis, the phallic mother exists only by virtue of the castration-anxious son; in *Frankenstein*'s judgment, the hysteric father (Victor Frankenstein gifted with his laboratory—the womb of theoretical reason) cannot produce a daughter. Here the language of racism—the dark side of imperialism understood as social mission— combines with the hysteria of masculism into the idiom of (the withdrawal of) sexual reproduction rather than subject-constitution. The roles of masculine and feminine individualists are hence reversed and displaced. Frankenstein cannot produce a "daughter" because "she might become ten thousand times more malignant than her mate . . . [and because] one of the first results of those sympathies for which the demon thirsted would be children, and a race of devils would be propagated upon the earth who might make the very existence of the species of man a condition precarious and full of terror" (*F*, p. 158). This particular narrative strand also launches a thoroughgoing critique of the eighteenth-century European discourses on the origin of society through (Western Christian) man. Should I mention that, much like Jean-Jacques Rousseau's remark in his *Confessions*, Frankenstein declares himself to be "by birth a Genevese" (*F*, p. 31)?

In this overly didactic text, Shelley's point is that social engineering should not be based on pure, theoretical, or natural-scientific reason alone, which is her implicit critique of the utilitarian vision of an engineered society. To this end, she presents in the first part of her deliberately schematic story three characters, childhood friends, who seem to represent Kant's three-part conception of the human subject: Victor Frankenstein, the forces of theoretical reason or "natural philosophy"; Henry Clerval, the forces of practical reason or "the moral relations of things"; and Elizabeth Lavenza, that aesthetic judgment—"the aerial creation of the poets"—which, according to Kant, is "a suitable mediating link connecting the realm of the concept of nature and that of the concept of freedom . . . (which) promotes . . . *moral* feeling" (*F*, pp. 37, 36).[26]

This three-part subject does not operate harmoniously in *Frankenstein*. That Henry Clerval, associated as he is with practical reason, should have as his "design . . . to visit India, in the belief that he had in his knowledge of its various languages, and in the views he had taken of its society, the means of materially assisting the progress of European colonization and trade" is proof of this, as well as part of the incidental imperialist sentiment that I speak of above (*F*, pp. 151–52). I should perhaps point out that the language here is entrepreneurial rather than missionary:

> He came to the university with the design of making himself complete master of the Oriental languages, as thus he should open a field for the plan of life he had marked out for himself. Resolved to pursue no inglorious career, he turned his eyes towards the East as affording scope for his spirit of enterprise. The Persian, Arabic, and Sanskrit languages engaged his attention. [*F*, pp. 66–67]

But it is of course Victor Frankenstein, with his strange itinerary of obsession with natural philosophy, who offers the strongest demonstration that the multiple perspectives of the three-part Kantian subject cannot co-operate harmoniously. Frankenstein creates a putative human subject out of natural philosophy alone. According to his own miscued summation:

"In a fit of enthusiastic madness I created a rational creature" (*F*, p. 206). It is not at all farfetched to say that Kant's categorical imperative can most easily be mistaken for the hypothetical imperative—a command to ground in cognitive comprehension what can be apprehended only by moral will—by putting natural philosophy in the place of practical reason.

I should hasten to add here that just as readings such as this one do not necessarily accuse Charlotte Brontë the named individual of harboring imperialist sentiments, so also they do not necessarily commend Mary Shelley the named individual for writing a successful Kantian allegory. The most I can say is that it is possible to read these texts, within the frame of imperialism and the Kantian ethical moment, in a politically useful way. Such an approach presupposes that a "disinterested" reading attempts to render transparent the interests of the hegemonic readership. (Other "political" readings—for instance, that the monster is the nascent working class—can also be advanced.)

Frankenstein is built in the established epistolary tradition of multiple frames. At the heart of the multiple frames, the narrative of the monster (as reported by Frankenstein to Robert Walton, who then recounts it in a letter to his sister) is of his almost learning, clandestinely, to be human. It is invariably noticed that the monster reads *Paradise Lost* as true history. What is not so often noticed is that he also reads Plutarch's *Lives*, "the histories of the first founders of the ancient republics," which he compares to "the patriarchal lives of my protectors" (*F*, pp. 123, 124). And his *education* comes through "Volney's *Ruins of Empires*," which purported to be a prefiguration of the French Revolution, published after the event and after the author had rounded off his theory with practice (*F*, p. 113). It is an attempt at an enlightened universal secular, rather than a Eurocentric Christian, history, written from the perspective of a narrator "from below," somewhat like the attempts of Eric Wolf or Peter Worsley in our own time.[27]

This Caliban's education in (universal secular) humanity takes place through the monster's eavesdropping on the instruction of an Ariel— Safie, the Christianized "Arabian" to whom "a residence in Turkey was abhorrent" (*F*, p. 121). In depicting Safie, Shelley uses some commonplaces of eighteenth-century liberalism that are shared by many today: Safie's Muslim father was a victim of (bad) Christian religious prejudice and yet was himself a wily and ungrateful man not as morally refined as her (good) Christian mother. Having tasted the emancipation of woman, Safie could not go home. The confusion between "Turk" and "Arab" has its counterpart in present-day confusion about Turkey and Iran as "Middle Eastern" but not "Arab."

Although we are a far cry here from the unexamined and covert axiomatics of imperialism in *Jane Eyre*, we will gain nothing by celebrating the time-bound pieties that Shelley, as the daughter of two antievangelicals, produces. It is more interesting for us that Shelley differentiates the

Other, works at the Caliban/Ariel distinction, and *cannot* make the monster identical with the proper recipient of these lessons. Although he had "heard of the discovery of the American hemisphere and *wept with Safie* over the helpless fate of its original inhabitants," Safie cannot reciprocate his attachment. When she first catches sight of him, "Safie, unable to attend to her friend [Agatha], rushed out of the cottage" (*F*, pp. 114 [my emphasis], 129).

In the taxonomy of characters, the Muslim-Christian Safie belongs with Rhys' Antoinette/Bertha. And indeed, like Christophine the good servant, the subject created by the fiat of natural philosophy is the tangential unresolved moment in *Frankenstein*. The simple suggestion that the monster is human inside but monstrous outside and only provoked into vengefulness is clearly not enough to bear the burden of so great a historical dilemma.

At one moment, in fact, Shelley's Frankenstein does try to tame the monster, to humanize him by bringing him within the circuit of the Law. He "repair[s] to a criminal judge in the town and . . . relate[s his] history briefly but with firmness"—the first and disinterested version of the narrative of Frankenstein—"marking the dates with accuracy and never deviating into invective or exclamation. . . . When I had concluded my narration I said, 'This is the being whom I accuse and for whose seizure and punishment I call upon you to exert your whole power. It is your duty as a magistrate' " (*F*, pp. 189, 190). The sheer social reasonableness of the mundane voice of Shelley's "Genevan magistrate" reminds us that the absolutely Other cannot be selfed, that the monster has "properties" which will not be contained by "proper" measures:

> "I will exert myself [he says], and if it is in my power to seize the monster, be assured that he shall suffer punishment proportionate to his crimes. But I fear, from what you have yourself described to be his properties, that this will prove impracticable; and thus, while every proper measure is pursued, you should make up your mind to disappointment." [*F*, p. 190]

In the end, as is obvious to most readers, distinctions of human individuality themselves seem to fall away from the novel. Monster, Frankenstein, and Walton seem to become each others' relays. Frankenstein's story comes to an end in death; Walton concludes his own story within the frame of his function as letter writer. In the *narrative* conclusion, he is the natural philosopher who learns from Frankenstein's example. At the end of the *text*, the monster, having confessed his guilt toward his maker and ostensibly intending to immolate himself, is borne away on an ice raft. We do not see the conflagration of his funeral pile—the self-immolation is not consummated in the text: he too cannot be contained by the text. In terms of narrative logic, he is "lost in darkness and distance"

(*F*, p. 211)—these are the last words of the novel—into an existential temporality that is coherent with neither the territorializing individual imagination (as in the opening of *Jane Eyre*) nor the authoritative scenario of Christian psychobiography (as at the end of Brontë's work). The very relationship between sexual reproduction and social subject-production— the dynamic nineteenth-century topos of feminism-in-imperialism—remains problematic within the limits of Shelley's text and, paradoxically, constitutes its strength.

Earlier, I offered a reading of woman as womb holder in *Frankenstein*. I would now suggest that there is a framing woman in the book who is neither tangential, nor encircled, nor yet encircling. "Mrs. Saville," "excellent Margaret," "beloved Sister" are her address and kinship inscriptions (*F*, pp. 15, 17, 22). She is the occasion, though not the protagonist, of the novel. She is the feminine *subject* rather than the female individualist: she is the irreducible *recipient*-function of the letters that constitute *Frankenstein*. I have commented on the singular appropriative hermeneutics of the reader reading with Jane in the opening pages of *Jane Eyre*. Here the reader must read with Margaret Saville in the crucial sense that she must *intercept* the recipient-function, read the letters *as* recipient, in order for the novel to exist.[28] Margaret Saville does not respond to close the text as frame. The frame is thus simultaneously not a frame, and the monster can step "beyond the text" and be "lost in darkness." Within the allegory of our reading, the place of both the English lady and the unnamable monster are left open by this great flawed text. It is satisfying for a postcolonial reader to consider this a noble resolution for a nineteenth-century English novel. This is all the more striking because, on the anecdotal level, Shelley herself abundantly "identifies" with Victor Frankenstein.[29]

I must myself close with an idea that I cannot establish within the limits of this essay. Earlier I contended that *Wide Sargasso Sea* is necessarily bound by the reach of the European novel. I suggested that, in contradistinction, to reopen the epistemic fracture of imperialism without succumbing to a nostalgia for lost origins, the critic must turn to the archives of imperialist governance. I have not turned to those archives in these pages. In my current work, by way of a modest and inexpert "reading" of "archives," I try to extend, outside of the reach of the European novelistic tradition, the most powerful suggestion in *Wide Sargasso Sea*: that *Jane Eyre* can be read as the orchestration and staging of the self-immolation of Bertha Mason as "good wife." The power of that suggestion remains unclear if we remain insufficiently knowledgeable about the history of the legal manipulation of widow-sacrifice in the entitlement of the British government in India. I would hope that an informed critique of imperialism, granted some attention from readers in the First World, will at least expand the frontiers of the politics of reading.

1. My notion of the "worlding of a world" upon what must be assumed to be uninscribed earth is a vulgarization of Martin Heidegger's idea; see "The Origin of the Work of Art," *Poetry, Language, Thought,* trans. Albert Hofstadter (New York, 1977), pp. 17–87.

2. See Charlotte Brontë, *Jane Eyre* (New York, 1960); all further references to this work, abbreviated *JE,* will be included in the text.

3. See Jean Rhys, *Wide Sargasso Sea* (Harmondsworth, 1966); all further references to this work, abbreviated *WSS,* will be included in the text. And see Mary Shelley, *Frankenstein; or, The Modern Prometheus* (New York, 1965); all further references to this work, abbreviated *F,* will be included in the text.

4. I have tried to do this in my essay "Unmaking and Making in *To the Lighthouse,*" in *Women and Language in Literature and Society,* ed. Sally McConnell-Ginet, Ruth Borker, and Nelly Furman (New York, 1980), pp. 310–27.

5. As always, I take my formula from Louis Althusser, "Ideology an Ideological State Apparatuses (Notes towards an Investigation)," *"Lenin and Philosophy" and Other Essays,* trans. Ben Brewster (New York, 1971), pp. 127–86. For an acute differentiation between the individual and individualism, see V. N. Vološinov, *Marxism and the Philosophy of Language,* trans. Ladislav Matejka and I. R. Titunik, Studies in Language, vol. 1 (New York, 1973), pp. 93–94 and 152–53. For a "straight" analysis of the roots and ramifications of English "individualism," see C. B. MacPherson, *The Political Theory of Possessive Individualism: Hobbes to Locke* (Oxford, 1962). I am grateful to Jonathan Rée for bringing this book to my attention and for giving a careful reading of all but the very end of the present essay.

6. I am constructing an analogy with Homi Bhabha's powerful notion of "not-quite/ not-white" in his "Of Mimicry and Man: The Ambiguity of Colonial Discourse," *October* 28 (Spring 1984): 132. I should also add that I use the word "native" here in reaction to the term "Third World Woman." It cannot, of course, apply with equal historical justice to both the West Indian and the Indian contexts nor to contexts of imperialism by transportation.

7. See Roberto Fernández Retamar, "Caliban: Notes towards a Discussion of Culture in Our America," trans. Lynn Garafola, David Arthur McMurray, and Robert Márquez, *Massachusetts Review* 15 (Winter–Spring 1974): 7–72; all further references to this work, abbreviated "C," will be included in the text.

8. See José Enrique Rodó, *Ariel,* ed. Gordon Brotherston (Cambridge, 1967).

9. For an elaboration of "an inaccessible blankness circumscribed by an interpretable text," see my "Can the Subaltern Speak?" *Marxist Interpretations of Culture,* ed. Cary Nelson (Urbana, Ill., forthcoming).

10. See Elizabeth Fox-Genovese, "Placing Women's History in History," *New Left Review* 133 (May–June 1982): 5–29.

11. Rudolph Ackerman, *The Repository of Arts, Literature, Commerce, Manufactures, Fashions, and Politics,* (London, 1823), p. 310.

12. See Terry Eagleton, *Myths of Power: A Marxist Study of the Brontës* (London, 1975); this is one of the general presuppositions of his book.

13. See Sandra M. Gilbert and Susan Gubar, *The Madwoman in the Attic: The Woman Writer and the Nineteenth-Century Literary Imagination* (New Haven, Conn., 1979), pp. 360–62.

14. Immanuel Kant, *Critique of Practical Reason, The "Critique of Pure Reason," the "Critique of Practical Reason" and Other Ethical Treatises, the "Critique of Judgement,"* trans. J. M. D. Meiklejohn et al. (Chicago, 1952), pp. 328, 326.

15. I have tried to justify the reduction of sociohistorical problems to formulas or propositions in my essay "Can the Subaltern Speak?" The "travesty" I speak of does not befall the Kantian ethic in its purity as an accident but rather exists within its lineaments as a possible supplement. On the register of the human being as child rather than heathen, my formula can be found, for example, in "What Is Enlightenment?" in Kant, *"Foundations of the Metaphysics of Morals," "What Is Enlightenment?" and a Passage from "The Metaphysics of Morals,"* trans. and ed. Lewis White Beck (Chicago, 1950). I have profited from discussing Kant with Jonathan Rée.

16. Jean Rhys, in an interview with Elizabeth Vreeland, quoted in Nancy Harrison, *An Introduction to the Writing Practice of Jean Rhys: The Novel as Women's Text* (Rutherford, N. J., forthcoming). This is an excellent, detailed study of Rhys.

17. See Louise Vinge, *The Narcissus Theme in Western European Literature Up to the Early Nineteenth Century,* trans. Robert Dewsnap et al. (Lund, 1967), chap. 5.

18. For a detailed study of this text, see John Brenkman, "Narcissus in the Text," *Georgia Review* 30 (Summer 1976): 293–327.

19. See, e.g., Thomas F. Staley, *Jean Rhys: A Critical Study* (Austin, Tex. 1979), pp. 108–16; it is interesting to note Staley's masculist discomfort with this and his consequent dissatisfaction with Rhys' novel.

20. I have tried to relate castration and suppressed letters in my "The Letter As Cutting Edge," in *Literature and Psychoanalysis; The Question of Reading: Otherwise,* ed. Shoshana Felman (New Haven, Conn., 1981), pp. 208–26.

21. This is the main argument of my "Can the Subaltern Speak?"

22. See Barbara Johnson, "My Monster/My Self," *Diacritics* 12 (Summer 1982): 2–10.

23. See George Levine, *The Realistic Imagination: English Fiction from Frankenstein to Lady Chatterley* (Chicago, 1981), pp. 23–35.

24. Consult the publications of the Feminist International Network for the best overview of the current debate on reproductive technology.

25. For the male fetish, see Sigmund Freud, "Fetishism," *The Standard Edition of the Complete Psychological Works of Sigmund Freud,* ed. and trans. James Strachey et al., 24 vols. (London, 1953–74), 21:152–57. For a more "serious" Freudian study of *Frankenstein,* see Mary Jacobus, "Is There a Woman in This Text?" *New Literary History* 14 (Autumn 1982): 117–41. My "fantasy" would of course be disproved by the "fact" that it is more difficult for a woman to assume the position of fetishist than for a man; see Mary Ann Doane, "Film and the Masquerade: Theorising the Female Spectator," *Screen* 23 (Sept.–Oct. 1982): 74–87.

26. Kant, *Critique of Judgement,* trans. J. H. Bernard (New York, 1951), p. 39.

27. See [Constantin François Chasseboeuf de Volney], *The Ruins; or, Meditations on the Revolutions of Empires,* trans. pub. (London, 1811). Johannes Fabian has shown us the manipulation of time in "new" secular histories of a similar kind; see *Time and the Other: How Anthropology Makes Its Object* (New York, 1983). See also Eric R. Wolf, *Europe and the People without History* (Berkeley and Los Angeles, 1982), and Peter Worsley, *The Third World,* 2d ed. (Chicago, 1973); I am grateful to Dennis Dworkin for bringing the latter book to my attention. The most striking ignoring of the monster's education through Volney is in Gilbert's otherwise brilliant "Horror's Twin: Mary Shelley's Monstrous Eve," *Feminist Studies* 4 (June 1980): 48–73. Gilbert's essay reflects the absence of race-determinations in a certain sort of feminism. Her present work has most convincingly filled in this gap; see, e.g., her recent piece on H. Rider Haggard's *She* ("Rider Haggard's Heart of Darkness," *Partisan Review* 50, no. 3 [1983]: 444–53).

28. "A letter is always and *a priori* intercepted, . . . the 'subjects' are neither the senders nor the receivers of messages. . . . The letter is constituted . . . by its interception" (Jacques Derrida, "Discussion," after Claude Rabant, "Il n'a aucune chance de l'entendre," in *Affranchissement: Du transfert et de la lettre,* ed. René Major [Paris, 1981], p. 106; my translation). Margaret Saville is not made to appropriate the reader's "subject" into the signature of her own "individuality."

29. The most striking "internal evidence" is the admission in the "Author's Introduction" that, after dreaming of the yet-unnamed Victor Frankenstein figure and being terrified (through, yet not quite through, him) by the monster in a scene she later reproduced in Frankenstein's story, Shelley began her tale "on the morrow . . . with the words 'It was on a dreary night of November'" (*F,* p. xi). Those are the opening words of chapter 5 of the finished book, where Frankenstein begins to recount the actual making of his monster (see *F,* p. 56).

Theories of Africans: The Question of Literary Anthropology

Christopher L. Miller

Une caravane traverse l'étendue infinie et morne de ces plaines, caravane de négriers, le plus souvent poussant devant eux de lamentables théories d'hommes, de femmes, d'enfants couverts d'ulcères, étranglés par le carcan, mains ensanglantées par les liens.

A caravan traversed those dismal and endless plains: slave traders driving wretched files ["theories"] of men, women, and children, covered with open sores, choked in iron collars, their wrists shackled and bleeding.

—YAMBO OUOLOGUEM, *Le Devoir de violence*

Literary criticism at the present moment seems ready to open its doors once again to the outside world, even if that world is only a series of other academic disciplines, each cloistered in its own way. For the reader of black African literature in French, the opening comes none too soon. The program for reading Camara Laye, Ahmadou Kourouma, and Yambo Ouologuem should never have been the program prescribed for Rousseau, Wordsworth, or Blanchot. If one is willing to read a literature that might not be a rewriting of Hegel (or even of Kant), and if the negative knowledge of recent theoretical criticism is questioned in the universality of its applications, then what is really open to a Western reader of non-Western literature? Claiming a break with his/her own culture and critical upbringing, can he/she read the Other, the African, as if from an authentically

All translations are by the author unless otherwise indicated.

African point of view, interpreting Africa in African terms, perceiving rather than projecting?

The goal of breaking through the nets of Western criticism, of reading African literature in a nonethnocentric, nonprojective fashion, will remain both indisputably desirable and ultimately unattainable. No matter how many languages I learn or ethnologies I study, I cannot make myself into an African. The Western scholar's claim to mastery of things African, albeit motivated by xenophilia rather than xenophobia, risks subjugation of the object to a new set of Western models. J. P. Makouta-M'Boukou rightly scolds Western critics who refuse to take into account the distance between themselves and African culture, and who read African literature only in function of their own cultural context.[1] Wole Soyinka, more forbiddingly, complains: "We black Africans have been blandly invited to submit ourselves to a second epoch of colonisation—this time by a universal-humanoid abstraction defined and conducted by individuals whose theories and prescriptions are derived from the apprehension of *their* world and *their* history, *their* social neuroses and *their* value systems."[2]

On the other hand, the fact of being biologically or culturally African neither guarantees nor necessarily permits any sort of purely authentic "African" reading, in a relation of total oneness with its text or with Africa itself—as we will see in examining recent critiques of Negritude. The question thus becomes a practical one of establishing guidelines for a kind of reading that lets the Other talk without claiming to be possessed of the Other's voice. It becomes evident from the start that contact with African literature will involve contact with, even dependence on, anthropology. The facts and interpretations of traditional African cultures— defined as those elements which precede or escape from European influence—are most likely to be found in texts which are labeled as ethnographic or anthropological. If one is to let the Other have its true dimensions, to stretch and displace the categories of a Western approach and not simply be, in Baudelaire's phrase, "un Orient de l'Occident," if one is to break the shell of self-reflexivity and Eurocentrism, then "theory"— European literature turning on itself—would do well to let itself be displaced by anthropology. This paper is intended as a programmatic reflection

1. See J. P. Makouta-M'Boukou, *Introduction à l'étude du roman négro-africain de langue française* (Abidjan, Ivory Coast, 1980), p. 9.
2. Wole Soyinka, *Myth, Literature, and the African World* (Cambridge, 1976), p. x.

Christopher L. Miller, Charles B. G. Murphy Assistant Professor of French and of African and Afro-American Studies at Yale University, is author of *Blank Darkness: Africanist Discourse in French* (1985). He is working at present on a study of francophone black African literature, for which he will have a Fulbright Africa Research grant.

on the relation between theory, anthropology, and the interpretation of African literature, as a call for a methodology that will only be elaborated in future work. I will therefore concentrate here on an examination of the historical relationship between black literature in French and a body of anthropological texts that influenced that literature.[3]

Allow me to be the first to question my own characterization of theory as self-reflexivity. But therein lies the question: can one think with theoretical rigor, can one rise above or dig below surface "themes" to the point at which literature is unveiled in a state of pure and rarefied, disseminative meaning, without at the same time obliterating difference itself, which may well reside or find its contact point in surface themes? The opposition between theory and difference should be a false one: from Blanchot and Bataille to Derrida and de Man, concepts such as alterity, deferral, adjournment, and difference itself occupy a privileged position. De Man's formula for describing allegory, to take one example, as "renouncing the nostalgia and the desire to coincide" seems to be the very model of a nonimperialistic *tolerance* of difference.[4] The subject renounces any claim to possession or totalization, permitting the Other to be itself. Yet in that phrase we see the roots of an intellectual problem: renouncing the claim to *have coincided* with the Other allows the Other to be different and apart from the subject, but when the subject renounces even the *desire* to coincide, the question of *knowing* the Other becomes problematic. Can knowledge be knowledge without coinciding, without on some level claiming appropriation and possession? Recent theories of "difference" have relegated difference to the realm of the purely theoretical. When, in the context of de Man's article "Semiology and Rhetoric," Archie Bunker asks Edith, "What's the difference?" (between lacing his bowling shoes "over" or "under"), the question is purely rhetorical. As de Man comments, " 'What's the difference?' *did not ask for difference* but means instead 'I don't give a damn what the difference is.' . . . Grammar allows us to ask the question, but the sentence by means of which we ask it may deny the very possibility of asking."[5]

3. I have been influenced in this undertaking by James Clifford's "On Ethnographic Authority," *Representations* 1 (Spring 1983): 118–46; by V. Y. Mudimbe's *L'Odeur du père: Essai sur les limites de la science et de la vie en Afrique noire* (Paris, 1982); and by Michèle Duchet's *Anthropologie et histoire au siècle des lumières: Buffon, Voltaire, Rousseau, Helvétius, Diderot* (Paris, 1971). Other relevant works include: Dan Sperber, *Le Savoir des anthropologues: Trois essais* (Paris, 1982); Clifford Geertz, *The Interpretation of Cultures: Selected Essays* (New York, 1973); and Paul Désalmand, *Sciences humaines et philosophie en Afrique: la différence culturelle* (Paris, 1978).

4. Paul de Man, "The Rhetoric of Temporality," in *Interpretation: Theory and Practice,* ed. Charles S. Singleton (Baltimore, 1969), p. 191.

5. De Man, "Semiology and Rhetoric," *Allegories of Reading: Figural Language in Rousseau, Nietzsche, Rilke, and Proust* (New Haven, Conn., 1979), p. 10; my emphasis. Archie Bunker

But suppose we *had* to give a damn what the difference is, even faced with all the "vertiginous possibilities of referential aberration" associated with literature? How can we proceed from a rhetorical "What's the difference?" to an *anthropological* (?) "What is different?" without jettisoning the wisdom of the former for ,the benefits of the latter? The challenge now is to formulate a model of knowledge which, while remaining conscious of the lessons of rhetorical theory, recognizes European theory as a *local phenomenon.*

Readers with strong theoretical backgrounds recognize that knowledge—particularly Western knowledge of Africa—far from being simply *lux et veritas,* can most often be revealed as a corrosive project of appropriation, wherein the Western reader projects desires onto the Other. Once the African text has surrendered its meaning, a treaty is signed, written by the Western critic who thereby influences not only reception of the present work but also publication of future African works, still largely published in Paris. The interpretive tie between reader and text is also a bond of enslavement. This negative model of interpretation then becomes a force of its own, enjoining the Western reader to assess only that of which he/she can be sure—his/her own reading processes. Readings are only readings of readings, and so on. Paradoxically, the only positive object of knowledge left to be trusted is not an object at all, but the solitary subject, paralyzed by its own power.

An illustrative example comes from classroom experience, from a discussion of Cheikh Hamidou Kane's novel *L'Aventure ambiguë.* The culture depicted by Kane, that of the Diallobé of Senegal, has been Islamic for centuries; the novel is concerned with the ambiguities involved in choosing between adherence to the old culture and surrender to the new one, that of French colonialism. The portrait of one of the principal characters, La Grande Royale, is itself already a "reading" of her face as a text:

> On la nommait la Grande Royale. . . . On ne voyait d'elle que le visage . . . qui était comme une page vivante de l'historie du pays des Diallobé. Tout ce que le pays compte de tradition épique s'y lisait. Les traits étaient tout en longueur. . . . Tout le reste disparaissait sous la gaze qui, davantage qu'une coiffure, prenait ici une signification de symbole. L'Islam refrénait la redoutable turbulence de ces traits, de la même façon que la voilette les enserrait. Autour des yeux et sur les pommettes, sur tout ce visage,

---

actually (in an episode of "All in the Family") went on to say: "I didn't say 'What's the difference—explain it to me,' I said 'What's the difference—Who the hell cares?' " Barbara Johnson has referred to this passage from de Man in her "Gender Theory and the Yale School," in *Rhetoric and Form: Deconstruction at Yale,* ed. Robert Con Davis and Ronald Schleifer (Norman, Okla., 1985), pp. 101–12.

il y avait comme le souvenir d'une jeunesse et d'une force sur
lesquelles se serait apposé brutalement le rigide éclat d'un souffle
ardent.

> They called her the Most Royal Lady. She was sixty years old,
> and she would have been taken for scarcely forty. Nothing was to
> be seen of her except her face . . . [which] was like a living page
> from the history of the Diallobé country. Everything that the country
> treasured of epic tradition could be read there. All the features
> were in long lines. . . . All the rest disappeared under the gauze,
> which, more than a coiffure would have done, took on here a
> symbolic meaning. Islam restrained the formidable turbulence of
> those features, in the same way that the little veil hemmed them
> in. Around the eyes and on the cheeks, over all this countenance,
> there was, as it were, the memory of a youth and a force upon
> which the rigid blast of an ardent breath was later brutally to
> blow.[6]

The passage leaves no doubt that it is concerned with the violent silencing
of one culture by another. That which represses is named as Islam; "all
the rest," hidden behind the veil, is identified two pages later as "un fond
de paganisme," a pagan substratum, the pre-Islamic culture of the Diallobé
which has not been completely erased after centuries of inculcation. A
student well trained in theory objected, however, to this interpretation
of the blank face behind the veil on the grounds that such an interpretation
was a mere "inscription" of outside information onto the text. Such
inscription or projection is indeed to be guarded against, but then this
text is not a blank, nor does it allow a blank to exist in tranquillity; the
text itself inscribes a certain historical and cultural message onto the
emptiness of La Grande Royale's face. My student's reluctance to go
beyond the veil was motivated by laudable impulses—the desire to leave
the Other alone, a refusal to reduce the text to a mere illustration—but
her reading of the veil as only a veil, a trope about tropes, excluded the
possibility of perceiving the traits that are there behind the veil, the traits
which make up a portrait of *difference*.

What becomes of difference in a methodology that trusts only self-
reflexivity? The impulse to leave the Other alone rejoins the impulse to
obliterate the Other on the ground they have in common: the inability
to describe something outside the self, to see, in Clifford Geertz's words,
"ourselves among others, as a local example of the forms human life has
locally taken." This is an ability without which Geertz says "objectivity is
self-congratulation and tolerance a sham."[7]

6. Cheikh Hamidou Kane, *L'Aventure ambiguë* (Paris, 1961), pp. 34, 35; *Ambiguous
Adventure*, trans. Katherine Woods (New York, 1963), pp. 20–21. I have altered the translation.
    7. Geertz, *Local Knowledge* (New York, 1983), p. 16.

The reader of African literature seeking a happy model of knowledge, turning to anthropology for transparent translations of the African difference, finds a field preoccupied with—guess what?—the imperialism of knowledge and the recourse to self-reflexivity. First of all, what is anthropology? The etymological meaning barely begins to tell the story: "the science of man" sounds like the self studying the self. In fact, the history of anthropology has appeared to adhere more to the *Oxford English Dictionary*'s third definition: "the study of man *as an animal*," implying both difference and inequality. Man as an animal is primitive man, man excluded from progress and development, stuck in time at the zero point where time begins and has no meaning. Man as an animal represents a general threat or challenge not only to the meaning of time but to meaning in general. The reliance of primitive man on oral rather than written communication makes his own systems of meaning more difficult for us to pin down and analyze. His reliance on orality must be reenacted by the inquiring anthropologist, who must learn the language, listen and report, with all the implicit risks of distortion involved in the child's game of telephone. Studying man as an animal is an act of redemption, of elevation, by which the primitive is translated out of his static, amorphous, oral condition, into books and articles which make sense.

The problem is that books that make sense out of African cultures have not generally been African books. Black Africa is now referred to as "animist" in religious culture, and there is no animist Bible or Koran, no written codification of beliefs with index and table of contents produced by the culture itself. The natural impulse is for the Western scholar to seek and produce such codifications. Titles such as *La Bible noire* and *La Philosophie bantoue,* even *Oedipe noir* and *The Black Decameron*, reveal an impulse to assimilate and Westernize in the process of explaining and making known. No one would call *La Chanson de Roland, The White Sundiata*!

Unlike a literary anthropology of the Middle Ages, in which the term "anthropology" designates a purely retrospective approach,[8] a literary anthropology of francophone African literature must face up to the substantial interference that has taken place between that literature and the institutionalized discipline of anthropology. It has been a complex, often messy relationship. A few cautionary tales are therefore in order, concerning the history of academic questions with ramifications in the everyday life of colonialism. Placide Tempels' *Bantu Philosophy* is an example of a text that would no longer be considered real anthropology but which had status and influence in its time, and whose ghostly presence keeps returning in debates over African philosophy and literature. *Bantu Philosophy* is a telling illustration of how the desire to explain and excuse African culture can lead the well-meaning Western writer to obliterate

8. See R. Howard Bloch, *Etymologies and Genealogies: A Literary Anthropology of the French Middle Ages* (Chicago, 1983).

Africa with kindness. Father Tempels was a Belgian missionary in the Belgian Congo. He begins his work by blaming the misunderstanding between Europe and Africa on a European failure to recognize the African worldview as a valid philosophy. We must, he writes, "understand their metaphysic"; "the gulf between Africans and Whites will remain and widen so long as *we* do not meet them in the wholesome aspirations of their own ontology."[9] All questions of behavior and belief in Africa can be answered by "a single principle, knowledge of the Inmost Nature of beings, that is to say, . . . their Ontological Principle" (*BP*, p. 23). That "Ontological Principle" is identified later as a "single value: vital force." African life can be explicated in terms of a balance of forces, African cultural formations as mechanisms for maintaining that balance. It is by this worldview that the Bantu differs *essentially* from the European, and I would not like to comment on the truth value of his analysis but rather on the uses to which he quickly puts it, that of better controlling Bantu behavior.

Tempels allows that there is a negative in all this: "This explains what has, indeed, been true, that the thing which most inhibits pagans from conversion to Christianity and from giving up magical rites is the fear of attenuating this vital energy through ceasing to have recourse to the natural powers which sustain it" (*BP*, p. 32). The good news is that the Bantu is basically monotheistic, believing in a single creator god (among others), and that "metaphysics . . . is within the capacity of every Bantu" (*BP*, p. 49). But now faced with an essentially different civilization, what becomes of the *mission civilisatrice* and the project of assimilation? Tempels advocates that the colonial project be redirected, to "educate them to discover . . . the ancient elements of truth ever present in their traditions," because "European civilization imparted to the Bantu is a mere superficial garb which has no deep impact upon their souls" (*BP*, pp. 113–14). Tempels therefore proposes a new *philosophical* colonialism based on a profound understanding of Bantu essence, readily available in his book of 120 pages.

> The Bantu can be educated if we take as a starting point their imperishable aspiration towards the strengthening of life. If not, they will not be civilized. Their masses will founder, in even greater numbers, in *false applications of their philosophy;* that is to say, in degrading 'magical' practices; and meanwhile the others, the **évolués,** will make up a class of pseudo-Europeans, without principles, character, purpose, or sense. . . . It is in Christianity alone that the Bantu will find relief for their secular yearning and a complete satisfaction of their deepest aspirations. . . . *Christianity*

9. Placide Tempels, *Bantu Philosophy*, trans. Colin King (Paris, 1959), pp. 16, 18; my emphasis. All further references to this work, abbreviated *BP*, will be included in the text.

> . . . *is the only possible consummation of the Bantu ideal.* [Pp. 120–21; my italics][10]

Once the essence is identified, the missionary/anthropologist/philosopher can determine the truth or falsehood of its application and judge the native's art of living. The new colonialism is thus far more insidious than the old slash-and-burn variety. "Tolerance" of difference is at its most pernicious here: I understand your essential difference from me, and will make you live up to it with an imposed program of separate development. Apartheid, it should be pointed out, is of course "nothing" but a theory of *separate,* that is, differentiated, development and of "tolerance" of an enforced difference.[11] As Aimé Césaire writes of *La Philosophie bantoue,* "Everyone wins: big corporations, colonial settlers, the government, excepting the Bantu, of course."[12] Tempels' text is the most striking example of miscarried anthropology and philosophy since Gérard de Nerval's conclusion that Islam is "une sorte de secte chrétienne."[13] Why, then, bother with Western interpretations and codifications of African culture at all? Why not read Africa on its own? There are two responses to this question.

African literature in French, through the fact of being written in French, has been or was imbued with a certain French culture or even *Kultur.* The inventors of black francophone literature—René Maran, Léopold Sédar Senghor, and Aimé Césaire—were educated in the French system and were more accustomed to expressing themselves in French than in Martinican creole or Senegalese Wolof. The birthplace of black francophone literature is more Paris than Fort-de-France or Dakar, and it is now easy to recognize in Negritude—the concept and the literary

10. The translator points out in a footnote: "Fr. 'idéal', but Du. 'heimwee': homesickness, nostalgia!"

11. See Vincent Crapanzano, "Waiting," *New Yorker,* 18 Mar. 1985, p. 97: "Apartheid . . . is an extreme case of the Western predisposition to classify and categorize just about everything in essentialist terms."

12. Aimé Césaire, *Discours sur le colonialisme* (Paris, 1955), p. 37; for sustained critiques of Tempels, see F. Eboussi Boulaga, "Le Bantou problématique," *Présence africaine* 66, no. 2 (1968): 5: "voici vingt ans, un livre révélait au monde que le bantou était le Monsieur Jourdain de la philosophie: il en faisait sans le savoir"; and Paulin Hountondji, *Sur la "philosophie africaine"* (Paris, 1977), p. 46: "*La Philosophie bantoue* [fit] feu de tout bois, en projetant massivement dans l'âme bantu ses propres rêveries métaphysiques, quitte à les renforcer par quelques descriptions ethnographiques sommaires propres à faire illusion." See also V. Y. Mudimbe, "Niam M'Paya: aux sources d'une pensée africaine," *L'Odeur du père,* pp. 125–34. For a defense of Tempels, see Meinrad P. Hebga, "Eloge de l'ethnophilosophie,' " *Présence africaine* 123, no. 3 (1982): 20–41.

13. "Il faut conclure . . . que l'islamisme ne repousse aucun des sentiments élevés attribués généralement à la société chrétienne. Les différences ont existé jusqu'ici beaucoup plus dans la forme que dans le fond des idées; les musulmans ne constituent en réalité qu'une sorte de *secte chrétienne*" (Gérard de Nerval, *Voyage en Orient, Oeuvres,* 2 vols. [Paris, 1960–61], 2:628).

movement—the signs of alienation from the author's native past: nostalgia and, so to speak, the desire to coincide again, to bring the past back. This perception is a consequence of hindsight and need not be seen to diminish the accomplishments of Negritude.

We know as a fact of literary history that Negritude was informed by a particular anthropology and by one very particular anthropologist, Leo Frobenius (a German, active in the first half of this century). Senghor writes in his preface to a Frobenius anthology in French "nul mieux que Frobenius ne révéla l'Afrique au monde *et les Africains à eux-mêmes* (no one better than Frobenius revealed Africa to the world *and Africans to themselves*)"[14]—creating a strange echo with Césaire's heroic figure of Patrice Lumumba in *Une Saison au Congo,* who claims "je parle et je rends l'Afrique à elle-même (I speak and return Africa to herself)."[15]

Senghor writes of Frobenius:

> Je ne saurais mieux faire que de dire ici, les leçons que nous avons tirées de la lecture de Frobenius, et surtout de ses deux ouvrages fondamentaux, traduits en français: *Histoire de la civilisation africaine* et *Le Destin des civilisations.* Quand je dis 'nous', il s'agit de la poignée d'étudiants noirs qui, dans les années 1930, au Quartier latin, à Paris, lancèrent . . . le mouvement de la *Négritude.* [*LF,* p. vii][16]
>
> Frobenius fut véritablement le moteur spirituel de l'émancipation de l'Afrique noire: sa vision idéaliste d'une Afrique encore pure, non contaminée par les influences extérieures, était pour nous . . . un aliment qui attisait notre ferveur.[17]

> I can do no better than to state here the lessons that we drew from our reading of Frobenius, and especially from his two basic works, translated into French as *Histoire de la civilisation africaine* and *Le Destin des civilisations.* When I say "we" I mean the handful of black students who, in the 1930s, in the Latin Quarter, launched the *Negritude* movement.
>
> Frobenius was truly the moving spiritual force in the emancipation of black Africa: his idealistic vision of a still-pure Africa, not yet contaminated by outside influences, nourished our fervor.

14. Léopold Sédar Senghor, "Les Leçons de Leo Frobenius," in *Leo Frobenius 1873/ 1973: Une Anthologie,* ed. Eike Haberland (Wiesbaden, 1973), p. vii; all further references to this work, abbreviated *LF,* will be included in the text.

15. Césaire, *Une Saison au Congo* (Paris, 1973), p. 94.

16. Senghor refers to the two works by Frobenius elsewhere as "sacred books" and compares his reaction to that of St. Paul on the road to Damascus (*Liberté III: Négritude et civilisation de l'universel* [Paris, 1977], pp. 13, 340; all further references to *Liberté III,* abbreviated *L,* will be included in the text).

17. Senghor, "Les Leçons de Léo Frobenius" (a different article from the preface to the *Anthologie,* but bearing the same title), *Présence africaine* 111, no. 3 (1978): 147–48.

What, then, is Frobenius' uncontaminated Africa? It is a place of "perfect order," which, at the time of the European discoveries, echoed a strangely European sense of *Gemütlichkeit:* "carefully designed streets, lined with trees for mile after mile as far as the eye can see . . . nothing but magnificent fields . . . crowds of people dressed in silk and velvet; great States, *where the smallest detail bears witness to a perfect order"* (*LF,* p. 66). Visiting the Kasai region of the Congo in 1906, Frobenius finds something like an "esthetocracy" in which "each cup, each pipe, each spoon is a work of art." My point is of course not that Frobenius was inaccurate in his physical description of African civilization, rather that his writing *rewards* Africa for conforming to a European image of civilization, for acting as a mirror in which a European can contemplate a European idea of beauty. The totality of African art is the cornerstone of Frobenius' anthropology—art is everything and everything is art; therefore art is *functional* and wastes no time or energy on false seductiveness: "There is nothing that tries to seduce through softness and sensitivity . . . everything is functional, rough, austere, tectonic [Teutonic?]" (*LF,* p. 69).[18] This is *the* essence of African art and African being for Frobenius: the essence preexists the art in which it is found; it *governs* ("il *régit* toute l'Afrique"), it manifests itself, it releases itself.[19] His verb *beherrschen,* which may be accurately translated as "command" or "govern," cannot help but recall Hegel's famous chapter on the master (*Herr*) and the slave (*Knecht*): the master is "consciousness that exists for itself," but can only exist "through an other"; the other, the slave, is "consciousness repressed within itself."[20] Note that it is a style posited as a totality by Frobenius' discourse that rules over Africa; as with Tempels' philosophy, Africans themselves are *subject* to, even subjugated by, an essence discovered by an outsider, of which, like Monsieur Jourdain and his "prose," they may be wholly unaware: this is Hegel's "consciousness repressed."[21]

Frobenius goes on to say, "It [this style] must have been born and must have crystallized itself a very long time ago, and it has preserved itself ever since in *all its originality"* (*LF,* p. 69; emphasis mine). This analysis leaves him "strengthened with this intimate knowledge of the

18. The original German reads: "Alles ist zweckmäßig, herb, streng, tektonisch!" (Frobenius, "Die Kunst Afrikas," *Der Erdball* 3 [1931], p. 90).

19. "Wer sich ihm bis zum vollen Verständnis genähert hat, der wird bald erkennen, daß er als Ausdruck des Wesens ganz Afrika *beherrscht"* (Frobenius, "Die Kunst Afrikas," p. 90; my emphasis).

20. G. W. F. Hegel, *Phänomenolgie des Geistes* (Frankfurt am Main, 1970), pp. 113–20.

21. It is this notion of African philosophy as a *mentality,* as "une vision du monde spontanée, collective et implicite," that Hountondji attacks in Tempels' work, to replace it with "l'analyse explicite, personelle, laborieuse qui prend cette vision du monde pour objet" (*Sur la "philosophie africaine,"* p. 65). Hountondji himself describes this transition as one out of a state of *enslavement* ("ce renoncement tragique à penser par nous-mêmes et pour nous-mêmes: l'esclavage" [p. 44]).

African essence" (*LF*, p. 69). That perfect preservation or mummification of an essentialized style—a style that is an essence—makes it a perfect primitivism. Nothing has changed of this essence, nor can it ever change; it can still be discovered, studied, and mastered. Frobenius uncovers this essence not as would Gobineau, to denigrate, but rather to assimilate and redeem. It becomes the basis of a theory whereby a *Euro-African* civilization can be posited in Southeast Europe and Northeast Africa, a theory based on comparisons of cave paintings. Europe and Africa share common roots; it's just that "the vital sentiment . . . has become completely foreign to us, whereas it continues to inspire vast ethnic groups of Africa" (*LF*, p. 75).

One would like to avoid a facile interpretive hindsight or retrospective indignation; one should admit that when Frobenius wrote "the idea of the barbarous Negro is a European invention" (*LF*, p. vii), the idea was brave and revolutionary. But one is compelled to look into the ideology and cultural baggage that Senghor in particular took on when he was seduced by Frobenius' positive valorization of African civilization.

For Senghor, any bridge between two civilizations is one more contribution to "la civilisation de l'universel" and is therefore to be encouraged. But Senghor reads Frobenius not on an intercontinental or global level, but as a particular link between Negritude and *Germanity*. In two articles, one from 1961 and the other from 1972, Senghor expands on Frobenius' theory of the fundamental unity and affinity between black African and German thought. Frobenius wrote: "L'Occident créa le réalisme anglais et le rationalisme français; l'Est, la mystique allemande. . . . L'accord, avec les civilisations correspondantes en Afrique, est complet (The West created English realism and French rationalism; the East, German mysticism. . . . The accord, with corresponding civilizations in black Africa, is complete)" (*LF*, p. xi).

Senghor speaks of his childhood fascination with things German ("maints traits de bravoure, de noblesse d'âme, que l'on soulignait à l'occasion de leurs actions guerrières me séduisaient . . . [I was seduced by the numerous acts of bravery, of nobility of the soul, which were emphasized at the time of their actions in battle . . .]" [*L*, p. 339]), and tells of his exposure to the Romantic poets, the philosophers and ethnographers, and principally to Frobenius. What did Germanity offer to an African intellectual? "Une saisie en profondeur des choses . . . la faculté de répondre à l'appel du réel, de vibrer aux ondes de l'Autre, du Toi (A grasp of things in their depths . . . the ability to answer the call of the real, to echo the vibrations of the Other, of the intimate Thou)" (*L*, pp. 13, 14). German and African civilizations are those "qui n'ont pas encore perdu l'équilibre entre l'âme et l'entendement (which have not yet lost the equilibrium between the soul and reason)" (*L*, p. 340). Senghor writes that after his demobilization in 1942, "je me suis plongé, de nouveau, dans la philosophie allemande en commençant par Marx et Engels, pour finir où j'aurais dû commencer: par Hegel, auquel j'ai ajouté Husserl et Heidegger (I immersed myself, again, in German philosophy, starting with Marx and Engels, winding up where I should have started: with Hegel, to which I added Husserl and Heidegger)" (*L*, p. 342).[22]

If I began by promising to talk of a literature that is not a rewriting of Hegel, something has obviously gone wrong. For the younger generation of post-Independence African writers, Senghor's reliance on Frobenius' anthropology could *only* have led to cultural assimilation and the erasure of difference, for it was a sign of alienation in the first place. A particularly harsh and quotable critique is Stanislas Adotevi's *Négritude et négrologues:*

> La négritude est un donné de la conscience réfléchie, c'est l'aliénation intellectuelle du nègre. . . . On ne peut se mettre à la fenêtre et se voir passer dans la rue. . . . La négritude c'est la dernière-née d'une idéologie de domination. . . . C'est la manière noire d'être blanc. . . . C'est l'aboutissement de plusieurs décades d'*ethnologie*. . . . La négritude est sur le plan politique ce que *La Philosophie bantoue* est idéologiquement pour l'Afrique. Senghor c'est le Père Tempels mis en mouvement, pour la même cause et dans la même mésaventure.[23]

> Négritude is a notion of reflexive consciousness, the intellectual alienation of the Negro. . . . You can't stand at the window and watch yourself go by in the street. . . . Négritude is the last-born child of an ideology of domination . . . it's the black way of being white. . . . It is the end product of many decades of ethnology. . . . Négritude is to politics what *Bantu Philosophy* is to ideology for Africa. Senghor is Father Tempels on the field of action, for the same cause and in the same misadventure.

For Adotevi, "Eurocentrism commands all anthropological discourse." A newer generation of Africanist anthropology has confronted the problem of Eurocentrism, and one would need to appraise Adotevi's stance in light of, for example, the theories of Geertz, work by Victor Turner, Robert Farris Thompson, and the self-reflexive "ethnopsychoanalytic" work of Paul Parin, Fritz Morgenthaler, and Goldy Parin-Matthèy.[24] But

---

22. I am not aware of any comment by Senghor on the following passage from Hegel: "Africa proper, as far as History goes back, has remained—for all purposes of connection with the rest of the World—shut up; it is the Gold-land compressed within itself—the land of childhood, which lying beyond the day of self-conscious history, is enveloped in the dark mantle of Night. . . . In Negro life the characteristic point is the fact that consciousness has not yet attained to the realization of any substantial objective existence—as for example, God, or Law" (*The Philosophy of History,* trans. J. Sibree [New York, 1956], pp. 91, 93).

23. Stanislas Adotevi, *Négritude et négrologues* (Paris, 1972), pp. 101, 207, 153, 54.

24. See Victor Turner, *The Forest of Symbols: Aspects of Ndembu Ritual* (Ithaca, N.Y., 1967); Robert Farris Thompson, *Flash of the Spirit: American and Afro-American Art and Philosophy* (New York, 1984); Paul Parin, Fritz Morgenthaler, and Goldy Parin-Matthèy,

for our purposes here, we must ask where Adotevi's moment of total rejection leaves us in relation to the body of francophone black African literature.

First, as I have indicated, it leaves us with an important project of tracing the influence and penetration of European aesthetics and ideology on particularly the early productions of African literature in French. This is a project of literary anthropology, but in a different sense from the one I mean to outline presently, for in analyzing the traces of Europeanism in African literature one has still not confronted the real challenge: that of reading something much further removed from one's own sphere.

But that first project, it should be pointed out, engenders a second, equally important one, that of reading the post-Independence literary productions which themselves critique the anthropological bias of their precursors. Such a text, for example, as Ouologuem's *Le Devoir de violence* from 1968, a novel in which we find "Fritz Shrobenius," "explorer, tourist and ethnographer," a lampoon of Frobenius:

> [Shrobenius voulait] ressusciter, sous couleur d'autonomie culturelle, un univers africain qui ne correspondait à plus rien de vivant. . . . il voulait trouver un sens métaphysique à tout. . . . Gesticulant à tout propos, il étalait son "amitié" pour l'Afrique et son savoir orageux avec une assurance de bachelier repêché. Il considérait que la vie africaine était art pur . . .

> [Shrobenius had] a groping mania for resuscitating an African universe—cultural autonomy, he called it—which had lost all living reality. . . . He was determined to find a metaphysical meaning in everything. . . . Gesticulating at every word, he displayed his love of Africa and his tempestuous knowledge with the assurance of a high school student who had slipped through his final examinations by the skin of his teeth. African life, he held, was pure art . . .[25]

Ouologuem's response to false images of cultural identity is to undermine the notion of identity itself, to construct a universe in which all bonds of unity are bonds of enslavement, including the bond between Ouologuem's writing and the European texts that he plagiarized.[26] Reading *Le Devoir de violence* will contribute to the formulation of an African literary anthropology only by showing where it can go wrong.

Fear Thy Neighbor as Thyself: Psychoanalysis and Society among the Anyi of West Africa, trans. and ed. Patricia Klamerth (Chicago, 1980).

25. Yambo Ouologuem, *Le Devoir de violence* (Paris, 1968), p. 102; trans. Ralph Manheim, *Bound to Violence* (London, 1971), p. 87.

26. See my "Trait d'union: Injunction and Dismemberment in Yambo Ouologuem's *Le Devoir de violence*," *L'Esprit créateur* 23 (Winter 1983): 62–73.

Another novel that appeared in 1968 strikes me as both a model anthropological text in its own right and as a good proving ground for an interpretive approach that is informed by anthropology. Ahmadou Kourouma's *Les Soleils des indépendances*[27] is anthropological in the sense that it teaches its reader how to interpret cultural signs within its own text; it plays both anthropologist and native informant. The novel starts from an identifiable cultural base: the Malinké ethnic group of Guinea and the Ivory Coast, descended from the Mali Empire founded by Sundiata Kéita in the thirteenth century. This is to all appearances the first African novel to dare to appropriate and remold the French language to suit local conditions. Spoken African French is not identical to spoken Parisian French, but in writers like Camara Laye, one is at pains to find any difference, any Africanisms in the prose. *Les Soleils* vibrates with the rhythms of African speech, committing numerous *barbarismes,* and teaching the reader—who is assumed not to be Malinké—Malinkéisms. On the first page: "disons-le en Malinké . . . l'ère des Indépendances (les soleils des Indépendances, disent les Malinkés) [to put in Malinké . . . the era of Independence (the suns of Independence, the Malinké say)]" (*LS,* p. 1; p. 3). The Malinké language gets its revenge on French in phrases like: "la nuit mal dormie"; "elle se conduisait . . . en pleine musulmane"; "asseoir le deuil"; "les soudains déclenchements et extinction du tinta-marre."[28] These are *calques,* traces, imperfect translations of Malinké, which one can interpret as a belated concession to the power of the African mother tongue, thereby constituting a significant moment in the political history of the Franco-African signifier.[29] It is ironic that Malinké language and culture gain such power within French discourse in a context describing the death and destruction of that culture in post-Independence Africa. It is also ironic that this creolized novel, seemingly such a powerful solution to the problem of writing in the language of

27. See Ahmadou Kourouma, *Les Soleils des indépendances* (Montreal, 1968; Paris, 1970); trans. Adrian Adams, *The Suns of Independence* (New York, 1981); all further references to this work, abbreviated *LS,* and with page numbers to the original and this translation, will be included in the text.

28. "The badly-slept night"; "She behaved like a full Muslim woman"; "to seat mourning"; "sudden sharp bursts of din." These translations—my own, except for the last phrase, which is from the Adams translation (p. 120)—cannot fully convey the violence done to standard French by Kourouma's prose.

29. The history of the anglophone signifier is quite different, in that one of the first African writers to gain wide recognition was Amos Tutuola, author of *The Palm-Wine Drinkard,* whose prose style started off as genuinely "naive" and poorly assimilated to the norms of English, meeting with critical acclaim in the West and skepticism in Africa. See Adebayo Williams, "The Crisis of Confidence in the Criticism of African Literature," *Présence africaine* 123, no. 3 (1982): 82–83: "with due and sincere respect to his enormous native talents, it is our view that Tutuola is a quaint anomaly . . . his ambition and middling education dislocate him from the oral tradition to which he properly belongs."

the colonizer, has not yet proved to be the foundation of a new order in the production of African literature in French.[30]

Readings in anthropology, including one particularly interesting study by a Malinké, reveal a complex and profoundly ambivalent attitude toward the *word*—the spoken word, the only kind of word in Malinké culture until the beginning of the Islamic conquests. Speech is categorized according to the part of the body in which it originates, in expressions similar to our "speak from the heart" or "lip service."[31] The hierarchy equates trustworthiness with interiority. A special subcaste of people are the guardians and manipulators of the word—they are the *jeli, les gens de la parole,* popularly known as *griots. Griots* are one of several subdivisions of the *nyamakala* caste, neither noble nor slave but ambiguous between the two. Nobles must guard against excessive speech so as to avoid contamination by contact with it; they must respect silence and secrecy, using a *griot* linguist who alone may listen to them and speak loudly for them, "car un Mansa ne parle pas comme un crieur public (for a Mansa [emperor] does not speak like a town crier)."[32] This attitude is also observed by the *griots* regarding their role as oral historians, repositories of genealogies:

> Le Manding garde jalousement ses secrets; il est des choses que le profane ignorera toujours car les griots, leurs dépositaires, ne les livreront jamais. . . . Malheureux, n'essaye point de percer le mystère que le Manding te cache . . . ne cherche point à connaître ce qui n'est point à connaître.

> Mali keeps its secrets jealously. There are things which the uninitiated will never know, for the griots, their depositaries, will never betray them. . . . Never try, wretch, to pierce the mystery which Mali hides from you. . . . Do not seek to know what is not to be known.[33]

So we are faced with an attitude toward the word which forbids unveiling completely its attitude toward the word. A novel such as Kourouma's *Les Soleils* enacts this hermeneutic by both revealing and teasing:

30. Few, if any, other francophone writers seem to have adopted Kourouma's technique entirely; not even Kourouma himself has followed up on *Les Soleils*. Henri Lopes, a Congolese novelist, claims in an interview to have used the technique, but the novel he seems to be referring to (*La Nouvelle romance* [Yaoundé, Cameroon, 1976]) shows nowhere near the degree of creolization of French by Africanisms. See Lopes, interviewed in "Ecriture noire en question," *Notre Librairie* 65 (July–Sept. 1982), p. 12.

31. See Sory Camara, *Les Gens de la parole* (Paris, 1976), pp. 237–42; and Dominique Zahan, *La Dialectique du verbe chez les Bambara* (Paris, 1963), pp. 17–28.

32. Djibril Tamsir Niane, *Soundjata; ou, L'épopée mandingue* (Paris, 1960), p. 140; trans. G. D. Pickett, *Sundiata: An Epic of Old Mali* (London, 1965), p. 77.

33. Here the *griot* relating the epic refused to tell any more (Niane, *Soundjata,* p. 150; trans. pp. 83–84).

on the one hand explaining things, and on the other reminding us we are outsiders—"vous ne le savez pas parce que vous n'êtes pas Malinké (you do not know this, because you are not Malinké)" (*LS,* p. 147; p. 98). The point is well taken and reminds the reader of basic academic problems such as the reliability of sources to complement the novel's own anthropological lessons. The most factual anthropologists, old-timers like Maurice Delafosse, not given to tortured introspection regarding their impact on the natives, may be the most dated and ethnocentric. The most sophisticated—such as Dominique Zahan, author of *Pensée, religion, et spiritualité africaines* and *La Dialectique du verbe chez les Bambara*—make one wonder if anything African is left under their web of convoluted, "Hautes Etudes" discourse. On a question as important and interesting as the etymology of the word *jeli, griot* in Malinké, we find wildly contradictory hypotheses and simply don't know whom to believe.[34] To make matters worse, Africans are now telling us that they may have deliberately misled anthropologists in the past, to protect the integrity of their cultures.[35] Even confining oneself to a single culture, then, the task is not as simple as finding the great book of Malinké culture with a full and accurate index.

A literary anthropology of Malinké fictions in French would have to address the question of the traditional attitude toward the word—with all the problems of sources and reliability and risks of ethnocentrism that involves—and that attitude in connection to the written word in French. Is the African writer of French a latter-day *griot,* and if so what does that mean? Camara Laye, a Malinké born into the *nyamakala* caste (his father was a smith; see the opening passages of *L'Enfant noir*), insisted that his act of writing reproduced his father's activity as a smith and sculptor, that through deformation of materials, be it gold or the word, both "let the heart speak." He goes on to compare himself to a *griot* as a manipulator of rhythms toward the end of *truth.*[36] But a simple production of truth

---

34. Zahan theorizes: "le mot *dyeli* ou *dyali* concernerait tout d'abord l'action de remonter le cours du temps par la parole. . . . le griot serait, à proprement parler, l'artisan du retour en arrière de la parole" (*La Dialectique du verbe,* p. 125); this appealing, Proustian hypothesis is rejected by Hugo Zemp, who sees in *jelí* a link with the word for blood (see "La légende des griots malinké," *Cahiers d'etudes africaines* 6, no. 4 [1966]: 630–32); Zemp's idea is in turn refuted by Sory Camara, who sees in *jàlí* (the older form of *jelí*) the "action of lodging, of offering hospitality" (*Gens de la parole,* p. 101). All three scholars offer corroboration from the social fabric of Malinké life.

35. "Ce procédé de 'mise dans la paille', consistant à fournir à quelqu'un une affabulation improvisée lorsqu'on ne peut lui dire la vérité, fut en effet inventé à partir du moment où l'autorité coloniale envoya ses agents ou ses représentants pour faire des recherches ethnologiques sans accepter de vivre les conditions requises. Bien des ethnologues en furent plus tard les victimes inconscientes. . . . Combien d'entre eux s'imaginèrent avoir tout compris d'une chose, alors que ne l'ayant pas vécue, ils ne pouvaient la connaître vraiment" (A. Hampaté Ba, "La Tradition vivante," in *Histoire générale de l'Afrique,* vol. 1, *Méthodologie et préhistoire africaine,* ed. J. Ki-Zerbo [Paris, 1980], pp. 204–5).

36. "Interview avec Camara Laye: Propos recueillis par Jacqueline Leiner," *Présence francophone* 10 (Spring 1975): 153–67.

seems hardly guaranteed to one who manipulates taboo materials (releasing the dangerous forces of *nyama*) such as gold or the word in Malinké culture. While orality is perceived in Western metaphysics as the immediacy of the voice, in the Malinké tradition orality is already a duplicitous betrayal of *silence*. *Les Soleils* states: "Rien en soi n'est bon, rien n'est mauvais. C'est la parole qui transfigure un fait en bien ou le tourne en mal (Nothing is good or evil in itself. It is speech that turns a thing into good or evil)" (*LS*, p. 109; p. 72).

This is the type of question that a literary anthropology would be able to elucidate. "Literary anthropology" must stand, on the one hand, for an approach that is influenced by the "facts" of ethnography and, on the other, for a willingness to adopt modes of interpretation that might come out of the culture in question. For the Western reader, this means venturing beyond the codes of established interpretive technique (categories such as *langue/parole,* signifier/signified, even oral/literate), and it means facing a challenge to their universality. It also means taking the risk of being wrong.

Before concluding, it may be helpful to describe briefly a debate within African intellectual circles which runs parallel to our concerns here. The development of an African literary anthropology calls for a study of "traditional" Africa in conjunction with "modern" writings in Western languages; the problems involved in any recourse to tradition have been brought out in the debate over "African philosophy." On one side of this dispute are the "ethnophilosophers," Tempels and those who do not reject him, devoted to describing an African worldview which is first and foremost *different* from that of Europe. The difference of Africa is founded on the study of "ethnic realities"; the status of its intellectual product derives from its independence. For "ethnophilosophers" (the name is obviously not of their own design), "pure" philosophy (as practiced by their adversaries) can be described like this: "appliquer sur nos sociétés africaines les formes pures de la pensée universelle providentiellement et définitivement dégagées par les philosophes des Livres (to apply to our African societies pure forms of universal thought providentially and definitively revealed by philosophers of Books)."[37] Those philosophers of the Books (European books), critics of ethnophilosophy, most importantly Hountondji and Marcien Towa, advocate a radical departure from the "ghetto" of ethnic difference, a *prise de conscience* by the African of contemporary rather than traditional reality: "Nous devons à tout prix libérer notre pensée du ghetto Africaniste où on a voulu l'enfermer (We must at all costs liberate our thought from the Africanist ghetto where some have sought to lock it up)"; "Nous avons à nous affirmer dans le

37. Hebga, "Eloge de l'"ethnophilosophie,' " p. 32.

monde actuel . . . une telle décision . . . exige pour aboutir une rupture
. . . radicale avec notre passé (We must affirm ourselves in the world as
it is . . . such a decision . . . if it is to lead anywhere, requires a radical
break with our past)."[38] A counterpart in the world of the novel is Ous-
mane Sembene, whose radical heroes in such works of socialist realism
as *O Pays! mon beau peuple* and *L'Harmattan* advocate a sharp awareness
of global political reality, along with a harsh skepticism directed at "retro-
grade" traditions.[39]

For this school, Africa's failure to resist European conquest is a sign
of almost ontological, certainly philosophical, weakness: the backward
gaze of the ethnophilosopher (or the Negritude poet), by concentrating
on the specificity of Africa's cultural difference, "runs the risk of saving
precisely that which caused our defeat" (*E*, p. 41). Only one path remains
open, that of surrendering identity and difference as a price to be paid
for gaining power and equality:

> La volonté d'être nous-mêmes . . . nous accule finalement à la
> nécessité de nous transformer en profondeur, de nier notre être
> intime pour devenir l'autre. [*E*, p. 41]

> Pour nous approprier le secret de l'Europe, savoir un esprit nouveau
> et étranger, nous devons révolutionner le nôtre de fond en comble,
> ce faisant nous devenons assurément semblables à l'Européen. [*E*,
> p. 48]

> The will to be ourselves . . . brings us face to face with the necessity
> to transform ourselves profoundly, to negate our inner being in
> order to become the other.

> In order to appropriate for ourselves Europe's secret, that is, this
> new and foreign spirit, we must revolutionize our own spirit com-
> pletely; in so doing we will assuredly become like the European.

For Towa, to be different, to have an identity, is to be a slave: "Nous
devons nourrir à l'égard de tout culte de la différence et de l'identité
une méfiance systématique; sans quoi nous courons le risque de nous

38. Hountondji, *Sur la "philosophie africaine,"* p. 49; Marcien Towa, *Essai sur la problématique philosophique dans l'Afrique actuelle* (Yaoundé, Cameroon, 1971), p. 41; all further references to Towa's *Essai*, abbreviated *E*, will be included in the text.

39. The hero of Sembene's *O pays! mon beau peuple* (Paris, 1957), Oumar, "se disait: 'Si un jour nous arrivons à sortir de cette ignorance, nous rirons de nous-mêmes.' . . . Il fut conduit devant Sa Majesté [the traditional king]. C'était un homme qui devait vivre perpétuellement assis. Ses reins étaient cachés par la masse de chair qui débordait de chaque flanc. . . . Oumar se demandait si cet homme était en mesure de réfléchir" (p. 105). Compare Kwasi Wiredu, *Philosophy and an African Culture* (Cambridge, 1980): "There is an urgent need . . . for the kind of analysis that would identify and separate the backward aspects of our culture from those aspects worth keeping" (p. 41).

confirmer dans la servitude (In regard to all worship of difference and identity, we must cultivate a systematic skepticism, without which we run the risk of confirming our own servitude)."[40] In order to gain the "secret of the West," one renounces the secrets of Africa. The anti-ethnophilosophers ask rhetorically, "What is African?" (compare "What's the difference?")—meaning that an essentialized, *metaphysical* Africanity is a trap;[41] to which the ethnophilosopher responds rhetorically, "What is rational?"—meaning that even "pure" European philosophy (in which the "secret" resides) is riddled with myth, ethnography, theology, and biology, and is no guarantor of anything.[42]

Hountondji and Towa's philosophy, which refuses the name "African," may be compared to "theory" as I have discussed it here. Both are rigorous systems based on Western books; both provide the certainty of a preordained system; both risk the loss of identity and difference, the assimilation of Africa into the categories of the West. The "radical praxis" of the African philosopher is aimed at a gain of power for Africa, but only by assuming that the West does indeed have a philosophical "secret" that permitted it to conquer the world, rather than seeing that conquest as a historical flash in the pan, the result of a temporary accident rather than a recuperable secret. Of course it must also be argued that, secret or not, European imperialism has changed the terms of any African discourse forever and must be dealt with. But why should it be that the West, by virtue of its sheer power, has the only secret worth preserving? Surely traditional Africa had and has its own. Whatever radical praxis the present may require, the imprint of the past—of identity, of difference, of the hundreds of African ethnic cultures—should not be ignored.

No one would want literary theory to occupy a similar position in the interpretation of African literature, as a body of texts and knowledge that wholly displaces local concerns. The literary anthropology I have called for here is of course related to the project of ethnophilosophy, if only in the sense that any attention paid to "tradition" leads one back to the time before the European conquests, before the "secret" got out, into a world of fragmented ethnicity, orality, and folklore. For some this may represent a ghetto, a jail of difference, a relegation to quaintness. At its extreme, this is the danger: interpreting any African text only in terms of its author's ancestor's beliefs and customs. No attempt to describe Africa's difference—as "primitive," "animist," "prelogical," "collective," "rhythmic," or whatever, seems immune from connotations and taints

40. Towa, *L'Idée d'une philosophie négro-africaine* (Yaoundé, Cameroon, 1979), p. 67.

41. "Nous ruinons, en somme, la conception mythologique dominante de l'africanité et revenons à l'évidence toute simple, toute banale, que l'Afrique est avant tout un continent, et le concept d'Afrique un concept géographique, empirique, non un concept métaphysique" (Hountondji, *Sur la "philosophie africaine,"* p. 72).

42. See Hebga, "Eloge de l'"ethnophilosophie,' " p. 28.

of ethnocentrism when seen in retrospect. By defining the Other's difference, one is forced to take into account, or to ignore at one's peril, the shadow cast by the self. But without some attention to the African past, some effort to describe the Other, how can we accurately read the African present? There are in fact two ways to lose identity, be it one's own or someone else's: as Césaire wrote: "Il y a deux manières de se perdre: par ségrégation murée dans le particulier ou par dilution dans l'"universel' (There are two ways to lose oneself: by segregation in the particular or by dilution in the 'universal')."[43]

The study of black African literature in French requires an approach that is sensitive both to local, "African," ethnic differences and to the homogenizing effects of the French language. If a literary anthropology of Africa can be formulated, it will be through addressing questions such as the question of the word in traditional Malinké society versus the word written in French. The part that "theory" has to play therein should be cautiously determined by asking to what degree it is appropriate. Another way to pose the problem is to ask, "Are tropes African?"—when we have pinpointed the relation between metaphor and metonymy in a novel like *Les Soleils des indépendances,* have we learned anything new, or have we domesticated the text to our own cognitive system, subjugated it to our "theories"? My epigraph from *Le Devoir de violence* serves as a reminder, by bringing back an ancient usage of the word *théorie:* "groupe de personnes qui s'avancent les unes derrière les autres; [in Antiquity], Députation envoyée par une ville à une fête solonelle" (*Petit Robert;* the *Oxford English Dictionary* lists this as a "specialized usage": "a body of *Theors* sent by a state to perform some religious rite or duty"). Ouologuem's "theory" of Africans is a vision of the African holocaust, Africans being led in bondage toward a new world, a reminder that any link can be a link in a chain of enslavement.

Europeans have been making "theories" of Africans for centuries. My feeling is that the most fruitful path for the Western critic of African literature—the *Theor*—is not to play it safe and "stay home," nor to "leave home without it" and pretend to approach African literature with a virgin mind, but to balance one against the other, by reconsidering the applicability of all our critical terms and by looking to traditional African cultures for terms they might offer.

43. Césaire, *Lettre à Maurice Thorez* (Paris, 1956), p. 15.

"On the Threshold of Woman's Era": Lynching, Empire, and Sexuality in Black Feminist Theory

Hazel V. Carby

> If the fifteenth century discovered America to the Old World, the nineteenth is discovering woman to herself. . . .
>
> Not the opportunity of discovering new worlds, but that of filling this old world with fairer and higher aims than the greed of gold and the lust of power, is hers. Through weary, wasting years men have destroyed, dashed in pieces, and overthrown, but to-day we stand on the threshold of woman's era, and woman's work is grandly constructive. In her hand are possibilities whose use or abuse must tell upon the political life of the nation, and send their influence for good or evil across the track of unborn ages.
> —FRANCES E. W. HARPER, "Woman's Political Future"

> The world of thought under the predominant man-influence, unmollified and unrestrained by its complementary force, would become like Daniel's fourth beast: "dreadful and terrible, and *strong* exceedingly;" "it had great iron teeth; it devoured and brake in pieces, and stamped the residue with the feet of it;" and the most independent of us find ourselves ready at times to fall down and worship this incarnation of power.
> —ANNA JULIA COOPER, *A Voice from the South*

My purpose in this essay is to describe and define the ways in which Afro-American women intellectuals, in the last decade of the nineteenth century, theorized about the possibilities and limits of patriarchal power through its manipulation of racialized and gendered social categories and practices. The essay is especially directed toward two academic constituencies: the practitioners of Afro-American cultural analysis and of feminist historiography and theory. The dialogue with each has its own peculiar form, characterized by its own specific history; yet both groups are addressed in an assertion of difference, of alterity, and in a voice characterized by an anger dangerously self-restrained. For it is not in the nature of Caliban to curse; rather, like Caliban, the black woman has learned from the behaviour of her master and mistress that if accommodation results in a patronizing loosening of her bonds, liberation will be more painful.

On the one hand, Afro-American cultural analysis and criticism have traditionally characterized the turn of the century as the age of Booker T. Washington and W. E. B. Du Bois. Afro-American studies frame our response to that period within a conceptual apparatus limiting historical interpretation to theories of exceptional male intellectual genius as exemplified in the texts *Up from Slavery* and *The Souls of Black Folk.* I wish to reconsider the decade of the 1890s as the "woman's era" not merely in order to insert women into the gaps in our cultural history (to compete for intellectual dominance with men) but to shift the object of interpretation from examples of individual intellectual genius to the collective production and interrelation of forms of knowledge among black women intellectuals. The intellectual discourse of black women during the 1890s includes a wide variety of cultural practices. This essay, however, will concentrate on the theoretical analyses of race, gender, and patriarchal power found in the essays of Anna Julia Cooper, the journalism of Ida B. Wells, and the first novel of Pauline Hopkins.

On the other hand, feminist theory and its academic practice, "women's studies," appear if not content with, then at least consistent in, their limited concern with a small minority of the women of the planet: those white, middle-class inhabitants of the metropoles. Although feminist scholarship has made the histories of these women visible, it has done so by reconstituting patriarchal power on another terrain rather than by promising a strategy for its abolition. This leaves us with the same complaint as our nineteenth-century black foremothers: feminist theory supports and reproduces a racist hierarchy. Feminist investigations of nineteenth-century women writers actively ignore nonwhite women; some of the most recent, exciting, and innovative thinking on sexuality relegates black women to a paragraph and secondary sources. Ellen DuBois and Linda Gordon, in their essay "Seeking Ecstasy on the Battlefield: Danger and

---

Hazel V. Carby is assistant professor of English at Wesleyan University. She is the coauthor of *The Empire Strikes Back: Race and Racism in Seventies Britain* and the author of *Uplifting as They Write: The Emergence of the Afro-American Woman Novelist* (forthcoming, 1986).

Pleasure in Nineteenth-Century Feminist Sexual Thought," argue that "the black women's movement conducted a particularly militant campaign for respectability, often making black feminists spokespeople for prudery in their communities," without direct reference to one of these black feminists or their work. Their subject is "how feminists conceptualized different sexual dangers, as a means of organizing *resistance* to sexual oppression"; their motivation is to be able to examine how these strategies changed and to learn what historical understanding can be brought to contemporary feminist campaigns.[1] I hope that a discussion of Cooper, Wells, and Hopkins in the context of the black women's movement will direct readers to consider more seriously how black feminists conceptualized the possibilities for resisting sexual oppression than the dismissal implied in "prudery" allows.

The decade of the 1890s was a time of intense activity and productivity for Afro-American women intellectuals. It opened with the publication of Frances Harper's *Iola Leroy*, Cooper's *Voice from the South*, and Wells' *Southern Horrors: Lynch Law in All Its Phases*.[2] In 1893, as part of the World's Columbian Exposition, the World's Congress of Representative Women met in Chicago. Among others, Hallie Q. Brown, Anna Julia Cooper, Fannie Jackson Coppin, Sarah J. Early, Frances Harper, Fannie Barrier Williams, and Frederick Douglass—six black women and one black man—addressed the gathering. Harper told her audience that she felt they were standing "on the threshold of woman's era"; in 1894, *Woman's Era* was the name chosen for the journal run by the Woman's Era Club in Boston.[3] The club movement grew rapidly among Afro-American women and culminated in the first Congress of Colored Women of the United States, which convened in Boston in 1895. In 1896, the National Federation of Colored Women and the National League of Colored Women united in Washington, D.C., to form the National Association of Colored Women (NACW). For the first time, black women were nationally organized to confront the various modes of their oppression.[4]

The decade opened and closed with the publication of novels by black women: Harper's *Iola* and the first of Hopkins' four novels, *Contending Forces* (1900). Both authors intended that their texts contribute to the struggle for social change in a period of crisis for the Afro-American community. Their novels were meant to be read as actively attempting to change the structure of the Afro-American culture of which they were a part. As an integral part of a wider movement among black women intellectuals, these books both shaped and were shaped by strategies for resisting and defeating oppression. Organizing to fight included writing to organize. The novels do not merely reflect constituencies but attempt to structure Afro-American struggles in particular directions; both are loci of political and social interests that try to form, not just reveal, their constituencies. Afro-American women were attempting to define the political parameters of gender, race, and patriarchal authority and were constantly engaged with these issues in both fiction and nonfiction. The formation of the NACW provided a forum for the exchange of ideas among Afro-American women intellectuals, within a structure that disseminated information nationally. Black women's clubs provided a support for, but were also influenced by, the work of their individual members. Hopkins, for example, read from the manuscript of *Contending Forces* to the members of the Woman's Era Club in Boston; in turn, those members were part of the constituency that Hopkins tried to mobilize to agitate against Jim Crow segregation and the terrorizing practices of lynching and rape.

As intellectuals, these women organized around issues that addressed all aspects of the social organization of oppression. Arrival at the threshold of woman's era did not lead to concentration on what could be narrowly construed as women's issues—whether domestic concerns or female suffrage. Cooper characterized the opportunity this way: "To be a woman of the Negro race in America, and to be able to grasp the deep significance of the possibilities of the crisis, is to have a heritage . . . unique in the ages" (*V*, p. 144). Cooper saw the responsibility of the black woman to be the reshaping of society: "Such is the colored woman's office. She must stamp weal or woe on the coming history of this people" (*V*, p. 145). To illustrate the process of exchange of ideas within the discourse of the woman's era, I will concentrate on one object of analysis: a theory of internal and external colonization developed in the works of Cooper and Wells and finally figured in the fiction of Hopkins.

As indicated in the epigraphs to this essay, both Harper and Cooper associated imperialism with unrestrained patriarchal power. Prefiguring Hopkins, Harper and Cooper reassessed the mythology of the founding fathers in terms of rampant lust, greed, and destruction: they portray white male rule as bestial in its actual and potential power to devour lands and peoples. Cooper developed a complex analysis of social, political, and economic forces as being either distinctly masculine or feminine in their orientation and consequences. She saw an intimate link between internal and external colonization, between domestic racial oppression and imperialism. While her critique of imperialism and institutionalized domestic racism is a particularly good example of her larger theories of masculine and feminine practices and spheres of influence, it is important to stress that her categories were not dependent on biological distinction. Cooper made it clear in her application of such analyses that women could conform to masculinist attitudes and practices and men could display womanly virtues.

Cooper saw the imperialist or expansionist impulse, with its ideology of racial categorization, as a supreme manifestation of patriarchal power. She argued that the source of such flagrant abuse had to be questioned, challenged, and opposed:

Whence came this apotheosis of greed and cruelty? Whence this sneaking admiration we all have for bullies and prize-fighters? Whence the self-congratulation of "dominant" races, as if "dominant" meant "righteous" and carried with it a title to inherit the earth? Whence the scorn of so-called weak or unwarlike races and individuals, and the very comfortable assurance that it is their manifest destiny to be wiped out as vermin before this advancing civilization? [*V,* p. 51]

Cooper refers to Lowell's *Soul of the Far East,* an imperialist treatise which predicted the death of all Asian peoples and cultures " 'before the advancing nations of the West.' " She indicts the author as a "scion of an upstart race" who felt confident that, with the stroke of a pen, he could consign "to annihilation one-third the inhabitants of the globe—a people whose civilization was hoary headed before the parent elements that begot his race had advanced beyond nebulosity" (*V,* p. 52). The world under a dominant male influence is compared to the beast from the Book of Daniel, devouring all before it and demanding that it be worshiped as an incarnation of power. The complementary force, the female influence, is unable to restrain "the beast"; the rampant will to dominate and despise the weak is also present in the racist attitudes of white women. Cooper saw patriarchal power revealed in the imperialist impulse, but she also saw that that power was nurtured and sustained at home by an elite of white women preoccupied with maintaining their caste status (see *V,* pp. 86–87).

Cooper felt strongly that the only effective counter to patriarchal abuse of power—the feminine—had to be developed through the education of women. Education held possibilities for the empowerment of women, who could then shape the course of a future society which would exercise sensitivity and sympathy toward all who were poor and oppressed. White women, however, rarely exercised their power in sympathy with their black sisters. Cooper was well aware of this, and some of her most vituperative work attacks the exclusionary practices and discourse of white women's organizations which presumed to exist for and address the experiences of "women." Cooper challenged white women, as would-be leaders of reform, to revolutionize their thinking and practices. She challenged them to transform their provincial determination to secure gender and class interests at the expense of the rights of the oppressed (see *V,* pp. 123–24).

These gender and class interests were disguised when the issue of justice began to be displaced by debates about the dangers of social equality—debates that concerned the possible status of subject peoples abroad as well as the position of blacks in the United States. Cooper recognized—and condemned as fallacious—the concept of social equality with its implications of forced association between the races. This was not the social justice which blacks demanded. On the contrary, Cooper asserted, forced association was the manacled black male and the raped black woman, both internally colonized. Social equality masked the real issue: autonomy and the right to self-determination.

Cooper understood that the smoke screen of social equality obscured questions of heritage and inheritance which appeared in the figure of "blood" and gained consensual dominance both North and South (see *V*, pp. 103–4). She became convinced that the key to understanding the unwritten history of the United States was the dominance of southern "influence, ideals, and ideas" over the whole nation. Cooper saw that the manipulative power of the South was embodied in the southern patriarch, but she describes its concern with "blood," inheritance, and heritage in entirely female terms and as a preoccupation that was transmitted from the South to the North and perpetuated by white women. The South represented not red blood but blue:

> If your own father was a pirate, a robber, a murderer, his hands are dyed in red blood, and you don't say very much about it. But if your great great great grandfather's grandfather stole and pillaged and slew, and you can prove it, your blood has become blue and you are at great pains to establish the relationship. . . . [The South] had blood; and she paraded it with so much gusto that the substantial little Puritan maidens of the North, who had been making bread and canning currants and not thinking of blood the least bit, began to hunt up the records of the Mayflower to see if some of the passengers thereon could not claim the honor of having been one of William the Conqueror's brigands, when he killed the last of the Saxon Kings and, red-handed, stole his crown and his lands. [*V*, pp. 103–4]

Ridicule effectively belittles and undermines the search for an aristocratic heritage and proof of biological racial superiority; it also masks a very serious critique of these ideologies that Hopkins was to develop in her fiction. The juxtaposition of "red" with "blue" blood reveals the hidden history of national and nationalist heritage to be based on the principles of murder and theft—piracy. Hopkins drew from this analysis of the methods of expansionism, as it applied to the colonization of the Americas and to the imperialist ventures of the United States, as she demystified the mythological pretensions of the American story of origins in her fiction.

By linking imperialism to internal colonization, Cooper thus provided black women intellectuals with the basis for an analysis of how patriarchal power establishes and sustains gendered and racialized social formations. White women were implicated in the maintenance of this wider system of oppression because they challenged only the parameters of their domestic confinement; by failing to reconstitute their class and caste interests, they reinforced the provincialism of their movement. Ultimately, however, Cooper placed her hopes for change on the possibility of a transformed woman's movement. She wanted to expand the rubric defining the concerns of women to encompass an ideal and practice that could inspire a movement for the liberation of all oppressed peoples, not just a movement for the defence of parochial and sectional interests in the name of "woman" (see *V*, p. 125).

The pen of Ida B. Wells was aimed at a different target—lynching, as a practice of political and economic repression. Wells' analysis of the relation between political terrorism, economic oppression, and conventional codes of sexuality and morality has still to be surpassed in its incisive condemnation of the patriarchal manipulation of race and gender.[5] Her achievement drew upon the support of club women but also provided the impetus for the formation of antilynching societies. *Southern Horrors*, on the one hand, was dedicated to the Afro-American women of New York and Brooklyn, whose contributions had made publication of the pamphlet possible. On the other hand, Wells claimed in her autobiography that the meetings to organize her first antilynching lecture and the forum itself were "the real beginning of the club movement among the colored women" in the United States.[6] The gathering of black women from Philadelphia, New York, Boston, and other cities indicated that organization was already embryonic. The meeting on one particular issue, lynching, was a catalyst for the establishment of numerous clubs and a general movement that would extend beyond any one single issue.

Wells established in *Southern Horrors* that the association between lynching and rape was strictly a contemporary phenomenon; she argued that there was no historical foundation for that association, since "the crime of rape was unknown during four years of civil war, when the white women of the South were at the mercy of the race which is all at once charged with being a bestial one" (*SH*, p. 5). She indicted the miscegenation laws, which, in practice, were directed at preventing sexual relations between white women and black men. The miscegenation laws thus pretended to offer "protection" to white women but left black women the victims of rape by white men and simultaneously granted to these same men the power to terrorize black men as a potential threat to the virtue of white womanhood. Wells asserted that "there are many white women in the South who would marry colored men if such an act would not place them at once beyond the pale of society and within the clutches of the law." The miscegenation laws, in her opinion, only operated against "the legitimate union of the races" (*SH*, p. 6). In her publications and speeches, Wells increasingly used evidence from the white press—statistics on lynchings and reports that substantiated her claims that black male/white female sexual relationships were encouraged by white women. Wells used the white press in this way not only to avoid accusations of falsification or exaggeration but also because she wanted to reveal the contradictions implicit in the association of lynching with the rape of white women. She wanted to condemn the murderers out of their own mouths (see *RR,* p. 15).

Wells recognized that the Southerners' appeal to Northerners for sympathy on the "necessity" of lynching was very successful. It worked, she thought, through the claim that any condemnation of lynching constituted a public display of indifference to the "plight" of white womanhood. Wells demonstrated that, while accusations of rape were made in only one-third of all lynchings, the cry of rape was an extremely effective way to create panic and fear. Lynching, she argued, was an institutionalized practice supported and encouraged by the established leaders of a community and the press they influenced. The North conceded to the South's argument that rape was the cause of lynching; the concession to lynching for a specific crime in turn conceded the right to lynch any black male for any crime: the charge of rape became the excuse for murder. The press acted as accomplices in the ideological work that disguised the lesson of political and economic subordination which the black community was being taught. Black disenfranchisement and Jim Crow segregation had been achieved; now, the annihilation of a black political presence was shielded behind a "screen of defending the honor of [white] women" (*SH,* p. 14). Those that remained silent while disapproving of lynching were condemned by Wells for being as guilty as the actual perpetrators of lynching.

The lesson the black community should learn, Wells argued, was to recognize its economic power. The South owed its rehabilitation to Northern capital, on the one hand, and to Afro-American labor, on the other: "By the right exercise of his power as the industrial factor of the South, the Afro-American can demand and secure his rights." But economic power was only one force among the possible forms of resistance, she concluded: "a Winchester rifle should have a place of honor in every black home" (*SH,* p. 23). Wells knew that emancipation meant that white men lost their vested interests in the body of the Negro and that lynching and the rape of black women were attempts to regain control. The terrorizing of black communities was a political weapon that manipulated ideologies of sexuality. Wells analysed how ideologies of manhood—as well as of citizenship—were embodied in the right to vote. The murder of blacks was so easily accomplished because they had been granted the right to vote but not the means to protect or maintain that right. Thus, Wells was able to assert that the loss of the vote was both a political silencing and an emasculation which placed black men outside the boundaries of contemporary patriarchal power. The cry of rape, which pleaded the necessity of revenge for assaulted white womanhood, attempted to place black males "beyond the pale of human sympathy" (*RR,* p. 12). Black women were relegated to a place outside the ideological construction of "womanhood." That term included only white women; therefore the rape of black women was of no consequence outside the black community.

Wells' analysis of lynching and her demystification of the political motivations behind the manipulation of both black male and female and white female sexuality led her into direct confrontation with women like Frances Willard, president of the Woman's Christian Temperance Union, who considered themselves progressive but refused to see lynching as an institutionalized practice. Willard's attitude and Wells' conclusion that Willard was "no better or worse than the great bulk of white Americans on the Negro questions" are indicative of the racism that Cooper condemned in white women's organizations (*RR*, p. 85). As Harper also pointed out, there was not a single black woman admitted to the southern WCTU. What Cooper called the white woman's concern with caste was evident in the assumption of many "progressive" white women that rape actually *was* the crime to which lynching was the response.[7]

For Cooper, imperialism linked all those oppressed under the domination of the United States. Patriarchy, for her, was embodied in these acts of violence; therefore she ultimately placed her focus and hopes for the future on a transformed woman's movement. Wells, in her analysis of lynching, provided for a more detailed dissection of patriarchal power, showing how it could manipulate sexual ideologies to justify political and economic subordination. Cooper had failed to address what proved central to the thesis of Wells—that white men used their ownership of the body of the white female as a terrain on which to lynch the black male. White women felt that their caste was their protection and that their interests lay with the power that ultimately confined them. Although Cooper identified the relation between patriarchal power and white women's practice of racial exclusion, she did not examine and analyse what forged that relation. She preferred to believe that what men taught women could be unlearned if women's education was expanded. Wells was able to demonstrate how a patriarchal system, which had lost its total ownership over black male bodies, used its control over women to attempt to completely circumscribe the actions of black males. As black women positioned outside the "protection" of the ideology of womanhood, both Cooper and Wells felt that they could see clearly the compromised role of white women in the maintenance of a system of oppression.

Black women listened, organized, and acted on the theses of both Wells and Cooper, but very few white women responded to their social critiques. Cooper was right to argue that a transformed woman's movement, purged of racism, would have provided a liberating experience for white women themselves. But racism led to concession, to segregated organizations, and, outside the antilynching movement, to a resounding silence about—and therefore complicity in—the attempt to eliminate black people politically, economically, and, indeed, physically.

Pauline Hopkins shared this very real fear that black people were threatened with annihilation. She addressed her plea to "all Negroes, whether Frenchmen, Spaniards, Americans or Africans to rediscover their history as one weapon in the struggle against oppression."[8] Hopkins challenged the readers of her work to bear witness to her testimony concerning the international dimensions of the crisis.

> The dawn of the Twentieth century finds the Black race fighting for existence in every quarter of the globe. From over the sea Africa stretches her hands to the American Negro and cries aloud for sympathy in her hour of trial. . . . In America, caste prejudice has received fresh impetus as the "Southern brother" of the Anglo-Saxon family has arisen from the ashes of secession, and like the prodigal of old, has been gorged with fatted calf and "fixin's."[9]

As a black intellectual, Hopkins conceived of her writing as an inspiration to political action, a pattern for encouraging forms of resistance and agitation, and an integral part of the politics of oppression.

Hopkins regarded fiction in particular as a cultural form of great historical and political significance. In the preface to her first novel, *Contending Forces* (1900), she asserted its "religious, political and social" value and urged other black writers to *"faithfully portray the inmost thoughts and feelings of the Negro with all the fire and romance which lie dormant in our history."*[10] History is the crucial element in Hopkins' fiction: current oppressive forces, she argued, must be understood in the context of past oppression. "Mob-law is nothing new. . . . The atrocity of the acts committed one hundred years ago are duplicated today, when slavery is supposed no longer to exist" (*CF*, pp. 14, 15). This thesis is a cornerstone of *Contending Forces*. Drawing upon the theoretical perspectives of women like Cooper and Wells as well as the central concerns of the black woman's movement as a whole, Hopkins figures lynching and rape as the two political weapons of terror wielded by the powers behind internal colonization.

Contending Forces opens with a brief recounting of family history. Charles Montfort, a West Indian planter, decides to move his family and estate of slaves from Bermuda to North Carolina in response to the increasing agitation in the British Parliament for the abolition of slavery. Montfort acts to protect his commercial interests and profits. Hopkins is careful to remove any motivation or intention on his part that could be attributed to cruelty or personal avariciousness. Thus she establishes the economic basis of slavery as the primary factor in this decision which precipitates all the events and conditions in the rest of the text. Once the Montfort estate has been established in North Carolina, the focus of the novel gravitates toward Grace Montfort and the suspicion, which becomes rumor, that her blood is "polluted" by an African strain. Hopkins utilizes what Cooper had identified as the American obsession with "pure blood" and reveals its mythological proportions. It is actually irrelevant whether Grace Montfort is a black or a white woman. Her behaviour is classically that of "true womanhood"—but her skin is a little too "creamy." The reader is not apprised of her actual heritage; what is important is the mere suspicion of black blood. This results in the social ostracism of her whole family, while Grace herself, denied her station on the pedestal of virtue, becomes the object of the illicit sexual desire of a local landowner, Anson Pollock. The possibility that Grace might be black leads directly to the murder of Charles Montfort, the rapes of Grace and her black foster sister Lucy, and the enslavement of the two Montfort sons, Jesse and Charles.

Grace Montfort rejects the advances of Pollock, who then plots to avenge his wounded pride and satisfy his sexual obsession. Under the pretence of quelling an imminent rebellion by Montfort's slaves, Pollock uses the "committee on public safety"—in fact, a vigilante group—to raid the Montfort plantation. Montfort himself is quickly dispatched by a bullet in the brain, leaving Grace prey to Pollock. In a graphic and tortured two-page scene, Hopkins represents a brutal rape in a displaced form: Grace is whipped by two members of the "committee." Her clothes are ripped from her and she is "whipped" alternately "by the two strong, savage men." Hopkins' replacement of the phallus by the "snaky leather thong" is crude but effective, and the reader is left in no doubt about the kind of outrage that has occurred when "the blood stood in a pool about her feet" (*CF*, p. 69).

Grace commits suicide, in the tradition of outraged virtue, and Pollock takes Lucy, Grace's black maid and slave, as his mistress instead. But the actual and figurative ravishing of "grace" at the hand of Southern brutality establishes the link that Hopkins is drawing between rape and its political motivation as a device of terrorism. Both Charles and Grace Montfort are punished because they threatened to break the acceptable codes that bound the slave system. The possibility of miscegenation represented the ultimate violation of the white woman's social position and required the degradation of the transgressor and the relegation of her offspring to the status of chattel. The two sons represent two possible histories. Charles junior is bought and eventually grows up "white" in Britain. Jesse escapes into the black communities of Boston and, later, New Hampshire; he is the ancestor of the black family which is the main subject of the novel.

This preliminary tale acts as an overture to the main body of *Contending Forces*, containing the clues and themes that will eventually provide the resolutions to the crises of relations between the main characters. Living in Boston at the turn of the century, the Smith family inherits this tale of its ancestors: the tale appears remote from their everyday lives but is retained in the naming of the children. Ma Smith, her husband dead, runs a lodging house with her son, William Jesse Montfort, and her daughter, Dora Grace Montfort. The two other main characters are both lodgers, John P. Langley, engaged to Dora, and Sappho Clark, a woman who is mysteriously hiding her personal history. All these characters cannot move forward into the future until their relation to the past is revealed. Hopkins displaces a direct attack on the increasing separation of the races onto issues of inheritance, heritage, and culture—issues where bloodlines between the races are so entangled that race as a biological category is subordinated to race as a political category. The historical importance of rape is crucial to the construction of Hopkins' fictionalized history: it is through the rapes of Grace and Lucy that the two races share an intertwined destiny.

Shifting contemporary debates about race from the biological to the political level was a crucial move for Hopkins to make in her fiction. At the height of debate about the consequences of colonizing overseas territories, Hopkins attempted to disrupt imperialist discourse concerning empires composed primarily of nonwhite peoples. The grounds of imperialist argument derived their problematic from the experience of the internal colonization of native American Indians and Africans. At the moment when black Americans were again being systematically excluded from participation in social institutions, the status of people who lived in what the United States now deemed its "possessions" was an integral component of the contemporary discourse on race. "Mixing blood" was seen as a threat to the foundations of North American civilization.[11]

Hopkins intended to disrupt this imperialist discourse through the figuration of an alternative set of historical consequences. The degradation of a race is not represented as being the result of amalgamation but of an abuse of power—the use of brutality against an oppressed group equates with savagery, in Hopkins' terms. She quotes Ralph Waldo Emerson on her title page and again in the body of the text: "*The civility of no race can be perfect whilst another race is degraded.*" The link that Hopkins establishes between Britain and the West Indies makes visible a colonial relationship that enables her to direct a critique of imperial relations to an American readership. Hopkins carefully demonstrates that blacks are a colonized people for whom it is a necessity that history be rewritten. The histories of the externally colonized and the internally colonized are interwoven in many ways but primarily through questions of rightful inheritance. In Hopkins' fictional world, one consequence of external colonization is that a debt must be paid from the profits of the slave trade and Charles Montfort's plantation. For the purposes of this essay, however, I want to concentrate on Hopkins' presentation of the two main weapons of terror of internal colonization: lynching and rape.

At the heart of the text are two tales told at a public gathering by Luke Sawyer, who is black. In the first, a lynching is the central focus of concern; in the second, a rape. Both tales confirm the privileging of these two acts in Hopkins' thesis of "contending forces." The first history that Luke tells is of his father, whose success in trade resulted in competition with white traders, threats on his life, and, ultimately, a mob attack on his home and family. His act of self-defence—firing into the mob—is punished by lynching; the women are whipped and raped to death, the two babies slaughtered.

The second tale follows from the first. Luke escapes into the woods and is found by a black planter, Beaubean, who rescues him and takes him into his home to raise as a son. Beaubean has a wealthy and politically influential white half brother, who assumes a stance of friendship toward the whole family but particularly toward Beaubean's daughter, Mabelle. At the age of fourteen, Mabelle is kidnapped by this uncle, raped, and left a prisoner in a brothel. After weeks of searching, Beaubean finds Mabelle and confronts his brother with the crime—only to be asked "What does a woman of mixed blood, or any Negress, for that matter, know of virtue?" (*CF*, p. 261). Beaubean is offered a thousand dollars by his brother which he rejects with a threat to seek justice in a federal court. Beaubean's threat is promptly met with mob action: his house is set on fire and its occupants shot. Luke escapes with Mabelle and places her in a convent.

Hopkins concentrates on the practices of oppression—the consequences of white supremacy—in reconstructing the history of her characters. The predominance of mulattoes and octoroons in the novel is not intended to glorify the possibilities of the black race if only it would integrate with (and eventually lose itself within) the white.[12] On the contrary, Hopkins states categorically in this novel and throughout her work that "miscegenation, either *lawful* or *unlawful*, we *do not want*" (*CF*, p. 264). The presence of racially mixed characters throughout the text emphasizes particular social relations and practices and must be understood historically. Such characters are often the physical consequences of a social system that exercised white supremacy through rape. Use of the mulatto figure, as a literary device, has two primary functions: it enables an exploration of the relation between the races while, at the same time, it expresses the relation between the races. It is a narrative mechanism of mediation frequently used in a period when social convention dictated an increased and more absolute distance between black and white. The figure of the mulatto allows for a fictional representation and reconstruction of the socially proscribed. Hopkins' particular use of such figuration is intended, in part, to demythologize concepts of "pure blood" and "pure race." More important, however, it is an attempt to demonstrate the crucial role of social, political, and economic interests in determining human behaviour by negating any proposition of degeneracy through amalgamation. Hopkins transposes contemporary accusations that miscegenation is the inmost desire of the nonwhite peoples of the earth by reconstructing miscegenation as the result of white rape.

Hopkins saw clearly that the threat to white supremacy was not black sexuality but the potential of the black vote. Rape, she argued, should be totally separated from the issue of violated white womanhood and then recast as part of the social, political, and economic oppression of blacks:

> "Lynching was instituted to crush the manhood of the enfranchised black. Rape is the crime which appeals most strongly to the heart of the home life. . . . *The men who created the mulatto race, who recruit its ranks year after year by the very means which they invoked lynch law to suppress,* bewailing the sorrows of violated womanhood!
> No; it is not rape. If the Negro votes, he is shot; if he marries a white woman, he is shot . . . or lynched—he is a pariah whom the National Government cannot defend. But if he defends himself and his home, then is heard the tread of marching feet as the Federal troops move southward to quell a 'race riot.' " [*CF*, pp. 270–71]

The analysis of rape and its links to lynching as a weapon of political terror is, obviously, shaped by the arguments and indictments of Wells. In Hopkins' fictional reconstruction of the social relations between white and black, the two parts of the text move across generations and thus, through historical knowledge, invalidate the understanding of cause and effect then being reasserted through white patriarchal supremacy. Hopkins offers her readers an alternative story of origins where the characters are not holistic creations but the terrain on which the consequences of the authorial assertion of history are worked through. This can be clearly seen in the creation of Sappho Clark, the dominant female figure in the text, who has two identities.

The disguise—that which hides true history—is Sappho, the poet of Lesbos, who was admired and loved by both men and women, though her erotic poetry was addressed to women. The Sappho of *Contending Forces* embodies the potential for utopian relationships between women and between women and men; she represents a challenge to a patriarchal order. To Dora, whose duties running the boarding house confine her to a domestic existence, Sappho is the independent woman who, in their intimate moments together, talks of the need for suffrage and the political activity of women (see *CF*, p. 125). Sappho disrupts Dora's complacency— Dora will "generally accept whatever the men tell me as right"—and leads her to reassess the importance of friendships with women. But Sappho as an ideal of womanhood does not exist except as a set of fictional possibilities. In order to function, to work and survive, Sappho's younger self, Mabelle Beaubean, a product of miscegenation and the subject of rape, has had to bury her violated womanhood and deny her progeny. Like Sappho of Lesbos, Sappho Clark has a child, "whose form is like / gold flowers."[13] But unlike Sappho of Lesbos, Mabelle exists in a patriarchal order, her body is colonized, her child the fruit of rape. Sappho Clark journeys toward the retrieval of a whole identity, one which will encompass a combination of the elements of Sappho and Mabelle. Such an identity leads to an acceptance of a motherhood which, like that of Sappho of Lesbos, does not require that a male occupy the space of father.

The most significant absence in the network of social forces is the black father. In narrative, the father is a figure that mediates patriarchal control over women; in most texts by nineteenth-century black women, this control is exercised by white men who politically, socially, and economically attempt to deny patriarchal power to black men. The absent space in fiction by black women confirms this denial of patriarchal power to black men, but Hopkins uses that space to explore the possibilities of alternative black male figures. Black men are depicted in peer relations, as brothers, or as potential partners/lovers. Women are not seen as the subject of exchange between father and husband; neither are their journeys limited to the distance between daughter and wife. As partners, sexual or nonsexual, the narrative impulse is toward utopian relations between black men and black women.

Nineteenth-century black feminists cannot be dismissed simply as "spokespeople for prudery in their communities." Their legacy to us is theories that expose the colonization of the black female body by white male power and the destruction of black males who attempted to exercise any oppositional patriarchal control. When accused of threatening the white female body, the repository of heirs to property and power, the black male, and his economic, political, and social advancement, is lynched out of existence. Cooper, Wells, and Hopkins assert the necessity of seeing the relation between histories: the rape of black women in the nineties is directly linked to the rape of the female slave. Their analyses are dynamic and not limited to a parochial understanding of "women's issues"; they have firmly established the dialectical relation between economic/political power and economic/sexual power in the battle for control of women's bodies.

A desire for the possibilities of the uncolonized black female body occupies a utopian space; it is the false hope of Sappho Clark's pretend history. Black feminists understood that the struggle would have to take place on the terrain of the previously colonized: the struggle was to be characterized by redemption, retrieval, and reclamation—not, ultimately, by an unrestrained utopian vision. Sappho could not deny the existence of the raped Mabelle but, instead, had to reunite with the colonized self. Thus, these black feminists expanded the limits of conventional ideologies of womanhood to consider subversive relationships between women, motherhood without wifehood, wifehood as a partnership outside of an economic exchange between men, and men as partners and not patriarchal fathers. As DuBois and Gordon have argued so cogently, we have "150 years of feminist theory and praxis in the area of sexuality. This is a resource too precious to squander by not learning it, in all its complexity."[14]

But let us learn *all* of it, not only in its complexity but also in its difference, and so stand again on the "threshold of woman's era"—an era that can encompass all women.

1. Ellen Carol DuBois and Linda Gordon, "Seeking Ecstasy on the Battlefield: Danger and Pleasure in Nineteenth-Century Feminist Sexual Thought," in *Pleasure and Danger: Exploring Female Sexuality*, ed. Carole S. Vance (Boston, 1984), pp. 34, 33.

2. See Frances E. W. Harper, *Iola Leroy; or, Shadows Uplifted* (Philadelphia, 1892), and Anna Julia Cooper, *A Voice from the South; By a Black Woman of the South* (Xenia, Ohio, 1892); all further references to this work, abbreviated *V*, will be included in the text. See also Ida B. Wells-Barnett, *On Lynchings: Southern Horrors; A Red Record; Mob Rule in New Orleans* (New York, 1969); all further references to *Southern Horrors* and *A Red Record*, respectively abbreviated *SH* and *RR*, are to this collection and will be included in the text. These were preceded by a novel by Emma Dunham Kelley ("Forget-me-not" [Emma Dunham Kelley], *Megda* [Boston, 1891]) and followed by the publication of a short story by Victoria Earle (Victoria Earle Matthews, *Aunt Lindy: A Story Founded on Real Life* [New York, 1893]) and a survey by Gertrude Mossel (Mrs. N. F. [Gertrude] Mossell, *The Work of the Afro-American Woman* [Philadelphia, 1894]).

3. Harper, "Woman's Political Future," in *World's Congress of Representative Women*, ed. May Wright Sewell, 2 vols. (Chicago, 1894), 1:433–34.

4. This paragraph draws upon material from my forthcoming book, *Uplifting as They Write: The Emergence of the Afro-American Woman novelist*.

5. Wells' pamphlet *Southern Horrors: Lynch Law in All Its Phases* was published in 1892; *A Red Record: Tabulated Statistics and Alleged Causes of Lynchings in the United States, 1892–1893–1894* was published in 1895; and *Mob Rule in New Orleans* was published in 1900. All three have been reprinted; see Wells, *On Lynchings* (New York, 1969). My account of some of her arguments is oversimplified and extremely adumbrated.

6. Wells, quoted in Alfreda M. Duster, ed., *Crusade for Justice: The Autobiography of Ida B. Wells* (Chicago, 1970), p. 81.

7. See Bettina Aptheker, ed., *Lynching and Rape: An Exchange of Views*, American Institute for Marxist Studies Occasional Paper 25 (San Jose, Calif., 1977), p. 29.

8. Pauline Hopkins, "Toussaint L'Overture," *Colored American Magazine* 2 (Nov. 1900): 10, 24.

9. Hopkins, "Heroes and Heroines in Black," *Colored American Magazine* 3 (Jan. 1903): 211.

10. Hopkins, *Contending Forces: A Romance Illustrative of Negro Life North and South* (1900; Carbondale, Ill., 1978), pp. 13, 14; all further references to this work, abbreviated *CF*, will be included in the text.

11. See Robert L. Allen, *Reluctant Reformers: Racism and Social Reform Movements in the United States* (Garden City, N.Y., 1975), and Christopher Lasch, *The World of Nations: Reflections on American History, Politics, and Culture* (New York, 1973), pp. 70–79.

12. Gwendolyn Brooks misunderstands Hopkins to be arguing for integration; see Brooks, afterword to Hopkins, *Contending Forces*, pp. 403–9.

13. Sappho, fragment 132, quoted in Sarah B. Pomeroy, *Goddesses, Whores, Wives, and Slaves: Women in Classical Antiquity* (New York, 1975), p. 54.

14. DuBois and Gordon, "Seeking Ecstasy on the Battlefield," p. 43.

Thresholds of Difference: Structures of Address in Zora Neale Hurston

Barbara Johnson

In preparing to write this paper, I found myself repeatedly stopped by conflicting conceptions of the structure of address into which I was inserting myself. It was not clear to me what I, a white deconstructor, was doing talking about Zora Neale Hurston, a black novelist and anthropologist, or to *whom* I was talking. Was I trying to convince white establishment scholars who long for a return to Renaissance ideals that the study of the Harlem Renaissance is not a trivialization of their humanistic pursuits? Was I trying to contribute to the attempt to adapt the textual strategies of literary theory to the analysis of Afro-American literature? Was I trying to rethink my own previous work and to re-referentialize the notion of difference so as to move the conceptual operations of deconstruction out of the realm of abstract linguistic universality? Was I talking to white critics, black critics, or myself?

Well, all of the above. What finally struck me was the fact that what I was analyzing in Hurston's writings was precisely, again and again, her strategies and structures of problematic address. It was as though I were asking her for answers to questions I did not even know I was unable to formulate. I had a lot to learn, then, from Hurston's way of dealing with multiple agendas and heterogeneous implied readers. I will focus here on three texts that play interesting variations on questions of identity and address: two short essays, "How It Feels to Be Colored Me"[1] and "What White Publishers Won't Print,"[2] and a book-length collection of folktales, songs, and hoodoo practices entitled *Mules and Men*.[3]

One of the presuppositions with which I began was that Hurston's work was situated "outside" the mainstream literary canon and that I, by implication, was an institutional "insider." I soon came to see, however, not only that the insider becomes an outsider the minute she steps out of the inside but also that Hurston's work itself was constantly dramatizing and undercutting just such inside/outside oppositions, transforming the plane geometry of physical space into the complex transactions of discursive exchange. In other words, Hurston could be read not just as an *example* of the "noncanonical" writer but as a commentator on the dynamics of any encounter between an inside and an outside, any attempt to make a statement about difference.

One of Hurston's most memorable figurations of the inside/outside structure is her depiction of herself as a threshold figure mediating between the all-black town of Eatonville, Florida, and the big road traveled by passing whites:

> The front porch might seem a daring place for the rest of the town, but it was a gallery seat for me. My favorite place was atop the gate-post. Proscenium box for a born first-nighter. Not only did I enjoy the show, but I didn't mind the actors knowing that I liked it. I usually spoke to them in passing. . . .
>
> They liked to hear me "speak pieces" and sing and wanted to see me dance the parse-me-la, and gave me generously of their small silver for doing these things. . . . The colored people gave no dimes. They deplored any joyful tendencies in me, but I was their Zora nevertheless. ["CM," pp. 152–53]

The inside/outside opposition here opens up a reversible theatrical space in which proscenium box becomes center stage and small silver passes to the boxholder-turned-actor.

Hurston's joyful and lucrative gatepost stance between black and white cultures was very much a part of her Harlem Renaissance persona and was indeed often deplored by fellow black artists. Langston Hughes, who for a time shared with Hurston the problematic patronage of the wealthy Charlotte Mason, wrote of Hurston:

> Of th[e] "niggerati," Zora Neale Hurston was certainly the most amusing. Only to reach a wider audience, need she ever write books—

Barbara Johnson is professor of French and comparative literature at Harvard University. She is the author of *Défigurations du langage poétique* and *The Critical Difference,* translator of Jacques Derrida's *Dissemination,* and editor of *The Pedagogical Imperative: Teaching as a Literary Genre.*

because she is a perfect book of entertainment in herself. In her youth she was always getting scholarships and things from wealthy white people, some of whom simply paid her just to sit around and represent the Negro race for them, she did it in such a racy fashion. . . . To many of her white friends, no doubt, she was a perfect "darkie."[4]

"Representing the Negro race for whites" was nevertheless in many ways the program of the Harlem Renaissance. While Hurston has often been read and judged on the basis of personality alone, her "racy" adoption of the "happy darkie" stance, which was a successful strategy for survival, does not by any means exhaust the representational strategies of her *writing.*

Questions of identity, difference, and race-representation are interestingly at issue in the 1928 essay entitled "How It Feels to be Colored Me," in which the gatepost passage appears. Published in *World Tomorrow,* a white journal sympathetic to Harlem Renaissance writers, the essay is quite clearly a response to the unspoken question inevitably asked by whites of the black artist. Since any student of literature trained in the European tradition and interested in Hurston out of a concern for the noncanonical is implicitly asking her that same question, a close reading of that essay is likely to shed light on what is at stake in such an encounter.

The essay is divided into a series of vignettes, each of which responds to the question differently. The essay begins, "I am colored but I offer nothing in the way of extenuating circumstances except the fact that I am the only Negro in the United States whose grandfather on the mother's side was *not* an Indian chief" ("CM," p. 152). Collapsed into this sentence are two myths of black identity, the absurdity of whose juxtaposition sets the tone for the entire essay. On the one hand, it implies that being colored is a misdemeanor for which some extenuation must be sought. On the other hand, it implies that among the stories Negroes tell about themselves the story of Indian blood is a common extenuation, dilution, and hence effacement of the crime of being colored. By making *lack* of Indian blood into an extenuating circumstance and by making explicit the absurdity of seeking extenuating circumstances for something over which one has no control, Hurston is shedding an ironic light both on the question ("How does it feel to be colored you?") and on one possible answer ("I'm not 100 percent colored"). Hurston is saying in effect, "I am colored but I am different from other members of my race in that I am not different from my race."[5]

While the first paragraph thus begins, "I am colored," the second starts, "I remember the very day that I *became* colored" ("CM," p. 152; my emphasis). The presuppositions of the question are again undercut. If one can become colored, then one is not born colored, and the definition of "colored" shifts. Hurston goes on to describe her "pre-colored" childhood spent in the all-black town of Eatonville, Florida. "During this period," she writes, "white people differed from colored to me only in that they rode through town and never lived there" ("CM," p. 152). It was not that there was no difference, it was that difference needed no extenuation.

> But changes came in the family when I was thirteen, and I was sent to school in Jacksonville. I left Eatonville, the town of the oleanders, as Zora. When I disembarked from the river-boat at Jacksonville, she was no more. It seemed that I had suffered a sea change. I was not Zora of Orange County any more, I was now a little colored girl. I found it out in certain ways. In my heart as well as in the mirror, I became a fast brown—warranted not to rub nor run. ["CM," p. 153]

In this sea change, the acquisition of color is a *loss* of identity: the "I" is no longer Zora, and "Zora" becomes a "she." "Everybody's Zora" had been constituted not by *an* Other but by the system of otherness itself, the ability to role-play rather than the ability to play any particular role. Formerly an irrepressible speaker of pieces, she now becomes a speaker of withholdings: "I found it out in certain ways."

The acquisition of color, which is here a function of motion (from Eatonville to Jacksonville), ends up entailing the fixity of a correspondence between inside and outside: "In my heart as well as in the mirror, I became a fast brown—warranted not to rub nor run." But the speed hidden in the word "fast," which belies its claim to fixity, is later picked up to extend the "color = motion" equation and to transform the question of race into the image of a road race:

> The terrible struggle that made me an American out of a potential slave said "On the line!" The Reconstruction said "Get set!"; and the generation before said "Go!" I am off to a flying start and I must not halt in the stretch to look behind and weep. ["CM," p. 153]

Later, however, "I am a dark rock surged upon"—a stasis in the midst of motion ("CM," p. 154).

The remainder of the essay is dotted with sentences playing complex variations on the title words "feel," "color," and "me":

> But I am not tragically colored.
>
> I do not always feel colored.
>
> I feel most colored when I am thrown against a sharp white background.
>
> At certain times I have no race, I am *me*.
>
> I have no separate feelings about being an American citizen and colored. ["CM," pp. 153, 154, 155]

The feelings associated with being colored are, on the one hand, the denial of sorrow and anger ("There is no great sorrow dammed up in my soul"; "Sometimes I feel discriminated against, but it does not make me angry" ["CM," pp. 153, 155]) and, on the other, the affirmation of strength and excitement ("I have seen that the world is to the strong regardless of a little pigmentation more or less"; "It is quite exciting to hold the center of the national stage" ["CM," p. 153]). Each case involves a reversal of implicit white expectations: I am not pitiful but powerful; being colored is not a liability but an advantage. "No one on earth ever had a greater chance for glory. . . . The position of my white neighbor is much more difficult" ("CM," p. 153).

There is one point in the essay, however, when Hurston goes out of her way to conform to a stereotype very much in vogue in the 1920s. The passage bears citing in its entirety:

> Sometimes it is the other way around. A white person is set down in our midst, but the contrast is just as sharp for me. For instance, when I sit in the drafty basement that is The New World Cabaret with a white person, my color comes. We enter chatting about any little nothing that we have in common and are seated by the jazz waiters. In the abrupt way that jazz orchestras have, this one plunges into a number. It loses no time in circumlocutions, but gets right down to business. It constricts the thorax and splits the heart with its tempo and narcotic harmonies. This orchestra grows rambunctious, rears on its hind legs and attacks the tonal veil with primitive fury, rending it, clawing it until it breaks through to the jungle beyond. I follow those heathen—follow them exultingly. I dance wildly inside myself; I yell within, I whoop; I shake my assegai above my head, I hurl it true to the mark *yeeeeooww!* I am in the jungle and living in the jungle way. My face is painted red and yellow and my body is painted blue. My pulse is throbbing like a war drum. I want to slaughter something—give pain, give death to what, I do not know. But the piece ends. The men of the orchestra wipe their lips and rest their fingers. I creep back slowly to the veneer we call civilization with the last tone and find the white friend sitting motionless in his seat, smoking calmly.
>
> "Good music they have here," he remarks, drumming the table with his fingertips.
>
> Music. The great blobs of purple and red emotion have not touched him. He has only heard what I felt. He is far away and I see him but dimly across the ocean and the continent that have fallen between us. He is so pale with his whiteness then and I am *so* colored. ["CM," p. 154]

"Feeling" here, instead of being a category of which "colored" is one example, becomes instead a *property* of the category "colored" ("He has only heard what I felt"). While the passage as a whole dramatizes the image of the exotic primitive, its relation to expectations and presuppositions is not as simple as it first appears. Having just described herself as feeling "most colored when I am thrown against a sharp white background," Hurston's announcement of having it "the other way around" leads one to expect something other than a description of "feel[ing] most colored." Yet there is no other way around. The moment there is a juxtaposition of black and white, what "comes" is color. But the colors that come in the passage are skin *paint,* not skin complexion: red, yellow, blue, and purple. The "tonal veil" is rent indeed, on the level at once of color, of sound, and of literary style. The move into the jungle is a move into mask; the return to civilization is a return to veneer. Either way, what is at stake is an artificial, ornamental surface.

Hurston undercuts the absoluteness of the opposition between white and black in another way as well. In describing the white man as "drumming the table with his fingertips," Hurston places in his body a counterpart to the "war drum" central to the jungle. If the jungle represents the experience of the body as such, the surge of bodily life external to conscious knowledge ("give pain, give death to what, I do not know"), then the nervous gesture is an alienated synecdoche for such bodily release.

In an essay entitled "What White Publishers Won't Print" written for *Negro Digest* in 1950, twenty-two years after "How It Feels to Be Colored Me," Hurston again takes up this "jungle" stereotype, this time to disavow it. The contrast between the two essays is significant:

> This insistence on defeat in a story where upperclass Negroes are portrayed, perhaps says something from the subconscious of the majority. Involved in western culture, the hero or heroine, or both, must appear frustrated and go down to defeat, somehow. Our literature reeks with it. It is the same as saying, "You can translate Virgil, and fumble with the differential calculus, but can you really comprehend it? Can you cope with our subtleties?"
>
> That brings us to the folklore of "reversion to type." This curious doctrine has such wide acceptance that it is tragic. One has only to examine the huge literature on it to be convinced. No matter how high we may *seem* to climb, put us under strain and we revert to type, that is, to the bush. Under a superficial layer of western culture, the jungle drums throb in our veins. ["WP," p. 172]

There are many possible explanations for Hurston's changed use of this image. For one thing, the exotic primitive was in vogue in 1928, while this was no longer the case in 1950. For another, she was addressing a white readership in the earlier essay and a black readership here. But the most revealing difference lies in the way the image is embedded in a structure of address. In the first essay, Hurston describes the jungle feeling as an art, an *ability* to feel, not a reversion. In the second, the jungle appears as a result of "strain." In the first, Hurston can proclaim

"I am this"; but when the image is repeated as "you are that," it changes completely. The content of the image may be the same, but its interpersonal use is different. The study of Afro-American literature as a whole poses a similar problem of address: any attempt to lift out of a text an image or essence of blackness is bound to violate the interlocutionary strategy of its formulation.

"What White Publishers Won't Print" is a complex meditation on the possibility of representing difference in order to erase it. Lamenting the fact that "the average, struggling, non-morbid Negro is the best-kept secret in America," Hurston explains the absence of a black *Main Street* by the majority's "indifference, not to say scepticism, to the internal life of educated minorities." The revelation to the public of the Negro who is "just like everybody else" is "the thing needed to do away with that feeling of difference which inspires fear and which ever expresses itself in dislike" ("WP," pp. 173, 170, 171, 173). The thing that prevents the publication of such representations of Negroes is thus said to be the public's *in*difference to finding out that there *is* no difference. Difference is a misreading of sameness, but it must be represented in order to be erased. The resistance to finding out that the Other is the same springs out of the reluctance to admit that the same is Other. If the average man could recognize that the Negro was "just like him," he would have to recognize that he was just like the Negro ("WP," p. 171). Difference disliked is identity affirmed. But the difficulty of pleading for a representation of difference *as* sameness is exemplified by the almost unintelligible distinction in the following sentence:

> As long as the majority cannot conceive of a Negro or a Jew feeling and reacting inside just as they do, the majority will keep right on believing that people who do not feel like them cannot possibly feel as they do. ["WP," p. 171]

The difference between difference and sameness can barely be said. It is as small and as vast as the difference between "like" and "as."

Hurston ends "How It Feels to Be Colored Me," too, with an attempt to erase difference. She describes herself as "a brown bag of miscellany" whose contents are as different from each other as they are similar to those of other bags, "white, red, and yellow" ("CM," p. 155). The outside is no guarantee of the nature of the inside. The last sentence of the article, which responds distantly to the title, is "Who knows?" ("CM," p. 155).

By the end of the essay, then, Hurston has conjugated a conflicting and ironic set of responses to her title. Far from answering the question of "how it feels to be colored me," she deconstructs the very grounds of an answer, replying "Compared to what? As of when? Who is asking? In what context? For what purpose? With what interests and presuppositions?" What Hurston rigorously shows is that questions of difference and identity are always a function of a specific interlocutionary situation— and the answers, matters of strategy rather than truth. In its rapid passage from image to image and from formula to formula, Hurston's *text* enacts the questions of identity as a process of *self*-difference that Hurston's *persona* often explicitly denies.

It is precisely that self-difference, however, that Hurston will assert as the key to her anthropological enterprise in *Mules and Men.* In discussing Hurston's folktale anthology, I will focus less on the tales themselves than on Hurston's multilayered envelope of address, in which such self-differentiations are most obvious and functional. In the opening lines of her introduction to the volume, Hurston writes:

> I was glad when somebody told me, "You may go and collect Negro folk-lore."
> In a way it would not be a new experience for me. When I pitched headforemost into the world I landed in a crib of negroism. . . . But it was fitting me like a tight chemise. I couldn't see it for wearing it. It was only when I was off in college, away from my native surroundings, that I could see myself like somebody else and stand off and look at my garment. Then I had to have the spy-glass of Anthropology to look through at that. [*MM*, p. 3]

The journey away to school does not confer color and fixed identity as it did in "How It Feels to Be Colored Me" but rather sight and self-division. "Seeing" and "wearing" (significantly, not seeing and being) cannot coincide, and we cannot always be sure which side of the spy-glass our narrator is standing on. The ambiguity of the inside/outside opposition involved in "see[ing] myself like somebody else" is dramatized in many ways in Hurston's collection of folktales, songs, and hoodoo practices, resulting in a complex interaction between the authority of her spy-glass and the rhetorical nature of her material.

Mules and Men is a book with multiple frames: it begins with a preface by Franz Boas, Hurston's teacher, and ends with a glossary and appendix. As we have seen, Hurston's own introduction begins with a paraphrase of Psalm 122 which replaces the Biblical "they" with an unnamed "somebody," and it ends by placing itself geographically just outside the town line of Eatonville:

> So I rounded Park Lane and came speeding down the straight stretch into Eatonville. . . .
> Before I enter the township, I wish to make acknowledgments to Mrs. R. Osgood [Charlotte] Mason of New York City. She backed my falling in a hearty way, in a spiritual way, and in addition, financed the whole expedition in the manner of the Great Soul that she is. [*MM*, p. 6]

And part 1 begins:

As I crossed the Maitland-Eatonville township line [*MM*, p. 9]

That line is the line between the two ends of the spy-glass, but it is also supposed to stand as the line between the theoretical introduction and the tales. Yet Hurston has already told the first tale, a folktale she remembers as she drives, a tale of creation and of the unequal distribution of "soul." Hence, not only does the first tale subvert the opposition between theory and material, but the tale itself comments doubly upon the acknowledgment to Mrs. Mason: what Mrs. Mason backed is called a "falling"—both a postcreational Fall and a losing hand in the "Georgia Skin Game" often referred to in the text. And since the story is about God's promise to redistribute "soul" more equally in the future, it sheds an ironic light on the designation of Hurston's wealthy patron as a "Great Soul."

Hurston does, however, offer some theoretical remarks in her introduction:

> Folk-lore is not as easy to collect as it sounds. The best source is where there are the least outside influences and these people, being usually under-privileged, are the shyest. They are most reluctant at times to reveal that which the soul lives by. And the Negro, in spite of his open-faced laughter, his seeming acquiescence, is particularly evasive. You see we are a polite people and we do not say to our questioner, "Get out of here!" We smile and tell him or her something that satisfies the white person because, knowing so little about us, he doesn't know what he is missing. The Indian resists curiosity by a stony silence. The Negro offers a feather-bed resistance. That is, we let the probe enter, but it never comes out. It gets smothered under a lot of laughter and pleasantries.
>
> The theory behind our tactics: "The white man is always trying to know into somebody else's business. All right, I'll set something outside the door of my mind for him to play with and handle. He can read my writing but he sho' can't read my mind. I'll put this play toy in his hand, and he will seize it and go away. Then I'll say my say and sing my song." [*MM*, pp. 4–5]

The shifts and reversals in this passage are multiple. Hurston begins as an outsider, a scientific narrative voice that refers to "these people" in the third person, as a group whose inner lives are difficult to penetrate. Then, suddenly, she leaps into the picture she has just painted, including herself in a "we" that addresses a "you"—the white reader, the new implied outsider. The structure of address changes from description to direct address. From that point on it is impossible to tell whether Hurston the narrator is *describing* a strategy or *employing* one. Is her book something set "outside the door" for the white man to "play with and handle," or is the difficulty of penetrating the featherbed resistance being described in order to play up her own privileged skill and access to its inner secrets? In any event, theory is here on the side of the withholder.

The text itself is a frame narrative recounting Hurston's *quest* for folktales along with the folktales themselves. It is a tale of the gathering of tales, or "lies," as they are called by the tellers (*MM*, p. 9). Hurston puts herself in a position to hear the tales only to the extent that she herself "lies." When she tells the townspeople that she has come to collect their "lies," one of them exclaims, "Aw shucks, . . . Zora, don't you come here and tell de biggest lie first thing. Who you reckon want to read all them old-time tales about Brer Rabbit and Brer Bear?" (*MM*, p. 10). Later, when Hurston leaves Eatonville to gather more tales, she is snubbed as an outsider because of her car and expensive dress until she lies and says that she is a bootlegger fleeing from justice. With her loss of difference comes a flood of tales. The strategy to obtain the material becomes indistinguishable from the material obtained.

This is not to say that the anthropological frame is entirely adequate to its task of accurate representation. The following tale can be read as a questioning of the framing activity:

> Ah know another man wid a daughter.
> The man sent his daughter off to school for seben years, den she come home all finished up. So he said to her, "Daughter, git yo' things and write me a letter to my brother!" So she did.
> He says, "Head it up," and she done so.
> "Now tell 'im, 'Dear Brother, our chile is done come home from school and all finished up and we is very proud of her.'"
> Then he ast de girl "Is you got dat?"
> She tole 'im "yeah."
> "Now tell him some mo'. 'Our mule is dead but Ah got another mule and when Ah say (clucking sound of tongue and teeth) he moved from de word.'"
> "Is you got dat?" he ast de girl.
> "Naw suh," she tole 'im.
> He waited a while and he ast her again, "You got dat down yet?"
> "Naw suh, Ah ain't got it yet."
> "How come you ain't got it?"
> "Cause Ah can't spell (clucking sound)."
> "You mean to tell me you been off to school seben years and can't spell (clucking sound)? Why Ah could spell dat myself and Ah ain't been to school a day in mah life. Well jes' say (clucking sound) he'll know what yo' mean and go on wid de letter." [*MM*, pp. 43–44]

The daughter in the tale is in a situation analogous to that of Hurston: the educated student returns home to transcribe what her forebears utter orally. She has learned a notation system that considers itself complete but that turns out to lack a sign for (clucking sound). The "inside" is here commenting on the "outside," the tale commenting on the book as a whole. It is not by chance that this should be a tale precisely about mules and men. The noncoextensiveness of oral signs and written signs is a problem very much at the heart of Hurston's enterprise. But lest one fall into a simple opposition between the tale's orality and the transcriber's literacy, it is well to note that the orality/literacy relation is the very *subject* of the tale, which cannot be appreciated by those who, like the father *in* the tale, cannot write. Its irony is directed both ways.

Despite Boas' prefatory claim that Hurston has made "an unusual contribution to our knowledge of the true inner life of the Negro," the nature of such "knowledge" cannot be taken for granted (*MM*, p. x). Like Hurston's representation of "colored me," her collection of folktales forces us to ask not "Has an 'inside' been accurately represented?" but "What is the nature of the dialogic situation into which the representation has been called?" Since this is always specific, always a play of specific desires and expectations, it is impossible to conceive of a pure inside. There is no universalized Other, no homogeneous "us," for the self to reveal itself *to*. Inside the chemise is the other side of the chemise: the side on which the observer can read the nature of his or her own desire to see.

Mules and Men ends, unexpectedly, with one final tale. Hurston has just spent 150 pages talking not about folktales but about hoodoo practices. Suddenly, after a break but without preamble, comes the following tale:

> Once Sis Cat got hongry and caught herself a rat and set herself down to eat 'im. Rat tried and tried to git loose but Sis Cat was too fast and strong. So jus' as de cat started to eat 'im he says "Hol' on dere, Sis Cat! Ain't you got no manners atall? You going set up to de table and eat 'thout washing yo' face and hands?"
>
> Sis Cat was mighty hongry but she hate for de rat to think she ain't got no manners, so she went to de water and washed her face and hands and when she got back de rat was gone.
>
> So de cat caught herself a rat again and set down to eat. So de Rat said, "Where's yo' manners at, Sis Cat? You going to eat 'thout washing yo' face and hands?"
>
> "Oh, Ah got plenty manners," de cat told 'im. "But Ah eats mah dinner and washes mah face and uses mah manners afterwards." So she et right on 'im and washed her face and hands. And cat's been washin' after eatin' ever since.
>
> I'm sitting here like Sis Cat, washing my face and usin' my manners. [*MM*, pp. 251–52]

So ends the book. But what manners is she using? Upon reading this strange, unglossed final story, one cannot help wondering who, in the final analysis, has swallowed what. The reader? Mrs. Mason? Franz Boas?

Hurston herself? As Nathan Huggins writes after an attempt to determine the sincerity of Hurston's poses and self-representations, "It is impossible to tell from reading Miss Hurston's autobiography who was being fooled."[6] If, as Hurston often implies, the essence of telling "lies" is the art of conforming a narrative to existing structures of address while gaining the upper hand, then Hurston's very ability to fool us—or to fool us into *thinking* we have been fooled—is itself the only effective way of conveying the rhetoric of the "lie." To turn one's own life into a trickster tale of which even the teller herself might be the dupe certainly goes far in deconstructing the possibility of representing the truth of identity.

If I initially approached Hurston out of a desire to re-referentialize difference, what Hurston gives me back seems to be difference as a suspension of reference. Yet the terms "black" and "white," "inside" and "outside," continue to matter. Hurston suspends the certainty of reference not by erasing these differences but by foregrounding the complex dynamism of their interaction.

1. See Zora Neale Hurston, "How It Feels to Be Colored Me," *World Tomorrow* 11 (May 1928): 215–16; rpt. in *I Love Myself When I Am Laughing and Then Again When I Am Looking Mean and Impressive: A Zora Neale Hurston Reader,* ed. Alice Walker (Old Westbury, N.Y., 1979), pp. 152–155; all further references to this work, abbreviated "CM," will be to this edition and will be included in the text.

2. See Hurston, "What White Publishers Won't Print," *Negro Digest* 8 (Apr. 1950): 85–89; rpt. in *I Love Myself When I Am Laughing,* pp. 169–73; all further references to this work, abbreviated "WP," will be to this edition and will be included in the text.

3. See Hurston, *Mules and Men* (1935; Bloomington, Ind., 1978); all further references to this work, abbreviated *MM,* will be included in the text.

4. Langston Hughes, *The Big Sea: An Autobiography* (New York, 1963), pp. 238–39.

5. This formulation was suggested to me by a student, Lisa Cohen.

6. Nathan Irvin Huggins, *Harlem Renaissance* (London, 1971), p. 133.

Racism's Last Word

Jacques Derrida

Translated by Peggy Kamuf

Translator's Note.—"Racism's Last Word" is a translation of "Le Dernier Mot du racisme," which was written for the catalog of the exhibition Art contre/against Apartheid. The exhibition was assembled by the Association of Artists of the World against Apartheid, headed by Antonio Saura and Ernest Pignon-Ernest, in co-operation with the United Nations Special Committee against Apartheid. Eighty-five of the world's most celebrated artists contributed paintings and sculpture to the exhibition, which opened in Paris in November 1983. In addition, a number of writers and scholars were invited to contribute texts for the catalog. "Le Dernier Mot du racisme" serves in particular to introduce the project of the itinerant exhibition, which the organizers described briefly in their preface to the catalog:

> *The collection offered here will form the basis of a future museum against apartheid. But first, these works will be presented in a traveling exhibition to be received by museums and other cultural facilities throughout the world. The day will come—and our efforts are joined to those of the international community aiming to hasten that day's arrival—when the museum thus constituted will be presented as a gift to the first free and democratic government of South Africa to be elected by universal suffrage. Until then, the Association of Artists of the World against Apartheid will assume, through the appropriate legal, institutional and financial structures, the trusteeship of the works.*

A somewhat modified version of "Racism's Last Word" was originally published in the bilingual catalog of the exhibition.

*   *   *

APARTHEID—may that remain the name from now on, the unique appellation for the ultimate racism in the world, the last of many.

May it thus remain, but may a day come when it will only be for the memory of man.

A memory in advance: that, perhaps, is the time given for this exhibition. At once urgent and untimely, it exposes itself and takes a chance with time, it wagers and affirms beyond the wager. Without counting on any present moment, it offers only a foresight in painting, very close to silence, and the rearview vision of a future for which *apartheid* will be the name of something finally abolished. Confined and abandoned then to this silence of memory, the name will resonate all by itself, reduced to the state of a term in disuse. The thing it names today will no longer be.

But hasn't *apartheid* always been the archival record of the unnameable?

The exhibition, therefore, is not a presentation. Nothing is delivered here in the present, nothing that would be presentable—only, in tomorrow's rearview mirror, the late, ultimate racism, the last of many.

1

THE LAST: or *le dernier* as one sometimes says in French in order to signify "the worst." What one is doing in that case is situating the extreme of baseness, just as, in English, one might say "the lowest of the . . ." It is to the lowest degree, the last of a series, but also that which comes along at the end of a history, or in the last analysis, to carry out the law of some process and reveal the thing's truth, here finishing off the essence of evil, the worst, the essence at its very worst—as if there were something like a racism par excellence, the most racist of racisms.

THE LAST as one says also of the most recent, the last to date of all the world's racisms, the oldest and the youngest. For one must not forget that, although racial segregation didn't wait for the name *apartheid* to come along, that name became order's *watchword* and won its title in the political code of South Africa only at the end of the Second World War. At a time when *all* racisms on the face of the earth were condemned,

Jacques Derrida, professor of philosophy at the Ecole des Hautes Etudes en Sciences Sociales in Paris, is the author of, among other works, *Of Grammatology, Writing and Difference, Margins of Philosophy,* and *Dissemination.* **Peggy Kamuf** teaches French at Miami University, Ohio. She is the author of *Fictions of Feminine Desire.*

it was in the world's face that the National party dared to campaign *"for the separate development of each race in the geographic zone assigned to it."*

Since then, no tongue has ever translated this name—as if all the languages of the world were defending themselves, shutting their mouths against a sinister incorporation of the thing by means of the word, as if all tongues were refusing to give an equivalent, refusing to let themselves be contaminated through the contagious hospitality of the word-for-word. Here, then, is an immediate response to the obsessiveness of this racism, to the compulsive terror which, above all, forbids contact. The white must not let itself be touched by black, be it even at the remove of language or symbol. Blacks do not have the right to touch the flag of the republic. In 1964, South Africa's Ministry of Public Works sought to assure the cleanliness of national emblems by means of a regulation stipulating that it is "forbidden for non-Europeans to handle them."

APARTHEID: by itself the word occupies the terrain like a concentration camp. System of partition, barbed wire, crowds of mapped out solitudes. Within the limits of this untranslatable idiom, a violent arrest of the mark, the glaring harshness of abstract essence (*heid*) seems to speculate in another regime of abstraction, that of confined separation. The word concentrates separation, raises it to another power and sets separation itself *apart:* "apartitionality," something like that. By isolating being apart in some sort of essence or hypostasis, the word corrupts it into a quasi-ontological segregation. At every point, like all racisms, it tends to pass segregation off as natural—and as the very law of the origin. Such is the monstrosity of this political idiom. Surely, an idiom should never incline toward racism. It often does, however, and this is not altogether fortuitous: there's no racism without a language. The point is not that acts of racial violence are only words but rather that they have to have a word. Even though it offers the excuse of blood, color, birth—or, rather, *because* it uses this naturalist and sometimes creationist discourse—racism always betrays the perversion of a man, the "talking animal." It institutes, declares, writes, inscribes, prescribes. A system of marks, it outlines space in order to assign forced residence or to close off borders. It does not discern, it discriminates.

THE LAST, finally, since this last-born of many racisms is also the only one surviving in the world, at least the only one still parading itself in a political constitution. It remains the only one on the scene that dares to say its name and to present itself for what it is: a legal defiance taken on by *homo politicus,* a juridical racism and a state racism. Such is the ultimate imposture of a so-called state of law which doesn't hesitate to base itself on a would-be original hierarchy—of natural right or divine right, the two are never mutually exclusive.

This name apart will have, therefore, a unique, sinister renown. *Apartheid* is famous, in sum, for manifesting the lowest extreme of racism, its end and the narrow-minded self-sufficiency of its intention, its eschatology, the death rattle of what is already an interminable agony, something like the setting in the West of racism—but also, and this will have to be specified below, racism as a Western thing.

2

In order to respond to this singularity or, better yet, to fling back an answer, the singularity right here of another event takes its measure. Artists from all over the world are preparing to launch a new satellite, a vehicle whose dimensions can hardly be determined except as a satellite of humanity. Actually, it measures itself against *apartheid* only so as to remain in no measure comparable with that system, its power, its fantastic riches, its excessive armament, the worldwide network of its openly declared or shamefaced accomplices. This unarmed exhibition will have a force that is altogether other, just as its trajectory will be without example.

Its movement does not yet belong to any given time or space that might be measured today. Its flight rushes headlong, it commemorates in anticipation—not its own event but the one that it calls forth. Its flight, in sum, is as much that of a planet as of a satellite. A planet, as the name indicates, is first of all a body sent wandering on a migration which, in this case, has no certain end.

In all the world's cities whose momentary guest it will be, the exhibition will not, so to speak, take place, not yet, not *its* place. It will remain in exile in the sight of its proper residence, its place of destination to come— and to create. For such is here the *creation* and the work of which it is fitting to speak: South Africa beyond *apartheid,* South Africa in memory of *apartheid.*

While this might be the cape to be rounded, everything will have begun with exile. Born in exile, the exhibition already bears witness against the forced assignment to "natural" territory, the geography of birth. And if it never reaches its destination, having been condemned to an endless flight or immobilized far from an unshakable South Africa, it will not only keep the archival record of a failure or a despair but continue to *say* something, something that can be heard today, in the present.

This new satellite of humanity, then, will move from place to place, it too, like a mobile and stable habitat, "mobile" and "stabile," a place of observation, information, and witness. A satellite is a guard, it keeps watch and gives warning: Do not forget *apartheid,* save humanity from this evil, an evil that cannot be summed up in the principial and abstract iniquity of a system. It is also daily suffering, oppression, poverty, violence, torture inflicted by an arrogant white minority (16 percent of the population, controlling 60 to 65 percent of the national revenue) on the mass of the black population. The information that Amnesty International compiled on political imprisonment in South Africa and on the whole of the judicial and penal reality is appalling.[1]

Yet, what can be done so that this witness-satellite, in the truth it exposes, is not taken over and controlled, thus becoming another technical device, the antenna of some new politico-military strategy, a useful machinery for the exploitation of new resources, or the calculation in view of more comprehensive interests?

In order better to ask this question, which awaits an answer only from the future that remains inconceivable, let us return to immediate appearances. Here is an exhibition—as one continues to say in the old language of the West, "works of art," signed "creations," in the present case "pictures" or "paintings," "sculptures." In this collective and international exhibition (and there's nothing new about that either), pictural, sculptural idioms will be crossing, but they will be attempting to speak the other's language without renouncing their own. And in order to effect this translation, their common reference henceforth makes an appeal to a language that cannot be found, a language at once very old, older than Europe, but for that very reason to be invented once more.

3

Why mention the European age in this fashion? Why this reminder of such a trivial fact—that all these words are part of the old language of the West?

Because it seems to me that the aforementioned exhibition exposes and commemorates, indicts and contradicts the whole of a Western history. That a certain white community of European descent imposes *apartheid* on four-fifths of South Africa's population and maintains (up until 1980!) the *official* lie of a white migration that preceded black migration is not the only reason that *apartheid* was a European "creation." Nor for any other such reason: the name of *apartheid* has managed to become a sinister swelling on the body of the world only in that place where *homo politicus europaeus* first put his signature on its tattoo. The primary reason, however, is that here it is a question of state racism. While all racisms have their basis in culture and in institutions, not all of them give rise to state-controlled structures. The judicial simulacrum and the political theater of this state racism have no meaning and would have had no chance outside a European "discourse" on the concept of race. That discourse belongs to a whole system of "phantasms," to a certain representation of nature, life, history, religion, and law, to the very culture which succeeded in giving rise to this state takeover. No doubt there is also here—and it bears repeating—a contradiction internal to the West and to the assertion of its rights. No doubt *apartheid* was instituted and maintained against the British Commonwealth, following a long adventure that began with England's abolition of slavery in 1834, at which time the impoverished Boers undertook the Long Trek toward the Orange Free State and the Transvaal. But this contradiction only confirms the occidental essence of the historical process—in its incoherences, its compromises, and its stabilization. Since the Second World War, at least if one accepts the givens of a certain kind of calculation, the stability of the Pretoria regime has been prerequisite to the political, economic, and strategic equilibrium of Europe. The survival of Western Europe depends on it. Whether one is talking about gold or what are called strategic ores, it is known to be the case that at least three-fourths of the world's share of them is divided between the USSR and South Africa. Direct or even indirect Soviet control of South Africa would provoke, or so think certain Western heads of state, a catastrophe beyond all comparison with the malediction (or the "bad image") of *apartheid*. And then there's the necessity of controlling the route around the cape, and then there's also the need for resources or jobs that can be provided by the exportation of arms and technological infrastructures—nuclear power plants, for example, even though Pretoria rejects international control and has not signed any nuclear nonproliferation treaty.

Apartheid constitutes, therefore, the first "delivery of arms," the first product of European exportation. Some might say that this is a diversion and a perversion, and no doubt it is. Yet somehow the thing had to be possible and, what is more, durable. Symbolic condemnations, even when they have been official, have never disrupted diplomatic, economic, or cultural exchanges, the deliveries of arms, and geopolitical solidarity. Since 1973, *apartheid* has been declared a "crime against humanity" by the General Assembly of the United Nations. Nevertheless, many member countries, including some of the most powerful, are not doing all that's required (that's the least one can say) to put the Pretoria regime in a difficult situation or to force it to abolish *apartheid*. This contradiction is sharpest no doubt in today's France, which has provided more support for this exhibition than anywhere else.

Supplementary contradictions for the whole of Europe: Certain Eastern European countries—Czechoslovakia and the USSR, for example—maintain their economic trade with South Africa (in phosphoric acids, arms, machinery, gold). As for the pressures applied to Pretoria to achieve the relaxation of certain forms of *apartheid,* in particular those that are called petty and that forbid, for instance, access to public buildings, one must admit that these pressures are not always inspired by respect for human rights. The fact is, *apartheid also* increases nonproductive expenditures (for example, each "homeland" must have its own policing and administrative machinery); segregation hurts the market economy, limits free enterprise by limiting domestic consumption and the mobility and training of labor. In a time of unprecedented economic crisis, South Africa has to reckon, both internally and externally, with the forces of a liberal current according to which *"apartheid* is notoriously inefficient from the point of view of economic rationality."[2] This too will have to remain in memory: if one day *apartheid* is abolished, its demise will not be credited only to the account of moral standards—because moral standards should not count or keep accounts, to be sure, but also because, on the scale which is that of a worldwide computer, the law of the marketplace will have imposed another standard of calculation.

4

The theologico-political discourse of *apartheid* has difficulty keeping up sometimes, but it illustrates the same economy, the same intra-European contradiction.

It is not enough to invent the prohibition and to enrich every day the most repressive legal apparatus in the world: in a breathless frenzy of obsessive juridical activity, two hundred laws and amendments were enacted in twenty years (Prohibition of Mixed Marriage Act, 1949; Immorality Amendment Act [against interracial sexual relations], Group Areas Act, Population Registration Act, 1950; Reservation of Separate Amenities [segregation in movie houses, post offices, swimming pools, on beaches, and so forth], Motor Carrier Transportation Amendment Act, Extension of University Education Act [separate universities], 1955; segregation in athletic competition has already been widely publicized).

This law is also founded in a theology and these Acts in Scripture. Since political power originates in God, it remains indivisible. To accord individual rights "to immature social communities" and to those who "openly rebel against God, that is, the communists" would be a "revolt against God." This Calvinist reading of Scripture condemns democracy, that universalism "which seeks the root of humanity in a set of worldwide sovereign relations that includes humanity in a whole." It points out that "Scripture and History each demonstrate that God requires Christian States."[3]

The charter of the Institute for National Christian Education (1948) sets out the only regulations possible for a South African government. It prescribes an education

> in the light of God's word . . . on the basis of the applicable principles of Scripture.

> For each people and each nation is attached to its own native soil which has been allotted to it by the Creator. . . . God wanted nations and peoples to be separate, and he gave separately to each nation and to each people its particular vocation, its task and its gifts. . . .

Christian doctrine and philosophy should be practiced. But we desire even more than this: the secular sciences should be taught from the Christian-National perspective on life. . . . Consequently, it is important that teaching personnel be made up of scholars with Christian-National convictions. . . . Unless [the professor] is Christian, he poses a danger to everyone. . . . This guardianship imposes on the Afrikaner the duty of assuring that the colored peoples are educated in accordance with Christian-National principles. . . . We believe that the well-being and happiness of the colored man resides in his recognition of the fact that he belongs to a separate racial group.

It happens that this political theology inspires its militants with an original form of anti-Semitism; thus the National party excluded Jews up until 1951. This is because the "Hebrewistic" mythology of the Boer people, coming out of its nomadic origins and the Long Trek, excludes any other "Chosen People." None of which prevents (see above) all sorts of worthwhile exchanges with Israel.

But let us never simplify matters. Among all the domestic contradictions thus exported, maintained, and capitalized upon by Europe, there remains one which is not just any one among others: *apartheid* is upheld, to be sure, but also condemned in the name of Christ. There are many signs of this obvious fact. The white resistance movement in South Africa deserves our praise. The Christian Institute, founded after the slaughter in Sharpeville in 1961, considers *apartheid* incompatible with the evangelical message, and it publicly supports the banned black political movements. But it should be added that it is this same Christian Institute which was, in turn, banned in 1977, not the Institute for National, Christian Education.

All of this, of course, is going on under a regime whose formal structures are those of a Western democracy, in the British style, with "universal suffrage" (except for the 72 percent of blacks "foreign" to the republic and citizens of "Bantustans" that are being pushed "democratically" into the trap of formal independence), a relative freedom of the press, the guarantee of individual rights and of the judicial system.

5

What is South Africa? We have perhaps isolated whatever it is that has been concentrated in that enigma, but the outline of such analyses has neither dissolved nor dissipated it in the least. Precisely because of this concentration of world history, what resists analysis also calls for another mode of thinking. If we could forget about the suffering, the humiliation, the torture and the deaths, we might be tempted to look at this region of the world as a giant tableau or painting, the screen for some geopolitical computer. Europe, in the enigmatic process of its globalization and of its paradoxical disappearance, seems to project onto this screen, point by point, the silhouette of its internal war, the bottom line of its profits and losses, the double-bind logic of its national and multinational interests. Their dialectical evaluation provides only a provisional stasis in a precarious equilibrium, one whose price today is *apartheid.* All states and all societies are still willing to pay this price, first of all by making someone else pay. At stake, advises the computer, are world peace, the general economy, the marketplace for European labor, and so on. Without minimizing the alleged "reasons of state," we must nevertheless say very loudly and in a single breath: If that's the way it is, then the declarations of the Western states denouncing *apartheid* from the height of international platforms and elsewhere are dialectics of denegation. With great fanfare, they are trying to make the world forget the 1973 verdict—"crime against humanity." If this verdict continues to have no effect, it is because the customary discourse on man, humanism and human rights, has encountered its effective and as yet unthought limit, the limit of the whole system in which it acquires meaning. Amnesty International: "As long as *apartheid* lasts, there can be no structure conforming to the generally recognized norms of human rights and able to guarantee their application."[4]

Beyond the global computer, the dialectic of strategic or economic calculations, beyond state-controlled, national, or international tribunals, beyond the juridico-political or theologico-political discourse, which any more serves only to maintain good conscience or denegation, it was, it will have to be, it is necessary to appeal unconditionally to the future of another law and another force lying beyond the totality of this present.

This, it seems to me, is what this exhibition affirms or summons forth, what it signs with a single stroke. Here also is what it must give one to read and to think, and thus to do, and to give yet again, beyond the present of the institutions supporting it or of the foundation that, in turn, it will itself become.

Will it succeed? Will it make of this very thing a work? Nothing can be guaranteed here, by definition.

But if one day the exhibition wins, yes, *wins* its place in South Africa, it will keep the memory of what will never have been, at the moment of these projected, painted, assembled works, the presentation of some present. Even the future perfect can no longer translate the tense, the time of what is being written in this way—and what is doubtless no longer part of the *everyday current,* of the cursory sense of history.

Isn't this true of any "work"? Of that truth which is so difficult to put into words? Perhaps.

The exemplary history of "Guernica" (name of the town, name of a hell, name of the work) is not without analogy to the history of this exhibition, to be sure; it may even have inspired the idea for the exhibition. *Guernica* denounces civilized barbarism, and from out of the painting's exile, in its dead silence, one hears the cry of moaning or accusation. Brought forward by the painting, the cry joins with the children's screams and the bombers' din, until the last day of dictatorship when the work is repatriated to a place in which it has never dwelled.

To be sure: still it was the work, if one may say so, of a single individual, and also Picasso was addressing—not only but also and first of all—his own country. As for the lawful rule recently reestablished in Spain, it, like that of so many countries, continues to participate in the system which presently assures, as we have been saying, the survival of *apartheid*.

Things are not the same with this exhibition. Here the single work is multiple, it crosses all national, cultural, and political frontiers. It neither commemorates nor represents an event. Rather, it casts a continuous gaze (paintings are always gazing) at what I propose to name a continent. One may do whatever one wishes with all the senses of that word.

Beyond a continent whose limits they point to, the limits surrounding it or crossing through it, the paintings gaze and call out in silence.

And their silence is just. A discourse would once again compel us to reckon with the present state of force and law. It would draw up contracts, dialecticize itself, let itself be reappropriated again.

This silence calls out unconditionally; it keeps watch on that which is not, on that which is not yet, and on the chance of still remembering some faithful day.

1. See *Political Imprisonment in South Africa: An Amnesty International Report* (London, 1978).

2. Howard Schissel, "La Solution de rechange libérale: comment concilier défense des droits de l'homme et augmentation des profits" [The liberal alternative as solution: how to reconcile the defense of human rights with increase in profits], *Le Monde diplomatique*, Oct. 1979, p. 18. For the same tendency, cf. René Lefort, "Solidarités raciales et intérêts de classe: composer avec les impératifs de l'économie sans renoncer au 'développement séparé'" [Racial solidarity and class interests: meeting economic imperatives without renouncing "separate development"], *Le Monde diplomatique*, Oct. 1979, pp. 15–16. For the same "logic" from the labor-union point of view, see Brigitte Lachartre, "Un Système d'interdits devenu gênant" [A system of prohibitions become a nuisance], *Le Monde diplomatique*, Oct. 1979, pp. 16–17, and Marianne Cornevin, *La République sud-africaine* (Paris, 1972).

3. *The Fundamental Principles of Calvinist Political Science*, quoted in Serge Thion, *Le Pouvoir pâle: Essai sur le système sud-africain* (Paris, 1969).

4. See *Political Imprisonment in South Africa*.

No Names Apart: The Separation of Word and History in Derrida's "Le Dernier Mot du Racisme"

Anne McClintock and Rob Nixon

Jacques Derrida's "Le Dernier Mot du Racisme" ("Racism's Last Word," pp. 329–38) leaves no doubt as to his signal opposition to the South African regime.[1] Certainly the essay is tendered as a call to action, an urgent injunction to "save humanity from this evil" *apartheid;* besides exposing the "truth" of *apartheid,* its purpose is to "fling back an answer" (*riposter*). If, then, Derrida seeks not merely to prize open certain covert metaphysical assumptions but also to point to something *beyond* the text, in this case the abolition of a regime, then the strategic value of his method has to be considered seriously. This entails, in particular, pondering the political implications of both his extended reflection on the word *apartheid* and his diffuse historical comments.

   As it stands, Derrida's protest is deficient in any sense of how the discourses of South African racism have been at once historically constituted and politically constitutive. For to begin to investigate how the representation of racial difference has functioned in South Africa's political and economic life, it is necessary to recognize and track the shifting character of these discourses. Derrida, however, blurs historical differences by conferring on the single term *apartheid* a spurious autonomy and agency: "The word concentrates separation. . . . By isolating being apart in some sort of essence or hypostasis, the word corrupts it into a quasi-

---

1. The English translation of the title—"Racism's Last Word"—does not quite do justice to the original. "The Last Word in Racism" might have been a preferable rendition, at least keeping in play Derrida's double sense of *apartheid* as not merely the last remaining word of racism but also racism's apogee.

ontological segregation" (p. 331). Is it indeed the word, *apartheid,* or is it Derrida himself, operating here in "another regime of abstraction" (p. 331), removing the word from its place in the discourse of South African racism, raising it to another power, and setting separation itself apart? Derrida is repelled by the word, yet seduced by its divisiveness, the division in the inner structure of the term itself which he elevates to a state of being.

The essay's opening analysis of the word *apartheid* is, then, symptomatic of a severance of word from history. When Derrida asks, "Hasn't *apartheid* always been the archival record of the unnameable?" (p. 330), the answer is a straightforward no. Despite its notoriety and currency overseas, the term *apartheid* has not always been the "watchword" of the Nationalist regime (p. 330). It has its own history, and that history is closely entwined with a developing ideology of race which has not only been created to deliberately rationalize and temper South Africa's image at home and abroad, but can also be seen to be intimately allied to different stages of the country's political and economic development. Because he views *apartheid* as a "unique appellation" (p. 330), Derrida has little to say about the politically persuasive function that successive racist lexicons have served in South Africa. To face the challenge of investigating the strategic role of representation, one would have to part ways with him by releasing that pariah of a word, *apartheid,* from its quarantine from historical process, examining it instead in the context of developing discourses of racial difference.

1

The word *apartheid* was coined by General Jan Smuts at the Savoy Hotel, London on 27 May 1917 but had barely any currency until it rose to prominence as the rallying cry of the Nationalist party's victorious electoral campaign of 1948. Derrida has reflected on the word's "sinister renown," but as far back as the mid-fifties the South Africans themselves began to recognize that the term *apartheid* had become sufficiently stigmatized to be ostentatiously retired. The developing history of South African racial policy and propaganda highlights the inaccuracy of Derrida's claim that South African racism is "the only one on the scene that dares

Anne McClintock is a Ph.D. candidate in English at Columbia University. She is working on a dissertation on race and gender in British imperial culture and is the author of a monograph on Simone de Beauvoir. **Rob Nixon,** in the same program at Columbia, is working on the topics of exile and Third World-metropolitan relations in the writing of V. S. and Shiva Naipaul.

to say its name and present itself for what it is" (p. 331). For in striving both to win greater legitimacy for itself and to justify ideologically the Nationalist bantustan policy,[2] South African racism has long since ceased to pronounce its own name: *apartheid,* the term Derrida misleadingly calls "the order's *watchword*" (*mot d'ordre*) (p. 330), was dismissed many years back from the lexical ranks of the regime. From the 1950s onward, the Nationalist party has radically rephrased its ideology, first tempering the grim rhetoric of *apartheid* into talk of "separate development," then into the even more insidious language of "multinationalism" and "self-determination," and most recently into the self-congratulatory discourse of "democratic federalism." These changes in the language of racism are closely, though not always symmetrically, allied to changes in Nationalist party policy.

F. A. van Jaarsveld, an apologist for the Nationalist regime, divides South African racial policy since 1948 into three phases. From 1948 until 1958, he argues, there was the "ideological, doctrinaire and negative" phase of *apartheid,* a period he admits was "severely racist." Second, between 1958 and 1966, this mellowed into the "homeland phase of separate development," a phase he characterizes as one of "internal de-colonisation." Third, the period from 1966 onward has seen what he considers to have been "the unobtrusive dismantling of *apartheid,*" "the movement away from discrimination," "the elimination of color as a determinant," and the introduction of "democratic pluralism."[3] As a very general way of periodizing changes in the *official discourse,* van Jaarsveld's schema may be instructive. But if one is to understand the political role that the regime's justificatory ideology has played, one must expose the contradiction between the uneven, somersaulting evolution of the official discourse in a "democratic" direction and the actual process of deepening brutalization and oppression which it belies.

Prior to the unexpected Afrikaner victory in 1948, South African society had been rife with racial discrimination, but much of it had been ad hoc rather than legislated. From 1948 onward, however, the official policy of *apartheid* ensured in a doctrinaire, unapologetic fashion that the old colonial racist edifice was buttressed with more methodical legislation. That *apartheid* came to supplant the earlier English term "segregation" was symptomatic of the waning influence of English speakers in political life; ever since 1949, the leadership and bureaucracy have been securely in Afrikaans hands. The 1950s were an era of strident *baasskap* ("mastery" or "domination"), but as early as 1953 a certain defensiveness began to creep into the regime's representation of its policies.

---

2. We here follow the practice of using the term "bantustan" in place of the more glamorous and euphemistic "homelands."

3. Our translation from the Afrikaans. F. A. van Jaarsveld, *Die Evolusie Van Apartheid* (Cape Town, 1979), pp. 1–2.

The attempts by Prime Minister D. F. Malan to rationalize the language of *apartheid* can be seen to prefigure the movement toward abandoning a rhetoric of *racial* for one of *national* difference:

> Europe, itself the matrix of Christian civilization, is the out-standing example of apartheid. The map resembles a Joseph's coat of some twenty-five sections, each represented by its own nationality, and for the most part also its own race with its own tongue and its own culture. . . . Apartheid is accepted in Europe as natural, self-explanatory, and right.[4]

Such efforts to improve South Africa's image abroad were, however, hampered by the word *apartheid* itself, which was already dragging a train of sinister connotations. It was in 1958, with the election of Dr. Hendrik Verwoerd as prime minister, that a truly decisive turn took place in the rhetoric and ideology of South African racism. References in the official discourse of the regime to the inferiority of blacks to whites started to be phased out, and the country was no longer referred to as "multiracial" (which would imply a single political entity) but as "multinational." White leaders were careful to speak of the "peoples" of South Africa, not the "people," and, most important, the rhetorically more benign "separate development" came to replace *apartheid*. Here is Dr. Verwoerd's plodding, patronizing explication of the new language before a group of black councillors:

> "Separateness" means: something for oneself. The other word refers to what is bigger still, viz. "development", which means growth. . . . Development is growth brought about by man creating something new in a continuing process. Therefore, separate development means the growth of something for oneself and one's nation, due to one's own endeavours.[5]

The ingeniously bipartisan phrase, "separate development," expresses in miniature the acute schizophrenia which marked both the ideology and practice of South African racism under Verwoerd, proclaiming to the world at large that there would be changes and whispering to the white folks at home that there would be no changes at all.

Verwoerd's attempts to whitewash the rhetoric of racism were closely bound to his Promotion of Bantu Self-Government Act of 1959, which involved the extension and deepening of the migrant labor system into the bantustan policy. After 1959, under Verwoerd, the restructuring of

4. D. F. Malan, *Die Burger*, 6 Mar. 1953, quoted in Martin Legassick, "Legislation, Ideology and Economy in Post-1948 South Africa," in *South African Capitalism and Black Political Opposition*, ed. Martin J. Murray (Cambridge, Mass., 1982), p. 505 n. 74.

5. Quoted in M. T. W. Arnheim, *South Africa after Vorster* (Cape Town, 1979), p. 23.

the bantustans gathered momentum, overlapping broadly with the ideological shift from *apartheid* to "separate development." From 1963 until
1964 there was a major overhaul of the urban areas legislation in order
to provide a more powerful apparatus for channeling the flow of labor
and controlling its every movement. Under Vorster in 1966 the system
was deepened. General Circular No. 25 of 12 December 1967 became
the basis for massive forced removals and resettlements. As the circular
noted:

> As soon as they [Bantu] become, for some reason or another, no
> longer fit for work or superfluous in the labour market, they are
> expected to return to their country of origin or the territory of
> their national unit where they fit in ethnically.[6]

Since the development of the bantustan policy, the Nationalist party
has strained to couch its policies in the language of *nationalities* rather
than that of *color,* creating the impression that South Africa's difficulties
are the same as those of modern Europe and that it could overcome
them similarly. As one cabinet minister put it:

> The problem in South Africa is basically not one of race, but
> of nationalism, which is a world-wide problem. There is a White
> nationalism, and there are several Black nationalisms. . . . My Gov-
> ernment's principal aim is to make it possible for each nation,
> Black and White, to achieve its fullest potential, including sovereign
> independence, so that each individual can enjoy all the rights and
> privileges which his or her community is capable of securing for
> him or her.[7]

Verwoerd's replacement of the alienating racial language of *apartheid*
with the more conciliatory rhetoric of multinationalism was sustained by
Prime Minister B. J. Vorster. But neither Verwoerd nor his successor
managed to create a perfectly watertight discourse of multinationalism,
caulked against any seepage of racism. For the dominant ideology of
race in white South Africa proved so insistent that it could not be suppressed
entirely, even at the level of discourse. Despite the Nationalists' contention
that their new egalitarian ideology of multiple nations had supplanted
the purportedly outmoded ideology of race, it was manifest that the two
ideologies coexisted, often in grinding contradiction, as dramatized by
references to "biologically demarcated tribal states."[8] Contradictions aside,
the general drive toward a more palatable idiom continued and, during

6. Quoted in Legassick, "Legislation, Ideology and Economy," p. 496.
7. R. F. Botha, *The Star*, 2 July 1976, quoted in No Sizwe, *One Azania, One Nation: The National Question in South Africa* (London, 1979), p. 12.
8. J. A. Coetzee, quoted ibid., p. 85.

the latter years of Vorster's rule (from roughly 1970 onward), the discourse of multinationalism graduated, in turn, into the even more desperately appeasing rhetoric of "plural democracy." The pace of this discursive transformation has increased markedly under Vorster's successor, P. W. Botha. By the end of 1981, South Africa had implemented the bantustan policy so relentlessly that the majority of the country's blacks had been officially declared citizens either of the four "independent" states or of the six "self-governing" territories. In the ideological realm, too, the Nationalist regime had moved well beyond Verwoerd—by now its official discourse had, as far as possible, been purged of open references to race.

Under Botha, the domestic and international campaign to gain acceptance for the Nationalists' wretched, inequitable partitioning of the land has been conducted not so much in the solicitous rhetoric of multiple nationalities as in the new proud language of democratic federalism. Verwoerd's was a language of promises, of "nations" to be; Botha's is the language of achievement, of an allegedly full-blown "confederation of independent states." In the words of one government publication:

> . . . 20 years ago it was postulated that . . . the need for segregation or discrimination, as a protective measure for Whites, would begin to fall away, since the Black peoples would . . . have their own bases for political hegemony and sovereignty.[9]

The pages of such publications resound with choice phrases from Botha's new lexicon: "the policy of multinational development [is] assuming the dimensions of what may be called a plural democracy—i.e. a democratic solution to the plural population structure of South Africa."[10] In this vein, the Department of Bantu Administration and Development (BAD) was rechristened Plural Relations and Development, and the names of other state departments were similarly disinfected. And in an attempt to ground the rhetoric of "plural democracy" in a less political, more homely idiom, Botha persistently describes his regime's relation to the black pseudostates within South Africa's borders as one of "good neighborliness," a phrase that banishes all thought of race and racism, and offers in its stead images of the lending and borrowing of lawn mowers in an atmosphere of suburban goodwill.

If an examination of South Africa's representation of racial difference is to be at all politically enabling, the changing hegemonic functions of the word *apartheid* and its kindred terms must be investigated in the context of an active, social language. Here, with Gareth Stedman Jones, we should underscore the prefigurative capacity of political discourses,

9. *South Africa 1983: Official Yearbook* (Johannesburg, 1983), p. 210.
10. *South Africa 1979: Official Yearbook of the Republic of South Africa* (Johannesburg, 1979), p. 211.

their power not merely to address preexistent constituencies but to re-constitute them, or even to generate new ones.[11] While the new discourses of South African racism may seem pitifully transparent, they have proved far from innocuous in bracing and rationalizing policies at home and in marketing them abroad. Conveniently for the Nationalists, their latest set of vocabulary—that of democratic federalism—is consonant with the political idiom of the country they need most urgently to impress: the United States. Reagan, for his part, has capitalized on this correspon-dence, at times even hinting that beneath their common language the two countries may have comparable histories—all the more reason for sympathy and patience. Complaining of "a failure to recognize . . . the steps they [the South Africans] have taken and the gains they have made" in moving toward the abolition of racial discrimination, Reagan has de-clared, "As long as there's a sincere and honest effort being made, based on our own experience in our own land, it would seem to me that we should be trying to be helpful."[12] In following a diplomatic course eu-phemistically described as one of "constructive engagement," then "quiet diplomacy," and most recently "active constructive engagement," Reagan and his subordinates in the State Department too often have given credit to the claims of that insidious Nationalist idiom which conveys the illusion of bodying forth democratic progress, reform, and "self-determination." This complicity between the Reagan administration and Botha's regime reached a new pitch with the State Department endorsement of South Africa's constitutional changes. Far from paving the way for full democracy, this new constitution sealed the disenfranchisement of the country's black majority and centralized power to an unprecedented degree, granting Botha personally, as state president, frightening authority. Yet George Shultz could say of this very constitution:

> We have tailored our programs, our diplomatic exchanges, and our rhetoric to the facts. Let us be candid with each other. Changes are occurring. . . . South Africa's white electorate has given solid backing to a government that defines itself as committed to evo-lutionary change.[13]

As the past two years have shown, white South Africa's endorsement of Botha's new constitution did not open the sluice gates of *political* reform. But it has proved a pivotal event in the development of a legit-imating *language* of reform. For the centerpiece of the new constitution

11. See Gareth Stedman Jones, *Languages of Class: Studies in English Working Class History 1832–1982* (Cambridge, 1983), pp. 23–24.

12. Ronald Reagan, "Interview with the President: Question-and-Answer Session with Walter Cronkite of CBS News, Mar. 3, 1981," *Weekly Compilation of Presidential Documents* 17, 10:235.

13. George Shultz, *Department of State Bulletin* 84, 2085 (Apr. 1984): 12.

is the notion of "power-sharing," whereby select Indians and Coloreds are admitted as junior members to the previously all-white parliament and govern the country in unison with the whites. With the advent of this attempt to disperse the regime's opponents by coopting the Indians and Coloreds, the resilient ideological opposition between white and nonwhite became more unpronounceable than ever. If the Coloreds and Indians were to be persuaded that they were entitled to white privileges, they could not be lumped together with the disenfranchised blacks under the category "nonwhites." So the opposition was (theoretically) to be between a "power-sharing" nonblack alliance and the blacks. Of course, the ruse has failed politically. Nevertheless, the discursive reforms remain and are gauged to present policy as pragmatic, reasonable, and transcendent of mere racial ideology.

The latest phase in Botha's attempts to institute a nonracial language has corresponded not only to the strategy of coopting Coloreds and Indians but also to the regime's unprecedented concern with persuading both foreign investors and the liberal, predominantly English-speaking capitalists at home that the old brittle racism has been rationalized into a flexible responsiveness to the "law" of the marketplace. Correspondingly, the regime's most pressing crisis—how to appease the millions of urban blacks barred from power under the constitution—has been transformed, through Botha's new technocratic language, into a crisis which has nothing to do with blacks, with South African racism, or even with politics. Where in the mid-seventies the Nationalists would talk of the need to remove unproductive, unwanted "foreign citizens" (that is, blacks) from the cities, the crisis is now couched as a purely structural one of a generic Third World sort; it is, in Botha's favorite catchphrase, a problem of "orderly urbanization."

2

Derrida's indictment of Western complicity with South Africa is possibly the most valuable contribution of "Le Dernier Mot," but his passionate condemnation remains troubling for a number of reasons which stem largely from his blindness to the unfolding of the racial discourses in their historical context. Rightly denouncing the discrepancy between rhetorical condemnations of South Africa and the West's economic and strategic stakes in shoring up the regime, Derrida suggests that pressure on South Africa for liberal reform may be prompted by motives less ennobling than concern for human rights. Far from being the flower of humanist outrage, liberal protest may be nothing more than an economic reflex of "the law of the marketplace" (p. 335). But Derrida's apparently pragmatic and economistic argument—that "segregation hurts the market economy, limits free enterprise by limiting domestic consumption and the mobility and training of labor" (p. 334)—is less a "fact" than it is a very frayed liberal strand of controversy that has been tightly woven into the center of political and economic debate on South Africa since the 1930s. This controversy bears directly on the Nationalist's bantustan policy, in turn the only context in which one can understand the laborious ideological efforts the Nationalists have made to replace the racial language of black and white with a language of national difference.

Very simply, two rival interpretations of South African history have emerged over the past few decades. The debate turns on whether the rational forces of capital are in contradiction with the irrational, archaic policies of white racism, or whether *apartheid* can profitably coexist with modern capitalism. The liberal-reformist school, which emerged during an optimistic period of uninterrupted growth in the 1930s, has argued that *apartheid*'s cumbersome racial laws serve only to hamper the forward-thrusting momentum of the country's capitalist economy. Since the 1950s it has been a liberal tenet of faith that the "progressive force" of an efficient market economy will inevitably compel South Africa to slough off the heavy trappings of white racism and spell the demise of *apartheid*.[14]

In the late fifties and early sixties, in the wake of the African nationalist movements, the Sharpeville massacre of 1960, and the Treason Trial, and throughout a decade of brutality, bannings, torture, and crushed resistance, a powerful counterargument began to be raised. The "revisionist" school (living for the most part in exile) has argued that *apartheid* and modern capitalism are bound in a flourishing blood brotherhood, a pragmatic and flexible alliance which is collaborative and of spectacular mutual benefit. The revisionists argue, against Derrida, that far from hurting the market economy, "racial policy is an historical product . . . designed primarily to facilitate rapid capital accumulation, and has historically been used thus by all classes with access to state power in South Africa."[15] They charge that South Africa's "economic miracle" cannot be explained on economic grounds alone, as the liberals would have it, but must be seen in terms of a shifting alliance between capital and racial ideology which has, to be sure, created acute internal tensions, but which has nevertheless successfully safeguarded both economic privilege and white racial supremacy.[16]

14. The liberal reformist literature is legion. Some representative examples are: Monica Wilson and Leonard Thompson, eds., *The Oxford History of South Africa*, 2 vols. (New York, 1971); Leo Marquard, *Liberalism in South Africa* (Johannesburg, 1965); and M. C. O'Dowd, "The Stages of Economic Growth and the Future of South Africa," in *Change, Reform and Economic Growth in South Africa*, ed. Lawrence Schlemmer and Eddie Webster (Johannesburg, 1978), p. 28–50.

15. Dan O'Meara, "The 1946 African Mine Workers' Strike and the Political Economy of South Africa," in *South African Capitalism*, p. 362.

16. The revisionists, however, do not present a monolithic front. See David Yudelman, "Industrialization, Race Relations and Change in South Africa: An Ideological and Academic

The Nationalist bantustan policy, central to any understanding of this debate, places in perspective not only Derrida's assertion that *"apartheid also* increases nonproductive expenditures (for example, each 'homeland' must have its own policing and administrative machinery)" (p. 334) but also the changes in the racial discourses of successive regimes as outlined above. It is misleading to claim, as Derrida does, that "no doubt *apartheid* was instituted and maintained against the British Commonwealth" (p. 333). A color-caste system became deeply entrenched after the abolition of slavery in 1834 through vagrancy laws, a pass law, and the Masters and Servants ordinances (1841, 1856, and 1873) preventing strikes and desertion. Moreover, as early as the mid-nineteenth century two British governors, George Grey in the Cape and Theophilus Shepstone in Natal, had recognized the bounty to be reaped from creating native reserves from which white farmers could draw labor at will. The discovery of diamonds (1867) and gold (1886) dramatically increased the need for more African workers, and hut and land taxes were levied on African farmers to force them to enter the white wage economy. An intricate system of labor controls subsequently developed, laying the ground for modern *apartheid*. The Land Acts of 1913 and 1936 allocated to blacks thirteen percent of the most arid and impoverished land, reserving for whites (sixteen percent of the population) eighty-seven percent of fertile and productive South Africa. The bantustans consist of eighty-one scattered pieces of land divided along artificial "ethnic" lines, where people live under conditions of deprivation that are barely possible to describe. There is virtually no running water or electricity and health conditions are disastrous, with malnutrition and disease resulting in an infant mortality rate of 220 per thousand. According to Nationalist policy this meager thirteen percent of the land is to be the destined home of all South Africa's black people—seventy-two percent of the population.

The reserve system came to serve two major functions. It coerced into existence a malleable and immiserated black migrant force to guarantee a constant, controlled source of labor. At the same time it drove the costs of reproducing labor as low as possible. Since it was argued that black workers could supplement their wages with food grown in the reserves, "family" wages rather than individual wages were paid. These were forced lower than the minimum needed to eke out a precarious survival, thereby reaping disproportionate profits for white farmers, industries, and mines. The system yields a number of other advantages. The bantustans are

---

Debate," *African Affairs: Journal of the Royal African Society* 74 (Jan. 1975): 82–96. See also Harold Wolpe, "Capitalism and Cheap Labour-power in South Africa: From Segregation to Apartheid," *Economy and Society* 1 (Nov. 1972): 425–55; Frederick A. Johnstone, "White Prosperity and White Supremacy in South Africa Today," *African Affairs: Journal of the Royal African Society* 69 (1970): 124–40; and Barbara Rogers, *White Wealth and Black Poverty: American Investments in Southern Africa* (Westport, Conn., 1976), pp. 60–83.

not only a constant source of cheap labor: they are also the places to which are banished the aged, the sick and broken people who are no longer fit to serve the needs of whites; professionals who are not "needed" in South Africa; strikers and dissidents; and, most critically, women and dependent children ("superfluous appendages" in the official terminology). The bantustan system bears most cruelly on women. Very limited job opportunities, low wages, and the fact that urban residence leases are given only to men make circumstances for women seeking work in urban South Africa especially difficult. This, together with forced removals, has meant that by 1982 fifty-seven percent of all black South African women were living in the bantustans under appalling conditions. Critical employment problems can also be shifted onto the shoulders of black bantustan governments as their own "national" problems to be solved outside South Africa. Similarly, social welfare becomes the responsibility of the bantustans which do not figure in official employment, health, or census statistics, but which are de facto economically impotent and politically at the beck and call of South Africa.

In 1948, the year the Nationalists came to power, South Africa was at a turning point in its economic development. The primary economy based on the gold and diamond mines was replaced by an economy based on the secondary industry of manufacturing. The paradox was that gold mining and farming had traditionally battened off a migrant black work force drawn from the reserves. The manufacturing industry, on the other hand, required a more skilled and stable black urban work force. The changes in the economy generated a major dilemma: who was to fill the new semiskilled roles created by mechanization? Manufacturing needed semiskilled operatives for factory work, but the central problem was that the uninhibited substitution of cheap black labor in place of white workers would not only give black labor some measure of bargaining power but would also bring black workers into direct competition with the white workers who had helped bring the Nationalists to power. Indeed, after the price of gold fell in the wake of World War I, miners had cut costs by substituting cheaper black labor for the more expensive whites, a state of affairs white workers had always feared deeply. Strikes and violent unrest among white workers erupted in 1922 (the Rand Revolt), resulting in a compromise between white workers and capital which limited certain jobs to whites (the infamous "color bar") and prohibited the formation of legal black unions. Thus white workers came to constitute a labor aristocracy militantly committed to preserving their privileges against the encroachment of black labor. Traditionally, the electoral triumph of the Nationalists in 1948 has been seen as a victory of backward racism over liberal British capitalism. But the Nationalists were in fact borne to power on an alliance of white mine workers, petit bourgeois and professional Afrikaners, and Afrikaans farmers. Thus, as Ruth Milkman points out, "while the Nationalist government was strongly committed to challenging the power of the British mining capitalists, it never opposed the development of South African capitalism."[17] It was rather a question of who was to control the process.

After 1948 the Nationalists chose a route which gives the clearest sense of how *apartheid* policy has adapted itself to the double goal of retaining access to black labor for manufacturing while protecting white cultural and political power. In apparent conflict with the manufacturing industry's need for a stable, urban work force, they chose to expand the system of migrant labor. It is in the context of this extremely profitable compromise between capital and *apartheid* that the allied changes in the justificatory Nationalist ideologies can be seen.

In 1952 the reserves were systematized on a national basis by the Orwellian Natives (Abolition of Passes and Coordination of Documents) Act, which bars from urban areas blacks who are not "ministering to the needs of whites." The system was enforced by a ruthless and constantly refined machinery of state legislation: through the hated passes which blacks have to carry at all times, by the registration of all black workers through labor bureaus which can terminate employment at their own discretion, by laws binding farm workers to their jobs and making desertion a crime, by the job reservation system, by the mesh of influx control legislation which makes it illegal for blacks to stay in a white urban area for more than seventy-two hours without government permits, and by forced removals to the bantustans.

The linchpin of Nationalist policy became the gradual enforcement of black citizenship in the bantustans, with the intention of depriving blacks forever of the right to demand the benefits of South African citizenship while not forgoing their labor. As the Minister of Bantu Development put it in a 1978 speech: "if our policy is taken to its full logical conclusion as far as the black people are concerned, there will not be one black man with South African citizenship."[18] Since 1960, the government has forcibly resettled 3.5 million Africans and effectively deprived 8 million of their citizenship by means of statutes carefully worded to avoid defining citizenship on racial grounds.

In the mid-seventies radical governments came to power in Angola and Mozambique, internal and external resistance increased, and large-scale civil unrest culminated in the Soweto riots of 1976. Certain elements in big business and the military began to press for labor policy changes that would relieve some of the tension by creating a black middle-class elite with a stake in shoring up the capitalist state. In 1979 the government-appointed Wiehahn and Riekert Commissions set the stage for a renewed

17. Ruth Milkman, "Apartheid, Economic Growth, and U.S. Foreign Policy in South Africa," in *South African Capitalism,* p. 427.
18. Quoted in Kevin Danaher, *In Whose Interest? A Guide to U.S.–South Africa Relations* (Washington, D.C., 1984), p. 31.

compromise between capital and state *apartheid*. The Wiehahn Commission proposed the legal recognition of black unions which would bring them into the industrial conciliation system while tightly curtailing their activity through legal restrictions, vetoes, prohibitions on political activity, arrests, detentions, and murders. The Riekert "reforms" amounted to a refinement of state labor control by means of two principal factors: controlling jobs and limiting housing to certain privileged groups of urban African workers. As Kevin Danaher puts it:

> At no time were the proposed reforms intended to improve the lot of the African majority. Rather, the changes were designed to 1) meet the needs of the white business community for a more well-regulated African workforce, and 2) divide the African workers into several distinct strata with a hierarchy of rights and wealth, thus dividing Africans along class as well as ethnic lines.[19]

Ultimately, the alliance between capital and *apartheid* was refined, not undermined, and the overall goals of *apartheid* remained the same. As the Riekert report declared: "Every black person in South Africa . . . is a member of his specific nation. . . . The fundamental citizenship rights may only be enjoyed by a Bantu person within his own ethnic homeland."[20]

In this way, the bantustan system, constantly refined and strengthened, has buttressed the capitalist economy while simultaneously serving the ideological purpose of justifying Nationalist claims that their policy is no longer one of racial discrimination but of safeguarding the sovereignty of distinct "nations." The deliberate efforts to fragment the black community into mutually antagonistic "ethnic" communities, into those with limited residence rights and those without, feed the perverse argument that South Africa is indeed a "working democracy." By pointing to the ten bantustans, the government can claim that "numerically the White nation is superior to all other nations in South Africa. . . . It demonstrates the folly of saying that a minority government is ruling others in South Africa."[21]

The progressive force/revisionist debate has a number of crucial implications which are left out of Derrida's account. The crux of the matter for the liberals is that the triumph of the impersonal "law of the market" over racial ideology will take an evolutionary rather than a revolutionary course and will be aided and abetted by deepening capital

---

19. Ibid., p. 15.
20. Quoted ibid., p. 19.
21. *HAD* 11 (13 Oct. 1966), quoted in Legassick, "Legislation, Ideology and Economy," p. 506 n. 88.

investment—that is, they believe that one can invest one's way to nonracial democracy. For the revisionists, on the other hand, as Martin Legassick points out, there is something troubling in the a priori faith (which Derrida appears to endorse) that such beneficial fruits as the demise of *apartheid* might be borne from the mere fact of capitalist growth alone.[22] Of paramount importance, moreover, is the influence of the debate on foreign investment policies toward South Africa. Derrida's optimistic vision of *apartheid* brought to its knees by a liberalizing capitalism has been staunchly defended by many in the South African business community; by Michael O'Dowd, for example, for whom capitalism is an "equalizing" factor with a "strong tendency" to overcome the color bar.[23] Indeed, if Derrida takes to its logical conclusion his argument that *apartheid* may be abolished by the imposition of the "law of the market," he will find himself in the position of advocating accelerated international investment in order to hasten the collapse of the regime.

But the business community's faith in the logic of capitalism has lost much of its clout over the years for, as Greenberg points out, "the historical record on African living standards is reasonably clear: nearly a century of capitalist development between 1870 and 1960 brought almost no gains to the African majority." Despite South Africa's "economic miracle," the "basic pattern of income inequality and racial income shares has proved remarkably stable in this century," and the discrepancy in living standards remains staggeringly disproportionate by almost any international standard.[24]

3

It must be emphasized that to question the strength of Derrida's method is not to question his commitment to change in South Africa. His repugnance for the policies of the Pretoria regime is never in doubt. However, we have argued that for anyone concerned with the cultural component in national and international politics, it is crucial to supplement the kind of symbolic vigilance embodied in the Exhibition with another kind of watchfulness entirely absent from "Le Dernier Mot," an alertness to the protean forms of political persuasion. For most of the essay, Derrida allows the solitary word *apartheid* to absorb so much of his attention that the changing discourses of South African racism appear more static and monolithic than they really are. Paradoxically, what is most absent from Derrida's essay is an attentiveness to racial and class difference: his insights

22. See Legassick, "Legislation, Ideology and Economy," p. 468.
23. See Stanley B. Greenberg, "Economic Growth and Political Change: The South African Case," *The Journal of Modern African Studies* 19 (Dec. 1981): 669.
24. Ibid., pp. 678, 680.

are premised on too uniform a conception of South Africa's discourses of racial difference, while his historical comments are too generalized to carry strategic force.

To remedy these shortcomings, an alternative approach is required, one which integrates discursive, political, economic, and historical analyses. The lineaments of such a method are traced by Stedman Jones when he enjoins us

> to study the production of interest, identification, grievance and aspiration within political languages themselves. We need to map out these successive languages . . . both in relation to the political languages they replace and laterally in relation to rival political languages with which they are in conflict. . . . It is clear that particular political languages do become inapposite in new situations. How and why this occurs involves the discovery of the precise point at which such shifts occur as well as an investigation of the specific political circumstances in which they shift.[25]

For an analysis of racial representation, at least, this would mean abandoning such favored monoliths of post-structuralism as "logocentrism" and "Western metaphysics," not to mention bulky homogeneities such as 'the occidental essence of the historical process" (p. 334) and a "European 'discourse' on the concept of race" (p. 333). Instead one would have to regard with a historical eye the uneven traffic between political interests and an array of cultural discourses—a traffic at times clandestine, at times frank, at times symmetrical, at times conflicting and rivalrous, but at all times intimate. Derrida's call to fling back an answer to *apartheid* is inspiring, but until one recognizes, with Dan O'Meara, that "racial policy is open to a sequence of somersaults, deviations, and permutations which endlessly confuse those who regard it as the product of a monolithic racial ideology," and until one embeds the analysis of racial policy in the dense everyday life of South Africa, such calls to action will remain of limited strategic worth.[26]

[December 1984]

---

25. Stedman Jones, *Languages of Class*, p. 22.
26. Dan O'Meara, "The 1946 African Mine Workers' Strike," p. 363.

But, beyond . . .
(Open Letter to Anne McClintock and Rob Nixon)

Jacques Derrida

Translated by Peggy Kamuf

Dear Anne McClintock and Rob Nixon,

We have never met but, after reading your "response," I have a sense of something familiar, as if our paths had often crossed at colloquia or in some other academic place. So I hope you will not mind my addressing you directly—in order to tell you without delay how grateful I am to you and to avoid speaking of you in the third person. Whenever I take part in a debate or, which is not often, in a polemic, I make it a point to quote extensively from the text I am discussing, even though this is not standard practice. Since I am going to be doing that here, by addressing you directly I will save the space (and I'm thinking also of *Critical Inquiry*'s hospitality) otherwise needed for lengthy formulas such as: "Anne McClintock and Rob Nixon go so far as to write . . . , " "the authors of 'No Names Apart' claim that . . . , " "my interlocutors have not understood that . . . , " and so forth.

Yes, that's right, I am grateful. You have brought useful details to the attention of ill-informed readers. Many who want to fight *apartheid* in South Africa still know little of the history of this state racism. No doubt you will agree with me on this point: the better informed, the more lucid, and, I dare say, the more competent the fight, the better it will be able to adjust its strategies. I am also grateful to the editors of *Critical Inquiry*. By publishing your article and inviting me to respond to it, they have chosen to continue the debate that I began here in a modest way. Despite the duly celebrated liberalism and pluralism which open the pages of this excellent journal to the most diverse and opposed intellectual currents, it has in the main been devoted until now to theoretical research such as goes on for the most part in especially academic environments. Now, here is a case where this journal has organized and given free rein to a discussion on a violently political issue, one which has the appearance at least of being barely academic. I am very pleased with this development and even congratulate myself for having been the occasion for it. But I must add, to the credit of certain American colleagues and students, that *apartheid* is becoming a serious issue on several campuses [see "Postscript" below], and I regret that the same is not the case elsewhere, in other countries. Given this, academic journals have the obligation to speak about it; it is even in their best interest. Initially, my short text was not intended for *Critical Inquiry* (and in a moment I will come back to this criterion of "context" which your reading entirely neglects). Nevertheless, I agreed to its republication in *Critical Inquiry* with this in mind: to engage a reflection or provoke a discussion about *apartheid* in a very visible and justly renowned place—where, in general, people talk about other things.

Reading you, I very quickly realized that you had no serious objections to make to me, as I will try to demonstrate in a moment. So I began to have the following suspicion: what if you had only pretended to find something to reproach me with in order to prolong the experience over several issues of this distinguished journal? That way, the three of us could fill the space of another twenty or so pages. My suspicion arose since you obviously agree with me on this one point, at least: *apartheid,* the more it's talked about, the better.

But who will do the talking? And how? These are the questions.

Because talking about it is not enough. On such a grave subject, one must be serious and not say just anything. Well, you, alas, are not always as serious as the tone of your paper might lead one to think. In your impatient desire to dispense a history lesson, you sometimes say just anything. The effect you want to produce is quite determined, but in order to arrive at it, you are willing to put forward any kind of countertruth, especially when, in your haste to *object,* you *project* into my text whatever will make your job easier. This is a very familiar scenario, as I will try to demonstrate as briefly as possible.

Jacques Derrida, professor of philosophy at the Ecole des Hautes Etudes en Sciences Sociales in Paris, is the author of, among other works, *Of Grammatology, Writing and Difference, Margins of Philosophy,* and *Dissemination.* **Peggy Kamuf** teaches French at Miami University, Ohio. She is the author of *Fictions of Feminine Desire.*

1

As you ought to have realized, I knew well before you did that an eight-page text accompanying an art exhibit couldn't be a historical or anthropological treatise. By reason of its context and its dimensions (which I was not free to choose), by reason also of its style, it could only be an *appeal,* an appeal to others and to other kinds of action. You're quite right when you say "such calls to action will remain of limited strategic worth" (p. 353). I had no illusions in this regard and I didn't need to be reminded of it by anyone. What I, on the other hand, must recall to your attention—and I will remind you of it more than once—is that the text of an *appeal* obeys certain rules; it has its grammar, its rhetoric, its pragmatics. I'll come back to this point in a moment, to wit: as you did not take these rules into account, you quite simply *did not read* my text, in the most elementary and quasi-grammatical sense of what is called *reading*.

As for the original context of "Racism's Last Word,"[1] the catalog of an exhibit, I regret that you didn't read the careful note placed in introduction to Peggy Kamuf's excellent translation. It's true, of course, that if you *had* taken it into account, you would not have written anything, this debate would not have taken place and that would have been too bad. On "limited strategic worth," we're in total agreement, alas. Yet you know, these things are always more complicated, more difficult to evaluate, more overdetermined than people think. My very modest contribution is part of a complex ensemble which I have neither the time nor the space to reconstitute. And even if I could, its limits are by definition not fixed and are in the process of shifting at the very moment I am writing to you. These overdeterminations should be of interest to historians, politologists, or activists who are eager to go beyond abstraction and partial perspectives, who, like you, are concerned not to dissociate words and history. If I had done nothing more than provoke the present debate in a place of high academic visibility, induce the article which I am now about to discuss, and get the attention of a certain number of influential and competent readers, the interest of "such calls to action" "will remain of limited strategic worth," no doubt about that, but it would be far from nil. As for its limits, they are no more restricted than those of a "response," yours, which not only *supposes* the appeal to which it responds in its own fashion but also, without appealing to any action, is content to chronicle

1. Translator's note.—I might acknowledge receipt here of Anne McClintock's and Rob Nixon's suggested revision to this translated title. In fact, however, I had already considered and rejected "The Last Word in Racism" for reasons which may now have become ironic. To me, the cliché "the last word in . . . " suggested pop fashions or fads. What is more, it is often used ironically to undercut the very finality it seems to announce. I wanted to avoid these associations in order not to undermine, however subliminally, the sense and force of Jacques Derrida's appeal: that *apartheid* remain the final name of racism.

the word "apartheid," while advising that, rather than making history, we all ought to become more like historians. I quote from your conclusion: "Instead," you say, "one would have to regard with an historical eye the uneven traffic between political interests and an array of cultural discourses" (p. 353). By the way, that's *also* what I did, as I will remind you in a moment, but without stopping there. In this domain, as in all domains, no one strategy is sufficient; there is, by definition, no ideal and absolute strategy. We have to multiply the approaches and conjugate efforts.

My "appeal" had to be launched according to a certain mode and in a determined context. You take no account of them. Isn't this a serious mistake on the part of those who constantly invoke the relations between words and history? If you had paid attention to the context and the mode of my text, you would not have fallen into the enormous blunder that led you to take a *prescriptive* utterance for a *descriptive* (theoretical and constative) one. You write for example (and I warned you that I was going to cite you often): "Because he views *apartheid* as a 'unique appellation,' Derrida has little to say about the politically persuasive function that successive racist lexicons have served in South Africa" (p. 340). But I never considered (or "viewed") *apartheid* as a "unique appellation." I wrote something altogether different, and it is even the first sentence of my text: "*Apartheid*—que cela reste le nom désormais, l'unique appellation au monde pour le dernier des racismes. Qu'il le demeure mais que vienne un jour . . . ," which Peggy Kamuf translates in the most rigorous fashion: "APARTHEID—may that remain . . . May it thus remain, but may a day come . . . " (p. 330). This translation is faithful because it respects (something you either could not or would not do) the grammatical, rhetorical, and pragmatic specificity of the utterance. The latter is not an historian's assertion concering the lexicon of the South African racists or the past vicissitudes of the word *apartheid*. It is an appeal, a call to condemn, to stigmatize, to combat, to keep in memory; it is not a reasoned dictionary of the use of the word *apartheid* or its pseudonyms *in the discourse of the South African leaders*. One may think such an appeal is just too pathetic, one may judge its strategic force limited, but does one have the right to treat it as one would an historian's observation? To do so would be proof either that one didn't know how to read (by which I mean how to distinguish a subjunctive, with the value of an imperative, from an indicative) or else that one was ready to shortchange the ethics, to say nothing of the politics, of reading or discussion. What is more, although it is not limited by the form of descriptive observation, my "appeal" in no way contradicts the historian's truth. Whatever may have been the vicissitudes of the word *apartheid* and especially of the desperate efforts of the Pretoria regime's propagandists and officials to rid themselves of it (to rid themselves of the word, and not the thing, of *their* word and not *their* thing!), no one can deny that *apartheid* designates today in the eyes of the whole world, beyond all possible equivocation or pseudonymy, the last state racism on the entire planet. I wanted therefore simply to formulate a wish: may this word *become* and *remain* (subjunctive! optative or jussive mode!) "the unique appellation" destined to maintain the memory of and stigmatize this state racism. It was not a thesis on the genealogy of a word but an appeal, a call to action, as you put it, and first of all an ethical appeal, as indicated by that which, in both ethics and politics, passes by way of memory and promising, and thus by way of language and denomination. Besides (and here I am speaking as a historian, that is, in the *indicative*), whatever efforts the ideologues and official representatives of South Africa may have made to efface this embarrassing word from *their* discourse, whatever efforts *you* may make to keep track of their efforts, the failure is not in doubt and historians can attest to it: the word *apartheid* remains and, as I hope or expect, it will remain the "unique appellation" of this monstrous, unique, and unambiguous thing. You say "Derrida is repelled by the word" (p. 340). No, what I find repulsive is the thing that history has now linked to the word, which is why I propose keeping the word so that the history will not be forgotten. Don't separate word and history! That's what you say to those who apparently have not learned this lesson. It is the South African racists, the National party, the Verwoerds and the Vorsters who ended up being afraid of the word (*their* word!), to whom it began to appear too repulsive because it had become so overseas. It's you, and not me, who also seem to be frightened by this word because you propose that we take seriously all the substitutes and pseudonyms, the periphrases and metonymies that the official discourse in Pretoria keeps coming up with: the tireless ruse of propaganda, the indefatigable but vain rhetoric of dissimulation. To counter it, I think the best strategy is to keep the word, the "unique appellation" that the South African racists and certain of their allies would like to make people forget. No doubt one should also pay attention to the rhetorical contortions of the ideologues and official politicians of *apartheid.* But should we, because they wish it, abandon the word *apartheid* and no longer consider it to be the most accurate word with which to designate this political reality, yesterday's and today's?

I could limit myself to this remark about grammar or pragmatics. In your haste, you took or pretended to take a subjunctive to be an indicative, a jussive or optative utterance to be an assertion, an appeal to be a thesis. At the same time, you took no account of what was nevertheless *realistic* in my appeal, you missed the way, even in my syntax, the performative was articulated with the constative (forgive me for using this language). In sum, I asked for a promise: let this "unique appellation" "remain," which means that it *already is* this unique appellation. Who can deny it? The official ideologues of South Africa can denegate it, but they cannot deny that they are now *alone* in no longer using this word. And if I ask that we keep the word, it is only for the future, for memory, in men's and women's memory, for when the thing will have disappeared.

Thus, my appeal is indeed an appeal because it calls for something which is not yet, but it is still strategically realistic because it refers to a massively present reality, one which no historian could seriously put in question. It is a call to struggle but also to memory. I never separate promising from memory.

Here, then, is a first point. I could stop at this: you confused two verbal modes. Whether or not they are fighting against *apartheid,* whether or not they are activists, historians must be attentive to rhetoric, to the type and status of utterances, at the very least to their grammar. No good strategy otherwise. Yet, I don't regret your reading error, however elementary it might be. As everything in your paper follows from this misreading which begins with the first sentence—what am I saying? with the first two words ("APARTHEID—may . . . ")—just a moment's lucidity would have prevented your bringing out these documents on South African policy, *Critical Inquiry* would not have opened its pages to this debate, and that would have been too bad.

So I could stop there, but to prolong the conversation, I will point out still some other mistakes, just the most serious and spectacular ones.

2

Another question of reading, still just as elementary and directly linked to the preceding one. You write: "The essay's opening analysis of the word *apartheid* is, then, symptomatic of a severance of word from history. When Derrida asks, 'hasn't *apartheid* always been the archival record of the unnameable?', the answer is a straightforward no. Despite its notoriety and currency overseas, the term *apartheid* has not always been the 'watchword' of the Nationalist regime" (p. 340). Once again you mistake the most evident meaning of my question. It did not concern the use of the word *by* the Nationalist regime but its *use value* in the world, "its notoriety and currency overseas," as you so rightly put it. The word "always" in my text referred to this notoriety and there is little matter here for disagreement. But I never said that *apartheid* had "always" been the *literal* "watchword" *within* the Nationalist regime. And I find the way you manage to slip the "always" out of *my* sentence ("but hasn't *apartheid* always been the archival record of the unnameable?") and into *yours* ("the term *apartheid* has not always been the 'watchword' of the Nationalist regime") to be less than honest. To be honest, you would have had to quote the whole sentence in which I myself speak of the "watchword" as such. I do so precisely in order to say that this "watchword" has a complex history, with its dates and places of emergence and disappearance. I knew this before reading you and I emphasized it despite the brevity of my text. Here, then, is *my* sentence—if you don't mind, I will quote myself whenever you have not done so or whenever you manipulate the quotations:

> For one must not forget that, although racial segregation didn't wait for the name *apartheid* to come along, the name became order's *watchword* and won its title in the political code of South Africa only at the end of the Second World War. At a time when *all* racisms on the face of the earth were condemned, it was in the world's face that the National party dared to campaign *"for the separate development of each race in the geographic zone assigned to it."* [Pp. 330–31]

This sentence, among others, gives a clear enough indication, I hope, of the historical concern with which I approached the question in general, and the question of the name *apartheid* in particular.

And while we're on the subject of this word, I would like to understand the meaning of a certain "but" in a passage I am going to cite at length. Its logic totally escapes me. You write:

> The word *apartheid* was coined by General Jan Smuts at the Savoy Hotel, London on 27 May 1917 [I knew it was in London, but I thought it was at the Lord Russell Hotel. Are you sure about the Savoy? Check it. This is one point of history on which you would have taught me something.] but had barely any currency until it rose to prominence as the rallying cry of the Nationalist party's victorious electoral campaign of 1948. [This is exactly[2] what I was recalling, incorrigible historian that I am, in the sentence I just cited above. You might have mentioned that.] Derrida has reflected on the word's "sinister renown," *but* [my emphasis, J. D.] as far back as the mid-fifties the South Africans themselves began to recognize that the term *apartheid* had become sufficiently stigmatized to be ostentatiously retired. [P. 340]

So what? [In English in the text.] Why this "but"? Has the word *apartheid* effaced its "sinister renown" because the South Africans wanted to retire it from circulation and precisely because of its "sinister renown"? It so happens that in spite of their efforts to "retire" this "sufficiently stigmatized" term, the renown has not been effaced: it has gotten more and more sinister. This is history, this is the relation between words and history. It's the thing and the concept they should have retired, and not just the word, if they had wanted to put an end to the "sinister renown." So why this "but"? What objection is it making? Should I have said nothing about

2. Translator's note.—The exactness is still more striking when one recalls that Derrida's term *mot d'ordre,* translated as "watchword," could also have been rendered by McClintock's and Nixon's term: "rallying cry."

the "sinister renown" because the South African Nationalists deemed it advisable to clean up their lexicon?

The unfortunate thing is that your entire text is organized around the incredible "logic," if one can call it that, of this "but"; it is even oriented by the stupefying politics of this "but." You are asking that we regulate our vocabulary by the lexical strategies of the South African regime! For, immediately after the passage just cited, you go on to write:

> The developing history of South African racial policy and propaganda highlights the inaccuracy of Derrida's claim that South African racism is "the only one on the scene that dares to say its name and present itself for what it is." For in striving both to win greater legitimacy for itself and to justify ideologically the Nationalist bantustan policy, South African racism has long since ceased to pronounce its own name: *apartheid,* the term Derrida misleadingly calls "the order's *watchword*" (*mot d'ordre*), was dismissed many years back from the lexical ranks of the regime. [Pp. 340–41]

What do you want? That everyone stop *considering* that *apartheid* is—and remains, as far as I know, still today—the watchword, the rallying cry, the concept, and the reality of the South African regime? And even that everyone stop *saying* it, on the pretext that the South African racists deem it more prudent to utter it no more, this word which you yourselves recognize to be the "proper name" of this racism, the word it has given itself, "its own name" ("South African racism" you clearly say, "has long since ceased to pronounce its own name: *apartheid* . . . " [p. 341])? Come on, you're not being very serious, either as historians or as political strategists. Where would we be, where would all those struggling against *apartheid* be if they had considered that *apartheid* ceased to be the watchword of the South African regime on the day that, as you put it so well, "the Nationalist party . . . radically rephrased its ideology"! (p. 341). Because that happened in 1950, it would have been necessary to stop talking about *apartheid* from then on! Thanks all the same for your strategic advice and your reminder of historical reality! You speak of a "quarantine from the historical process" but it's you, coming on the heels of the Nationalist regime, who want to put the word *apartheid* in quarantine! I, on the other hand, insist that we continue to use the word, so that we may remember it, in spite of all the verbal denegations and lexical stratagems of the South African racists. I, on the contrary, insist that we remember this: whether or not the term is pronounced by South African officials, *apartheid* remains the *effective* watchword of power in South Africa. Still today. If *you* think, on the other hand, that it's necessary to take account of the diplomatic prudence or the lexical ruses of this power to the point of no longer speaking of *apartheid* as a watchword, well, then you're going to have to ask the whole world to go along with you and not just me. Historical reality, dear comrades, is that in spite of all the lexicological contortions you point out, those in power in South Africa have not managed to convince the world, and first of all because, still today, they have refused to change the real, effective, fundamental meaning of their watchword: *apartheid*. A watchword is not just a name. This too history teaches us, as you should know since you're so concerned with history. A watchword is also a concept and a reality. The relation among the reality, the concept, and the word is always more complex than you seem to suppose. The South Africans in power wanted to keep the concept and the reality while effacing the word, an evil word, *their* word. They have managed to do so in *their* official discourse, that's all. Everywhere else in the world, and first of all among black South Africans, people have continued to think that the word was indissolubly—and legitimately— welded to the concept and to the reality. And if you're going to struggle against this *historical* concept and this *historical* reality, well, then you've got to call a thing by its name. What would have happened if throughout the world—in Europe, in Africa, in Asia, or in the Americas—people had sworn off speaking of racism, anti-Semitism, or slavery on the pretext that the offenders never spoke of these things or did *not* use those words, better yet *no longer* used those words? In the best hypothesis and assuming one didn't want to accuse it of simple complicity with the adversary, such a strategy would have been both childish and disastrous.

So I stand by what I said. One must be attentive, and I was, to the word, to the watchword, and to their history. One must be attentive to what links words to concepts and to realities but also to what can dissociate them. Now if even as it kept the concept and the reality, the power in South Africa has tried to get rid of the word, nobody has been fooled. The concept and the reality persist, under other names, and South African racism, I repeat, "is the only one on the scene that dares to say its name and present itself for what it is," which is to say a state racism, the only one in the world today which does not hide its face. When I wrote that it "dares to say its name," I wanted to recall simply this: *apartheid* may have disappeared since 1950 from official speech or from the dispensaries of propaganda as if by magic, but this changes nothing in the fact ("facts are stubborn," you know) that the system of *apartheid* is not only practiced but *inscribed in the constitution* and in an impressive judicial apparatus. In other words, it is *declared, assumed, publicly approved*. To speak one's name, in politics (as history has shown over and over), is not simply to make use of a substantive but to present oneself as such, for what one is, in complex discourses, the texts of the law or of socioeconomic, even police and "physical" practices. In politics, as history should have taught you, a "watchword" is not limited to a lexicon. You confuse words and history. Or rather, you make poor distinctions between them.

What would have happened if I had followed your "strategic" advice? I would not have called for a fight against the state racism named *apartheid* (so named at the outset by its inventors!); instead I would have cautiously murmured as you do: "Careful, don't say *apartheid* anymore, you no longer have the right to use this word in order to name the watchword of South African racism because those who instituted the word, the concept, and the thing have not 'pronounced' the word since 1950"! Or maybe this: "Don't say *apartheid* anymore, but know that since 1948 there have been 'three phases' of racial policy in South Africa. Only the first of these (1948–58) would have been an 'ideological, doctrinaire, and negative' phase; the second (1958–66) is the one that 'mellowed into the homeland phase of separate development,' 'internal decolonisation'; the third, since 1966, would correspond to 'the unobtrusive dismantling of *apartheid,*' 'the movement away from discrimination,' 'the elimination of color as a determinant' and the introduction of 'democratic pluralism.'" Should I have said all that each time in place of the word *apartheid?* All that, which is to say what? Well, what you say by citing F. A. van Jaarsveld, "an apologist for the Nationalist regime," for the "periodizing changes in the *official discourse*" and for "the regime's justificatory ideology" (p. 341). Should I have been content to reproduce this official discourse? It is, in fact, the only one you cite at any length—the point of view of blacks being less represented in your text than that of *apartheid*'s partisans, even if you must admit that their "ruse has failed politically" (p. 346).

I'm still trying to imagine what I should have written if I had been carefully following your "strategic" advice. Perhaps I should have said: You know, *apartheid* is no longer the right word, even *racism* is no longer the right word because ever since "the development of the bantustan policy," " 'the problem in South Africa is basically not one of race, but of nationalism, which is a world-wide problem. There is White nationalism, and there are several Black nationalisms'" (p. 343). Unfortunately, if I had done that, I would have been quoting you quoting Verwoerd or Vorster, or else at best I would have written a paper on the ideological strategies of state racism in South Africa. But I would not have said the essential thing, to wit: *apartheid,* as a state racism and under the name initially chosen by the Nationalist party, then in control in South Africa, has been and remains the effective and official practice, still today, in spite of all the denegations and certain softening touches to the facade (which, by the way, I also mentioned). And *apartheid* must be fought as such. Once again, it's a question of context and of "pragmatics": I wrote a brief text for an exhibit entitled "Art against Apartheid" and not a paper on Verwoerd's and Vorster's rhetoric, whatever interest there may be in knowing the resources of this discourse. And despite the constraints on the length of my text, I also spoke of the secondary transformations of *apartheid* (p. 334), of the discourse, the culture, what I call the "official lie," the "judicial simulacrum," and the "political theater" (p. 333) that organize the racist and nationalist ideology in South Africa (see in particular parts 3 and 4). If *you* think *apartheid* has effectively given way to one nationalism among others, then you ought to have said so. If you don't think that's the case, well, then I don't see what objection you can have with me.

3

In spite of the brevity of my text, I never made do with what you call "such favored monoliths of post-structuralism as 'logocentrism' and 'Western metaphysics,'" not to mention bulky homogeneities such as 'the occidental essence of the historical process' and a 'European "discourse" on the concept of race'" (p. 353). To be sure, I said, and I'll say it again, that the history of *apartheid* (its "discourse" and its "reality," the totality of its *text*) would have been impossible, unthinkable without the European concept and the European history of the state, without the European discourse on race—its scientific pseudoconcept and its religious roots, its modernity and its archaisms—without Judeo-Christian ideology, and so forth. Do you think the contrary? If so, I'd like to see the demonstration. That said, you would have shown a little more honesty if you had noted that, far from relying on "monoliths" or "bulky homogeneities," I constantly emphasized heterogeneity, contradictions, tensions, and uneven development. "Contradiction" is the most frequently occurring word in my text. You force me to quote myself again. I spoke of "a contradiction internal to the West and to the assertion of its rights" (p. 333). I even wrote that one is right to insist on these contradictions ("and it bears repeating" [p. 333]) and that one must never simplify ("but let us never simplify matters" [p. 336]). Is that what you call monolithism? In spite of the brevity of my text, I multiplied the examples of "contradiction" in the theologico-political discourse, of the strategic "contradiction" of the West, of economic contradiction (see pp. 335, 334). Is that a sign of monolithic thinking and a preference for homogeneity? This will surely have been the first time I have met with such a reproach, and I fear you deserve it more than I do.

4

To what level of bad faith must one stoop in order to palm off on me the credo of unbridled capitalism by implying that, in my view, it would suffice to let the law of the marketplace work to put an end to *apartheid*? You have the nerve, for example, to write the following: "The revisionists argue, against Derrida [!!!], that far from hurting the market economy, 'racial policy is an historical product . . . designed primarily to facilitate rapid capital accumulation, and has historically been used thus by all classes with access to state power in South Africa'" (p. 347). *On the contrary,* I have always thought that there was some truth—it's stating the obvious—in this "revisionist" view. If, however, I *also* said that, despite the apparent contradiction, "*apartheid also* increases nonproductive expenditures (for example, each 'homeland' must have its own policing and administrative machinery); segregation hurts the market economy, limits free enterprise by limiting domestic consumption and the mobility and training of labor" (p. 334), I did so because it's true and *especially* as a reminder that, if *apartheid* is abolished one day, it will not be for purely moral reasons. You force me to quote myself again, the passage immediately following the sentence you have just read:

> In a time of unprecedented economic crisis, South Africa has to reckon, both internally and externally, with the forces of a liberal current according to which "*apartheid* is notoriously inefficient from the point of view of economic rationality" [I'm not speaking here, this is a quote]. This too will have to remain in memory: if one day *apartheid* is abolished, its demise will not be credited only to the account of moral standards—because moral standards should not count or keep accounts, to be sure, but also because, on the scale which is that of a worldwide computer, the law of the marketplace will have imposed another standard calculation. [Pp. 334–35]

After you had read that, it is quite simply indecent to make me out to be pleading *for* capitalism or suggesting that laws of the marketplace ought to be allowed free rein because *all by themselves* they would take care of *apartheid.* You have the nerve nonetheless to do just that. Your argument at this point reaches such a degree of bad faith that I even wondered whether I ought to continue our dialogue in these conditions and respond to *Critical Inquiry*'s generous invitation. You actually go so far as to speak of "Derrida's optimistic vision of *apartheid* brought to its knees by a liberalizing capitalism . . . " and you continue: "Indeed, if Derrida takes to its logical conclusion his argument that *apartheid* may be abolished by the imposition of the 'law of the market,' he will find himself in the position of advocating accelerated international investment in order to hasten the collapse of the regime"! (p. 352). To be sure, I defy you to find the least hint in my text of such an "optimistic vision" (even supposing that it is optimistic!). Had I such a "vision," I would not have written anything "against *apartheid.*" I would have thought: *laissons faire le capital!* That said, here again things are complex, heterogeneous, and contradictory, whether you like it or not. *Apartheid* can *at the same time* serve the interests of capitalist accumulation *and* get in the way of capitalist development. One has to distinguish here among different phases and *various* capitalisms or different, even contradictory sectors of capitalism. No more than logocentrism and the West, capitalism is not

a monolith or a "bulky homogeneity." Have you ever heard of the contradictions of capitalism? Is it really that difficult for you to imagine how
apartheid might serve capitalism in certain conditions and impede free
enterprise at some other moment, in other conditions? You see, I fear
you have a simple, homogeneistic, and mechanistic vision of history and
politics.

5

One last point with which perhaps I should have begun. It's about
your first paragraph, that little word "beyond" which you underline ("*beyond*
the text") and what you call my "method." Once again, it's best that I
quote you: "If, then, Derrida seeks not merely to prize open certain
covert metaphysical assumptions but also to point to something *beyond*
the text, in this case the abolition of a regime, then the strategic value
of his method has to be considered seriously" (p. 339).

I am not sure I clearly understand the extent of what you mean by
my "method." If you mean my "method" in this text against *apartheid*,
in the appeal that I launch and in my treatment of the word *apartheid*,
I have just answered you and told you what I think of *your* methods. But
if you are suggesting that my "method" in this specific case reveals all
that my "method" in general and elsewhere could learn from your lessons,
well in that case, there are one or two more things I will have to add. I
am led to think that you mean to contest, beyond the precise context of
apartheid, the "strategic value" of my "method" *in general* by the allusions
or insinuations tied to the word "text" ("*beyond* the text" is no doubt, and
I'll come back to this in a moment, a clever, oh so clever nod in the
direction of something I once said: there is nothing beyond the text), by
the use of the word "post-structuralism" (which I myself have never used
but which is commonly applied to me), or by words such as "logocentrism,"
"Western metaphysics," and so forth.

A serious response here would take hundreds and hundreds of pages,
and we mustn't abuse *Critical Inquiry*'s hospitality. Know, however, that
these pages are already written. If you wish to continue our correspondence
privately, I will give you some exact references.

But one thing at least I can tell you now: an hour's reading, beginning
on any page of any one of the texts I have published over the last twenty
years, should suffice for you to realize that *text,* as I use the word, is not
the book. No more than writing or trace, it is not limited to the *paper*
which you cover with your graphism. It is precisely for strategic reasons
(set forth at length elsewhere) that I found it necessary to recast the
concept of text by generalizing it almost without limit, in any case without
present or perceptible limit, without any limit that *is.* That's why there
is nothing "*beyond* the text." That's why South Africa and *apartheid* are,

like you and me, part of this general text, which is not to say that it can be read the way one reads a book. That's why the text is always a field of forces: heterogeneous, differential, open, and so on. That's why deconstructive readings and writings are concerned not only with library books, with discourses, with conceptual and semantic contents. They are not simply analyses of discourse such as, for example, the one you propose. They are also effective or active (as one says) interventions, in particular political and institutional interventions that transform contexts without limiting themselves to theoretical or constative utterances even though they must also produce such utterances. That's why I do not go *"beyond the text,"* in this *new* sense of the word text, by fighting and calling for a fight against *apartheid,* for example. I say "for example" because it also happens that I become involved with institutional and academic politics or get myself imprisoned in Czechoslovakia for giving seminars prohibited by the authorities. Too bad if all this strikes you as strange or intolerable behavior on the part of someone whom you, like others, would like to believe remains enclosed in some "prison-house of language." Not only, then, do I not go "beyond the text," in this new sense of the word text (no more than anyone else can go beyond it, not even the most easy-to-recognize activists), but the strategic reevaluation of the concept of text allows me to bring together in a more consistent fashion, in the most consistent fashion possible, theoretico-philosophical necessities with the "practical," political, and other necessities of what is called deconstruction. The latter, by the way, has never presented itself as a method, for essential reasons that I explain elsewhere (once again, if you care to write to me, I'll send you the references).

This letter is too long. In order to hasten its conclusion, I will give you my opinion in two words:

1. Your "response" is typical. It reflects an incomprehension or "misreading" that is widespread, and spread about, moreover, for very determined ends, on the "Left" and the "Right," among those who think they represent militantism and a progressivist commitment as well as among neoconservatives. It is in the interest of one side and the other to represent deconstruction as a turning inward and an enclosure by the limits of language, whereas in fact deconstruction *begins by* deconstructing logocentrism, the linguistics of the word, and this very enclosure itself. On one side and the other, people get impatient when they see that deconstructive practices are also and first of all political and institutional practices. They get impatient when they see that these practices are perhaps more radical and certainly less stereotyped than others, less easy to decipher, less in keeping with well-used models whose wear and tear ends up by letting one see the abstraction, the conventionalism, the academism, and everything that separates, as you would say, words and history. In a word, verbalism. On one side and the other, on one hand and on the other hand (but you see now how the two hands join and

maintain each other [comme les deux mains se tiennent, maintenant]), there is an interest in believing, in pretending to believe, or simply in making others believe that the "text" which concerns "deconstructionists" (this is the first time I use this word and I do so, as others have done, to go quickly) can be found neatly in its place on some library shelves. That being the case, in order to act (!) in the area of *real* politics, in history (!), these poor "deconstructionists" should go *"beyond* the text," into the field, to the front! As you do, I suppose.

Well, it so happens that the text which various deconstructions are speaking of today is not at all the *paper* or the *paperback* with which you would like to identify it. If there is nothing *"beyond* the text," in this new sense, then that leaves room for the most open kinds of political (but not just political) practice and pragmatics. It even makes them more necessary than ever. But that is no reason—on the contrary—to give up reading the books and writings still to be found in libraries. It is no reason to read quickly or badly or to stop learning how to read otherwise other texts—especially if one wants to better adjust one's political strategies. It is thus no reason to continue to spread the most uneducated interpretations and the crudest prejudices about "deconstruction," the "text," or "logocentrism." It is no reason to go on manipulating them as you do, to keep rolling them along in a primitive fashion, after having erected them into monolithic menhirs.

2. So, you share the impatience of those who would like texts to remain in the libraries, who would like text to signify "book." And you want this order maintained: let all those who concern themselves with texts understood in this latter sense (the "deconstructionists"!) remain in their compartments, better yet in their departments! Let no "deconstructionists" concern themselves with politics since, as we all know, don't we, deconstruction, differance, writing, and all that are (in the best of cases) politically neutral, ahistorical! Those people are not to concern themselves with politics because we always believed that they never did, that they left such things to the qualified, conscious, and organized activists whom we clearly are according to that *good old tradition* [in English in the text] which anyone can easily recognize. Otherwise, you seem to be saying, what would be left for *us* to do? Let the theoreticians of literature concern themselves with literature, philosophers with philosophy, historians with history, Africanists with Africa, and we, the activists, with politics! There, that's the best strategy! When a "deconstructionist," as one says, concerns himself with *apartheid,* even if he is on the "good" side, his strategy is all wrong, he's getting mixed up with things that are none of his business because he's going *"beyond* the text"! He exceeds the limits of his competence, leaves his own territory! "The strategic value of his method has to be considered seriously"!

In short, you are for the division of labor and the disciplined respect of disciplines. Each must stick to his role and stay within the field of his competence, none may transgress the limits of his territory. Oh, you wouldn't go so far as to wish that some sort of *apartheid* remain or become the law of the land in the academy. Besides, you obviously don't like this word. You are among those who don't like this word and do not want it to remain the "unique appellation." No, in the homelands of academic culture or of "political action," you would favor instead reserved domains, the separate development of each community in the zone assigned to it.

Not me.

Cordially,

Jacques Derrida
6 February 1986

Postscript (April 1986): I am rereading the translation of this letter while in the United States, at several universities (Yale, Harvard, Columbia) which have seen an intensification of demonstrations against *apartheid:* the divestiture movement, "shantytowns," student arrests, and so on. I want to reiterate my admiration and solidarity. Such courageous demonstrations on campuses are also signs of strategic lucidity because the problem of *apartheid* is surely an *American problem,* as are so many others. *In a first sense,* this means that its evolution will depend from now on in large measure on American pressure. These signs of lucidity are carried by an energy and perseverance which cannot be explained *simply* by the economy of necessarily ambiguous motivations. Some might be tempted in effect to seek there the mechanism and dynamic of bad conscience. The latter is always quicker to arise among intellectuals and at the university, especially in universities obliged to manage their capital. For here again, and *in a second sense, apartheid* would be an *American problem.* According to this insufficient but necessary hypothesis, *apartheid* might have to be put at some remove, expulsed, objectified, held at a distance, prevented from returning (as a ghost returns), parted with, treated, and cured *over there,* in South Africa. *Apartheid* might bear too great a resemblance to a segregation whose image continues at the very least to haunt American society. No doubt, this segregation has become more urban, industrial, socioeconomic (the frightening percentage of young black unemployed, for example), less immediately racial in its phenomenon. But this might recall much more, by some of its features, the South African hell.

"Race," Writing, and Culture

Tzvetan Todorov

Translated by Loulou Mack

For the past ten years, most of my work has dealt with the problems arising from the perception of "the other" (whether this other be collective or individual). For this reason, when Henry Louis Gates, Jr. asked me to comment on the contributions to an issue of *Critical Inquiry* devoted to the relationship between "race" and writing, I accepted without hesitation, even though I am personally more familiar with the subject as it pertains to French rather than to British or American literary and intellectual history. What I did not realize at the time I accepted Gates' invitation was that despite this proximity created by the frequentation of a similar theme, a major difference subsisted: I belong to a different critical tradition (European rather than American or British), and my reactions are determined as much by this difference as by the proximity. Thus, the pages I am setting out to write not only deal with cultural difference; they are also a living illustration of it.

"Racism" is the name given to a type of behavior which consists in the display of contempt or aggressiveness toward other people on account of physical differences (other than those of sex) between them and oneself. It should be noted that this definition does not contain the word "race," and this observation leads us to the first surprise in this area which contains many: whereas racism is a well-attested social phenomenon, "race" itself does not exist! Or, to put it more clearly: there are a great number of physical differences among human groups, but these differences cannot be superimposed; we obtain completely divergent subdivisions of the human species according to whether we base our description of the "races" on an analysis of their epiderms or their blood types, their genetic heritages or their bone structures. For contemporary biology, the concept of "race" is therefore useless. This fact has no influence, however, on racist behavior: to justify their contempt or aggressiveness, racists invoke not scientific analyses but the most superficial and striking of physical characteristics (which, unlike "races," do exist)—namely, differences in skin color, pilosity, and body structure.

Thus, it is with good cause that the word "race" was placed in quotes in the title of this issue: "races" do not exist. I am less sure, however, that all the contributors managed to avoid postulating the existence, behind this word as behind most words, of a thing. In his introduction Gates remarks that "race, in these usages, pretends to be an objective term of classification, when in fact it is a dangerous trope," and he goes on to describe as follows the goal of the special issue: "to deconstruct, if you will, the ideas of difference inscribed in the trope of race, to explicate discourse itself in order to reveal the hidden relations of power and knowledge inherent in popular and academic usages of 'race' " ("Writing 'Race' and the Difference It Makes," pp. 5, 6). Up to this point, I agree with him, even if I cannot help pointing out (cultural difference *oblige*) the insistent allusions to certain contemporary critical theories ("deconstruct" and "difference," "power" and "knowledge")—allusions which furnish proof that the author of these lines possesses a particular *knowledge* and thereby sets up a particular *power* relationship between himself and the reader. This, however, is not the problem. The problem arises on page 15, when the same author declares, "We must, I believe, analyze the ways in which writing relates to race, how attitudes toward racial differences generate and structure literary texts by us *and* about us." What bothers me about this sentence is not so much that "generate" and "structure" allude to yet another critical theory as that its author seems to be reinstating what he himself referred to as the "dangerous trope" of "race": if "racial differences" do not exist, how can they possibly influence literary texts?

Racist attitudes have always existed, but they have not always had the same amount of influence. By virtue of another irony, racism (like sexism) becomes an increasingly influential social phenomenon as societies approach the contemporary ideal of democracy. A possible explanation of this fact might be that in traditional, hierarchical societies, social differences are acknowledged by the common ideology; hence, physical differences play a less crucial role. In such societies, it is more important

---

Tzvetan Todorov works at the Centre National de la Recherche Scientifique in Paris. His most recent book in translation is *The Conquest of America* (1984). *Criticism of Criticism* is forthcoming. **Loulou Mack** is a free-lance writer and translator living in Paris.

to know who are masters and who are slaves than whose skin is light and whose is dark. In democratic societies, however, things happen quite differently. Although actual equality does not prevail, the ideal of equality becomes a commonly shared value; differences (perhaps somewhat attenuated) continue to exist, but the social ideology refuses to acknowledge them. Hence emphasis is placed on apparently irrefutable and "natural" physical differences. It was the abolition of slavery which led to the rise of racism in the United States: we attribute to "race" what we no longer have the right to attribute to social difference.

Another surprise is the relationship between racism and science. Anyone can observe two sets of variables: on the one hand human beings differ in physical appearance, and on the other they differ in social behavior. Racism begins when one proceeds to reason that the two series cannot possibly be independent of one another; the first must vary *as* the second, or vice versa. Now, this is a typically scientific mode of reasoning, since science consists in the effort to replace chaos with order. It is therefore not surprising to discover that the advent of the natural sciences in the eighteenth century was accompanied by the appearance of the first theories concerning "races." Today, a distinction is made between *racism*, which is a ubiquitous form of behavior, and *racialism*, or theories of race, whose heyday extended from the middle of the eighteenth through the middle of the twentieth centuries. Racism and racialism are both distinct and interrelated. If the neighbor on my landing tells me, in a confidential tone of voice, that "Blacks stink," it is not because she has read Gobineau; she knows nothing about theory, and her racism has not the least scientific pretension. In contemporary France, racialism is quasi-inexistent—virtually no one in the scientific world believes in the superiority of the white race—while racism thrives more than ever—a political party recently won ten percent of the popular vote on an exclusively racist platform. When, on the other hand, racism uses racialism to justify itself, the results are catastrophic: this was precisely the case of Hitler's racism.

Here it is worth making a slight digression concerning the historical origins of racialism. Several authors in the present issue see racialism as a consequence of Enlightenment philosophy and humanism. This affirmation seems to me not only inaccurate but dangerous. I admit, however, that it is necessary to decide exactly what is meant by the term "Enlightenment." This is not always an easy matter to settle, from an historical point of view. Buffon and Condorcet were both close to the group of *Encyclopédistes*, yet the former was in favor of slavery and the latter against it: should one conclude that the Enlightenment was pro- or antislavery? The same contradiction sometimes arises within the writings of one and the same author: for example, Kant is racist (and sexist) in his *Observations on the Feeling of the Beautiful and the Sublime* but egalitarian in his *Foundations of the Metaphysics of Morals;* which of the two texts belongs to the Enlightenment? If one makes the effort to get beyond historical contingencies and reconstruct an "ideal type" of the Enlightenment, its ideology can only be described, for a number of reasons, as universalist and egalitarian—as far removed as possible from racialism—and the ideology propounded by naturalists such as Buffon as opposed to the main current of Enlightenment philosophy. This opposition became very clear-cut in the course of the nineteenth century: those who defended and promoted racialism—Gobineau, Hippolyte-Adolphe Taine, Gustave Le Bon—were the self-declared enemies of the Enlightenment, the French Revolution, and the ensuing democratic model of government. (There was a famous exchange of polemical letters between Gobineau and Alexis de Tocqueville on this very subject.)

This reference to nineteenth-century racialism leads me to another difficulty. Gobineau believed that races could be distinguished by differences in blood, but he was the only one to hold this belief. All the other racialist thinkers realized that too much mixing among populations had already gone on for it to be possible to speak of purity of blood. They did not give up the notion of race for all that, but rather transformed a physical category into a cultural one: for example, Joseph Renan speaks of "linguistic races," Taine of "historical races," and Le Bon of "psychological races." The word "race" thus became virtually synonymous with what we ourselves call "culture," and nineteenth-century racialism subsists today in the idea of cultural difference.

One might almost conclude that some aspects of racialism were not all bad. A great many pages in Taine, and even in Gobineau, can be read today as descriptions of cultural differences among populations. All one would have to do in order to "recycle" these authors would be to subject their works to a double "cleansing" process, first eliminating their now confusing references to "race" and physical differences (replacing them with "culture" and its derivatives) and then criticizing their oversimplified classifications and their glaring ethnocentric value judgments—which does not, by any means, imply that we should renounce making value judgments concerning a culture other than our own.

This raises yet another problem: racialism has affinities both with relativism and with universalism. It is relativistic in relation to facts, denying, ultimately, the "basis of a shared humanity" (Gates, p. 13) (or reducing it to the mere possibility of intermarriage), and affirming the existence of a discontinuity among the different "races." However, it is universalistic in relation to values: these are considered to be the same everywhere, and it is the existence of a single set of criteria which allows certain "races" to be deemed superior and others inferior. The ideology of cultural difference, which in our day and age has replaced that of racialism, has inherited this ambiguity and finds itself similarly threatened by both excessive universalism and excessive relativism.

The excessive universalism takes the form of refusing cultural differences in the name of the unicity of the human species and the diversity of individuals. We are so busy battling stereotypes in the description of

Others that we end up refusing these Others any specificity at all. It is true that "the Orient" is far too broad a category, including as it does both Syria and Japan; it is also true that the very existence of such a category teaches us a great deal about the obsessions of scholars and world travelers. But does this mean that there is no such thing as a Japanese culture or Near Eastern traditions—or that this culture and these traditions are impossible to describe? Do the past attempts at describing them tell us about *nothing* except the observers' prejudices, or do they transmit, despite these prejudices, *something* of the societies observed?

Still, it is the dangers of excessive relativism which seem to me particularly acute at the present time. Universalism has acquired a bad reputation by getting itself compromised in realizations which did not live up to its ambitions. The so-called universality of many theoreticians of the past and present is nothing more nor less than unconscious ethnocentrism, the projection of their own characteristics on a grand scale. What has been presented as universality has in fact been a fair description of white males in a few Western European countries. This failure, however, should not lead us to abandon the idea itself, for such an abandonment would lead us to renounce the very idea of shared humanity, and this would be even more dangerous than ethnocentric universalism. Rather, the restricted universality of the past should be opened up as much as possible, until it is able to account for both the diversity of cultures and the differences which exist within one and the same culture.

This is why, in my opinion, a statement such as the following is excessively pessimistic: "Genuine and thorough comprehension of Otherness is possible only if the self can somehow negate or at least severely bracket the values, assumptions, and ideology of his culture. . . . However, this entails in practice the virtually impossible task of negating one's very being, precisely because one's culture is what formed that being" (Abdul R. JanMohamed, "The Economy of Manichean Allegory: The Function of Racial Difference in Colonialist Literature," p. 84). It is not true that in changing cultures one changes one's very being: human beings are not trees, and they can be uprooted without provoking such dramatic consequences. My culture is not a negligible quantity, but neither is it all. We are not only separated by cultural differences; we are also united by a common human identity, and it is this which renders possible communication, dialogue, and, in the final analysis, the comprehension of Otherness—it is possible precisely because Otherness is never radical. This implies not that the task is simple but that if we allow ourselves to believe in its feasibility, we can acquire an ever deeper understanding of Others. Affirming the existence of incommunicability among cultures, on the other hand, presupposes adherence to a racialist, apartheid-like set of beliefs, postulating as it does insurmountable discontinuity within the human species.

The Spanish language is famous for having two verbs which mean "to be": *ser* and *estar,* the former evoking essence and the latter existence. The absence of this distinction in most other languages makes it all the more difficult accurately to apprehend cultural differences: the present tense of the verb "to be" is ambiguous, and in order to perceive distinction clearly we must resort to the past tense. It is legitimate to affirm that a given population, or even a given segment of that population, *was* like this or that: these generalizations neglect a certain amount of individual variation (one can always find a German who behaves very differently from "the Germans"), but they are nonetheless useful. However, it is not legitimate to affirm that a given population *is* like this or that (in terms of essence, and no longer of existence): culture is learned, and it can therefore be unlearned; sometimes a new culture can then be relearned. Germans are either made or not made; in any case they are not born.

All of the above has to do with the question of "race." But what does writing have to do with it?

Theoretically, there are two possible relationships between the two subjects: either "race" explains writing or the other way around. In the first case, it is held that differences in literary works can be attributed to racial differences between their authors. In the second case, it is held that literature—and possibly criticism as well—can reveal to us certain truths concerning "races" or racism.

Oddly enough, none of the texts in the present issue adopts the former point of view. Perhaps this is because deterministic thinking, of which this would be an example, is an unpopular stance among contemporary critics. We do not like to use reality to explain literature; rather, we consider that it is literature which explains reality. (It is worth pointing out here that just as racial totalitarianism collapsed relatively quickly while social totalitarianism remains alive and well, racial determinism is unfashionable in literary criticism while social determinism is considered acceptable.) Nonetheless, I was somewhat surprised to see that, despite the hundreds of footnotes which weigh down these pages, not a single reference was made to the critical school of thought which long attempted to explain literary differences by racial differences. Taine is mentioned (see Gates, p. 3), but I suspect that his reader did not get much beyond the introduction to his *History of English Literature* since the portrait he draws of it is a rather poor likeness. There is not one word concerning the evolution of criticism in Nazi Germany—a case which cannot be said to lack interest, since literary historians such as Josef Nadler, Franz Koch, Clemens Lugowski, Heinz Kindermann, and others attempted to bring literary studies into harmony with the racial theories of the Führer. My surprise can doubtless be attributed to the cultural differences between Europe and the United States: a European, even a mere Bulgarian, never dares talk about anything without first having presented a five-hundred-page summary of the authors who have already dealt with the same subject.

The question of the determination of literary texts by "race" is in fact not anachronistic, if only because the word "race," as we have seen, has so often been used to mean "culture." This aspect of the problem is mentioned in the introduction to the issue, but only as it relates to criticism (and not to literature itself). However, I am not sure I quite grasp Gates' intention in these passages. On the one hand, he approvingly quotes the following statement of Anthony Appiah: "It is not necessary to show that African literature is fundamentally the same as European literature in order to show that it can be treated with the same tools" (quoted in Gates, p. 14). It is true enough that analytic concepts strive for universality (even though they never achieve it in practice); to exclude any nation's literature from one's analysis would be a form of discrimination. Naturally, it may turn out that the original concept is incapable of fully accounting for the new facts, in which case it should be either modified or else replaced by a new concept—but one which will in any case have just as much of a universal aspiration. Concepts are a little bit like workers: in order to measure their real value, one has to know what they can do, not where they come from.

However, the same author had declared on the preceding page: "I once thought it our most important gesture to *master* the canon of criticism, to *imitate* and *apply* it, but I now believe that we must turn to the black tradition itself to develop theories of criticism indigenous to our literatures" (Gates, p. 13). Is this not to say that the content of a thought depends on the color of the thinker's skin—that is, to practice the very racialism one was supposed to be combatting? This can only be described as cultural apartheid: in order to analyze black literature, one must use concepts formulated by black authors. And just how far should this imperative—that only birds of a feather can think together—be carried? In order to analyze football players, should we use only "indigenous" concepts and theories? Should we judge Renaissance texts using nothing but Renaissance concepts, and medieval texts by medieval concepts?

Almost all of the essays in the present volume explore the second of the two possible relationships between "race" and writing: they attempt to comprehend "race" and racist behavior as they appear in written texts. It may be useful at this point to make a new distinction, dividing the essays into two groups.

The first group, which makes up nearly two-thirds of the volume, analyzes the image of the Other in European literature; the choice field of study is English literature in the nineteenth and early twentieth centuries. This concentration is probably due to the institutional affiliation of the authors (English departments), but I cannot help regretting the absence of a greater variety in the selection of examples (yet another effect of my own status as cultural outsider). I would have enjoyed reading analyses not only of literary texts but also of political, scientific, and philosophical writings on the question of "race" during the same period, since the subject we are interested in is ideology, the dividing line between fiction and nonfiction grows rather fuzzy, and it is clear that these texts had considerable influence on one another, no matter to what genre they belonged. (In this respect, Sander L. Gilman's essay ["Black Bodies, White Bodies: Toward an Iconography of Female Sexuality in Late Nineteenth-Century Art, Medicine, and Literature," pp. 223–61] is the only exception.) I would have liked to learn more about the images of "races" other than the black—the yellow, for example, or the white as seen by nonwhites. Finally, I was surprised, not to say shocked, by the lack of any reference to one of the most odious forms of racism: anti-Semitism. Given the fact that the Nazis' "final solution" to the "Jewish problem" led to the greatest racial massacre in the history of humankind, its absence from the volume suggests that the authors chose to "actively ignore" it, to borrow an expression used by Hazel V. Carby in a different context ("'On the Threshold of Woman's Era': Lynching, Empire, and Sexuality in Black Feminist Theory," p. 302).

The danger inherent in this type of study seems to me to be two-fold. On the one hand, the subject matter is largely composed of stereotypes: racial Others are either noble savages or filthy curs, rarely anything in between; and in any case, whether they are judged to be inferior (as by those authors who worship civilization) or superior (as by those who embrace primitivism), they are radically opposed to European whites. This results in what JanMohamed calls a "manichean allegory," namely, "a field of diverse yet interchangeable oppositions between white and black, good and evil, superiority and inferiority," and so forth (JanMohamed, p. 82). The risk entailed is that this manichean writing might elicit a similarly manichean interpretation, with good and evil simply having switched places. On your right, the disgusting white colonialists; on your left, the innocent black victims. The buzzword "imperialism," pronounced on any and every pretext, seems to me to have exactly this oversimplifying effect. Are expressions such as "imperialist narrativization of history," "the axiomatics of imperialism," "the discursive field of imperialism," or "the epistemic fracture of imperialism" really very enlightening? Gayatri Chakravorty Spivak, from whose essay ("Three Women's Texts and a Critique of Imperialism," pp. 262–80) I have taken these quotes, uses the word "imperialism" almost as often as others use "deconstruction" and to fulfill a similar function (even though one of the words is laudatory and the other derogatory.) It is a sort of philosophers' stone designed to transform the base metal of discourse into pure gold; the word's effectiveness is of a comparable nature as well. The more nuanced studies of Mary Louise Pratt ("Scratches on the Face of the Country; or, What Mr. Barrow Saw in the Land of the Bushmen," pp. 138–62) and Patrick Brantlinger ("Victorians and Africans: The Genealogy of the Myth of the Dark Continent," pp. 185–222) give us a better idea of what it means to analyze the "image of the Other."

The second danger, which is less flagrant and less easy to avoid, arises not from the manicheism of binary oppositions but rather from the facility with which we choose the right side. Racialist and colonialist authors of the nineteenth century, in promulgating racism, were completely in accordance with popular opinion of their time. Critics in the final decades of the twentieth century, in condemning racism, resemble their predecessors even as they contradict them: they too are in accordance with popular opinion. Today, it is not an act of outstanding merit or courage to declare, from within university classrooms or publications, that one is against racism. In proudly describing ourselves as antiracists, we can give ourselves a good conscience at almost no expense. What else, then, do I recommend that we do? Certainly not endorse the racist credo just for the sake of making a more unconventional choice, but, at the very least, become aware of the problem and carefully question the commonplaces of contemporary good conscience. If we do this, we are likely to make some unexpected discoveries. The certainties of the modern age, whether they concern "races" or anything else, should not be swallowed whole. Is it really so very obvious, as JanMohamed seems to believe, that a "representation is sympathetic and, therefore, informative" (p. 106), or that "every desire is at base a desire to impose oneself on another" (JanMohamed, pp. 106, 105)? A peremptory style does not suffice to make a statement true. One might also refrain from suggesting that writers like J. M. Coetzee be more didactic than they are (see JanMohamed, p. 92).

The second group of essays includes the contributions of Appiah, Carby, and Barbara Johnson. These texts share several characteristics which distinguish them from the rest. In the first place, all of them are devoted to writings by Afro-American authors. In the second place, they explore not the victimizers' but the victims' perception of "race" and racism. Third, they analyze not the image of the Other (an object), but the Other—so declared by the whites—as a writing subject. These three characteristics (perhaps especially the third) converge to produce a single effect: of all the essays in the volume, these are the ones from which I learned the most.

Carby's contribution is somewhat weakened by the fact that the author does not allow her own voice to be heard but contents herself with describing the (admittedly impressive) works of three black women writers: Anna Julia Cooper, Ida B. Wells, and Pauline Hopkins. This essay does, however, raise an important question. Black feminists at the end of the nineteenth century who fought for the dignity of both women and blacks were considered by some contemporary critics as "spokespeople for prudery in their communities" (quoted in Carby, p. 303). Not only is such a judgment overhasty, as Carby says; it also points up a very real conflict: how is it possible to reconcile the demand for equality and dignity, which is a moral exigency, with the modern demand for freedom, which defends the individual's right to do as he or she pleases and considers everything moral as "prudery"? Should we really allow morals to remain the prerogative of a self-proclaimed "majority"?

Appiah's essay, which is a thought-provoking reading of W. E. B. Du Bois' works on racism, and which seems to me exemplary from every point of view, also raises a more general problem. Appiah, as we have already seen, objects to the idea of "black," "white," and "yellow" analytic concepts, and he is right to do so. However, it does not necessarily follow that all "methods"—or rather, all angles of approach chosen by critics—are equally appropriate for dealing with "race" and racism in texts. There is something futile about approaching these texts, which speak of tortures and lynchings, passionate love and hatred, with a critical apparatus that precludes any interrogation concerning their truth and values, or which combats the very idea of seeking truth and values. This, however, is just what the better part of contemporary criticism does. "Under Saussurian hegemony, we have too easily become accustomed to thinking of meaning as constituted by systems of differences purely internal to our endlessly structured *langues*"; "post-structuralism is not a step forward here" (Appiah, pp. 35, 37 n. 13). It might be worth our critical while to meditate on the attitude of Du Bois himself, who "throughout his life . . . was concerned not just with the meaning of race but with the truth about it" (Appiah, p. 22).

This brings me to the essay by Johnson, who describes herself as "a white deconstructor," thus indicating her adherence to racialist beliefs in the relationship between skin color and thought quality ("Thresholds of Difference: Structures of Address in Zora Neale Hurston," p. 317). Johnson analyzes with a great deal of acuity the fabulous works of Zora Neale Hurston; the conclusion she comes to is that she has met up with a soul sister—a black deconstructor. "To turn one's own life into a trickster tale of which even the teller herself might be the dupe certainly goes far in deconstructing the possibility of representing the truth of identity. . . . What Hurston gives me back seems to be difference as a suspension of reference" (Johnson, p. 328). For my part, I was somewhat disappointed to find that all the author under study could do was confirm the pre-suppositions of the author studying her; monotony would seem to be inherent in the work of deconstructors. Hurston's books, as Johnson shows, are indeed overflowing with irony, paradox, and ambiguity (to use a somewhat dated critical vocabulary); but does this mean that their author practiced suspension of reference and renounced seeking for the truth? To put the question differently: is there really no middle ground between worshiping dogmas as immutable truth and abandoning the idea of truth itself? The same goes for values: racism and sexism, totalitarianism and atomic weapons are very serious issues; only within the confined atmosphere of universities, where we tend to forget about the rest of the world, is it possible to flirt with skeptical or relativistic suspension of values. The profession of criticism requires more of us—and I am convinced that Johnson would agree with me (her very presence in this volume is a step in that direction), although she would hesitate to say so, for fear of contradicting the tenets to which she presently adheres.

One last remark: in his introduction, Gates raises the question of what the particular act of publishing a volume like this one means. In a world in which "scores of people are killed every day in the name of differences ascribed only to race," he writes, "the gesture that we make here seems local and tiny" (Gates, p. 6). However, a little further on, his text has a more optimistic ring to it: the new ways of reading, he says, "can indeed be brought to bear upon relationships that extend far beyond the confined boundaries of a text" (Gates, p. 17). My impression as a reader is that the volume falls somewhat short of this very legitimate goal. Johnson suggests a reason for this, though probably unintentionally, when she asks herself who the potential addressees of her study might be: "Was I talking to white critics, black critics, or myself?" (Johnson, p. 317). There is no doubt but that one is always talking to oneself when one writes; but is it totally impossible to imagine that among the other addressees there might be people who are neither black nor white nor yellow nor red critics—who are simply not critics at all? Must we really write exclusively for members of our own profession?

Only physicists can read other physicists, true. But the distinguishing feature of the humanities and the social sciences, including literary criticism, is that their object, being people, arouses people's most ardent interest; it would therefore be appropriate that specialists in these disciplines make their discourse accessible and interesting. This does not imply that they should lower their standards or make concessions to the public: Plato never did this, nor did Freud, and yet they were read by nonphilosophers and nonpsychoanalysts. Our critical writings, smothered beneath an erudite apparatus of footnotes and references, rife with a jargon better adapted for conveying to our colleagues which army we belong to than for conveying to our readers what we are talking about, have little chance of getting "beyond the confined boundaries" of our profession. Zora Neale Hurston is admirable not only for having asked herself "How It Feels to Be Colored Me," but also for having made her readers laugh; it is quite understandable that her readership is larger than that of critical journals. Perhaps critics could learn something, in this respect, not from physicists, but from those who furnish them their subject matter: writers?

Caliban's Triple Play

Houston A. Baker, Jr.

One legacy of post-Enlightenment dualism in the universe of academic discourse is the presence of two approaches to *notions of duality* championed by two differing camps. One camp might arbitrarily be called debunkers; the other might be labeled rationalists. The strategies of the camps are conditioned by traditional notions of inside and outside. Debunkers consider themselves outsiders, beyond a deceptive show filled with tricky mirrors. Rationalists, by contrast, spend a great deal of time among mirrors, listening to explanations from the overseers, attempting to absorb sideshow language, hoping to provide acceptable analytical accounts. If debunkers are intent on discovering generative and, presumably, hidden ideological inscriptions of a given discourse—its situation on what Amiri Baraka calls the "real side" of economic exchange and world exploitative power—rationalists are concerned to study discursive *products,* to decode or explain them according to forms and formulas that claim to avoid general views or judgments of ideology. Differentiating the camps also is what might be called a thermal gradient: the heat of the debunker's passion is palpable. It is unnecessary to command him, in the manner of the invisible man's tormentor, to "Get hot, boy! Get hot!" Rationalists, by contrast, do not radiate. They appear to have nothing personal at stake and remain coolly instructive and intelligently unflappable in their analyses.

This tale of an Enlightenment legacy, as I have told it, contrasts a debunking body and a rationalist soul. As I have suggested in my opening sentence, however, what is at issue is not so much two actual and substantially distinctive camps as two metonyms for dual approaches to a common *subject*—namely, notions of duality. My claim is that the Enlightenment reflexivity of academic discourse, devoted to, say, "the Other" and conceived in dualistic terms of *self-and-other,* expresses itself as an opposition. Those whom I have called debunkers gladly accept the Other's sovereignty as a bodily and aboriginal donnée; rationalists work to discover the dynamics of "othering" engaged in by a self-indulgent Western soul. The difficulty of producing useful analytical or political results for either camp is occasioned by their joint situation within a post-Enlightenment field (indeed, one might say, after the manner of deconstruction, a field full of Western metaphysical folk).

That is to say, the framing of the matter of "Otherness" in traditional dualistic terms means that the framer, or the person who accepts such *framing* (with all the implications of ascribed *culpability*), cannot ever see an a priori picture, hear a "native" sound, or begin speaking at unengaged margins of a discourse radically overdetermined by the dualism of self-and-other. Here, of course, I do not mean to insert a myth of "origins." There is no need to spring that metaphysical trap. Nor am I invoking, when I talk of the "prerational," ideas of *la pensée sauvage.* Rather, I am suggesting that what I call "supraliteracy"—the committed scholar's "vernacular" invasion and transcendence of fields of colonizing discourse in order to destroy whitemale hegemony—is, perhaps, a way beyond traditional dualities. What appears with supraliteracy is not a double frame or framing, but a triple play that changes a dualistic Western joke and opens a space for the sui generis and liberating sound of the formerly yoked. But I am anticipating conclusions before engaging the project that led to these reflections. That project is *Critical Inquiry*'s special issue, *"Race," Writing, and Difference,* guest edited by Henry Louis Gates, Jr. I will offer only a selective response to the issue, avoiding detailed engagement with each of the volume's twelve essays.

1

Selectivity prompts me to begin by noting the seemingly divided aims that mark the editor's statement of his project in the introduction ("Writing 'Race' and the Difference It Makes," pp. 1–20). The editor commences his introductory tale by suggesting that the Enlightenment

Houston A. Baker, Jr. is the Albert M. Greenfield Professor of Human Relations at the University of Pennsylvania. He is a poet whose recent volume *Blues Journeys Home* appeared in 1985. He is also the author of a number of studies of Afro-American literature and culture, including the forthcoming *Modernism and the Harlem Renaissance.*

defined rationality as a code of conduct whose visible sign and signature were writing. To be without writing was to be irrational, uncivilized, an inhabitant of a plane of living *different* from civilization. Enlightenment writers, according to Gates, inscribed this difference as racial differentiation—as *race*. (We hear tones of the debunker at work.) He goes on to discuss the Afro-American poet Phillis Wheatley and her achievement and certification in literacy (by white Boston gentlemen) as an example of the racially uncivilized subject writing her way into rationality. His argument, if it can be said to be distinctively oriented, is language-bound. It holds that race is an always, already Western *metaphor* of difference. As such, it is tantamount to an epiphenomenon that can be replicated, with a difference, by the racially confined subject, producing an escape through metaphor. Wheatley gains a "write of way" to Western civility through her mastery of Western metaphor. To comprehend her progress, Gates implies, the critic must be a debunker, recognizing that all critical theories and approaches contain ideological subtexts. A critic of Afro-American literature must have, therefore, his or her own unique, black, *vernacular* ideological grounding if he or she wishes to provide an adequate reading of, say, Wheatley.

But at the same instant that he calls for a vernacular model, Gates proclaims that he is gratified by commentators and scholars who are currently addressing issues of Otherness, difference, and race in sophisticated, analytical terms made available by scientific, social scientific, and expressive cultural modes of analysis in the academy. (Shades of the rationalist start to close around the full-spoken editor.) "If the contributors, in all their diversity," he writes, "might agree on one matter, it would be this: one important benefit of the development of subtle and searching modes of 'reading' is that these can indeed be brought to bear upon relationships that extend far beyond the confined boundaries of a text" (Gates, p. 17). I believe that what Gates intends by "reading" is a transcendent academic (rationalist?) discourse which escapes pitfalls of error and anachronism not through its devotion to the "vernacular" but rather through its allegiance to putatively achievable and supposedly empirical "scientific" models. In a sense (but not a cruel one), I am suggesting that Gates remains a prisoner to the Enlightenment dualism that he debunks at the outset of his introduction.

An ideological fissure thus yawns at the beginning of *"Race," Writing, and Difference.* "Subtle" modes of contemporary analysis, the editor implies, will somehow unify a group of commentators on issues as traditionally divisive as race and Otherness. At the same instant, he suggests that *only* individualizing vernacular models can make sense of such issues. There is confusion.

I believe Gates' enthusiasm for academic address and his belief in the possibilities of a wholly empirical discourse are sustaining forces for his championship of the current academic scene. The vernacular seems to become almost a tag. And, in truth, there is virtually no trace of it in the volume's first essay, Anthony Appiah's "The Uncompleted Argument: Du Bois and the Illusion of Race" (pp. 21–37). Appiah's essay presents W. E. B. Du Bois' shifting perspectives on "race" as an occasion for reviewing current, scientific findings on that subject.

In a sense, one might say that Appiah's essay effects a shift from Gates' directly recommended vernacular ideological model to the "subtle" academic discourse that is implicitly championed at the close of the introduction. The shift is equivalent to a move from one linguistic orientation to another. Leaving behind the possibilities of an ideological proof upon vernacular pulses, Appiah biologically engages issues of Otherness and race at the mitochondrial level. Carefully reviewing evidence provided by evolutionary biologists, he analytically demonstrates that Du Bois' notions of "race" are founded upon a mistake. Biology, anthropology, and the human sciences in general all believed, in former times, that there was such a phenomenon as "race." Current genetic research demonstrates that there is no such thing. There are only populations whose intrapopulation variability is scarcely smaller than variations across populations. Francis Galton and his descendants to the contrary notwithstanding, all thought of a scientific basis for "race" is mistaken.

Along the way in his essay, Appiah invokes philosophical criteria of "racial" identity and difference in order to reduce Du Bois' assertions of a "common" Afro-American racial history and identity to affective wishes. Clearly, Appiah is one who has journeyed among mirrors and captured the language of the overseers. For one is patently aware in reading his essay that one is in the presence of eloquence—an elegant mind analyzing. Yet, there is also a feeling that our response might be akin to that of the indigenous people pictured on the cover of *"Race," Writing, and Difference.*

The cover portrays the British explorer David Livingstone as a saint reading to inhabitants of whatever turf it is he has just invaded. One of the inhabitants leans forward eagerly; the other looks unutterably depressed. We hear the leaning native exclaim, "He is teaching us! He is teaching us!" The depressed native may be thinking, "This is all very well and good, Dr. Livingstone, but what about the fact that *your* privileges are accorded by a book that even in its mistaken forms has never granted and will never grant me, in *my* aboriginal form, similar privileges?" In the presence of Appiah's essay, one wants to exclaim, "He is teaching us! He is teaching us!" But depression quickly sets in when one realizes that what Appiah—in harmony with his privileged evolutionary biologists—discounts as mere "gross" features of hair, bone, and skin are not, in fact, discountable. In a world dramatically conditioned both by the visible and by a perduring discursive formation of "old" (and doubtless mistaken) racial enunciative statements, such gross features always make a painfully significant difference—perhaps, *the only* significant difference where life and limb are concerned in a perilous world.

In short, Appiah's eloquent shift to the common ground of subtle academic discourse is instructive but, ultimately, unhelpful in a world where New York cab drivers scarcely ever think of mitochondria before refusing to pick me up. (Ah, those much maligned New York operators! There are others, of course. I once heard a Philadelphia driver exclaim, on seeing two black men dressed in handsome business suits emerging from the terminal, "I don't go there! Wherever they're going, I don't go there.")

2

An anecdote. Not long ago, my family and I were in a line of traffic moving along Chestnut Street in Philadelphia. On the corner, six or seven cars ahead of us, was a deranged, shabbily clad, fulminating white street person shouting obscenities at passengers and drivers. His vocabulary was the standard repertoire of SOBs and sons and mothers directed at occupants of the cars ahead, but when we came in view (gross features and all), he produced the standard "Goddamned niggers! Niggers! Niggers!" Now, if even a mad white man in the City of Brotherly Love knows that race, defined as gross features, makes all the difference in this world, what is it that Professor Appiah and evolutionary biology have done? What are they *teaching* us?

I want to suggest that, at the very least, they are implying that homogeneity is the law of the universe at a time when a violent reinforcement and retrenchment of whitemale hegemony dictates the dismantling of quotas meant to repair damages done by old (and scientifically sanctioned) differentiations, of revolutionary initiatives (such as women's and black studies) predicated upon accepted and championed differences, and of federal support systems grounded on policies that forthrightly acknowledge manifest (and scientifically sanctioned) racial differences. The scenario they seem to endorse reads as follows: when science apologizes and says there is no such thing, all talk of "race" must cease. Hence "race," as a recently emergent, unifying, and forceful sign of difference *in the service* of the "Other," is held up to scientific ridicule as, ironically, "unscientific." A proudly emergent sense of ethnic diversity in the service of new world arrangements is disparaged by whitemale science as the most foolish sort of anachronism.

For example, at a recent symposium at the University of Pennsylvania, two of that university's leading anthropologists insisted that talk of "racial" difference as a *positive* aspect of Afro-American life sounded like biology "some two hundred years ago." Complementing their smug condescension was, of course, a myopic and racist insensitivity that kept them from realizing that the discourse set in motion in the name of science "two hundred years ago" contained no Afro-American speaking subjects. Further, they left the symposium immediately after their presentations, patently (indeed, almost blissfully, it would seem) ignorant of the practical vulnerability of their claims. That is to say, if things are so beneficially and empirically changed (presumably by science) in our present era, why are there no black evolutionary biologists at the University of Pennsylvania— or black anthropologists in their own department?

No, what the anthropologists heard was not two-hundred-year-old talk, but inversive discourse—talk designed to take a bad joke of "race" (produced, in large measure, by *their* discipline) and turn it into a unifying discourse. This discourse would produce a black *group* initiative contrary to the interests of the academically isolated whitemales who have always done whatever was necessary (fudging data in twin studies and so forth) to make science work. I do not want to sound entirely like an intemperate debunker. I am not interested simply in taking pot shots at "science." Rather, I am suggesting that science, as Mary Louise Pratt so brilliantly demonstrates in her essay "Scratches on the Face of the Country; or, What Mr. Barrow Saw in the Land of the Bushmen" (pp. 138–62), is simply one system in a series of "interlocking information orders" that often subserve state power.

Pratt demonstrates—convincingly, I think, in the foremost essay of *"Race," Writing, and Difference*—that in European travel narratives, a whitemale I/Eye always narrates the landscapes of invaded territories in a manner that produces self-effacing accounts of endlessly proliferating nature. What never appears in such narrations is the I/Eye itself, or the indigenous inhabitants as people in functional relationship to the landscape. Instead, an objective voice domesticates and normalizes the landscape, recording it with an eye always in the service of European "science." Suppressed terms that interlock with "science"—implicit systems that are coextensive with it—include "politics," "economics," and "the State." The I/Eye as an organ and agent of state power—an advance prospector revealing dramatic economic advantages available from a pliant landscape— is always bracketed. Similarly, the indigenous people are bracketed— separated from chapters of landscape narration into descriptive chapters labeled "manners-and-customs of the natives."

Pratt designates the types of narratives I have just described as "informational." Their limitation is their dryness; "science," even as an ideologically loaded enterprise cleverly in the service of imperialism, is "boring." Hence there is a need for a contrasting narrative. If an informational narrative instantiates state power, then, Pratt suggests, the "experiential" account of the individual whitemale missionary bringing civilization to the natives projects a sentimental individualism of hearth and home onto an alien landscape. The overriding project for both types of narrative, however, is *ethnography*—a writing of the "Other" out of relationship to his or her native ground and into the sexual, commercial, voyeuristic fantasies of imperialism.

When Pratt delivered a version of her essay at the 1985 Georgetown University Conference in Literary Criticism, she noted that both the Central Intelligence Agency's instruction manual for agents and the recent report by the Secretary of Education entitled "To Reclaim a Legacy" are forms of "informational" discourse designed to instantiate state power and bracket the natives. Clearly, then, the import of Pratt's essay is to debunk—in my sense of the term. Her deeply intelligent and witty awareness of the necessity to deconstruct a disastrous scientific "objectivity" and "informational" neutrality as covers for state power and oppression bring her essay into harmony with what I would call vernacular rhythms. Her work is unabashedly political and undeniably persuasive in its presentation of inscribed difference, differences that are truly never born but always *made* by state science alone. A world of oppression, a *sound* of conflict between invaders and the indigenous, a voyeuristic and narcissistic exploitation of world resources in opposition to the everyday life of indigenous cultures are stunningly revealed by the essay.

Now I want to suggest that in all likelihood Pratt's is the type of work that will make a difference where "difference" is concerned in the future. "Science," by contrast, will more than likely continue to march to stately drums. In harmony with Pratt's account, we might think of such "scientific" Afro-American academicians as Thomas Sowell, Glenn Loury, and William J. Wilson as prospectors on the new frontiers of an urban "dark continent"—"native" territories constituted by the black inner city. Applying their "science," such explorers narrate the landscape and suggest that "racial" differentiations have been dramatically exaggerated, have, in fact, led to supportive policies (like luxurious tropical trees) that undermine the self-help capacities of the "natives." The proper thing to do—in the office of the natives' "own good"—is to civilize their territory. Gentrification and black genocide go hand in hand with the "science" of Sowell and others. They are capitalism's—the state's—new Livingstones in blackface. And, indeed, "race"—as an "old" discursive formation predicated on gross features—plays a major role in their work. Pratt helps make sense of these new and conservative blackmale explorers by constructing a model that demonstrates (by easy inference) that she herself has journeyed all about, around, and through the territories of the big show, constructing a "real side" context for her work and allying herself, I believe, with a discernible ideology of liberation.

With other commentators in *"Race," Writing, and Difference,* one sometimes has the feeling that an imitation of science—conceived as a neutral, rationalist presentation of "facts" or a rigorous cataloging of "instances"—is the only end. This end, lacking as it is in what might be called "real side" referentiality and present-day political sensitivity, leads to frighteningly embarrassing moments such as Sander L. Gilman's "Black Bodies, White Bodies: Toward an Iconography of Female Sexuality in

Late Nineteenth-Century Art, Medicine, and Literature" (pp. 223–61). The only thing that can be said about this "scientific" presentation with its simplistically contextualized illustrations and weak connectives is that it offers a fine illustration of Pratt's "manners-and-customs" category, presenting yet again, and so dreadfully embarrassingly, a whitemale confessional. "Look what we have done," it naughtily delights, rubbing its hands and looking pruriently sidewise. Patrick Brantlinger's "Victorians and Africans: The Genealogy of the Myth of the Dark Continent" (pp. 185–222) is less indicting, but nonetheless a whitemale confessional. Brantlinger offers a catalog of whitemale texts that take Africa and the Africans as their subject, telling us that, indeed, it was whitemales who "darkened" the continent of Africa. Significantly, only at the very end, as a tag paragraph in "manners-and-customs" style, is there any mention of brilliant African voices as always already counterforces to whitemale nonsense.

In a universe of dualistic academic discourse, one does not always find on the contrastive side of whitemale confessionals the kind of demolition effort Pratt's work represents. Rather, there is often only the confessional *manqué* of the colonial subject, as it were. Speaking the very language and employing the shrewd methods of the overseers, such reverse efforts have been called "protest" writing by, among others, James Baldwin. Edward W. Said in "An Ideology of Difference" (pp. 38–58) and Gayatri Chakravorty Spivak in "Three Women's Texts and a Critique of Imperialism" (pp. 262–80) provide the voice of the "submerged" subject: the cadences of, in the instance of Said, a newly emergent Palestinian nationalism, the visage and implications, in the case of Spivak, of the "native" woman suppressed even by contemporary modes of radical feminist criticism. What is most striking about Said's and Spivak's efforts, I believe, is their engagement with what I call a "hermeneutics of overthrow." They attempt—by bringing to bear all the canny presentational dynamics of the overseers—to prove that "A" is *as good as* "B" and to induce shame in defenders of "B" who have made other axiological choices.

For example, Spivak's argument is that the suppressed "native" woman is as important as, say, Jane Eyre. But as long as she preserves the middle ground of "as good as," the primary text of "B" (*Jane Eyre*) will be timelessly taken up. And how can one convince "B" to alter his or her axiology by implicitly, always, reinstating—even in the language and tone of criticism that one employs—the basis for such an evaluation? Similarly, Said presents a case for the Palestinians by summoning all the texts of Jewish defense, apology, invective, and disparagement. It is difficult to hear a Palestinian voice separate from the world of Jewish discourse. (Of course, Jews are not likely to feel this way, and will probably call for Said's head on a platter. But that is the necessary reaction of well-financed client states.) Protest, Baldwin argues, preserves the always already arrangements of power. I add that the confessional *manqué* may be the alternative and, indeed, sustaining voice of the whitemale confessional.

3

What seems present in *"Race," Writing, and Difference* is a firm inscription of the duality suggested by the venerable Western trope of Prospero and Caliban—figures portrayed in terms of self-and-other, the West and the Rest of Us, the rationalist and the debunker, the colonizer and the indigenous people. Language, writing, ideology, race, and a host of other Western signs are conveniently given resonance and force (in the office of a definition of *civilization*) by the simple iconography of the conquering magician Prospero and his enslaved and "deformed" island subject Caliban.

One question, of course, for anyone taking up issues (such as race and writing) implicit in this iconography is how does one escape, or explode, its simplistic duality? There is a need to explode the duality, for it often leads merely to an endless rehearsing of evidence (such as the "scientific" proof that Caliban's tribe is not really "racially" deformed, but merely populationally *different*). Or, it promotes the colonial subject's borderlining, his or her heroic and literate stance between two worlds, as, say, a graduated recipient of the varsity Western "W" for writing. He then speaks in the manner of the West Indian writer Derek Walcott, saying, "I who am poisoned with the blood of both, / Where shall I turn, divided to the vein? / . . . how choose / Between this Africa and the English tongue I love?"[1] When this Walcottian dilemma is absent, there may sound instead the gross polemics of a nationalism that militaristically asserts the superiority of Caliban. This is "protest" with a vengeance. What never emerges, however, from such strategies of response to the Prospero/Caliban iconography is the *sound* of Caliban, or a consideration of what the full politics of "deformation" and "mastery" surrounding him amount to.

For me, the signal shortcoming of *"Race," Writing, and Difference* is the paucity of Caliban's sound. The issue chooses instead to repeatedly sound (perhaps, of academic necessity) "subtle" phonics of academic discourse. There is scarcely a vernacular problematic to be found. I want to attempt, therefore, as I move toward a conclusion, to attempt to sound the problematics of "deformation."

In order to do so, I take up, somewhat in the middle I'm afraid, an argument that I develop at some length in my forthcoming book, *Modernism and the Harlem Renaissance*. Discussing the work of guerrillas who fight

---

1. Derek Walcott, "A Far Cry from Africa," in *Three Thousand Years of Black Poetry*, ed. Alan Lomax and Raoul Abdul (New York, 1970), p. 115.

invading armies and the dynamics of gorillas who *soundingly* resist territorial invasion, I introduce the phrase the "deformation of mastery" and go on to define it in terms of what ethologists call "display."

The deformation of mastery is fully at work in gorilla "display." Man—the master of "civilization"—enters forests and triggers a response. The display is described by Colin Groves:

> The full display is extremely impressive and quite terrifying except to another gorilla. . . . [The gorilla] stands or sits on the ground, and begins to hoot. Suddenly he stops; unexpectedly he turns his head, plucks a leaf with his lips and holds it between them . . . the hoots get faster and faster, the gorilla rises on his hindlegs. . . . Still standing erect, he runs sideways a few yards, bringing himself up short and slapping and tearing at the vegetation with great sideways sweeps of the arms. At last, as if to bring the display to a final close, he thumps the ground with the open palm of one or both hands, and drops back onto all fours.[2]

Such displays present the type of allaesthetic mask that Hugh Cott calls *phaneric*.[3] Rather than concealing or disguising in the manner of the *cryptic* mask (a colorful mastery of codes), the phaneric mask is meant to advertise. It distinguishes rather than conceals. It secures territorial advantage and heightens a group's survival possibilities.

The guerrilla's deformation is made possible by his superior knowledge of the landscape and the loud assertion of possession that he makes. It is, of course, the latter—the "hoots" of assurance that remain incomprehensible to intruders—that produce a notion (in the intruder's mind and vocabulary) of "deformity." An "alien" *sound* gives birth to notions of the indigenous—say, Africans or Afro-Americans—as *deformed*.

Two things, then, can be stated about the dynamics of deformation: first, the indigenous comprehend the territory within their own vale/veil more fully than any intruder. ("The kingdom is divided into many provinces or districts, in one of the most remote and fertile of which, I was born, in the year 1745, situated in a charming fruitful *vale*, named Essaka." Thus writes Olaudah Equiano the African. And W. E. B. Du Bois provides echoes in his own prefatory words to a guerrilla literacy: "And, finally, need I add that I who speak here am bone of the bone and flesh of the flesh of them that live within the Veil?").[4] The vale/veil, one might assert, is for the indigenous *language* itself.

2. Colin Groves, *Gorillas* (New York, 1970), pp. 38–39.

3. See Hugh B. Cott, "Animal Form in Relation to Appearance," in *Aspects of Form: A Symposium on Form in Nature and Art*, ed. Lancelot Law Whyte (London, 1951), pp. 121–56. Cott's essay treats variability of form (essentially either disguise or display) as a mechanism of biological survival.

4. Olaudah Equiano, *The Life of Olaudah Equiano, or, Gustavas Vassa, the African*, in *Great Slave Narratives*, ed. Arna Bontemps (Boston, 1969), p. 5, my emphasis; W. E. B.

Second, the indigenous *sound* appears monstrous and deformed *only* to the intruder. In the popular domain, the intruder's response is King Kong (or Mr. T); in literature, the trope most frequently visited by "alien" writers and their adversaries is the hooting deformed of Shakespeare's *The Tempest*.

Caliban, like a maroon in Jamaican hills or Nat Turner preparing his phaneric exit from the Great Dismal Swamp of the American South, focuses a drama of deformation that authors such as George Lamming, James Baldwin, and, of course, William Melvin Kelley have found suggestive for their own situations. What then of deformity/deformation and Caliban?

If one claims, following a post-structuralist line, that to possess the "gift" of language is to be possessed, then one immediately situates him- or herself in a domain familiar to the diaspora. *Possession* operates both in the spirit work of voodoo and in the dread slave and voodoo economics perpetuated by the West. What is involved in possession, in either case, is supplementarity—the immediately mediating appearance, as specter or shadow, of a second and secondary "self." In specifically diasporic terms, "being possessed" (as slave, but also as a BEING POSSESSED) is more than a necessary doubling or inscribed "Otherness" of the *con-scripted* (those who come, as necessity, *with* writing). For in the diaspora, the possessed are governed not simply by *script* but also by productive conditions that render their entire play a *tripling*.

Caliban speaks his possession as a metacurse:

> You taught me language; and my profit on 't
> Is, I know how to curse. The red plague rid you
> For learning me your language![5]

Caliban's utterance is "meta" because its semantics are marked by economies (implied or explicit) of *ob-scenity*—they speak *against* the scene of an intruder's tongue. Not "self" discovery, but the impossibility of feeling anything other than cursed by language is the sense of Caliban's utterance. For his self-assurance is not at issue. He has always known the forms (the morphology) of his indigenous vale, reminding the intruding Prospero of his role in showing "thee all the qualities o' th' isle, / The fresh springs, brine-pits, barren place and fertile" (1. 2. 339–41). Further, he scarcely lacks self-certainty regarding transformations wrought by the Western magician's intrusion. He and Prospero are alike "kings" victimized by *usurpation*, which is, in effect, the force and theme that moves the action

---

Du Bois, *The Souls of Black Folk*, in *Three Negro Classics*, ed. John Hope Franklin (New York, 1965), p. 209.

5. William Shakespeare, *The Tempest*, act 1, sc. 2, ll. 365–67; all further references to this work will be included in the text.

of the play. The preeminent reason that Caliban is the metatactician of *The Tempest,* however, is his morphophonemics—his situation vis-à-vis sound variations ("sounds and sweet airs")—which are truly foundational.

In his essay *Nature,* Ralph Waldo Emerson writes: "Nature is the vehicle of thought."[6] On Caliban's island, there could be no signifying whatsoever were it not for the indigenous inhabitant's instruction in the language (veil/vale) of nature. Seeking a new master, Caliban ebulliently promises the island's semantics to the scurrilous Stephano: "I'll show you the best springs"; "I prithee, let me bring thee where crabs grow. . . . Show thee a jay's nest, and instruct thee how / To snare the nimble marmoset" (2. 2. 160, 167–70). Sycorax's son is the adept instructor in natural "forms."

"Every appearance in nature," continues Emerson, "corresponds to some state of the mind, and that state of the mind can only be described by presenting that natural appearance as its picture."[7] The icons or pictures of Caliban's island reflect the usurpations of the Renaissance West—a social world of displaced knowledge-seekers that mocked (to distraction) honestly salvific people like Gonzalo. A shared nature *as* language—as a fruitful ecology of communication—was, thus, subjected to usurpation by men who refused to brook difference. Tyranny demanded self-sameness and subjugation, appropriated labor—even from the seemingly suitable suitor. (Ferdinand becomes the "Other" in the woodpile to qualify as Miranda's groom.) The "tempest," then, is, veritably, a havoc wreaked by mastery; it disrupts "natural" order, blunts "sounds and sweet airs, that give delight, and hurt not" (3. 2. 134). The Western Renaissance "storm" displaces, in fact, the witch as worker of sounding magic and releases, in her place, the comprador spirit Ariel who aids Prospero's male manipulations.

The tripling of Caliban vis-à-vis writing as supplementarity is implicit in Gonzalo's vision of *difference:* "I would by contraries / Execute all things"; "All things in common Nature should produce . . . treason, felony, / Sword, pike, knife, gun, or need of any engine, / Would I not have" (2. 1. 143–44, 155–58). In brief, the "fool" would have the isle wisely pre-Prosperian, revising or deforming the contraries of Western civilization in order to return to a "natural" signification. Such a world would witness Caliban not as student of "culture as a foreign language" (CFL, as it were), but rather as an instructor in a first voice, resonant with "a thousand twangling instruments" *in* nature. Caliban's position as metacurser derives from his knowledge that his cursedness is a function of his own largesse as signifier, as a man in tune with *first* meanings. "Curs'd be I that did so!" is his judgment on his willingness to barter his signs for the white magician's language.

    6. Ralph Waldo Emerson, "Nature," in *American Poetry and Prose,* ed. Norman Foerster (Boston, 1962), p. 467.
    7. Ibid.

The West Indian novelist George Lamming argues that Prospero gives Caliban language and, thus, controls his conceptual field through a dubious gift.[8] And James Baldwin seems to accept Lamming's point of view when he writes:

> The Negro problem [meaning, surely, the actual *sound* of a sui generis life in America] is nearly inaccessible. It is not only written about so widely; it is written about so badly. It is quite possible to say that the price the Negro pays for becoming articulate is to find himself, at length, with nothing to be articulate about. ("You taught me language," says Caliban to Prospero, "and my profit on't is I know how to curse.")[9]

Baldwin, like Lamming, asserts that the field of vision surrounding those considered "deformed" is overdetermined by the assumption that *sounds* of protective display are crude protests, or laments.

There is a sense, however, in which we are compelled to see what Baldwin, Lamming, and others consider a dilemma as the motivating challenge of *writing* as a project in and for itself. For the original island dweller—son of Sycorax—is aware of a cursed "self" cursing a notion of "self" that assumes that sounds of the phaneric mask are, like the conditions of language itself, alienating and fearful. This awareness, of course, calls into question the intruder's very definitions of "self" (worth). What batters our ears—if Caliban is newly interpreted—is the three-personed god of "natural" meanings, morphophonemics, and, most important, meta-morphoses. The Afro-American spokesperson who would perform a deformation of mastery shares the task of Sycorax's son insofar as he or she must transform an obscene situation, a tripled metastatus, into a signal self/cultural expression. The birth of such a self is never simply a coming into being, but always, also, a release from a BEING POSSESSED. The practice of a phaneric, diasporic expressivity is both a metadiscourse on linguistic investiture and a lesson in the metaphorical "worm holing," as it were—the tunneling out of the black holes of possession and "tight places" of old clothes, into, perhaps, a new universe. Black writers, one might say, are always on *display*, writing a black renaissance and righting a Western Renaissance that was, in the words of Ralph Ellison's preacher in *Invisible Man*, "most black, brother, most black." Language, insists

8. For a discussion of Lamming's perspective, see Janheinz Jahn, *Neo-African Literature: A History of Black Writing* (New York, 1969), p. 240. Jahn's own perspective adds considerable interest to the Calibanistic problematic. For a discussion of this problematic in relationship to Afro-American slave narratives, see my own discussion, "Autobiographical Acts and the Voice of the Southern Slave" in *The Journey Back: Issues in Black Literature and Criticism* (Chicago, 1980), pp. 27–52.

9. James Baldwin, *Notes of a Native Son* (Boston, 1962), p. 6. *Notes* appeared originally in 1955.

Jacques Derrida, is a "possibility founded on the general possibility of writing."[10]

4

    Caliban's triple play consists in what I described earlier as *supraliteracy;* it is a maroon or guerrilla action carried out *within* linguistic territories of the erstwhile masters, bringing forth *sounds* that have been taken for crude hooting, but which are, in reality, racial poetry. In recent weeks, I have heard lectures by both Afro-American and Caribbean scholars at the highest ranks of the Western academy. These lectures unfailingly privileged what I have called racial poetry for their explanatory models. Robert Hill, who is the brilliant editor of the Marcus Garvey papers, insisted that West Indian reggae music and a theory of the black audience are de rigueur if one would understand the life and work of Garvey, who was one of the foremost black, mass leaders of the twentieth century. And Clayborne Carson, editor of the papers of Martin Luther King, Jr., insisted that one can only consider the leadership of King as an "anomaly," for he was a leader chosen from "outside." This perspective is available only if one surveys vernacular dimensions of an ongoing black liberation struggle in America, a struggle that takes its force from such grassroots leaders as Robert Moses and Ella Baker. Further, Carson insists that it is only possible to see the civil rights movement as a "brief" flash upon the United States scene—as a short-range activity designed to secure legislation—if one fails to explore the ongoing "poetry" of liberation expressed in the timeless struggle of Afro-Americans for black community empowerment.

    I call such formulations as those of Hill and Carson *supraliterate* because it seems to me they invade the linguistic territories of traditional academic disciplines and "masters" with sounds of the vale/veil. What rises before Caliban is not a cursed status but rather a realization that his situation in a simple iconography forestalls a just reading of his "natural" situation. I believe that many Afro-American academics today find themselves in tenured (indeed, even "chaired") situations where they are not only compelled (given the conservative offensives enjoined by even some of their "racial" compeers) but also affectively inclined to execute a triple play.

    My conclusion should include mention, of course, of the concrete example of triple playing Gates offers in his vernacular perspective on Afro-American literature and culture entitled (with all the flair of racial poetry) *The Signifying Monkey.* Further, the conclusion should note that

10. Jacques Derrida, *Of Grammatology*, trans. Gayatri Chakravorty Spivak (Baltimore, 1976), p. 52.

Gates has executed a signal and substantial triple play with *"Race," Writing, and Difference* by invading the territories of the Western Enlightenment and appropriating to his own *vale* the entire panoply of issues held in trust for so many years by whitemales. If we fail to hear long choruses of Caliban's triple playing in the issue, still the collection creates an occasion for several signifying black academics—those who have already journeyed back to the *vale* and asked their mommas and daddies what did they do to be so very black and to sound such funky blues—to sound racial poetry in the courts of the civilized. Such soundings, I believe, augur new world arrangements, because the answers given by the mommas asked (and the black daddies, too) is, "You's different, son, and the future."

Caliban's triple play clears the (U.S.) bases in Third World geographies, providing space for poetry, a song, a sound rather than a sight, cite, or site for further Western duels—and dualities.

The Hegemonic Form of Othering; or, The Academic's Burden

Harold Fromm

I knew I was in for trouble, that the going would be rough, when I removed the wrapper from the *"Race," Writing, and Difference* issue of *Critical Inquiry* and observed the word "race" in quotation marks. Something deep was clearly brewing. And any doubts were quickly removed when I turned to the opening remarks of Henry Louis Gates, Jr. "Who," he asked me, "has seen a black or a red person, a white, yellow, or brown?" ("Writing 'Race' and the Difference It Makes," p. 6). *There* was a question that spelled trouble, a glove in the face if I ever saw one. Here I was, crude, unregenerate, lacking the hypersensitivity that prevents someone like Gates from making such infra dig distinctions; here I was, daring to use words *without* quotation marks, actually believing that I referred to something identifiable when I spoke of black people, Americans, musicians, and whatnot, and being told that it was all just my own narcissistic and preemptive fantasy. Here I was, faced with the impossible choice of keeping permanently quiet or of perpetuating ruthless violence—of denying the individuality of all of God's creation—not only by referring to knives, cats, my brother, or Indians, but simply by referring at all. But why, I wondered, was only the word "race" in quotation marks? Why not every single word in the entire issue of *Critical Inquiry*? For to refer, it seems, is to colonize, to take things over for one's own brutal use, to turn everything else into a mere Other. There was Gates engaging in the academic's favorite pastime, *épater les bourgeois*, and here was I, a hopeless bourgeois, just asking for a put-down.

Things were bad enough; guilt feelings were settling in. I had begun to equate thought with sin, naming with killing (we murder to dissect, you know); even the act of *being* made me uneasy: I felt that I was taking up someone else's air, inadvertently stepping on ants, killing bacteria in my own body by taking antibiotics, turning vegetables into Others by eating them. Then I began to read Mary Louise Pratt's essay on European colonizing of Africa (a subject, by the way, that looks to be a veritable capitalism of academic industry these days) and saw little ground for hope. How could I begin to understand what complex moral standards are operating in today's academia?

"Any reader recognizes here," Pratt tells us after quoting a passage describing John Barrow's travels into Africa,

> a very familiar, widespread, and stable form of "othering." The people to be othered are homogenized into a collective "they," which is distilled even further into an iconic "he" (the standardized adult male specimen). This abstracted "he"/"they" is the subject of verbs in a timeless present tense, which characterizes anything "he" is or does not as a particular historical event but as an instance of a pregiven custom or trait. . . . Through this discourse, encounters with an Other can be textualized or processed as enumerations of such traits. ["Scratches on the Face of the Country; or, What Mr. Barrow Saw in the Land of the Bushmen," p. 139]

After reading this and the ensuing remark to the effect that such description "could serve as a paradigmatic case of the ways in which ideology normalizes, codifies, and reifies" (Pratt, p. 140), I was puzzled. Although Pratt was agreeing with Gates, wasn't she, in the very act of characterizing colonial characterizing, engaged in the same practice as Barrow? And when Pratt remarked that "during the so-called opening up of central and southern Africa to European capitalism . . . such explorer-writers were the principal producers of Africa for European imaginations— producers, that is, of ideology in connection with the European expansionist project there" (Pratt, pp. 140–41), wasn't she failing to see that in the very act of "producing" her essay she was, like Gates, engaged in the opening up of certain texts to academic capitalism and its own—her own—expansionist project? Was she not ruthlessly reducing a complex world to a simple commodity (without even bothering with quotation

---

Harold Fromm is an independent scholar who has taught for many years in university English departments. He has published articles on Leonard and Virginia Woolf as well as on literary theory, politics, and professionalism. His most recent work concerns the Brontës.

marks) for academic consumption, which, when successfully "produced," would lead to promotions, professional recognition, salary increases, establishing of dogma, and the general colonizing of the minds of graduate students eager to cut it with their sahibs?

As I read on I became increasingly uneasy and embarrassed by what seemed to be one *double entendre* after another. "Unheroic, unparticularized, without ego, interest, or desire of its own," Pratt continues, with increasing, but insufficient, irony, "it [colonial discourse] seems able to do nothing but gaze from a periphery of its own creation, like the self-effaced, noninterventionist eye that scans the Other's body" (Pratt, p. 143). "To the extent that it strives to efface itself," this Foucauldian melodrama continues, "the invisible eye/I strives to make those informational orders natural, to find them there uncommanded, rather than assert them as the products/producers of European knowledges or disciplines" (Pratt, p. 144). Surely, I kept feeling, Pratt could hardly have failed to imagine for a moment the word "academic" in place of "European" in the above and all similar passages. Such sensitivity to the pure passivity of the Other so brutalized and "hegemonized" over by European exploitation could hardly fail also to sense the applicability of these observations to—their interchangeability, in fact, with—her own academic colonization. But no, irony can only go so far.

Speaking of the "reveries" of nineteenth-century writings about exploration, Pratt comments: "They are determined, in part, by highly generalized literary conventions" (Pratt, p. 145). And when I looked over Pratt's own essay, I could see again how well her descriptions of descriptions served to describe her own production. For what are such terms as *discourse, textualized, paradigmatic, seen/scene, site/sight, capitalist mode of production, Other, narration, hegemonic, Bahktinian, gaze,* if not the "highly generalized literary conventions" of today's self-aggrandizing, colonizing academic, who tells us we are crude to think there are really such creatures as blacks, whites, or whatnots, but who guiltlessly goes right along telling us about sights/sites (as though some essence really underlay the arbitrary sounds of two words and as though this were not just the latest academic sort of fun and games), about "capitalist production" (where do we find it?), about "textuality" and "carnival" (Pratt neglects to use that one, I must admit).

Although *Critical Inquiry*'s *"Race"* issue contains a good deal of moral instruction, "Physician, heal thyself" perhaps ought to be the first moral exhortation of the day. Against a more generalized background of Stanley Fish telling us that we are already perfect now (a better account than his of antiprofessionalism can be found in Bruce Robbins' "Professionalism and Politics" in *Profession 85*) and a horde of academic Marxists who are increasingly difficult to distinguish from yuppies, our professional humanist robes really do need to be sent out to the cleaners. They are beginning to smell. The pontifications of Gates and Pratt—and others like them—can't do much good for anybody except Gates and Pratt. For are they not just academic members of the Evangelical Guru and Guilt Industry that tells its members "I'm okay, you're okay, the rest of the world's rotten" while their garages fill up with Rolls Royces or their vitas with grants?

A Reply to Harold Fromm

Mary Louise Pratt

Harold Fromm argues that my essay exemplifies a kind of academic colonization, a form of exploitation in which raw material (in this case travel books) is processed into prestige, money, and influence. Other writers, including Foucault, have used this metaphor of colonization to describe intellectual expansionism in the academy, the apparent momentum toward bringing more and more of the world into the academy's purview. I imagine there are few humanists who have not questioned their work along these lines, who have not felt a twinge at the thought that they are building their fame and fortune (or at least their livelihood) on the work of others or acquiring professional capital by opening up previously unscrutinized territories.

Though I doubt it has put a Rolls Royce in anybody's garage, the criticism industry is a reality not to be overlooked. Academics have a responsibility to stay self-aware and self-critical about their own and their profession's interests. All academic activity has a careerist dimension, but it obviously cannot be explained by that dimension alone, and in this sense Fromm's point is simply reductive. But of course it is not *all* academic activity that Fromm is objecting to, only some and notably mine.

The image of academic colonization suggests one has stepped beyond some legitimate borders and laid claim to territory rightfully inhabited by others. Whose world was invaded by my essay, or by the *"Race," Writing, and Difference* issue in general? Mr. Fromm's, evidently. Fromm wants a world where words stand still and refer, and don't get changed. In particular, to use his own examples, he wants a world where blacks are blacks, whites are whites, Americans are Americans, knives are knives, brothers are brothers, and Indians are Indians (Is it the wild west? or maybe just Chicago).

This is precisely the world the *Critical Inquiry* issue set out to intervene in, and in that sense Fromm's reaction is to be welcomed. Part of the project of the issue was to destabilize fixed, naturalized meaning systems around race and other lines of hierarchical differentiation. Many of the essays, including mine, sought this end by historicizing such systems, pointing up their constructedness, their means of legitimation, and so on.

It was an interventionist project, to be sure; however, the name for such interventions is not colonialism, it is critique—or, if you like, critical inquiry. They are attempts to change the culture one lives in. Fromm feels the issue left him with "the impossible choice of keeping permanently quiet or perpetuating ruthless violence . . . simply by referring at all" (p. 396). But these are not his only choices—for one thing, he has chosen to respond, and his response is not ruthlessly violent. For another, his ideas might change, maybe despite himself—the words certainly will.

Much of Fromm's response consists of his simply quoting my text in disgust, as if he had no (critical) language of his own. When that language does surface at the end of the piece, I could not help hearing in its evocation of the "horde of academic Marxists" in bad-smelling robes the echoes of all those European travelers looking at the Bushmen. I wondered whether, face to face, Fromm would be likely to load his rifle or start handing out tobacco. Perhaps he would pull out a Bible. Alternatively, I wondered whether we couldn't all think of something completely different.

Mary Louise Pratt is an associate professor in the Department of Spanish and Portuguese and the Program in Comparative Literature at Stanford University. She is the author of *Toward a Speech-Act Theory of Literary Discourse*.

Talkin' That Talk

Henry Louis Gates, Jr.

The editors of *Critical Inquiry* and I decided to bracket the word "race" in our title after much discussion and debate, and only after an extended correspondence with Tzvetan Todorov. We decided to do so to underscore the fact that "race" is a metaphor for something else and not an essence or a thing in itself, apart from its creation by an act of language.

Why is this gesture necessary? Why is it not merely cute to remind one's readers that even adjectives such as red, yellow, brown, and black are also metaphors when applied to the so-called color of people? Harold Fromm's response to these gestures, as amusing as it intended itself to be, only reveals the necessity of undermining the habit, in the West, of accounting for the Other's "essence" in absolute terms, in terms that *fix* culturally defined differences into transcendent, "natural" categories or essences. The essays collected in *"Race," Writing, and Difference* show that "race" is not a thing. For, if we believe that races exist as things, as categories of being already "there," we cannot escape the danger of generalizing about observed differences between human beings as if these differences were consistent and determined, a priori. The history of Western discourse on "race" is replete with deductions and presumptions ascertained by "reason" rather than by observation and empiricism; "racial reasoning," one might say, is reasoning from causes to effects without reference to experience, in terms of a fixed essence. When authors of African descent began to publish imaginative literature in English in the eighteenth century, for example, they confronted a collective and racist text of themselves which Europeans had invented. This helps us to understand why so very much Anglo-African writing—whether Phillis Wheatley's elegies, or Olaudah Equiano's autobiography, or Ignatius Sancho's epistles—directly addressed European fictions of the African in an attempt to *voice* or speak the African into existence in Western letters. When the African walked into the court of Western letters, she or he was judged in advance by a fixed racist subtext, or pretext, which the African was forced to confront, confirm, or reject. Given that these fictions of racial essence were sanctioned by "science," the Africans had little hope indeed of speaking themselves free of European fantasies of their "Otherness."

Our decision to bracket "race" was designed to call attention to the fact that "races," put simply, do not exist, and that to claim that they do, for whatever misguided reason, is to stand on dangerous ground. Fromm understands this all too well, it seems, judging from the satirical tone of his response. Were there not countries in which the belief in racial essences dictates social and political policy, perhaps I would have found Fromm's essay amusing and our gesture merely one more token of the academic's tendency to create distinctions which common sense alone renders unnecessary. The joke, rather, is on Fromm: one's task is most certainly *not* to remain "permanently quiet"; rather, our task is to utilize language more precisely, to rid ourselves of the dangers of careless usages of problematic terms which are drawn upon to delimit and predetermine the lives and choices of human beings who are not "white." Fromm's response only reinforces Todorov's worry about not bracketing "race" every time it occurs in our texts, because "race" (as each essay subtly shows) simply does not exist.

Todorov argues that "racism" is "a type of behavior which consists in the display of contempt or aggressiveness toward other people on account of physical differences (other than those of sex) between them and oneself" (p. 370). The problem with this definition is that it depends upon the "display" of "contempt" or "aggressiveness" for its effect. Afro-American history is full of examples of "racist" benevolence, paternalism, and sexual attraction which are not always, or only, dependent upon contempt or aggression. Todorov implies that the only racists are those who act with malice for reasons attributable to purportedly essential biological differences. I would say that "racism" exists when one generalizes about the attributes of an individual (and treats him or her accordingly). Such generalizations are based upon a predetermined set of causes or effects thought to be shared by all members of a physically defined group

Henry Louis Gates, Jr. is professor of English, comparative literature, and African studies at Cornell University. He has edited several books and has written *Figures in Black* and *The Signifying Monkey*.

who are also assumed to share certain "metaphysical" characteristics: "Skip, sing me one of those old Negro spirituals that you people love so dear," or "You people sure can *dance,*" or even "Black people play basketball so remarkably well because of their peculiar muscular system coupled with a well-defined sense of rhythm." These are racist statements, certainly, which can have rather little to do with aggression or contempt in *intent,* even if the effect is contemptible (but often "well-intentioned"). It is the penchant to *generalize* based upon essences perceived as *biological* which defines "racism." Todorov's behavioral definition also ignores a host of instances in which behavior is only a second-order reflection of attitude. His definition is curiously limited, and limiting, because it depends upon *physical characteristics* rather than upon the purported nature of a transcendent "metaphysical" *character.* The racist's error is one of *thought,* not merely, or only, of behavior.

Todorov's objection to our failure to bracket "race" every time it appears in the issue is somewhat surprising. The editors of *Critical Inquiry* and I argued at length about doing so. We decided, however, that our point would be made most efficiently and effectively in the issue's title and in my introduction. Thereafter, each time the words "race" or "racial" appeared, we expected our readers to bracket the terms themselves. Since each essay, in its own way, demonstrates that "race" is not a thing, perhaps each essayist chose not to bracket the term so as to achieve this effect more subtly.

Whereas Fromm would upbraid me for placing quotation marks around "race," then, Todorov wonders aloud if I have forgotten my own admonitions about the dangers of misusing this term and reintroduced it into my essay without thinking about it! I find it amusing to respond to both criticisms at once, even if I can take neither too seriously. Todorov, however, raises a more substantial matter which I should like to address squarely.

Todorov questions my belief that "we must turn to the black tradition itself to develop theories of criticism indigenous to our literatures." He accuses me of presupposing, thereby, that "the content of a thought depends on the color of the thinker's skin" (p. 376). If so, he continues, then I am at fault for saying implicitly that "only birds of a feather can think together," and thereby I "practice the very racialism one was supposed to be combatting." This, he concludes, "can only be described as cultural apartheid: in order to analyze black literature, one must use concepts formulated by black authors" (p. 376). Todorov's reasoning here seems to me specious. It is intended, it seems, to show that I am unwittingly guilty of the very "racialism" that I condemn: "if 'racial differences' do not exist," he asks, then "how can they possibly influence literary texts?" (p. 371). Todorov is being disingenuous here, and is guilty of shallow thinking about a serious problem for all theorists of so-called "noncanonical" literatures. Todorov attempts nothing less than a neocolonial recuperation of the sense of difference upon which a truly *new* criticism of world literature must be granted.

The term that I use to qualify my assertion is *attitudes:* "how attitudes toward [pointed or purported] racial differences generate and structure texts by us *and* about us" ("Writing 'Race' and the Difference It Makes," p. 15). There is no question that representations of black character-types in European and American literature have a history—and a life—of their own, generating repetitions, revisions, and refutations. Within African and Afro-American literature, there can be no question that the *texts* that comprise these traditions repeat, refute, and revise key, canonical tropes and topoi peculiar to those *literary* traditions.

The term that is unstated in my sentence is "textual": we must turn to the black *textual* tradition itself to develop theories of criticism indigenous to our literatures. I believed that when I wrote that sentence; I believe it even more firmly now, especially since confronted with this remark of Todorov's: "In order to analyze football players, should we use only 'indigenous' concepts and theories?" (p. 376).

It is naive to think that the theorists of Afro-American or African literature can utilize theories of criticism generated by critics of European or American literature without regard for the textual *specificity* of those theories. Since Todorov has learned something from Anthony Appiah's essay, I can do no better than to cite Appiah once again, on what he rather cleverly has called "the Naipaul fallacy," a passage which Todorov for some reason conveniently ignores: "nor should we endorse a *more sinister line* . . . : the post-colonial legacy which requires us to show that African literature is worthy of study precisely (but only) because it is fundamentally the same as European literature" (quoted in Gates, p. 14; my emphasis). Appiah then concludes with devastating impact that we must not ask "the reader to understand Africa by embedding it in European culture" (quoted in Gates, p. 15).

Why would Todorov ignore these crucial segments of Appiah's argument, which I quote with great favor? Precisely because he wishes to debunk my position, hoping to unveil its supposed "racialism," and because he has failed to understand the necessity of a task which Appiah, Houston Baker, Wole Soyinka, and I (among others) believe to be absolutely essential if there is to be created something that is validly "African" in contemporary literary theory. To deny us the right even to make the attempt is either for Todorov to be engaged in bad faith, or to be implicated in one more instance of what Appiah calls the "post-colonial legacy."

I have never written, or thought, that "the content of a thought depends on the color of the thinker's skin" (p. 376). Only a fool—and a racialist—would think that. Since I am well known in the profession for encouraging students and critics of all ethnic and cultural groups to write about black literature, I find Todorov's attempt to be amusing quite disturbing. Since Todorov has decided what it is I think, perhaps I should state my position bluntly.

Theories of criticism are text-specific: the New Critics tended to explicate the metaphysical poets, the structuralists certain forms of narrative, and deconstructionists found their ideal field of texts among the Romantics. While each school of criticism claims for itself what Todorov calls "a universal aspiration," in practice European and American critics tend to write about European and American writers of one specific sort or another. (Todorov, to his credit, mentions Chester Himes' *For Love of Imabelle* as an example of the thriller in *The Poetics of Prose,* but only in passing. Sartre's fantasies of "the being" of "the" African in *Black Orpheus* are racialist, as is his consideration of Richard Wright's "split" audience in *What Is Literature?* A passing nod, and racialist musings, however, are at least *something;* Todorov and Sartre are among the very few [white] critics in this century who have even *read* the works of the black traditions.) This observation has been made so many times before that it is a commonplace of the history of criticism. Why does Todorov choose to parody this point? So that he can claim that I am a racialist.

My position is clear: to theorize about black literatures, we must do what all theorists do. And that is to read the texts that comprise our literary tradition, formulate (by reasoning from observed facts) useful principles of criticism from within that textual tradition, then draw upon these to read the texts that make up that tradition. *All* theorists do this, and we must as well. Todorov's position—let me call it the neocolonial position—pretends that "where [analytical concepts] come from" is irrelevant to the literary critic (p. 376). My position is that for a critic of black literature to borrow European or American theories of literature regardless of "*where they come from*" is for that critic to be trapped in a relation of intellectual indenture or colonialism. (Please note, M. Todorov, that I wrote "critic of black literature," and not "black critic.") One must *know* one's textual terrain before it can be explored; one must know one's literary tradition before it can be theorized about.

What can be at all controversial—or "racialist"—about my position? I believe that Todorov finds it problematic because it implies that what European or American critics pretend or claim to be their subject—the wondrous institution of "literature"—in practice means only the branch of that vast institution occupied by "white" authors. To discourage us from reading our own texts in ways suggested by those very texts is to encourage new forms of neocolonialism. To attempt such readings is neither to suggest that "black" texts have no "white" antecedents nor that the Western literary and critical traditions have no relevance for critics of "other" literatures. Several aspects of formal literary language-use seem to be common to all formal literatures: for instance, the structure of a metaphor, *style indirect libre,* even the *skaz* of the Russian Formalists, it seems obvious to me, are the same in "noncanonical" literatures. My method does not mean that we have to reinvent the wheel. No, we turn to our literary tradition to define its specificity, to locate what I call its *signifying black difference*. The critic of black literature who does not do this is the critic destined to recapitulate unwittingly the racist stereotype of Minstrel Man, a Tzvetan Todorov in black face. And who would want to look so foolish?

Todorov upbraids us for not charting the history of the critical schools of thought which attempted to explain literary differences by racial differences, specifically the work of Josef Nadler, Franz Koch, Clemens Lugowski, and Heinz Kindermann. While such an exposition and critique of their work would have been appropriate as an essay, it was thought by the editors to be inappropriate in my introduction, since I was attempting there to sketch the effects of accounting for *black* literary differences by "racial" differences in the works of white racialist critics. My references to Taine, as I state, are taken from Walter Jackson Bate's introduction to his excerpts from *The History of English Literature*. (I treat Taine at length in the forthcoming second volume of *Black Letters and Western Criticism*.) I cited Bate only to suggest to the acute and sensitive reader the origins of his unfortunate and racialist statement (which serves as my first epigraph) about "the progressive trivialization of topics" (such as "The Trickster Figure in Chicano and Black Literature") which scholars now discuss at the annual gatherings of the Modern Language Association. Bate believes that such topics have helped to create what for him is "the crisis in English studies," but these, for many of us, constitute the beginnings of the *salvation* of English studies, which heretofore have been by white people, about white people, and for white people. I am sorry that the point I sought to make escaped Todorov. I was engaged in a black cultural game, M. Todorov, one known as "signifying." I was *signifying upon* Bate, as my black readers would know from their familiarity with this coded exchange. As Louis Armstrong said, "If you have to ask . . . !"

Finally, Todorov wonders why so many of our authors "see racialism as a consequence of Enlightenment philosophy and humanism. This affirmation seems to me not only inaccurate but dangerous" (p. 372). I cannot speak for other essayists who make this affirmation, but I can state why it is true when we examine the instance of the *author* of African descent and the European critical reception to his or her work. (Todorov, by the way, has much homework to do if he *really* believes, as he says he does, that "It was the abolition of slavery which led to the rise of racism in the United States" [p. 372]. Racism, rather, is *simultaneous* with "racial" slavery.) For in the Enlightenment even the most "egalitarian" thinkers argued that the production of imaginative literature was necessary for the African to demonstrate her or his equality of "mental capacity" with the European. To be antislavery was not the same thing as not being a racist: one could very well oppose slavery yet believe black people to be *innately* or *naturally* inferior. To make this affirmation, as Todorov does, and to seek to valorize the Enlightenment is not only historically inaccurate but dangerous. As I try to show in my book, *Black Letters and the Enlightenment,* racism and—dare I say it?—*logocentrism* marched arm in arm to delimit black people in perhaps the most pernicious way of all: to claim that they were subhuman, that they were "a different species of men," as Hume put it so plainly, because they could not "write" literature. Did Kant stop being a racist, stop thinking that there existed a natural, predetermined relation between "stupidity" and "blackness" (his terms) just because he wrote *Foundations of the Metaphysics of Morals*? Hardly! Indeed, one might say that Kant's *Observations on the Feeling of the Beautiful and Sublime* functions to deconstruct, for the black reader, Kant's *Foundations,* revealing it to be just one more example of the remarkable capacity of European philosophers to conceive of "humanity" in ideal terms (white, male), yet despise, abhor, colonize, or exploit human beings who are not "ideal." Todorov's position is a classic example of Baker's definition of the "rationalist" who "claims to avoid general views or judgments of ideology," when all along he has reproduced an ideology of egalitarianism and universalism which seeks to bracket the *soundings* of the critical voice of the Other—why else question our attempt to redefine "theory" in our own images, in our own voices? How *else* are we to define theories of our own literatures but to step out of the discourse of the white masters and speak in the critical language of the black vernacular? I agree with Baker that this challenge confronts Edward Said and Gayatri Spivak, just as it confronts Baker and Gates. We see it as a problem, as an opportunity, as possibility, while they do not . . . *yet.* To adopt Todorov's ideology of egalitarianism and universalism is to allow our discourse to be incorporated into the discourse of Europe and then to be naturalized (seemingly) and colonized. Great danger lurks there. It was Soyinka who advised us to beware of the neocolonial wolf, dressed in the sheep's clothing of "universality."

*   *   *

As for Houston "Caliban" Baker's *own* "triple play," let me, first, thank him for the twin compliments about the import of *Critical Inquiry*'s willingness to open its pages, as Derrida says so clearly, to subjects not addressed heretofore, and, second, for his kind words about my own "vernacular" theory of literature, expounded upon in *The Signifying Monkey.* But let me state clearly that my call for vernacular theories of the Other was intended, as I state it to be, as an example of where he and I found it necessary and fruitful to turn to escape the neocolonialism of the "egalitarian criticism" of Todorov and company, whose claims to "the universal" somehow always end up lopping off our arms, legs, and pug noses, muffling the peculiar timbres of our voices, and trying to straighten our always already kinky hair, and not to the essays that comprise the text of *"Race," Writing, and Difference*. But Caliban is nothing if not a debunker.

With Caliban, we can say:

> You taught me language; and my profit on 't
> Is, we know how to debunk: the red plague gird you,
> For learning us your criticism!

No, Houston, there are no vernacular critics collected here; nor did you expect there to be. Todorov's response forces me to realize that the discursive dualism that you criticize is still urgently needed. For we must attack the racism of egalitarianism and universalism in as many languages as we can utter. Todorov can't even hear us, Houston, when we talk *his* academic talk; how he gonna hear us if we "talk *that* talk," the talk of the black idiom? Maybe you think we should give up, but I am still an optimist. Things is just gettin' innerestin', as LeRoi says.

Index

TEXAS WOMAN'S UNIVERSITY LIBRARY